Contemporary Authors®

ISSN 0010-7468

Contemporary Authors®

A Bio-Bibliographical Guide to
Current Writers in Fiction, General Nonfiction,
Poetry, Journalism, Drama, Motion Pictures,
Television, and Other Fields

volume 242

THOMSON

GALE

Detroit • New York • San Francisco • San Diego • New Haven, Conn. • Waterville, Maine • London • Munich

Contemporary Authors, Vol. 242

Project Editor
Julie Mellors

Editorial
Michelle Kazensky, Joshua Kondek, Lisa Kumar, Tracey Matthews, Mary Ruby

Permissions
Jacqueline Key, Sue Rudolph, Kim Smilay

Imaging and Multimedia
Lezlie Light, Kelly A. Quin

Composition and Electronic Capture
Carolyn Roney

Manufacturing
Drew Kalasky

LIBRARY OF CONGRESS CATALOG CARD NUMBER 62-52046

ISBN 0-7876-7871-6
ISSN 0010-7468

This title is also available as an e-book.
ISBN 1-4144-1002-6
Contact your Thomson Gale sales representative for ordering information.

Printed in the United States of America
10 9 8 7 6 5 4 3 2 1

Contents

Indexing note: All *Contemporary Authors* entries are indexed in the *Contemporary Authors* cumulative index, which is published separately and distributed twice a year.

As always, the most recent Contemporary Authors cumulative index continues to be the user's guide to the location of an individual author's listing.

Preface

Contemporary Authors (*CA*) provides information on approximately 120,000 writers in a wide range of media, including:

- Current writers of fiction, nonfiction, poetry, and drama whose works have been issued by commercial publishers, risk publishers, or university presses (authors whose books have been published only by known vanity or author-subsidized firms are ordinarily not included)

- Prominent print and broadcast journalists, editors, photojournalists, syndicated cartoonists, graphic novelists, screenwriters, television scriptwriters, and other media people

- Notable international authors

- Literary greats of the early twentieth century whose works are popular in today's high school and college curriculums and continue to elicit critical attention

A *CA* listing entails no charge or obligation. Authors are included on the basis of the above criteria and their interest to *CA* users. Sources of potential listees include trade periodicals, publishers' catalogs, librarians, and other users of the series.

How to Get the Most out of *CA*: Use the Index

The key to locating an author's most recent entry is the *CA* cumulative index, which is published separately and distributed twice a year. It provides access to *all* entries in *CA* and *Contemporary Authors New Revision Series* (*CANR*). Always consult the latest index to find an author's most recent entry.

For the convenience of users, the *CA* cumulative index also includes references to all entries in these Thomson Gale literary series: *Authors and Artists for Young Adults, Authors in the News, Bestsellers, Black Literature Criticism, Black Literature Criticism Supplement, Black Writers, Children's Literature Review, Concise Dictionary of American Literary Biography, Concise Dictionary of British Literary Biography, Contemporary Authors Autobiography Series, Contemporary Authors Bibliographical Series, Contemporary Dramatists, Contemporary Literary Criticism, Contemporary Novelists, Contemporary Poets, Contemporary Popular Writers, Contemporary Southern Writers, Contemporary Women Poets, Dictionary of Literary Biography, Dictionary of Literary Biography Documentary Series, Dictionary of Literary Biography Yearbook, DISCovering Authors, DISCovering Authors: British, DISCovering Authors: Canadian, DISCovering Authors: Modules* (including modules for Dramatists, Most-Studied Authors, Multicultural Authors, Novelists, Poets, and Popular/ Genre Authors), *DISCovering Authors 3.0, Drama Criticism, Drama for Students, Feminist Writers, Hispanic Literature Criticism, Hispanic Writers, Junior DISCovering Authors, Major Authors and Illustrators for Children and Young Adults, Major 20th-Century Writers, Native North American Literature, Novels for Students, Poetry Criticism, Poetry for Students, Short Stories for Students, Short Story Criticism, Something about the Author, Something about the Author Autobiography Series, St. James Guide to Children's Writers, St. James Guide to Crime & Mystery Writers, St. James Guide to Fantasy Writers, St. James Guide to Horror, Ghost & Gothic Writers, St. James Guide to Science Fiction Writers, St. James Guide to Young Adult Writers, Twentieth-Century Literary Criticism, 20th Century Romance and Historical Writers, World Literature Criticism,* and *Yesterday's Authors of Books for Children.*

A Sample Index Entry:

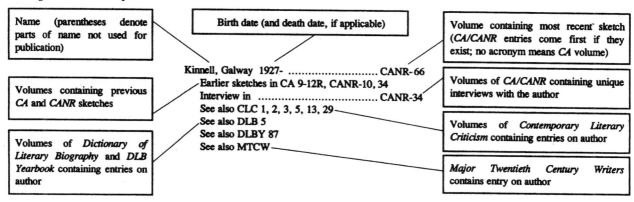

How Are Entries Compiled?

The editors make every effort to secure new information directly from the authors; listees' responses to our questionnaires and query letters provide most of the information featured in *CA*. For deceased writers, or those who fail to reply to requests for data, we consult other reliable biographical sources, such as those indexed in Thomson Gale's *Biography and Genealogy Master Index,* and bibliographical sources, including *National Union Catalog, LC MARC,* and *British National Bibliography.* Further details come from published interviews, feature stories, and book reviews, as well as information supplied by the authors' publishers and agents.

An asterisk (*) at the end of a sketch indicates that the listing has been compiled from secondary sources believed to be reliable but has not been personally verified for this edition by the author sketched.

What Kinds of Information Does An Entry Provide?

Sketches in *CA* contain the following biographical and bibliographical information:

- **Entry heading:** the most complete form of author's name, plus any pseudonyms or name variations used for writing

- **Personal information:** author's date and place of birth, family data, ethnicity, educational background, political and religious affiliations, and hobbies and leisure interests

- **Addresses:** author's home, office, or agent's addresses, plus e-mail and fax numbers, as available

- **Career summary:** name of employer, position, and dates held for each career post; resume of other vocational achievements; military service

- **Membership information:** professional, civic, and other association memberships and any official posts held

- **Awards and honors:** military and civic citations, major prizes and nominations, fellowships, grants, and honorary degrees

- **Writings:** a comprehensive, chronological list of titles, publishers, dates of original publication and revised editions, and production information for plays, television scripts, and screenplays

- **Adaptations:** a list of films, plays, and other media which have been adapted from the author's work

- **Work in progress:** current or planned projects, with dates of completion and/or publication, and expected publisher, when known

- **Sidelights:** a biographical portrait of the author's development; information about the critical reception of the author's works; revealing comments, often by the author, on personal interests, aspirations, motivations, and thoughts on writing

- **Interview:** a one-on-one discussion with authors conducted especially for *CA*, offering insight into authors' thoughts about their craft

- **Autobiographical essay:** an original essay written by noted authors for *CA*, a forum in which writers may present themselves, on their own terms, to their audience

- **Photographs:** portraits and personal photographs of notable authors

- **Biographical and critical sources:** a list of books and periodicals in which additional information on an author's life and/or writings appears

- **Obituary Notices** in *CA* provide date and place of birth as well as death information about authors whose full-length sketches appeared in the series before their deaths. The entries also summarize the authors' careers and writings and list other sources of biographical and death information.

Related Titles in the *CA* Series

Contemporary Authors Autobiography Series complements *CA* original and revised volumes with specially commissioned autobiographical essays by important current authors, illustrated with personal photographs they provide. Common topics include their motivations for writing, the people and experiences that shaped their careers, the rewards they derive from their work, and their impressions of the current literary scene.

Contemporary Authors Bibliographical Series surveys writings by and about important American authors since World War II. Each volume concentrates on a specific genre and features approximately ten writers; entries list works written by and about the author and contain a bibliographical essay discussing the merits and deficiencies of major critical and scholarly studies in detail.

Available in Electronic Formats

GaleNet. *CA* is available on a subscription basis through GaleNet, an online information resource that features an easy-to-use end-user interface, powerful search capabilities, and ease of access through the World-Wide Web. For more information, call 1-800-877-GALE.

Licensing. *CA* is available for licensing. The complete database is provided in a fielded format and is deliverable on such media as disk, CD-ROM, or tape. For more information, contact Thomson Gale's Business Development Group at 1-800-877-GALE, or visit us on our website at www.galegroup.com/bizdev.

Suggestions Are Welcome

The editors welcome comments and suggestions from users on any aspect of the *CA* series. If readers would like to recommend authors for inclusion in future volumes of the series, they are cordially invited to write the Editors at *Contemporary Authors*, Thomson Gale, 27500 Drake Rd., Farmington Hills, MI 48331-3535; or call at 1-248-699-4253; or fax at 1-248-699-8054.

Contemporary Authors Product Advisory Board

The editors of *Contemporary Authors* are dedicated to maintaining a high standard of excellence by publishing comprehensive, accurate, and highly readable entries on a wide array of writers. In addition to the quality of the content, the editors take pride in the graphic design of the series, which is intended to be orderly yet inviting, allowing readers to utilize the pages of *CA* easily and with efficiency. Despite the longevity of the *CA* print series, and the success of its format, we are mindful that the vitality of a literary reference product is dependent on its ability to serve its users over time. As literature, and attitudes about literature, constantly evolve, so do the reference needs of students, teachers, scholars, journalists, researchers, and book club members. To be certain that we continue to keep pace with the expectations of our customers, the editors of *CA* listen carefully to their comments regarding the value, utility, and quality of the series. Librarians, who have firsthand knowledge of the needs of library users, are a valuable resource for us. The *Contemporary Authors* Product Advisory Board, made up of school, public, and academic librarians, is a forum to promote focused feedback about *CA* on a regular basis. The six-member advisory board includes the following individuals, whom the editors wish to thank for sharing their expertise:

- **Anne M. Christensen,** Librarian II, Phoenix Public Library, Phoenix, Arizona.

- **Barbara C. Chumard,** Reference/Adult Services Librarian, Middletown Thrall Library, Middletown, New York.

- **Eva M. Davis,** Youth Department Manager, Ann Arbor District Library, Ann Arbor, Michigan.

- **Adam Janowski, Jr.,** Library Media Specialist, Naples High School Library Media Center, Naples, Florida.

- **Robert Reginald,** Head of Technical Services and Collection Development, California State University, San Bernadino, California.

- **Stephen Weiner,** Director, Maynard Public Library, Maynard, Massachusetts.

International Advisory Board

Well-represented among the 120,000 author entries published in *Contemporary Authors* are sketches on notable writers from many non-English-speaking countries. The primary criteria for inclusion of such authors has traditionally been the publication of at least one title in English, either as an original work or as a translation. However, the editors of *Contemporary Authors* came to observe that many important international writers were being overlooked due to a strict adherence to our inclusion criteria. In addition, writers who were publishing in languages other than English were not being covered in the traditional sources we used for identifying new listees. Intent on increasing our coverage of international authors, including those who write only in their native language and have not been translated into English, the editors enlisted the aid of a board of advisors, each of whom is an expert on the literature of a particular country or region. Among the countries we focused attention on are Mexico, Puerto Rico, Germany, Luxembourg, Belgium, the Netherlands, Norway, Sweden, Denmark, Finland, Taiwan, Singapore, Spain, Italy, South Africa, Israel, and Japan, as well as England, Scotland, Wales, Ireland, Australia, and New Zealand. The sixteen-member advisory board includes the following individuals, whom the editors wish to thank for sharing their expertise:

- **Lowell A. Bangerter,** Professor of German, University of Wyoming, Laramie, Wyoming.

- **Nancy E. Berg,** Associate Professor of Hebrew and Comparative Literature, Washington University, St. Louis, Missouri.

- **Frances Devlin-Glass,** Associate Professor, School of Literary and Communication Studies, Deakin University, Burwood, Victoria, Australia.

- **David William Foster,** Regent's Professor of Spanish, Interdisciplinary Humanities, and Women's Studies, Arizona State University, Tempe, Arizona.

- **Hosea Hirata,** Director of the Japanese Program, Associate Professor of Japanese, Tufts University, Medford, Massachusetts.

- **Jack Kolbert,** Professor Emeritus of French Literature, Susquehanna University, Selinsgrove, Pennsylvania.

- **Mark Libin,** Professor, University of Manitoba, Winnipeg, Manitoba, Canada.

- **C. S. Lim,** Professor, University of Malaya, Kuala Lumpur, Malaysia.

- **Eloy E. Merino,** Assistant Professor of Spanish, Northern Illinois University, DeKalb, Illinois.

- **Linda M. Rodríguez Guglielmoni,** Associate Professor, University of Puerto Rico—Mayagüez, Puerto Rico.

- **Sven Hakon Rossel,** Professor and Chair of Scandinavian Studies, University of Vienna, Vienna, Austria.

- **Steven R. Serafin,** Director, Writing Center, Hunter College of the City University of New York, New York City.

- **David Smyth,** Lecturer in Thai, School of Oriental and African Studies, University of London, England.

- **Ismail S. Talib,** Senior Lecturer, Department of English Language and Literature, National University of Singapore, Singapore.

- **Dionisio Viscarri,** Assistant Professor, Ohio State University, Columbus, Ohio.

- **Mark Williams,** Associate Professor, English Department, University of Canterbury, Christchurch, New Zealand.

CA Numbering System and Volume Update Chart

Occasionally questions arise about the *CA* numbering system and which volumes, if any, can be discarded. Despite numbers like "29-32R," "97-100" and "241," the entire *CA* print series consists of only 293 physical volumes with the publication of *CA* Volume 242. The following charts note changes in the numbering system and cover design, and indicate which volumes are essential for the most complete, up-to-date coverage.

CA First Revision
- 1-4R through 41-44R (11 books)
  Cover: Brown with black and gold trim.
  There will be no further First Revision volumes because revised entries are now being handled exclusively through the more efficient *New Revision Series* mentioned below.

CA Original Volumes
- 45-48 through 97-100 (14 books)
  Cover: Brown with black and gold trim.
  101 through 242 (142 books)
  Cover: Blue and black with orange bands.
  The same as previous *CA* original volumes but with a new, simplified numbering system and new cover design.

CA Permanent Series
- *CAP*-1 and *CAP*-2 (2 books)
  Cover: Brown with red and gold trim.
  There will be no further Permanent Series volumes because revised entries are now being handled exclusively through the more efficient *New Revision Series* mentioned below.

CA New Revision Series
- CANR-1 through CANR-147 (147 books)
  Cover: Blue and black with green bands.
  Includes only sketches requiring significant changes; **sketches are taken from any previously published CA, CAP, or CANR volume.**

If You Have:	You May Discard:
CA First Revision Volumes 1-4R through 41-44R and *CA Permanent Series* Volumes 1 and 2	*CA* Original Volumes 1, 2, 3, 4 Volumes 5-6 through 41-44
CA Original Volumes 45-48 through 97-100 and 101 through 242	**NONE:** These volumes will not be superseded by corresponding revised volumes. Individual entries from these and all other volumes appearing in the left column of this chart may be revised and included in the various volumes of the *New Revision Series*.
CA New Revision Series Volumes *CANR*-1 through *CANR*-147	**NONE:** The *New Revision Series* does not replace any single volume of *CA*. Instead, volumes of *CANR* include entries from many previous *CA* series volumes. All *New Revision Series* volumes must be retained for full coverage.

A Sampling of Authors and Media People Featured in This Volume

Walden Bello

Bello is the author of over a dozen books critiquing globalization and the effects of U.S. government policies on the rest of the world, especially Asia and the Pacific Rim. A professor of sociology, Bello has been a long-time activist, fighting first the martial-law government of Ferdinand Marcos in his native land, and then resisting and critiquing the monetary policies of international agencies and groups such as the World Bank, World Trade Organization (WTO), and International Monetary Fund (IMF). Bello's writing and editing has spanned several decades, and he is the recipient of the 2003 Right Livelihood Award.

James Frey

Frey became a public figure when it was revealed that his memoir of addiction and recovery, *A Million Little Pieces,* is mostly fictionalized. Talk-show host Oprah Winfrey, who had chosen the book for her popular book club, apologized to her viewers for initially defending Frey's purported memoir. Although Frey's book was officially removed from the Oprah Book Club, ironically, sales of *A Million Little Pieces* soared shortly thereafter. Frey has more recently published another alleged memoir, titled *My Friend Leonard.*

Michel Gondry

French director Gondry was initially well-respected for his music-video and advertising work. By 2001 he was working on his first feature film. Gondry solidified his reputation as one of the most innovative film directors of the early twenty-first century through two critically acclaimed movies: *Human Nature,* released in 2001, and the Academy Award-winning *Eternal Sunshine of the Spotless Mind,* released in 2004. Gondry has also authored several screenplays, and critics agree that Gondry's uniqueness comes from his tendency to approach subjects in a highly individual way.

Mireille Guiliano

Guiliano is a native of France who lives in the United States and has worked for many years in the wine, spirits, and luxury-goods industries. Her book *French Women Don't Get Fat: The Secret of Eating for Pleasure* is a best-selling diet and exercise book based on her experience with French cuisine and lifestyle. The book expresses Guiliano's philosophy on eating and enjoying life sensibly to prevent weight gain, and it is also partly a memoir of the author's life.

Gordon Lightfoot

Lightfoot has been called an unpretentious singer and songwriter, but despite his simple arrangements, his evocative ballads have made him one of the most popular and enduring folk singers of the late twentieth century. He has often sung of Canadian history and culture, and is known for the hundreds of songs he has written both alone and with other artists. In 2003 his lifetime of work was acknowledged by a number of hall of fame inductions and with a tribute album.

Marcia Muller

Novelist Muller has been instrumental in creating an audience for private eye fiction that features a female protagonist. She began writing fiction at the age of twelve, but her career as a successful author emerged slowly. In 1977 Muller created the character of Sharon McCone, a San Francisco legal investigator who differs from some of her counterparts in that she is more apt to use her wits than her gun, and McCone has been featured in more than twenty of her novels. Muller also edited many short-story anthologies with her husband, writer Bill Pronzini, and has collaborated with Pronzini to produce a number of novels. An autobiographical essay by Muller is included in this volume of *CA.*

Eva Sallis

Australian author Sallis is a writer of fiction, nonfiction, and poetry. A frequent traveler to the Middle East, Sallis is fluent in Arabic. She is cofounder of Australians against Racism, an organization that works to increase public awareness and knowledge of the many experiences of refugees and asylum seekers throughout the world. Sallis also served as coeditor, with Sonja Dechian and Heather Miller, of *Dark Dreams: Australian Refugee Stories.* The book is an anthology of thirty-seven stories all written by refugees between the ages of eleven and twenty years old.

Brooke Shields

Actor and author Shields is an award-winning performer in films, on stage, and on television. She has also been a fashion model, a television producer, and frequent celebrity guest on a variety of television programs and specials. In 2003 Shields took on what she considered her most important role: that of mother to daughter Rowan Francis Henchy. After the birth, Shields was confused by her feelings of depression and alienation from her newborn. She was diagnosed with and treated for severe postpartum depression and anxiety. She recounts her experience and her eventual recovery in *Down Came the Rain: My Journey through Postpartum Depression.*

Acknowledgments

Grateful acknowledgment is made to those publishers, photographers, and artists whose work appear with these authors's essays. Following is a list of the copyright holders who have granted us permission to reproduce material in this volume of *CA*. Every effort has been made to trace copyright, but if omissions have been made, please let us know.

Photographs/Art

Muller, Marcia: Photographs courtesy of Marcia Muller. Reproduced by permission.

Muller, Marcia: Photograph by Tom Graves. Reproduced by permission of Tom Graves.

A

ADAMS, Marie 1945-

PERSONAL: Born September 3, 1945, in Gravelbourg, Saskatchewan, Canada; daughter of Neil Bendixon (a mechanic) and Germaine (a homemaker; maiden name, Jeannotte) Bekker; married Rodney Adams, November 3, 1963; children: Lorelei Brown, Jeffrey, Melanie. *Ethnicity:* "Danish-French." *Education:* University of Saskatchewan, B.Ed.; York University, B.A.; University of Toronto, Ed.D., 1996. *Hobbies and other interests:* Travel.

ADDRESSES: Home—520 Sunset Beach Rd., Richmond Hill, Ontario L4E3J7, Canada. *E-mail*—m. adams@aci.on.ca.

CAREER: Educator. Centennial College, Scarborough, Ontario, Canada, professor, 1981—, General Arts and Science coordinator, 1988-95, acting chair, 1992. Parents for Youth, Toronto, group psychotherapist, 1993-98.

WRITINGS:

Our Son, a Stranger: Adoption Breakdown and Its Effects on Parents, McGill-Queens's University Press (Montreal, Quebec, Canada), 2003.

BIOGRAPHICAL AND CRITICAL SOURCES:

ONLINE

Marie Adams Home Page, http://www.marieadams. com (May 30, 2005).

ADAMS, Mary
See PHELPS, Elizabeth Stuart

*   *   *

ALCOVER, Joan 1854-1926

PERSONAL: Born May 3, 1854, in Palma de Mallorca, Spain; died March 26, 1926, in Palma de Mallorca, Spain; married Rosa Pujol i Guarch, 1881 (died, 1887); married Maria del Haro i Rosselló; children: Pere, Teresa, Gaieta, Maria, Pau.

CAREER: Writer.

AWARDS, HONORS: Jocs Florals de Barcelona prize for poetry, 1909; Premi Fastenrath, 1919, for *Poemes bíblics*; the poem "La Balanguera," set to music by Amadeu Vives, became the anthem of Mallorca.

WRITINGS:

Art i literatura, Llibreria L'Avenç (Barcelona, Spain), 1904.
Humanització de l'art i alters escrits, Editorial Moll (Palma de Mallorca, Spain), 1988.

POETRY

Nuevas poesias, Amengual y Muntaner (Palma de Mallorca, Spain), 1892.

Meteoros: poemas, apólogos y cuentos, Juan Gili (Barcelona, Spain), 1901.

Poesies, Oliva de Vilanova (Barcelona, Spain), 1921.

Cap al tard, poesies, Editorial Moll (Palma de Mallorca, Spain), 1941.

Poemes bíblics, Impremta "Mossen Alcover" (Palma de Mallorca, Spain), 1942.

Poesies completes, Biblioteca Selecta (Barcelona, Spain), 1948.

Obres completes, Biblioteca Selecta (Barcelona, Spain), 1951.

Ideari de Joan Alcover, Editorial Moll (Palma de Mallorca, Spain), 1954.

Jardí desolat: antologia poètica, Edicions de la Magrana (Barcelona, Spain), 2000.

Author of prologues to *Joan M. Guasch,* Edicions Lira (Barcelona, Spain), 1924, and *Miguel S. Oliver: Estudio biográfico.* Contributor to literary reviews, including *Revista Balear, Museo Balear,* and *El Isleño.*

Alcover's work has been translated into Spanish, Basque, Italian, and French.

ADAPTATIONS: Alcover's work was put to music by Amadeu Vives and Emili Vendrell and recorded by mezzo soprano Maria del Mar Bonet.

SIDELIGHTS: Joan Alcover was a poet, essayist, and politician. In his poems, written primarily in Catalan, one finds an aesthetic interpretation of the pain he suffered on the death of his wife and children. Like his contemporary Miguel Costa Llobera and other members of the Mallorca school, he found in the Spanish landscape symbolic parallels with his particular states of mind. Nonetheless, he was not attracted by the more extreme elements of modernism but rather identified with the expressive restraint and formal rigor of the incipient movement of Noucentisme and the French movement of Parnassianism.

Alcover's literary theory was based on sincerity of feeling and clarity in poetic form. Some of his poems have been translated into different languages and set to music, including "La Balanguera," which was put to music by Amadeu Vives and which, in 1996, was declared the official anthem of Mallorca. Beginning in 1972 Alcover began publishing poems in both Catalan and in Spanish in the literary reviews *Revista Balear,*

Museo Balear, and *El Isleño.* As a contributor to *Columbia Dictionary of Modern European Literature* wrote, "Like other poets of [Mallorca], Alcover had a true gift of form. . . . Alcover expressed a deeply felt personal bereavement in elegies of consummate beauty."

Mainly concerned with form, meter, rhyme, and strophe, Parnassianism and Noucentisme denied Romanticism's strong emotions and hyperbole. The styles suited the somber group who formed the Catalan Renaissance. Following a period ending around 1900, Alcover abandoned his experiment with bilingualism and devoted himself to expressing himself in Catalan. The death of his daughter Teresa in 1899 also contributed to his evolving an elegiac and sincere form of expression. This sincerity was a hallmark of his entire career as a poet and writer and can be seen in his dedication of an essay on aesthetics, in 1921, to Russian author Leo Tolstoy. In his last collection, *Poemes bíblics,* Alcover probes deeply into the tragedy of the human condition in a series of imagined "visions" by biblical figures. Through the personas of Abigail, Saul, David, Rebecca, and Agar, the collection becomes an expression of the human condition.

BIOGRAPHICAL AND CRITICAL SOURCES:

BOOKS

Columbia Dictionary of Modern European Literature, second edition, Columbia University Press (New York, NY), 1980.

Gayà, Miguel, *Contribució a l'epistolari de Joan Alcover,* Editorial Barcino (Barcelona, Spain), 1964.

PERIODICALS

Catalan Review, June, 1987, Kristine Doll, "Toward a Revaluation of Joan Alcover's Elegies," p. 69.

ONLINE

Catalan Writers Web site, http://www.catalanwriters.com/ (February 28, 2002), biography of Joan Alcover.

Escriptors.com, http://www.escriptors.com/ (February 28, 2002), biography of Joan Alcover.*

AMICK, Steve 1964-

PERSONAL: Born February 16, 1964, in Ann Arbor, MI; son of Bob and Connie Amick; married Sharyl Burau, December 6, 2003. *Education:* St. Lawrence University, B.A.; George Mason University, M.F.A.

ADDRESSES: Home—Ann Arbor, MI. *Agent*—Artists Literary Group, 27 W. 20th St., 10th Fl., New York, NY 10011.

CAREER: Writer. College writing instructor, 1989-93; freelance advertising copywriter, 1995-2004. Also works as an artist, playwright, musician, and songwriter.

AWARDS, HONORS: Dan Rudy Prize, George Mason University, 1989; Clio Award, 1996, for copywriting associated with an advertisement titled "Itchy Satan Jews Gun"; Sokolov scholarship, Bread Loaf Writers' Conference, 1999; Best Playwright, CollaberAction Sketchbook Play Festival (Chicago, IL), 2001; named Ann Arbor's Best Writer, *Current* magazine reader's poll, 2005.

WRITINGS:

(And illustrator of maps) *The Lake, the River & the Other Lake* (novel), Pantheon Books (New York, NY), 2005.

Also contributor of short stories and essays to the periodicals *McSweeney's, Southern Review, New England Review, Playboy, New York Times* and *Story,* and the anthology *The Sound of Writing.*

PLAYS

Jazz Genius (short play), produced in Chicago, IL, 2001.
We Were Soldiers (short play), produced in Chicago, IL, 2002.
Mr. Smarty-Pants (two-act play), produced in Chicago, IL, 2002.

LYRICIST; SOUND RECORDINGS

(With the His Own Worst Enemies) *Your Mother/Dead Horse,* Ratman Records, 1999.
There's Always Pie, 2005.

SIDELIGHTS: Steve Amick's first novel, *The Lake, the River & the Other Lake,* was published in 2005. The book is set in Amick's home state of Michigan, in the fictional town of Weneshkeen, which is located in the state's lower peninsula. Weneshkeen is a resort town, divided between the year-round residents and the tourists who flock to its lakes during the summer. As in all tourist towns, some of the locals resent the dichotomy of being a vacation destination. At the core of Amick's novel is the character Roger Drinkwater, a Native-American Vietnam veteran who has decided not just to complain about the tourists but to fight back. Sick of jet skiers nearly running over him while he takes his morning swim across the lake, he declares a guerrilla war on the jet skiers. "This smart, punchy first novel is a smalltown soap opera," declared a *Publishers Weekly* contributor. The reviewer went on to call the novel "bitterly comic and surprisingly meaty." David A. Berona, in his review of the novel for *Library Journal,* stated: "Amazingly rich and colorful, the writing flows so smoothly that one's only regret might be that the novel has to end."

Amick told *CA:* "I was profoundly inspired by the example of Rob Petrie on *The Dick Van Dyke Show.* I first saw it when I was two or three years old, and Rob Petrie seemed like a great guy with a very pretty wife, who had a lot of fun. Everything he did stemmed from his brain, his creative imagining: the beautiful wife, the lovely home, the cute kid, Ritchie. It seemed like a very admirable way to make a living. You kiss your wife, go into the office, roll up your shirt sleeves, and build something. It was a fun job, but a job. The importance of craft and revision was a key element to all the writers' room scenes, and I really think that demystification—that writing was a process, not ivory tower magic that you wait for—sunk in.

"Additionally, my mother was a grade-school teacher before she got married, so she was very big on reading and telling us simple, true stories about her own youth. Later, I had several very good teachers in the public schools who steered me, pretty early on, toward writing as a possible career.

"The most surprising thing that I have learned as a writer is that specificity leads to universality. It seems counterintuitive, but the more concrete and specific the detail, the more vivid and believable the scene. The reader is then no longer straining to picture it and so can focus all attention on what is going on emotionally.

Therefore, it becomes easier for the reader to empathize and connect—even if the particularities of the characters and events are personally foreign to the reader. I'm amazed by this every time.

"The other thing I've learned, which also surprises me with its simplicity, is the idea that at the heart of the most intriguing and even complex stories, two relative strangers 'make friends.' It sounds hokey, and I'm not saying that's the primary story, but I think there's something basic in our humanity that likes to see this—even if it's just one character acknowledging some fact about the other character that he didn't know at the beginning, or making some offhand joke that shows he remembered something personal about the other. We are, primarily, tribal animals, and I suppose this has something to do with it."

BIOGRAPHICAL AND CRITICAL SOURCES:

PERIODICALS

Kirkus Reviews, February 15, 2005, review of *The Lake, the River & the Other Lake,* p. 187.
Library Journal, April 1, 2005, David A. Berona, review of *The Lake, the River & the Other Lake,* p. 83.
New York Times Books Review, June 5, 2005, review of *The Lake, the River & the Other Lake,* p. 13.
Publishers Weekly, March 14, 2005, review of *The Lake, the River & the Other Lake,* p. 43.
San Francisco Chronicle, May 15, 2005, review of *The Lake, the River & the Other Lake,* p. B2.
Washington Post Book World, June 12, 2005, review of *The Lake, the River & the Other Lake,* p. 6.

ONLINE

Ann Arbor Book Festival Web site, http://www.aabookfestival.org/ (June 24, 2005), brief profile of author.
Steve Amick Home Page, http://www.steve-amick.com (June 24, 2005).
WinningWriters.com, http://www.winningwriters.com/ (June 24, 2005), "2002 War Poetry Contest Finalist: Steve Amick."

*   *   *

ANDERSON, Brian C. 1961-

PERSONAL: Born 1961; married; children: two sons. *Education:* Boston College, B.A., M.A.; University of Ottawa, Ph.D.

ADDRESSES: Home—Westchester County, NY. *Office*—Manhattan Institute, City Journal, 52 Vanderbilt Ave., New York, NY 10017.

CAREER: Writer, editor, and scholar.

American Enterprise Institute, Washington, DC, research associate in social and political studies; *Crisis,* literary editor; Manhattan Institute (think tank), New York, NY, scholar and senior editor of quarterly periodical *City Journal.*

WRITINGS:

POLITICAL SCIENCE

(Editor) *The Pope in America,* Crisis Books (Notre Dame, IN), 1996.
Raymond Aron: The Recovery of the Political, Rowman & Littlefield (Lanham, MD), 1997.
(Editor) Michael Novak, *On Cultivating Liberty,* Rowman & Littlefield (Lanham, MD), 1999.
South Park Conservatives: The Revolt against Liberal Media Bias, Regnery (Washington, DC), 2005.

Contributor to *First Things, Public Interest, Wilson Quarterly, New York Post, New York Daily News, New York Sun, Los Angeles Times, Wall Street Journal,* and *Washington Times.* Author of introduction, with Daniel Mahoney, to *Thinking Politically,* English-language translation of *Le Spectateur Engage* by Raymond Aron. Co-editor of "Aron Project" series, Transaction Publishers, and "Religion, Society, and Politics in the New Millennium" series, Lexington Publishers.

SIDELIGHTS: Brian C. Anderson has long been active in conservative-leaning intellectual circles. He has become well known to many in that milieu as the senior editor of *City Journal,* a New York-based quarterly magazine that focuses on urban policy issues. Anderson's best-known book, *South Park Conservatives: The Revolt against Liberal Media Bias,* is an expanded version of an article titled "We're Not Losing the Culture Wars Anymore," which Anderson wrote for *City Journal* in 2003. The article was described on the *Brothers Judd* Web site as "one of the best pieces of recent years on the rise of a conservative media counter-culture."

The phrase "South Park Republican" originated with Andrew Sullivan, a selectively conservative blogger who used the term to describe people similar to himself: not stereotypical, straight-laced conservatives, but people who have a great disdain for modern liberalism. The moniker refers to a popular animated television series for adults, *South Park,* that was known for tackling serious political issues with aggressively non-politically correct humor. In *South Park Conservatives* Anderson examines the rise of television programs such as *South Park* and other media with an anti-liberal bent, including Fox News; Regnery, a publishing house that focuses on books by conservative authors; popular right-wing radio talk-show host Rush Limbaugh; programs hosted by comedians Dennis Miller and Colin Quinn; and the well-read conservative and libertarian "blogosphere," including Glenn Reynolds's *Instapundit* and Scott Ott's satiric *Scrappleface.* "The book offers a fascinating history of the rise of these more conservative media outlets," noted a reviewer on the *Brothers Judd* Web site. Mark Radulich, writing for the *Pop and Politics* Web site, stated that the book also functions as "a who's who guide to new conservatism in mainstream news and politics." *Weekly Standard* contributor Jordan Fabian praised *South Park Conservatives* as "more than just the run of the mill liberals-control-the-media shtick. Anderson's reporting style . . . and articulate judgments make his book a quick and refreshing read."

Anderson is also the author of *Raymond Aron: The Recovery of the Political,* an examination of the political philosophies of the mid-twentieth-century French thinker. Although Aron's works remain popular in his native country, it is little known in the United States. "Writing with great clarity of style from a stance of interpretive charity, Anderson helps us to sort out Aron's enormous oeuvre," Jean Bethke Elshtain explained in *First Things.* Aron was reluctant to espouse one particular, concrete political philosophy, particularly Stalinism (which he soundly rejected) or the purportedly anti-political literary philosophies of Jean-Paul Sartre and some of Aron's other French contemporaries. Anderson explains this reluctance as the logical result of Aron's belief that human beings cannot know enough about the way in which society works to fashion the perfect world envisioned by many such theorists. Elshtain went on to comment Anderson's "discussion of Aron's 'critique of ideology' contains powerful moments, as does Anderson's unpacking of one of Aron's chief passions and

concerns, the world of international and diplomatic relations." *Review of Politics* contributor Sanford Lakoff also praised *Raymond Aron* as being written "with considerable skill and nuance."

BIOGRAPHICAL AND CRITICAL SOURCES:

PERIODICALS

First Things, November, 1998, Jean Bethke Elshtain, review of *Raymond Aron: The Recovery of the Political,* p. 52.

Review of Politics, fall, 1998, Sanford Lakoff, review of *Raymond Aron,* p. 799.

Weekly Standard, May 9, 2005, Jordan Fabian, review of *South Park Conservatives: The Revolt against Liberal Media Bias,* p. 43.

ONLINE

Brothers Judd Web site, http://www.brothersjudd.com/ (April 15, 2005), review of *South Park Conservatives,* and interview with author.

Manhattan Institute for Policy Research Web site, http://www.manhattan-institute.org/ (June 24, 2005), "Brian C. Anderson."

Pop and Politics Web site, http://www.popandpolitics.com/ (April 22, 2005), Mark Radulich, review of *South Park Conservatives.*

*   *   *

ANTHONY, Carl Sferrazza

PERSONAL: Male.

ADDRESSES: Home—Los Angeles, CA. *Agent*—c/o Author Mail, William Morrow & Company, 10 E. 53rd St., 7th Fl., New York, NY 10022.

CAREER: Writer and editor. Former speechwriter for First Lady Nancy Reagan, 1985-86; *George* magazine, former contributing editor. Producer, *The Reagans* (Television film), 2003.

WRITINGS:

First Ladies: The Saga of the Presidents' Wives and Their Power, William Morrow (New York, NY), Volume 1: *1789-1961,* 1990, Volume 2: *1961-1990,* 1991.

America's Most Influential First Ladies, foreword by Betty Ford, Oliver Press (Minneapolis, MN), 1992, revised edition, Oliver Press (Minneapolis, MN), 2003.

As We Remember Her: Jacqueline Kennedy Onassis, in the Words of Her Family and Friends, Harper-Collins (New York, NY), 1997.

Florence Harding: The First Lady, the Jazz Age, and the Death of America's Most Scandalous President, William Morrow (New York, NY), 1998.

America's First Families: An Inside View of Two Hundred Years of Private Life in the White House, Touchstone (New York, NY), 2000.

The Kennedy White House: Family Life and Pictures, 1961-1963, Simon & Schuster (New York, NY), 2001.

(Editor) *"This Elevated Position—": A Catalogue and Guide to the National First Ladies' Library and the Importance of First Lady History,* National First Ladies' Library (Canton, OH), 2003.

Heads of State, Bloomsbury (New York, NY), 2004.

Nellie Taft: The Unconventional First Lady of the Ragtime Era, William Morrow (New York, NY), 2005.

Contributor to *New York Times, Los Angeles Times, Washington Post, Vanity Fair, American Heritage, Smithsonian, American Heritage,* and *Town and Country.* Also author of screenplays; contributor to television movie *The Reagans,* 2003.

SIDELIGHTS: Carl Sferrazza Anthony is the author of numerous books about the men and women who have inhabited the White House, from Martha Washington to Hillary Rodham Clinton. His first book, *First Ladies: The Saga of the Presidents' Wives and Their Power,* is a two-volume set that examines every first lady from 1789 to 1990. Anthony provides biographies of the women, but also focuses on their role in the political process and the often unrecognized power that first ladies possess and have frequently used. "The author makes history entertaining," Genevieve Stut-

taford noted in a *Publishers Weekly* review of the first volume, yet still "provides a comprehensive, instructive view" of his subjects.

Anthony is also the author of in-depth biographies of individual first ladies, including Florence Harding and Nellie Taft. Both early-twentieth-century first ladies are notable for being powerful forces in their own right and for working hard to help their sometimes-reluctant husbands attain the highest political office in the country. In *Florence Harding: The First Lady, the Jazz Age, and the Death of America's Most Scandalous President* Anthony digs deeply into the infamous personal lives of both Florence and her husband, President Warren G. Harding. Before she married Harding, Florence had an illegitimate baby, was divorced, and had been a self-supporting single mother; for his part, Warren seduced Florence's female friends and fathered two illegitimate children of his own. It was Florence's ambition that pushed Warren into the presidency, and presidential historians have generally concluded that he was not well suited for the office. He "ran the country during a time of baroque corruption and excess that the book also engagingly chronicles," Gina Bellafante noted in *Time.* Florence, however, took to her role as first lady with a progressive spirit: she held pioneering press conferences for female reporters, helped to bring about the creation of a separate federal prison system for women, and supported civil rights for women and minorities. In this "massive, incredibly detailed study of the Hardings," as Edward Goedeken described the 660-page work in *Library Journal,* Anthony also acquits Florence of the long-standing rumor that she poisoned her husband. Instead, Anthony attributes Harding's fatal 1923 heart attack to the family's dependence on homeopathic medicine. *Florence Harding* is a "riveting, defining biography of the indefatigable spouse of the twenty-ninth president," Brad Hooper concluded in *Booklist.*

Anthony takes on Taft in *Nellie Taft: The Unconventional First Lady of the Ragtime Era.* Like Florence Harding, Taft's behavior scandalized some in Washington: she drank beer, smoked cigarettes, and played cards. Taft also espoused progressive causes, particularly women's rights, during her time as first lady, but she was hampered in her efforts by a crippling stroke she suffered during her husband's first year in office. "The best part of [Anthony's] narrative covers Taft's successful quest for recovery," wrote a *Publishers Weekly* contributor. A *Kirkus Reviews* critic deemed

Nellie Taft "a pleasing biography" and "a vivid portrait" of this first lady.

America's First Families: An Inside View of Two Hundred Years of Private Life in the White House was published at the time of the two-hundredth anniversary of the White House's construction. In thematically arranged chapters, Anthony discusses the ways first families, from John and Abigail Adams to Bill and Hillary Clinton, navigated Inauguration Day, family relationships, and the constant struggle to maintain some semblance of privacy while living in the very public White House. "Drawing on extensive research, the author provides a wealth of entertaining anecdotes and trivia," noted a *Publishers Weekly* contributor, adding that Anthony's "intimate miscellany" is "great for browsing."

In the years after former First Lady Jacqueline Kennedy Onassis's death from cancer in 1994, Anthony published two books looking back on her life and her years in the White House: *As We Remember Her: Jacqueline Kennedy Onassis, in the Words of Her Family and Friends* and *The Kennedy White House: Family Life and Pictures, 1961-1963.* The latter book is notable for the many previously unpublished pictures among its 300 photographs, mostly candid shots of Kennedy Onassis, President John F. Kennedy, and their children relaxing and playing like any other family. In the accompanying "sensitive yet revealing narrative," as Jill Ortner described it in *Library Journal,* Anthony provides an equally intimate picture of the Kennedy's family life, discussing the way they spent their vacations and holidays and how they chose to raise their children. It is "a domestically detailed and staunchly apolitical history," declared a *Publishers Weekly* contributor.

BIOGRAPHICAL AND CRITICAL SOURCES:

PERIODICALS

Booklist, May 1, 1998, Brad Hooper, review of *Florence Harding: The First Lady, the Jazz Age, and the Death of America's Most Scandalous President,* p. 1496; January 1, 1999, review of *Florence Harding,* p. 776; November 1, 2000, Vanessa Bush, review of *America's First Families: An Inside View of Two Hundred Years of Private Life in the White House,* p. 513.

Entertainment Weekly, July 24, 1998, Megan Harlan, review of *Florence Harding,* p. 70.
Kirkus Reviews, July 15, 2001, review of *The Kennedy White House: Family Life and Pictures, 1961-1963,* p. 989; February 15, 2003, review of *Nellie Taft: The Unconventional First Lady of the Ragtime Era,* p. 205.
Library Journal, May 1, 1998, Edward Goedeken, review of *Florence Harding,* p. 110; October 1, 2000, Jill Ortner, review of *America's First Families,* p. 120; August, 2001, Jill Ortner, review of *The Kennedy White House,* p. 130; April 1, 2005, Cynthia Harrison, review of *Nellie Taft: The Unconventional First Lady of the Ragtime Era,* p. 103.
Publishers Weekly, July 13, 1990, Genevieve Stuttaford, review of *First Ladies: The Saga of the Presidents' Wives and Their Power, 1789-1961,* p. 48; March 8, 1991, Genevieve Stuttaford, review of *First Ladies: The Saga of the Presidents' Wives and Their Power, 1961-1990,* p. 64; April 13, 1998, review of *Florence Harding,* p. 58; October 23, 2000, review of *America's First Families,* p. 67; October 29, 2001, review of *The Kennedy White House,* p. 57; February 28, 2005, review of *Nellie Taft,* p. 55.
Time, July 20, 1998, Ginia Bellafante, review of *Florence Harding,* p. 65.

ONLINE

Triangle.com, http://www.triangle.com/ (April 24, 2005), Gil Troy, "Thoroughly Pre-Modern Nellie."
Washingtonian Online, http://www.washingtonian.com/ (June 24, 2005), Courtney Rubin, review of *America's First Families.**

*   *   *

ARDEN, William
See LYNDS, Dennis

*   *   *

ARMSTRONG, Kevin D. 1973-

PERSONAL: Born August 15, 1973, in Kingston, Ontario, Canada; son of Paul (a cardiologist) and Beverly (a teacher; maiden name, Dawson) Armstrong. *Ethnicity:* "Anglo." *Education:* Queen's University,

B.A., 1996, master's certificate, 1998. *Religion:* "Miscellaneous." *Hobbies and other interests:* Windsurfing, music, wine.

ADDRESSES: Home—115 Osland Dr., Edmonton, Alberta T6R 2A2, Canada. *Agent*—Denise Bukowski, The Bukowski Agency, 14 Prince Arthur Ave., Toronto, Ontario M5R 1A9, Canada. *E-mail*—kevarm@telus. net.

CAREER: Writer. First mate on sailing yacht, 1997-98, 2000-01.

AWARDS, HONORS: Western Magazine Award, Western Magazine Association, 2001, and Journey Prize, Canadian Writer's Trust/McClelland and Stewart, 2001, both for "The Cane Field."

WRITINGS:

Night Watch (short stories), Penguin Putnam (New York, NY), 2002.

WORK IN PROGRESS: A novel set in Micronesia.

SIDELIGHTS: Kevin D. Armstrong told *CA:* "My primary motivations for writing? Giving characters the freedom to act—for better or worse—without my own moral or fearful constraints, and hoping their experience teaches me something. Travel inspires through paradox: each individual and culture is unique, yet I find a universality of human struggle and desire. Story crystallizes this axiom, and, among other things, facilitates further communication. My chosen subjects stem from experiences I have witnessed/heard about that open the door to character and the narrative each one subsequently chooses. Usually, I start with some vague objective in mind: getting there provides the challenges and the excitement, because this objective often changes the nearer to the end I get."

BIOGRAPHICAL AND CRITICAL SOURCES:

PERIODICALS

Booklist, July, 2003, Carrie Bissey, review of *Night Watch,* p. 1862.

Kirkus Reviews, June 15, 2003, review of *Night Watch,* p. 817.
Publishers Weekly, July 28, 2003, review of *Night Watch,* p. 78.

*   *   *

ASHER, Neal 1961-
(Neal L. Asher)

PERSONAL: Born 1961, in Billericay, Essex, England; married; wife's name, Caroline.

ADDRESSES: Home—Essex, England. *Agent*—c/o Author Mail, Tor Books, 175 5th Ave., New York, NY 10010.

CAREER: Author. Also worked as milling machine operator and programmer of computerized machine tools, 1979-87; worked in landscaping, 1987-2003.

AWARDS, HONORS: British Fantasy Society Award nominatee, 1999, for stories "Sucker" and "Mason's Rats III"; *SF Review* Best Book designation, 2002, for *The Skinner.*

WRITINGS:

FICTION

Mindgames: Fool's Mate (novella), Gordon McGregor Paperback, 1992.
The Parasite (novella), Tanjen (Leicester, England), 1996.
The Engineer (short story collection), Tanjen (Leicester England), 1998.
Mason's Rats (short story collection), Kimota Publishing (Preston, England), 1999.
Runcible Tales (short story collection), Piper's Ash (Chippenham, Wiltshire, England), 1999.
Africa Zero (novella), Cosmos Books, 2001.
Gridlinked (novel), Pan Macmillan (London, England), 2001, Tor Books (New York, NY), 2003.
The Skinner (novel), Pan Macmillan (London, England), 2002, Tor Books (New York, NY), 2004.
The Line of Polity (novel), Pan Macmillan (London, England), 2003.

Cowl, Tor Books (London, England), 2004 Tor Books (New York, NY), 2005.

Brass Man (novel), Tor Books (London, England), 2005.

The Voyage of the Sable Keech (novel), Tor Books (London, England), 2006.

Contributor of short stories to numerous magazines, and to the anthology, *Spectrum 8.*

Asher's work has been translated into German.

SIDELIGHTS: British science-fiction and fantasy author Neal Asher worked variously as a machinist and gardener while his short stories and novellas were published in magazines and small-press editions in England. In 2000 all that changed with a three-book contract that resulted in a loose trilogy of novels comprised of *Gridlinked, The Line of Polity,* and *Brass Man.* Other novels by Asher include *Cowl* and *The Skinner.* Eventually published in the United States, Asher's stories and novels, set in different worlds and often involving time travel and confrontations with aliens, are, according to Duncan Lawie writing for *The Zone,* "highly readable, fast paced and gripping books with subtly complex plots and well realised settings." They also include a great deal of violence; not only are humans ripped apart, but their robotic artificial-intelligence (AI) partners also meet unpleasant fates.

Beginning his writing career as a teenager, Asher published his first short story in 1989. Novellas and short story collections made up his published work until publication of *Gridlinked* in 2001. These more recent short stories provided inspiration for many of Asher's novels. For example, the idea of the Runcible, a teleportation mechanism, was introduced in *Runcible Tales,* and later reprised for the novels *Gridlinked* and *The Line of Polity.* The novel *The Skinner* owes its plot to "Scatterjay" and "Snairls," two stories in the collection *The Engineer.* The title novella of this collection is about the galactic recovery of an ancient escape pod from a long-dead civilization. When put into some water, the crab-like occupant of the pod begins to create elaborate nanotechnology instruments looking exactly like humans. These human reproductions also have a built-in memory of a huge selection of now-ancient videos. The same collection also introduces Polity, an empire in a far-distant universe that has also been used in Asher's novels. John D. Owen, reviewing

The Engineer for *Infinity Plus* online, presciently stated: "If Asher could flesh out his stories into full-blown works, I'm sure that he would find himself many more readers."

In *Gridlinked* Asher posits Polity, an interstellar government in the distant future that rules the universe in a basically benevolent manner. When separatist terrorists on the planet Cheyne III rebel against the central government, it is the job of super agent Ian Cormac of Earth Central Security to infiltrate the terrorist network and put an end to their bombings. In Cormac's attempts to stop the group, the sister of the terrorist leader, Arian Pelter, is killed. Then Cormac is summoned to an even more urgent mission. Traveling through the teleporting "runcible" machine, he arrives at the planet Samarkand, where the entire population has been killed. Here Cormac has to deal with the ancient and powerful Dragon, and combat psychopaths, mercenaries, and androids while investigating the cause of this planetary holocaust. Meanwhile, he also has to watch his back against the vengeance-seeking terrorist Pelter. Throughout the novel, the emphasis is on action. As Asher told Lawie, "What kind of fiction am I writing? I'm writing action-centred science fiction with big boys' toys and alien creatures and so forth. I don't want to get that wrapped up in the psychology."

Lisa DuMond, writing for *SFSite.com,* praised the "gritty, gloves-off voice" of *Gridlinked* and described action-hero Cormac as "a battle-scarred veteran, an almost indestructible agent for the Polity, his abilities almost super-human." This amazing ability is partly the result of Cormac being "gridlinked," that is, connected to the AI that runs the entire society. Cormac has been gridlinked for far longer than is recommended; on his mission to Samarkand, he goes off the link and attempts to also regain part of his humanity. Shaun Green, writing for *Yet Another Book Review Web site,* found *Gridlinked* a "highly enjoyable read, and [it] serves as an excellent introduction to the Polity." Green also noted that Asher "has flung all of the requisite elements of a dynamic and highly enjoyable space opera into this novel."

The world of Polity and the adventures of Cormac are continued in *The Line of Polity* and *Brass Man.* Tomas L. Martin, writing in *SF Crows Nest* online, called the second novel in the series, a hefty 663-page book, "lengthy but satisfying." The scope is far wider in *The*

Line of Polity than in *Gridlinked.* Here Cormac is on the trail of a larger-than-life villain named Skellor. However, once again Cormac's initial mission is curtailed when he receives word that his old nemesis, Dragon, has been spotted near the planet Masada, where a revolt against the ruling clergy is brewing. Cormac sets off in a spaceship for the distant planet and a battle with the powerful alien, not suspecting that his enemy Skellor has stowed away on the same ship and is now fortified by nanotechnology and AI, making him a deadly rival for Cormac. Martin went on to call *The Line of Polity* "a compelling story." Similarly, Graham Connor, reviewing the same novel for *Concatenation* online described it as "purist escape," and also noted that the book is "fast paced with a clean, if somewhat violent style." Asher's third book about Polity, *Brass Man,* appeared in 2005, and once again Cormac is on the trail of the bad guys. Skellor returns in this novel as one of those malevolent characters, as is Mr. Crane, a golem whose brass armor gives the book its title. Writing for the online *Agony Column Book Reviews and Commentary,* Rick Kleffel called *Brass Man* "grand science fiction adventure, bristling with ideas, action, excitement and wit." Martin, writing in *SF Crows Nest,* dubbed the same novel an "exhilarating new space epic."

With *The Skinner* Asher deals with a separate world, the planet Spatterjay, where a virus has made all life forms able to resist any damage and gives them virtual immortality. The planet, mostly water, is ruled by the Old Captains, and life forms include a grisly assortment, including giant leeches. Three visitors arrive on this planet, one of whom is Keech, a long-dead policeman kept alive cybernetically. Keech hopes to track down a group of pirates. Erlin is another arrival; infected by the Spatterjay virus, she is also in effect immortal and has come looking for one of the Old Captains. The third visitor is Janer, employed by a hornet hive mind. These three, however, have little idea of the malevolence awaiting them on Spatterjay. A *Publishers Weekly* reviewer found *The Skinner* a "rousing space opera," and also noted: "Asher will definitely appeal to connoisseurs of sophisticated adventure-oriented SF." More praise came from Regina Schroeder, writing for *Booklist,* who felt "Asher beautifully realizes the background to this wild adventure." A critic for *Kirkus Reviews* concluded: "The whole impressive, ingenious enterprise hurtles along at a high-octane clip while swinging with nonchalant abandon between horror and comedy." Keech, from *The Skinner,* is reprised in the 2006 title, *The Voyage of the Sable Keech.*

Asher presents a stand-alone title with *Cowl,* a time-travel book with a twist. Set in the future, the novel opens amid a war between two super-human races, the Umbrathane and the Heliothane. Cowl, a modified Heliothane, has changed sides, and is sent back in time by the Umbrathanes. The Heliothanes now want to kill Cowl, and thus he faces not only enemies in the past worlds he travels through, but also from his own time. One of these threats is Tack, a programmed assassin, sent by the Heliothanes. A critic for *Kirkus Reviews* commended the "crackling energy and slam-bang action" of the novel, but also noted that "absent noteworthy or appealing characters, [it is] hard to care about what comes next." Other reviewers had less-qualified praise. A contributor for *Publishers Weekly,* for example, called *Cowl* "an excellent read," and further noted that the title "should increase the author's growing reputation." Jackie Cassada, writing for *Library Journal,* concluded that "fans of techno-military sf should find this tale satisfying."

BIOGRAPHICAL AND CRITICAL SOURCES:

PERIODICALS

Booklist, February 15, 2004, Regina Schroeder, review of *The Skinner,* p. 1047.
Entertainment Weekly, April 23, 2004, Noah Robischon, "SF 101," review of *The Skinner,* p. 86.
Kirkus Reviews, December 15, 2003, review of *The Skinner,* p. 1492; March 15, 2005, review of *Cowl,* p. 322.
Library Journal, May 15, 2005, Jackie Cassada, review of *Cowl,* p. 111.
Publishers Weekly, January 26, 2004, review of *The Skinner,* p. 235; April 4, 2005, review of *Cowl,* p. 47.

ONLINE

Agony Column Reviews and Commentary, http://trashotron.com/agony/ (April 14, 2005), Rick Kleffel, review of *Brass Man.*
AuthorTrek.com, http://www.authortrek.com/ (August 11, 2005), Kevin Patrick Mahoney, "Neal L. Asher Interview."
ComputerCrowsNest.com, http://www.computercrows nest.com/ (August 11, 2005), Tomas L. Martin, "Neal Asher Interview."

Concatenation Web site, http://www.concatenation.org/ (August 11, 2005), Graham Connor, review of *The Line of Polity.*

Infinity Plus, http://www.infinityplus.co.uk/ (July 11, 1998), John D. Owen, review of *The Engineer.*

Neal Asher Home Page, http://www.nealasher.com (August 11, 2005).

SF Crows Nest, http://www.sfcrowsnest.com/ (August 11, 2005), Tomas L. Martin, review of *The Line of Polity;* Tomas L. Martin, review of *Brass Man.*

SFSite.com, http://www.sfsite.com/ (August 11, 2005), Lisa DuMond, "A Conversation with Neal Asher."

Yet Another Book Review Web site, http://www.yetanotherbookreview.com/ (August 11, 2005), Shaun Green, review of *Gridlinked.*

Zone, http://www.zone-sf.com/ (August 11, 2005), Duncan Lawie, "Neal Asher: A Couple of Pints at the Quart Pot."*

*   *   *

ASHER, Neal L.
See ASHER, Neal

*   *   *

ASLAN, Reza

PERSONAL: Born in Iran; immigrated to United States. *Education:* Santa Clara University, B.A.; Harvard University, Master of Theological Studies; University of Iowa, M.F.A.; University of California, Santa Barbara, doctoral candidate. *Religion:* Islam.

ADDRESSES: Home—Santa Barbara, CA; New Orleans, LA. *Agent*—c/o Author Mail, Random House, 1745 Broadway, New York, NY 10019. *E-mail*—contact@rezaaslan.com.

CAREER: Writer. Friends' Committee on National Legislation, Washington, DC, former legislative assistant; University of Iowa, Iowa City, former visiting assistant professor of Islamic and Middle East studies; Iowa Writers' Workshop, former Truman Capote fellow in fiction.

MEMBER: World Conference on Religion and Peace (president of Harvard chapter).

WRITINGS:

No God but God: The Origins, Evolution, and Future of Islam, Random House (New York, NY), 2005.

Contributor to popular and scholarly periodicals.

SIDELIGHTS: Reza Aslan, an Iranian who now lives in the United States, is the author of *No God but God: The Origins, Evolution, and Future of Islam.* The book sprang from the classes Aslan taught about religion in general and Islam in particular at the University of Iowa. "I was genuinely surprised at how popular these courses were and the hunger that people had to learn about the things I was talking about," particularly after the September 11 terrorist attacks, Aslan told *Blog Critics.org* interviewer Keith Gottschalk. *No God but God* was written in part to help non-Muslim Americans understand Islam, but the book also has another purpose. As Aslan explained to Gottschalk, the book is also written for "first and second generation Muslims growing up in America as I did. . . . I wanted to explain to them that Islam is not an exotic religion of the past but a modern religion that can be adaptable."

Aslan starts at the beginning of the history of Islam, explaining what religious life was like in the Middle East before Mohammed, and then continues through to the present day. However, he reads the most recent two centuries of Muslim history differently than many scholars. To Aslan, the Western colonization of Muslim lands in the 1800s sparked a "Reformation" in Islam, as the residents and rulers of these Muslim lands were forced to confront the technological superiority of Western Christian countries. Aslan sees the recent spate of terrorism, ostensibly aimed at Western nations, as a continuation of this intrafaith struggle between Islam's conservative and modernizing factions. Aslan concludes the book with a plea for Muslims to endorse the progressive side of Islam and for Middle Eastern countries to embrace a Muslim form of democracy.

Aslan makes several arguments that may not sit well with more conservative modern Muslims. He blames the current conservative state of Islam on the clerical establishment, which, he claims, perverted the original Muslim state Mohammed established in Medina. According to Aslan, this community was progressive, egalitarian, and tolerant, a state of affairs Aslan says is well supported by the Quran. However, in the decades after Mohammed's death 700,000 "hadith"—brief stories that purport to record events in Mohammed's life and things he said—were created. Most of these hadith, Aslan argues, "were unquestionably fabricated by individuals who sought to legitimize their own particular beliefs and practices by connecting them with the Prophet." Aslan places the roots of the misogyny of modern Islam, for example, squarely in these apocryphal hadith. Thus, he argues, the progressive side of the current intra-Muslim struggle conforms more closely to the faith's original ideals.

Although *No God but God* is a work of history, Aslan's background as a fiction writer is apparent in his use of "vivid details and like-you-were-there, present-tense narration," John Green noted in *Booklist*. *Houston Chronicle* contributor William Grimes also commented on Aslan's writing skill, praising *No God but God* as "grippingly narrated and thoughtfully examined . . . a literate, accessible introduction to Islam."

BIOGRAPHICAL AND CRITICAL SOURCES:

BOOKS

Aslan, Reza, *No God but God: The Origins, Evolution, and Future of Islam,* Random House (New York, NY), 2005.

PERIODICALS

Booklist, March 1, 2005, John Green, review of *No God but God: The Origins, Evolution, and Future of Islam,* p. 1114.
Houston Chronicle, May 27, 2005, William Grimes, "Struggle for Islam's Soul: Is the West a Bystander in an Internal Religious Rivalry?"
Library Journal, March 1, 2005, Gary P. Gillum, review of *No God but God,* p. 90.
Publishers Weekly, February 14, 2005, review of *No God but God,* p. 73.

ONLINE

Agonist, http://www.agonist.org/ (April 29, 2005), Sean-Paul Kelley, interview with Aslan.

Alternet, http://www.alternet.org/ (April 28, 2005), Lakshmi Chaudhry, "The Future of Islam."
Blog Critics.org, http://blogcritics.org/ (April 8, 2005), Keith Gottschalk, interview with Aslan.
Reza Aslan Home Page, http://www.rezaaslan.com (June 24, 2005).*

*   *   *

AUSEON, Andrew 1976-

PERSONAL: Born 1976, in Columbus, OH; married Sarah Zogby; children: Samara Ruth. *Education:* Ohio University, B.A. (creative writing); Vermont College, M.F.A. (creative writing for children and young adults). *Hobbies and other interests:* Travel.

ADDRESSES: Home—Baltimore, MD. *Agent*—c/o Author Mail, Harcourt International, 6277 Sea Harbor Dr., Orlando, FL 32887.

CAREER: Writer. PhotoAssist, Inc., photo editor, 1999-2002; The History Factory, senior researcher, 2002-04; Words & Numbers, Baltimore, MD, currently editor and staff writer.

MEMBER: Society of Children's Book Writers and Illustrators.

WRITINGS:

Funny Little Monkey, Harcourt (Orlando, FL), 2005.

SIDELIGHTS: An M.F.A. graduate of Vermont College who has traveled to over twenty countries, Andrew Auseon published his first book, the young-adult novel *Funny Little Monkey,* in 2005.

In what a *Publishers Weekly* reviewer called a "darkly comic debut novel," Auseon introduces readers to mild-mannered main character Arty Moore. Arty is mere shadow in contrast to his much larger and quite intimidating twin brother Kurt. Raised by a single mother, with a father who serves as a poor role model in his career as a bank robber, the boys have always found themselves at odds. Now, as a freshman at Millard Fillmore High, Arty's luck seems to be changing when he makes two new friends: the beautiful, wealthy overachiever Leslie Dermott, and Kerouac, the ringleader of a rebellious group of kids. With his friends' help, Arty is able to finally put his bullying brother in his place, while at the same time adjusting to life in high school. The *Publishers Weekly* critic wrote that Auseon "taps into the painful experience of high school, leavened with healthy doses of hyperbole, hope and wry humor," while Susan W. Hunter noted in *School Library Journal* that Arty "steps up and uses an outrageous fabrication to resolve the final crisis in this offbeat coming-of-age story."

BIOGRAPHICAL AND CRITICAL SOURCES:

PERIODICALS

Booklist, April 15, 2005, Jennifer Hubert, review of *Funny Little Monkey,* p. 1447.
Columbus Dispatch, November 6, 2005, Nancy Gilson, "Novel Explores Sophomoric Cruelty of High School."
Kirkus Reviews, June 1, 2005, review of *Funny Little Monkey,* p. 632.
Publishers Weekly, July 11, 2005, review of *Funny Little Monkey,* p. 94.
School Library Journal, June, 2005, Susan W. Hunter, review of *Funny Little Monkey,* p. 147.
Voice of Youth Advocates, June, 2005, Jazmine Nazek, review of *Funny Little Monkey,* p. 133.

ONLINE

Andrew Auseon Home Page, http://www.andrew auseon.com (November 6, 2005).

*   *   *

AUSLANDER, Shalom

PERSONAL: Male; married; children: one.

ADDRESSES: Agent—c/o Author Mail, Simon & Schuster, 1230 Avenue of the Americas, New York, NY 10020. *E-mail*—shalom@shalomauslander.com.

CAREER: Writer. Former advertising copy writer, now an advertising executive.

WRITINGS:

(With Jerry Beck) *I Tawt I Taw a Puddy Tat: Fifty Years of Sylvester and Tweety,* Henry Holt (New York, NY), 1991.
Beware of God (short stories), Simon & Schuster (New York, NY), 2005.

Contributor to *This American Life,* for National Public Radio.

WORK IN PROGRESS: A memoir, tentatively titled *Serving Time in the Big House of the Lord.*

SIDELIGHTS: Shalom Auslander drew on his childhood in an Orthodox Jewish family and his subsequent rejection of that culture for his first book of short stories, *Beware of God.* "It wasn't religion that made me leave," he explained to *Next Book* online interviewer Sara Ivry, "and it wasn't just family. It was a combination of being in something of a stereotypical but also rather dysfunctional family, combined with a religion, or a form of a religion, that allowed for nothing."

The fourteen stories in *Beware of God* are surrealist satires of devout Jewish belief that "investigate the meaning of faith and spirituality while making the reader laugh out loud," according to Megan Walton for *Bookslut.com.* In "God Is a Big Happy Chicken," the late Yankel Morgenstern enters heaven and finds that, as the title suggests, God is a thirty-foot-tall, perfectly content chicken. "The Metamorphosis" features a young yeshiva student who wakes up to find himself inhabiting a very large, very hairy, and very definitely gentile body. A modern man is commanded to build an ark in "Prophet's Dilemma" and, to his surprise, finds the project much easier than it seems. Home Depot sells everything he needs, and "there was absolutely nothing you could tell Home Depot Man you were building that would surprise him, that would get any reaction from him at all, for that matter, aside from the usual skepticism about your choice of building materials."

Other stories wonder what would happen if members of the animal kingdom found religion. For the title character of "Bobo the Self-Hating Chimp," the realization that he feels shame totally shatters him. In "Waiting for Joe" two pious hamsters believe that their owner will return and take care of them if they worship him the right way, but they are unable to agree on what the right way is. This theme of religious strife reappears in "It Ain't Easy Bein' Supremey," about two golems who, instead of making their creator's life easier as he had intended, fight constantly about the true meaning of his commands to them. *Small Spiral Notebook* online contributor Katie Weekley declared "It Ain't Easy Bein' Supremey" to be "one of the funniest stories in the collection."

One of the most commented-upon tales in *Beware of God* is "Holocaust Tips for Kids," written from the perspective of a modern-day child who is frightened that the Nazis will return but who resolutely plans how to escape and survive if they do. A *Kirkus Reviews* contributor described this piece as "a marvelously twisted catalogue of grisly historical facts mixed with juvenile naivete and fear," and *Onion A.V. Club* reviewer Tasha Robinson thought that "*Beware of God* hits its high mark with 'Holocaust Tips for Kids.'" Robinson continued: "Auslander is a clever, sharp writer. . . . In his better stories, he clearly illustrates how people let beliefs get in the way of their understanding, and at his absolute best, he shows how much emotional harm that lack of understanding can cause."

Although many of Auslander's tales are likely to be disquieting to devout believers, Auslander insists that he is not as anti-God as his title might indicate. "I do [believe in God]," he told Ivry, "because I don't want not to. . . . I have a hard time believing the opposite, believing that me and my wife finding each other and our love and our child are accidents. It would be hard to live thinking that things are that random."

BIOGRAPHICAL AND CRITICAL SOURCES:

BOOKS

Auslander, Shalom, *Beware of God,* Simon & Schuster (New York, NY), 2005.

PERIODICALS

Booklist, March 1, 2005, Debi Lewis, review of *Beware of God,* p. 1140.
Kirkus Reviews, January 15, 2005, review of *Beware of God,* p. 63.
Publishers Weekly, February 28, 2005, review of *Beware of God,* p. 42.
Tikkun, May-June, 2005, review of *Beware of God,* p. 81.

ONLINE

Bookslut.com, http://www.bookslut.com/ (April, 2005), Megan Walton, review of *Beware of God.*
Jewish.com, http://jewish.com/ (April 5, 2005), Lawrence Goodman, review of *Beware of God.*
Next Book, http://www.nextbook.org/ (March 24, 2005), Sara Ivry, "Dogs and Monsters."
Onion A.V. Club Web site, http://www.theonionavclub.com/ (March 30, 2005), Tasha Robinson, review of *Beware of God.*
Shalom Auslander Home Page, http://www.shalomauslander.com (June 24, 2005).
Small Spiral Notebook, http://www.smallspiralnotebook.com/ (June 24, 2005), Katie Weekley, review of *Beware of God.*

B

BAILEY, Jerry 1957-

PERSONAL: Born August 29, 1957, in Dallas, TX; married.

ADDRESSES: Office—c/o Jockeys Guild, 250 W. Main St., Lexington, KY 40507-1714. *E-mail*—info@ jerrybailey.com.

CAREER: Professional jockey, beginning 1974.

AWARDS, HONORS: Winner of Belmont Stakes, 1991, riding Hansel, 2003, riding Empire Maker; winner of Preakness Stakes, 1991, riding Hansel, 2000, riding Red Bullet; George Woolf Award, Jockey's Guild, 1992; Mike Venezia Award, New York Racing Association, 1993; winner of Kentucky Derby, 1993, riding Sea Hero, 1997, riding Grindstone; named to Racing Hall of Fame, 1995.

WRITINGS:

(With Tom Pedulla) *Against the Odds: Riding for My Life* (autobiography), G.P. Putnam's Sons (New York, NY), 2005.

SIDELIGHTS: In *Against the Odds: Riding for My Life,* explained a *Kirkus Reviews* contributor, "An ace jockey gives a sincere, straightforward account of his alcoholism and his sensational career." That jockey, Jerry Bailey, describes his lifelong appreciation of horses and riding and the early success he achieved as a jockey in his autobiography, but he also discusses the alcoholism that held him back from achieving true greatness in the sport. Justifiably fearful that owners would not let him ride the best horses if they knew about his drinking, Bailey kept that part of his life secret from all but his closest friends and family. Finally, at the insistence of his wife, he gave up drinking in 1989 and began the truly remarkable phase of his career. Bailey has gone on to win the Kentucky Derby, Preakness, and Belmont Stakes; while riding Cigar he won sixteen races in a row, making Cigar the richest thoroughbred in history. Both his struggles and triumphs are recounted in *Against the Odds,* "an inspiring book that would appeal not only to racing fans but also to families coping with substance abuse," according to *Library Journal* contributor Patsy Gray. A *Publishers Weekly* reviewer found the book somewhat "cliche-ridden" but also called it "an often poignant memoir of the triumph of the human spirit."

BIOGRAPHICAL AND CRITICAL SOURCES:

BOOKS

Bailey, Jerry, and Tom Pedulla, *Against the Odds: Riding for My Life,* G.P. Putnam's Sons (New York, NY), 2005.

PERIODICALS

Booklist, March 15, 2005, Dennis Dodge, review of *Against the Odds,* p. 1257.

Kirkus Reviews, March 1, 2005, review of *Against the Odds,* p. 269.

Library Journal, April 15, 2005, Patsy Gray, review of *Against the Odds,* p. 96.

Publishers Weekly, March 7, 2005, review of *Against the Odds,* p. 59.

Sports Illustrated, November 6, 2000, William Nack, "Silky Smooth," p. 74; April 25, 2005, Richard Deitsch, "Q&A: Jerry Bailey," p. 22.

ONLINE

ESPN Web site, http://www.espn.go.com/ (July 5, 2005), Kenny Mayne, "Q&A with Jerry Bailey."*

*   *   *

BAKER, Marilyn 1929-2001

PERSONAL: Born September 13, 1929, in San Francisco, CA; died November 12, 2001, in Palm Springs, CA; children: Jeff.

CAREER: Journalist and author. Reporter, KQED-TV and KPIX-TV, San Francisco, CA. Humane Society of the Desert, Palm Springs, CA, former executive director and member of board.

AWARDS, HONORS: Emmy awards for local news, 1974, 1975; awards from United Jewish Women's Council, National Academy of Television Arts and Sciences, and American Women in Radio and Television.

WRITINGS:

(With Sally Brompton) *Exclusive! The Inside Story of Patricia Hearst and the SLA,* Macmillan (New York, NY), 1974.

Also author and editor of magazines on business and pets. Creator of pet information Web site.

SIDELIGHTS: Marilyn Baker covered many major stories during her long career in print and broadcast journalism. After beginning her career as a newspaper journalist, she joined KPIX-TV in San Francisco in 1974. She is best known for her award-winning investigation of the kidnapping of newspaper heiress Patty Hearst by the militant group known as the Symbionese Liberation Army (SLA), and expanded her initial reportage of the case into the book *Exclusive! The Inside Story of Patricia Hearst and the SLA.*

Hearst, a descendant of newspaper tycoon William Randolph Hearst, was kidnapped from her Berkeley, California apartment by the SLA in 1974. She alleged that her captors, radical leftists, then brainwashed her and forced her to denounce the capitalist "crimes" of her family. She was also forced, she claimed, to participate in a series of robberies. Hearst traveled across the country with the SLA until September 18, 1975, when she was apprehended by FBI agents in San Francisco. She went on trial and was convicted in March, 1976 of bank robbery and felonious use of firearms. She served three years of a seven-year sentence and was released in February, 1979. Baker, according to an obituary in *San Francisco Chronicle,* covered the Hearst story "with flair and flamboyance."

Baker was also involved with investigating the controversial Zebra serial murder case, when seventy-one whites in the San Francisco area were killed by black extremists between 1972 and 1974. She developed a reputation as an aggressive journalist who did not shirk controversy. Her stories on guns and on Santa Cruz won local Emmy awards. After her retirement, Baker moved to Palm Springs, California, where she became executive director and board member of the Humane Society of the Desert.

BIOGRAPHICAL AND CRITICAL SOURCES:

PERIODICALS

Detroit News, October 17, 1974.
New York Times Book Review, November 17, 1974.
Saturday Review, October 5, 1974.

OBITUARIES

PERIODICALS

San Francisco Chronicle, November 30, 2001.*

BAKER, Robert Allen, Jr. 1921-2005

OBITUARY NOTICE— See index for *CA* sketch: Born June 27, 1921, in Blackford, KY; died of congestive heart failure, August 8, 2005, in Lexington, KY. Psychologist, educator, and author. Baker was well known for his work in debunking paranormal and other strange occurrences, which he explained as phenomena with psychological origins. His skepticism for everything from religious zealotry to ghosts began when he was growing up in Kentucky. Although his parents took him to church, his father once told him that religious fervor could go too far on occasion. His interest in eerie occurrences as a young man led him to investigate spooky sounds emanating from a local cave, where he discovered that the noise originated from wind blowing through a cracked rock. With the onset of World War II, Baker enlisted in the U.S. Army Air Forces and became a cryptographer; at the same time, his fascination with psychology grew, and he read avidly on the subject. With the war over, he studied psychology at the University of Kentucky, earning a B.S. in 1948, followed by an M.S. in 1949. He then went to Stanford University to complete a doctorate in 1952. His first job was on the staff of the Lincoln Laboratory at the Massachusetts Institute of Technology, which was involved in military research. His involvement in military work continued at Fort Knox, where he was a scientist at the Human Resources Research Office in the mid-1950s; he became a senior staff scientist from 1956 to 1960 and was group leader throughout the 1960s. It was here that he became more seriously involved in studying claims of ghostly haunting. Baker soon discovered that such mysterious incidents usually stemmed from psychological issues suffered by witnesses. In one case, for example, a woman who claimed to be haunted by a three-year-old girl was suffering from grief over not being able to bear children. Baker suggested she adopt, and the ghost quickly disappeared. When budget cuts led to trimmed staff at Fort Knox, Baker was hired at the University of Kentucky as a professor and chair of the psychology department. Remaining at the university until his 1988 retirement, Baker continued his research into the psychological origins of everything from ghosts to UFO abductions, repeatedly showing how all these paranormal and alien events could be traced to the mental traumas suffered by those who claimed to see such things. Baker also debunked the validity of such practices as hypnosis, which he said was all a matter of relaxation and suggestion techniques that proved nothing, and he criticized the overuse of medication for mental patients. Baker wrote and edited number of books, including such edited works as *They Call It Hypnosis* (1990), *Hidden Memories: Voices and Visions from Within* (1992; 2nd edition, 1996), *Missing Pieces* (1992), *Mind Games* (1996), and *Child Sexual Abuse and False Memory Syndrome* (1998). An active member of several psychology associations (he served as president of the Kentucky Psychological Association), Baker was also the author of *Psychology in the Wry* (1963) and *Psychology for Man* (1981).

OBITUARIES AND OTHER SOURCES:

PERIODICALS

Seattle Times, August 14, 2005, p. A23.
Times (London, England), September 15, 2005, p. 67.
Washington Post, August 12, 2005, p. B5.

*   *   *

BAKER, Rosalie F. 1945-

PERSONAL: Born February 8, 1945; married Charles F. Baker III (a writer and publisher); children: one son.

*ADDRESSES: Home—*150 Page St., New Bedford, MA 02740. *E-mail—*cfbakeriii@meganet.net.

CAREER: Author, editor, and publisher. Formerly worked as a teacher; Ivy Close Publishing Company, cofounder with husband, Charles F. Baker III, beginning 1980; *Classical Calliope* (now *Calliope* magazine), co-editor and writer, beginning 1981.

AWARDS, HONORS: (With Charles F. Baker III; for *Calliope* magazine) Best New Magazine designation, *Library Journal,* 1991; EdPress Golden Lamp Award, 1998.

WRITINGS:

(With husband, Charles F. Baker III) *The Classical Companion,* 1988.

(With Charles F. Baker III) *Myths and Legends of Mount Olympos,* illustrated by Joyce Audy Zarins, Cobblestone (Peterborough, NH), 1992.

(With Charles F. Baker III) *Classical Ingenuity: The Legacy of the Ancient Greek and Roman Architects, Artists, and Inventors,* 1992.

(With Charles F. Baker III) *Ancient Greeks: Creating the Classical Tradition,* Oxford University Press (New York, NY), 1997.

(With Charles F. Baker III) *Ancient Romans: Expanding the Classical Tradition,* Oxford University Press (New York, NY), 1998.

(With Charles F. Baker III) *Ancient Egyptians: People of the Pyramids,* Oxford University Press (New York, NY), 2001.

In a Word: 750 Words and Their Fascinating Stories and Origins, illustrated by Tom Lopes, Cobblestone (Peterborough, NH), 2003.

(Coauthor with Charles Baker) Winfred Rembert, *Don't Hold Me Back: My Life and Art,* Cricket Books (Chicago, IL), 2003.

(With Charles F. Baker III) *Companion to Ancient Greece,* Oxford University Press (New York, NY), 2005.

Work anthologized in *Of Cabbages and Kings 1991: The Year's Best Magazine Writing for Kids,* Bowker, 1991. Contributor to educational materials, including textbooks for Harcourt Brace and Cobblestone Publishing; contributor of articles to numerous publications, including *Cricket, Calliope, Odyssey,* and *Boston Globe.*

SIDELIGHTS: Writer, teacher, and editor Rosalie F. Baker, together with her husband Charles F. Baker III, co-founded *Classical Calliope* magazine in 1981. Now simply known as *Calliope,* the magazine fulfills Baker's goal as a publisher: to heighten awareness among middle-school and high-school students of the importance and influence of Greek and Roman civilizations on modern society. In addition to her work on the award-winning magazine, Baker is also the author of several nonfiction titles focusing on ancient civilizations, among them *Ancient Egyptians: People of the Pyramids* and *Ancient Romans: Expanding the Classical Tradition.* In addition to each of these books, which have been coauthored with her husband, Baker has also penned *In a Word: 750 Words and Their Fascinating Stories and Origins,* an illustrated guide to etymology.

In *Ancient Egyptians* the coauthors chronicle the lives of twenty-eight famous Egyptians, organizing their subjects by historical period. In addition to the biographies—largely of ancient ruling kings and queens—Baker includes three appendices outlining the five names of each ruler, a list of foreign rulers other than native Egyptians, and lastly, a conclusive time line of the Egyptian civilization. "The text is readable and should be accessible to most students," commented a *Booklist* reviewer, while Cynthia M. Sturgis wrote in *School Library Journal* that *Ancient Egyptians* should serve as "a useful addition for report writers and subject enthusiasts."

Ancient Romans adopts a similar format, this time exploring forty individuals, including: emperors, high-ranking state officials, writers, and generals throughout Rome. Noting that the Bakers describe Roman society and culture "without sensationalizing its brutal aspects," *Booklist* contributor Randy Meyer added that the volume "admits the violent legacy of warfare and assassination while affirming the political and academic achievements that laid the foundation for our own culture."

Baker once commented: "When my husband and I founded the magazine *Classical Calliope* (now *Calliope*) in 1981, a chief goal was to heighten awareness among young people of the importance and merits of studying Greek and Roman civilization. We felt that one of the ways to accomplish this goal would be to include a department that focused on the origins of English words derived from Greek and Latin. Since the first *Calliope* issue in January of 1981, we have done just that—even after we expanded the scope of *Calliope* from classical civilizations to world history. Today, the department is called 'Fun with Words.'

"For years, we considered a book that would take all the word origins and expressions we had included in *Calliope* and arrange them somehow in book form. Our son, Chip and his friend, Jennifer Parker, took on the project when they worked for us as college interns. They created a mock-up of the potential designs, chose the words to include, and presented their idea of introducing fun facts to complement words, at spaced intervals, throughout the book. Everyone loved their ideas—and so, the work of collating and editing, as well as researching the facts, began. It was a great family project!"

BIOGRAPHICAL AND CRITICAL SOURCES:

PERIODICALS

Booklist, August, 1997, Karen Hutt, review of *Ancient Greeks: Creating the Classical Tradition,* p. 1889; September 15, 1997, review of *Ancient Greeks,* p. 262; May 1, 1998, Mary Ellen Quinn, review of *Ancient Romans: Expanding the Classical Tradition,* p. 1550; June 1, 1998, Randy Meyer, review of *Ancient Romans,* p. 1738; February 1, 2002, review of *Ancient Egyptians: People of the Pyramids,* p. 958.

Bulletin of the Center for Children's Books, December, 2001, review of *Ancient Egyptians,* p. 129.

Reference and Research Book News, February, 1998, review of *Ancient Greeks,* p. 21; August, 1998, review of *Ancient Romans,* p. 27.

School Library Journal, September, 1997, Cynthia M. Sturgis, review of *Ancient Greeks,* p. 228; August, 1998, David N. Pauli, review of *Ancient Romans,* p. 169; November, 2001, Cynthia M. Sturgis, review of *Ancient Egyptians,* p. 168; November, 2001, review of *Ancient Egyptians,* p. 168.

ONLINE

Oxford University Press Web site, http://www.oup.com/ (November 6, 2005).

*   *   *

BANDELIN, Oscar J. 1964-

PERSONAL: Born August 31, 1964. *Education:* University of Washington, Seattle, B.A., 1986, M.A.I.S., 1990, Ph.D., 1998. *Politics:* Independent. *Religion:* Protestant.

ADDRESSES: Home—17702 S.E. May Valley Rd., Renton, WA 98059. *E-mail*—bandelin@nwlink.com.

CAREER: Writer. University of Washington, instructor, 1999, guest lecturer, 2000, visiting scholar, 2003-05; American Councils for International Education Regional Scholar Exchange Program to Moscow, Russia, program officer, 2000. Four Creeks Unincorpo-

rated Area Council, at-large representative, 2000-03, president, 2002-03; May Valley Environmental Council, executive committee, 2000-03. Salvatori fellow, Heritage Foundation, Washington, DC, 1994-96.

WRITINGS:

Return to the NEP: The False Promise of Leninism and the Failure of Perestroika, Praeger (Westport, CT), 2002.

*   *   *

BARI, Ruth Aaronson 1917-2005

OBITUARY NOTICE—See index for *CA* sketch: Born November 17, 1917, in Brooklyn, NY; died of complications from Alzheimer's disease, August 25, 2005, in Rockville, MD. Mathematician, educator, and author. Best known for her work in the field of algebra, Bari was professor emeritus of mathematics at George Washington University. Her interest in math began in high school, where she studied independently because math was not a subject young girls were encouraged to pursue at the time. Despite this, she proved her talent in algebra by earning a medal from her school at graduation. Bari continued to study math at Brooklyn College, where she earned a B.A. in 1939. She then took a master's at Johns Hopkins University and planned to get her doctorate there as well, but when male students started returning from World War II she was effectively pushed out of the program. While her husband was in the Marines, she took work as a college math instructor and technical assistant at Bell Telephone Laboratories to support her family. Bari then spent most of the next twenty years focusing on being a wife and mother. After her children had grown, however, her husband encouraged her to return to school, which she did. She completed her Ph.D. in mathematics at the University of Maryland in 1966. Impressed by her doctoral thesis, several colleges offered Bari employment; she selected George Washington University, where she was quickly promoted to full professor. Bari remained at the university until she retired in 1988. She was coeditor of the book *Graphs and Combinatorics: Proceedings* (1974). Having felt the effects of chauvinism in the past, Bari campaigned for equitable salaries for women and men at her university during the 1970s. She also contributed to mathematics education by starting a master's program in teaching mathematics.

OBITUARIES AND OTHER SOURCES:

BOOKS

Math & Mathematicians: The History of Math Discoveries around the World, Volume 3, UXL (Detroit, MI), 2002.

PERIODICALS

Washington Post, August 30, 2005, p. B5.

*   *   *

BARKIN, Jill
     See JOHNSON, Susan

*   *   *

BARRON, John 1930-2005
     (John Daniel Barron)

PERSONAL: Born 1930, in Wichita Falls, TX; died of pulmonary failure, February 24, 2005, in VA; married; wife's name Patricia; children: Lisa, Kelly. *Education:* University of Missouri, M.A.; studied Russian at Naval Postgraduate School.

CAREER: Washington Star, Washington, DC, investigative reporter, 1957-65; *Reader's Digest,* Washington, DC, reporter, 1965-91. *Military service:* U.S. Navy, 1953-57; served as an intelligence officer in Berlin, Germany.

AWARDS, HONORS: George Polk Award (with Paul Hope), 1964; Raymond Clapper Award, 1964; Sir James Goldsmith Award for international journalism, 1985; Attorney General's Award for Meritorious Public Service, 1987; Washington Newspaper Guild Award; American Political Science Association Award.

WRITINGS:

KGB: The Secret Work of Soviet Secret Agents, Reader's Digest Press (New York, NY), 1974.
(With Anthony Paul) *Murder of a Gentle Land: The Untold Story of a Communist Genocide in Cambodia,* Reader's Digest Press (New York, NY), 1977.
MIG Pilot: The Final Escape of Lieutenant Belenko, Reader's Digest Press (New York, NY), 1980.
KGB Today: The Hidden Hand, Reader's Digest Press (New York, NY), 1983.
Breaking the Ring, Houghton (Boston, MA), 1987.
Operation Solo: The FBI's Man in the Kremlin, Regnery Publishing (Washington, DC), 1996.

ADAPTATIONS: Breaking the Ring was adapted as an audiobook, Brilliance Corp. (Grand Haven, MI), 1987.

SIDELIGHTS: Journalist John Barron served in the U.S. Navy during the 1950s, and he spent two of those years in Berlin as an intelligence officer. With his cold-war spying experience behind him, Barron became an investigative reporter with the *Washington Star.* One of his early stories was on the scandalous ethics and financial dealings of Bobby Baker, advisor to then Vice President Lyndon B. Johnson, and he covered the 1960s civil rights movement. When his story on the arrest of White House aide Walter Jenkins for sexual activity in a YMCA bathroom was suppressed under pressure, Barron left the paper and joined the staff of *Reader's Digest.* Barron wrote many notable exposés, including coverage of the Internal Revenue Service abuse of taxpayers that led to Senate hearings. In 1980 his coverage of the drowning death of Mary Jo Kopechne at Chappaquiddick was largely responsible for the end of Massachusetts Senator Edward Kennedy's presidential aspirations.

Barron's bestselling first book, *KGB: The Secret Work of Soviet Secret Agents,* includes the names of more than 1,500 KGB agents worldwide. He wrote it over four years as he spoke with KGB defectors and Western intelligence sources. He was assisted by Yuri Ivanovich Nosenko, a KGB major who escaped first to Switzerland, then to the United States in 1964, and who offered his help to Barron.

Several years later, with coworker Anthony Paul, Barron wrote *Murder of a Gentle Land: The Untold Story of a Communist Genocide in Cambodia,* which documents the mass murders committed by the notorious Pol Pot regime. Barron also became a leading expert on communism. He was sued and attempts were made to discredit him, but former Soviet agents visited him at his office to tell their stories, which aided Barron in writing articles for the publication, as well as providing additional background for his books. He traveled worldwide, and his reporting was considered judicious.

KGB Today: The Hidden Hand contains Barron's account of the career of double agent Stanislav Levchenko. Joseph Sobran wrote in the *National Review* that "Barron writes a narrative that sucks the reader in the way a vacuum sucks confetti. The story of Levchenko's work for the KGB in Japan and his tortured defection to the United States is a masterpiece of factual storytelling." Barron next wrote *Breaking the Ring,* about the members of the John Walker spy ring, which included Walker's brother, his son, and Jerry Whitworth, who had access to U.S. Navy secrets, including encryption methods. The ring stole Navy encryption codes and sold them to the Soviet Union. If the United States had gone to war with the Soviets during the 1970s, U.S. messages would not have been secure.

Barron retired in 1991 but continued to write. His *Operation Solo: The FBI's Man in the Kremlin,* called a "bombshell of a book" by *National Review* contributor William A. Rusher, is a biography of Morris Childs (1902-1991), an American Communist Party leader in the 1930s who became a double agent and worked for the Federal Bureau of Investigation (FBI). Before he died in 1991, Morris was interviewed by Barron, who learned of the decades over which Morris, his wife, Eva, and his brother, Jack Childs, made more than fifty trips to the Soviet Union and other Communist countries and supplied critical information to the FBI. Morris became disillusioned with the party in 1945, when he was removed as editor of the communist *Daily Worker* newspaper. After a period of illness, he was recruited by the FBI and once again became active in the Party. He eventually came to know Khrushchev, Brezhnev, Mao, Chou EnLai, Castro, and other top communist leaders around the world. U.S. President Ronald Reagan bestowed the Medal of Freedom on Morris Childs and Jack Childs (posthumously) for their contributions on behalf of the United States.

BIOGRAPHICAL AND CRITICAL SOURCES:

PERIODICALS

Booklist, February 15, 1996, Gilbert Taylor, review of *Operation Solo: The FBI's Man in the Kremlin,* p. 967.

National Review, July 8, 1983, Joseph Sobran, review of *KGB Today: The Hidden Hand,* p. 872; July 31, 1987, William Murchison, review of *Breaking the Ring,* p. 46; March 11, 1996, William A. Rusher, review of *Operation Solo,* p. 64.

Orbis, fall, 1996, William A. Rusher, review of *Operation Solo,* p. 627.

Publishers Weekly, February 5, 1996, review of *Operation Solo,* p. 74.

OBITUARIES

PERIODICALS

Human Events, March 14, 2005, p. 14.
Washington Post, March 9, 2005, p. B6.

ONLINE

National Review Online, (March 14, 2005), John J. Miller, "He Shot down Commies."

*   *   *

BARRON, John Daniel
   See BARRON, John

*   *   *

BARTLETT, Anne

PERSONAL: Married; husband's name, Russell (a minister); children: four. *Education:* Attended Flinders University; University of Adelaide, M.A., Ph.D. candidate.

ADDRESSES: Agent—Joy Harris Literary Agency, 156 5th Ave., Ste. 617, New York, NY 10010. *E-mail*—anne@annebartlett.com.au.

CAREER: Freelance writer and editor. Has worked as a writer-in-residence at schools and a creative-writing instructor for universities; knitter for clothing designers.

WRITINGS:

Daisy Bates: Keeper of Totems (biography; for children), Reed Library (Carlton, Victoria, Australia), 1997.

(Editor, with others) *Iron Lace: An Anthology of Writing by Students from the 1997 Graduate Diploma in Creative Writing, the University of Adelaide,* University of Adelaide (Adelaide, South Australia, Australia), 1998.

The Aboriginal Peoples of Australia (nonfiction; for children), Lerner (Minneapolis, MN), 2002.

(With Garnett Ian Wilson) *The Chairman: The Story of Garnett Ian Wilson OAM,* Australian Scholarly Publishing (Melbourne, Victoria, Australia), 2004.

Knitting (novel), Houghton Mifflin (Boston, MA), 2005.

SIDELIGHTS: Australian writer Anne Bartlett is best known in the United States for her novel *Knitting,* but before that work was published she wrote two children's books about her country's history. The first of these books, *Daisy Bates: Keeper of Totems,* is a biography of the nineteenth-century Irish immigrant to Australia who became famous for her anthropological work with the Australian Aborigines. The second, *The Aboriginal Peoples of Australia,* includes an overview of the geography and environment of Australia and the history and culture of the aborigines, all "neatly divided into categories," Gillian Engberg noted in *Booklist.* The book also "provides a fairly straightforward look at the treatment of Aboriginal peoples by the Australian government," Jeanette Larson commented in *School Library Journal.*

Bartlett's first novel, *Knitting,* tells the story of two widows. The elder, Sandra Fildes, is an academic who is considered an expert in the history of textiles; the younger, Martha McKenzie, is a former professional knitter who found that knitting with deadlines and constraints drained what was formerly her favorite hobby of its pleasure. Now, she supports herself as a cleaning lady in a church and knits just for the love of the craft. The two strike up an unlikely friendship across class and generational lines after they are the only two good Samaritans who stop and help a man who falls. At first, this friendship helps Sandra to cope with the loss of her husband, who died only a year before: she finds in Martha a project that helps her to occupy her time and keep her mind off of her pain.

However, when Sandra commissions Martha to help her mount an exhibition of historical knitted garments both the friendship and Martha's sanity are threatened.

Knitting was praised by several critics. For example, *Library Journal* reviewer Robin Nesbitt declared it to be "an enthralling story about the healing power of friendship, enriched by knitting details," and a *Kirkus Reviews* contributor deemed it "a brief, sweetly winning tale" and "a spirited feminist take sure to find favor with women's book groups." Aside from feminist underpinnings, some critics recognized theological undercurrents in the novel as well. Bartlett explained on her Web site, "The novel was partly a subterranean attempt to define women's work and to explore the tension I've always felt between different types of work."Each of the women personifies one type: Sandra, the career-woman, works for money and prestige, while Martha pursues her vocation for knitting purely for love and enjoyment and does not expect to earn anything else from it. *Knitting* "is not autobiographical," Bartlett explained, "but at the same time I think the different characters probably do represent different parts of myself which I was trying to get to co-operate rather than be in conflict."

Bartlett told *CA:* "I have written since I was a child, and always loved books, reading and writing. My work is greatly influenced by the Australian landscape, both rural and urban, and also by my interest, both personally and as a pastor's wife, in the experience of grief and grieving.

"I used to try and write in a linear fashion, but I have found that accumulating a series of fragments is an easier process. This means that in the difficult phase of first draft I'm not too burdened by the huge task ahead—I can just write what I feel like on the day, and it doesn't necessarily have to connect with work from the day before. When I have a reasonable pile of fragments I put them all out to see if some kind of story is emerging, and go on from there.

"I try to make a book work at several levels, the surface story, but also with other layers of meaning that make it interesting for the reader. I have a painter friend, Dieter Engler, who says a painting is best if it 'lets out its secrets slowly,' and I think that a good book needs to do the same, lingering in the mind for further reflection."

BIOGRAPHICAL AND CRITICAL SOURCES:

PERIODICALS

Booklist, October 15, 2001, Gillian Engberg, review of *The Aboriginal Peoples of Australia,* p. 405.

Kirkus Reviews, January 15, 2005, review of *Knitting,* p. 65.

Library Journal, March 1, 2005, Robin Nesbitt, review of *Knitting,* p. 74.

Publishers Weekly, February 2, 2004, John F. Baker, "Houghton Executive Editor Jane Rosenman Preempted a First Novel by Australia's Anne Bartlett called *Knitting,* the Story of an Unlikely Friendship between Two Women Whose Lives Are Defined by Wool," p. 14.

School Library Journal, March, 2002, Jeanette Larson, review of *The Aboriginal Peoples of Australia,* p. 241.

ONLINE

Anne Bartlett Home Page, http://www.annebartlett. com.au (June 25, 2005).

Bookreporter.com, http://www.bookreporter.com/ (June 25, 2005), Norah Piehl, review of *Knitting.*

Christianity Today Online, http://www.christianity today.com/ (October 17, 2005), Cindy Crosby, review of *Knitting.*

*   *   *

BASTID, J.P.
    See MANCHETTE, Jean-Patrick

*   *   *

BEAL, Timothy K. 1963-
    (Timothy Kandler Beal)

PERSONAL: Born 1963, in Hood River, OR; married Clover Reuter (a Presbyterian minister); children: Sophie, Seth. *Education:* Seattle Pacific University, B.A., 1986; Columbia Theological Seminary, M.Div, 1991; Emory University, certificate in women's studies and Ph.D., 1995. *Hobbies and other interests:* Travel.

ADDRESSES: Home—Shaker Heights, OH. *Office*—Department of Religion, Case Western Reserve University, 10900 Euclid Ave., Cleveland, OH 44106-7112. *E-mail*—timothy.beal@case.edu.

CAREER: Professor and writer. Emory University, Atlanta, GA, teaching assistant, 1993; archaeological excavation at Tell Nimrin, Jordan, assistant site director, 1993; Columbia Theological Seminary, Decatur, GA, adjunct professor in Hebrew exegesis, 1993-94; Eckerd College, St. Petersburg, FL, assistant professor of religious studies and adjunct faculty member in women's and gender studies and environmental studies, 1994-99; Case Western Reserve University, Cleveland, OH, Harkness associate professor of Biblical literature, 1999-2002, Harkness professor of Biblical literature, 2002-04, then Florence Harkness professor of religion, 2004—, associate director, 2002-03, then director, 2003—, of Baker-Nord Center for the Humanities. University of Glasgow, honorary lecturer at Centre for the Study of Literature, Theology, and the Arts, 1997. Lecturer; co-director (with Tod Linafelt) of *Bible and Pop Culture: A Multimedia CD-ROM Project for Teaching in Biblical Studies.*

AWARDS, HONORS: Fellow, Consortium for the Advancement of Private Higher Education, 1996-98; senior faculty fellow, Case Western Reserve University/Ohio Board of Regents Challenge Program, 2001; Professor of the Year Award, Alphi Phi, Case Western Reserve University chapter, 2000-01; Award for Teaching Excellence, Northeast Ohio Council on Higher Education, 2004; grant, Presidential Initiative Fund.

WRITINGS:

NONFICTION

The Book of Hiding: Gender, Ethnicity, Annihilation, and Esther, Routledge (New York, NY), 1997.

(Editor, with David M. Gunn) *Reading Bibles, Writing Bodies: Identity and the Book,* Routledge (New York, NY), 1997.

(With Tod A. Linafelt) *God in the Fray: A Tribute to Walter Brueggemann,* Fortress Press (Minneapolis, MN), 1998.

(With Tod A. Linafelt) *Ruth and Esther,* edited by David W. Cotter, Liturgical Press (Collegeville, MN), 1999.

Religion and Its Monsters, Routledge (New York, NY), 2002.

(With William E. Deal) *Theory for Religious Studies,* Routledge (New York, NY), 2004.

Roadside Religion: In Search of the Sacred, the Strange, and the Substance of Faith (memoir), Beacon Press (Boston, MA), 2005.

(Editor, with Tod A. Linafelt) *Mel Gibson's Bible: Religion, Popular Culture, and The Passion of the Christ,* University of Chicago Press (Chicago, IL), 2006.

Contributor to periodicals, including *Church Divinity, Biblical Interpretation, Semeia, Chronicle of Higher Education, Cleveland Plain Dealer, Hedgehog Review,* and *Washington Post.* Contributor to books, including *Reading between the Texts: Intertexuality and the Hebrew Bible,* edited by Danna Nolan Fewell, Westminster/John Knox Press (Louisville, KY), 1992; *The Feminist Companion to Esther, Judith, and Susanna,* edited by Athalya Brenner, Sheffield Academic Press (Sheffield, England), 1995; *The Dictionary of Biblical Interpretation,* Volume 2, edited by John H. Hayes, Abingdon (Nashville, TN), 1998; *The Dictionary of Biblical Interpretation,* Volume 1, edited by Hayes, Abingdon, 1999; *Imag(in)ing Otherness: Filmic Visions of Living Together,* edited by David Jaspar and S. Brent Plate, American Academy of Religion/ Oxford University Press (Oxford, England), 1999; *Handbook for Postmodern Biblical Interpretation,* edited by Andrew K.M. Adam, Chalice (St. Louis, MO), 2000; *Strange Fire: Reading the Hebrew Bible after the Holocaust,* edited by Tod Linafelt, New York University Press (New York, NY), 2000; *Professing in the Postmodern Academy: Faculty and the Future of Church-Related Colleges,* edited by Stephen R. Hayenes, Baylor University Press (Waco, TX), 2002; *A Shadow of Glory: Reading the New Testament after the Holocaust,* edited by Linafelt, Routledge (New York, NY), 2002; *Constructs of Ancient Israel: The Bible and Its Social Worlds,* edited by David M. Gunn and Paula McNutt, Continuum (New York, NY), 2002; *Relating to the Text: Form Critical and Interdisciplinary Insights on the Bible,* edited by T. Sandoval and C. Mandolfo, Continuum (Sheffield, England), 2003; *Derrida and Religion: Other Testaments,* edited by Kevin Hart and Yvonne Sherwood, Routledge, 2004; *Sanctified Aggression: Violent Legacies of Biblical, Jewish, and Christian Vocabularies,* edited by Jonneke Bekkenkamp and Yvonne Sherwood, Continuum (Sheffield, England), 2004; *Levianas and Biblical Studies,* edited by Tamara Eskenazi and Gary A.

Phillips, Society of Biblical Literature (Atlanta, GA), 2004; and *Renovare Study Bible,* edited by Richard Foster, Walter Brueggemann, and Eugene Peterson, Harper San Francisco (San Francisco, CA), 2005. Coeditor, with Linafelt, *Afterlives of the Bible,* University of Chicago Press, 2003—; editorial assistant, *Literary Currents in Biblical Interpretation,* Westminster John Knox Press, 1991-94. *Journal for the Study of the Old Testament,* member of editorial board, 2000—; *Postscripts,* member of editorial board, 2004—.

WORK IN PROGRESS: The White Supremacist Bible.

SIDELIGHTS: A professor of religion, Timothy K. Beal has written and edited books on the Bible, Biblical issues, and religion in general. As a professor, he has also taught on similar topics. His primary classes include Biblical studies, the theory and methodology of religious studies, and related issues.

One of Beal's first books is on the Old Testament's book of Esther. Titled *The Book of Hiding: Gender, Ethnicity, Annihilation, and Esther,* the work analyzes and interprets the text using postmodern critical theory. Beal uses a literary approach and looks at the Masoretic text, rather than the more common Greek text, of Esther. Sidnie White Crawford, writing in the *Catholic Biblical Quarterly,* acknowledged that Beal's reading of Esther in *The Book of Hiding* might have limited appeal to readers, but noted: "Beal, nevertheless, is bridging the gap between postmodern theory and biblical scholarship. His approach promises to yield fresh new insights into the biblical text."

Several years later, Beal cowrote another work on Esther with Tod Linafelt. For *Ruth and Esther* Beal wrote the commentary on the book of Esther while Linafelt commented on the book of Ruth. In his section, Beal offers a literary analysis and interpretation of the Old Testament book, again using the Masoretic text. He highlights themes of Esther such as hiding and writing, and studies the artistic qualities of the text.

Writing in the *Catholic Biblical Quarterly,* Linda Day felt that the authors should have written a joint introduction to bring together *Ruth and Esther* thematically. However, Day commented positively on Beal's contribution, stating that his "analysis is generally sound, and the lenses through which he views the story are well chosen. He is not afraid to point out the strangeness of the Scroll and the complexities within it." *Interpretation* contributor Joan E. Cook voiced a similar opinion, calling the book "an informative and insightful discussion of the literary and theological features of the book of Esther."

Beal's work also explores other issues related to the Bible and religion. One book discusses where religion and popular culture meet. In *Religion and Its Monsters*, he offers a theory about what monsters are, why people like them, and the mediums that feature monsters such as films and books. Beal relates these monsters to religion, God, and the Bible. He also explores the idea that God can be a part of the monsters people create and how God's actions can be seen as hideous. A primary argument that Beal makes is that monsters like Dracula are a way of dealing with the unknown in ritualistic fashion. Writing in *Commonweal*, William Jordan noted that "Beal reminds us that heaven and earth are full of monsters, and that grappling with them—and sometimes transforming them—has always been one of the principal tasks of religion."

Critics commented positively on Beal's style of writing in *Religion and Its Monsters*. As *Library Journal* reviewer Sandra Collins noted, "an informal, chatty style makes this more accessible than academic, although it is well researched." In addition, Jana Riess stated in *Publishers Weekly* that the book is "brilliant, twisted, [and] imaginative."

Beal's memoir, *Roadside Religion: In Search of the Sacred, the Strange, and the Substance of Faith*, was written as a result of a Beal family road trip in 2002. Beal visited several religious locations around the United States with his wife and two children. One visit was to Richard Greene, a man making his own ark, just like Noah of the Bible. Greene believes that God has asked this of him and he has made it his life' work to honor the request. Another visit featured the biggest collection of rosaries in the world, located in the state of Washington. Several places were entertainment oriented such as Virginia's Holy Land and Kentucky's Biblical Mini-Golf course.

One critic noted the effect the experience had on Beal. Richard N. Osting noted in the *Journal Star* of Peoria, Illinois, that "reflecting on his travels, Beal says that

people like himself who forsake evangelicalism 'don't tend to revisit that particular culture or theological tradition with much sympathy.' Yet he had to recapture some of the old warmth to understand what he was observing."In the book, Beal's treatment of his subjects was also positively commented on. *Booklist* reviewer June Sawyers stated, "The book is full of good humor, and Beal doesn't patronize the creators of these attractions but accords them respect and dignity."

BIOGRAPHICAL AND CRITICAL SOURCES:

BOOKS

Beal, Timothy K., *Roadside Religion: In Search of the Sacred, the Strange, and the Substance of Faith*, Beacon Press (Boston, MA), 2005.

PERIODICALS

Booklist, April 15, 2005, June Sawyers, review of *Roadside Religion,* p. 1415.
Catholic Biblical Quarterly, July, 2000, Sidnie White Crawford, review of *The Book of Hiding: Gender, Ethnicity, Annihilation, and Esther,* p. 510; January, 2001, Linda Day, review of *Ruth and Esther,* p. 117.
Commonweal, March 8, 2002, William Jordan, "Mysterium tremendum," review of *Religion and Its Monsters,* p. 23.
Interpretation, April, 2001, Joan E. Cook, review of *Ruth and Esther,* p. 188.
Journal Star (Peoria, IL), May 7, 2005, Richard N. Osting, "Oddities—Author's Odyssey Uncovers Ten 'Strange' Religious Sites in Nine States," p. E8.
Library Journal, December, 2001, Sandra Collins, review of *Religion and Its Monsters,* p. 131.
New York Times Book Review, June 5, 2005, Sarah Ferrell, "Cross Country: A Professor of Religion Investigates Unusual Pilgrimage Sites throughout Rural America," p. 38.
Publishers Weekly, November 12, 2001, Jana Riess, review of *Religion and Its Monsters,* p. S16.

ONLINE

Case Western Reserve University Web site, http://www.case.edu/ (June 29, 2005), biography of Timothy K. Beal.*

BEAL, Timothy Kandler
   See BEAL, Timothy K.

*   *   *

BEARD, Philip 1963-

PERSONAL: Born 1963; married; wife's name, Traci; children: Cali, Phoebe, Madelynne. *Education:* Attended Colgate University; University of Pittsburgh, LAW degree, 1988, education degree, 2000. *Hobbies and other interests:* Coaching varsity golf.

ADDRESSES: Home—Aspinwall, PA. *Agent*—Jane Dystel, Dystel & Goderich Literary Management, 1 Union Square West, Ste. 904, New York, NY 10003. *E-mail*—author@philipbeard.net.

CAREER: Stonecipher, Cunningham, Beard & Schmitt (law firm), Pittsburgh, PA, partner, 1990-2000, member of counsel, 2000—.

WRITINGS:

Dear Zoe (novel), Viking (New York, NY), 2005.

SIDELIGHTS: Philip Beard's first novel, *Dear Zoe,* is told in the form of letters written by the protagonist, a fifteen-year-old girl named Tess De Nunzio, to her stepsister Zoe. The letters are Tess's way of dealing with the tragedy of Zoe's death, a tragedy for which she was partly responsible. On the morning of September 11, 2001, Tess was watching four-year-old Zoe play in the yard when she heard the news of the terrorist attacks on the World Trade Center. Running inside to get more information from the television, she left Zoe unattended and the little girl ran into the street, where she was struck by a car—the driver of which was also distracted by the news of the disaster. Tess's mother is overcome with grief, and eventually the teen-aged girl comes to feel so alienated from her mother and her caring, sensitive stepfather that she goes to live with her biological father, a carefree sort who lives on the edge of the law.

Dear Zoe is a reflection of how the deep personal tragedy of Zoe's death is overshadowed by the greater tragedy that happened at the same instant. It is also a coming-of-age story, relating Tess's experimentation with drugs and sex. Several reviewers commented on the author's success at creating an authentic persona for Tess. Keddy Ann Outlaw, a contributor to *Library Journal,* stated that Tess's "plucky, spirited voice deserves a wide audience." Cristina Rouvalis, reviewing the book for the *Pittsburgh Post-Gazette,* found many "charming" elements in the book, but added that "it never sugar-coats the depths of a young girl's despair." Kristine Huntley, assessing the novel for *Booklist,* called it "a piercing look at how a family recovers from a devastating loss."

Dear Zoe was many years in the making. Beard began writing the book long before the September 11 attacks, and had finished a version of it, but it was rejected by one publisher after another. He was advised to change the viewpoint of the story and do away with the epistolary style, which he eventually did. The book then faced many more rejections, and Beard decided to go ahead and invest money in self-publishing the book as he had originally written it. He was very close to completing that project when a publisher approached him with a deal for the earlier version. By the time it was published, Beard had reworked it to include the September 11 references.

Beard, a lawyer as well as an author, was asked by *Bookreporter* online interviewers Carol Fitzgerald and Shannon McKenna how his legal training influenced his writing. The author answered, "Although the end-product is certainly different, the skill sets of both crafts are entirely consistent. In both genres, you define your conflicts early, let them play out against one another, and then hope that you have made your case convincingly or eloquently enough to convince your audience. Whether as a lawyer or novelist, I'm trying to make someone believe in a reality I have created, to care about it enough to stay with me until the end, and, if I'm really lucky, to make them remember it."

BIOGRAPHICAL AND CRITICAL SOURCES:

PERIODICALS

Booklist, February 1, 2005, Kristine Huntley, review of *Dear Zoe,* p. 940.
Entertainment Weekly, March 25, 2005, Jennifer Reese, review of *Dear Zoe,* p. 76.

Kirkus Reviews, January 15, 2005, review of *Dear Zoe,* p. 65.

Library Journal, February 15, 2005, Keddy Ann Outlaw, review of *Dear Zoe,* p. 113.

Pittsburgh Post-Gazette, March 13, 2005, Cristina Rouvalis, review of *Dear Zoe.*

Publishers Weekly, April 19, 2004, John F. Baker, "Rep to the Rescue," p. 12; January 24, 2005, Bridget Kinsella, "Philip Beard: Dear Zoe," p. 117, review of *Dear Zoe,* p. 218.

ONLINE

Bookreporter, http://www.bookreporter.com/ (March 25, 2005), Carol Fitzgerald and Shannon McKenna, interview with Philip Beard.

Penguin Group Web site, http://us.penguingroup.com/ (July 6, 2005), interview with Philip Beard.

Philip Beard Home Page, http://www.philipbeard.net (July 5, 2005), Maryglenn McCombs, interview with Philip Beard.*

*   *   *

BECKERMAN, Michael 1951-
(Michael Brim Beckerman)

PERSONAL: Born August 2, 1951, in New York, NY; son of Bernard (a professor and writer) and Gloria (a professor and poet; maiden name, Brim) Beckerman; married Karen P. Beckerman; children: Charles, Bernard, Anne. *Education:* Hofstra University, B.A., 1973; Columbia University, Ph.D., 1982.

ADDRESSES: Home—2 Cornelia St., Apt. 605, New York, NY 10014. *E-mail*—michael.beckerman@nyu. edu.

CAREER: Writer and educator. University of California, Santa Barbara, professor of music, 1992-2002; New York University, NY, professor of music, 2002—, department chair, 2004.

WRITINGS:

(Editor) *Dvorak and His World,* Princeton University Press (Princeton, NJ), 1993.

Janacek as Theorist, Pendragon Press (Stuyvesant, NY), 1995.

(Editor) *Janacek and His World,* Princeton University Press (Princeton, NJ), 2003.

New Worlds of Dvorak: Searching in America for the Composer's Inner Life, W.W. Norton (New York, NY), 2003.

WORK IN PROGRESS: Idyllic Sounds, expected 2005.

SIDELIGHTS: Michael Beckerman told *CA:* "I write to explore two basic things: (1) The relationship between music and the rest of the world (2) The relationship between writing and the rest of the world.

"I am also trying to find the technology to make musical sound as accessible as art reproductions."

BIOGRAPHICAL AND CRITICAL SOURCES:

PERIODICALS

American Music Teacher, February-March, 2004, Jane Ann Wilson, review of *Janacek and His World,* p. 91.

Library Journal, September 1, 2003, Larry Lipkis, review of *Janacek and His World,* p. 170.

Notes, September, 2003, Paul Christiansen, review of *New Worlds of Dvorak: Searching in America for the Composer's Inner Life,* p. 167.

*   *   *

BECKERMAN, Michael Brim
See BECKERMAN, Michael

*   *   *

BECKMAN, Ludvig 1970-

PERSONAL: Born May 30, 1970, in Stockholm, Sweden; son of Staffan and Gunilla Beckman; children: Amanda. *Ethnicity:* "Caucasian." *Education:* Uppsala University, B.A., 1994, Ph.D., 2000. Attended Oxford University, 1997-98.

ADDRESSES: Home—Valhallaväagen 20, 114 22 Stockholm, Sweden. *Office*—Department of Political Science, Stockholm University, 102 10 Stockholm, Sweden. *E-mail*—ludvig.beckman@statsvet.su.se.

CAREER: Writer. Uppsala University, Uppsala, Sweden, researcher, 2000-04; Stockholm University, Stockholm, Sweden, assistant professor, 2004—.

WRITINGS:

The Liberal State and the Politics of Virtue, Transaction Publishers (New Brunswick, NJ), 2001.
(Editor, with Emil Uddhammar) *Virtues of Independence and Dependence on Virtues,* Transaction Publishers (New Brunswick, NJ), 2002.

Contributor of articles to scholarly journals, including *Journal of Value Inquiry, Medicine, Philosophy, and Health Care, Theoretical Medicine and Bioethics, Human Reproduction,* and *Genetic Ethics.*

*   *   *

BELLO, Walden 1945-
    (Walden F. Bello)

PERSONAL: Born 1945, in Manila, Philippines. *Education:* Ateneo de Manila University, A.B.; Princeton University, M.A., Ph.D.

ADDRESSES: Office—Department of Sociology, College of Social Sciences and Philosophy, University of the Philippines, Diliman, Quezon City 1101, Philippines. *E-mail*—W.Bello@focusweb.org.

CAREER: University of the Philippines, professor of sociology and public administration, 1992—; Focus on the Global South, founder, executive director, 1995—. Visiting professor, University of California at Los Angeles. Human rights activist; Anti-Martial Law Coalition, coordinator; Philippines Human Rights Lobby, Washington, DC, founder. Food First, board member; Green Peace Southeast Asia, former chair of the board;

AWARDS, HONORS: New California Media Award for Best International Reporting, 1998; Chancellor's Award, University of the Philippines, 2000, for *A Siamese Tragedy: Development and Disintegration in Modern Thailand;* Right Livelihood Award, 2003.

WRITINGS:

NONFICTION

(Editor, with others) *Modernization: Its Impact in the Philippines,* five volumes, Ateneo de Manila University Press (Quezon City, Philippines), 1967–71.
(Editor, with Severina Rivera) *The Logistics of Repression and Other Essays: The U.S. Assistance in Consolidating the Martial Law Regime in the Philippines,* Friends of the Filipino People (Washington, DC), 1977.
(With David Kinley and Elaine Elinson) *Development Debacle: The World Bank in the Philippines,* Institute for Food and Policy (San Francisco, CA), 1982.
(With John Harris and Lyuba Zarsky) *Nuclear Power in the Philippines: The Plague That Poisons Morong!,* Third World Studies Center, University of the Philippines (Quezon City, Philippines), 1983.
(With Peter Hayes and Lyuba Zarsky) *American Lake: Nuclear Peril in the Pacific,* Penguin Books (New York, NY), 1986.
(With Stephanie Rosenfeld) *Dragons in Distress: Asia's Miracle Economies in Crisis,* Institute for Food and Development (San Francisco, CA), 1990.
People and Power in the Pacific: The Struggle for the Post-Cold War Order, foreword by Renato Constantino, Foundation for Nationalist Studies (Quezon City, Philippines), 1992.
(With Shea Cunningham and Bill Rau) *Dark Victory: The United States, Structural Adjustment, and Global Poverty,* Food First Books (Oakland, CA), 1994, 2nd edition, foreword by Susan George, 1999.
(Editor, with Jenina Joy Chavez-Malaluan) *APEC, Four Adjectives in Search of a Noun,* Manila People's Forum on APEC (Quezon City, Philippines), 1996.
(With Shea Cunningham and Li Kheng Po) *A Siamese Tragedy: Development and Disintegration in Modern Thailand,* Zed Books (New York, NY), 1998.

(Editor, with Nicola Bullard and Kamal Malhotra) *Global Finance: New Thinking on Regulating Speculative Capital Markets,* Zed Books (New York, NY), 2000.

The Future in the Balance: Essays on Globalization and Resistance, edited and with a preface by Anuradha Mittal, Food First Books (Oakland, CA), 2001.

Deglobalization: Ideas for a New World Economy, Zed Books (New York, NY), 2002.

(With Herbert Docena, Marissa de Guzman, and Mary Lou Malig) *The Anti-Development State: The Political Economy of Permanent Crisis in the Philippines,* Focus on the Global South/University of the Philippines (Quezon City, Philippines), 2004.

Dilemmas of Domination: The Unmaking of the American Empire, Metropolitan Books (New York, NY), 2005.

Also contributor to numerous journals and periodicals, including the *Bangkok Post.* Contributor to books, including *A Movement of Movements: Is Another World Really Possible?,* edited by Tom Mertes, Verso (New York, NY), 2004.

SIDELIGHTS: Walden Bello is the author of over a dozen books critiquing globalization and the effects of U.S. government policies on the rest of the world, especially Asia and the Pacific Rim. A professor of sociology at the University of the Philippines, Bello has been a long-time activist, fighting first the martial-law government of Ferdinand Marcos in his native land, and then resisting and critiquing the monetary policies of international agencies and groups such as the World Bank, World Trade Organization (WTO), G-8, and International Monetary Fund (IMF). Bello is the recipient of the 2003 Right Livelihood Award. In awarding the prize, the selection committee, as reported on the *Right Likelihood Award* Web site, commended Bello as "one of the leading critics of the current model of economic globalisation, combining the roles of intellectual and activist." The selection committee further noted that, "through a combination of courage as a dissident, with an extraordinary breadth of published output and personal charisma, [Bello] has made a major contribution to the international case against corporate-driven globalisation."

Bello's writing and editing has spanned several decades, and deals with topics specifically Philippine in nature, but also with larger global issues. His politi-

cal activism led him to research IMF and World Bank loans to the Philippines that were in effect underwriting the Marcos regime. Breaking into the headquarters of the World Bank in Washington, DC, Bello made off with several thousands pages of documents that demonstrated World Bank involvement in support of the Marcos dictatorship. These he used in his 1982 book, *Development Debacle: The World Bank in the Philippines,* a work that helped to politicize the residents of the Philippines. Ultimately Marcos was brought down in 1986 by a people's movement. Thereafter, Bello examined the new Asian economies, writing his *Dragons in Distress: Asia's Miracle Economies in Crisis,* several years before those markets collapsed. Since that time, the crux of Bello's more recent work has been a critique of the manner in which developing countries have, in his opinion, become dominated by foreign capital and an examination of alternatives to such subjugation. Additionally, he has examined the ecological fallout of globalization, and since the terrorist attacks of September 11, 2001, he has also taken a sharp look at U.S. foreign policy around the world.

With the 1998 *A Siamese Tragedy: Development and Disintegration in Modern Thailand* Bello "depicts various disappointments and adverse side-effects in Thailand's economic development model of the last forty years or so," according to Nick J. Freeman in *ASEAN Economic Bulletin.* Philip Hirsh, reviewing that title in *Geographical Journal,* called it a "penetrating—if polemical—analysis of one country's experience." Bello and his fellow authors examine aspects from the damming of rivers and subsequent environmental degradation to the advent of the AIDS crisis as indicative of the failure of fast-track capitalist development in Thailand. Written before the 1997 economic crash in Thailand, the book provides a prescient introduction to the problems besetting other Asian countries as well.

With *The Future in the Balance: Essays on Globalization and Resistance* Bello gathers together what Susanne Martikke, writing in *World Watch,* called "scathing critiques of globalization." Here Bello takes on the WTO, the IMF, and World Bank, characterizing them as bankrupt institutions, doing more harm than good in developing countries. Speaking with Jerry Harris of *Race and Class,* Bello outlined some of his complaints about globalization: "The loss of place, the loss of one national economy and of having some space from the volatility of growth. The loss of sense that the state could act as a protective mechanism vis à vis the global economy, the feeling that corporations have completely taken over. That is what we're talking about." With *Deglobalization: Ideas for a New World Economy* he delivers some alternatives to what he sees as outmoded globalization; as Theresa Wolfwood noted in a *Briarpatch* review, "We need to decommission the financial institutions while we build a pluralist system of governments." Bello further argues that development should be based on human needs and environmental concerns rather than solely on growth, as in the Western model. Wolfwood concluded, "This short concise volume is a guidebook no activist should travel without."

Bello also tackles the United States' role in the world in his 2005 title, *Dilemmas of Domination: The Unmaking of the American Empire.* For Bello, U.S. foreign policy in the Middle East and the invasion of Iraq are mistakes that will result in the end of American hegemony in the world and cause the rise of other economic powers, such as China, to take its place. Much of the world, according to Bello, is turning against American imperial designs. A critic for *Kirkus Reviews* found Bello's position "resonantly and assuredly" argued, as well as "provocative and useful." Similarly, a reviewer for *Publishers Weekly* thought *Dilemmas of Domination* to be a "concise and thoughtful global South perspective on America's military, economic, and political realities." Writing for *Booklist,* Brendan Driscoll also found the book a "a provocative, well-researched polemic."

BIOGRAPHICAL AND CRITICAL SOURCES:

PERIODICALS

Arena, February, 2001, Dave Gilbert, "In the Philippines: Estrada and After," p. 15.

ASEAN Economic Bulletin, April, 2001, Nick J. Freeman, review of *A Siamese Tragedy: Development and Disintegration in Modern Thailand,* p. 94.

Asia Africa Intelligence Wire, October 8, 2003, "Alternative Nobel Prize Awarded to Walden Bello."

Booklist, February 15, 2005, Brendan Driscoll, review of *Dilemmas of Domination: The Unmaking of the American Empire,* p. 1039.

Briarpatch, December, 2002, Theresa Wolfwood, review of *Deglobalization: Ideas for a New World Economy,* p. 29.

Geographical Journal, September, 2001, Philip Hirsch, review of *A Siamese Tragedy,* p. 280.

Kirkus Reviews, December 15, 2004, review of *Dilemmas of Domination,* p. 1174.

Publishers Weekly, January 31, 2005, review of *Dilemmas of Domination,* p. 56.

Race and Class, April-June, 2002, Jerry Harris, "Notes for a New Economy: An Interview with Walden Bello."

World Watch, January-February, 2002, Susanne Martikke, review of *The Future in the Balance: Essays on Globalization and Resistance,* p. 39.

ONLINE

Right Livelihood Award Web site, http://www.right livelihood.org/ (August 12, 2005), "Walden Bello (2003)."

University of the Philippines Web site, http://www.upd. edu.ph/ (August 12, 2005), "Dr. Walden Bello Receives 2003 Right Livelihood Award."*

*   *   *

BELLO, Walden F.
See BELLO, Walden

*   *   *

BENARDE, Scott R. 1953-

PERSONAL: Born March 31, 1953 in Lansing, MI. *Ethnicity:* "Russian-Jewish." *Education:* University of Massachusetts, B.A., 1975; University of Missouri, M.A., 1977. *Religion:* Jewish.

ADDRESSES: Home—12645 Colony Preserve Dr., Boynton Beach, FL 33436. *Office*—Jewish Community Center of the Greater Palm Beaches, 3151 N. Military Trail, West Palm Beach, FL 33436. *E-mail*—scottbenarde@aol.com.

CAREER: Writer. *Evening Herald,* Rock Hill, SC, reporter, 1978-79; *Fort Lauderdale News,* Fort Lauderdale, FL, feature writer and pop music columnist, 1980-87; *Palm Beach Post,* West Palm Beach, FL, pop music columnist, feature writer, and copy editor, 1987-99. Also has presented lectures throughout the country, including "Jews and Blues and Rock 'n' Roll: A Musical History Tour" and "The Holocaust and Rock 'n' Roll."

WRITINGS:

Stars of David: Rock 'n' Roll's Jewish Stories, Brandeis University Press (Hanover, NH), 2003.

Contributor of articles on music and travel to numerous newspapers and magazines.

SIDELIGHTS: Scott R. Benarde told *CA:* "I first got into writing (poetry, songwriting) in high school and college as a way to express myself to myself, family, and close friends. Writing as a career didn't occur to me until it was time to graduate college and find a way to make a living. I tried journalism school as an experiment and found it suited my personality as a crusader for truth and justice. I also saw journalism as a great job for someone who didn't know what they wanted to be when they grew up as it allowed you to write about people in every profession and was rarely boring or repetitive. (Sure, deadlines were the same, but the subjects and the approach to a story, review, or column didn't have to be.)

"Writing *Stars of David: Rock 'n' Roll's Jewish Stories* combined three strong influences and passions in my life: Journalism, Judaism, and rock 'n' roll. I feel that no matter what I've done as a journalist until now, or what I will ever do, doing this book was one of my raisons d'etre. It was meant to be that I do this book to chronicle the Jewish contribution to music of the rock era and illuminate Judaism's surprising influence on the music and the people who made/make it.

"I view my book as really a social history book as well as a book about popular music and/or Judaism, of interest to those of any faith who love the music of the rock era. It was the most arduous, ambitious undertaking of my career, one of those projects that might not have been tackled had I known the amount of time, dedication, and frustration involved. I guess that's one reason I'm so proud of *Stars.*"

BIRCHFIELD, D.L. 1948-
(Don L. Birchfield)

PERSONAL: Born July 10, 1948, in Atoka County, OK; son of Richard Lee Birchfield (a farmer, steelworker, minister, and missionary) and Lavenia McDaniel (a cosmetologist and missionary). *Ethnicity:* "Choctaw, Chickasaw, Welsh, Scots, Black, Dutch." *Education:* Mesa College, A.A., 1968; Western State College of Colorado at Gunnison, B.A., 1971; University of Oklahoma College of Law, J.D., 1975. Attended University of Colorado, University of Denver, U.S. Marine Corps Officer Candidate School, and Oklahoma City Community College. *Religion:* "Choctaw."

ADDRESSES: Office—c/o Cherry Weiner Literary Agency, 28 Kipling Way, Manalapan, NJ 07726. *E-mail*—BarkingPup@aol.com.

CAREER: Author and professor of Native American studies. Attorney-at-law, 1976-83; freelance writer and editor, 1983-96; Cornell University, Ithaca, NY, former instructor in English and American Indian studies, 1996-98; University of Lethbridge, Alberta, Canada, associate professor of Native American studies, 2001—. University of New Mexico, Albuquerque, visiting associate professor of Native American studies, 1998-99; University of Wisconsin, Green Bay, adjunct associate professor of humanistic studies and fiction writing, 2000-01.

AWARDS, HONORS: Hazel Butler Garms U.S. History Award, Daughters of the American Revolution, 1967; R.C. Walker Award, *Daily Sentinel* (Atlantic City, NJ), 1967; Balfour Award, 1968; fellowship in fiction writing, Jackson Hole Writers Conference, 1994; Outstanding Ability in Teaching Award, Cornell University American Indian Science and Engineering Society, 1997; named Writer of the Year, Wordcraft Circle of Native Writers, 1997, for *The Encyclopedia of North American Indians;* Louis Littlecoon Oliver Memorial Prose Award, Native Writers' Circle of the Americas at the University of Oklahoma, 1997, for *The Oklahoma Intelligence Test and Other New and Collected Elementary, Epistolary, Autobiographical, and Oratorical Essays;* named Writer of the Year, Wordcraft Circle of Native Writers, 2004, and Spur Award for Best First Novel, Western Writers of America, 2005, both for *Field of Honor;* University of Lethbridge Book Awards, 2004, for *Raintree Biographies* and "Native Peoples" series.

WRITINGS:

FOR ADULTS

(Coeditor) *Durable Breath: Contemporary Native American Poetry,* Salmon Run Press (Anchorage, AK), 1994.

The Oklahoma Intelligence Test: New and Collected Elementary, Epistolary, Autobiographical, and Oratorical Choctologies, Greenfield Review Press (Greenfield Center, NY), 1998.

Field of Honor (novel), University of Oklahoma Press (Norman, OK), 2004.

Black Silk Handkerchief: A Hom-Astubby Mystery (novel), University of Oklahoma Press (Norman, OK), 2006.

JUVENILE NONFICTION

Jim Thorpe, World's Greatest Athlete, Modern Curriculum Press (Parsippany, NJ), 1994.

Tecumseh, Leader, Modern Curriculum Press (Parsippany, NJ), 1994.

(Reteller) *Rabbit: American Indian Legends,* additional text by Vic Warren, illustrated by Diana Magnuson, Scholastic (New York, NY), 1996.

(Editor) *The Encyclopedia of North American Indians,* eleven volumes, Marshall Cavendish (New York, NY), 1997.

Acoma: The Sky City, Macmillan/McGraw-Hill (New York, NY), 1999.

Crazy Horse, Raintree Steck-Vaughan (Austin, TX), 2003.

Apache, Gareth Stevens Publishers (Milwaukee, WI), 2003.

Sioux, Gareth Stevens Publishers (Milwaukee, WI), 2003.

Sacagawea, Raintree Steck-Vaughan (Austin, TX), 2003.

Seminole, Gareth Stevens Publishers (Milwaukee, WI), 2003.

(With Sabrina Crewe) *The Trail of Tears,* Gareth Stevens Publishers (Milwaukee, WI), 2004.

Navajo, Gareth Stevens Publishers Milwaukee, WI), 2004.

Comanche, Gareth Stevens Publishers (Milwaukee, WI), 2004.

Cheyenne, Gareth Stevens Publishers (Milwaukee, WI), 2004.

Cherokee, Gareth Stevens Publishers (Milwaukee, WI), 2004.

RETELLER

How the People Found a Home, Macmillan/McGraw-Hill (New York, NY), 1997.

The Man Searching for the Sun, Macmillan/McGraw-Hill (New York, NY), 1997.

How the Mice Stole Fire, Macmillan/McGraw-Hill (New York, NY), 1999.

When the Sun Fell from the Sky, Macmillan/McGraw-Hill (New York, NY), 1999.

OTHER

Contributor of short stories to anthologies, including *Earth Song, Sky Spirit: Stories of the Contemporary Native American Experience,* Anchor (New York, NY), 1993; and *Blue Dawn, Red Earth: Contemporary Native American Storytellers,* Anchor, 1996. Contributor of poems to anthologies, including *A Multicultural Reader: Collection One,* Perfection Learning (Logan, IA), 2002. Contributor of articles to reference books, including *Gale Encyclopedia of Multicultural America,* Thomson Gale (Detroit, MI), 1995; *Peoples of the World,* Marshall Cavendish (New York, NY), 1999; *Native American Tribes,* Thomson Gale, 1999; and *Rain Forest Encyclopedia,* Marshall Cavendish, 2001. Editor of *OKC Camp Crier,* 1987-88; General editor of *The Encyclopedia of North American Indians;* guest coeditor of special issue of *Callaloo;* editorial consultant to university presses. Contributor of articles, short stories, creative nonfiction, poetry, and reviews to periodicals, including *Roundup, News from Indian Country, Studies in American Indian Literatures, Raven Chronicles, Moccasin Telegraph, Four Directions, Eclectic Literary Forum, Aboriginal Landscapes,* and *Native Press Research Journal.*

WORK IN PROGRESS: The Choctaw Nation: A History, for University of New Mexico Press; *Bridle Fee: A Hom-Astubby Mystery,* volume two in the "Hom-Astubby Mystery" series, for University of Oklahoma Press; a university textbook providing an introduction to Native American studies; and "a third volume in the 'Hom-Astubby Mystery' series; an historical novel reevaluating the most forgotten presidential election in U.S. history; a murder mystery set in the world of the U.S. Chess Federation, Swiss-system, weekend chess tournaments; other novels and academic projects."

SIDELIGHTS: A member of the Choctaw Nation, D.L. Birchfield is a teacher of fiction and Native American studies at a Canadian university. He has also authored numerous nonfiction titles for juvenile readers dealing with topics in Native American history and served as editor for the eleven-volume *The Encyclopedia of North American Indians.* Writing for adults, he produced the 2004 novel *Field of Honor.*

Birchifield's many books for younger readers include several volumes in the "Native American Peoples" series from the publishers Gareth Stevens. Each thirty-two-page book deals with a specific nation of Native Americans, providing historical background, sidebars, highlighted information, and numerous color illustrations. Reviewing *Cherokee, Cheyenne,* and *Comanche,* S.K. Joiner, writing for *School Library Journal,* commented that "each book is full of information for reports." In a review of other books in the series, including Birchfield's *Apache,* Joiner further noted that they are "solid sources for both current and historical information about each nation." Writing for the "Raintree Biographies" Series, Birchfield traces the major incidents in the life of a famous Native American leader in his *Crazy Horse.* Sue Sherif, writing for *School Library Journal,* felt the books in the series "offer quick overviews of the lives of these American icons." Serving as editor, Birchfield oversaw the production of the eleven volumes of *The Encyclopedia of North American Indians.* Despite its name, the volumes also deal with indigenous people of Mexico, Central and South America, and even Greenland and the Caribbean. Birchfield enlisted forty Native Americans to take part in the project, an effort to bring the lives of Native Americans out of the dry history books and into the modern world. This "unique undertaking," as a *Booklist* contributor described the project, includes plentiful illustrations with alphabetical entries geared for readers from the middle grades to young adult. The same *Booklist* reviewer felt that "entries present basic information in a readable format," and that Birchfield "has taken care to blend contemporary and historical illustrations." Overall, this reviewer concluded, *The Encyclopedia of North American Indians* is "an extremely useful addition." Similarly, John Burch, writing in *Library Journal,* called the work "lavishly illustrated," and praised the "multicultural perspective that will enhance the juvenile or general reference collections of any library."

Birchfield has also turned his hand to adult fiction. His *Field of Honor* is a "mix of biting satire and science fiction," according to *Booklist* reviewer Deborah Donovan. The novel follows the adventures and misadventures of McDaniel, a Marine and half Choctaw, who hides out in Oklahoma after having deserted during the Vietnam War. In Oklahoma he discovers an underground (literally) community of Choctaw who have fled into subterranean caverns to escape the destruction of their culture by the dominant white culture above ground. In this society, McDaniel learns of the extent of destruction to his native community. Though Donovan called Birchfield's first novel "over-the-top," she also felt his "message is impossible to ignore."

Birchfield told *CA:* "As a high school sophomore in the early 1960s I became intensely aware of the vicarious pleasures I derived from reading fiction, when I sustained a badly broken leg in sophomore football practice that curtailed many of my activities, and after I had broken away from my parents' new religion (after having practically lived at church for five years, after my parents had become neophyte converts when I was ten years old—old enough to remember life before church). At that time, when I was fifteen, I decided (as a long-range goal and as an avocation) that I wanted to find out if I could learn how to write fiction. Accordingly, on my own, throughout high school, I haunted libraries, reading books on the craft of fiction, and *Writer's Digest* and *Writer* magazines. I studied *Writer's Market* and read biographical sketches of writers (such as in *CA*), and autobiographies by writers. I paid the most attention to what writers had to say about their careers.

"I don't labor under any illusions that any of my novels might change the world in any way, but I have some things to say, and I want readers to be entertained. So I strive to try to seduce a reader into wanting to turn the pages. I try to enable readers to lose themselves, vicariously, in a fictional world where they will want to find out what happens next, and, along the way, become aware that I am sharing my view of some things.

"In *Field of Honor,* I tried to communicate what that process of disillusionment felt like. The vehicle for that was to take an exaggerated caricature of a teenager from the early sixties (with an exaggerated 1950s American worldview), put him in isolation for more than a decade, and then thrust him into the world of the mid-1970s with his 1950s mental constellation still intact, where he would be an out-of-place coming-of-age baby boomer (having missed all the watershed moments of his generation—the Kennedy assassinations, Vietnam War, civil rights movement, urban riots, Watergate, etc). He's a character I would hope baby boomers might connect with emotionally, and root for, while fearing it is surely going to end badly for him, because he represents what we used to be, long ago, and we know what happened to us. He's too out of place in the mid-1970s, and what he tries to do in the book is dangerous. My generation learned that the hard way, but this guy possesses some remarkable qualities that might make him equal to the task, and I'd hope that possibility might remind us of how we were in those coming-of-age moments when we possessed some remarkable qualities that made us willing to put ourselves on the line. I'd hope it might speak to other baby boomers, and that other generations might come away from it having learned something about what it was like to be a baby boomer, at least for many of us.

"I was astonished to learn that I could write humor—satire. For me it was a cathartic discovery because my writing was propelled by anger, bordering on rage, at having learned the history of what the United States has done to my Choctaw people. That my literary response to that has turned out to be humor has been the biggest surprise of my life. I credit the catharsis of humor with preserving my sanity and prolonging my life. Otherwise, I would have burned out, or stressed out, or simply disintegrated, long ago.

"I've also been more than a little surprised at producing novels for adults, as my ambition at the outset, as a teenager, was pretty much limited to hoping to write YA novels in the juvenile outdoor adventure tradition of authors such as Stephen W. Meader and Jim Kjelgaard, having grown up spending a lot of time in the remote backwoods of the Choctaw country of southeastern Oklahoma and knowing that world very well (where my Choctaw relatives lived literally at the end of the road in the Ouachita Mountains, didn't own cars, didn't have electricity or running water or indoor toilets, cooked on a wood-burning stove and still lived a subsistence lifestyle largely dependent on hunting and fishing).

"I cut my teeth on genre fiction as a preteen and a teenager and have never seen any conflict in employing genre-fiction techniques in attempting to write stories that are otherwise not genre fiction. Those

techniques are, as a matter of craft, extremely difficult to master, but I believe an author has an obligation to employ every trick known to the craft to seduce a reader into turning the pages. I don't agree with some academics who scoff at those techniques. I don't disparage the fiction many of them write, much of it experimental in ways that will only have a limited appeal. What they do is important and helps all of us, but many of them have little choice but to publish in journals that have 700 libraries for subscribers, and few readers. I would rather have readers.

"I had the luxury of writing rough drafts of novels, then putting them aside for years while I thought about the storylines and matters of craft related to that, before taking any of them up again and trying to execute any revisions. I did that again and again, at intervals, for a long time. In the meantime, I tried to learn how to write poetry, short stories, plays, reviews, literary criticism, nonfiction, creative nonfiction, anything from which I might learn something about writing, and I published a lot of that in small journals. In my reading I looked for anything that might show me how something might be done that might solve some problem that had me hung up in some novel I was writing, discovering potential solutions in works ranging from *The Clouds* by Aristophanes, to *The Crucible* by Henry Miller.

"I've learned that one of the most effective creative tools for me is to burden a novel with artificial limitations that I don't like and that I don't want to deal with. Forcing myself to try to figure out ways to overcome those limitations has sometimes led to creative solutions that I never otherwise would have imagined, which can have the power of being transformational for a story, suggesting other revisions that can end up making it truly distinctive. It's a long, difficult process, but my hope is that at some point in any of my novels a reader familiar with my work would have an awareness that nobody else could have written that novel.

"I can't begin to tell you how much it meant to me just to get my first novel published, let alone for it to be well received. For all those many years, I was aware that if the things I was trying to do didn't work out, I'd have no one to blame but myself, because I'd insisted on trying to figure out how to do it on my own, mostly when I was a teenager. There were a lot of times during those long years that I had ample reason to second-guess myself."

BIOGRAPHICAL AND CRITICAL SOURCES:

BOOKS

The Oklahoma Intelligence Test: New and Collected Elementary, Epistolary, Autobiographical, and Oratorical Choctologies, Greenfield Review Press (Greenfield Center, NY), 1998.

PERIODICALS

Bloomsbury Review, May-June, 1996, review of *Rabbit: American Indian Legends,* p. 15.
Booklist, September 1, 1997, review of *The Encyclopedia of North American Indians,* p. 164; January 1, 2000, Dona Helmer, review of *The Encyclopedia of North American Indians,* p. 960; May 1, 2004, Deborah Donovan, review of *Field of Honor,* p. 1544.
Library Journal, May 1, 1997, John Burch, review of *The Encyclopedia of North American Indians,* p. 96.
School Library Journal, March, 2003, Sue Sherif, review of *Crazy Horse,* p. 214; September, 2003, S.K. Joiner, review of *Apache,* p. 222; May, 2004, S.K. Joiner, reviews of *Cherokee, Cheyenne,* and *Comanche,* p. 162; June, 2004, Susan Shaver, review of *The Trail of Tears,* p. 158.
Small Press Review, winter, 1995, Julie Parson-Nesbitt, review of *Durable Breath: Contemporary Native American Poetry,* p. 80.

ONLINE

Wordcraft Circle Web site, http://www.wordcraftcircle. org/ (August 13, 2005), "D.L. (Don) Birchfield, Choctaw."

*   *   *

BIRCHFIELD, Don L.
    See BIRCHFIELD, D.L.

*   *   *

BIRKS, Jane 1958-

PERSONAL: Born November 9, 1958, in Broken Hill, New South Wales, Australia; daughter of Brian (an exploration geology manager) and Dorothy (a teacher; maiden name, Gould) Hawkins; married Peter Birks, (an educator) August 18, 1979; children: Jared, Cody. *Ethnicity:* "Caucasian." *Education:* Griffith University, B.Ed., 1982; Queensland University of Technology, graduate diploma in teacher-librarianship, 1993; University of Southern Queensland, M.Ed., 2004. *Hobbies and other interests:* Travel, cooking and eating, sailing.

ADDRESSES: Home—36 Camfield St., Alexandra Headland, Queensland 4572, Australia. *E-mail*—jbirks@bigpond.com.

CAREER: Writer. Education Queensland, Queensland, Australia, teacher, 1979-88, teacher-librarian, 1989-98; Zayed University, Dubai, United Arab Emirates, academic librarian, 1999-2003; University of the Sunshine Coast, Queensland, lecturer in higher education (internet courses), 2004—. Basic and Beyond Computer Education, director, 1996-98.

MEMBER: Australian Library and Information Association.

AWARDS, HONORS: Online Learning Course Developer Award, Education Queensland, 2004.

WRITINGS:

(With Fiona Hunt) *Hands-On Information Literacy Activities,* Neal-Schuman Publishers (New York, NY), 2003.

Contributor to *Expectations of Librarians in the Twenty-first Century,* edited by Karl Bridges, Greenwood Press (Westport, CT), 2003. Contributor of articles to professional journals, including *Portal: Libraries and the Academy.* Also author of Which Literacy? (professional learning course).

WORK IN PROGRESS: Numerous children's picture books, including *Up the Beach;* research on the way different groups and/or individuals take up or adapt to an internet learning environment in higher education.

SIDELIGHTS: Jane Birks *CA:* "I enjoy writing and the collaborative effort involved in joint publications. My writing has resulted from my work. My first book,

Hands-On Information Literacy Activities, was written as a result of a team effort to support young-adult learners and was published in order to share useful information with others. I often feel driven and can set myself a task which I will work at virtually without a break until it's completed. I like to keep moving forward and being productive."

*   *   *

BISHOP, Holley 1966(?)-

PERSONAL: Born c. 1966. *Hobbies and other interests:* Beekeeping.

ADDRESSES: Home—New York, NY; CT. *Agent*—c/o Author Mail, Free Press, 1230 Avenue of the Americas, New York, NY 10020.

CAREER: Writer. Has worked as a literary agent.

WRITINGS:

Robbing the Bees: A Biography of Honey, the Sweet Liquid Gold That Seduced the World, Free Press (New York, NY), 2005.

SIDELIGHTS: Holley Bishop is a former literary agent and part-time beekeeper. Her first book, *Robbing the Bees: A Biography of Honey, the Sweet Liquid Gold That Seduced the World,* reflects her passion for bees and their most famous product. Her interest in bees and honey was sparked by a neighbor who kept a couple of hives on his property. Before long she had begun to learn the ancient art and science of beekeeping, and had some hives of her own. *Robbing the Bees* details the many ancient references to honey. For instance, royal seals in Egypt featured representations of bees, as did Greek coins and the coat of arms of Napoleon. The insects' cooperative way of life, in which the individuals are important only for their contributions to the hive as a whole, has long been a subject of fascination to philosophers and sociologists, while the geometric, intricate structure of their hives inspired the likes of renowned architect Frank Lloyd Wright.

Bishop's book explains how a bee anatomy is perfectly adapted to mesh with a flower's in order to facilitate pollination. The insects' pollen-collecting abilities are enhanced by the static electricity they create as they fly—up to 450 volts of it. The author also offers a profile of Donald Smiley, one of the approximately two thousand professional beekeepers in the United States. The long hours, hard work, and relatively low profit margin typical of beekeeping mean that one must be truly dedicated to make it a profession. In recent years, parasites fatal to bee populations have presented serious challenges to beekeepers, although declines in natural populations have presented new business opportunities. Some beekeepers travel with their hives to farms that hire them to ensure good crop pollination. In addition to detailing history, lore, and factual information about bees and beekeeping, the author also includes a section of honey-based recipes and information about the medicinal uses of bee products.

Booklist reviewer Nancy Bent called *Robbing the Bees* an "eminently readable" book, noting that in her descriptions of modern bee culture, Bishop's "journalistic ear for local culture is put to good use." A *Publishers Weekly* writer commented that the author is, at times, weighed down by her attempt to include so much information. Yet she concluded that, "her combination of engrossing natural history and down-home reportage make this a fitting homage to one of nature's most admirable creatures."

BIOGRAPHICAL AND CRITICAL SOURCES:

PERIODICALS

Booklist, March 1, 2005, Nancy Bent, review of *Robbing the Bees: A Biography of Honey, the Sweet Liquid Gold That Seduced the World,* p. 1124.
Forbes, March 14, 2005, Susan Adams, review of *Robbing the Bees,* p. 117.
Kirkus Reviews, January 15, 2005, review of *Robbing the Bees,* p. 93.
Newsday, May 15, 2005, Kerry Fried, review of *Robbing the Bees.*
Publishers Weekly, February 14, 2005, review of *Robbing the Bees,* p. 61.

ONLINE

Bookreporter, http://www.bookreporter.com/ (July 7, 2005), review of *Robbing the Bees.**

BJORNERUD, Marcia

PERSONAL: Female.

ADDRESSES: Home—Appleton, WI. *Office*—Department of Geology, Lawrence University, P.O. Box 599, Appleton, WI 54912. *E-mail*—marcia.bjornerud@lawrence.edu.

CAREER: Lawrence University, Appleton, WI, professor of geology and chair of geology department.

WRITINGS:

Reading the Rocks: The Autobiography of the Earth, Basic Books (New York, NY), 2005.

SIDELIGHTS: A geologist with a particular expertise in how mountains are formed, Marcia Bjornerud is the author of *Reading the Rocks: The Autobiography of the Earth,* a geological history "that will instill an appreciation for the dynamism and comparative uniqueness of our planet," according to *Booklist* reviewer Gilbert Taylor. Bjornerud describes the major theories and recent developments in this complex field, as well as intriguing asides, such as the theory that the oceans were once entirely frozen and the fact that a small zircon found in Australia is the oldest object native to planet Earth. "Bjornerud chronicles the watersheds in Earth's history from the primordial supernova that seeded the nascent solar nebula to the man-made cataclysms of global warming," explained a *Publishers Weekly* reviewer, who added that at present humanity produces sixteen times as much carbon dioxide as volcanoes produce. At the same time, she sets forth the remarkable powers of renewal and recycling that the Earth has displayed over its long history, allowing it to regulate itself through redistribution of elements among the oceans, the interior, and the atmosphere. A *Kirkus Reviews* contributor particularly praised "Bjornerud's plain-English approach," which makes her work easily accessible to the average reader.

BIOGRAPHICAL AND CRITICAL SOURCES:

PERIODICALS

Booklist, March 15, 2005, Gilbert Taylor, review of *Reading the Rocks: The Autobiography of the Earth,* p. 1252.

Kirkus Reviews, March 1, 2005, review of *Reading the Rocks,* p. 269.
Publishers Weekly, February 28, 2005, review of *Reading the Rocks,* p. 50.
Science News, June 11, 2005, Cait Goldberg, review of *Reading the Rocks,* p. 383.

ONLINE

Perseus Books Web site, http://www.perseusbooks group.com/ (July 5, 2005), brief biography of Marcia Bjornerud.*

*   *   *

BLUE, Howard 1941-

PERSONAL: Born October 7, 1941, in New York, NY; married Deborah Goldberg (a teacher and writer); children: Tanya, Julie, Elise. *Education:* Stony Brook University, B.A., 1963; Long Island University, M.A., 1970. *Politics:* Progressive. *Hobbies and other interests:* Genealogy, hiking.

ADDRESSES: Home—1951 Valentines Rd., Westbury, NY 11590. *E-mail*—khovard@verizon.net.

CAREER: Writer. Union Free School District, No. 4, Northport, NY, social studies teacher, 1966-98; Foreign Visitors Exchange Program with Israel and Russia, coordinator, 1987-94. Copake (NY) Citizens for Fair Taxation, cofounder.

AWARDS, HONORS: Fulbright Seminar Award, Israel, 1986; National Endowment for the Humanities fellowship, 1993; Ray Stanich Award, Friends of Old Time Radio, 2003.

WRITINGS:

Words at War: World War II-Era Radio Drama and the Postwar Broadcasting Industry Blacklist, Scarecrow Press (Lanham, MD), 2002.

Contributor of translations to *An Anthology of Russian Literature,* edited by Nicholas Rzhevsky, M.E. Sharpe (Armonk, NY), 1996.

WORK IN PROGRESS: Twenty Radio and Television Shows That Helped Change America.

SIDELIGHTS: Howard Blue told *CA:* "My first major writing project was a master's thesis about Nikita Khrushchev. Ironically, thirty years later I was able to donate a copy of it to a scholarly institute at Brown University, headed by Khrushchev's son, Sergei.

"My overall interest in writing was influenced by some great experiences that my former students and I had interviewing interesting people. I had my students interview a cousin of Anne Frank, a former German World War I U-boat sailor, a local veteran of the Spanish Civil War, and other witnesses to history. To enable them to interview a Canadian World War I veteran of trench warfare and the copilot of the airplane that dropped the atomic bomb on Hiroshima, both of whom lived far from us, I set up telephone interviews using a speakerphone. My writings, like many of the best lessons that I prepared when teaching, are driven by a concern for international understanding and social justice. I studied a great deal of Russian literature in my younger years. Tolstoy and his grand view of life had a big impact on me."

"I can be compulsive when writing nonfiction. Heed the warnings that one must take breaks when sitting at a computer. My back and I learned the hard way!

"*Words at War: World War II—Era Radio Drama and the Postwar Broadcasting Industry Blacklist* discusses both World War II radio propaganda and the postwar broadcasting industry blacklist. I originally planned it as an anthology of World War II propaganda radio, from four countries: Britain, the Soviet Union, Nazi Germany, and the USSR. I did some research in Moscow and in the BBC archives in England. But I changed the book's focus when I realized both how much American material there was out there and that there would be greater interest in a history of radio drama. I wrote *Words at War* partly to demonstrate the influence of propaganda during a crucial time in American history and partly to make a plea for the Bill of Rights about which many Americans seem to have rather ambiguous feelings.

"My interest in the Golden Age of Radio, part of the theme of *Words at War,* was revived while listening to BBC radio drama every evening during a 1973 sabbatical leave in London.

"I tried (unsuccessfully) to get my first book, a history of Amnesty International, published almost thirty years ago. It took me all that time to finally get one published. Part of the reason is that there's a tough market for books. My advice: Keep pluggin."

BIOGRAPHICAL AND CRITICAL SOURCES:

PERIODICALS

Journal of Popular Culture, August, 2004, John M. O'Toole, review of *Words at War: World War II-Era Radio Drama and the Postwar Broadcasting Industry Blacklist,* p. 225.

*   *   *

BONDURANT, Matt
(Matthew Bondurant)

PERSONAL: Male. *Education:* James Madison University, M.A., 1993; Florida State University, Ph.D., 2003.

ADDRESSES: Home—Alexandria, VA. *Office*—George Mason University, Department of English, Robinson A487, 4400 University Dr., MSN 3E4, Fairfax, VA 22030. *Agent*—Alex Grass, Trident Media Group, 41 Madison Ave., 36th Fl., New York, NY 10010. *E-mail*—mbondura@gmu.edu; bondurantmr@hotmail.com.

CAREER: George Mason University, Fairfax, VA, professor of literature, 1997—; British Museum, London, England, steward, 2002; has also worked for Associated Press and National Public Radio.

AWARDS, HONORS: Kingsbury fellow, Florida State University; two Bread Loaf scholarships; Walter E. Dakin fellow in fiction, Sewanee Writers Conference; Bernice Slote Award for Best Story by a New Writer.

WRITINGS:

The Third Translation (novel), Hyperion (New York, NY), 2005.

Fiction editor for literary magazines, including *Southeast Review* and *Appalachee Review.* Contributor to periodicals, including *Glimmer Train, New England Review, Prairie Schooner,* and *Hawaii Review.*

The Third Translation was published in Spanish, Italian, Portugese, Russian, Catalan, German, French, and Serbian.

SIDELIGHTS: Matt Bondurant's novel debut, *The Third Translation,* revolves around an ancient Egyptian relic known as the Stela of Paser. The stela is a funerary stone, broken in two and with some of its edges missing. The hieroglyphics on it have mystified scholars throughout the ages, and Walter Rothschild, a middle-aged American Egyptologist, has been hired by the British Museum to clear up the puzzle at last. Yet as his contracted time with the museum draws to a close, Rothschild has still not solved the riddle. The quest becomes more urgent when a young woman he meets seduces him in the museum and steals a valuable text for which Rothschild is responsible. As he seeks to retrieve the stolen document and clear his name, he is also pursued by a cultish group that wants to make use of his specialized knowledge of translation. He soon finds not only his reputation and career at stake, but his life as well.

Bondurant himself worked at the British Museum, where he became fascinated with the real-life Stela of Paser. Allison Block, a reviewer for *Booklist,* noted that the author's "extensive research has paid off in a literary page-turner whose characters are as compelling and complex as the Stela itself." *Washington Examiner* critic Charles Devilbiss gave the book a strong recommendation, describing the novel as "an ingeniously literate and incandescent historical thriller that mixes linguistic cryptology and translation with gripping success in unexpected and ingenious ways." Devilbiss was especially impressed with Bondurant's use of language, which he called "absolutely remarkable in its breadth. The words coalesce like the vivid lines of the glyphs themselves, to the point where you see them rise before you, a swirl of joyous wording that is rarely matched." Devilbiss concluded, "Bondurant has proven himself a master scribe here, and this text deserves to be read as closely and safeguarded as long as the sacred writings so intrinsic to his masterful work."

BIOGRAPHICAL AND CRITICAL SOURCES:

PERIODICALS

Booklist, February 15, 2005, Allison Block, review of *The Third Translation,* p. 1058.
Kirkus Reviews, January 15, 2005, review of *The Third Translation,* p. 66.
Publishers Weekly, January 24, 2005, Natalie Danford, "Most Likely, to Succeed," p. 26, review of *The Third Translation,* p. 218.

ONLINE

Matt Bondurant Home Page, http://www.matt bondurant.com (July 5, 2005).
Third Translation Web site, http://www.thirdtranslation. com/ (July 5, 2005).
Washington Examiner Online, http://dcexaminer.com/ (July 7, 2005), Charles Devilbiss, review of *The Third Translation.*

*   *   *

BONDURANT, Matthew
  See BONDURANT, Matt

*   *   *

BORDEWICH, Fergus M. 1948(?)-

PERSONAL: Born c. 1948, in New York, NY; son of LaVerne Madigan (a government aid agency administrator).

ADDRESSES: Agent—c/o Author Mail, Amistad Press, 10 E. 53rd St., 7th Fl., New York, NY 10022. *E-mail*—fergus@valstar.net.

CAREER: Writer and journalist.

WRITINGS:

Cathay: A Journey in Search of Old China (nonfiction), introduction by Jan Morris, Prentice-Hall (New York, NY), 1991.

Peach Blossom Spring: Adapted from a Chinese Tale (folklore), illustrated by Yang Ming-Yi, Green Tiger Press (New York, NY), 1994.

Killing the White Man's Indian: Reinventing of Native Americans at the End of the Twentieth Century (nonfiction), Doubleday (New York, NY), 1996.

My Mother's Ghost (memoir), Doubleday (New York, NY), 2001.

Bound for Canaan: The Epic Story of the Underground Railroad, America's First Civil Rights Movement (nonfiction), Amistad (New York, NY), 2005.

Contributor to *New York Times, Smithsonian, American Heritage, Atlantic Monthly, Harper's,* and *Reader's Digest.*

SIDELIGHTS: Fergus M. Bordewich has written books on a number of nonfiction subjects, including the Underground Railroad, the contemporary state of Native-American culture and identity, and his own mother's work among the Native Americans. He has traveled widely as a journalist and published many articles in periodicals about American history, human rights, and other issues. Growing up in Yonkers, New York, he lived near a neighborhood that was said to have a great heritage of activity in the Underground Railroad, a network of safe-houses set up by concerned people in the years prior to the U.S. Civil War, through which escaped slaves from the South were able to make their way north to safety in Canada. Later in life, he researched the area near his home and found that most of the stories were not based in fact, but these tales of the Underground Railroad remained an inspiration to Bordewich nevertheless. The importance of helping downtrodden people was demonstrated to him early by his mother, who, although she was of Irish descent, was a tireless worker for the rights of Native Americans. She traveled throughout the country in her position as director of the Association on Bureau of Indian Affairs, and her son frequently went with her, learning firsthand about the life of modern Native Americans.

Bordewich addressed the question of Native-American identity in his book *Killing the White Man's Indian: Reinventing of Native Americans at the End of the Twentieth Century.* His aim was to clarify the distorted image of Native Americans in the 1990s. Bordewich posits that the white man's culture has always used the Native Americans as a means to define what is

good and bad about Western culture. He gives examples of this, and also demonstrates the ways in which Native Americans themselves have played into these cultural stereotypes. He states that Native Americans have been portrayed as either noble, spiritually superior, natural people or as brutal, ignorant savages, depending on what ends need to be met by the characterization. Bordewich argues that neither of these images is correct or timely, and he seeks to offer an accurate picture of the Native American today.

Assessing this book in *Social Science Journal,* Thomas J. Hoffman commented that Bordewich's "style is that of a journalist: he tells stories, interprets them, and then comments on their implications. Therein lies the deceptive charm . . . and the fatal flaw of this work." In Hoffman's opinion, Bordewich does not succeed in his quest to offer a balanced discussion of the issue of tribal sovereignty, but instead lets his bias against this concept show through. "Bordewich is a fine storyteller," the critic concluded, "and an occasionally subtle advocate of certain social and political positions. He has presented some stories of some real, flesh and blood Indians. However, although his intent was to do so, he has not removed distortion from the American imagination." On the other hand, *Booklist* contributor Ray Olson gave unequivocal praise to the author for his "hefty, engrossing" book and his in-depth, even-handed examination of Native-American culture.

Bordewich recalls his mother's vibrant life and her horrible death in his memoir *My Mother's Ghost.* As a young person, the author saw his mother, LaVerne Madigan, as an heroic figure. Brilliant, energetic, and determined to bring justice to oppressed people, she earned a college degree at a time when few women did so, worked to help interred Japanese Americans during World War II, and eventually took charge of a national relief agency for Native Americans. After Bordewich, who was then fourteen years old, begged her to go horseback riding with him one day, she was killed in a violent accident. The trauma and guilt linked to her demise has cast a shadow over Bordewich's life. He followed in his mother's footsteps, confronting the Ku Klux Klan as a civil rights worker, but eventually fell into depression and alcoholism. "Bordewich's pace remains as steady as his unflinching reporter's eye as he recounts his own remarkable life, then sets about dismantling the myths of his ancestors in an effort to exorcise his mother's ghost," explained Amber Nimocks in the *Fort Worth Star-*

Telegram. Booklist reviewer Patricia Monaghan called *My Mother's Ghost* a "gripping, unforgettable memoir" that proves the author to be "a master of pacing, sensuous detail, and filmlike narrative."

In *Bound for Canaan: The Underground Railroad and the War for the Soul of America* Bordewich takes a penetrating look at the secret network that helped so many slaves to reach freedom. He describes many of the people who made this system work, both famous and obscure. Charles L. Lumpkins, a *Library Journal* reviewer, recommended this book as "a rich, spellbinding, and readable narrative." A *Publishers Weekly* reviewer echoed that praise, calling *Bound for Canaan* "a clear, utterly compelling survey of the Railroad." Numerous reviewers pointed out the author's skill in showing the complex interplay between abolitionists, slaves, freed blacks, and other parties involved in making the Railroad work, as well as his ability to make his characters and their era come alive. The *Publishers Weekly* reviewer concluded: "All emerge as fully realized characters, flawed but determined people doing what they believed was right."

BIOGRAPHICAL AND CRITICAL SOURCES:

BOOKS

Bordewich, Fergus M., *My Mother's Ghost,* Doubleday (New York, NY), 2001.

PERIODICALS

American Heritage, April, 2001, review of *My Mother's Ghost,* p. 14.
Booklist, June 1, 1994, Hazel Rochman, review of *Peach Blossom Spring: Adapted from a Chinese Tale,* p. 1835; February 15, 1996, Ray Olson, review of *Killing the White Man's Indian: Reinventing of Native Americans at the End of the Twentieth Century,* p. 970; November 15, 2000, Patricia Monaghan, review of *My Mother's Ghost,* p. 589; February 1, 2005, Vernon Ford, review of *Bound for Canaan: The Underground Railroad and the War for the Soul of America,* p. 933.
Current Anthropology, August-October, 1998, Les W. Field, review of *Killing the White Man's Indian,* p. 583.

Fort Worth Star-Telegram, February 28, 2001, Amber Nimocks, review of *My Mother's Ghost.*
Hollywood Reporter, April 11, 2005, Gregory McNamee, review of *Bound for Canaan,* p. 28.
Kirkus Reviews, January 15, 2005, review of *Bound for Canaan,* p. 94.
Library Journal, February 1, 2005, Charles L. Lumpkins, review of *Bound for Canaan,* p. 95.
New Republic, July 8, 1996, Richard White, review of *Killing the White Man's Indian,* p. 37.
Publishers Weekly, December 21, 1990, Genevieve Stuttaford, review of *Cathay: A Journey in Search of Old China,* p. 371; May 16, 1994, review of *Peach Blossom Spring,* p. 63; January 1, 1996, review of *Killing the White Man's Indian,* p. 63; November 6, 2000, review of *My Mother's Ghost,* p. 80; January 31, 2005, review of *Bound for Canaan,* p. 56.
Social Science Journal, January, 1999, Thomas J. Hoffman, review of *Killing the White Man's Indian,* p. 185.

ONLINE

Fergus Bordewich Home Page, http://www.fergus bordewich.com (July 8, 2005).*

*   *   *

BOTTIGLIA, William F. 1912-2005
(William Filbert Bottiglia)

OBITUARY NOTICE—See index for *CA* sketch: Born November 23, 1912, in Bernardsville, NJ; died August 19, 2005, in Needham, MA. Educator and author. Bottiglia was a retired professor of Italian and French literature who was particularly noted for his studies on eighteenth-century French writer Voltaire. After completing a master's degree at Princeton University in 1935, he taught French and Italian there for five years. During World War II, he remained stateside as a general manager at the J. & S. Tool Company. in New Jersey. In 1948 he returned to academia as an assistant English professor at St. Lawrence University for a year. He then spent eight years as a professor and department chair in the Romance languages and literatures department at Ripon College. Bottiglia joined the Massachusetts Institute of Technology in 1956, where he later became head of the department of foreign literatures and linguistics from 1964 to 1973, and professor of management and humanities at the Sloan School of Management in 1973. He retired from teaching in 1991. During his career, Bottiglia produced two books on Voltaire: *Voltaire's Candide: Analysis of a Classic* (1959; revised edition, 1964) and the edited *Voltaire: A Collection of Critical Essays* (1968). Later, from 1997 to 1999, he completed a four-volume novel titled *Heroic Symphony.*

OBITUARIES AND OTHER SOURCES:

PERIODICALS

MIT Tech Talk, September 21, 2005, p. 6.

ONLINE

Massachusetts Institute of Technology News Office Web site, http://web.mit.edu/newsoffice/ (September 12, 2005).

*   *   *

BOTTIGLIA, William Filbert
    See BOTTIGLIA, William F.

*   *   *

BOUNDS, Gwendolyn 1971-
    (Wendy Bounds)

PERSONAL: Born August 29, 1971, in Durham, NC; partner of Kathryn Kranhold. *Education:* Graduated from University of North Carolina, Chapel Hill.

ADDRESSES: Home—Garrison, NY; New York, NY. *Office*—Wall Street Journal, 200 Liberty St., New York, NY 10281. *E-mail*—email@gwendolynbounds.com.

CAREER: Wall Street Journal, New York, NY, columnist, 1993—.

WRITINGS:

(As Wendy Bounds; with Ruth Hanessian) *Birds on the Couch: The Bird Shrink's Guide to Keeping Polly from Going Crackers and You out of the Cuckoo's Nest,* Crown (New York, NY), 1998.

Little Chapel on the River: A Pub, a Town, and the Search for What Matters Most, Morrow (New York, NY), 2005.

SIDELIGHTS: September 11, 2001 began as a normal day for *Wall Street Journal* columnist Gwendolyn Bounds and her partner, who were getting ready for work in their home across the street from the World Trade Center. The terrorist attacks severely damaged their apartment and sent them scrambling for temporary housing. Several weeks later, the couple found their way to the Hudson River Valley town of Garrison and a small Irish pub named Guinan's. Bounds began jotting down the stories of the bar's regulars and her own memories of growing up in small-town North Carolina. The resulting narrative, *Little Chapel on the River: A Pub, a Town, and the Search for What Matters Most,* was published in 2005. In an interview with *USA Today* contributor Bob Minzesheimer, Bounds shared the inspiration for the book's title: "Coming to Guinan's was something of a religion, with its own customs, community and rites of passage." She further commented that she wanted the book's style to "feel like the pace inside a bar where people are coming and going."

Library Journal contributor Maria Kochis commented that, "in the era of big box stores, chain restaurants, and the proliferation of cloned communities, this debut about a family-owned pub in Garrison, NY, on the Hudson River will be perceived as timely and meaningful." A *Publishers Weekly* reviewer wrote: "It modestly reminds us that in this uncertain world, when you come to a place that speaks to you, you should hold it dear and treasure it while it lasts." Mary Ann Smyth, writing for the *BookLoons* Web site, called the book "heartwarming and sensitively told," adding that "Bounds makes the camaraderie that drew patrons to Guinan's—to incorporate the store and pub into their lives—believable and endearing." Kim Hughes, a contributor to the *Toronto Star,* described *Little Chapel on the River* as "a tender, heartfelt love letter" and Bounds' writing style as "refreshingly uncluttered." *Week* magazine online columnist Dennis Smith called it "a beautifully told tale that shows how people come to know one another—talking, laughing, and learning."

In addition to her ongoing column with the *Wall Street Journal,* Bounds has contributed to numerous North Carolina newspapers, she has also collaborated with bird psychologist Ruth Hanessian to produce 1998's

Birds on the Couch: The Bird Shrink's Guide to Keeping Polly from Going Crackers and You out of the Cuckoo's Nest. A guide for the bird owner on controlling unruly pet behavior, *Birds on the Couch* was described by *Booklist* reviewer Nancy Bent as "full of practical advice" and "entertaining reading."

BIOGRAPHICAL AND CRITICAL SOURCES:

PERIODICALS

Booklist, June 1, 1998, Nancy Bent, review of *Birds on the Couch: The Bird Shrink's Guide to Keeping Polly from Going Crackers and You out of the Cuckoo's Nest,* p. 1694.
Library Journal, May 15, 2005, Maria Kochis, review of *Little Chapel on the River: A Pub, a Town, and the Search for What Matters Most,* p. 132.
Publishers Weekly, April 25, 2005, review of *Little Chapel on the River,* p. 46.

ONLINE

BookLoons, http://www.bookloons.com/ (September 22, 2005), Mary Ann Smyth, review of *Little Chapel on the River.*
Toronto Star Online, http://www.thestar.com/ (September 19, 2005), Kim Hughes, "A Refuge from a Tragic Storm," review of *Little Chapel on the River.*
USA Today Online, http://www.usatoday.com/ (July 7, 2005), Bob Minzesheimer, "One 'Little Chapel' Beer Changed Author's Life."
Week Online (http://www.theweekmagazine.com/ (September 16, 2005), Dennis Smith, review of *Little Chapel on the River.**

*   *   *

BOUNDS, Wendy
See BOUNDS, Gwendolyn

*   *   *

BOYDEN, Joseph 1966-

PERSONAL: Born 1966, in Ontario, Canada; son of Raymond Wilfred Boyden (a physician) and a teacher; married; wife's name, Amanda (a trapeze artist, contortionist, educator and writer). *Education:* York University, B.A., 1991; University of New Orleans, M.F.A.

ADDRESSES: Home—Ontario, Canada; New Orleans, LA. *Office*—Department of English, 127 Liberal Arts Bldg., University of New Orleans, New Orleans, LA 70148. *Agent*—Nicole Winstanley, Westwood Creative Artists, 94 Harbord St., Toronto, Ontario M5S 1G6, Canada. *E-mail*—jboyden@uno.edu.

CAREER: Northern College, James Bay, Ontario, Canada, former instructor in communications; University of New Orleans, New Orleans, LA, teacher of writing and literature.

AWARDS, HONORS: Canada Council for the Arts grant.

WRITINGS:

Born with a Tooth (short stories), Cormorant Books (Toronto, Ontario, Canada), 2001.
Three-Day Road (novel), Viking (New York, NY), 2005.
She Takes You Down (fiction), Weidenfeld & Nicolson (London, England), 2006.

Contributor to periodicals, including *Potpourri, Cimarron Review, Blue Penny Quarterly,* and *Panhandler.*

SIDELIGHTS: Joseph Boyden is a Canadian citizen who divides his time between his Ontario homeland and New Orleans, Louisiana. Although he has taught at the University of New Orleans for many years and has a deep attachment to the city, his fiction is more concerned with life in northern Ontario. In fact, the author has said that the distance between the setting of his stories and his base in New Orleans somehow facilitates his writing. His first book, *Born with a Tooth,* is a collection of short stories set in the remote lands of Ontario, where many of his characters have grown up on Indian reserves. Boyden did not have that experience personally, but his heritage does include ancestors from various Canadian tribes. "I'm Irish, Scottish and Métis (most people don't know what that means but it's Indian mixed with European blood, usually French and Indian, but in my case it's a little bit of French and more Scottish), and Mi'kmaq on my father's side. They're an east coast tribe in Canada," he told Susan Larson in the *Times-Picayune.* "But here's where it gets complicated. I have friends who've grown up on reserves and experienced horrible racism and all the trials and tribulations of being Indian. But my father raised us Irish-Catholic, and the Indian thing was really not discussed. . . . When I look at myself in the mirror I don't say I'm Indian. I don't want to come off as such a wannabe." Still, his familiarity with Native Canadian culture is evident in *Born with a Tooth,* according to Cheryl Petten in *Wind Speaker.* "Boyden is a talented writer," she asserted. "His characters are well put together—real, believable, human. By the end of the book, you feel like you know these people. You feel like you have been to these places with them, and have watched as bits of their lives have unfolded before you."

Boyden's first novel, *Three-Day Road,* also features characters of Native-Canadian extraction, and it addresses their part in World War I. Specifically, the story focuses on two Cree youths whose wilderness know-how is the foundation for their training as deadly efficient soldiers. The two long-time friends, who are very different in their natures, function as a sniper team, but things begin to go awry as they become addicted to narcotics, and to killing. Taking ever-greater risks in order to perfect the marksmanship in which he takes such pride, Elijah eventually slides into madness, and this leads to an act of outright murder. Xavier, meanwhile, watches his friend's disintegration helplessly, and returns from the war broken in spirit and body.

Three-Day Road allowed the author to indulge a personal passion for military history and also to pay tribute to his family experience. As Boyden explained to Larson, he came from a military family, and his father "was the most highly decorated doctor in the British Empire in World War II." About the book, *Library Journal* reviewer David Keymer stated, "In straightforward, concrete prose, first novelist Boyden evokes a ghastly poetry of death." A *Publishers Weekly* reviewer called the novel "a powerful tale of two young men numbed by the horrors and brutality of trench warfare. Boyden vividly portrays the chaos, fear, cowardice and courage of infantrymen."

BIOGRAPHICAL AND CRITICAL SOURCES:

PERIODICALS

Booklist, March 15, 2005, David Pitt, review of *Three-Day Road,* p. 1263.
Bookseller, April 16, 2004, p. 28.

Kirkus Reviews, February 15, 2005, review of *Three-Day Road,* p. 189.
Library Journal, May 15, 2005, David Keymer, review of *Three-Day Road,* p. 104.
Publishers Weekly, March 21, 2005, review of *Three-Day Road,* p. 35.
Times-Picayune (New Orleans, LA), May 10, 2005, Susan Larson, "Author Makes His Home in Orleans; Not Your Average Joseph."
Toronto Life, May, 2005, Ken Hunt, "One for the Road: Author Joseph Boyden Is Can-Lit's Newest Hot Property," p. 116.
Wind Speaker, November 21, 2001, Cheryl Petten, review of *Born with a Tooth,* p. 18.

ONLINE

Minnesota Public Radio Web site, http://news.minnesota.publicradio.org/ (May 24, 2005), Euan Kerr, interview with Joseph Boyden.*

*　　*　　*

BRADLEY, Ernestine 1935-

PERSONAL: Born 1935, in Passau, Germany; daughter of Sepp Misslbeck; immigrated to United States, 1957; naturalized U.S. citizen, 1963; married Robert Schlant (a physician; divorced); married Bill Bradley (a politician), 1974; children: (first marriage) Stephanie; (second marriage) Theresa Anne. *Education:* Emory University, B.A., Ph.D.

ADDRESSES: Home—NJ. *Office*—New School University, 66 W. 12th St., New York, NY 10011.

CAREER: Pan American Airlines, flight attendant, beginning 1957; Montclair State College, Montclair, NJ, former professor of German and comparative literature; New School University, New York, NY, part-time faculty member; has also worked for a film production company.

WRITINGS:

NONFICTION

Hermann Broch, Twayne (Boston, MA), 1978, published with a foreword by Michael P. Steinberg, University of Chicago Press (Chicago, IL), 1986.

(Editor with J. Thomas Rimer) *Legacies and Ambiguities: Postwar Fiction and Culture in West Germany and Japan,* Woodrow Wilson Center Press (Washington, DC), 1991.

The Language of Silence: West German Literature and the Holocaust, Routledge (New York, NY) 1999.

The Way Home: A German Childhood, an American Life, Pantheon Books (New York, NY), 2005.

SIDELIGHTS: Ernestine Bradley chronicles her remarkable life in her memoir *The Way Home: A German Childhood, an American Life.* The book's first half recounts the author's youth in Germany, including the years of Nazi rule, while the second relates her move to the United States and her ascent to the public stage as the wife of Bill Bradley, a former basketball star and Democratic hopeful in the presidential election of 2000.

Bradley grew up in the towns of Passau and Ingolstadt. Her descriptions of these places are "vivid and often warm," according to Edward Morris, who interviewed Bradley for *Bookpage.com.* That warmth is expressed even though Bradley suffered considerably as a child. Morris noted that Bradley's mother dominates these memories, even as she dominated her daughter's life. Her mother became pregnant out of wedlock, but did not tell the child's father, who left to join the German military. She then married a local man, and Ernestine grew up believing that he was her real father. When she was eight years old, her biological father returned, and her mother's marriage ended.

The period following the end of World War II was a very difficult one for that Germany's citizens, economically as well as emotionally and intellectually. There was a "stifling atmosphere of denial" about the Nazi regime and its atrocities, according to Helen Thorpe, a writer for *New York.* Troubled by her home life as by well as her country's heritage, Bradley left as soon as she could, her means of escape a job as a flight attendant for Pan American Airlines. In 1958, she came to the United States, and soon after that she left her job to marry an American doctor. She continued to travel and study, eventually earning multiple degrees, and had a daughter before her marriage ended. Bradley became a respected professor of comparative literature, authoring two books about Hermann Broch, an Austrian philosopher, and one book on German novelists and their treatment of the Jewish Holocaust. The

last-named book, *The Language of Silence: West German Literature and the Holocaust,* is "elegantly written and devoid of the sort of jargon that mars many academic works," according to Sara Mosle in *Harper's Bazaar.*

In 1970 she met Bill Bradley, who at the time was a professional basketball player with the New York Knicks. They met at a game only to discover that they lived in the same apartment building. In 1974 they were married. Four years later Bradley ran for a seat in the U.S. Senate and won. In 2000 he mounted a campaign for the Democratic presidential nomination. Ernestine Bradley's position as a potential first lady stirred up considerable interest; if her husband had been elected, she would have been only the second foreign-born First Lady. Bradley campaigned energetically for her husband when he sought the Democratic nomination, just as she had during his Senate campaign.

Reviewing Ernestine Bradley's autobiography, a *Publishers Weekly* writer said that *The Way Home* stands as a "fine portrait of a childhood spent in wartime and an adult's search for true identity." Carol Haggas, a *Booklist* reviewer, especially liked the way Bradley analyzes her difficult and ambiguous relationship with her mother, showing how those sorts of tension can carry on far into a person's adult life. "Unflinchingly honest, Bradley mines the most sensitive and complex parts of her life with brutal candor," Haggas added. In addition to detailing her childhood, her coming of age in postwar Germany, and her adult careers and marriages, Bradley also includes an open and honest recounting of her diagnosis with breast cancer and her subsequent treatment. Haggis concluded that this book is a "stirring tale" of courage, sacrifice, and triumph.

BIOGRAPHICAL AND CRITICAL SOURCES:

BOOKS

Bradley, Ernestine, *The Way Home: A German Childhood, an American Life,* Pantheon Books (New York, NY), 2005.

PERIODICALS

Booklist, February 1, 2005, Carol Haggas, review of *The Way Home: A German Childhood, an American Life,* p. 921.

Gazette (Cedar Rapids, IA), August 5, 1999, Steve Gravelle, "Ernestine Bradley Points to Polls."

Harper's Bazaar, March, 2000, Sara Mosle, interview with Ernestine Bradley, p. 400.

Kirkus Reviews, January 15, 2005, review of *The Way Home,* p. 95.

Library Journal, Jill Ortner, March 15, 2005, review of *The Way Home,* p. 92.

Newsweek, September 13, 1999, Lynette Clemetson, "The Importance of Ernestine," p. 28; January 24, 2000, Matt Bai, "A Daughter's Hard Questions," p. 50.

New York, January 10, 2000, Helen Thorpe, "Bill Bradley's Secret Weapon."

People, February 21, 2000, "One Shall Be First," p. 50.

Publishers Weekly, February 7, 2005, review of *The Way Home,* p. 56.

ONLINE

Bookpage, http://www.bookpage.com/ (July 7, 2005), Edward Morris, interview with Ernestine Bradley.

Hill News Online (Washington, DC), http://www.hillnews.com/ (April 5, 2005), Betsy Rothstein, "Ernestine Bradley Finds 'Home,' amid Husband's Career."*

*   *   *

BRALLIER, Kate

PERSONAL: Born in New York, NY; married. *Education:* Attended Yale University and University of California at Irvine. *Hobbies and other interests:* Travel.

ADDRESSES: Agent—Kay McCauley, The Pimlico Agency, Inc., P.O. Box 20447, Cherokee Station, New York, NY 10021.

CAREER: Senior editor at a publishing house in New York, NY.

WRITINGS:

Seal Island (romance novel), Tom Doherty Associates (New York, NY), 2005.

WORK IN PROGRESS: Another romance.

SIDELIGHTS: Kate Brallier's debut novel, *Seal Island,* is a paranormal romance set in the "down East" area of Maine. It is a region Brallier knows well, since she spent her childhood summers there, living with her family in tents overlooking the Penobscot Bay. According to *Booklist* reviewer Diana Tixier Herald, "a delicious gothic feel permeates this debut." Despite the gothic atmosphere, however, the story is set in modern times, and concerns a Manhattan woman named Cecilia, who loses her job and home in New York and must take up residence in a seaside cottage on an island in Maine. Celia has inherited the place from a cousin, Allegra, who was recently murdered. Cecilia did not know Allegra well, but upon reaching the island she discovers that she had many things in common with the dead woman. She befriends a seal that Allegra raised, and also begins a relationship with a neighbor, a man who, as in the British "selkie" stories, might be a seal that has turned into a human.

Commenting on Brallier's ability to weave together many genres, Harriet Klausner wrote in *MBR Bookwatch* that the story seems to begin as a contemporary romance, but develops into a mystery and ultimately adds an element of fantasy. She added, "Fans will appreciate this modern day romance with an iota of a mystery that climaxes as a fantasy suspense thriller." *Seal Island* was recommended as a "gentle" romance by a reviewer for *Publishers Weekly,* who added that the story's "slightly old-fashioned take on love exudes a leisurely and timeless charm."

BIOGRAPHICAL AND CRITICAL SOURCES:

PERIODICALS

Booklist, March 1, 2005, Diana Tixier Herald, review of *Seal Island,* p. 1148.

MBR Bookwatch, March, 2005, Harriet Klausner, review of *Seal Island.*

Publishers Weekly, January 24, 2005, review of *Seal Island,* p. 227.

ONLINE

Kate Brallier Home Page, http://www.katebrallier.com (June 22, 2005).*

BREMER, Arthur H. 1950-
(Arthur Herman Bremer)

PERSONAL: Born August 21, 1950, in Milwaukee, WI; son of William (a truck driver) and Sylvia Bremer. *Education:* Attended Milwaukee Technical College.

ADDRESSES: Home—Maryland Correctional Institution—Hagerstown, 18601 Roxbury Rd., Hagerstown, MD 21746.

CAREER: Convicted felon. Story Elementary School, Milwaukee, WI, former janitor; Milwaukee Athletic Club, Milwaukee, former busboy.

WRITINGS:

An Assassin's Diary, introduction by Harding Lemay, Harper's Magazine Press (New York, NY), 1973.

SIDELIGHTS: Arthur H. Bremer was a troubled young man when he attempted to assassinate one of the most prominent segregationists in the South. On May 15, 1972, he shot governor of Alabama and then-presidential candidate George C. Wallace, striking him in the spine. Wallace was paralyzed from the waist down, but he survived.

In March of 1972, Bremer began keeping a diary of his attempt to assassinate a politician, but at that time he had not decided whether to shoot Wallace or pursue President Richard Nixon. The diary was read in full as evidence in Bremer's trial, and the next year it was published as *An Assassin's Diary,* complete with Bremer's spelling errors. In this work, Bremer revealed that he had hoped to assassinate President Nixon during a visit to Ottawa, Ontario, Canada, in April of 1972, but he was foiled by Nixon's tight security. The first half of the original diary, although lost, was recovered from a landfill in 1980.

Wallace was wary of assassination attempts, even speaking from behind a bulletproof podium in Laurel, Maryland, the day he was shot. He often wore a bulletproof vest as well, but that day the weather was warm and he decided to forego it. After his speech, Wallace stepped out from behind the podium and, as was his custom, walked through the crowd to shake his supporters' hands. When he walked by Bremer and stretched out his arm to shake the man's hand, Bremer shot him. Wallace, the victim Bremer had called a "segregationist dinosaur," died in 1998 of cardiac arrest, several years after he forgave his attacker. Although the diary indicated that Bremer was antisocial and psychopathic, he was deemed not to be psychotic and was sentenced to fifty-three years in the Maryland Correctional Institution.

Bremer's diary became one of the inspirations for Martin Scorsese's film *Taxi Driver,* about a mentally ill Vietnam veteran who attempts to assassinate a presidential candidate. That film, in turn, inspired another notorious assassination attempt, John Hinckley's shooting of President Ronald Reagan in 1980.

BIOGRAPHICAL AND CRITICAL SOURCES:

BOOKS

Bremer, Arthur H., *An Assassin's Diary,* introduction by Harding Lemay, Harper's Magazine Press (New York, NY), 1973.
World of Criminal Justice, two volumes, Thomson Gale (Detroit, MI), 2002.

PERIODICALS

Atlanta Journal-Constitution, September 15, 1998, "Wallace Gunman Seeking Parole," p. 7.
Insight on the News, November 29, 1999, Timothy W. Maier, James P. Lucier, "Possible Conspiracy in Wallace Assassination Attempt?," p. 6.

ONLINE

Public Broadcasting Service Web site, http://www.pbs.org/ (June 25, 2005), *American Experience:* "Portrait of an Assassin: Arthur Bremer."*

*   *   *

BREMER, Arthur Herman
See BREMER, Arthur H.

BRICKNER, Balfour 1926-2005

OBITUARY NOTICE— See index for *CA* sketch: Born November 18, 1926, in Cleveland, OH; died of lung cancer, August 28, 2005, in New York, NY. Rabbi, educator, activist, broadcaster, and author. Considered a liberal Zionist, Brickner was a prominent Reform rabbi who was outspoken on causes ranging from abortion to war. The son of Zionist parents, Brickner later became a disciple of Free Synagogue founder Stephen Samuel Wise. He also served in the U.S. Navy during World War II, afterward completing his undergraduate work at the University of Cincinnati in 1948. Studying to be a rabbi at Hebrew Union College Jewish Institute of Religion, he was ordained in 1952. That year, he founded Temple Sinai in Washington, DC, where he served as rabbi until 1961. During this time he also taught at the American University's Jewish Chautauqua Society. After moving to New York City in 1961, he became codirector of the National Commission on Social Action at the Union of American Hebrew Congregation. In 1978 he was also named its director, and he remained in that post until the late 1990s. By the 1960s, Brickner had already become an active voice in the country; he was involved in the civil rights movement and anti-war protests during the Vietnam War. In 1980 Brickner took the job of senior rabbi at his mentor's Free Synagogue, and he led the congregation there for the next dozen years before retiring in 1991. As a leader in Reform Judaism, Brickner was unafraid to state his opinions, even when they were controversial. One of the most debated issues he took up pertained to the state of Israel. Although Brickner believed that there should be a Jewish state, he also voiced sympathy for the Palestinians and protested vehemently against the Israeli government's policies of expanding its territory into Palestinian areas. Brickner was also viewed as controversial because of his pro-abortion stance; he was the founder of Religious Leaders for a Free Choice. His opinions came to be widely known in America during the 1980s when he hosted the radio program *Adventures in Judaism,* which was syndicated nationally. On the other hand, Brickner's was also a unifying voice; he tried to bridge gaps between religions by promoting strengthened ties between Judaism, Christianity, and other beliefs. He also encouraged his congregation to participate more in decision making at the Free Synagogue. Brickner was the author of several books, including *As Driven Sands: The Arab Refugees, 1948-68* (1969), the cowritten *Searching the Prophets for Values* (1981), and his last book, *Finding God in the Garden: Backyard Reflections on Life, Love, and Compost* (2002).

OBITUARIES AND OTHER SOURCES:

PERIODICALS

Los Angeles Times, September 2, 2005, p. B11.
New York Times, September 1, 2005, p. C18.
Washington Post, September 1, 2005, p. B6.

*   *   *

BRODEUR, Adrienne 1967(?)-

PERSONAL: Born c. 1967.

ADDRESSES: Home—New York, NY. *Agent*—c/o Author Mail, Random House, 1745 Broadway, New York, NY 10019. *E-mail*—adrienne@gotomancamp.com.

CAREER: Editor and novelist. *Paris Review,* reader; *Zoetrope: All-Story,* San Francisco, CA, founding coeditor, then editor-in-chief, 1997-2002.

AWARDS, HONORS: National Magazine Award for best fiction, 2001.

WRITINGS:

(Editor, with Samantha Schnee) *Francis Ford Coppola's Zoetrope All-Story* (short story collection), introduction by Coppola, Harcourt (San Diego, CA), 2000.
(Editor, with Samantha Schnee) *Francis Ford Coppola's Zoetrope All-Story 2* (short story collection), introduction by Coppola, Harcourt (Orlando, FL), 2003.
Man Camp (novel), Random House (New York, NY), 2005.

WORK IN PROGRESS: A novel to be titled *Motherload.*

SIDELIGHTS: Adrienne Brodeur is the cofounder, with filmmaker Francis Ford Coppola, of the award-winning literary journal *Zoetrope: All-Story.* In addition to its oversize, tabloid format and use of newsprint, the journal is distinguished by its connection to Coppola's American Zoetrope studios, which purchases the film rights for the stories and plays published in the magazine. Reviewing the early editions for *Library Journal*, Eric Bryant found it "an impressive work that will be welcome wherever short fiction is popular." The journal features both established names and new voices, as well as a wide array of styles and themes. There is also an overarching idea. As Brodeur told an interviewer in *Reveries*, "I think the things that separate out *Zoetrope* are that we have stories that have great voices, that have real narrative arc. They're what I would call a classic story—you really go somewhere in a *Zoetrope* story. We don't have sort of small, experimental, little slice of life, thoughts-on-the-potato type of stories." At the same time, there are more meditative nonfiction pieces, such as Salman Rushdie's essay on the transition of his novel *Midnight's Children* into a movie. A number of critics were pleased with the results. Reviewing the first collection, *Francis Ford Coppola's Zoetrope: All-Story*, *Library Journal* contributor Shana C. Fair found it "perfect for summer reading." Similarly, *Publishers Weekly* reviewer Jeff Zalesky asserted, "Almost every entry's a winner. (How often can you say that?)."

After leaving the magazine in 2002, Brodeur decided to write her own fiction full time. The result was her debut novel, *Man Camp*. Set in her native New York, Brodeur's novel centers on a biologist named Lucy and on Martha, an actress. In her own way, each character deals with the hazards of modern love. While Lucy is somewhat disenchanted by her attentive but insecure boyfriend, Martha is tired of meeting men who seem to lack a certain masculine spark. The two decide to set up a seminar to train men in the old-fashioned art of manliness, but they soon discover that their one-day session is not enough, so they turn to an old friend of Lucy's, a West Virginia dairy farmer named Cooper. The three agree to set up Man Camp as a way to train Manhattanites in the finer points of carpentry, horsemanship, and chivalry. Before long, however, the trio find themselves dealing with unexpected difficulties as Martha seems increasingly drawn to Cooper and Lucy surprises herself by feeling pangs of jealousy. At the same time, Martha is not entirely enjoying herself, explained a critic in *Kirkus Reviews*, "because Cooper's mother is a steel magnolia doing her damnedest to thwart Martha's romance with her son." A *Publishers Weekly* contributor described the results of Brodeur's first attempt at fiction as a "cleanly written, brainy chick-lit tale" in which "the women learn they can't necessarily apply sociobiology to human romance."

BIOGRAPHICAL AND CRITICAL SOURCES:

PERIODICALS

Cosmopolitan, July, 2005, Sara Bodnar, review of *Man Camp*, p. 490.

Kirkus Reviews, May 1, 2005, review of *Man Camp*, p. 490.

Library Journal, November 15, 1998, Eric Bryant, review of *Zoetrope: All-Story* (magazine), p. 98; May 1, 2000, Shana C. Fair, review of *Francis Ford Coppola's Zoetrope All-Story*, p. 111.

Publishers Weekly, June 16, 2003, Jeff Zalesky, review of *Francis Ford Coppola's Zoetrope All-Story 2*, p. 52; May 9, 2005, review of *Man Camp*, p. 37.

Reveries, February, 2002, interview with Adrienne Brodeur.

USA Today, May 26, 2005, Bob Minzesheimer, review of *Man Camp*, p. D6.

Washington Post Book World, May 21, 2000, Jennifer Howard, review of *Francis Ford Coppola's Zoetrope All-Story*, p. 10.

ONLINE

Man Camp Web site, http://www.gotomancamp.com/ (June 27, 2005), brief biography of Adrienne Brodeur.

*   *   *

BROGAN, Jan 1958(?)-

PERSONAL: Born c. 1958, in Clifton, NJ; married Bill Santo; children: Lannie, Spike. *Education:* Boston University, B.A.

ADDRESSES: Home—Westwood, MA. *Agent*—c/o Author Mail, Warner Books, 1271 Avenue of the Americas, New York, NY 10020. *E-mail*—jan@janbrogan.com.

CAREER: News Tribune, Waltham, MA, former staff member; *Worcester Telegram and Gazette,* Worcester, MA, former staff writer; *Providence Journal-Bulletin,* Providence, RI, former staff writer; *Boston Globe,* Boston, MA, currently correspondent. Has also taught mystery writing at Cape Cod Writer's Center, Boston Learning Society, Brown University Learning Community, and Providence, RI Learning Connection.

MEMBER: Mystery Writers of America, Sisters in Crime (New England), PEN New England.

AWARDS, HONORS: Gerald Loeb award for distinguished financial writing; Editors' Choice award, *Drood Review of Mystery,* 2001, for *Final Copy.*

WRITINGS:

Final Copy (mystery novel), Larcom Press (Prides Crossing, MA), 2001.
A Confidential Source (mystery novel), Mysterious Press (New York, NY), 2005.

Contributor to periodicals, including *Ladies' Home Journal, Forbes, Boston,* and *Improper Bostonian.*

SIDELIGHTS: Jan Brogan is a journalist with a long and distinguished career with New England newspapers. Similarly, the protagonist of her debut mystery novel is a journalist in Boston, but there the parallels end. Instead, as Pamela H. Sacks explained in the Worcester, Massachusetts, *Telegram & Gazette,* protagonist Addy McNeil is "a reporter with a foundering career, a drug habit and some questionable journalistic values." In *Final Copy* former star investigative reporter McNeil is struggling with a sinking career and an addiction to sleeping pills. At the same time, Boston is struggling with a slow down in the biotech industry and the resulting recession. When she is assigned to investigate the murder of a prominent venture capitalist, McNeil finds herself delving into the hidden intrigues of the region's biotech industry and uncovering emotional wounds from her own past, particularly her continued attraction to an ex-boyfriend, another venture capitalist, who happens to be the prime suspect in the case.

Brogan introduces a different heroine, Hallie Ahern, in *A Confidential Source,* but there are some similarities to her first protagonist. Like McNeil, Ahern is trying to resuscitate her journalistic career, but she has fallen considerably farther than McNeil. After an affair with a source who ultimately uses her, Ahern leaves her high-profile position at a prestigious Boston newspaper and finds herself working at the small bureau of Rhode Island's largest daily newspaper. Lacking confidence in her own judgment, she is reluctant to take on any major stories, but then she witnesses the shooting death of a local deli owner. Before long, her reporters' instincts propel her to investigate the victim's background, and she soon discovers his gambling debts and mob connections. From there, she finds herself reporting on the issues of gambling addiction. At the same time, Rhode Island prepares for a referendum legalizing casinos in Providence, a referendum strongly supported by the corrupt mayor and just as strongly opposed by a local talk-show host who begins to help Ahern in her investigations. A further complication is Hallie's own growing addiction to gambling, from state lotteries to casinos.

A *Kirkus Reviews* contributor described *A Confidential Source* as a novel that is "smoothly told, with welcome insight into compulsive gamblers and insider jabs at newsroom politics." Similarly, *New York Times Book Review* contributor Marilyn Stasio found that "Brogan's brooding analysis of the gambling itch that leaves so many people rubbed raw is especially persuasive with a narrator like Hallie." In contrast, *Booklist* contributor David Wright felt that "Brogan's sophomore effort lacks much of the investigative detail and psychological acuity of its predecessor," but a reviewer for *MBR Bookwatch* deemed the novel "a well thought out thriller that is full of misdirection, especially a believable unexpected u-turn that will surprise an elated audience."

Brogan told *CA:* "Once I learned to write, I wanted to be a writer. The mystery writer who inspires me most is Scott Turow. The humanity he brings to each and every character deepens the story well beyond the mystery plot. I write five days a week and rewrite extensively. I take detailed notes between the drafts and my second draft takes almost as long as the first.

"The most surprising thing I've learned as a writer is how difficult the business is. This is no career for sissies. My favorite book is my first, *Final Copy,* which is more personal because I explore (or should I say exploit) my own feelings about losing a beloved brother too early in life. It also skillfully weaves several plots together and shocks most readers with its conclusion.

"In both books, I try to show that the news business is subjective from the moment the editor makes the assignment. Errors and misjudgements are unavoidable in the competitive environment of a newspaper and deadline pressure. There is no real truth, just that day's version of the truth. I also create a flawed protagonist, because brilliant sleuths bore me. I'm not just in the external obstacles, but the internal obstacles we all face in trying to solve any problem."

BIOGRAPHICAL AND CRITICAL SOURCES:

PERIODICALS

Booklist, February 15, 2005, David Wright, review of *A Confidential Source,* p. 1063.

Boston Globe, May 19, 2005, David J. Montgomery, "In 'Source,' A Reporter's Investigation Fails to Turn up Satisfying Results," p. D7.

Chicago Tribune, April 17, 2005, Dick Adler, review of *A Confidential Source,* p. 3.

Kirkus Reviews, March 1, 2005, review of *A Confidential Source,* p. 260.

Library Journal, December 1, 2004, Ann Kim, review of *A Confidential Source,* p. 96.

MBR Bookwatch, April, 2005, review of *A Confidential Source.*

New York Times Book Review, April 24, 2005, Marilyn Stasio, "A Funny Thing Happened," p. 21.

Publishers Weekly, March 21, 2005, review of *A Confidential Source,* p. 38.

Telegram & Gazette (Worcester, MA), November 16, 2001, Pamela H. Sacks, "Reporter Switches to Mystery," p. C1.

ONLINE

Armchair Interviews, http://www.armchairinterviews. com/ (July 6, 2005), biography of Jan Brogan.

Jan Brogan Home Page, http://www.janbrogan.com (July 6, 2005).

Time Warner Bookmark, http://www.twbookmark.com/ (July 6, 2005), biography of Jan Brogan.

Who-Dunnit, http://www.who-dunnit.com/ (July 6, 2005), biography of Jan Brogan.

BROWNE, L. Virginia

PERSONAL: Female.

ADDRESSES: Agent—c/o St. Martin's Griffin, 175 5th Ave., New York, NY 10010. *E-mail*—cleoandtyrone@ yahoo.com.

CAREER: Author and screenwriter.

WRITINGS:

The Wade Inheritance (novel), Harcourt (Boston, MA), 1977.

Sioux City (screenplay), Cabin Fever Entertainment, 1994.

(With Linda Hamner) *Letters from Cleo and Tyrone: A Feline Perspective on Love, Life, and Litter,* illustrated by Steve Feldman, St. Martin's Griffin (New York, NY), 2000.

Writer for soap operas, including *Edge of Night,* American Broadcasting Companies, Inc. (ABC), *Days of Our Lives,* National Broadcasting Company (NBC), and *Another World,* NBC. Also author of teleplays.

WORK IN PROGRESS: With Linda Hamner, an original online serial for Warner Bros.

SIDELIGHTS: For sidelights, please see HAMNER, Linda (Elin).

BIOGRAPHICAL AND CRITICAL SOURCES:

PERIODICALS

Cats, May, 2001, Sally Rosenthal, review of *Letters from Cleo and Tyrone: A Feline Perspective on Love, Life, and Litter,* p. 62.

Kirkus Review, September 15, 2000, review of *Letters from Cleo and Tyrone.*

Publishers Weekly, October 16, 2000, review of *Letters from Cleo and Tyrone,* p. 51.

ONLINE

Cleo and Tyrone Home Page, http://www.cleoand
tyrone.com/ (September 16, 2003).*

*   *   *

BRUNI, Frank 1965(?)-

PERSONAL: Born c. 1965. *Education:* University of
North Carolina, Chapel Hill, B.A., 1986; Columbia
Graduate School of Journalism, M.S. (high honors),
1988.

ADDRESSES: Office—New York Times Company, 229
W. 43rd St., New York, NY 10036.

CAREER: Detroit Free Press, Detroit, MI, reporter and
movie critic, 1990-95; *New York Times,* New York, NY,
reporter, 1995-98, San Francisco bureau, 1998,
Washington bureau, 1998-2002, Rome, Italy, bureau,
2002-04, New York, restaurant critic, 2004—.

MEMBER: Phi Beta Kappa.

AWARDS, HONORS: Pulitzer traveling fellowship; Pulitzer Prize finalist, for "Twisted Love"; George Polk
Award for metropolitan reporting (co-recipient), 1996.

WRITINGS:

(With Elinor Burkett) *A Gospel of Shame: Children,
    Sexual Abuse, and the Catholic Church,* Viking
    (New York, NY), 1993.
(With Elinor Burkett) *Consumer Terrorism: How to
    Get Satisfaction When You're Being Ripped Off,*
    HarperPerennial (New York, NY), 1997.
*Ambling into History: The Unlikely Odyssey of George
    W. Bush,* HarperCollins (New York, NY), 2002.

SIDELIGHTS: Journalist Frank Bruni was a Pulitzer
Prize finalist for his investigative reporting while on
the staff of the *Detroit Free Press.* During that period
in his career, he wrote his first book, *A Gospel of
Shame: Children, Sexual Abuse, and the Catholic
Church,* with *Miami Herald* reporter Elinor Burkett.

This study of pedophile priests and the hierarchy that
covered up their sins against the children of the
Catholic Church offers factual and explicit descriptions
of the crimes committed and the statistical probability
of the numbers of priests who have, or will, abuse
young children. Bruni and Burkett condemn the
Church for being more concerned with protecting its
image than the children and families who followed its
teachings, calling the Church's position "the ultimate
betrayal of faith." Donald E. Messer wrote in *Christian
Century* that the authors "are to be commended for
forcing us to face the ugly consequences of clergy
sexual misconduct and the reprehensible silence and
strategies of a church unwilling to face its responsibility or live up to its gospel."

In 1995 Bruni took a position with the *New York Times,*
and from 1998 to 2002, he worked at the newspaper's
Washington bureau, where he covered the first
presidential election of George W. Bush and Bush's
early years in the White House. His observations of
the president are collected in *Ambling into History:
The Unlikely Odyssey of George W. Bush,* a volume
that benefits from a close relationship between the
president and the reporter the Texas-based president
sometimes called "Frankie Boy" or "Panchito" (the
Spanish version of the nickname). Ben Macintyre
noted in the *New York Times Book Review* that the verb
of the title "precisely summons up an unhurried
candidate whose vaunted lack of concern with the
process was his hallmark, who seemed to wander into
office with a sense of awe, ambivalence, entitlement
and detached amusement."

The book is anecdotal, documenting Bush's
mispronunciations, mannerisms, temperament, and
reactions to the power of the presidency. As Bruni
wrote, "The Bush I knew was part scamp and part
bumbler, a timeless fraternity boy and heedless cutup,
a weekday gym rat and weekend napster, an adult with
an inner child that often brimmed to the surface or
broke through." Bruni notes Bush's tendency to touch
male reporters. He says that Bush put his fingers in
Bruni's ears, grabbed him by the neck, and pinched
his cheeks. "So perhaps it shouldn't surprise that Bruni
becomes smitten, dishing to readers that Bush was far
more charming in off-the-record gab sessions than his
guarded public persona would suggest," wrote Ryan
Lizza in *Washington Monthly.*

Among those reviewers who found fault with the book
was Eric Alterman, who wrote in the *American Pros-*

pect that *Ambling into History* "contains nary a word about health care, Social Security, tax cuts, the Middle East conflict, missile defense, or God forbid, global warming. . . . We learn precisely how many seconds the Bushes danced at each of the inaugural balls but precious little that would prepare us to understand what the president might be doing the next day when he went to work."

Despite the president's casual behavior, Bruni eventually began to see a more serious side to Bush and observed qualities that overcame his initial impression. This was particularly true following the attacks of September 11, 2001. "Only later," wrote Bruni, "when I watched him in the aftermath of the terrorist attacks, did I also see something true and meaningful in his description of his outlook on the presidency and life, an explanation for his ability to ride out storms that might lay waste to someone with a less keen sense of destiny and less ready acceptance of fate." Lizza noted that, as *Ambling into History* concludes, Bruni "paints Bush as a 'vibrant, probing leader' who 'was turning into one of the most interesting presidents in decades.' His thesis seems to be that by November of 2001, Bush had matured into a true president . . . hence the 'odyssey' of the book's title."

BIOGRAPHICAL AND CRITICAL SOURCES:

BOOKS

Bruni, Frank, and Elinor Burkett, *A Gospel of Shame: Children, Sexual Abuse, and the Catholic Church,* Viking (New York, NY), 1993.

Bruni, Frank, *Ambling into History: The Unlikely Odyssey of George W. Bush,* HarperCollins (New York, NY), 2002.

PERIODICALS

American Prospect, May 20, 2002, Eric Alterman, review of *Ambling into History: The Unlikely Odyssey of George W. Bush,* p. 33.

Booklist, October 1, 1993, Gary Young, review of *A Gospel of Shame: Children, Sexual Abuse and the Catholic Church,* p. 220.

Business Week, April 15, 2002, review of *Ambling into History,* p. 20.

Business Wire, April 8, 2004, "The *New York Times* Names Frank Bruni Restaurant Critic and Eric Asimov Chief Wine Critic," p. 5752.

Chicago Tribune, March 20, 2002, Kevin Canfield, review of *Ambling into History,* Tempo section, p. 5.

Christian Century, April 6, 1994, Donald E. Messer, review of *A Gospel of Shame,* p. 361.

Economist, March 23, 2002, review of *Ambling into History.*

Houston Chronicle, March 23, 2002, Elizabeth Bennett, review of *Ambling into History.*

Library Journal, March 15, 2002, Michael A. Genovese, review of *Ambling into History,* p. 95.

Nation, June 3, 2002, Eric Alterman, review of *Ambling into History,* p. 10.

Nation's Restaurant News, September 20, 2004, Bret Thorn, "Former Foreign Correspondent Trades in Political Beat for Seat at Dinner Table," p. 46.

New York Times Book Review, March 31, 2002, Ben Macintyre, review of *Ambling into History,* p. 8.

Publishers Weekly, October 4, 1993, review of *A Gospel of Shame,* p. 62.

Washington Monthly, March, 2002, Ryan Lizza, review of *Ambling into History,* p. 55.

Washington Post Book World, March 3, 2002, Christopher Caldwell, review of *Ambling into History,* p. 1.

ONLINE

Dream of Italy Web site, http://www.dreamofitaly.com/ (June 26, 2005), interview with Bruni.

Salon.com, http://www.salon.com/ (March 4, 2002), Noam Scheiber, review of *Ambling into History.**

*   *   *

BRYSON, John 1923-2005

OBITUARY NOTICE— See index for *CA* sketch: Born October 12, 1923, in Brownwood, TX; died of complications from heart disease, August 10, 2005, in Brookings, OR. Photographer, journalist, actor, and author. Bryson was a highly respected photojournalist whose photos of celebrities and world leaders graced such magazines as *Life, People,* and *Time.* After studying at the University of Texas at Austin and serving in the U.S. Army Air Forces during World War II, he joined *Life* magazine as a correspondent and bureau chief in Atlanta. Over the next several years, he moved around the country—from Chicago to Los Angeles to Boston to New York City—as he continued to work for *Life.* In 1955, however, Bryson decided to become a freelance photojournalist. As such, he took on assignments not only for his old magazine, but also for *Paris Match, Look, Time, McCall's,* and the *Saturday Evening Post,* among others. Over the years, he developed a talent for gaining the trust of Hollywood celebrities, who allowed him to take pictures of their day-to-day lives. Among Bryson's famous subjects were stars Marilyn Monroe, John Wayne, Katharine Hepburn, Frank Sinatra, and Elizabeth Taylor as well as author Ernest Hemingway, painter Salvador Dali, and industrialist Armand Hammer. He also took photographs of world leaders, including U.S. President John F. Kennedy and USSR leader Nikita Khrushchev. Bryson became so well connected in Hollywood that he was approached by directors to appear in their films. He consequently held roles in several movies, including *Convoy, The Getaway, Grand Prix,* and *The Osterman Weekend.* A number of Bryson's photos were collected in the books *The World of Armand Hammer* (1985) and *The Private World of Katharine Hepburn* (1990).

OBITUARIES AND OTHER SOURCES:

PERIODICALS

Chicago Tribune, August 14, 2005, section 4, p. 7.
Los Angeles Times, August 12, 2005, p. B11.
New York Times, August 13, 2005, p. A25.

*   *   *

BUNDY, Carol 1958-

PERSONAL: Born 1958; children: two sons.

ADDRESSES: Home—Cambridge, MA. *Agent*—Geri Thoma, Elaine Markson Agency, 44 Greenwich Ave., New York, NY 10011.

CAREER: Script writer and biographer.

WRITINGS:

The Nature of Sacrifice: A Biography of Charles Russell Lowell, Jr. (biography), Farrar, Straus & Giroux (New York, NY), 2005.

Author of film scripts.

SIDELIGHTS: Carol Bundy became interested in her great-great-great uncle, Charles Russell Lowell, when Lowell's sword and saddlebags were discovered while clearing out the attic of the family house, and she tells his story in the biography *The Nature of Sacrifice: A Biography of Charles Russell Lowell, Jr.* Charles Lowell was born into one of the less-prosperous branches of the Lowell family, which wielded great wealth and power in nineteenth-century Boston. Nevertheless, he was still considered a prominent citizen and became valedictorian of his class at Harvard University. He became passionately devoted to the abolition of slavery, and helped to found one of the first regiments made up of African-American soldiers. Despite the difficulty of enduring his father's bankruptcy and his own personal struggle with tuberculosis, Lowell was quick to step forward for service when the U.S. Civil War broke out, serving in a variety of positions. Eventually he became the commander of a cavalry brigade, and he was killed in the Battle of Cedar Creek, Virginia.

Bundy deserves "high praise for her thoroughness, relative readability . . . and the admirable lack of psychobabble in her analysis of motives and relationships," commented Roland Green in *Booklist.* The reviewer further credited the author with creating a good collective portrait of Boston society during that era, as well as with painting a well-realized portrait of her subject. A *Publishers Weekly* writer praised Bundy for doing "an excellent job" of telling Lowell's story and "explaining the ethic of selfless sacrifice out of which he emerged. This in an admirable life of an admirable man."

BIOGRAPHICAL AND CRITICAL SOURCES:

PERIODICALS

Booklist, March 1, 2005, Roland Green, review of *The Nature of Sacrifice: A Biography of Charles Russell Lowell, Jr.,* p. 1134.

Boston Globe, April 24, 2005, Michael Kenney, review of *The Nature of Sacrifice.*

Kirkus Reviews, January 1, 2005, review of *The Nature of Sacrifice,* p. 28.

Library Journal, February 1, 2005, Theresa McDevitt, review of *The Nature of Sacrifice,* p. 93.

Publishers Weekly, January 31, 2005, review of *The Nature of Sacrifice,* p. 59.

Washington Post, August 7, 2005, Edwin Yoder, review of *The Nature of Sacrifice.*

*   *   *

BURK, Martha 1941-
(Martha Gertrude Burk)

PERSONAL: Born October 18, 1941, in Tyler, TX; daughter of Ivan Lee Burk (an oil company engineer) and Dorothy May Dean (a dress-business owner); married Eddie C. Talley (a pharmacist), September 2, 1960 (divorced, 1985); married Ralph Estes (a professor), 1986; children: (first marriage) Edward, Mark. *Education:* University of Houston, B.S., 1962; University of Texas at Arlington, M.S., 1968, Ph.D., 1974.

ADDRESSES: Office—National Council of Women's Organizations, 1050 17th St., NW, Ste. 250, Washington, DC 20036.

CAREER: Licensed psychologist. University of Texas at Arlington, research director of Graduate School of Social Work, 1974-76, assistant professor of management, 1976-79; A.U. Software, Inc., Wichita, KS, cofounder and partner, 1981-90; Center for the Advancement of Public Policy, cofounder, president, 1990. National Organization for Women, former president of Wichita chapter and member, national board of directors, 1988-90; National Council of Women's Organizations, Washington, DC, chair; National Task Force on Pay Equity, member, 1993. Guest on television and radio programs, including *Today Show, Lou Dobbs Moneyline, CNN Financial, Bloomberg News, Crossfire,* and *News Hour with Jim Lehrer.* Consultant on discrimination prevention. Member of official U.S. delegations to international conferences in Iceland, Lithuania, Estonia, and China.

AWARDS, HONORS: Named among Women of the Year, *Ms.* magazine, 2003.

WRITINGS:

Cult of Power: Sex Discrimination in Corporate America and What Can Be Done about It (nonfiction), Scribner (New York, NY), 2005.

Syndicated columnist. Contributor to periodicals, including *Louisville Courier Journal, Los Angeles Daily News, Ms. Magazine, Working Woman, Business Woman,* and *Washington Post.* Editorial advisor, *Ms.*

SIDELIGHTS: Martha Burk is a women's rights activist who attracted national attention when she challenged the men-only membership policy of the Augusta National Golf Club in 2002. The elite club, located in Georgia, annually hosts the prestigious Masters Tournament, so Burk's accusation that the association was guilty of discrimination was headline news. Her cause touched off a storm of media coverage that lasted for months. Burk did not succeed in forcing Augusta National to change its policy, but she looked at the situation positively nevertheless, predicting that her actions would, at least, generate more consciousness on the issue. Burk shared her views and ideas about discrimination in *Cult of Power: Sex Discrimination in Corporate America and What Can Be Done about It,* published in 2005.

Burk grew up in Pasadena, Texas. A top student, she finished high school at the age of sixteen, then married and had children while earning her bachelor's degree. As the years went by, she became increasingly dissatisfied with her roles as wife and mother, and returned to school. She eventually earned a master's degree and a Ph.D. in experimental psychology, yet as she conducted her job search, her experiences convinced her that male applicants had a decided advantage over females. Burk eventually developed an educational software program that became the foundation for her own company—a company so successful that she was able to resign from her teaching position and devote herself full-time to political activism.

Burk's first marriage ended in divorce, and she later married Ralph Estes, an accounting professor with a strong political bent. The couple moved to Wichita, where Burk became head of the local chapter of the National Organization for Women. In 1990, the couple moved to Washington, DC, where they established the

Center for the Advancement of Public Policy, which seeks to eliminate prejudice, sexism, and discrimination in the workplace, government, and other organizations. Burk also became chair of the National Council of Women's Organizations (NCWO), an umbrella entity that takes in more than 200 women's groups.

When Burk read an article about the Augusta National's mens-only membership around the time of the 2002 Masters Tournament, she was annoyed enough to write to the club's president, William W. "Hootie" Johnson, chiding him for the club's ban on women and urging him to do away with it. The Augusta Club is one of the most elite private clubs in the United States, with a membership that includes some of the most powerful business leaders in the country. Women may only play on the course at the invitation of a member. Johnson not only replied to her letter, he released a statement to the media about it, stating in part that women would one day be asked to join the club, but that the club would not be dictated to by outside interests. Burk was soon caught up in a media frenzy and bombarded with requests for interviews. The NCWO began to pressure CBS, the television network broadcasting the tournament, to use its influence in the matter, and a letter-writing campaign was begun to media sponsors and members of the club.

Burk and Johnson exchanged harsh words in the press for several months. The Augusta National eventually released CBS and tournament sponsors from their contracts for the 2003 Masters Tournament, creating a twenty-million-dollar shortfall in broadcasting costs that the club agreed to cover. After Burk announced her intention to stage protests when the tournament was held. The local sheriff refused to grant the NCWO a permit to protest outside the main gates of the club, so these demonstrations took place a half-mile up the road. Despite the uproar, Augusta National remained a mens-only club. A federal court later ruled that there was no reason to force the protests away from the main gates, giving NCWO the right to stage new protests for future tournaments. NCWO also began investigating gender-bias claims at companies whose executives belong to Augusta National, acting on their belief that the sex discrimination at the club extends to many of the businesses where members work. In 2005, this effort resulted in a class action lawsuit against the Smith-Barney division of Citigroup.

In *Cult of Power* Burk analyzes the reasons why there are so few women in the top ranks of the power elite,

and offers concrete solutions to correct the problem. Though the author has been accused by some of being unreasonable in her demands, her book shows that Burk is "no ideologue," reported a writer for *Kirkus Reviews*. "Rather, she evenhandedly addresses all the important questions. . . . She strikes a perfect balance between the personal and impersonal, seeming variously tough, feisty, and self-critical, yet conveying all these qualities through the most occasional asides." In addition, a *Publishers Weekly* critic stated, "With a terrific story on which to hang her recommendations, Burk achieves a rare hybrid of activism and entertainment."

BIOGRAPHICAL AND CRITICAL SOURCES:

BOOKS

Newsmakers, Issue 1, Thomson Gale (Detroit, MI), 2004.

PERIODICALS

Booklist, March 15, 2005, Barbara Jacobs, review of *Cult of Power: Sex Discrimination in Corporate America and What Can Be Done about It,* p. 1249.
Broadcasting & Cable, March 21, 2005, "Burk Plans Golf Outing," p. 6.
Columbia Daily Tribune (Columbia, MO), April 1, 2005, Nate Carlisle, "Activist Touts Women's Issues."
Golf World, April 23, 2004, Ryan Herrington, "Thirteenth-Hour Ruling: While Not in Time to Affect the '04 Masters, a Federal Court Agrees Martha Burk's '03 Protest Was Illegally Restricted," p. 7; August 6, 2004, "Burk Gets Last Laugh on Augusta," p. 9; August 27, 2004, Ron Sirak, "Golf & Sexism: Sources Say Female Employees at the PGA Tour Ask NCWO to Look into Tour's Equal Opportunity Practices," p. 5.
Kirkus Reviews, January 1, 2005, review of *Cult of Power,* p. 29.
Miami Herald, April 12, 2005.
Orlando Sentinel, February 14, 2005, Myriam Marquez, "Lesson from Carly Fiorina: Women Have a Long Way to Go."
PR Newswire, February 10, 2005, "Burk Says Gender a Factor in Fiorina Firing"; March 31, 2005, "Martha Burk Comments on New Wall Street Sex Bias Suit."

Publishers Weekly, March 7, 2005, review of *Cult of Power,* p. 63.

UPI NewsTrack, October 26, 2004, "Burk Calls on Coors to Resign Augusta."

UPI Perspectives, February 3, 2005, Jackie L. Franzil, "Businesswomen Gather on Capitol Hill,"; April 7, 2005, Dar Haddix, "Martha Burk Targets Masters Sponsors."

ONLINE

Center for Individual Freedom Web site, http://cfif.org/ (October 3, 2002), "Martha Burk Is out of Bounds in Attack on Augusta."

Hall of Hypocrisy Online, http://www.augusta discriminates.org/ (July 7, 2005), "About Martha Burk."

Intellectual Conservative Online, http://www. intellectualconservative.com/ (April 23, 2004), Carey Roberts, "Martha Burk's Holy War on Corporate America."

Martha Burk Home Page, http://www.marthaburk.org (July 7, 2005).

*   *   *

**BURK, Martha Gertrude
See BURK, Martha**

C

CAMON, Ferdinando 1935-

PERSONAL: Born November 14, 1935, in Padua, Italy; married Gabriella Imperatori (a journalist), 1962; children: Alessandro, Alberto.

ADDRESSES: Agent—c/o Garzanti Editore, Via Gasparotto 1, 20124, Milan, Italy. *E-mail*—fercamon@libero.it.

CAREER: Writer and critic.

AWARDS, HONORS: Viareggio prize, for *Liberare l'animale;* Premio Strega, for *Un altare per la madre;* Pen Club Prize, for *Mai visti sole e luna;* Premio Selezione Campiello, for *La donna dei fili;* Premio Elsa Morante, for *Il Super-Baby;* Premio Giovanni Verga, for *La cavallina, la ragazza e il diavolo.*

WRITINGS:

Il mestiere di poeta, Lerici (Milan, Italy), 1965.

La moglie del tiranno, Lerici (Milan, Italy), 1969, enlarged edition published as *Il mestiere di scrittore: conversazioni critiche,* Garzanti (Milan, Italy), 1973.

Il quinto stato, preface by Pier Paolo Pasolini, Garzanti (Milan, Italy), 1970, translated by John Shepley as *The First Estate,* Marlboro Press (Marlboro, VT), c. 1970.

La vita eterna, Garzanti (Milan, Italy), 1972, translated by John Shepley as *Life Everlasting,,* Marlboro Press (Marlboro, VT, c. 1972.

Liberare l'animale (poems), Garzanti (Milan, Italy), 1973.

Letteratura e classi subalterne, Marsilio (Venice, Italy), 1974.

Occidente (first novel in "Cycle of Terror" sequence), Garzanti (Milan, Italy), 1975.

Avanti popolo, Garzanti (Milan, Italy), 1977.

Un altare per la madre, Garzanti (Milan, Italy), 1978, translated by David Calicchio as *Memorial,,* Marlboro Press (Marlboro, VT), c. 1979.

La malattia chiamata uomo (first novel in "Cycle of the Family" sequence), Garzanti (Milan, Italy), 1981, translated by John Shepley as *The Sickness Called Man,* Marlboro Press (Marlboro, VT), 1992.

Storia di Sirio: parabola per la muova generazione (second novel in "Cycle of Terror" sequence), Garzanti (Milan, Italy), 1984, translated by Cassandra Bertea as *The Story of Sirio: A Parable,* Marlboro Press (Marlboro, VT), 1985.

La donna dei fili (second novel in "Cycle of the Family" sequence), Garzanti (Milan, Italy), 1986.

(Editor) Primo Levi, *Autoritratto di Primo Levi,* Nord-Est (Padua, Italy), 1987, published as *Conversazione con Primo Levi,* Garzanti (Milan, Italy), 1991, translated by John Shepley as *Conversation with Primo Levi,* Marlboro Press (Marlboro, VT), 1989.

I miei personaggi mi scrivono, Nord-Est (Padua, Italy), 1987.

(Editor) *Alberto Moravia: io e il mio tempo,* Nord-Est (Padua, Italy), 1988.

Romanzi della pianura (collected works; includes revised versions of *Il quinto stato* and *La vita eterna*), Garzanti (Milan, Italy), 1988.

Il canto delle balene (first novel in "Cycle of the Couple" sequence), Garzanti (Milan, Italy), 1989.

Il Super-Baby (second novel in "Cycle of the Couple" sequence), Rizzoli (Milan, Italy), 1991.

Il santo assassino: dichiarazioni apocrife, Marsilio (Venice, Italy), 1991.

Mai visti sole e luna (novel), Garzanti (Milan, Italy), 1994.

La terra é di tutti, Garzanti (Milan, Italy), 1996.

Dal silenzio delle campagne: tori, mucche, diavoli, contadini, drogati, mercanti di donne e serial-killer: scene e raccontini in versi (poems), preface by Fernando Bandini, Garzanti (Milan, Italy), 1998.

La cavallina, la ragazza e il diavolo: racconto campes-tre (novel), Garzanti (Milan, Italy), 2004.

Also author of preface to *L'ossessione e il fantasma: il teatro di Pasolini e Moravia,* by Enrico Groppali, Marsilio, 1979. Contributor to periodicals, including *Stampa, Giorno, Corriere della Sera,* and *L'Unità.*

"SAGA OF THOSE WHO ARE LAST" TRILOGY; NOVELS

Il quinto stato, Garzanti (Milan, Italy), 1970, revised edition, 1988, translated by John Shepley as *The Fifth Estate,* Marlboro Press (Marlboro, VT), 1987.

La vita eterna, Garzanti (Milan, Italy), 1972, revised edition, 1988, translated by John Shepley as *Life Everlasting,* Marlboro Press (Marlboro, VT), 1987.

Un altare per la madre, Garzanti (Milan, Italy), 1978, translated by David Calicchio as *Memorial,* Marlboro Press (Marlboro, VT), 1983.

ADAPTATIONS: Movie adaptations of *Occidente* and *Un altare per la madre* were produced by Italian Radiotelevision; *La malattia chiamata uomo* was staged in Paris every evening for four years and was filmed by Claude Miller.

SIDELIGHTS: Novelist Ferdinando Camon has made a name for himself both in his native Italy and internationally as an insightful author of novels focusing on the Italian peasant classes and on psychological fiction. His "Saga of Those Who Are Last" trilogy has been acclaimed for its lyrical style and unsentimental look into the disappearing culture of agrarian communities in northern Italy. Camon is also well known for novels that probe the inner lives of ordinary urban characters, many of whom find help adapting to a rapidly changing modern society through psychoanalysis. Among these novels are *The Story of Sirio: A Parable* and *Il canto delle balene.*

In his early books, such as *Il mestiere di poeta* and *La moglie del tiranno,* Camon earned a reputation as an insightful interviewer. Interviewing such literary figures as Pier Paolo Pasolini and Alberto Moravia, Camon helped pioneer a technique in which inter-viewer and interviewee both contribute to the dialogue on an equal footing. Thus, according to *Dictionary of Literary Biography* essayist Angela M. Jeannet, "the dialogue is doubly revealing, for Camon conveys the sense of his own contribution to the exchange, not only by the aptness of his questions but also by the original-ity of his views and familiarity with the dilemmas and pleasures inherent in the process of writing."

Camon made a tremendous splash with his debut novel, *Il quinto stato,* the first book in the "Saga of Those Who Are Last" trilogy, which was later translated as *The Fifth Estate.* Because the bourgeoisie make up the third estate and the proletariat the fourth, the fifth estate refers to the peasant classes. These people have been ignored by many writers, though some, such as Alessandro Manzoni and Carlo Levi, have addressed their issues. Camon's subjects are the lower-class farming people who inhabit the Po Valley of Padua. Knowing only hard work and family as they strive to eek out a difficult life, they have become victimized by the world around them, as war and technology have destroyed their time-honored ways. Camon does not romanticize this lifestyle or its people, but he does lament the way they have been treated by outsiders. "Being a victim in Camon's world," explained Jeannet, "is to be caught in the labyrinth of history built by a foreign architect; it means becoming imprisoned in other people's versions of historical events."

Camon continues his trilogy with *La vita eterna* (translated as *Life Everlasting*) and *Un altare per la madre* (translated as *Memorial*). While in the first two books in the series the protagonist in many ways represents the entire group of people—the residents of the valley—*Memorial* is a much more personal vision; as *Publishers Weekly* reviewer Barbara A. Bannon called it "an elegy for the author's mother, a simple Italian peasant." In reviews of all the books in the trilogy, critics noted the beautiful lyricism of Camon's writing, but this becomes all the more intense in

Memorial, which describes in great detail how the narrator's father strives to erect an appropriate memorial for his dead wife. Commenting that the entire trilogy is an effort by Camon to memorialize "the old ways," *Washington Post Book World* critic Claudio G. Segrè called *Memorial,* "perhaps the most moving and successful of his books." While Segrè went on to say that he found the book flawed by its "pretentious and self-conscious" style, Jeannet praised Camon's effort in the entire trilogy as an honest attempt "to be faithful to human experience in all its diversity, especially when he lends a voice to those historically silent groups excluded from the literary tradition."

In addition to his fiction about northern Italian peasant life, Camon often writes psychological novels about characters struggling to deal with a separation from culture, the collapse of the family structure, or the battle of the sexes. For example, in *La malattia chiamata uomo,* which was later translated as *The Sickness Called Man,* the main character has to come to terms with deep wounds caused by being separated from his native culture. This is exacerbated by a world in which feminism and the decline of the family have left many without a traditional base of support. He undergoes therapy to try to deal with his personal issues. *World Literature Today* contributor Michela Montante called the book an "intimate story" of a patient-psychoanalyst relationship that "is also a stimulating and original work which examines civilization's discontents."

Politics and terrorism have also uprooted many people in disturbing ways. This is the subject of Camon's "Cycle of Terror" sequence, which includes the novels *Occidente* and *Storia di Sirio: parabola per la muova generazione,* the latter of which was translated as *The Story of Sirio.* The first book in the cycle, *Occidente,* is about the rise of neofascism in Europe. When the novel was adapted as a film in 1976, the author was sued by neofascist leader Franco Freda, who claimed that one of Camon's characters was an unflattering portrait of him; the suit was later dismissed. *The Story of Sirio* follows a young man's struggles after he rejects his upper-middle-class background in search of self-identity in the 1970s. Becoming a revolutionary activist, Sirio lands in jail, becomes addicted to drugs, and eventually seeks help via psychotherapy. A critic for the *Review of Contemporary Fiction* described the book as "a diatribe against capitalism, and a parable in defense of the 'young.'" James Marcus, writing in the *New York Times Book Review,* disliked the parable format, which he felt results in an overly "grave" tone

and "wooden" style, though the reviewer felt some blame could be placed on the "awkward translation." On the other hand, Rochelle Ratner asserted in her *Library Journal* review that *The Story of Sirio* is "an imaginative philosophical treatise on revolution."

Other aspects of modern life are addressed by Camon in such books as *Il Super-Baby,* which concerns the issue of artificial reproduction, and *Il canto delle balene,* a rather comical look at an unfaithful husband and his wife as they struggle with their sexual relationship. Camon has also not forgotten his interest in the working poor in northern Italy; this is the subject of his novel *Mai visti sole e luna.* His lament for the disappearance of a way of life is also expressed in his poetry collection *Dal silenzio delle campagne: tori, mucche, diavoli, contadini, droġati, mercanti di donne e serial-killer: scene e raccontini in versi.* Here, according to Giose Rimanelli in *World Literature Today,* "The ever-vigilant gaze of the writer is focused upon this landscape [of northern Italy]; it is a view at times grotesque or satirical, painted with dreamlike brushstrokes, with the dissatisfaction and the disillusionment and the bloodletting that mark the end of an illusion."

Camon told *CA:* "I write 'in revenge.' I want to avenge country folk who are illiterate; I want to avenge the poor and the ignorant, and give them immortal glory; I want to avenge the illiterate believers, and give them the triumph of altars; I want to avenge those who feel bad and undergo analysis, and describe the psychoanalyst sarcastically; I want to avenge the human victims of the terrorists' slaughters, and describe the terrorists' ignorance and delirium. I have succeeded in this. My novels on peasants are translated in about twenty countries, my novels on terrorism have helped in detecting the terrorists who exploded a bomb in a Bologna railway station (a hundred people killed). . . . Writing is power."

BIOGRAPHICAL AND CRITICAL SOURCES:

BOOKS

Dictionary of Literary Biography, Volume 196: *Italian Novelists since World War II, 1965-1995,* Thomson Gale (Detroit, MI), 1999.

PERIODICALS

Bloomsbury Review, March-April, 1988, Gregory McNamee, reviews of *The Fifth Estate, Memorial,* and *Life Everlasting,* p. 18.

Booklist, October 1, 1989, John Brosnahan, review of *Conversation with Primo Levi,* p. 253.

Library Journal, November 1, 1985, Rochelle Ratner, review of *The Story of Sirio: A Parable,* p. 101; May 15, 1988, Marcia G. Fuchs, reviews of *The Fifth Estate* and *Life Everlasting,* p. 91.

New York Times Book Review, December 22, 1985, James Marcus, review of *The Story of Sirio,* p. 18; January 24, 1988, Susan Zuccotti, "Without Sin, Without Time," review of *The Fifth Estate,* p. 16.

Publishers Weekly, September 9, 1983, Barbara A. Bannon, review of *Memorial,* p. 59; February 15, 1993, review of *The Sickness Called Man,* p. 217.

Review of Contemporary Fiction, fall, 1987, Jack Byrne, review of *The Story of Sirio,* p. 261.

Washington Post Book World, May 29, 1988, Claudio G. Segrè, "Ferdinando Camon and the Cycle of the Lowly," reviews of *Memorial, The Fifth Estate,* and *Life Everlasting,* p. 4.

World Literature Today, spring, 1980, Anthony Oldcorn, review of *Un altare per la madre,* pp. 265-266; spring, 1983, Michela Montante, review of *La malattia chiamata uomo,* p. 265; spring, 1987, Gaetano Iannace, review of *La donna dei fili,* p. 268; summer, 1990, Peter Cocozzella, review of *Il canto delle balene,* p. 446; spring, 1995, Rufus S. Crane, review of *Mai visti sole e luna,* p. 340; winter, 1997, C. Fantazzi, review of *Occidente,* p. 81; fall, 1997, Rocco Capozzi, review of *La terra é di tutti,* p. 767; summer, 1999, Giose Rimanelli, review of *Dal silenzio delle campagne: tori, mucche, diavoli, contadini, drogati, mercanti di donne e serial-killer: scene e raccontini in versi,* p. 506.

ONLINE

Ferdinando Camon Home Page, http://www.ferdinandocamon.it (July 26, 2005).

*   *   *

CAREY, Richard Adams 1951-

PERSONAL: Born October 18, 1951, in Hartford, CT; son of John Henry and Mary Jane (Farrell) Carey; married Lois Anne Kuglin, November 16, 1974; children: Ryan Adams, Kyle Anne. *Education:* Harvard College, B.A., 1973; Lesley College, M.Ed., 1984.

ADDRESSES: Office—Holderness School, Plymouth, NH 03264. *Agent*—c/o Author Mail, Counterpoint Press, 387 Park Ave. S., New York, NY 10016.

CAREER: Lower Kuckokwim School District, teacher in Kongiganak, AK, 1977-79, principal, 1979-84, principal in Chefornake, AK, 1988-89, director of Yupik studies in Bethel, AK, 1990-91; writer in Sandwich, NH, 1984-86, 1989-90; Moultonboro School District, NH, teacher, 1986-88; Holderness School, Plymouth, NH, director of communications, 1991-94. Member of board of directors, Sandwich Players, 1991-94.

AWARDS, HONORS: Notable Book award, 1992, for *Raven's Children.*

WRITINGS:

NONFICTION

Raven's Children: An Alaskan Culture at Twilight, Houghton Mifflin (Boston, MA), 1992.
Against the Tide: The Fate of the New England Fishermen, Houghton Mifflin (Boston, MA), 1999.
The Philosopher Fish: Sturgeon, Caviar, and the Geography of Desire, Counterpoint (New York, NY), 2005.

Contributor to professional journals.

SIDELIGHTS: Richard Adams Carey has chronicled disappearing ways of life in two of his books, *Raven's Children: An Alaskan Culture at Twilight* and *Against the Tide: The Fate of the New England Fishermen.* The former was drawn from his experiences among the indigenous people of Alaska; to research the latter, he worked on four different fishing boats sailing from the Cape Cod region of Massachusetts. In his third book, *The Philosopher Fish: Sturgeon, Caviar, and the Geography of Desire,* he examines the history of the sturgeon, a once-numerous species of fish whose population is now in danger.

Carey was living in Alaska, working as a teacher in Kongiganak, when in 1989, he spent a summer with two Yupik Eskimos, Oscar and Margaret Active. That summer provided the genesis for *Raven's Children,* a book that discusses traditional ways of life for the Eskimos and what the reality of contemporary life has become for them as ancient cultural values collide with modern problems such as alcoholism, poverty, and the difficulties of obtaining fishing permits. A *Publishers Weekly* reviewer called *Raven's Children* a "thoroughly researched, engagingly written sociological study," and noted: "Carey brings this world alive."

A culture of rugged fishermen has long been a part of New England's heritage, but by the late twentieth century that way of life had been virtually destroyed. Government regulations first allowed foreign trawlers to overfish the Atlantic waters off New England; when this practice was halted, super-efficient factory fishing boats financed by U.S. business interests moved in, aggressively depleting the fish stocks. During the 1970s, New England fishermen accounted for approximately twenty percent of the world's fish catch; more recently that figure has plummeted to two or three percent, largely because of dwindling fish populations. In *Against the Tide* Carey recounts his experiences with four fishermen on Cape Cod, each involved in a different aspect of the industry. He gives detailed information on the mechanics of fishing itself, as well as reflections on the loss of this part of American culture. According to Robert Finch, a reviewer for the *New York Times,* the book is "deep ecological journalism at its best, an effective and compassionate chronicle of a threatened way of life."

The sturgeon is a fish that can grow so large that it may have given rise to tales of the Loch Ness monster. It was once prized as a food by European royalty, but eventually fell into disfavor and was considered a "junk fish," suitable only for feeding to animals. Demand for the sturgeon has since risen dramatically; its eggs are considered the best form of caviar, with certain types being sold for as much as one hundred dollars an ounce. Even as sturgeon populations have subsequently plummeted, those who love their caviar remain willing to hunt the fish down, even if it means breaking the law to do so. Carey examines this desire and what it has done to fish stocks, and also takes a look at those who are struggling to save the sturgeon. His book is "a nonfiction page-turner," according to a reviewer for *Science News,* and a *Publishers Weekly* writer stated that in his story of the sturgeon, Carey imparts to his readers "a deeper understanding of the human species."

BIOGRAPHICAL AND CRITICAL SOURCES:

BOOKS

Carey, Richard Adams, *Raven's Children: An Alaskan Culture at Twilight,* Houghton Mifflin (Boston, MA), 1992.

PERIODICALS

Business Week, June 28, 1999, review of *Against the Tide: The Fate of the New England Fishermen,* p. 14E10.
Entertainment Weekly, March 4, 2005, Michelle Kung, review of *The Philosopher Fish: Sturgeon, Caviar, and the Geography of Desire,* p. 79.
Kirkus Reviews, January 1, 2005, review of *The Philosopher Fish,* p. 29.
Library Journal, June 15, 1999, Mary J. Nickum, review of *Against the Tide,* p. 103; April 1, 2005, Susan E. Brazer, review of *The Philosopher Fish,* p. 120.
Los Angeles Times, May 29, 2005, Kai Maristed, review of *The Philosopher Fish.*
New York Times, August 22, 1999, Robert Finch, review of *Against the Tide.*
Publishers Weekly, April 27, 1992, review of *Raven's Children,* p. 239; May 3, 1999, review of *Against the Tide,* p. 60; January 31, 2005, review of *The Philosopher Fish,* p. 58.
Science News, March 19, 2005, review of *The Philosopher Fish,* p. 191.*

*   *   *

CARMINES, Al 1936-2005
(Alvin Allison Carmines, Jr.)

OBITUARY NOTICE— See index for *CA* sketch: Born July 25, 1936, in Hampton, VA; died August 9, 2005, in New York, NY. Minister, composer, actor, singer, and author. A revolutionary creator of off-off-Broadway productions, the award-winning Carmines cofounded the Judson Poets' Theater in association with the Judson Memorial Church in New York City, where he was pastor. His boyhood love of music, singing, and dancing was combined with his Protestant faith. Although his talents earned him scholarship offers to several colleges, he decided to enter the ministry instead. After studying philosophy and English at Swarthmore College, where he earned a B.A. in 1958, he completed a B.D. at Union Theological Seminary in 1961. Two years later, he graduated with an S.T.M. from the seminary. Ordained a Baptist minister in 1960, he was hired in 1961 to be Howard Moody's assistant minister at Judson Memorial. It was Moody who asked Carmines, along with playwright and architect Robert Nichols, to start a theater in association with the church. Despite the affiliation, the two were allowed to write and produce plays without religious themes and messages. The Judson Poets' Theater became an influential fringe venue, creating daring, unconventional plays that shunned realism, experimented with musical form, and embraced what was then called "polymorphous perversity." Over the years, Carmines wrote about eighty musicals, ten of which were also performed off-Broadway. Carmines eventually became pastor at Judson, but had to leave his post in 1981 after suffering a brain aneurysm. He slowly recovered and then founded the Rauschenbusch Memorial Church in 1982. Among Carmines's plays are his *Village Voice* Off-Broadway ("Obie") Award-winning *What Happened* (1963), *Home Movies* (1964), and *In Circles* (1967); he also won an Obie award in 1979 for sustained achievement. Carmines, whose love of the works of Gertrude Stein resulted in five plays featuring Stein as a character, also wrote the controversial play *The Faggot* (1973), which earned him a Vernon Rice award for outstanding composer from Drama Desk.

OBITUARIES AND OTHER SOURCES:

PERIODICALS

New York Times, August 13, 2005, p. A25.

*   *   *

CARMINES, Alvin Allison, Jr.
    See CARMINES, Al

*   *   *

CARSWELL, Sue 1962-

PERSONAL: Born 1962. *Education:* University of Vermont, received degree.

ADDRESSES: Agent—c/o Author Mail, Random House, 1745 Broadway, 18th Fl., New York, NY 10019.

CAREER: American Broadcasting System, New York, NY, former senior story editor of *Good Morning America*; *People* magazine, former correspondent; *Vanity Fair,* New York, NY, currently researcher and reporter. Has also worked as a book editor for a publisher.

WRITINGS:

Faded Pictures from My Backyard: A Memoir, Ballantine Books (New York, NY), 2005.

Contributing editor to *O* magazine.

SIDELIGHTS: As a journalist and television producer, Sue Carswell has contributed to numerous stories. In *Faded Pictures from My Backyard: A Memoir* she tells her own story growing up next door to an orphanage for troubled children. Her father oversaw the school that served these orphans, but this proximity proved more of a hindrance than a help to Carswell's curiosity. Her father absolutely forbade his own children from mixing with his students, fearing they would be a bad influence. As a result, noted a *Publishers Weekly* reviewer, "Though Carswell seems obsessed with orphans, she doesn't include much information on the Home." Instead, much of the memoir concerns her mother, herself an orphan, and her own struggles with psychiatric problems that mirrored those of her father's charges. She also tracks down some of the orphans to see how they have fared in adulthood. The result is a combination of memoir and reporting that "sinks into bathos and mawkishness as often as it rises to limn a searing memory or tie a loose emotional end off neatly," according to *Booklist* contributor GraceAnne A. DeCandido. A *Kirkus Reviews* contributor noted the "somewhat incohesive" nature of the book, but also called it a "historical record of import."

BIOGRAPHICAL AND CRITICAL SOURCES:

BOOKS

Carswell, Sue, *Faded Pictures from My Backyard: A Memoir,* Ballantine Books (New York, NY), 2005.

PERIODICALS

Booklist, April 1, 2005, GraceAnne A. DeCandido, review of *Faded Pictures from My Backyard,* p. 1326.

Kirkus Reviews, March 1, 2005, review of *Faded Pictures from My Backyard,* p. 271.

People, May 9, 2005, Sue Corbett, review of *Faded Pictures from My Backyard,* p. 53.

Publishers Weekly, February 28, 2005, review of *Faded Pictures from My Backyard,* p. 51.*

*   *   *

CARTER, Betsy 1945-

PERSONAL: Born June 9, 1945, in New York, NY; married Malcolm Carter (divorced); married second husband, Gary Hoenig. *Education:* University of Michigan, B.A., 1967.

ADDRESSES: Agent—c/o Author Mail, Algonquin Books of Chapel Hill, P.O. Box 2225, Chapel Hill, NC 27515-2225. *E-mail*—bcarter@nyc.rr.com.

CAREER: Writer. McGraw Hill, New York, NY, editorial assistant, 1967-68; American Security and Trust, editor of company magazine, 1968-69; *Atlantic Monthly,* editorial assistant, 1969-70; *Newsweek,* New York, NY, researcher, 1971-73, assistant editor, 1973-75, associate editor, 1975-80; *Esquire,* New York, NY, senior editor, 1980-81, executive editor, 1981-82, senior executive editor, 1982-83, editorial director, 1983-85; *New York Woman,* creator and editor-in-chief, 1988; *New Woman,* New York, NY, editor-in-chief, 1994-97; *AARP's My Generation,* founding editor-in-chief, 1999-2003. Member of board of directors, National Alliance of Breast Cancer Organizations.

MEMBER: American Society of Magazine Editors (executive committee member, 1988-91, vice president, 1997).

WRITINGS:

Nothing to Fall Back On: The Life and Times of a Perpetual Optimist (autobiography), Hyperion (New York, NY), 2002.

The Orange Blossom Special (novel), Algonquin Books of Chapel Hill (Chapel Hill, NC), 2005.

Contributor to periodicals, including *Good Housekeeping, New York, AARP, Atlantic Monthly, Washington Post,* and *O.*

SIDELIGHTS: Betsy Carter has had many highs and lows in her life. In her career as a magazine editor, she has founded and run several high-profile titles, including *New York Woman, Esquire,* and *My Generation,* the last published by the American Association of Retired People. She was known as an accomplished professional, well-established at the top of the publishing world in New York City, when a terrible run of bad luck began after a taxicab in which she was riding became involved in an accident. As a result, Carter lost all of her teeth. Soon after that her marriage crumbled when her husband announced that he was gay, and her job was lost when the magazine she was working for folded. Her home burned down and she learned she had cancer. Carter reviews this terrible period in *Nothing to Fall Back On: The Life and Times of a Perpetual Optimist,* an autobiography that is "surprisingly upbeat," according to *Time* writer Andrea Sachs. Carter told Sachs that although her title implies a continuous positive outlook, it was not that simple, and no one who is going through difficult times should expect it to be. "I was not always cheerful," she told Sachs. To those who, like her, face overwhelming bad fortune, she advised, "Be easy on yourself. The last thing you need is that inner judge saying you shouldn't be losing control that way, why are you crying that much?"

The author alternates the story of her adult troubles with memories of growing up in the 1950s, as the child of refugees from Nazi Germany. In the course of addressing her adult problems, Carter writes "most poetically about confronting the reality of aging, ailing parents," commented a *Publishers Weekly* reviewer, who added that the author's "engaging account" of her struggle to overcome her many challenges "should gratify many readers." *Booklist* reviewer Carol Haggas called Carter's style "fresh, frank, and forthright" and termed her book "inspiring, witty, and refreshingly upbeat."

Carter tried her hand at fiction in the novel *The Orange Blossom Special,* published in 2005. The story begins in 1958, and features a young widow, Tessie Lockhart. Tessie works as a clerk in an Illinois dress shop, and although her husband has been dead for two and a half years, she still talks to him everyday. Finally, she seeks a fresh start, moving with her young daughter to Gainesville, Florida, a college town whose inhabitants will see many changes in the decade to come, as lives are touched by the Vietnam War, the civil rights movement, and the general social upheaval of the 1960s and 1970s. The story has many humorous aspects, such as Tessie's continued communication with her husband via something she calls "The Jerry Box," in which she drops notes to her late husband and waits for him to answer with a sign.

As Carter's story progresses, it takes on a more serious tone. The title refers to the first passenger train running from New York to Miami, and it is, in the words of the *Publishers Weekly* reviewer, "a not-so-subtle metaphor for the American dream and the forward march of history." That critic commented that the author's desire to provide historical sweep works to the detriment of her character development. Joanne Wilkinson in *Booklist,* however, found that the characters are drawn with "fresh, often idiosyncratic detail," making them "instantly engaging." A *Kirkus Reviews* contributor remarked that *The Orange Blossom Special* is an "odd mix of styles and themes, but nonetheless an endearing portrait of a place and time."

BIOGRAPHICAL AND CRITICAL SOURCES:

BOOKS

Carter, Betsy, *Nothing to Fall Back On: The Life and Times of a Perpetual Optimist,* Hyperion (New York, NY), 2002.

PERIODICALS

Booklist, July, 2002, Carol Haggas, review of *Nothing to Fall Back On: The Life and Times of a Perpetual Optimist,* p. 1816; March 1, 2005, Joanne Wilkinson, review of *The Orange Blossom Special,* p. 1136.
Folio: The Magazine for Magazine Management, October 1, 1995, Lorraine Calvacca, interview with Betsy Carter, p. 45.
Kirkus Reviews, May 15, 2002, review of *Nothing to Fall Back On,* p. 714; March 15, 2005, review of *The Orange Blossom Special,* p. 302.

O, August, 2002, Cathleen Medwick, review of *Nothing to Fall Back On,* p. 74.
People, June 27, 2005, Vick Boughton, review of *The Orange Blossom Special,* p. 49.
Publishers Weekly, May 9, 2005, review of *The Orange Blossom Special,* p. 44; July 15, 2002, review of *Nothing to Fall Back On,* p. 66.
Time, August 19, 2002, Andrea Sachs, "Still Here: A Leading Editor Describes Her Rebound from Stunning Woes," p. G14.*

*   *   *

CARTER, Nick
See LYNDS, Dennis

*   *   *

CASSIDY, Anne 1952-

PERSONAL: Born 1952, in London, England; married; children: one son.

ADDRESSES: Agent—c/o Author Mail, Scholastic, Ltd., 1-19 New Oxford St., London WC1A 1NU, England.

CAREER: Writer. Worked as a teacher in London, England for nineteen years; also worked in a bank.

AWARDS, HONORS: British Book Trust Teenage Book of the Year designation, and Whitbread Children's Book of the Year shortlist, both 2004, and Carnegie Children's Book Award shortlist, 2005, all for *Looking for JJ.*

WRITINGS:

FOR CHILDREN

Talking to Strangers, Adlib (Tarporley, England), 1994.
Spider Pie, illustrated by Bee Willey, Hamish Hamilton (London, England), 1995.
The Hidden Child (young-adult novel), Scholastic (London, England) 1997.

The Crying Princess, illustrated by Colin Paine, Franklin Watts (London, England), 2000, Picture Window Books (Minneapolis, MN), 2003.

Pippa and Poppa, illustrated by Philip Norman, Franklin Watts (London, England), 2000.

Cheeky Monkey, illustrated by Lisa Smith, Franklin Watts (London, England) 2000, published as *The Sassy Monkey,* Picture Window Books (Minneapolis, MN), 2005.

Jasper and Jess, illustrated by François Hall, Franklin Watts (London, England), 2001, Picture Window Books (Minneapolis, MN), 2003.

Tough Love (young-adult novel), Scholastic (London, England), 2001.

Naughty Nancy, illustrated by Desideria Guicciardini, Franklin Watts (London, England), 2002, Picture Window Books (Minneapolis, MN), 2005.

Missing Judy (young-adult novel), Scholastic (London, England), 2002.

Love Letters (young-adult novel), Scholastic (London, England), 2003.

Blood Money (young-adult novel), Hodder Children's (London, England), 2003.

Cleo and Leo, illustrated by Philip Norman, Picture Windows Books (Minneapolis, MN), 2003.

Looking for JJ, Scholastic (London, England), 2004.

Toby's Trousers, illustrated by Jan Lewis, Franklin Watts (London, England), 2004, Sea to Sea (North Mankato, MN), 2005.

The Best Den Ever, illustrated by Deborah Allwright, Franklin Watts (London, England), 2004.

(Reteller) *Snow White,* illustrated by Melanie Sharp, Franklin Watts (London, England), 2005.

Birthday Blues (young-adult novel), Scholastic (London, England), 2005.

The Queen's Dragon, illustrated by Gwyneth Williamson, Picture Window Books (Minneapolis, MN), 2005.

Jumping Josie, Sea to Sea (North Mankato, MN), 2005.

CRIME NOVELS

Big Girl's Shoes, Lion Tracks (London, England), 1990.

Driven to Death, Scholastic (London, England), 1994.

"EAST END MURDERS" SERIES; NOVELS

A Family Affair, Scholastic (London, England), 1995.

End of the Line, Scholastic (London, England), 1996.

No Through Road, Scholastic (London, England), 1996.

Accidental Death, Scholastic (London, England), 1996.

Brotherly Love, Scholastic (London, England), 1997.

Death by Drowning, Scholastic (London, England), 1999.

Dead Quiet, Scholastic (London, England), 2000.

SIDELIGHTS: The author of several teen thrillers in the "East End Murders" series as well as other young-adult novels known for their troubled protagonists and compelling plots, British writer Anne Cassidy explained to Madelyn Travis on the *Book Trust Web site* that she is attracted to "dark subjects." "I'm not interested only in whodunit, but in why something's done and how something's done and what effect it has on the people who did it," Cassidy added, in a discussion of her acclaimed novel *Looking for JJ.* In addition to her books for teens, Cassidy has also authored a number of books for entry-level readers.

Based on an actual incident that attracted worldwide attention—the murder of a young toddler by two ten-year-old British boys—*Looking for JJ* introduces another ten year old. Jennifer Jones is a lonely girl whose single mother focuses attention on her job rather than her daughter. Left with little supervision, JJ is drawn to the wrong sort: one of her two friends is a bully who ultimately eggs JJ and her equally weak-willed second friend into an act that has tragic consequences. Through its three main characters *Looking for JJ* focuses on "the power games that are going on, if you're at all soft or lonely or needy," Cassidy explained to Travis, adding of JJ and her friend that the two girls endure their friend's increasingly cruel behavior "just to fit in." Freed following a jail sentence for her participation in a horrific murder, JJ attempts to live life under a new name, but remains haunted by her past.

Other novels by Cassidy include *Tough Love,* which finds Gina falling for an older boy who seems to have his act together until he engages in gang violence and leaves Gina with an important choice to make. *Missing Judy* focuses on the aftermath of a young woman's abduction, as family and friends are left haunted by questions and inner terrors. While a teen is first flattered by the anonymous notes she receives, as *Love Letters* continues she realizes that she is actually being stalked, and *Blood Money* follows three teens who, after discovering a bag of cash and realizing that it is the lost property of a local drug dealer, are now faced with a moral dilemma in which several options could result in violence. Cassidy attempts to understand the thoughts of a young woman who abandons her newborn infant in *Birthday Blues,* another novel inspired by a prominent news story.

A devotee of crime fiction—particularly the novels of Ruth Rendell, Sue Grafton, John Harvey, and Scott Turow—Cassidy has also contributed several books to the detective genre with her "East End Murders" series. Including the novels *Death by Drowning, No Through Road,* and *Dead Quiet,* these books feature teen sleuth Patsy Kelly, an eighteen year old who works for her uncle's detective agency. "There's a lot more to these books than you'd think," Cassidy noted of crime fiction on her home page. "I love them. At their best they're thrilling and puzzling and—if they're well written—they tell you a lot about human nature and a darker side of life."

BIOGRAPHICAL AND CRITICAL SOURCES:

PERIODICALS

Magpies, May, 2002, review of *Naughty Nancy,* p. 29; September, 2005, review of *Birthday Blues,* p. 41.

School Librarian, May, 1995, review of *Talking to Strangers,* p. 76; May, 1996, review of *End of the Line,* p. 71; February, 1997, review of *Accidental Death,* p. 44; August, 1997, review of *The Hidden Child,* p. 157; spring, 2000, review of *Death by Drowning,* p. 43; autumn, 2002, review of *The Queen's Dragon,* p. 129, and *Missing Judy,* p. 154; winter, 2003, review of *Blood Money,* p. 207; spring, 2005, Rudolf Lowewnstein, review of *The Best Den Ever,* p. 19; summer, 2005, review of *Looking for JJ,* p. 99.

School Library Journal, November, 2004, Mary Elam, review of *Naughty Nancy,* p. 94; February, 2005, Melinda Piehler, review of *The Queen's Dragon,* p. 94.

ONLINE

Anne Cassidy Home Page, http://www.anne.cassidy4. users.btopenworld.com (October 6, 2005).

British Book Trust Web site, http://www.booktrusted. co.uk/ (November 6, 2005), Madelyn Travis, "No Hiding Place."

CASTILLO, Edmund L. 1924-2005

OBITUARY NOTICE— See index for *CA* sketch: Born November 13, 1924, in Toledo, OH; died of congestive heart failure, August 24, 2005, in Washington, DC. Naval officer, government official, and author. Castillo was a retired U.S. Navy captain, where he served as a public affairs officer, and later worked as spokesman for Fairfax County in Virginia. After graduating from Northwestern University in 1945, he was commissioned as an officer in the Naval Reserve just in time to see action in the Pacific theater during the last months of World War II. In 1949 he was commissioned in the regular navy and became a public affairs specialist. Castillo served until 1968, rising to the rank of captain. During this time, he held several posts, including press officer for the Department of Navy, officer-in-charge of the Navy Journalist School, and press officer of the Department of Defense. During his time in the navy, Castillo also wrote several nonfiction books for children, including *All about the United States Navy* (1961), *The Seabees of World War II* (1963), and *Flat-Tops—The Story of Aircraft Carriers* (1969). Castillo continued his education in the 1950s, earning a master's degree in communication from Boston University in 1954. After retiring from the U.S. Navy, he put his public relations experience to good use by becoming the spokesman for Fairfax County. Castillo also earned a Ph.D. in public administration from George Washington University in 1978. He left his job as spokesman in 1984 to become executive assistant to the county executive, retiring from public service in 1990.

OBITUARIES AND OTHER SOURCES:

PERIODICALS

Washington Post, September 13, 2005, p. B6.
Washington Times, September 9, 2005, p. B2.

*   *   *

CHASKEY, Scott 1950-
(Scott Allan Chaskey)

PERSONAL: Born April 17, 1950, in Toledo, OH; son of Harry William and Mary Isabelle (Pratt) Chaskey; married Megan Edith Boyd, June 3, 1982; children: Levin, Rowenna, Liam. *Education:* State University of New York–Binghamton, B.A., 1973; Antioch University, M.A., 1978.

ADDRESSES: Home—P.O. Box 27, Sag Harbor, NY 11963-0001. *Office*—Peconic Land Trust, P.O. Box 1776, Southampton, NY 11969-1776.

CAREER: Cliff farmer in Mousehole, Cornwall, England, 1978-89; Quail Hill Community Farm, Peconic Land Trust, Amagansett, NY, farmer and stewardship coordinator, 1991—. Teacher and poet-in-schools and museums; lecturer. Board member, Center for Whole Communities in Vermont.

MEMBER: Land Trust Alliance, Biodynamic Farming and Gardening Association, Northeast Organic Farmers Association (president).

AWARDS, HONORS: Fellowship, Virginia Center for Creative Arts, 1989; Gold Medal for Excellence in Horticulture, Long House Reserve.

WRITINGS:

This Common Ground: Seasons on an Organic Farm (memoir), Viking (New York, NY), 2005.

Also author of *A Book of Odes,* 1980, and *Stars Are Suns,* 1994.

SIDELIGHTS: Scott Chaskey is a farmer, writer, and educator. His work as the president of the Northeast Organic Farmers Association and as a pioneer of the community farming movement are part of his drive to find alternatives to conventional agricultural techniques in order to preserve Earth's ecological balance. His teaching is aimed at avoiding harm to the planet through the use of organic fertilizers, natural pesticides, and other techniques that are not used by large-scale agribusiness. In the community-farming model espoused by Chaskey, food is grown for members who pool their costs and share the harvest. Chaskey tells his own story in *This Common Ground: Seasons on an Organic Farm,* It is not a practical guide to farming, but a mixture of the author's observations and reflections on such things as garlic, compost, and wildlife. As a reviewer for *Publishers Weekly* commented, "The delight of his writing is his balancing of the poetry of farm life . . . with touches of humor." The reviewer advised that the book would be highly enjoyable for all who are interested in organic farming. *Booklist*

contributor George Cohen commended the author's tone, saying that "Chaskey's reverence for the land and its creatures is rare in today's society. We should all follow in his footsteps." A *Kirkus Reviews* writer called *This Common Ground* "nothing less than a vision, not original so much as eloquently expressed, of farming returned to its roots, and of the mighty pleasures it can give."

BIOGRAPHICAL AND CRITICAL SOURCES:

BOOKS

Chaskey, Scott, *This Common Ground: Seasons on an Organic Farm,* Viking (New York, NY), 2005.

PERIODICALS

Booklist, March 1, 2005, George Cohen, review of *This Common Ground,* p. 1142.
Kirkus Reviews, February 15, 2005, review of *This Common Ground,* p. 206.
Library Journal, April 15, 2005, Ilse Heidmann, review of *This Common Ground,* p. 110.
Publishers Weekly, March 28, 2005, review of *This Common Ground,* p. 69.

ONLINE

Center for Whole Communities Web site, http://www. wholecommunities.org/ (July 7, 2005), biographical information about Scott Chaskey.*

*   *   *

CHASKEY, Scott Allan
   See CHASKEY, Scott

*   *   *

CHIAPPONE, Richard

PERSONAL: Male.

ADDRESSES: Office—Alaska Quarterly Review, University of Alaska, Anchorage, 3211 Providence Dr., Anchorage, AK 99508. *E-mail*—afrac2@uaa.alaska. edu.

CAREER: University of Alaska, Anchorage, senior affiliate editor of *Alaska Quarterly Review* and adjunct professor at Kachemak Bay campus.

WRITINGS:

Water of an Undetermined Depth (stories), Stackpole Books (Mechanicsburg, PA), 2002.

Contributor to anthology *City Fishing,* Stackpole Books (Mechanicsburg, PA), 2002. Contributor to periodicals, including *Playboy, Alaska, Missouri Review, ZYZZYVA,* and *Gray's Sporting Journal.*

ADAPTATIONS: The short story "Raccoon" was adapted as a short film.

WORK IN PROGRESS: A feature-length screenplay.

SIDELIGHTS: Richard Chiappone's *Water of an Undetermined Depth* is a collection of stories in which fishing sometimes plays a part, as in "The Chubs," about a student who goes fishing with his factory-worker father. Most of the characters in the fourteen stories are men and include a plumber, Vietnam soldier, and retiree, the last who becomes stranded in a remote village while on a tropical vacation in "A Girl, the Jungle, Monkeys." The title story is a short tale about a father who is obsessed by the possibility of injury or death by accident, generated by his memories of the death of a childhood friend, when his daughter asks permission to go swimming at a local quarry with friends. *Library Journal* contributor Ellen R. Cohen called the stories "stark but well told." A *Publishers Weekly* reviewer said that "Chiappone's ironic humor differentiates this collection, and his strong voice bodes well for subsequent efforts."

BIOGRAPHICAL AND CRITICAL SOURCES:

PERIODICALS

Booklist, January 1, 2002, John Rowen, review of *City Fishing,* p. 793.
Library Journal, April 1, 2002, Nathan Ward, review of *City Fishing,* p. 117; February 1, 2003, Ellen R. Cohen, review of *Water of an Undetermined Depth,* p. 120.

Publishers Weekly, December 17, 2001, review of *City Fishing,* p. 79; January 6, 2003, review of *Water of an Undetermined Depth,* p. 39.

ONLINE

Kachemak Bay Writers' Conference Web site, http://writersconference.homer.alaska.edu/ (June 26, 2005), profile of Chiappone.*

*   *   *

CHILDERS, Mary 1952-
(Mary M. Childers)

PERSONAL: Born 1952. *Education:* Ph.D.

ADDRESSES: Home—Hanover, NH. *Agent*—c/o Author Mail, Bloomsbury Publishing, 175 5th Ave., Ste. 300, New York, NY 10010. *E-mail*—info@MaryChilders.org.

CAREER: Dartmouth College, Hanover, NH, adjunct assistant professor, director of Equal Opportunity and Affirmative Action program, and assistant to the president. Instructor at various colleges. Consultant, mediating conflict and providing discrimination prevention training. Guest on radio and television programs, including *McNeil-Lehrer News Hour* and *Diane Rehm Show.*

WRITINGS:

Welfare Brat: A Memoir, Bloomsbury Publishing (New York, NY), 2005.

Contributor to books, including *Radical Mothers: Activist Voices from Left to Right,* edited by Alexis Jetter, University Press of New England, 1997, and *Conflicts in Feminism,* edited by Marianne Hirsch and Evelyn Fox Keller, Routledge, 1990. Contributor of articles and essays to journals and periodicals.

SIDELIGHTS: Mary Childers delivers both a personal story and a slice of social history in her autobiography *Welfare Brat: A Memoir.* Childers was born in 1952, the third of several children. Her mother was a troubled woman who struggled with alcoholism. With no father figure, the large family struggled to survive in one of the few neighborhoods they could afford, the Bronx section of New York City. Once an elegant neighborhood of fine apartments and universities, the area was rapidly decaying, as long-time residents fled to the suburbs and crime took over. The family was mired in dysfunction and an attitude that ridiculed efforts to excel, or to escape poverty. Still, at an early age Childers was determined to achieve a different life from those she saw all around her, and she succeeded. Her book not only relates her personal story, but brings insight to the complex social issues within it. In addition, it serves as a portrait of an pivotal era in American history, when the decay of urban centers accelerated and became a serious problem.

A *Library Journal* reviewer, Dale Farris, praised this "heartfelt story of growing up white, Irish Catholic, and on welfare." A *Kirkus Reviews* writer noted that the author's narrative is highly engaging, particularly in recreating the tension she felt while watching her siblings succumb to the same forces that had blighted their parents' lives. "It all makes for raw, magnetic reading," added the reviewer, who concluded that the book is "a valuable piece of social history, as well as a potent personal tale."

BIOGRAPHICAL AND CRITICAL SOURCES:

BOOKS

Childers, Mary, *Welfare Brat: A Memoir,* Bloomsbury (New York, NY), 2005.

PERIODICALS

Boston Globe, May 15, 2005, Kate Bollick, review of *Welfare Brat.*
Kirkus Reviews, February 15, 2005, review of *Welfare Brat,* p. 207.
Library Journal, March 15, 2005, Dale Farris, review of *Welfare Brat,* p. 92.
Washington Post, July 12, 2005, Jonathan Yardley, review of *Welfare Brat.*

ONLINE

Bloomsbury USA Web site, http://www.bloomsburyusa. com/ (July 9, 2005), biographical information on Mary Childers.
Mary Childers Home Page, http://www.marychilders. org (October 18, 2005).

CHILDERS, Mary M.
    See CHILDERS, Mary

*   *   *

CHILDS, Faye

PERSONAL: Children: four children.

ADDRESSES: Agent—c/o St. Martin's Press, 175 5th Ave., New York, NY 10010.

CAREER: Founder and president of Blackboard, Columbus, OH, 1991—.

WRITINGS:

(With Noreen Palmer) *Going Off: A Guide for Black Women Who've Just about Had Enough,* St. Martin's Press (New York, NY), 2001.

SIDELIGHTS: Faye Childs is the founder of "Blackboard," a list of bestselling books written exclusively by African-American authors that has been a bi-weekly feature of *Essence* and other publications since its inception. Childs founded the list because black writers were not included on traditional lists, due to the fact that black-focused bookstores were not used in data collection. The list names the top five books in fiction and nonfiction in both hardcover and paperback. Booklists have long been followed by book buyers, and as more African-American buyers shop in ever-increasing numbers of black-focused bookstores, the market share for African-American authors has increased. The dollars spent by black book buyers nearly doubled during the 1990s, with ninety percent of books being bought by women. The "Blackboard" list plays a significant role in promoting African-American authors.

Childs co-wrote *Going Off: A Guide for Black Women Who've Just about Had Enough* with psychotherapist Noreen Palmer. They study the "triggers" that anger African-American women, such as discrimination, and others that create that response in all women, including betrayal, stress, and overwork. Childs and Palmer discuss ways to suppress and deal with anger and suggest counseling to women who have difficulty controlling their emotions on their own.

BIOGRAPHICAL AND CRITICAL SOURCES:

PERIODICALS

Publishers Weekly, April 23, 2001, review of *Going Off: A Guide for Black Women Who've Just about Had Enough,* p. 65.

ONLINE

Africana.com, http://www.africana.com/ (December 12, 2000), Njeru Waithaka, "Black Writers Cracking the Booklist."*

* * *

CHOTZI
See ROSEN, Jennifer

* * *

CLARKE, Stephen 1958-

PERSONAL: Born 1958.

ADDRESSES: Home—Paris, France. *Agent*—c/o Author Mail, Bantam Books, 20 Vauxhall Bridge Rd., London SW1V 2SA, England.

CAREER: Writer, journalist, and magazine editor.

WRITINGS:

A Year in the Merde (autobiographical fiction), Bloomsbury (New York, NY), 2005.

Also author of two self-published books, *Who Killed Beano* and *Beam Me up,* and of a film script, *The First Red Phone Box in Space.*

SIDELIGHTS: British writer Stephen Clarke went to live in Paris in 2002, keeping a journal of his experiences and impressions of life in the French capital. He transformed this journal into a novel, *A Year in the Merde.* The book was initially self-published by Clarke in Paris, where it was a local bestseller. Word-of-mouth praise led to such demand for the book that Clarke was approached by a major publisher. His humorous book has been frequently compared to Peter Mayle's bestseller *A Year in Provence.*

In the book, Clarke's alter ego is Paul West, a young Englishman sent to France to market a chain of British tearooms. He comically describes the frustrations of doing business with the French, and his dismissal from his job in the spring of 2003, in part because of anti-British sentiment following the invasion of Iraq. *Library Journal* reviewer Ravi Shenoy noted that "this laugh-out-loud yarn about West's colleagues . . . his romantic escapades, and French culture in general, will win Clarke many fans."

BIOGRAPHICAL AND CRITICAL SOURCES:

PERIODICALS

Kirkus Reviews, February 15, 2005, review of *A Year in the Merde,* p. 207.
Library Journal, April 1, 2005, Ravi Shenoy, review of *A Year in the Merde,* p. 115.
Publishers Weekly, March 28, 2005, review of *A Year in the Merde,* p. 66.

ONLINE

Fantastic Fiction, http://www.fantasticfiction.co.uk/ (July 7, 2005), review of *A Year in the Merde.*
Stephen Clarke Home Page, http://www.redgarage books.com (July 7, 2005).
Write Words Web site, http://www.writewords.org.uk/ (July 7, 2005), interview with Stephen Clarke.*

* * *

CLEVE, Anders 1937-1985
(Anders Zachris Cleve)

PERSONAL: Born July 25, 1937, in Helsinki, Finland; died March 26, 1985; married; children: two. *Education:* Earned M.A. degree.

CAREER: Taught history.

WRITINGS:

Dagen (poems), Söderström & Co. (Helsinki, Finland), 1955.

Det bara ansiktet, Söderström & Co. (Helsinki, Finland), 1956.

Gatstenar (stories), Söderström & Co. (Helsinki, Finland), 1959.

Vit eld; en paradoxal saga, Bonniers (Stockholm, Sweden), 1962.

Påskägget; en berettelse om vänskap, Bonniers (Stockholm, Sweden), 1966.

Labyrint, Söderström & Co. (Tammerfors, Finland), 1971.

Locknät, Söderström & Co. (Helsinki, Finland), 1981.

SIDELIGHTS: Finnish educator and writer Anders Cleve made his debut as a poet in 1955 with his collection *Dagen.* Several years later he published *Gatstenar,* a collection of short stories about life in Helsinki. Cleve has been an inspiration to more recent generations of Finnish and Swedish authors, and was one of the first writers to mix Finnish into an otherwise Swedish text. While some of the stories in *Gatstenar,* such as "Licentiaten," are written entirely in Swedish, "Kråkan—en individualist" mixes Finnish with Swedish, sometimes in the same sentence.

In 1919, when Finland drafted its national constitution, the Swedish-speaking Finns made up one fifth of the population, and the two extremely different languages were then given equal status by law. The Swedish-speaking Finns formed a minority group in Finland, yet often enjoyed a higher social position than did the Finnish-speaking population. The linguistic differences in Finland was a frequently occurring subject in Finnish-Swedish literature during the 1970s and 1980s, because these differences were closely related to issues of identity. While the younger generations became increasingly more tolerant of mixing Finnish with Swedish, Cleve was one of the first to introduce this feature to Finnish-Swedish literature.*

*   *   *

CLEVE, Anders Zachris
See CLEVE, Anders

COAKE, Christopher

PERSONAL: Born in IN; married Stephanie Lauer. *Education:* Ball State University, B.S.; Miami University (OH), M.A.; Ohio State University, M.F.A.

ADDRESSES: Home—Reno, NV. *Office*—Department of English, University of Nevada at Reno, Reno, NV 89557. *E-mail*—cjcoake@unr.edu.

CAREER: Writer and educator. University of Nevada, Reno, English department, assistant professor, 2005—.

WRITINGS:

We're in Trouble: Stories, Harcourt (Orlando, FL), 2005.

Contributor of stories to magazines, including *Gettysburg Review,* and to anthologies, including *Best American Mystery Stories 2004,* edited by Otto Penzler and Nelson DeMille, Houghton Mifflin, 2004.

WORK IN PROGRESS: Several novellas; a novel about a Colorado mining town; editing an anthology of stories relating to cancer.

SIDELIGHTS: Christopher Coake's 2005 debut collection, *We're in Trouble: Stories,* garnered the attention of numerous foreign publishers, making Coake, in the words of Sean Murphy, writing for the *Algonkian Writer Workshops* Web site, "a writer to watch out for."

Adam B. Vary, writing for *Entertainment Weekly,* stated that the theme central to Coake's initial collection is "love in the face of harrowing death," a theme which, according to Vary, the author tackles in a "wildly engaging" manner. Coake's story "All through the House," included in *We're in Trouble,* was also anthologized in the *Best American Mystery Stories 2004.* The story centers around a sheriff who has the task of investigating the murder of a local Indiana family. While being interviewed by a true-crime writer about the murders, the sheriff—a childhood friend of the killer, who later committed suicide—is reluctant to give all the details of the tragedy. Other tales in the collection include "In the Event," in which a man discovers that he must raise his godchild after the death of the child's parents, and "Cross-Country," about a road trip a man takes with his young child after being separated from his wife. Joanne Wilkinson, a reviewer for *Booklist,* stated that Coake's characters undergo transformations and the "painful truths they learn about themselves can be discomforting." Writing for *Library Journal,* Christopher Korenowsky concluded that the book contains "gripping reading from a talented newcomer." A reviewer for *Publishers Weekly* called *We're in Trouble* a "striking debut collection," and praised Coake's "unadorned but dramatic, economical prose."

BIOGRAPHICAL AND CRITICAL SOURCES:

PERIODICALS

Booklist, February 1, 2005, Joanne Wilkinson, review of *We're in Trouble: Stories,* p. 938.
Entertainment Weekly, April 15, 2005, Adam B. Vary, review of *We're in Trouble,* p. 89.
Kirkus Reviews, January 15, 2005, review of *We're in Trouble,* p. 67.
Library Journal, February 15, 2005, Christopher Korenowsky, review of *We're in Trouble,* p. 122.
Publishers Weekly, February 28, 2005, review of *We're in Trouble,* p. 42.

ONLINE

Algonkian Writer Workshop Web site, http://www.webdelsol.com/Algonkian/ (June 25, 2005), Sean Murphy, "An Interview with Christopher Coake."
Christopher Coake Home Page, http://www.christophercoake.com (June 25, 2005).
Christopher Coake Web log, http://www.christophercoake.blogspot.com/ (June 25, 2005).
Kacey Kowars Radio Show Web site, http://www.kaceykowarsshow.com/ (April 13, 2005), brief profile of author.

*   *   *

COLLINS, Michael
See LYNDS, Dennis

COMPTON, Jodi

PERSONAL: Born in CA.

ADDRESSES: Home—CA. *Agent*—Barney Karpfinger, Karpfinger Agency, 357 W. 20th St., New York, NY 10011.

CAREER: Author and journalist. Worked variously as an author of police procedurals and journalist. Associated Press, Minneapolis, MN, reporter;, subeditor of central CA newspaper.

WRITINGS:

"DETECTIVE SARAH PRIBEK" NOVEL SERIES

The Thirty-seventh Hour, Delacorte Press (New York, NY), 2004.
Sympathy between Humans, Delacorte Press (New York, NY), 2005.

SIDELIGHTS: Jodi Compton is the author of a series of police procedurals featuring Detective Sarah Pribek, a woman with a past who investigates missing persons for a sheriff's department in Minnesota. In Compton's 2004 debut title, *The Thirty-seventh Hour,* Pribek is investigating a case close to home, the disappearance of fellow detective Mike Shiloh, who also happened to be her husband. Shiloh and Pribek have been married for two months when he fails to turn up at an FBI training camp. While other police officers think the erratic Shiloh has simply run out on his new bride, Pribek doubts this is the situation and follows leads from Minnesota back to Utah, where Shiloh's family lives. Pribek also involves her partner, Genevieve Brown, in the hunt. For Brown, on leave and grieving after the brutal death of her daughter, this proves something of a life preserver, for the fact that her daughter's murderer has walked free on a technicality has affected her deeply. As Pribek continues her investigation, stories from the past come back to haunt the living.

A contributor for the *Mystery Reader* Web site called *The Thirty-seventh Hour* "a mystery that should not be missed." Jon Courtenay Grimwood observed in London's *Guardian Unlimited* that, "What begins as a slim and slightly unsatisfactory crime novel develops into an Old Testament unraveling of sin." A reviewer for *Publishers Weekly* called the novel "first-class, serious crime fiction," and in her review for *Booklist,* Connie Fletcher found *The Thirty-seventh Hour* a "nail-biter of a debut novel," and concluded: "Compton uses suspense as a powerful propellant." A critic for *Kirkus Reviews* warned readers to "watch this writer."

Compton followed her debut with *Sympathy between Humans,* once again featuring Pribek. In this installment, the female detective becomes the suspect in a murder case when she stonewalls over the killing of a low-grade hoodlum. A second plot line involves the investigation into the five-year-old disappearance of a famous writer's twin children. The writer, Marlinchen Hennessy, enlists Pribek's aid after other investigators have failed to come up with any leads. Part of the reason for the previous lack of success, Pribek soon discovers, is that Marlinchen has been less than reliable in the information she has supplied. The deeper Pribek gets into this missing-person's case, the darker the secrets she discovers about the Hennessy household. A contributor for *Kirkus Reviews* stated parts of the story "drift toward melodrama," but concluded, "Compton is clearly the goods." *Booklist* reviewer David Wright deemed Compton a "promising new voice in psychological suspense," while a contributor for *Publishers Weekly* felt her second book is a "multi-layered, touching tale of crimes and misdemeanors." Michelle Foyt, writing in *Library Journal,* praised *Sympathy between Humans* as a "first-rate sequel." A contributor for *MBR Bookwatch* called *Sympathy between Humans* "a strong thriller that will send readers seeking Sarah's previous appearance." Oline H. Cogdill, writing for the *South Florida Sun-Sentinel,* concluded that "Compton's penchant for sharply realized characters and believable situations elevates her burgeoning series. . . . [and] intelligently challenges the reader."

Speaking with Carol Fitzgerald, Joe Hartlaub, and Wiley Saichek of *Bookreporter.com,* Compton credited the initial success of her series to two things: "One, a lot of noir is about male characters, not female. Two, often those noir heroes live in L.A., in a studio apartment under a neon sign and drink whiskey neat and so on. A noir about a young female investigator who lives in Minnesota and is married seems to have caught readers off guard, and I'm sort of pleased about that."

BIOGRAPHICAL AND CRITICAL SOURCES:

PERIODICALS

Booklist, December 1, 2003, Connie Fletcher, review of *The Thirty-seventh Hour,* p. 650; February 1, 2005, David Wright, review of *Sympathy between Humans,* p. 944.

Kirkus Reviews, October 15, 2003, review of *The Thirty-seventh Hour,* p. 1252; January 15, 2005, review of *Sympathy between Humans,* p. 84.

Kliatt, May, 2004, Melody Moxley, review of *The Thirty-seventh Hour* (audiobook), p. 56.

Library Journal, December, 2003, Jetta Carol Culpepper, review of *The Thirty-seventh Hour,* p. 164; February 15, 2005, Michelle Foyt, review of *Sympathy between Humans,* p. 114.

MBR Bookwatch, April, 2005, review of *Sympathy between Humans.*

Publishers Weekly, October 27, 2003, review of *The Thirty-seventh Hour,* p. 43; February 14, 2005, review of *Sympathy between Humans,* p. 54.

San Jose Mercury News, January 21, 2004, John Orr, review of *The Thirty-seventh Hour.*

South Florida Sun-Sentinel, April 27, 2005, Oline H. Cogdill, review of *Sympathy between Humans.*

ONLINE

AllReaders.com, http://www.allreaders.com/ (June 26, 2005), Harriet Klausner, review of *The Thirty-seventh Hour.*

Bookreporter.com, http://www.bookreporter.com/ (January 16, 2004), Carol Fitzgerald, Joe Hartlaub, Wiley Saichek, "Jodi Compton Interview"; (March 11, 2005), Carol Fitzgerald, Joe Hartlaub, Wiley Saichek, "Jodi Compton Interview"; (June 26, 2005), Joe Hartlaub, review of *The Thirty-seventh Hour.*

BooksnBytes, http://www.booksnbytes.com/ (June 26, 2005), review of *The Thirty-seventh Hour.*

Guardian Online, http://www.books.guardian.co.uk/ (March 6, 2004), Jon Courtenay Grimwood, "Living in Sin," review of *The Thirty-seventh Hour.*

Mystery Reader Web site, http://www.themysteryreader.com/ (June 26, 2005), review of *The Thirty-seventh Hour.**

CONLON, Edward 1965-
(Marcus Laffey)

PERSONAL: Born 1965. *Education:* Graduated from Harvard University.

ADDRESSES: Agent—c/o Author Mail, Penguin Group, Riverhead Books Publicity, 375 Hudson St., New York, NY 10014.

CAREER: Writer and police detective. New York Police Department, officer, 1995-2001, detective, 2001—.

AWARDS, HONORS: Finalist for National Book Critics Circle Award, *Los Angeles Times* Book of the Year, and PEN/Martha Albright award, all 2004, all for *Blue Blood.*

WRITINGS:

Blue Blood (memoir), Riverhead Books (New York, NY), 2004.

Under pseudonym Marcus Laffey, published parts of *Blue Blood* in *New Yorker* under title "Cop Diaries," and contributed to *The Best American Essays 2001,* edited by Kathleen Norris and Robert Atwan, Houghton Mifflin, 2001.

ADAPTATIONS: Blue Blood was adapted as an audiobook by Recorded Books, 2004.

SIDELIGHTS: Edward Conlon is a Harvard University-educated police detective who works for the New York City Police Department (NYPD). In the late 1990s, under the pseudonym Marcus Laffey, he began publishing a series of articles on the daily life of a NYPD policeman, and in 2004 he collected these initial diary entries as the memoir *Blue Blood,* which, according to *Time* magazine reviewer Lev Grossman, "may be the best account ever written about life behind the badge." Conlon comes from a family of policemen and is conversant not only with current events occurring in the NYPD, but also with historical ones. As Terry D'Auray noted on *Trashotron.com, Blue Blood* tells of Conlon's years on the force, of the boring mundane work and of the dangerous and exciting moments, as well. As D'Auray further commented, the book "is not just a collection of recollections," however: "The reader learns a bit about the illustrious Tammany era, the Knapp Commission, Serpico, [and] the full story of the French Connection." Zac Unger, writing for the *Washington Post Online* noted, "Conlon is a cop's cop and his book, a dazzling epic of street life and rough camaraderie, is far more rewarding than any disgruntled Serpico-style tell-all could ever be." Conlon's work on the streets of the South Bronx introduced him to the seamier side of life as a policeman. As he told Leonard Picker in a *Publishers Weekly* interview: "I love case work, helping victims and catching bad guys. I have no interest in administration or management. I like robbery and traditional detective work because you have real victims— individual human beings who need you to help them."

In her review of *Blue Blood* for *Booklist,* Connie Fletcher noted, "readers are lucky Conlon gives them a pass into his world." A *Publishers Weekly* reviewer found Conlon's book a "gripping account," and further commented that *Blue Blood* provides a "compelling and detailed rendering of the daily grind of the average policeman." Sarah Jent, writing for *Library Journal,* termed the book "an insightful and revealing biography." Laura Italiano, a reviewer for *People,* felt Conlon's "respect for cop life is palpable."

BIOGRAPHICAL AND CRITICAL SOURCES:

BOOKS

Conlon, Edward, *Blue Blood,* Riverhead Books (New York, NY), 2004.

PERIODICALS

Booklist, February 15, 2004, Connie Fletcher, review of *Blue Blood,* p. 1002.
Entertainment Weekly, April 23, 2004, Gregory Kirschling, "Cop Talk," p. 42.
Kirkus Reviews, February 15, 2004, review of *Blue Blood,* p. 162.
Library Journal, April 1, 2004, Sarah Jent, review of *Blue Blood,* p. 103.

People, April 19, 2004, Laura Italiano, review of *Blue Blood,* p. 47; June 28, 2004, "Edward Conlon," p. 111.

Publishers Weekly, November 30, 1998, John F. Baker, "Talk of the City," p. 12; March 29, 2004, Leonard Picker, "An Ivy League Policeman on the Job" (interview), and review of *Blue Blood,* p. 53.

Time, April 19, 2004, Lev Grossman, "Rhapsody in Blue: Tales of Life on the Job from a Harvard-Educated Cop in the South Bronx," review of *Blue Blood,* p. 75.

ONLINE

Gothamist, http://www.gothamist.com/ (September 16, 2004), review of *Blue Blood.*

Trashotron.com, http://trashotron.com/ (May 10, 2004), Terry D'Auray, review of *Blue Blood.*

Washington Post Online, http://www.washingtonpost.com/ (June 26, 2005), Zac Unger, review of *Blue Blood.*

*   *   *

COOK, Robin 1946-2005
(Robin Finlayson Cook)

OBITUARY NOTICE— See index for *CA* sketch: Born February 28, 1946, in Belshill, Scotland; died of heart failure, August 6, 2005, in Iverness, Scotland. Politician and author. Cook was a prominent Labour Party leader in Britain who rose to the post of foreign secretary and later resigned as House of Commons leader in protest of Britain's policies in Iraq. Cook originally intended to become a Presbyterian minister, and he studied English literature at Edinburgh University. During his college years, however, he began to lose his religious faith and decided to pursue a political career instead. After university he became a school teacher; his left-leaning beliefs then led to work as a lecturer for the Workers' Educational Association. In the early 1970s he became chair of the Edinburgh City Council's housing committee; then, in 1974, he won the election to represent Edinburgh Central. As a member of British Parliament (MP), Cook was careful to prove himself as a moderate leftist, and by 1980 he had earned a post as deputy spokesman of economic affairs and the treasury. In 1983 Cook was chosen to the House of Commons' Shadow Cabinet and was as-

signed to be European spokesman, a vote of confidence from the Labour Party. Winning reelection in 1987, he was made spokesman of Shadow Social Services. Cook became a noted voice opposing conservative Tory Party leadership, and was recognized for his stalwart insistence on sticking by his principles when the *Spectator* named him Parliamentarian of the Year in 1991. When, in 1996, Cook opposed Prime Minister John Major's policy of arms sales to Iraq, he helped bring about the downfall of the Tories. This subsequently helped Labour Party candidate Tony Blair win the next election for prime minister. Blair rewarded Cook by appointing him foreign secretary in 1997, but Cook found it a difficult office to serve in. He was criticized for signing off on arms sales to Sierra Leone and Indonesia. An affair with Gaynor Regan that ended his first marriage also damaged his reputation, though he soon married Regan. On the other hand, he was credited with helping to modernize the Labour Party. Winning reelection to Parliament in 2001, Cook was removed from the foreign secretary post and made leader of the House of Commons. He made use of this position by expressing his views against Britain's policies in Iraq. Frustrated, he finally resigned in 2003 when he could no longer countenance Blair's continuing support for the Iraq war. Cook remained an MP, however, and had just won reelection when he suffered a heart attack while hiking in the Scottish highlands. Over the years, he published several books, including the coauthored *What Future in NATO?* (1978), *Life Begins at Forty: In Defence of the NHS* (1988), and the autobiography *The Point of Departure* (2004).

OBITUARIES AND OTHER SOURCES:

BOOKS

Cook, Robin, *The Point of Departure,* Simon & Schuster (New York, NY), 2004.

PERIODICALS

Los Angeles Times, August 7, 2005, p. B13.
New York Times, August 8, 2005, p. A17.
Times (London, England), August 8, 2005, p. 43.
Washington Post, August 7, 2005, p. C10.

*   *   *

COOK, Robin Finlayson
See COOK, Robin

CORLETT, William 1938-2005

OBITUARY NOTICE— See index for *CA* sketch: Born October 8, 1938, in Saltburn, Yorkshire, England; died August 16, 2005, in Sarlat, France. Author. Corlett was an actor and playwright who became best known for his young-adult books, ranging from fantasy to nonfiction and often addressing themes on homosexuality. Attending the Royal Academy of Dramatic Art in the mid-1950s, Corlett resolved to become a stage actor. He spent the late 1950s and much of the 1960s performing in plays across England and began writing his own plays as well. Among his early plays are *Another Round* (1963), *Flight of a Lone Sparrow* (1965), *Tinker's Curse* (1969), and *The Deliverance of Fanny Blaydon* (1971). As television gained an audience, he also wrote for this medium, penning movies and scripts for adult and children's television series. His work for television earned him three New York International Film and Television Festival gold awards, and he won two Writer's Guild awards for his contributions to the children's television series *The Paper Lads* in 1977. By the mid-1970s, however, Corlett was gaining even more attention as a novelist. A homosexual himself, his trilogy of young-adult novels, including *The Gate of Eden* (1974), *The Land Beyond* (1975), and *Return to the Gate* (1975), features a homosexual protagonist, a daring move when such topics were still not generally accepted. He later won fans with his fantasy trilogy, "The Magician's House" (1990-92), which he also adapted for television. The television versions, broadcast in 1999 and 2000, earned him Writers' Guild awards and nominations for both Emmy and British Academy of Film and Television Arts awards. Corlett, who also produced a number of religious nonfiction titles over the years, such as *The Question of Religion* (1978) and *The Buddha Way* (1979), again addressed the theme of homosexuality in his book *Now and Then* (1995) and the more light-hearted comedy *Two Gentlemen Sharing* (1997). His final work, *Kitty* (2004), is a bittersweet fantasy about a pair of dogs seeking a final resting place.

OBITUARIES AND OTHER SOURCES:

PERIODICALS

Guardian (London, England), August 24, 2005, p. 23.
Independent (London, England), August 23, 2005, p. 31.

COWLING, Maurice 1926-2005
(Maurice John Cowling)

OBITUARY NOTICE— See index for *CA* sketch: Born September 6, 1926, in London, England; died August 24, 2005, in Swansea, England. Journalist, historian, educator, and author. Cowling was an influential Cambridge history professor whose sometimes controversial views against liberal doctrine were said to influence several of England's conservative Tory leaders. After serving in the Queen's Royal Regiment from 1944 to 1948, he completed his master's degree at Jesus College, Cambridge, in 1952. He then taught at the college as a fellow for two years, but abruptly left to work in the British Foreign Office for a year. He then pursued a journalism career as a writer for the London *Times* from 1955 to 1956, and as a writer for the London *Daily Express* from 1955 to 1957. Some of his highly provocative articles never saw print, and philosophical differences with his editor led him to quit the *Express*. Cowling tried his hand at politics next, running unsuccessfully for Parliament in 1959 against former Minister of War Frederick Bellenger. Cowling then decided to go back to academia, returning to Cambridge as a lecturer in history in 1961 at Jesus College. He worked at Peterhouse College as a reader in history from 1963 until 1988, and was a fellow there from 1988 until his retirement in 1993. As a teacher, Cowling was very popular with his students, who found him humorous and provocative. It was Cowling's opinion that liberalism is a pariah on English society that aims to replace Christianity with a secular philosophy that all must follow. He criticized the ideals set down by British utilitarian philosopher John Stuart Mill, in particular, and all those who followed him. At one point, he even went so far as to assert that Britain's entry into World War II was a mistake that was designed primarily by the likes of such politicians as Winston Churchill for the sole purpose of maintaining power. Cowling's conservative views have been credited with influencing such politicians as Prime Minister Margaret Thatcher and Michael Portillo, the latter of whom served as defense secretary under Prime Minister John Major. Of the former, however, Cowling once asserted that Thatcher's extreme Toryism was distasteful to him. The historian expressed his views in a number of books, including *Mill and Liberalism* (1963), *The Impact of Hitler: British Politics and British Policy, 1933-1940* (1975), and the three-volume *Religion and Public Doctrine in Modern England* (1980, 1985, 2001).

OBITUARIES AND OTHER SOURCES:

PERIODICALS

Daily Telegraph (London, England), August 26, 2005.
Independent (London, England), September 6, 2005, p. 30.
Times (London, England), August 26, 2005, p. 72.

*   *   *

COWLING, Maurice John
    See COWLING, Maurice

*   *   *

CRANE, Frances 1896-1981

PERSONAL: Born 1896, in Lawrenceville, IL; died 1981; married Ned Crane; children: one daughter. *Education:* University of Illinois, Urbana, B.A.

CAREER: Author.

MEMBER: Phi Beta Kappa.

WRITINGS:

NOVELS

The Tennessee Poppy; or, Which Way Is Westminster Abbey?, Farrar & Rinehart (New York, NY), 1932.
The Reluctant Sleuth (mystery), Hammond (London, England), 1961.
Three Days in Hong Kong (mystery), Hammond (London, England), 1965.
Body beneath the Mandarin Tree (mystery), Hammond (London, England), 1965.
A Very Quiet Murder (mystery), Hammond (London, England), 1966.
Worse than a Crime (mystery), Hale (London, England), 1968.

"PAT AND JEAN ABBOTT" SERIES; MYSTERY NOVELS

The Turquoise Shop, Lippincott (Philadelphia, PA), 1941.
The Golden Box, Lippincott (Philadelphia, PA), 1942.

The Yellow Violet, Lippincott (Philadelphia, PA), 1942.
The Applegreen Cat, Lippincott (Philadelphia, PA), 1943.
The Pink Umbrella, Lippincott (Philadelphia, PA), 1943.
The Amethyst Spectacles, Random House (New York, NY), 1944.
The Indigo Necklace, Random House (New York, NY), 1945.
The Cinnamon Murder, Random House (New York, NY), 1946.
The Shocking Pink Hat, Random House (New York, NY), 1946.
Murder on the Purple Water, Random House (New York, NY), 1947.
Black Cypress, Random House (New York, NY), 1948.
The Flying Red Horse, Random House (New York, NY), 1950.
The Daffodil Blonde, Random House (New York, NY), 1950.
Murder in Blue Street, Random House (New York, NY), 1951, published as *Death in the Blue Hour,* Hammond (London, England), 1952.
The Polkadot Murder, Random House (New York, NY), 1951.
Murder in Bright Red, Random House (New York, NY), 1953.
13 White Tulips, Random House (New York, NY), 1953.
The Coral Princess Murders, Random House (New York, NY), 1954.
Death in Lilac Time, Random House (New York, NY), 1955.
Horror on the Ruby X, Random House (New York, NY), 1956.
The Ultraviolet Widow, Random House (New York, NY), 1956.
The Buttercup Case, Random House (New York, NY), 1958.
The Man in Gray, Random House (New York, NY), 1958, published as *The Gray Stranger,* Hammond (London, England), 1958.
Death-Wish Green, Random House (New York, NY), 1960.
The Amber Eyes, Random House (New York, NY), 1962.

SIDELIGHTS: Primarily a formula mystery author, Frances Crane wrote mysteries for over two decades, moving from the conventions of the late Golden Age "Had-I-But-Known" school to the fringes of modern crime novels. Most of her books feature Jean Abbott—Jean Holly prior to her marriage—who narrates the stories while her husband, Pat, is the strong silent detective. Though they live in San Francisco, many of the Abbotts' cases occur while they are on vacation; in fact, the books are often travelogues. Hints of spies or gangsters are usually kept vague. A murder occurs, usually offstage, and Jean becomes involved; Pat, who is in charge of the final scenes, catches the villain and explains how and why the murder occurred. His solution is based largely on points learned or discussed by Jean, but his reasoning process to uncover the murderer's identity is not given. The earlier books use Had-I-But-Known teasers to evoke suspense, but Crane dropped most of those by the late 1950s. And Crane moved with the times in other ways, introducing more naturalistic elements, drugs in *Death-Wish Green* and *The Coral Princess Murders,* and a retarded child in *The Amber Eyes.*

Crane's mysteries often drop the reader into the middle of a situation and then backtrack to show how the Abbotts got into it. A large eccentric family or close-knit group makes up the list of suspects, often not clearly differentiated. There is often a pair of young lovers toward whom Jean is sympathetic, even though at least one of them acts suspiciously. Pat seems to accept them at face value, forcing Jean to withhold some incriminating information. In the earlier books Jean is a prominent character. Her style is almost chatty, including detailed reporting of clothes and makeup. Later, she is primarily an observer.

Crane achieved her popularity as a mystery writer by using familiar themes, taking her readers to exotic places, and presenting a non-taxing, unthreatening tale for which all the loose threads are neatly tied by the end of each book.*

                    *   *   *

CREW, Cheryl Howard 1954(?)-
(Cheryl Howard)

PERSONAL: Born c. 1954, in CA; married Ron Howard (a film director), 1975; children: Reed, Paige, Jocelyn, Bryce.

ADDRESSES: Home—Armonk, NY. *Agent*—c/o Author Mail, St. Martin's Press, 175 5th Ave., New York, NY 10010.

CAREER: Writer.

AWARDS, HONORS: Eleanor Roosevelt Award, 2005, for *In the Face of Jinn.*

WRITINGS:

In the Face of Jinn (novel), St. Martin's Press (New York, NY), 2005.

SIDELIGHTS: Cheryl Howard Crew traveled to India, Pakistan, and Afghanistan in 1996-97 in order to research her first book. During her trip she stayed with Pakistani villagers and was smuggled into the remote Northwest frontier on the Pakistani-Afghan border. Her travels, which occurred before the U.S. invasion of Afghanistan, introduced her to some of the tribal life in Central Asia and the plight of women, who were subjugated under the rule of the Taliban and Afghan warlords. Her novel *In the Face of Jinn* tells the story of Christine Shepherd, who has an import business that requires her to travel to South Asia with her sister and partner Liz. On one of the trips, Liz disappears during a terrorist attack. Christine soon realizes that the Indian government is going to be of little help in finding her sister, so she sets out on her own search for both her sister and for the man who masterminded the terrorist attack. Traveling through India, Pakistan, and Afghanistan, Christine encounters the Taliban, warring tribal clans, and drug smugglers while fighting to survive as she is assaulted sexually and contracts a life-threatening illness.

In a review of *In the Face of Jinn* in *People,* Beth Perry noted that the author "deftly uses her knowledge of the area to create daunting images." A *Publishers Weekly* contributor wrote that "the nonstop action and gripping plot twists should keep readers entranced." Deborah Donovan commented in *Booklist* that "the sights, sounds, and smells of this harsh land leap from every page," and a *Kirkus Reviews* contributor noted: "The plausibility of her story relies on the generous personal detail the author brings to the landscape and characters, and especially to the ancient family customs and protocol of the people Christine encounters along the way."

BIOGRAPHICAL AND CRITICAL SOURCES:

PERIODICALS

Booklist, March 1, 2005, Deborah Donovan, review of *In the Face of Jinn,* p. 1136.

Daily Variety, April 21, 2005, Jonathan Bing, "I Dream of 'Jinn,'" p. 60.

In Style, April 4, 2005, Sarah Stebbins, "A Beautiful Time," p. 308

Kirkus Reviews, January 15, 2005, review of *In the Face of Jinn,* p. 74.

New Yorker, May 2, 2005, Lauren Collins, interview with author, p. 42.

People, May 23, 2005, Beth Perry, review of *In the Face of Jinn,* p. 56.

Publishers Weekly, March 28, 2005, review of *In the Face of Jinn,* p. 56.

Time, April 11, 2005, Rebecca Winters, "Mogul Wife Goes Undercover," p. 69.

USA Today, April 13, 2005, Carol Memmott, "Director's Wife Faces Danger to Write 'Jinn.'"

Women's Wear Daily, April 21, 2005, Marcy Medina, "Spice World," about book party for author, p. 4.

ONLINE

New York Social Diary Online, http://www.newyorksocialdiary.com/ (March 28, 2005), brief profile of author.*

*   *   *

CREWDSON, Michael

PERSONAL: Male.

ADDRESSES: Home—Brooklyn, NY. *Agent*—c/o Author Mail, Villard Books, 1745 Broadway, New York, NY 10019.

CAREER: Writer and naturalist.

WRITINGS:

NONFICTION

(With Margaret Mittelbach) *Wild New York: A Guide to the Wildlife, Wild Places & Natural Phenomena of New York City,* Crown (New York, NY), 1997.

(With Margaret Mittelbach) *Carnivorous Nights: On the Trail of the Tasmanian Tiger,* illustrations by Alexis Rockman, Villard Books (New York, NY), 2005.

Contributor of articles to publications, including the *New York Times* and *Newsday.*

SIDELIGHTS: Michael Crewdson and Margaret Mittelbach have written about various aspects of the natural world for major newspapers. They have also produced two book-length works. Their 1997 work *Wild New York: A Guide to the Wildlife, Wild Places & Natural Phenomena of New York City* is a field guide to an urban space. In 2005, the pair released the book *Carnivorous Nights: On the Trail of the Tasmanian Tiger,* a "spirited narrative of the authors' hunt for the presumed-extinct thylacine," according to a reviewer for *Science News.* The authors were inspired to search for the purportedly extinct Tasmanian tiger after seeing a stuffed version of the animal in New York's Museum of Natural History. The two traveled to Tasmania and braved the backcountry in the hopes of catching a glimpse of the animal; along the way they recorded their experiences with a variety of other animals. A *Science News* contributor praised the resulting book as both a "detailed nature guide and a humorous and engaging adventure story." Edell M. Schaefer, a reviewer for *Library Journal,* noted that *Carnivorous Nights* is "an irresistible work of armchair travel, not to be missed." Similarly, a reviewer for *Publishers Weekly* felt that "the authors' lively writing will keep readers' spirits high." A critic for *Kirkus Reviews* concluded the book "neatly and wonderfully sews together natural science and travel yarn."

BIOGRAPHICAL AND CRITICAL SOURCES:

PERIODICALS

Kirkus Reviews, February 15, 2005, review of *Carnivorous Nights: On the Trail of the Tasmanian Tiger,* p. 217.

Library Journal, April 1, 2005, Edell M. Schaefer, review of *Carnivorous Nights,* p. 121.

Publishers Weekly, March 14, 2005, review of *Carnivorous Nights,* p. 60.

Science News, May 14, 2005, review of *Carnivorous Nights,* p. 319.*

CROSS, Robert F. 1950-

PERSONAL: Born December 17, 1950, in Port Jervis, NY; son of Francis S. and Rita C. (a nurse) Cross; married September 24, 1983; wife's name Sheila L. (a physician). *Education:* Orange County Community College, A.A., 1971; State University of New York at Albany, B.S., 1973; State University of New York at New Paltz, M.A., 1976. *Politics:* Democrat. *Religion:* Roman Catholic. *Hobbies and other interests:* Sailing.

ADDRESSES: Office—City of Albany Department of Water and Water Supply, 35 Erie Blvd., Albany, NY 12203.

CAREER: Writer. *Catskills* magazine, feature writer, 1974-75; *New York Times,* New York, NY, correspondent, 1974-76; *Union Gazette,* Port Jervis, NY, reporter-photographer, 1974-76; *Wall Street Journal,* Albany, NY, statehouse correspondent, 1976-78; Ottaway Newspapers, Inc., Albany Statehouse Bureau, chief, 1976-78; New York State Department of Environmental Conservation, Albany, editor-writer, 1978-83, special assistant to the commissioner, 1983-85, executive assistant to the commissioner, 1985-87, assistant commissioner, 1987-89; City of Albany Department of Water and Water Supply, commissioner, 1996—; Albany Port District Commission, commissioner and chairman, 1998—. Destroyer Escorts Historical Museum, trustee on board of directors.

MEMBER: Franklin and Eleanor Roosevelt Institute, Minisink Valley Historical Society.

AWARDS, HONORS: New York State Publishers Award for Excellence, 1978, for distinguished state government reporting; Labor Management Achievement Award, Governor's Office of Employee Relations/ Civil Service Employees Association, 1986; Award of Recognition, New York State Office of Mental Retardation and Developmental Disabilities Client Employment Program, 1987.

WRITINGS:

Sailor to the White House: The Seafaring Life of FDR, Naval Institute Press (Annapolis, MD), 2003.

Contributor to periodicals, including *Naturalist's, Historic Nantucket,* and *Conservationist.*

WORK IN PROGRESS: Research and interviews for new book on World War II sailors aboard destroyers.

*   *   *

CROWE, John
See LYNDS, Dennis

*   *   *

CUNNINGTON, Yvonne 1955-

PERSONAL: Born October 17, 1955, in Malartic, Quebec, Canada; married John Cunnington. *Education:* University of Western Ontario, B.A., 1978, M.A. (journalism); McMaster University, M.A. (German), 1994. *Hobbies and other interests:* Gardening, garden and nature photography.

ADDRESSES: Home—959 Book Rd. W., Ancaster, Ontario L9G 3L1, Canada. *E-mail*—ycunnington@ sympatico.ca.

CAREER: Garden writer, photographer, and lecturer. *Canadian Living,* Toronto, Ontario, Canada, associate editor, 1980-84; *Maclean's,* Toronto, associate editor, 1986-88; freelance writer, 1988—. *Chatelaine,* contributing editor, 2000-04; Royal Botanical Gardens, Hamilton, Ontarioa, board of directors, 2004—gardening lecturer and instructor.

WRITINGS:

Clueless in the Garden: A Guide for the Horticulturally Helpless, Key Porter Books (Toronto, Ontario, Canada), 2003.

Contributor of articles on gardening and landscaping to magazines, including *Chatelaine, Gardening Life, Canadian Gardening,* and *Doctor's Review.*

SIDELIGHTS: Yvonne Cunnington told *CA:* "If there was an unlikely gardener, I was it. Growing up on a farm, where I helped tend a large vegetable plot, I thought that gardening was drudgery. I yearned for more refined pursuits where your hands stayed clean: so I chose journalism, and worked primarily for women's magazines.

"My wholesale conversion to gardening—and eventually to garden writing—began innocently enough in 1991 when my husband and I bought an older home in Hamilton, Ontario. Like the house, the backyard was in dire need of a makeover. In the process of turning it into a garden, I too was transformed.

"Since that time I have earned a certificate in landscape design, and worked as a freelance garden designer (1996-99). This I gave up when we moved to a ten-acre property in the country, which was also in dire need of a makeover. These days, I garden with flowering perennials and lots of ornamental grasses on a ten-acre property with many different garden areas. We host garden tours, including bus tours from the United States and Canada.

"As a garden writer, photographer, and lecturer, I'm passionate about plants and landscape design. I favor contemporary, easy-care, meadow-like garden styles that work with nature, rather than fighting it."

BIOGRAPHICAL AND CRITICAL SOURCES:

PERIODICALS

Gardening Life, August-September, 2003, review of *Clueless in the Garden: A Guide for the Horticulturally Helpless,* p. 12.

ONLINE

Yvonne Cunnington Home Page, http://www.flower-gardening-made-easy.com (May 30, 2005).

D

DANIEL, John 1948-

PERSONAL: Born 1948; son of Franz (a union organizer) and Zilla (A union organizer) Daniel; married; wife's name Marilyn. *Education:* Attended Reed College (Portland, OR).

ADDRESSES: Home—Canton, NY; Coast Range region, OR. *Agent*—c/o Author Mail, Shoemaker & Hoard, 1400 65th St., Ste. 250, Emeryville, CA 94608.

CAREER: Writer and educator. Oregon State University Center for Humanities, research and writing fellow; St. Lawrence University, Viebranz visiting writer. Also worked as a logger.

AWARDS, HONORS: Wallace Stegner fellow in poetry, Stanford University; creative writing fellowship, National Endowment for the Arts; Oregon Book Award for Literary Nonfiction, 1992, for *The Trail Home: Essays* and 1996, *Looking After: A Son's Memoir.*

WRITINGS:

BIOGRAPHY

The Trail Home: Essays, Pantheon Books (New York, NY), 1992.
Looking After: A Son's Memoir, Counterpoint (Washington, DC), 1996.
Winter Creek: One Writer's Natural History, Milkweed Editions (Minneapolis, MN), 2002.
Rogue River Journal: A Winter Alone, Shoemaker & Hoard (Emeryville, CA), 2005.

POETRY

Common Ground: Poems, Confluence Press (Lewiston, ID), 1988.
(Editor) *Wild Song: Poems of the Natural World,* illustrated by Deborah Randolph Wildman, University of Georgia Press (Athens, GA), 1998.

OTHER

Contributor of essays to *Oregon Rivers,* photographs by Larry Olson, foreword by David R. Brower, Westcliffe Publishers (Englewood, CO), 1997. Author of poetry collection, *All Things Touched by the Wind,* 1994. Contributor to periodicals, including *Southwest Review.*

SIDELIGHTS: John Daniel is a poet and essayist whose writing is often a product of having spent time in reflection, solitude, and nature. His 1992 collection, *The Trail Home: Essays,* deals with the natural beauty of the San Francisco Bay area, the relative merits of radical environmentalism, as well as approaching nature in a variety of ways—in the wild, in one's own garden, and even on television. A reviewer for *Publishers Weekly* found the essays in the collection "delightful," and concluded the work presents a "personal, contemplative and satisfying view of nature." With his 1996 book, *Looking After: A Son's Memoir,* the author composed an account of the four years he and his wife cared for his aged mother, who had been diagnosed with Alzheimer's. He recounts his attempts to try and reach a woman who had always been such a force in his life and relates the strain performing as a caretaker put on his marriage. According to a reviewer for *Publishers Weekly,* the memoir contains "graceful, poignant prose."

If *Looking After* is an homage to his mother, then Daniel's 2002 memoir, *Winter Creek: One Writer's Natural History,* is a tribute to Daniel's own youth. In the book Daniel details his move from the area around Washington, DC, to the West Coast and the influence particular writers have had on his development as an author. A critic for *Kirkus Reviews* praised the "reflective and polished text" in *Winter Creek,* while a contributor to *Publishers Weekly* commended the book's "vivid and thoughtful" prose.

A memoir of a different sort is served up in Daniel's 2005 book, *Rogue River Journal: A Winter Alone.* As the title suggests, Daniel spent the winter of 2000-2001 alone in an Oregon cabin. Free from the trappings of modern life, he tends his garden, lives off the land, and notes the wildlife that abounds near his remote cabin—and journals what he experiences during his period of isolation. The resulting memoir also contains ruminations on the life and works of his father, Franz Daniel, a labor organizer. A critic for *Kirkus Reviews* stated that "Daniel's time alone is potent, a dilation on the amusements and scorchings of the simple life, and a distillation of the strange, human group that was his family."

BIOGRAPHICAL AND CRITICAL SOURCES:

BOOKS

Daniel, John, *Looking After: A Son's Memoir,* Counterpoint (Washington, DC), 1996.
Daniel, John, *Rogue River Journal: A Winter Alone,* Shoemaker & Hoard (Emeryville, CA), 2005.
Daniel, John, *The Trail Home: Essays,* Pantheon Books (New York, NY), 1992.
Daniel, John, *Winter Creek: One Writer's Natural History,* Milkweed Editions (Minneapolis, MN), 2002.

PERIODICALS

Kirkus Reviews, May 1, 2002, review of *Winter Creek,* p. 632; February 15, 2005, review of *Rogue River Journal,* p. 208.

Publishers Weekly, May 11, 1992, review of *The Trail Home,* p. 64; September 9, 1996, review of *Looking After,* p. 71; June 3, 2002, review of *Winter Creek,* p. 80.

ONLINE

St. Lawrence University Web site, http://web.stlawu. edu/ (April 18, 2005), "John Daniel Closes out SLU Writers Series April 28."
Shoemaker & Hoard Web site, http://www.shoemaker hoard.com/ (June 27, 2005), brief profile of author.
University of Oregon Web site, http://lnf.uoregon.edu/ (June 27, 2005), brief profile of author.*

* * *

DANILOWITZ, Brenda

PERSONAL: Born in Kimberley, South Africa; daughter of Jack Frank (an attorney and professional cricket player) and Hannah Bergman; married Sorrel Danilowitz; children: Guy, Gideon.

ADDRESSES: Home—Orange, CT. *Office*—Josef and Anni Albers Foundation, 88 Beacon Rd., Bethany, CT 06524.

CAREER: Curator and art historian. University of the Witwatersrand, Johannesburg, South Africa, faculty member, 1980-86; Josef and Anni Albers Foundation, Bethany, CT, curator, 1990—.

WRITINGS:

(Editor, and author of introduction) *Anni Albers: Selected Writings on Design,* University Press of New England (Hanover, NH), 2000.
The Prints of Josef Albers: A Catalogue Raisonné, 1915-1976, Hudson Hills Press (New York, NY), 2001.

Contributor to *Between Union and Liberation: Women Artists in South Africa 1910-1994,* Ashgate Publishers (Burlington, VT), 2005. Contributor to periodicals, including *African Arts,* and to Web sites, including *Reece Galleries.*

SIDELIGHTS: Brenda Danilowitz works as an art historian and curator specializing in the study of African art. She has also taught art history at a number of universities, including the University of the Witwatersrand, Yale University, and the University of Connecticut. Since 1990, she has also served as chief curator at the Josef and Anni Albers Foundation, a nonprofit organization that promotes and preserves the art of German artists Josef and Anni Albers. Danilowitz was the editor of the 2000 book *Anni Albers: Selected Writings on Design.* The next year, she also wrote *The Prints of Josef Albers: A Catalogue Raisonné, 1915-1976.* This book features a selection of works by Josef Albers, who studied and taught at the famed Bauhaus. Danilowitz accompanies Albers's works with a detailed biographical essay about his life and career.

Critics responded positively to *The Prints of Josef Albers.* Many appreciated the book's thorough coverage of Albers's career. "This is the first work to fully catalog and examine his graphic contributions and is thus essential to complete any collection on Albers," wrote *Library Journal* contributor Kraig Binkowski. Other reviewers appreciated the quality of Danilowitz's biography of the artist. One *Publishers Weekly* contributor concluded that Danilowitz has "written a lucid introductory essay on the evolution of Albers's oeuvre."

BIOGRAPHICAL AND CRITICAL SOURCES:

PERIODICALS

Choice, December, 2001, M. Tulokas, review of *Anni Albers: Selected Writings on Design,* p. 671.
Library Journal, April 1, 2002, Kraig Binkowski, review of *The Prints of Josef Albers: A Catalogue Raisonné, 1915-1976,* p. 99.
Publishers Weekly, January 28, 2002, review of *The Prints of Josef Albers,* p. 284.

*   *   *

DANNEMARK, Francis 1955-

PERSONAL: Born April 13, 1955, in Macquenoise, Belgium; married; children: Thomas, Lucas, Noé. *Education:* Studied literature at Université de Louvain.

ADDRESSES: Home—Brussels, Belgium. *Office*—Editions le Castor Astral, 52 rue des Grille, 93500 Pantin, France. *E-mail*—francis.dannemark@swing.be.

CAREER: Editions le Castor Astral (publishing house), Pantin, France, editor. Founder, *La Vigie des Minuits Polaires* (literary review); organizer of literary festivals.

AWARDS, HONORS: Prix Charles Plisnier, 1991, for *Choses qu'on dit la nuit entre deux villes;* Prix Alexandre Vialatte, 1993, for *La longue promenade avec un cheval mort;* Prix Maurice Carême, 2001, for *La longue course: poèmes, 1975-2000.*

WRITINGS:

Heures locaales (poetry), Seghers (Paris, France), 1977.
Antartique (poetry), Le Castor Astral (Bordeaux, France), 1978.
Le voyage à plus d'un titre (novel), R. Laffont (Paris, France), 1981.
Périmètres (poetry), Dominique Bedou (Gourdon, France), 1981.
La nuit est la dernière image (novel), R. Laffont (Paris, France), 1982.
Les eaux territoriales (poetry), Dominique Bedou (Gourdon, France), 1983.
Mémoires d'un ange maladroit (novel), R. Laffont (Paris, France), 1984.
L'hiver ailleurs [and] *Sans nouvelles du paradis,* R. Laffont (Paris, France), 1988.
Choses qu'on dit la nuit entre deux villes (novel), R. Laffont (Paris, France), 1991.
Les agrandissements du ciel en bleu (novel), R. Laffont (Paris, France), 1992.
La longue promenade avec un cheval mort (novel), R. Laffont (Paris, France), 1993.
L'incomparable promenade (poetry), Cadex (Montpelier, France), 1993.
(With Étienne Reunis) *Zone de perturbations* (novel), Zulma (Cadeilhan, France), 1994.
Dans les jardins mouillés entre Arras et Bruxelles (poetry), Cadex (Saussines, France), 1995.
La tombe d'un jeu d'enfant, photographs by Bernard Kerger, Cadex (Montpelier, France), 1995.
Poèmes et letters d'amour, Cadex (Montpelier, France), 1997.

La grève des archéologues (novel), Le Castor Astral (Bordeaux, France), 1998.

Qu'il pleuve (novel), Le Castor Astral (Bordeaux, France), 1998.

La traversée des grandes eaux: huile de Teddy Magnus, Cadex (Montpelier, France), 1999.

(With Réjane Peigny) *Le jour se lève encore,* Cadex (Saussines, France), 1999.

La longue course: poèmes, 1975-2000, Le Castor Astral (Pantin, France), 2000.

Bel amour, chambre 204, ou l'autre moitié: une romance (novella), Le Castor Astral (Pantin, France), 2001.

33 voix (poetry; in thirty-three languages), Cadex (Saussines, France), 2002.

Les petites voix (novel), Belfond (Paris, France), 2003.

SIDELIGHTS: Since the mid-1970s, Francis Dannemark has published numerous poetry collections and novels. He is considered part of a wave of Belgian writers, including Eugène Savitzkya, Jean-Philippe Toussaint, and Paul Emond, whose styles are drawn from a variety of linguistic origins, atmospheres, and altered realities. Dannemark has readers all over the world and his work has achieved considerable renown within French literature.

Dannemark's *Les agrandissements du ciel en bleu* is a semi-autobiographical novel set in Belgium. Belgian writers at the end of the twentieth century were known for their strong feelings of aversion, fatalism, and despair toward their own country, in which they believed indifference smothered thought. Dannemark expresses these same sentiments in his novel, while at the same time offering a note of hope for the future. In the story the protagonist, Theo returns to Brussels after a long absence, encounters old friends who have become bourgeois and dull, and then rediscovers himself in a jazz café. American jazz becomes his salvation. He laments that Belgium is dull and that many of its citizens have nervous problems, but he decides that it is not all bad—after all, Belgium has twenty different breads, which he feels is worth something—and that he will return to the woman he formerly loved. Dannemark fills the book with wit and wisdom, according to reviewers, a technique *World Literature Today* critic Judith L. Greenberg found somewhat tedious; she commented, for instance, on the inclusion of sayings observed on bumper stickers and T-shirts, such as "Don't follow me, I'm lost too." Morsels of popular culture also fill the book, including

quotes from writers and movie stars such as Ingrid Bergman, and Dannemark features landscapes that remind him of artists' paintings. The concluding sentiment of the novel, according to Greenberg, is that "the only way to avoid more or less constant despair is to live each day as an entire world and to love someone."

Dannemark is suspicious of books about events or books founded on arguments that are too strong. He claims that each of his novels is associated very closely with a certain group of his poems. For him, the tie between the two is indispensable: poetry and prose are two approaches to the same thing, and pairing them results in a family of books very solidly joined together. Many of his works have titles involving water and rain, such as *Qu'il pleuve, Dans les jardins mouillés entre Arras et Bruxelles,* and *Les eaux territoriales,* while *La grève des archéologues* is set in the waters of Venice. Dannemark has said that he only noticed this commonality after he had written and titled his works, but that it goes along with his habitual conjoining of poetry and prose written on similar themes.

Living and writing in Belgium, Dannemark has published most of his books in France, including at publisher Le Castor Astral, where he works as an editor. This is in keeping with the typical practice of Belgian writers, who have by and large avoided claiming a national identity in favor of exposing their books to more readers by publishing in Paris instead of in their homeland. Some eighty percent of Belgian writers choose to have their work published in France; Jean-Jacques Brochier, editor of *Magazine littéraire,* once joked that half of all French authors in the 1990s were Belgian, referring to Dannemark, as well as such writers as Conrad Detrez, Dominique Rolin, and Hergé, the creator of Tintin. Dannemark has claimed that it took him a long time to accept that he is a writer. For years he refused to travel to Paris to meet in person with his own editor, finally making the trip for the first time after his fourth novel. He eventually came to terms with his career by likening being a writer to having blue eyes, a fact of life that must merely be accepted because it cannot be changed.

BIOGRAPHICAL AND CRITICAL SOURCES:

PERIODICALS

World Literature Today, autumn, 1992, Judith L. Greenberg, review of *Les agrandissements du ciel en bleu,* p. 688.

ONLINE

Cineature, http://cineature.lasecte.com/ (August 21, 2001), "Francis Dannemark."

FNAC, http://www.fnac.fr/ (August 21, 2001), interview with Francis Dannemark.

Frank 15 Online: Belgium, http://www.gyoza.com/ (August 21, 2001), Jean-Luc Outers, "Belgium: A Literature Apart."*

*　　*　　*

DART-THORNTON, Cecilia

PERSONAL: Married. *Education:* B.A. (with honors); diploma in education.

ADDRESSES: Home—Melbourne, Victoria, Australia. *Agent*—c/o Author Mail, Tor Books, 175 5th Ave., New York, NY 10010. *E-mail*—dartthornton@yahoo.co.uk.

CAREER: Writer. Worked in various positions until turning to writing full-time.

WRITINGS:

The Ill-Made Mute (first novel in "Bitterbynde" fantasy trilogy), Warner Books (New York, NY), 2001.

The Lady of the Sorrows (second novel in "Bitterbynde" fantasy trilogy), Warner Books (New York, NY), 2002.

The Battle of Evernight (third novel in "Bitterbynde" fantasy trilogy), Warner Books (New York, NY), 2003.

The Iron Tree (first novel in "Crowthistle Chronicles" fantasy series), Tor Books (New York, NY), 2005.

The Well of Tears (second novel in "Crowthistle Chronicles" fantasy series), Tor Books (New York, NY), 2006.

WORK IN PROGRESS: Weatherwitch, and *Fallowblade,* the third and fourth novels, respectively, in the "Crowthistle Chronicles" series, both for Tor Books.

SIDELIGHTS: Australian author Cecilia Dart-Thornton had been interested in writing stories since her youth. At an early age, her mother also shared her own love of science fiction and fantasy literature. As an adult, while working a variety of jobs and writing on the side, Dart-Thornton discovered an online writing workshop where participants could submit excerpts of their work; she began to workshop parts of the book manuscript she was currently working on. One of the Web site's moderators gave Dart-Thornton the contact details of a literary agent, and she has since become a prolific and popular fantasy/science-fiction author.

In 2001 the author published the first novel in the "The Bitterbynde" fantasy trilogy, titled *The Ill-Made Mute.* This story focuses on an unnamed protagonist who is an abandoned mute living on Erith, a world inhabited by supernatural creatures drawn from English and Celtic folklore and dominated by a society where the people are either privileged aristocrats or "lower" class. The nameless mute, who is disfigured because of exposure to poisonous plants, ends up in Isse Tower and is horribly abused. The character escapes as a stowaway on a "windship" and, when discovered, is forced to work as a dockhand. Eventually, the nameless one escapes once again when pirates attack the ship, meets up with the treasure-seeker Sianadh, who names the character Imrhien, and the two are off on an adventure that includes a battle with the forces of evil.

Dart-Thornton received much praise for her work on *The Ill-Made Mute.* Many reviewers found the author's debut to be a creative and gripping story, one that had much potential as the first in a trilogy. "A stunning, dazzling debut . . . tirelessly inventive, fascinating, affecting, and profoundly satisfying," commented one *Kirkus Reviews* contributor. Others found it a welcome addition to Dart-Thornton's genre. "For fans of mainstream fantasy, this is likely to be one of the high marks of the year," declared Don D'Ammassa in a review for *Science Fiction Chronicle.*

Dart-Thornton's second novel in the "Bitterbynde" trilogy is *The Lady of the Sorrows,* picks up with a young woman who has no memory of her past and is troubled by her inability to remember. Given a message for the king-emperor of Caermelor, she disguises herself as Lady Rohain in order to gain admission to court society. When she finally is able to meet with the king, she learns an amazing secret and also discovers that wicked creatures are pursuing her for an unknown reason.

The author enhances her plotline and story with actual myths and folklore, an aspect of her novel that appealed to many reviewers. "Dart-Thornton flavors her saga with retelling of traditional folktales and legends," observed *Library Journal* contributor Jackie Cassada. Other reviewers found the author's writing to be well researched and thought out. This second book in the trilogy is "a very intelligently written novel that draws heavily on legend, filled with fairies and other creatures of wonder," wrote Don D'Ammassa in *Science Fiction Chronicle.*

In 2003 Dart-Thornton published the third novel in her "Bitterbynde" trilogy, *The Battle of Evernight.* Readers discover that Tahquil, although mortal, once lived in the Fair Realm and holds the key to the Gate of Oblivion's Kiss. In order to end the war between the brother kings of the Faeran, Tahquil needs to cross the land of Erith and open the gate for them. In addition to the novel, the author provides summaries of the previous two novels as well as a short glossary and references.

Reviewers found *The Battle of Evernight* to be a satisfying conclusion to Dart-Thornton's science fiction trilogy. The author's use of folklore again gained attention and praise by critics. "Those who esteem the Irish and Scottish myths of faerie folk will be delighted by the magic folklore and tales within the tales that fill this book," wrote one *Publishers Weekly* contributor. Other reviewers lauded the author's creation of a strong main character who could support the hefty plotlines of three novels. "Dart-Thornton's epic fantasy features a courageous heroine determined to fulfill her destiny," observed Jackie Cassada in the *Library Journal.*

In 2005 Dart-Thornton began a new fantasy series, the "Crowthistle Chronicles." The four books—*The Iron Tree, The Well of Tears, Weatherwitch,* and *Fallowblade*—follow the story of a charmed young man named Jarrod, who is searching for his estranged father.

BIOGRAPHICAL AND CRITICAL SOURCES:

PERIODICALS

AAP General News Wire, December 3, 2004, Jenny Napier, "Fantasy Writer's Rise to Fame a Fairytale Come True," p. 1.

Booklist, April 15, 2001, Roland Green, review of *The Ill-Made Mute,* p. 1539; April 15, 2003, Roland Green, review of *The Battle of Evernight,* p. 1454.

Kirkus Reviews, March 1, 2001, review of *The Ill-Made Mute,* p. 299; March 1, 2002, review of *The Lady of the Sorrows,* p. 296; February 15, 2003, review of *The Battle of Evernight,* p. 276.

Library Journal, May 15, 2001, Jackie Cassada, review of *The Ill-Made Mute,* p. 167; April 15, 2002, Jackie Cassada, review of *The Lady of the Sorrows,* p. 127; April 15, 2003, Jackie Cassada, review of *The Battle of Evernight,* p. 129.

Magazine of Fantasy and Science Fiction, August, 2001, James Sallis, review of *The Ill-Made Mute,* p. 43.

MBR Bookwatch, February, 2005, Harriet Klausner, review of *The Iron Tree.*

Publishers Weekly, March 26, 2001, review of *The Ill-Made Mute,* p. 67; April 1, 2002, review of *The Lady of the Sorrows,* p. 58; March 24, 2003, review of *The Battle of Evernight,* p. 64.

Science Fiction Chronicle, April, 2001, Don D'Ammassa, review of *The Ill-Made Mute,* p. 35; April, 2002, Don D'Ammassa, review of *The Lady of the Sorrows,* p. 46.

Washington Post, June 24, 2001, Paul Di Filippo, review of *The Ill-Made Mute,* p. 13; February 20, 2005, Paul Di Filippo, review of *The Iron Tree,* p. 13.

ONLINE

Australian Broadcasting Corporation Web site, http://www.abc.net.au/ (May 6, 2002), "Australian Writer to Make U.S. Debut."

BookBrowser, http://www.bookbrowser.com/ (May 6, 2002), Harriet Klausner, review of *The Ill-Made Mute.*

Cecilia Dart-Thornton Home Page, http://www.dart thornton.com (July 15, 2005).

Greenman Review Online, http://www.greenman review.com/ (May 6, 2002), Michael M. Jones, review of *The Ill-Made Mute.*

Road to Romance, http://www.roadtoromance.dhs.org/ (May 6, 2002), autobiography of Cecilia Dart-Thornton; Sue Waldeck, review of *The Ill-Made Mute.*

SFRevu.com, http://www.sfrevu.com/ (May 6, 2005), Neal Asher, interview with Cecilia Dart-Thornton; John Berlyne, review of *The Ill-Made Mute.*

Time Warner Bookmark, http://www.twbookmark.com/ (June 20, 2005), biography of Cecilia Dart-Thornton.

* * *

de ANGELIS, Milo 1951-

PERSONAL: Born June 6, 1951, in Milan Italy; married Giovanni Secure (a poet), 1989; children: Danielle. *Education:* Attended University of Milan, 1970-74; University of Montpelier, graduated, 1976.

ADDRESSES: Agent—c/o Author Mail, Donzelli Editore, Via Mentana, 2b, 00185, Rome, Italy.

CAREER: Poet and translator. Founder of *Niebo* (journal); tutor in Greek and Latin.

WRITINGS:

Somiglianze (poems), Guanda (Milan, Italy), 1976, revised edition, 1990.
La corsa dei mantelli, Guanda (Milan, Italy), 1979.
Poesia e destino (poems), Cappelli (Bologna, Italy), 1982.
Millimetri (poems), Einaudi (Turin, Italy), 1983.
Terra del viso, Mondadori (Milan, Italy), 1985.
Distante un padre, Mondadori (Milan, Italy), 1989.
Cartina muta, Elytra, 1991.
Finite Intuition: Selected Poetry and Prose, translated by Lawrence Venuti, Sun & Moon Press (Los Angeles, CA), 1995.
Between the Blast Furnaces and the Dizziness: A Selection of Poems, 1970-1999, translated by Emanuel Di Pasquale, Chelsea Editions, 2004.

Work published in anthologies, including *Italian Poetry, 1960-1980: From Neo to Post Avant-garde,* edited by Adriano Spatola and Paul Vengelisti, Red Hill (San Francisco, CA), 1982; *New Italian Poets,* edited by Dana Gioia and Michael Palma, Story Line (Brownsville, OR), 1991; *Une autre anthologie,* edited by Henri Deluy, Fourbis (Paris, France), 1992; and *Anni '80: poesia italiana,* edited by Luca Cesari and Roberto Carifi, Jaca Book (Milan, Italy), 1993.

TRANSLATOR

Maurice Blanchot, *L'attesa l'oblio,* Guanda (Milan, Italy), 1978.
Charles Baudelaire, *I paradisi artificiali,* Guanda (Milan, Italy), 1983.
(And editor, with Marta Bertamini) Claudius Claudianus, *Il rapimento di Proserpina,* Marcos & Marcos (Milan, Italy), 1984.

SIDELIGHTS: Described as "a sophisticated experimentalist who has set out to reinvent poetry in postmodern terms" by Lawrence Venuti in *Dictionary of Literary Biography,* Milo de Angelis has written poems since he was a young man in the early 1970s. The function of poetry for de Angelis is "to stimulate thinking by pushing at the limits of language and transgressing cultural norms . . . always aware that their destruction is simultaneously tragic and creative, the end of existence and the careless proliferation of new beginnings," stated Venuti.

Among de Angelis's poetry collections are *Somiglianze* and *Millimetri.* Venuti noted that each work seeks to "challenge consciousness" and "break down" self-identity. *Millimetri* exhibits an "increase in the rapid discontinuity" of de Angelis's poetry, and by the late 1990s, the poet employed "symbolist" stylistic considerations in *Finite Intuition: Selected Poetry and Prose.* R. Watson wrote in *Chelsea* that de Angelis "sometimes achieves quite masterful effects, poems alive with a shifting mystery, a movement of compelling and intriguing power." *Finite Intuition* contains English translations of poetry and a number of essays that were originally published between 1976 and 1989.

John Taylor, writing in the *Antioch Review,* found the poems in *Between the Blast Furnaces and the Dizziness: A Selection of Poems, 1970-1999* to be "dense, [and] complex," and stated that, "as the title indicates, a first exposure can be dizzying." Taylor noted de Angelis's "daring juxtapositions of images, symbols, and obscure personal allusions. His cognitive leaps are many."

BIOGRAPHICAL AND CRITICAL SOURCES:

BOOKS

Affinati, Eraldo, *Patto giurato: la poesia de Milo de Angelis,* Tracce (Pescara, Italy), 1996.

Dictionary of Literary Biography, Volume 128: *Twentieth-Century Italian Poets,* Thomson Gale (Detroit, MI), 1993.

PERIODICALS

Antioch Review, fall, 2004, John Taylor, review of *Between the Blast Furnaces and the Dizziness: A Selection of Poems, 1970-1999,* p. 777.
Chelsea, issue 64, 1998, R. Watson, review of *Finite Intuition: Selected Poetry and Prose,* pp. 240-245.*

*   *   *

de BLASI, Marlena

PERSONAL: Born in Schenectady, NY; married Fernando de Blasi (a banker); children: two. *Education:* State University of New York at Albany, B.A.; also attended graduate school at New York University.

ADDRESSES: Home—Orvieto, Italy. *Agent*—c/o Author Mail, Algonquin Books of Chapel Hill, P.O. Box 2225, Chapel Hill, NC 27515.

CAREER: Has worked as a chef and partner of a café.

WRITINGS:

Regional Foods of Northern Italy: Recipes and Remembrances (cookbook), Prima (Rocklin, CA), 1997.
Regional Foods of Southern Italy (cookbook), Viking (New York, NY), 1999.
A Thousand Days in Venice: An Unexpected Romance (memoir), Algonquin Books of Chapel Hill (Chapel Hill, NC), 2002.
A Thousand Days in Tuscany: A Bittersweet Adventure (memoir), Algonquin Books of Chapel Hill (Chapel Hill, NC), 2004.

Contributor of restaurant reviews to periodicals.

SIDELIGHTS: Marlena de Blasi has long had a love for food. She was the co-owner and chef of a St. Louis café and has written about restaurants, food, and cooking for a number of different publications. Now making her home in Italy, de Blasi directs culinary tours of Tuscany and Umbria with her husband, Fernando de Blasi.

Drawing from her vast knowledge of Italian foods and cooking, de Blasi has written two cookbooks focusing on Italian cuisine: 1997's *Regional Foods of Northern Italy: Recipes and Remembrances* and 1999's *Regional Foods of Southern Italy.* Both cookbooks take care to describe the atmosphere, history, and people of Italy's many towns and cities as well as provide detailed recipes of traditional dishes from those regions. The recipes usually consist of ingredients accessible to the average cook.

In 2002 de Blasi published *A Thousand Days in Venice: An Unexpected Romance.* This memoir documents the author's blossoming romance with an Italian man she meets in Venice while on vacation with friends. The two begin a long-distance relationship, and soon Fernando asks de Blasi to move to Venice to be with him. The author's tales of life in Italy focus on the cuisine and culture of Venice, as well as the humorous challenges of a cross-cultural romantic relationship.

Many critics of *A Thousand Days in Venice* enjoyed the author's honest and revealing voice, which provides readers with a deep understanding of her experiences. "De Blasi relates it all in a voice at once worldly and sensuous, unsentimental and aware of what it means to have such good fortune," wrote one *Kirkus Reviews* contributor. Others lauded the author's detailed descriptions of everyday Italian life. In her account of the markets at the Rialto, "she conjures up vivid images of produce . . . and picturesque scenes of the vendors," observed a reviewer for *Publishers Weekly.*

In 2004 de Blasi picked up where she left off on her last memoir with the release of *A Thousand Days in Tuscany: A Bittersweet Adventure.* This memoir follows Fernando's and de Blasi's move from Venice to Tuscany, where the couple buys an old farmhouse and works to renovate it. The book is also replete with descriptions of the local cuisine and culture. Many of the chapters close with recipes the author has written about earlier on. Critics were again generally positive toward *A Thousand Days in Tuscany.* Some reviewers noted that although food is a strong focus of the book, the author conveys a deeper story about her adventures. "De Blasi is more than a sunny regional food writer—she digs into the meaning of life," wrote one *Publishers Weekly* contributor. On a similar note, others found the author's work rich with reflection and thought. According to a *Kirkus Reviews* contributor, de Blasi's book provided "an object lesson in living fully from a genuine sensualist unabashed by her emotions."

BIOGRAPHICAL AND CRITICAL SOURCES:

BOOKS

De Blasi, Marlena, *A Thousand Days in Venice: An Unexpected Romance,* Algonquin Books of Chapel Hill (Chapel Hill, NC), 2002.

De Blasi, Marlena, *A Thousand Days in Tuscany: A Bittersweet Adventure,* Algonquin Books of Chapel Hill (Chapel Hill, NC), 2004.

PERIODICALS

Booklist, July, 1999, Barbara Jacobs, review of *Regional Foods of Southern Italy,* p. 1905; October 1, 2004, Mark Knoblauch, review of *A Thousand Days in Tuscany,* p. 291.

Kirkus Reviews, March 15, 2002, review of *A Thousand Days in Venice,* p. 379; August 15, 2004, review of *A Thousand Days in Tuscany,* p. 785.

Library Journal, September 15, 2004, Sheila Kasperek, review of *A Thousand Days in Tuscany,* p. 72.

Publishers Weekly, June 7, 1999, review of *Regional Foods of Southern Italy,* p. 78; April 1, 2002, review of *A Thousand Days in Venice,* p. 62; July 26, 2004, review of *A Thousand Days in Tuscany,* p. 44.

ONLINE

Allen & Unwin Web site, http://www.allen-unwin.com/ (May 31, 2002).

Barnes & Noble Web site, http://www.barnesandnoble.com/ (June 20, 2005), biographical information on Marlena de Blasi.

Italian Food Forever, http://www.italianfoodforever.com/ (May 31, 2002), review of *Regional Foods of Southern Italy.*

Saga Online, http://www.saga.co.uk/ (June 20, 2005), William Langley, "The Food of Love."

WritersWrite.com, http://www.writerswrite.com/ (May 31, 2002), review of *Regional Foods of Southern Italy.**

* * *

DEEGAN, Mary Jo 1946-

PERSONAL: Born November 27, 1946, in Chicago, IL; daughter of William James (a firefighter) and Ida May (a clerical worker; maiden name, Scott) Deegan; partner of Michael Ray Hill (a geographer and sociologist) beginning May 1, 1982. *Ethnicity:* "Irish-American." *Education:* Lake Michigan College, A.S., 1966; Western Michigan University, B.S., 1969, M.A., 1971; University of Chicago, Ph.D., 1975. *Politics:* "Independent." *Religion:* Roman Catholic. *Hobbies and other interests:* Antiques, book collecting, photography.

ADDRESSES: Office—University of Nebraska, Department of Sociology, Lincoln, NE 68588.

CAREER: Writer. Kay Foods Corporation, Millburg, MI, food chemist, 1966; Laboratory Equipment Company, St. Joseph, MI, 1969; Western Michigan University, Kalamazoo, teaching and research assistant, sociology department, 1969-71; University of Nebraska, Lincoln, assistant professor of sociology, 1976-81, associate professor of sociology, 1981-90, professor of sociology, 1990—, women's studies committee, founding and continuing member, 1976—, graduate faculty member, 1976-78, graduate faculty fellow, 1978—. Kent County Mental Health Study, field director, 1971; Centennial College, fellow, 1980-81.

MEMBER: American Sociological Association, Harriet Martineau Sociological Society, Charlotte Perkins Gilman Society, International Wizard of Oz Club, Phi Kappa Theta.

AWARDS, HONORS: Distinguished Teaching Award, University of Nebraska, Lincoln, 1981; Outstanding Academic Book Award, *Choice,* 1988-89, for *Jane Addams and the Men of the Chicago School, 1892-1918;*

Distinguished Scholarly Career Award, American Sociological Association, 2002; Distinguished Scholarly Book Award, American Sociological Association, 2003, for *Race, Hull-House, and the University of Chicago: A New Conscience against Ancient Evils.*

WRITINGS:

Jane Addams and the Men of the Chicago School, 1892-1918, Transaction Books (New Brunswick, NJ), 1988.

American Ritual Dreams: Social Rules and Cultural Meanings, Greenwood Press (Westport, CT), 1989.

Race, Hull-House, and the University of Chicago: A New Conscience against Ancient Evils, Praeger (Westport, CT), 2002.

EDITOR

(With Nancy A. Brooks) *Women and Disability: The Double Handicap,* Transaction Books (New Brunswick, NJ), 1985.

(With Michael R. Hill) *Women and Symbolic Interaction,* Allen & Unwin (Boston, MA), 1987.

(With others) *A Feminist Ethic for Social Science Research,* Edwin Mellen Press (Lewiston, NY), 1988.

Women in Sociology: A Bio-Bibliographical Sourcebook, Greenwood Press (New York, NY), 1991.

Gilman, Charlotte Perkins, *With Her in Ourland,* Greenwood Press (Westport, CT), 1997.

The American Ritual Tapestry: Social Rules and Cultural Meanings, Greenwood Press (Westport, CT), 1998.

George Herbert Mead, *Play, School, and Society,* Peter Lang (New York, NY), 1999.

George Herbert Mead, *Essays in Social Psychology,* Greenwood Press (Westport, CT), 2001.

Charlotte Perkins Gilman, *The Dress of Women: A Critical Introduction to the Symbolism and Sociology of Clothing,* Greenwood Press (Westport, CT), 2002.

The New Woman of Color: The Collected Works of Fannie Barrier Williams, Northern Illinois Press (DeKalb, IL), 2002.

Ellen Gates Starr, *On Art, Labor, and Religion,* Transaction Books (New Brunswick, NJ), 2003.

Jane Addams, Emily Greene Balch, and Alice Hamilton, *Women at the Hague: The International Peace Congress of 1915,* Prometheus Press (Amherst, NY), 2003.

Mary Roberts Coolidge, *Why Women Are So,* Humanity Books (Amherst, NY), 2004.

Charlotte Perkins Gilman, *Social Ethics: Sociology and the Future of Society,* Praeger (Westport, CT), 2004.

Contributor of articles to books, including *Eros in the Mind's Eye: Sexuality and the Fantastic in Art and Film,* edited by Donald Palumbo, Greenwood Press (New York, NY), 1986; *On the Problem of Surrogate Parenthood: Analyzing the Baby M Case,* edited by Herbert Richardson, Edwin Mellen Press (Lewiston, NY), 1987; *Women's Power and Roles as Portrayed in Visual Images of Women in the Arts and Mass Media,* edited by Valerie Bentz and Philip E.F. Mayes, Edwin Mellen Press, 1993; *A Second Chicago School? The Development of a Postwar American Sociology,* edited by Gary Alan Fine, University of Chicago Press (Chicago, IL), 1995; *Identities and Issues in Literature,* edited by David R. Peck, Salem Press (Pasadena, CA), 1997; *Social Change for Women and Children,* edited by Vasilike Demos and Marcia Texler Segal, JAI Press (Greenwich, CT), 2000; and *Harriet Martineau: Theoretical and Methodological Perspectives,* edited by Michael R. Hill and Susan Hoecker-Drysdale, Routledge (New York, NY), 2001.

Contributor of articles to scholarly journals, including *Sociological Theory, Sociological Origins, American Sociologist, Disability Studies Quarterly, Environmental Ethics, ASA Footnotes, Teaching Sociology, Gender & Society, Journal of Women's History, Midwest Feminist Papers, Humanity and Society, Journal of Sociology and Social Welfare, Clinical Sociology, Women's Studies, Free Inquiry in Creative Sociology, Journal of the History of Sociology, Sociological Quarterly, Qualitative Sociology, International Journal of Symbology,* and *Sociology and Social Welfare.*

WORK IN PROGRESS: Multiple books on feminist pragmatism.

SIDELIGHTS: Mary Jo Deegan told *CA:* "I loved reading immediately. I spent my childhood in a small town, St. Joseph, Michigan, where I read the entire library of books available to young adults before I entered high school. When I turned eleven, the children's librarian took me 'upstairs' to the adult library so I could continue to read new books. I always knew I would be a writer because in my world they had the most important and glamorous job anyone could have. Although these childhood expectations have not led to fame, wealth, or glamour, I still believe writing is the most vital activity I could ever do. I have traveled widely in Europe and hold dual citizenship in the United States and Ireland, so I have experienced a number of cultures outside of America.

"I am a theorist who explains the ideas and activities of other intellectuals. I have written or introduced books about many significant American writers and leaders: Jane Addams, Emily Green Balch, Mary Roberts Coolidge, Charlotte Perkins Gilman, George Herbert Mead, and Fannie Barrier Williams. I also analyze American rituals, such as parades and sports, and the mass media, including films and television shows such as the *Wizard of Oz* and *Star Trek*. I find these rituals often enjoyable but incorporating social inequality and injustice into their very fabric. I also specialize in the analysis of physical disability and its social construction.

"All my work is part of the struggle of creating a more just society and a fulfillment of the ideals found in the documents shaping American life: the Constitution, Bill of Rights, and Declaration of Independence. I focus on the injustice created by racism, sexism, able-bodyism, and capitalism.

"I have been influenced by many teachers at Western Michigan University, where I earned bachelor's and master's degrees, and at the University of Chicago, where I earned a doctorate. The theorists Talcott Parsons and Victor Turner were especially important teachers and role models.

"I engage in extensive library research, including archival collections, for each book or essay. I try to write two pages a day every day. Sometimes this is on particular topics, but often I write bits and pieces on widely scattered ideas. I find that over time I have completed essays or books that require bringing all these parts together and I spend a lot of time making the connections between these smaller pieces of writing.

"My most productive writing is done during the periods I spend at our cottage near Lake Michigan, usually a month in the winter and the summertime. The lakeside gives me the serenity and inspiration I need to pull together my ideas and see the long vision of what I am saying about American values, lives, and leadership. This whole process is aided by my life partner, who is also an author and theorist, who supports my work continuously."

BIOGRAPHICAL AND CRITICAL SOURCES:

BOOKS

Feagin, Joe R., and Hernán Vera, *Liberation Sociology,* Westview Press (Boulder, CO), 2001.

PERIODICALS

Gender & Society, October, 1998, Beth B. Hess, review of *With Her in Ourland,* p. 605.
Social Forces, December, 1999, Penny Long Marler, review of *The American Ritual Tapestry: Social Rules and Cultural Meanings,* p. 848.
Utopian Studies, spring, 1998, Carol F. Kessler, review of *With Her in Ourland,* p. 225.

*   *   *

DEFFEYES, Kenneth S. 1931-

PERSONAL: Surname is pronounced "*dee*-phase"; born 1931, in OK; son of J.A. (an oil engineer) and Hazel Deffeyes. *Education:* Colorado School of Mines, B.S., 1952; Princeton University, M.S, Ph.D., 1958.

ADDRESSES: Office—Princeton University, B58A2 Guyot Hall, Princeton, NJ 08540. *E-mail*—deffeyes@ princeton.edu.

CAREER: Writer, petroleum geologist, educator, and consultant. Shell Oil, research geologist, 1952-53, 1958-62; Minnesota Fish and Game Commission, geologist, 1962-64; Oregon State University, oceanography department, instructor, 1964-67; Princeton University, geology professor, 1967-98; professor emeritus, 1998—. *Military service:* Served in U.S. Army Corps of Engineers Presidio, San Francisco, CA, 1952-53.

AWARDS, HONORS: Coolbaugh Award, Colorado School of Mines, for undergraduate work in chemistry.

WRITINGS:

(With Sheldon Judson and Robert B. Hargraves) *Physical Geology,* Prentice-Hall (Englewood Cliffs, NJ), 1976.
Hubbert's Peak: The Impending World Oil Shortage, Princeton University Press (Princeton, NJ), 2001.
Beyond Oil: The View from Hubbert's Peak, Hill and Wang (New York, NY), 2005.

Contributor of numerous articles to professional journals.

SIDELIGHTS: A professor emeritus at Princeton University, Kenneth S. Deffeyes is the author of two books on declining petroleum reserves worldwide. A geologist and petroleum engineer with Shell Oil before he became a professor at Princeton University in 1967, Deffeyes worked with M. King Hubbert, who forecasted that the United States would reach the peak of its oil production by the 1970s. Deffeyes was enough of a believer in the forecast that he left his lucrative position at Shell to take up teaching, believing oil reserves were on the decline. Deffeyes honors Hubbert with both his books. His 2001 title, *Hubbert's Peak: The Impending World Oil Shortage,* expands on Hubbert's theory that the quantity left in the United States' oil reserves, when calculated, forms a bell curve, which points to contracting oil reserves domestically. After Hubbert's death, it occurred to Deffeyes to apply this same sort of analysis to world oil supplies. Through equations used in Hubbert's original theory, Deffeyes was able to predict oil production would peak somewhere between 2004 and 2008, thereafter declining. In *Hubbert's Peak* Deffeyes applies a numbers-crunching model founded on the basis that a full ninety percent of oil-exploration drilling is unsuccessful, even when employing the most modern and sophisticated of methods. With a world dependent on oil, such a finding is understandably contentious, and some scientists hotly dispute Deffeyes's theories. Some sources, including the U.S. Geological Survey, put the level of oil extant in the world at a trillion times higher than Deffeyes. Ronald R. Charpentier, writing for *Science,* stated that "Deffeyes's projection of an imminent drop in world oil production is based,

however, on a questionable methodology." Specifically, Charpentier noted that Deffeyes does not mention miscalculations Hubbert made in the depletion of natural gas, and also that Hubbert's methodology should not be expanded beyond the situation in the United States. In his review of the book for *American Scientist,* Brian J. Skinner wrote that the author relates Hubbert's analysis with "engaging wit, humor and great insight." Addressing the controversy over the viability of Deffeyes's findings, Skinner concluded that "it's better to know what lies ahead than to be surprised too late to respond."

A contributor for *Business Week,* noting the author's credentials as a former Shell Oil researcher, commented, "Deffeyes is no tree-hugger." The same reviewer concluded that "The time to act is now, before the next wave of gas lines and rationing is upon us." Similarly, a critic for *Natural History* found *Hubbert's Peak* "sobering," and J.R. McNeill, writing for the *Wilson Quarterly,* concluded: "There are few things as important nowadays as the energy system, and few books on the subject as thought provoking as this one."

Deffeyes revisits his theories of declining oil production with his 2005 book, *Beyond Oil: The View from Hubbert's Peak.* In this book he reprises earlier arguments and expounds upon certain theories, delving into short-term solutions, the pros and cons of nuclear energy, gas and coal production, and the mining of oil shale. In his review of the book for *Booklist,* Gilbert Taylor found that Deffeyes gives the topic a "practical yet genial treatment," and a critic for *Kirkus Reviews* thought that Deffeyes presents a "timely, compelling argument."

BIOGRAPHICAL AND CRITICAL SOURCES:

PERIODICALS

American Scientist, January-February, 2002, Brian J. Skinner, review of *Hubbert's Peak: The Impending World Oil Shortage,* p. 82.
Booklist, February 1, 2005, Gilbert Taylor, review of *Beyond Oil: The View from Hubbert's Peak,* p. 925.
Business Record (Des Moines, IA), October 1, 2001, review of *Hubbert's Peak,* p. 15.

Business Week, November 19, 2001, "Energy Conservation: An Idea Whose Time Has Come Again," p. 26.

Kirkus Reviews, January 1, 2005, review of *Beyond Oil,* p. 31.

Natural History, November, 2001, review of *Hubbert's Peak,* p. 86.

Newsweek International, April 8, 2002, Fred Guterl, Adam Piore, and Sandy Edry, "The Energy Squeeze," p. 52.

Science, February 22, 2002, Ronald R. Charpentier, review of *Hubbert's Peak,* p. 1470.

Wilson Quarterly, autumn, 2001, J.R. McNeill, review of *Hubbert's Peak,* p. 150.

World Watch, March 2002, Seth Dunn, "Energy in an Insecure World," review of *Hubbert's Peak,* p. 33.

ONLINE

Hubbert Peak of Oil Production Web site, http://www.hubbertpeak.com/ (June 27, 2005), brief profile of author.

Princeton University Web site, http://www.princeton.edu/ (June 27, 2005), brief profile of author.*

*   *   *

de GRAZIA, Victoria

PERSONAL: Born in Chicago, IL; married Leonardo Paggi; children: Livia. *Education:* Smith College, B.A. (magna cum laude), 1968; Columbia University, Ph.D. (with distinction), 1976.

ADDRESSES: Office—Department of History, Columbia University, 2960 Broadway, New York, NY 10027-6902. *E-mail*—vd19@Columbia.edu.

CAREER: Writer, scholar, and educator. Cooper Union for the Advancement of Science and Art, adjunct instructor, 1972; Herbert H. Lehman College of the City University of New York, instructor, 1974-76, assistant professor of history, 1976-78; Rutgers University, Rutgers, NJ, assistant professor, 1977-80, associate professor, 1981-90, professor of history, 1991-94; project director of Rutgers Center for Historical Analysis, 1991-93; Columbia University, New York, NY, professor of history, 1993—, director of Institute for Research on Women and Gender, 1994-96; European University Institute, Fiesole, Italy, professor of history, 2003-2004. Visiting and guest professor at numerous universities. *Radical History Review,* member of founding collective.

MEMBER: Member of American Academy of Arts and Sciences.

AWARDS, HONORS: Fulbright fellow, 1968-69; Columbia University faculty fellow, 1969-73; best first manuscript prize, Society for Italian Historian Studies; Joan Kelly Prize, American Historical Association, 1992, and Primio Acquistoria, 1994, both for *How Fascism Ruled Women: Italy, 1922-1945*; Guggenheim fellowship; Jean Monnet fellowship

WRITINGS:

NONFICTION

The Culture of Consent: Mass Organization of Leisure in Fascist Italy (dissertation), Cambridge University Press (New York, NY), 1981.

How Fascism Ruled Women: Italy, 1922-1945, University of California Press (Berkeley, CA), 1992.

(Editor, with Ellen Furlough) *The Sex of Things: Gender and Consumption in Historical Perspective,* University of California Press (Berkeley, CA), 1996.

(Editor, with Sergio Luzzatto) *Dizionario del fascismo* (title means "Dictionary of Fascism"), 2 volumes, G. Einaudi (Turin, Italy), 2003.

Irresistible Empire: America's Advance through Twentieth-Century Europe, Belknap Press of Harvard University Press (Cambridge, MA), 2005.

Contributor of articles to numerous books and anthologies, and to journals and other periodicals, including *Journal of Modern History, New York Times, American Film,* and *American Studies Journal.* Member of board of editors of numerous publications, including *Journal of Modern History, Geneses, Contemporary European History,* and *Journal of Consumer Culture.*

SIDELIGHTS: A professor of history at Columbia University, Victoria de Grazia specializes in the contemporary history of Western Europe, focusing on consumer cultures, gender, and the history of family politics. Having grown up traveling between Italy and the United States, she has written with an insider's authority on aspects of both countries. Her doctoral thesis was published in 1981 as *The Culture of Consent: Mass Organization of Leisure in Fascist Italy,* and she returns to the theme of fascist Italy in her 1992 book, *How Fascism Ruled Women: Italy, 1922-1945.* That study reveals how the regime of Benito Mussolini prevented women from assuming a liberated place in Italian society, despite fascism's avowal of a policy of emancipation for women. In the book, de Grazia demonstrates how government, church, and commercial culture cooperated to define the woman of the time, maintaining the typical patriarchal model. A reviewer for *Publishers Weekly* called *How Fascism Ruled Women* a "noteworthy study," and further praised the author's "meticulous research and deep contemplation." The reviewer concluded that the book is an "important contribution to women's studies."

De Grazia worked with Ellen Furlough as coeditor of the 1996 title *The Sex of Things: Gender and Consumption in Historical Perspective,* a book of essays examining the connections of consumerism and women. De Grazia also wrote the introductions to the various sections of the book and contributed an article titled "Empowering Women as Citizen Consumers," which questions the idea of consumerism and its stereotyped feminist persona. Kevin H. White, writing for *Historian,* found the work an "excellent collection . . . maintained by a solid historical organization." As White also observed, "the authors and de Grazia have brought massive sophistication to their analysis." A reviewer for *Women's Studies* deemed *The Sex of Things* an "impressive collection," and went on to praise the "strong editorial voice of Victoria de Grazia [that] repeatedly urges the reader to question received notions about consumption." Whitney Walton, writing in the *Women's Review of Books,* also had favorable comments for the book and de Grazia's contributions to the work. Walton wrote that "de Grazia's introductions are valuable histories of consumption and gender," and concluded that *The Sex of Things* is "especially thought-provoking among the increasing number of works on the history of consumption."

De Grazia returns to the topic of consumerism with her 2005 work, *Irresistible Empire: America's Advance through Twentieth-Century Europe.* In this book she demonstrates how American mercantile power made

inroads in Europe during the twentieth century, and fundamentally altered the way of life on that continent. The time frame she covers is from World War I to September 11, 2001, but she approaches her subject thematically rather than chronologically, devoting chapters to the hegemony of Hollywood, for example, or to inroads made by Rotary Clubs in Europe. Her analysis attempts to show that by mid-century, Europe was as caught up in the mass-consumer society as was the United States. In his review for *Library Journal,* Scott H. Silverman called the book "brilliantly argued, based on a rich sampling of popular Culture." However, due to its academic prose style, Silverman concluded that would "appeal to only a very narrow, scholarly readership." A reviewer for *Publishers Weekly* observed that "de Grazia writes clearly, giving an uncommon perspective on the ways and means by which the U.S. and Europe drew close" following World War II. A critic for *Kirkus Reviews* found the work "smart and engaging," as well as a "lucid, accessible introduction to globalism and its discontents." Further praise came from Jean-Christophe Agnew in *Frontlist.* Agnew described the book as a "brilliant account of how the American standard of living defeated the European way of life and achieved the global cultural hegemony." Stephen Bayley, writing in London's *Independent Online,* called *Irresistible Empire* an "elegant" and "eloquent" work, "written with measure and cadences and care which have their roots in Old World learning rather than New World Write-Lite and its flashy neologisms."

BIOGRAPHICAL AND CRITICAL SOURCES:

PERIODICALS

Historian, spring, 1998, Kevin H. White, review of *The Sex of Things: Gender and Consumption in Historical Perspective,* p. 682.
Journal of Modern History, March, 1999, Judy Coffin, review of *The Sex of Things,* p. 177.
Kirkus Reviews, January 15, 2005, review of *Irresistible Empire: America's Advance through Twentieth-Century Europe,* p. 97.
Library Journal, April 15, 2005, Scott H. Silverman, review of *Irresistible Empire,* p. 101.
Publishers Weekly, December 20, 1991, review of *How Fascism Ruled Women: Italy, 1922-45,* p. 69; February 14, 2005, review of *Irresistible Empire,* p. 64.

Women's Review of Books, April, 1997, Whitney Walton, review of *The Sex of Things,* p. 18.

Women's Studies, July, 1997, review of *The Sex of Things,* p. 387.

ONLINE

Columbia University Web site, http://www.columbia.edu/ (June 28, 2005),author profile.

Frontlist Web site, http://www.frontlist.com/ (June 29, 2005), Jean-Christophe Agnew, review of *Irresistible Empire.*

Independent Online, http://enjoyment.independent.co.uk/ (May 27, 2005), Stephen Bayley, "Under the Axles of Evil," review of *Irresistible Empire.**

*   *   *

DeKKER, Carl
See LYNDS, Dennis

*   *   *

de KREMER, Raymond Jean Marie 1887-1964
(John Flanders, Jean Ray)

PERSONAL: Born July 8, 1887, in Ghent, Belgium; died September 17, 1964, in Ghent, Belgium.

CAREER: Journalist and writer. Worked in a variety of clerical positions.

WRITINGS:

UNDER PSEUDONYM JEAN RAY

Les croisière des ombres: histories hantées de terre et de mer, Nouvelles Éditions Oswald (Paris, France), 1932.

Malpertuis: histoire d'un maison fantastique (novel), Le Cri Éditions (Paris, France), 1943, translated into English by Iain White, Atlas 1998.

Ghouls in My Grave, Berkley (New York, NY), 1965.

Contes d'horreur et d'aventures, Union Générale d'Editions (Paris, France), 1972.

Les étoiles de la mort et autres aventures de Harry Dickson, Éditto-Service (Geneva, Switzerland), 1973.

Les cercles de l'épouvante, Librairie des Champs-Élysées (Paris, France), 1978.

Le livre des fantômes, Librairie des Champs-Élysées (Paris, France), 1979.

Visages et choses crépusculaires: nouvelles, Nouvelles Éditions Oswald (Paris, France), 1982.

Les aventures de Harry Dickson: le Sherlock Holmes américain, Corps 9 Éditions (Laferté-Milon, France), 1983.

Harry Dickson: l'intégrale, Club Neo (Paris, France), 1984.

La malédiction de Machrood: roman fantastique; suivi de onze histoires d'épouvante, Nouvelles Éditions Oswald (Paris, France), 1984.

Trois aventures inconnues de Harry Dickson, Nouvelles Éditions Oswald (Paris, France), 1984.

Visions nocturnes: contes fantastiques inédits, Nouvelles Éditions Oswald (Paris, France), 1984.

Le carrousel des maléfices, Nouvelles Éditions Oswald (Paris, France), 1985.

Les contes du whisky: suivis de la croisière des ombres, Neo (Paris, France), 1985.

Les dernier contes de Canterbury, Nouvelles Éditions Oswald (Paris, France), 1985.

(With Gérard Dôle, Albert van Hageland, and Alfred Roloff) *Terreur sur Londres,* Corps 9 Éditions (Laferté-Milon, France), 1985.

Les contes noirs du golf, Nouvelles Éditions Oswald (Paris, France), 1986.

L'île noire (novel), Nouvelles Éditions Oswald (Paris, France), 1986.

Harry Dickson: Les étoiles de la mort, suivi de le studio rouge, Diffusion France et Étranger Flammarion (Paris, France), 1995.

Harry Dickson [le Sherlock Holmes américain]: les illustres fils du zodiaque, suivi de: le vampire qui chante, Flammarion (Paris, France), 1997.

UNDER PSEUDONYM JOHN FLANDERS

Bestiaire fantastique, Marabout (Verviers, Belgium), 1974.

La cité de l'indicible peur, Marabout (Verviers, Belgium), 1977.

Le trou dans le mur et autres contes, Musée Noir (Brussels, Belgium), 1984.

Le grand nocturne: les cercles de l'épouvante, nouvelle, Actes Sud/Labor (Brussels, Belgium), 1989.

Jack-de-Minuit, [Brussels, Belgium], 1991.

Les cahiers de la biloque, Éditions du Noyé (Brussels, Belgium), 1991.

Les histoires étrangers de la biloque, [Brussels, Belgium], 1996.

Contributor of short stories to *Weird Tales.* Member of editorial boards for several Flemish magazines.

OTHER

Author, under pseudonyms, of *Terra d'aventures, La bataille d'Angleterre, La brume verte, La vallée du sommeil, Le croisière des ombres, Le gardiens du gouffre, La grebe noire: les meilleurs récits des maîtres de l'épouvante, Les aventures de Harry Dickson (une centaine de courts romans), Les contes du Fulmar, Les feux follets de Satan, Histoires noires et fantastiques,* and *Visions infernales.*

ADAPTATIONS: Malpertuis was filmed in 1972 by Harry Kuemel. Another film, *Le grande frousse,* was based on Ray's writings.

SIDELIGHTS: Writer Jean Ray claimed to be a sailor, smuggler, tarantula tamer, Dakota Indian, lion tamer, American bootlegger, gangster, or adventurer. In actuality Ray was Belgian Raymond Jean Marie de Kremer, who wrote in French using the pen name Jean Ray, and in Flemish using the pen name John Flanders. He was a prolific writer, producing more than twenty novels and story collections, as well as a great deal of other work; several of his stories, under the Flanders pseudonym, appeared in the famed pulp magazine *Weird Tales* in the 1930s. His first book, *Terra d'aventures,* was published in 1910, and his best-known and most highly regarded work is *Malpertuis: histoire d'un maison fantastique,* which is about Greek gods who are imprisoned and dying in an evil house.

Until age forty, Ray held various clerical positions, and he worked on the editorial boards of Flemish magazines. In 1927, when he was working in a stockbroker's office, money was found to be missing, and he was accused and sentenced to six years' imprisonment for embezzlement. After he was released,

he found it impossible to find a job, so he turned to writing anything that would pay, including scenarios for comic strips, journalistic stories, and children's stories. During the 1930s he wrote over a hundred stories in a mystery series called "Adventures of Harry Dickson, the American Sherlock Holmes." In the *Times Literary Supplement,* Richard Davenport-Hines wrote, "Hammering at an aged typewriter, working without pause for twenty-four hours until he had completed the tale, he Gothicized the traditional style of shilling shockers."

During World War II, the publication of cheap "pulp" magazines featuring horror and fantasy fiction was disrupted by paper shortages, and Ray turned to writing novels and novellas in French, including such titles as *La cité de l'indicible peur* and *Le livre des fantômes,* as well as *Malpertuis.* Ray's stories and novels revel in "wide-open terror," according to Lawrence Greenberg in the *St. James Guide to Horror, Ghost, and Gothic Writers,* and emphasize people who are caught up in vast and horrible forces that are awakened when they encounter other people. For example, in his story "The Cemetery Watchman" three men are hired to guard a mausoleum, and one of them finds that the other watchmen are not the ordinary men they seem to be; in the end, he meets the vampire duchess whose grave they are guarding. In "Mr. Glass Changes Direction" a shopkeeper kills customers he dislikes, and then meets a man named Mr. Sheep, who is responsible for a series of similar murders. They chat about their murderous activities until Mr. Glass murders Mr. Sheep, and continues to murder randomly until several months later, when he is killed by someone else. Greenberg noted that Ray's stories have a "bite of black humour," which usually comes from Ray's combinations of the mundane and the horrific.

Ray worked on *Malpertuis* for more than twelve years. In this novel, a dying sea captain discovers the ancient Greek gods, captures them, and brings them back to his mansion, which is called Malpertuis. The house is filled with bizarre side passages that lead to other dimensions. There, the sea captain employs a taxidermist who inserts the personalities of the gods into the bodies of ordinary people. Strange events occur, such as a sailor wandering into the house and falling in love with a woman who looks beautiful but is actually the Gorgon, an evil creature who turns men to stone when they look at her. Other events involve the interaction of the gods with ordinary people. As Greenberg noted, "there is no definitive ending. In fact, there are three of them and all are inconclusive."

BIOGRAPHICAL AND CRITICAL SOURCES:

BOOKS

Linkhorn, Renee, editor, *La Belgique telle qu'ell s'écrit: Perspectives sur les lettres belges de langue française,* Peter Lang (New York, NY), 1995.
Carion, Jacques, *Jean Ray: Un livre: Le grand nocturne,* Éditions Labor (Brussels, Belgium), 1986.
St. James Guide to Horror, Ghost, and Gothic Writers, St. James Press (Detroit, MI), 1998.

PERIODICALS

Presence Francophone, 1974, Christian Delcourt, "Thomas Owen et Jean Ray," p. 114.
Review of Contemporary Fiction, fall 1998, Gordon McAlpine, review of *Malpertuis: histoire d'un maison fantastique,* p. 253.
Times Literary Supplement, March 19, 1999, Richard Davenport-Hines, review of *Malpertuis,* p. 35.*

*   *   *

de la VALDÉNE, Guy W. 1944-

PERSONAL: Born May 8, 1944, in New York, NY; married Therese Anderson; children: Valerie Seifert, John. *Education:* Attended Cornell University, 1963, and University of Miami, 1964-65. *Politics:* Democrat.

ADDRESSES: Home—606 Robin Lane, Havana, FL 32333. *Agent*—Alice Martell, Martell Agency, 545 Madison Ave., New York, NY 10020. *E-mail*—afmartell@aol.com.

CAREER: Writer.

WRITINGS:

Making Game: An Essay on Woodcock, Willow Creek Press (Oshkosh, WI), 1985.

For a Handful of Feathers (nonfiction), Atlantic Monthly Press (New York, NY), 1995.
Red Stag (novel), Lyons Press (Guilford, CT), 2003.

WORK IN PROGRESS: A nature book on the grey partridge; a Southern novel.

*   *   *

de SANT'ANNA, Affonso Romano 1937-

PERSONAL: Born March 27, 1937, in Belo Horizonte, Brazil; son of Jorge Firmino and Maria Romano Sant'Anna; married Marina Colasanti, 1972; children: Fabiana, Alessandra. *Education:* University of Minas Gerais, Brazil, Ph.D., 1969.

ADDRESSES: Home—Apt. 1504, Rua Nascimento e Silva, 22421020 Rio de Janeiro, Brazil.

CAREER: University of California at Los Angeles, visiting lecturer, 1965-67; University of Iowa international writing program, visiting writer, 1968-69; Catholic University, Rio de Janeiro, Brazil, director of arts, 1973-76; University of Texas, Austin, visiting professor, 1977, 1989; University of Köln, Cologne, Germany, guest professor, 1978; Université d'Aix-en-Provence, Provence, France, associate professor, 1981-82; University of Rio de Janeiro, Rio de Janeiro, Brazil, professor, 1984-90; National Library of Rio de Janeiro, president, 1990-96.

MEMBER: Association for International Literary Critique, Iberian-American National Librarians Association (executive secretary, 1995-96), Brazilian Society for the Progress of Science, Society Mondiale pour la Paix, Association dos Amigos do Museu Historico National Rio.

WRITINGS:

(With Teresinha Alves Pereira, Silviano Santiago, and Domingos Muchon) *4 poetas,* Universidad de Mina Gerais (Belo Horizonte, Brazil), 1960.
O desemprêgo do poeta, Estánte Universitaria (Belo Horizonte, Brazil), 1962.

Canto e palavra, Edições Movimento Perspectiva, 1965.

Poesia viva; poemas de Affonso Romano de Sant'Anna, Civilização Brasileira (Rio de Janeiro, Brazil), 1968.

Drummond, o gauche no tempo, Lia Editor (Rio de Janeiro, Brazil), 1972, second edition published as *Carlos Drummond de Andrade: análise da obra,* Editora Documentário (Rio de Janeiro, Brazil), 1977.

(With Dirce Côrtes Riedel and Marlene de Castro Correia) *Autores para vestibular: estrutura e interpretação de textos: Aluísio Azevedo, Machado de Assis, Autran Dourado, Carlos Drummond de Andrade [e] Manuel Bandeira,* Editora Vozes (Petrópolis, Brazil), 1973.

Análise estrutural de romances brasileiros, Editora Vozes (Petrópolis, Brazil), 1973, seventh edition, Editora Vozes (Petrópolis, Brazil), 1989.

(Author of notes and introduction) Joaquim Manuel de Macedo, *A moreninha,* F. Alves (Rio de Janeiro, Brazil), 1975.

Poesia sobre poesia, Imago Editora (Rio de Janeiro, Brazil), 1975.

Por um novo conceito de literatura brasileira, Eldorado (Rio de Janeiro, Brazil), 1977.

A grande fala do indio guarani perdido na história e outras derrotas (moderno Popol Vuh), Summus Editorial (São Paulo, Brazil), 1978.

Música popular e moderna poesia brasileira (music criticism), Vozes (Petrópolis, Brazil), 1978.

Que país é este? e outros poemas (poems), Civilização Brasileira (Rio de Janeiro, Brazil), 1980, published as *Que país é este?,* Rocco (Rio de Janeiro, Brazil), 1990.

A morte da baleia, Berlendis & Vertecchia Editores (Rio de Janeiro, Brazil), 1981.

Estória dos sofrimentos, morte e ressurreição do Senhor Jesus Cristo na pintura de Emeric Marcier, Edições Pinakotheke (Rio de Janeiro, Brazil), 1983.

O canibalismo amoroso: o desejo e a interdição em nossa cultura através de poesia (criticism), Brasiliense (São Paulo, Brazil), 1984, fourth edition, Rocco (Rio de Janeiro, Brazil), 1993.

Política e paixão (nonfiction), Rocco (Rio de Janeiro, Brazil), 1984.

A Catedral de colônia e outros poemas (also see below), Rocco (Rio de Janeiro, Brazil), 1985.

Como se faz literatura, Editora Vozes (Petrópolis, Brazil), 1985.

Paródia, paráfrase & cia, second edition, Editora Atica (São Paulo, Brazil), 1985.

A mulher madura, Rocco (Rio de Janeiro, Brazil), 1986, third edition, 1987.

(With wife, Marina Colasanti) *O imaginário a dois: textos escolhidos,* Art Bureau (Rio de Janeiro, Brazil), 1987.

A poesia possível, Rocco (Rio de Janeiro, Brazil), 1987.

O homem que conheceu o amor, Rocco (Rio de Janeiro, Brazil), 1988, second edition, 1994.

(With Antônio Houaiss and Herculano Gomes Mathias) *Gente do aço,* photographs by Jamie Stewart-Granger, Siderurgia Brasileira (Rio de Janeiro, Brazil), 1989.

A raiz quadrada do absurdo, Rocco (Rio de Janeiro, Brazil), 1989.

(With Marina Colasanti) *Agosto 1991: estávamos em Moscou* (history), Melhoramentos (São Paulo, Brazil), 1991.

De que ri a Mona Lisa?, Roco (Rio de Janeiro, Brazil), 1991.

Os melhores poemas de Affonso Romano de Sant'Anna, selected by Donaldo Schüler, Global (São Paulo, Brazil), 1991.

Drummond, o gauche no tempo, Editora Record (Rio de Janeiro, Brazil), 1992.

O lado esquerdo do meu peito: livro de aprendiazgens, Rocco (Rio de Janeiro, Brazil), 1992.

Mistérios gozosos, Rocco (Rio de Janeiro, Brazil), 1994.

Fizemos bem em resistir: crônicas selecionadas, Rocco (Rio de Janeiro, Brazil), 1994.

Porta de colégio & outras crônicas, Ática (São Paulo, Brazil), 1995, fourth edition, 1997.

A vida por viver: crônicas, Rocco (Rio de Janeiro, Brazil), 1997.

Barroco, alma do Brasil, photographs by Pedro Oswaldo Cruz, Comunicação Máxima (Rio de Janeiro, Brazil), c. 1997, translated by Diane Grosklaus as *Baroque, the Soul of Brazil,* Comunicação Máxima, 1998.

A grande fala do índio guarani; e, A catedral de Colônia (poems), Rocco (Rio de Janeiro, Brazil), 1998.

(With Roberto M. Moura) *MPB: Caminhos da arte brasileira mais reconhecida no mundo,* Irmãos Vitale (Rio de Janeiro, Brazil), 1998.

Textamentos, Rocco (Rio de Janeiro, Brazil), 1999.

Intervalo amoroso: e outros poemas escolhidos (poems), L & PM Pocket (Porte Alegre, Brazil), 1999.

Barroco: do quadrado à elipse, Rocco (Rio de Janeiro, Brazil), 2000.

A sedução da palavra (essays), Letraviva (Brasília, Brazil), 2000.

Que fazer de Ezra Pound: ensaios (essays), Imago (Rio de Janeiro, Brazil), 2003.

Contributor to books, including *A legião estrangeira,* by Clarice Lispector, Editora Ática, 1977, ninth edition, 1990; *Liçõ de casa: exercīcios de imaginação,* edited by Julieta de Godoy Ladeira, Livraria Cultura Editora, 1978; *O livro do seminário, ensaios, bienal Nestlé de literatura Brasileira, 1982,* edited by Domício Proença Filho, L.R. Editores, 1983; *Crônicas mineiras,* Editora Atica, 1984; *1950 almanaque,* João Fortes Engenharia, 1985; *O Rosto do povo: foto-jornalismo,* Léo Christiano Editoria, 1986; *Hélio Pellegrino, a-Deus: psicanálise e religião: textos e depoimentos,* Voses, 1988; *Ouro: sua história, seus encantos, seu valor,* Salamandra, 1989; *Cartas a Mário de Andrade,* edited by Fábio Lucas, Editora Nova Fronteira, 1993; *Transformação,* Editora Diferença, 1993; *100 anos,* Eletricidade de São Paulo, 1993; *Epitafio para el siglo XX: antología,* Alcaldía de Caracas, 1994; *O livro ao vivo,* Centro Cultural Candido Mendes, 1995; *Gold: Its History, Its Charm, Its Value,* Salamandra, 1997; *Brasil e Portugal: 500 años de enlaces e desenlaces,* two volumes, Real Gabinete Português de Leitura do Rio de Janeiro, 2000-01; *Ao enctontro da palavra cantada: poesia, música e voz,* edited by Cládia Neiva de Matos, Elizabeth Travassos, and Fernanda Teixeira de Medeiros, 7Letras, 2001; and *Para entender o Brasil,* Alegro, 2001.

SIDELIGHTS: Affonso Romano de Sant'Anna is one of Brazil's most prominent and respected poets and literary critics. His poetry, anchored in the real world, often expresses the author's frustrations over the lost potential of his country, squandered by Brazil's politicians. Verses in such collections as *Que país é este? e outros poemas* address themes such as national identity and modern social problems in "language of the highest literary quality," according to Wilson Martins in a *World Literature Today* review. In Martins' view, de Sant'Anna's work shows him to be "the poet for whom Brazil has waited for so long."

De Sant'Anna has also been praised for his literary criticism. One example of this is his book *O canibalismo amoroso: o desejo e a interdição em nossa cul-*

tura através de poesia in which the author explores sexual attitudes of male Brazilian poets toward women during the nineteenth and twentieth centuries. As Bobby J. Chamberlain explained in another *World Literature Today* article, de Sant'Anna demonstrates that the poems by these writers betray how they "regard the female as an object on which the male poet—the subject of discourse—has projected his own desires and neuroses." Chamberlain especially praised de Sant'Annas analyses of the works by Vinícius de Moraes and Manuel Bandeira, and complimented the author for publishing "a vast store of new information on a hitherto neglected facet of Brazilian poetry." Another *World Literature Today* critic, Melvin S. Arrington, Jr., similarly lauded the work as "an intriguing guide to nineteenth-and early twentieth-century Brazilian poetry."

BIOGRAPHICAL AND CRITICAL SOURCES:

PERIODICALS

World Literature Today, summer, 1981, Wilson Martins, review of *Que país é este? e outros poemas,* p. 444; spring, 1985, Bobby J. Chamberlain, review of *O canibalismo amoroso: o desejo e a interdição em nossa cultura através de poesia,* pp. 253-254; winter, 1995, Melvin S. Arrington, Jr., review of *O canibalismo amoroso,* p. 126.*

*　　*　　*

DEWOSKIN, Rachel

PERSONAL: Born in Kyoto, Japan; married; children: one. *Education:* Columbia University, B.A. (with honors); Boston University, M.A., 2000. *Hobbies and other interests:* Karate and composing music (particularly rap songs).

ADDRESSES: *Home*—New York, NY; Beijing, China. *Office*—AGNI Magazine, Boston University Writing Program, 236 Bay State Rd., Boston, MA 02215.

CAREER: Writer, educator, and actor. *AGNI* magazine, associate poetry editor; Boston University, writing instructor.

Worked variously as a consultant and an account executive at a public relations firm in Beijing, China, and as an actor. Appeared in *Foreign Babes in Beijing* (Chinese soap opera), and *Restless* (movie), 2000.

AWARDS, HONORS: American Academy of Poets Award, 2000; Grolier Poetry Prize, 2002.

WRITINGS:

Foreign Babes in Beijing: Behind the Scenes of a New China (memoir), W.W. Norton (New York, NY), 2005.

Contributor of poetry and articles to *Boston Globe, Seneca Review, New Delta Review, Nerve, Boston, Ann Arbor Observer, Drumvoices Revue, Ploughshares,* and *Teachers and Writers.*

SIDELIGHTS: Rachel DeWoskin was born in Japan to a sinologist father and English-teacher mother, DeWoskin grew up mainly in Ann Arbor, Michigan, but spent summers in Taiwan and China. After graduating with honors from Columbia University in 1994, DeWoskin decided to return to China. She took a job at an American public-relations firm and was just getting settled in Beijing when a friend urged her to audition for a part in a new soap opera, *Foreign Babes in Beijing.* The show dealt with the adventures and misadventures of a pair of American students in China. Fluent in Mandarin, DeWoskin decided to give it a try and landed the part of Jessie. With 600 million viewers, the soap opera made DeWoskin a celebrity in Beijing. As Bob Young noted in *Transpacific,* the author's "life changed overnight: Suddenly, she was hounded by adoring crowds, signing endless autographs, posing for photos with locals, her face splashed all over Chinese entertainment magazines."

A full decade after her participation in the television show and having moved back to the United States, DeWoskin wrote an account of her time as an actress on a Chinese soap opera. The result was the 2005 memoir *Foreign Babes in Beijing: Behind the Scenes of a New China.* According to *Salon.com* reviewer Christine Smallwood, the book is "a diaristic account of her experiences abroad interwoven with musings on Chinese and American politics and pop culture."

Smallwood stated that DeWoskin had the "perspective to collapse the personal and political to great, and occasionally hilarious, effect." A critic for *Kirkus Reviews* found DeWoskin "a charming, rather humble narrator, and her prose is as gripping as the content." The same contributor went on to note that DeWoskin's "babe's-eye view turns out to be surprisingly substantive." *Library Journal* reviewer Susan G. Baird stated that the book is a "highly entertaining and enlightening memoir." Similarly, a reviewer for *People* called the book an "intelligent, funny memoir." In her review of the memoir for *Women's Wear Daily,* Vanessa Lawrence commented that the "book captures the city's bustle . . . the dynamics of her group of young Chinese hipsters grappling with sex, love and work."

DeWoskin, also a poet, told Smallwood she tried to maintain an objective approach in her book. "I tried not to generalize so much in the book. One of the things I came to think, not only while living there but also while writing the book, is that writers ask questions and propagandists answer them. So I never felt like I was in a position to answer questions about China particularly."

BIOGRAPHICAL AND CRITICAL SOURCES:

BOOKS

DeWoskin, Rachel, *Foreign Babes in Beijing: Behind the Scenes of a New China,* W.W. Norton (New York, NY), 2005.

PERIODICALS

Kirkus Reviews, February 15, 2005, review of *Foreign Babes in Beijing,* p. 209.
Library Journal, April 1, 2005, Susan G. Baird, review of *Foreign Babes in Beijing,* p. 116.
People, June 6, 2005, review of *Foreign Babes in Beijing,* p. 49.
Publishers Weekly, March 28, 2005, review of *Foreign Babes in Beijing,* p. 66.
Transpacific, October, 1996, Bob Young, "Foreign Babe in Beijing," p. 12.
Women's Wear Daily, May 9, 2005, Vanessa Lawrence, "The China Syndrome," review of *Foreign Babes in Beijing,* p. 20.

ONLINE

Boston University AGNI Web site, http://www.bu.edu/agni/ (June 29, 2005), brief profile of author.

GoldSea.com, http://goldsea.com/ (June 29, 2005), "White Babe in Beijing."

Salon.com, http://www.salon.com/ (May 17, 2005), Christine Smallwood, "China Girl."*

*   *   *

de ZENGOTITA, Thomas

PERSONAL: Male. *Education:* Columbia University, B.A., 1974, M.A., 1975, M.Phil., 1977, Ph.D., 1985.

ADDRESSES: Office—New York University, Draper Program, 14 University Pl., New York, NY 10003-6607.

CAREER: Writer, editor, and educator. New York University Draper Graduate Program, New York, NY, adjunct associate professor; Dalton School, instructor.

WRITINGS:

Mediated: How the Media Shapes Your World and the Way You Live in It, Bloomsbury (New York, NY), 2004.

Contributor of articles to magazines and journals, including *Nation, Shout,* and *Cultural Anthropology.* Contributor of fiction to *Fiction* and *Logos. Harper's* magazine, contributing editor.

SIDELIGHTS: A contributing editor to *Harper's,* writer Thomas de Zengotita often focuses on the media and its influences on culture and society. In his 2004 book *Mediated: How the Media Shapes Your World and the Way You Live in It,* de Zengotita takes the reader on a tour of how media—from television to the Internet—shapes people's reactions to events. According to the author, the media has permeated every corner of both the individual and collective consciousness. As a result, media influences not only how people choose a dish soap, but also shape their

idea of what is real. Thus, performance and reality have become fused, in de Zengotita's opinion. Reading this book is, according to Judith Stone, writing in *O,* "like spending time with a wild, wired friend." A critic for *Kirkus Reviews* called *Mediated* a "mostly pessimistic, mostly ironic extended commentary about the contemporary American experience." Vanessa Bush, writing in *Booklist,* found the book an "amazing look" at the ways in which perceptions are shaped by mass media, and concluded that the work is "completely absorbing, amusing and insightful." In her review for *Library Journal,* Audrey Snowden referred to the book as "smart, provocative, and funny."

BIOGRAPHICAL AND CRITICAL SOURCES:

PERIODICALS

Booklist, February 1, 2005, Vanessa Bush, review of *Mediated: How the Media Shapes Your World and the Way You Live in It,* p. 921.

Kirkus Reviews, January 1, 2005, review of *Mediated,* p. 30.

Library Journal, February 15, 2005, Audrey Snowden, review of *Mediated,* p. 141.

O, March, 2005, Judith Stone, "Losing Our Minds: A Provocative Look at the Way TV, Radio, E-Mail, and Ads Distort—and Replace—Reality," review of *Mediated,* p. 170.

Psychology Today, May-June, 2005, review of *Mediated,* p. 36.

ONLINE

New York University Web site, http://www.nyu.edu/ (June 30, 2005), brief profile of author.

What Is Enlightenment Web site, http://www.wie.org/ (June 30, 2005), brief profile of author.*

*   *   *

DICKINSON, Mrs. Herbert Ward
See PHELPS, Elizabeth Stuart

*   *   *

DONOHUE, John 1956-
(John J. Donohue)

PERSONAL: Born 1956, in Brooklyn, NY; married; wife's name Kathleen; children: Erin, Owen. *Education:* State University of New York at Stony Brook,

B.A., 1978, M.A., 1982, Ph.D., 1987. *Hobbies and other interests:* Martial arts; holds a black belt in kara-tedo and kendo; highland bagpipes.

ADDRESSES: Home—NY. *Office*—D'Youville College, 320 Porter Ave., Buffalo, NY 14201-9985. *E-mail*—donohuejj@yahoo.com.

CAREER: Author. University College, Adelphi University, Garden City, NY, instructor in humanities and social sciences, 1987-93, coordinator of student affairs, 1988-90, director of academic affairs, 1990-91, assistant dean, 1991-92, associate dean, 1992-93; State University of New York College at Morrisville, instructor of anthropology, 1993-95, dean of School of Liberal Arts, 1993-95; Medaille College, Buffalo, NY, professor of social science, 1995-2002, academic dean, 1995-97, vice president for academic affairs and academic dean, 1997-2000, acting executive vice president, 2000-01, acting president, 2001-02; D'Youville College, Buffalo, NY, professor of social science, 2002—, vice president for academic affairs, 2002—. *Journal of Asian Martial Arts,* associate editor. Speaker and commentator on martial arts at international conventions, and on television and radio.

MEMBER: American Anthropological Association, International Thriller Writers, Mystery Writers of America, Society of Martial Arts, American Council on Martial Arts (board member).

AWARDS, HONORS: American Library Association List of Best First Mysteries listee, 2003, for *Sensei.*

WRITINGS:

NONFICTION

(Editor, as John J. Donohue; with Peter Katopes and Daniel Rosenberg) *The Human Condition in the Modern Age,* Kendall/Hunt Publishing (Dubuque, IA), 1991, 2nd edition, 1996.
(As John J. Donohue) *The Forge of the Spirit: Structure, Motion, and Meaning in the Japanese Martial Tradition,* Garland Publishing (New York, NY), 1991.
(As John J. Donohue) *Warrior Dreams: The Martial Arts and the American Imagination,* Bergin and Garvey (Westport, CT), 1994.

(As John J. Donohue) *Herding the Ox: The Martial Arts as Moral Metaphor,* Turtle Press (Hartford, CT), 1998.
Complete Kendo, illustrations by Kathleen Sweeney, Turtle Publishers (Boston, MA), 1999.
(Editor) *The Overlook Martial Arts Reader,* second edition, Overlook Press (New York, NY), 2004.

Contributor of articles to martial arts journals.

NOVELS; "CONNOR BURKE" SERIES

Sensei, Thomas Dunne Books (New York, NY), 2003.
Deshi, Thomas Dunne Books (New York, NY), 2005.

SIDELIGHTS: John Donohue is a professor and administrator at a college in Buffalo, New York, and the author of a well-received series of martial arts thrillers. Donohue, who has a black belt in karate, has also written several nonfiction works dealing with the spiritual and cultural aspects of martial arts. Such a background proved invaluable when beginning his series featuring Connor Burke, who, like Donohue, is a martial arts student and a college professor. In the debut title, *Sensei,* Burke is enlisted by his detective brother Mickey to aid in the search for a serial killer. In this case, the victims are martial arts practitioners all across the country. It seems that there is a ronin, or rogue samurai, with a grudge, and Mickey needs his brother's insider knowledge of martial arts to help crack the case. Connor seeks the aid of the teacher, or sensei, Yamashita, to track down the killer, and this unlikely duo of sleuths works through a forest of clues to find the perpetrator in this "impressive" debut, as a critic for *Kirkus Reviews* dubbed *Sensei.* The same reviewer praised the "strong story, good writing, [and] colorful setting." Similarly, a contributor for *Publishers Weekly* noted that Donohue "crisply and elegantly blends Japanese martial arts and urban New York in his assured debut." *Booklist* reviewer David Pitt also had praise for this first novel, finding the characters "fresh and interesting," and the story itself "entirely absorbing."

With *Deshi* Donohue extends his initial novel into a series featuring Burke. Here the martial arts expert is once again enlisted by brother Mickey to help solve a series of murders. The first of these involves a Japanese-American businessman and practitioner of calligraphy who seems to have left an inked clue to the identity of his killer, who executed the calligrapher with a shot through the temple. Connor, working with Yamashita, once again succeeds in finding his way through a thicket of clues, this time leading to the Chinese secret service and a controversial lama. A critic for *Kirkus Reviews* was less impressed with this sequel, finding it "a talky disappointment more interested in proselytizing than storytelling." In the same vein, *Booklist* reviewer Pitt found *Deshi* less successful than its predecessor: "[It] seems formulaic by comparison," Pitt wrote. However, a contributor for *Publishers Weekly* thought Donohue's blend of Eastern philosophy and Western police methods will "appeal to all kinds of readers, not just martial arts aficionados," and called *Deshi* "intriguing."

BIOGRAPHICAL AND CRITICAL SOURCES:

PERIODICALS

Booklist, February 15, 2003, David Pitt, review of *Sensei*, p. 1052; February 15, 2005, David Pitt, review of *Deshi*, p. 1063.
Chicago Sun-Times, February 6, 2005, David Pitt, "They Deserve Better than Obscurity," review of *Deshi*, p. 11.
Kirkus Reviews, February 1, 2003, review of *Sensei*, p. 185; January 1, 2005, review of *Deshi*, p. 22.
Publishers Weekly, March 24, 2003, review of *Sensei*, p. 61; January 24, 2005, review of *Deshi*, p. 224.

ONLINE

D'Youville College Web site, http://depts.dyc.edu/ (June 30, 2005), "John Donohue."

*　　*　　*

DONOHUE, John J.
See DONOHUE, John

*　　*　　*

DOUTHAT, Ross Gregory 1979-

PERSONAL: Born 1979. *Education:* Graduated from Harvard University, 2002.

ADDRESSES: Agent—c/o Author Mail, Hyperion Books, 77 W. 66th St., 11th Fl., New York, NY 10023.

CAREER: National Review, research intern; *Atlantic Monthly,* Boston, MA, editorial analyst.

WRITINGS:

Privilege: Harvard and the Education of the Ruling Class, Hyperion (New York, NY), 2005.

SIDELIGHTS: An editorial analyst at the *Atlantic Monthly,* Ross Gregory Douthat is also an alumnus of Harvard University, and in his 2005 book, *Privilege: Harvard and the Education of the Ruling Class,* he provides a personal view of that institution and of the four years he spent there from 1998 to 2002. Ari Sigal, writing in *Library Journal,* found the book a "stark memoir" in that Douthat, though he enjoyed his time at Harvard, also has harsh criticism for the college and what he sees as its culture of elitism, grade inflation, mindless socializing, and careerism. As Douthat told Kathryn Jean Lopez for the *National Review Online:* "There's plenty of actual learning going on—but all too often, it feels optional, both because the environment of the place is career-focused rather than learning-focused, and because the curriculum makes it easy to skate through without being challenged." Speaking on the *Washingtonian Online* with Bill O'Sullivan, Douthat enlarged on this critique: "I don't want to pretend that there was some golden age in the past when everyone in elite colleges was just pursuing the life of the mind with no thought of personal gain." However, he noted, "I think that the pendulum has swung too far away from notions of idealism and service now, and toward careerism and success for success's sake." He went on to comment: "Today's elite universities are surprisingly depoliticized places," but Douthat believes this depoliticization has occurred because all members of the academy—including students, faculty, and administrators—"are primarily concerned with careerism and the bottom line, rather than with the older ideological debates." Politically conservative, Douthat confessed to Lopez that at times he wished he could socialize with Trotskyists, since "at least the Trotskyists cared about the important stuff."

Critical response to Douthat's memoir was generally positive. William F. Buckley, Jr., writing in the *National Review,* called *Privilege* a "satisfying account of the Harvard experience," while Sigal called it a "grim retrospective." Similarly, *Booklist* contributor Bryce Christensen found *Privilege* a "withering indictment of Harvard's institutional culture." A critic for *Kirkus Reviews* felt the same work is "quite thoughtful," and went on to praise the "controlled verve" of Douthat's writing.

BIOGRAPHICAL AND CRITICAL SOURCES:

BOOKS

Douthat, Ross Gregory, *Privilege: Harvard and the Education of the Ruling Class,* Hyperion (New York, NY), 2005.

PERIODICALS

Booklist, February 1, 2005, Bryce Christensen, "Harvard under Siege," review of *Privilege,* p. 922.
Kirkus Reviews, January 1, 2005, review of *Privilege: Harvard and the Education of the Ruling Class,* p. 31.
Library Journal, February 15, 2005, Ari Sigal, review of *Privilege,* p. 142.
National Review, March 28, 2005, William F. Buckley, Jr., "Blushing Crimson," review of *Privilege,* p. 44.

ONLINE

Biscuit Report, http://www.kafka.com/ (February 23, 2005), "Ross Douthat Is Bitter about Harvard."
Dartmouth Review Online, http://www.dartreview.com/ (April 8, 2005), Nicholas Desai, "Ross Douthat Explores Harvard: The Iviest of the Ivy League," review of *Privilege.*
National Review Online, http://www.nationalreview.com/ (May 26, 2005), Kathryn Jean Lopez, "Harvard Gone Wild."
Washingtonian Online, http://www.washingtonian.com/ (May 26, 2005), "*Washingtonian* Book Club: Featuring Ross Gregory Douthat."*

*   *   *

DOWLING, Vincent 1929-

PERSONAL: Born September 7, 1929, in Dublin, Ireland; immigrated to United States; naturalized U.S. citizen; son of William Francis (a sea captain) and Mai (Kelly) Dowling; married Brenda Mary Doyle (an

actor), 1952 (divorced); married Olwen Patricia O'Herlihy (an artist), 1975; children: (first marriage) Bairbre, Louise, Valerie, Rachel; (second marriage) Cian (son). *Education:* Attended St. Mary's College, Rathmines School of Commerce, and Brendan Smith Academy of Acting.

ADDRESSES: Office—Miniature Theatre of Chester, P.O. Box 722, Chester, MA 01011-0722.

CAREER: Standard Life Insurance Company, Dublin, Ireland, 1946-50; Brendan Smith Productions, Dublin, 1950-51; staff member, Roche-David Theatre Productions, 1951-53; Abbey Theatre, Dublin, actor, director, and associate director, 1953-76, artistic director, 1980s; Great Lakes Shakespeare Festival, Cleveland, OH, producing director, 1976-84; Solvang Theaterfest, artistic and producing director, 1984-86; College of Wooster, Wooster, OH, professor of theater, 1986-87; Pacific Conservatory of Performing Arts, Sacramento, CA, producing director; Miniature Theater of Chester, Chester, MA, founding director, 1990—. Actor in films, including *Boyd's Shop,* R.F.D. Productions, 1960; *Young Cassidy,* Metro-Goldwyn-Mayer, 1965; and *Guns in the Heather* (also known as *Spy Busters*), Buena Vista, 1968. For seventeen years played role of Christy Kennedy for radio program *The Kennedys of Castlerosse;* narrator of documentary video *Sons of Derry,* Cinema Guild, 1993, 1997. Producer of productions, including play *The Life and Adventures of Nicholas Nickelby,* 1982; and *Playboy of the Western World* broadcast on Public Broadcasting Service, 1982. Director of productions, including *A Moon for the Misbegotten,* produced in Buffalo, NY, 1989, and productions of Trinity Square Repertory Company, 1975-76, Meadow Brook Theatre, 1976-77, and Missouri Repertory Theatre, 1978-79. Co-founder, Jacob's Ladder Trail Business Association; International Artistic Directorate of the Globe Theatre, London, England, member.

AWARDS, HONORS: European Artist's Prize, Loyola University, 1969; Cleveland Critics Circle Award, 1982, for *The Life and Adventures of Nicholas Nickelby;* named Irishman of the Year, 1982; Wild Geese Award, 1988; Loyola Mellon Humanitarian Award, 1989; Walks of Life Award, Irish American Archives Society of Cleveland, 2000; D.F.A. from John Carroll University, College of Wooster, and Westfield State University; D.H.L. from Kent State University, 2003.

WRITINGS:

Astride the Moon: A Theatrical Life, Wolfhound Press (Dublin, Ireland), 2000.

A collection of Dowling's papers and video interviews are held by the Department of Special Collections and Archives at Kent State University.

PLAYS

The Fit-Ups, 1978.
Acting Is Murder, 1986.
A Life in the Day of an Abbey Actor, 1990.
Upstart Crow, 1995.

Also author of play *Do Me a Favourite!* Adaptor of *The Cherry Orchard* by Anton Chekhov and *Lysistrata* by Aristophanes. Writer and producer of one-man shows, including *Wilde about Oscar, Another Actor at the White House,* and *4P's.*

WORK IN PROGRESS: A second volume of autobiography.

SIDELIGHTS: Irish-born Vincent Dowling spent more than two decades as a director and actor with the Abbey Theatre, Ireland's national theater, in Dublin, and the majority of his more than one hundred acting roles were performed with the Abbey. Dowling, who immigrated to the United States in the 1970s, has produced, directed, and acted worldwide, including at the Kennedy Center for the Performing Arts and at the White House where, in 1981, he performed for then-President Ronald Reagan. The following year, he was invited to perform before the U.S. Congress. He has also brought many successful productions to New York, Paris, Moscow, and Florence.

In 1990, Dowling founded the Miniature Theater of Chester, in Chester, Massachusetts, where he now makes his home. The 150-seat theater is housed in the Chester Town Hall, and Dowling acted in the first production, *Mr. Dooley's America.* Dowling told *Variety* writer Markland Taylor that the theater expands the art scene of the Berkshires.

Dowling has mentored a great many young actors, including Roma Downey (*Touched by an Angel*) and Tom Hanks. He offered Hanks his first union job at the Great Lakes Shakespeare Festival. In the foreword of Dowling's memoir, *Astride the Moon: A Theatrical Life,* Hanks writes that "Vincent's the reason I'm an actor." In the book, Dowling writes of his childhood in Dublin during the 1930s and 1940s, where he was the sixth of seven children. His parents had a volatile relationship, and in a time when divorce was forbidden, his father left his mother, and they lived apart for fifty years. He writes that although his father was unsuccessful as a husband and father, he was a hard-working river captain who emphasized the power of the written word to his son.

Dowling also writes of his brother's participation in the Irish Republican Army (IRA), Irish politics, and his occasional disagreements with the Abbey's director, Ernest Blythe, a Northern Protestant and former minister in the Free State who auditioned potential actors and printed their names in Gaelic, while Dowling knew just enough Irish to get by. "Their skirmishes not only make fascinating reading," wrote C.L. Dallet in the *Times Literary Supplement,* "but belong in any discussion on the functions of art and culture and their all too frequent misuse as weapons for enforcing political hegemony." Dowling recounts his dual career as an actor and director and his many love affairs, including those he engaged in while he was married to his first wife, Brenda, an actor with whom he attended the Brendan Smith Academy of Acting at age sixteen. He writes of keeping several mistresses at a time and his inability to stop betraying Brenda, who was pregnant with their fourth child when the marriage ended. Dowling later married American Olwen Patricia O'Herlihy, with whom he has had one son.

BIOGRAPHICAL AND CRITICAL SOURCES:

BOOKS

Dowling, Vincent *Astride the Moon: A Theatrical Life,* Wolfhound Press (Dublin, Ireland), 2000.

PERIODICALS

Irish Literary Supplement, spring, 2002, David Krause, review of *Astride the Moon: A Theatrical Life,* p. 13.

New York Times, February 15, 1987, James W. Flannery, "An Irish Rover Comes Home to the Abbey," section 2, pp. 5, 31.

School Library Journal, September, 1997, Edward T. Sullivan, review of *Sons of Derry,* p. 163.

Times Literary Supplement, May 11, 2001, C.L. Dallat, review of *Astride the Moon.*

Variety, August 8, 1990, Markland Taylor, "Mass[a-chussetts] Director Makes Mini Theater," p. 56; September 24, 1990, review of *Playboy of the Western World,* p. 94.

ONLINE

Bookview Ireland, http://www.bookviewireland.ie/ (June 28, 2005), Pauline Ferrie, review of *Astride the Moon.*

Vincent Dowling Home Page, http://www. vincentdowling.com (June 28, 2005).*

*   *   *

DRUMMOND, Laurie Lynn 1956-

PERSONAL: Born 1956, in Bryan, TX. *Education:* Attended Ithaca College; Louisiana State University, B.A., M.F.A.

ADDRESSES: Office—Creative Writing Program, 5243 University of Oregon Eugene, OR 97403-5243. *E-mail*—lauried@darkwing.uoregon.edu.

CAREER: Author and educator. St. Edwards University, Austin, TX, adjunct instructor and assistant professor, 1991-2004; University of Oregon, Eugene, assistant professor of creative writing, 2004—. Ithaca Police Department, Ithaca, NY, police dispatcher, 1976-78; Louisiana State University Police Department, Crime Prevention Division, plainclothes officer, 1978-80; Baton Rouge Police Department, Baton Rouge, LA, uniformed police officer, 1980-85. Coordinating editor, Butterworth Legal Publishers Employment Law Division.

AWARDS, HONORS: Tennessee Williams Scholar in Fiction, Sewanee Writers' Conference, 1993; Association of Writers and Writing Programs Intro Award in Fiction; two Virginia Center for the Creative Arts fellowships; Walter E. Dakin fellow, Sewanee Writers' Conference, 2004; Violet Crown Texas Book Award in Fiction, and Jesse Jones Award for Best Book, Texas Institute of Letters, both 2004, both for *Anything You Say Can and Will Be Used against You;* Edgar Allan Poe Award for Best Short Story, Mystery Writers of America, and PEN/Hemingway Award finalist, both 2005, both for "Something about a Scar."

WRITINGS:

Anything You Say Can and Will Be Used against You (story collection), HarperCollins (New York, NY), 2004.

WORK IN PROGRESS: A novel, *The Hour of Two Lights,* for HarperCollins; a memoir, *Losing My Gun.*

SIDELIGHTS: Laurie Lynn Drummond is a former police officer whose 2004 short-story collection, *Anything You Say Can and Will Be Used Against You,* is a series of ten interlinking tales examining the life and work of female officers in the Baton Rouge Police Department, where Drummond herself was employed in the 1980s. A reviewer for *Publishers Weekly* thought that Drummond blends "Southern grace and urban brutality" in her "blistering fictional portraits." Three of the stories feature a fictional officer named Kathryn, who shoots a robbery suspect and then tries to save the badly injured man's life. Other tales focus on a traffic officer named Liz; an officer in Victim Services named Cathy; Sarah, who flees to New Mexico from her own past; and Mona, who has exhausted herself on the job. The *Publishers Weekly* reviewer went on to note that Drummond's "profiles in courage" offer continual surprises. Similar praise came from a critic for *Kirkus Reviews,* who felt Drummond's "prose . . . weighs like a gun in your palm." The same contributor felt Drummond successfully draws readers into her tales "with a marvelous command of fear and sensuous involvement." For Jo Ann Vicarel, writing in *Library Journal,* "this is an exceptional body of writing."

BIOGRAPHICAL AND CRITICAL SOURCES:

PERIODICALS

Kirkus Reviews, November 1, 2003, review of *Anything You Say Can and Will Be Used against You,* p. 1285.

Library Journal, November 15, 2003, Jo Ann Vicarel, review of *Anything You Say Can and Will Be Used against You,* p. 100.

Publishers Weekly, December 1, 2003, review of *Anything You Say Can and Will Be Used against You,* p. 39.

ONLINE

Laurie Lynn Drummond Home Page, http://www.lauriedrummond.com (July 3, 2005).

University of Oregon Creative Writing Program Web site, http://darkwing.uoregon.edu/~crwrweb/ (July 3, 2005), "Laurie Lynn Drummond."

*   *   *

DUNN, Anthony Taylor 1958-

PERSONAL: Born February 23, 1958, in New York, NY; son of Daniel (a corporate attorney) and Barbara (self-employed; maiden name, Taylor) Dunn; married Bonne Lynn (a photographer) August 29, 1987; children: Isabella Angeline. *Ethnicity:* "Caucasian." *Education:* Dean College, A.A., 1979; University of Maine, B.A., 1984. *Politics:* Democrat. *Religion:* Episcopalian.

ADDRESSES: Home—47 Micmac Lane, Machiasport, ME 04655. *E-mail*—info@anthonytaylordunn.com.

CAREER: Writer. FleetBoston Financial, Boston, MA, banker, 1995-2001.

WRITINGS:

Sunbathing on the Bottom of the Atlantic (poems), MK Publishing (St. Cloud, MN), 2005.

WORK IN PROGRESS: A children's book.

SIDELIGHTS: Anthony Taylor Dunn told *CA:* "I began writing poetry when I was working in Boston as a banker. I participated in Harold Bond's workshops at the Blacksmith House in Cambridge. Many of the narrative poems I wrote for my book, *Sunbathing on the Bottom of the Atlantic,* are set in Boston. I suppose I began writing out of a kind of psychic pain that forced me to break the silence and start writing. Poetry seemed to be the most direct means of precise expression because of its condensation of words. One never knows where poems come from—out of the air, perhaps—I simply chip away at the words that don't belong there to reveal the poem underneath. The overall tone of my collection is one of dark humor, playing against the themes of freedom, or lack of it, the act of writing poetry, and death. The styles of poetry I am drawn towards and like to write are narrative, free verse. I enjoy writing in the early morning, say around five, beginning in the dark, and by the time the sunlight reaches my desk, I've come up with something to work on."

BIOGRAPHICAL AND CRITICAL SOURCES:

ONLINE

Anthony Taylor Dunn Home Page, http://www.anthonytaylordunn.com (May 30, 2005).

*   *   *

DWYER, Gerald P., Jr. 1947-

PERSONAL: Born July 9, 1947, in Pittsfield, MA; son of Gerald P. (a chief petty officer in the U.S. Navy) and Mary Frances (a homemaker; maiden name, Weir) Dwyer; married Katherine M. Lepiane (a homemaker), January 15, 1966; children: Tamara K., Gerald P., III, Angela Marie, Michael James, Terence F. *Education:* University of Washington, B.B.A., 1969; University of Tennessee, M.A., 1973; University of Chicago, Ph.D., 1979. *Religion:* Roman Catholic. *Hobbies and other interests:* Sailing.

ADDRESSES: Home—2122 Maple Springs Way, Lawrenceville, GA 30043. *Office*—Federal Reserve Bank of Atlanta, 1000 Peachtree St. NE, Atlanta, GA 30309. *E-mail*—gdwyer@dwyerecon.com.

CAREER: Writer. Oak Ridge National Laboratory, research associate, 1972; Federal Reserve Bank of St. Louis, St. Louis, MO, junior economist, 1972-75, visiting scholar, 1987-89; Federal Reserve Bank of Chicago, Chicago, IL, economist, 1976-77; Texas A & M University, assistant professor of economics, 1977-81; Emory University, Atlanta, GA, assistant professor of economics, 1981-84, adjunct faculty, 2001; University of Houston, Houston, TX, associate professor of economics, 1984-89; Clemson University, Clemson, SC, professor of economics, 1989-99, acting head of economics department, 1992-93; Federal Reserve Bank of Atlanta, visiting scholar, 1995-97, finance team leader, 1997—, vice president, 1998—Commodity Futures Trading Commission, visiting financial economist, 1990; Federal Reserve Bank of Minneapolis, Institute for Empirical Macroeconomics, visiting scholar, 1995; Georgia State University, adjunct faculty, 1997; University of Georgia, adjunct faculty, 1999-2000, 2003; University of Rome, Tor Vergata, visiting professor, 2000—University of Carlos III, Madrid, Spain, visiting professor, 2005—. Also lecturer at University of Missouri, American Institute of Banking, St. Louis, and Belleville Area College, 1972-74.

Editorial board member, *Studies in Economics and Finance,* 1996-98, *Research in Banking and Finance,* 2000—, *Economic Inquiry,* 2002—, and *Journal of Financial Stability,* 2003—.

MEMBER: Society for Nonlinear Dynamics and Econometrics (treasurer, 1997-2003; president, 2003-05), American Economics Association, American Finance Association, Western Economics Association (executive committee member, 2005—), Association of Private Enterprise Education (executive committee member, 2002—), Beta Gamma, Phi Kappa Phi.

AWARDS, HONORS: Earhart Foundation fellowship, 1975-77; Intercollegiate Studies Institute fellowship, 1974-75.

WRITINGS:

(Coeditor) *Monetary Policy and Taiwan's Economy,* Edward Elgar (Northhampton, MA), 2002.

Contributor to *Monetary Unions and Hard Pegs: Effects on Trade, Financial Development, and Stability,* edited by Volbert Alexander, Jacques Mélitz, and George M. von Furstenberg, Oxford University Press (New York, NY), 2004. Contributor of numerous articles to scholarly journals, including *Journal of International Money and Finance, Journal of Economic Dynamics and Control, Managerial Finance, Journal of Money, Credit, and Banking, Economic Journal, Economic Inquiry, Journal of Monetary Economics, Economica, American Economic Review, Historical Methods, Behavioural Processes, Journal of Political Economy,* and *Research in Banking and Finance.* Contributor of articles to Federal Reserve Bank publications, including Federal Reserve Bank of St. Louis *Review* and Federal Reserve Bank of Atlanta *Economic Review.* Contributor of book reviews to journals, including *Journal of Economic History, Journal of Economic Literature,* and *Southern Economic Journal.*

WORK IN PROGRESS: Economics and Finance for Everyday Life; research on banking panics and economic growth and stagnation.

E

EICHLER, Selma

PERSONAL: Married; husband's name Lloyd.

ADDRESSES: Home—NY. Agent—Stuart Krichevsky, Stuart Krichevsky Literary Agency, Inc., 381 Park Ave. S., Ste. 914, New York, NY 10016.

CAREER: Freelance writer.

WRITINGS:

"DESIREE SHAPIRO" MYSTERY NOVELS

Murder Can Kill Your Social Life, Signet (New York, NY), 1994.

Murder Can Ruin Your Looks, Signet (New York, NY), 1995.

Murder Can Stunt Your Growth, Signet (New York, NY), 1996.

Murder Can Wreck Your Reunion, Signet (New York, NY), 1997.

Murder Can Spook Your Cat, Signet (New York, NY), 1998.

Murder Can Singe Your Old Flame, Signet (New York, NY), 1999.

Murder Can Spoil Your Appetite, Signet (New York, NY), 2000.

Murder Can Upset Your Mother, Signet (New York, NY), 2001.

Murder Can Cool Off Your Affair, Signet (New York, NY), 2002.

Murder Can Rain on Your Shower, Signet (New York, NY), 2003.

Murder Can Botch Up Your Birthday, Signet (New York, NY), 2004.

Murder Can Mess Up Your Mascara, Signet (New York, NY), 2005.

Murder Can Run Your Stockings, Signet (New York, NY), 2006.

Contributor to anthology And the Dying Is Easy, Signet (New York, NY), 2001.

ADAPTATIONS: Murder Can Spoil Your Appetite was adapted as an audiobook, Blackstone, 2001.

SIDELIGHTS: Selma Eichler's lighthearted mystery series, which Harriet Klausner described in Best Reviews online as "cerebral" and "cozy," features overweight Manhattan private investigator Desiree Shapiro. Shapiro is a likeable, forty-something woman who is unconcerned that her full-figured body is not socially acceptable; she enjoys a double scoop of Haagen Dazs ice cream as much as she does solving a mystery. Reviewers have noted that the murder mystery in each of Eichler's books is not always the most intriguing part of the story, as the author spends a good deal of time on Desiree's relationships, her interest in food, and her observations about living in New York City. For some critics, this has proved to be a sticking point. For example, Dawn Goldsmith, reviewing Murder Can Spoil Your Appetite for Crescent Blues Book Views, felt that the book is "bland." Other critics, however, enjoyed the author's laid-back style. For instance, in a Crescent Blues Book Views assessment of *Murder Can Singe Your Old Flame,* Stephen J. Metherell-Smith described the novel as a "kind of 'bare bones' mystery," while still finding it to be "an easy-to-read and enjoyable novel."

Reception of more recent "Desiree Shapiro" mysteries has often been positive. A critic for *Publishers Weekly,* reviewing *Murder Can Upset Your Mother,* praised "Eichler's all-too-human, wacky private investigator," as well as the book's "witty repartee and zany characters." Klausner, writing in *MBR Bookwatch,* declared that *Murder Can Mess Up Your Mascara* is "a fine Manhattan cozy that fans of the series will enjoy."

BIOGRAPHICAL AND CRITICAL SOURCES:

PERIODICALS

Baldwin Ledger (Baldwin City, KS), March 5, 1999, review of *Murder Can Wreck Your Reunion,* p. 13.
I Love a Mystery, June, 1996, review of *Murder Can Stunt Your Growth,* pp. 22-23.
MBR Bookwatch, February, 2005, Harriet Klausner, review of *Murder Can Mess Up Your Mascara.*
Publishers Weekly, December 21, 1998, review of *Murder Can Singe Your Old Flame,* p. 65; February 12, 2001, review of *Murder Can Upset Your Mother,* p. 189; February 25, 2002, review of *Murder Can Cool Off Your Affair,* p. 48; January 10, 2005, review of *Murder Can Mess Up Your Mascara,* p. 44.
Romantic Times, February, 2005, Cindy Harrison, review of *Murder Can Mess Up Your Mascara,* p. 82.

ONLINE

Best Reviews, http://thebestreviews.com/ (February 7, 2002), Harriet Klausner, review of *Murder Can Cool Off Your Affair.*
Book Browser, http://www.bookbrowser.com/ (January 24, 1998), Harriet Klausner, review of *Murder Can Spook Your Cat.*
Crescent Blues Book Views, http://www.crescentblues. com/ (May 6, 2002), Dawn Goldsmith, review of *Murder Can Spoil Your Appetite* and Stephen J. Metherell-Smith, review of *Murder Can Singe Your Old Flame.*

EIG, Jonathan

PERSONAL: Married; wife's name Jennifer; children: Lillian. *Education:* Northwestern University, B.A.

ADDRESSES: Home—Chicago, IL. *Agent*—c/o Author Mail, Simon and Schuster, 1230 Avenue of the Americas, New York, NY 10020. *E-mail*—jonathan@ jonathaneig.com.

CAREER: New Orleans Times-Picayune, reporter; *Dallas Morning News,* reporter; *Chicago* magazine, journalist, executive editor, 1995-2000; *Wall Street Journal,* senior special reporter, 2000—.

AWARDS, HONORS: Won numerous writing awards at *Chicago* magazine.

WRITINGS:

Luckiest Man: The Life and Death of Lou Gehrig, Simon and Schuster (New York, NY), 2005.

Contributor of articles to periodicals, including *Esquire, New Republic,* and *American Prospect.*

SIDELIGHTS: A senior special reporter for the *Wall Street Journal,* Jonathan Eig made his debut as a book author with the 2005 biography *Luckiest Man: The Life and Death of Lou Gehrig.* Writing in the *Pittsburgh Post-Gazette Online,* John Caroulis noted the difficulties inherent in writing an account of the life and death of one of baseball's most famous players, someone who played 2,130 consecutive games and hit 493 home runs in his career, before being struck by the debilitating disease that finally ended his life. Indeed, Caroulis noted, "Gehrig is more famous now as a victim of amyotrophic lateral sclerosis (ALS), a disease named for him, that killed him just before he turned thirty-eight, than for his prodigious baseball feats." Thus the prospective biographer must avoid the trap of hagiography, as well as of repeating the same apocryphal tales that so many other biographers of Gehrig, baseball's so-called "Iron Man," have passed on. According to Caroulis, Eig avoids making a myth of the man, providing instead "a full, compelling account of the Yankee first baseman." Caroulis also praised Eig's "impressive research," allowing him to paint a full portrait of this baseball legend, who during his lifetime had to live in the shadow of the great Babe Ruth. Eig provides a rounded picture of Gehrig through an extensive use of letters the baseball player wrote to various people during the course of his final illness. Though Gehrig's voice is not necessarily eloquent, it is honest and forthright, and Eig lets the athlete speak for himself much of the time.

Eig chronicles Gehrig's impoverished beginnings, his baseball scholarship to Columbia University, the courtship and marriage that went against his strong-willed mother's desires, his ascent in his chosen profession, and his final fight against ALS, a losing battle his doctors never let him would end in his death. A critic for *Kirkus Reviews* felt that Gehrig's decline is "one of the saddest . . . instances" of a young, popular athlete's death in all of sports history. The same contributor thought that "Eig crafts a portrait that goes far beyond the usual rendering," and his "account brings uncommon humanity to a legendary, golden sports hero." Further praise for this "meticulous biography" came from a *Publishers Weekly* reviewer who noted that "Eig find[s] lively anecdotes" and is able to describe "his story's medical aspects with powerful sensitivity." Wes Lukowsky, reviewing *Luckiest Man* in *Booklist*, observed that Eig is able to get behind the cliché image of Gehrig to add "a third dimension—heart—to our understanding of a legendary ballplayer." Similarly, Bill Ott, writing in *American Libraries*, commented that Eig "gives Gehrig back his multidimensionality."

BIOGRAPHICAL AND CRITICAL SOURCES:

PERIODICALS

American Libraries, April, 2005, Bill Ott, "Baseball When the Bodies Were Real," review of *Luckiest Man: The Life and Death of Lou Gehrig*, p. 86.
America's Intelligence Wire, July 28, 2003, John Gibson, "Interview with the *Wall Street Journal* critic Jonathan Eig."
Booklist, March 1, 2005, Wes Lukowsky, review of *Luckiest Man*, p. 1129.
Economist, May 7, 2005, review of "Struck Out: Sporting Heroes," review of *Luckiest Man*, p. 79.
Kirkus Reviews, January 15, 2005, review of *Luckiest Man*, p. 98.

Library Journal, December 1, 2004, Barbara Hoffert, review of *Luckiest Man*, p. 92.
Publishers Weekly, February 7, 2005, review of *Luckiest Man*, p. 51.
Sports Illustrated, April 11, 2005, Bill Syken, "The Rise of the Iron Horse," review of *Luckiest Man*, p. Z6.

ONLINE

Jonathan Eig Home Page, http://www.jonathaneig.com (July 4, 2005).
Pittsburgh Post-Gazette Online, http://www.post-gazette.com/ (January 21, 2005), John Caroulis, "Gehrig the Man, Not Legend, Emerges in New Biography," review of *Luckiest Man*.

*   *   *

EISEN, Adrienne

PERSONAL: Female. *Education:* Attended graduate writing program at Boston University.

ADDRESSES: Home—NY. *Agent*—c/o Author Mail, Eastgate Systems, Inc., 134 Main St., Watertown, MA 02472. *E-mail*—adrienneeisen@earthlink.net.

CAREER: Writer. Taught creative writing at Boston University; former editor for Artcommotion.com.

AWARDS, HONORS: New Media Invision Award.

WRITINGS:

Making Scenes (novel), Broadvision, 2001.

Also author of hypertext novels, including *Six Sex Scenes*, Alt-X Press, and *What Fits*, Eastgate. Contributor to online publications, including *Alt-X, Iowa Review Web*, and *Eastgate*.

SIDELIGHTS: Even before the popularity of e-novels on the Internet and other electronic media, author Adrienne Eisen had become an innovator of the hypertext novel for which she is now well known. Beginning her excursion into electronic publishing in 1992, Eisen explained to Jeffrey Yamaguchi in a *Bookmouth.com* interview that she started writing for CD-ROMs even before they were called CD-ROMs: "They were actually called CD-i back then, and no one could think of something to put on them. I had all this writing that didn't work as a linear novel, so I went to Philips Media—they invented CD-i—and said, 'Look, I wrote stuff for CD-i.' After that, I went to Boston University's graduate program for creative writing, and I wrote hypertext." Eisen's writing professors at the time did not seem to grasp the concept, and kept telling her to write in a linear form. However this practice proved beneficial, Eisen explained, because it "taught me how to adapt hypertext to print," which she eventually did with her first print novel, *Making Scenes.*

In a hypertext novel, readers can make decisions about where a story's plot goes by clicking on hyperlinks at certain points in the novel where the author has inserted them. Thus, a story can veer in unexpected directions depending, in part, on the whims of the reader. This type of writing is reflected in Eisen's *Making Scenes,* which can be approached linearly or non-linearly by the reader. As Beth Warrell explained in her *Booklist* review of the novel, "The story makes sense read front to back, but skipping around won't cause much confusion" because the story is a collection of scenes that can be read independent of each another. The basic plot of *Making Scenes* involves a young woman's adventures—often sexual—after she graduates from college. Suffering from bulimia and a troubled childhood during which she was the victim of incest, the heroine explores her identity and sexuality. Enjoying the "genuinely funny treatments of sex scattered throughout" the story, *Curve* reviewer Rachel Pepper found the vivid descriptions of bulimia and the "incestuous overtones" about the protagonist's past to be "disturbing." Nevertheless, she enjoyed the "character's smart-aleck, wise-girl tone." A *Publishers Weekly* contributor felt the scenes suffer from repetitiveness because of the nature of the book's background in hypertext. Although this results in a story that "isn't really going anywhere," the critic praised Eisen's "short, pithy scenes anchored by clever observation."

BIOGRAPHICAL AND CRITICAL SOURCES:

PERIODICALS

Booklist, March 1, 2002, Beth Warrell, review of *Making Scenes,* p. 1089.

Curve, August, 2002, Rachel Pepper, "Reads for Road-Trippers," p. 41.
Publishers Weekly, February 18, 2002, review of *Making Scenes,* p. 72.

ONLINE

Adrienne Eisen Home Page, http://www.adrienneeisen. com (July 6, 2005).
Alt-X Press, http://www.altx.com/ (July 6, 2005), review of *Making Scenes.*
Bookmouth.com, http://www.bookmouth.com/ (June 28, 2002), Jeffrey Yamaguchi, "An Interview with Hypertext Novelist Adrienne Eisen."*

*   *   *

EMENEAU, Murray Barnson 1904-2005

OBITUARY NOTICE— See index for *CA* sketch: Born February 28, 1904, in Lunenburg, Nova Scotia, Canada; died August 29, 2005, in Berkeley, CA. Linguist, educator, and author. Emeneau, a professor emeritus at the University of California at Berkeley, was acclaimed for his groundbreaking work in non-literary dialects in India and for his research on now-extinct native Californian languages. A brilliant student from an early age, he studied Latin, French, and German in high school, then proceeded to major in Greek and Latin at Dalhousie University. After earning a B.A. there in 1923, he attended Oxford University on a Rhodes scholarship, earning a second B.A. in 1926 and, in 1935, an M.A. Between these two degrees, he also completed a Ph.D. at Yale University in 1931. During the late 1920s, Emeneau was an instructor at Yale, and from 1931 to 1940 he worked there as a research scholar. During the 1930s he came under the influence of prominent linguist Edward Sapir, who encouraged Emeneau to travel to India and research dialects there. Emeneau did so, learning the Kota, Badaga, Kolami, and Toda languages, which led to such works as *Kota Texts* (1944-46), *A Dravidian Etymological Dictionary* (1961), *Studies in Indian Linguistics* (1968), the edited *Toda Songs* (1971), and *Toda Grammar and Texts* (1984). After joining the Berkeley faculty in 1940 as an assistant professor, Emeneau's next major project was the study of Vietnamese. This resulted in his writing a grammar book on the language, as well as penning several other related publications. By 1946 Emeneau was already a full professor of Sanskrit and general linguistics at Berkeley. While at the university, he also established the Survey of California Indian Languages; he spent several decades studying extinct native tongues. After retiring in 1971, when he received the prestigious Berkeley Citation from the university, Emeneau continued to publish for many more years. Among his last publications are *Sanskrit Studies: Selected Papers* (1988) and *Dravidian Studies: Selected Papers* (1994).

OBITUARIES AND OTHER SOURCES:

PERIODICALS

San Francisco Chronicle, September 12, 2005, p. B4.

ONLINE

Berkeley Linguistics Department Web site, http://www. linguistics.berkeley.edu/ (October 26, 2005).

* * *

ERDAL, Jennie

PERSONAL: Born in Fifeshire, Scotland; married David Erdal (second marriage); children: (first marriage) three. *Education:* Attended college.

ADDRESSES: Home—Scotland. *Agent*—c/o Author Mail, Doubleday, 1745 Broadway, New York, NY 10019.

CAREER: Author, ghostwriter, and translator. Quartet Books, London, England, Russian translator, editor, and ghostwriter, 1981-98.

WRITINGS:

Ghosting: A Double Life, Canongate Books (Edinburgh, Scotland), 2004, Doubleday (New York, NY), 2005.

Ghostwriter of twelve books, including two fiction titles, and numerous magazine and newspaper articles.

SIDELIGHTS: Jennie Erdal caused a publishing scandal in London in 2004 with her memoir, *Ghosting: A Double Life,* in which she detailed the dozen books she wrote for others, the numerous articles ghost-written for prestigious British periodicals, and the love letters she ghosted for flamboyant Lebanese publisher Naim Attallah, of Quartet Books. Beginning in 1981, the unassuming Scots-born Erdal began working for Quartet Books as a translator of Russian works. Soon Attallah, eager to gain respect in his adopted country and in his second language, had Erdal penning articles and interviews under his name, profiling personalities such as Claus von Bülow, the aristocrat accused of attempting to murder his wife; Hartley William, Lord Shawcross of Friston, the chief British prosecutor at the Nuremberg trials of Nazi leaders following World War II; and Laurens van der Post, a South African author and conservationist. Erdal even authored an article on Attallah's trip to China, though she had never been to that country herself. The arrangement worked well for Erdal, as she could remain at her home in Scotland and do the writing. Letters were also part of her ghosting activities, including love letters to Attallah's wife and missives to his son. Soon the arrangement broadened to include book-length works, among them two novels, one of them based on Attallah's idea of two women so close to one another that they share orgasms, even when separated by the Atlantic. Attallah shipped Erdal off to France's Dordogne region to work on the project, where she was kept a virtual prisoner until the book was completed. This arrangement paid the bills and was satisfactory for Erdal until her second husband began questioning the fifty calls per day she sometimes received from her demanding boss. In 1998 Erdal ended her association with Attallah and began writing under her own name. The result was not the novel she had imagined, but a memoir of her years working for the eccentric publisher.

Published both in the United Kingdom and in the United States, *Ghosting* understandably received most attention in England. Writing for the London *Guardian Online,* Blake Morrison noted that, instead of an actual memoir, Erdal creates a "character study [of Attallah] in the tradition of the realist novel." Morrison felt Erdal "succeeds by being merciless but also forgiving." For Morrison, "Erdal's account of their novelistic collaboration is the best (and funniest) part" of the book. Similarly, a reviewer for the *Economist Online* found "a rich vein of humour" in this "delightful book," and Lloyd Evans, in a London *Telegraph Online* review, found *Ghosting* "an unusually rich and entertaining memoir—hilarious, infuriating and unforgettable."

Reviewing the American edition of the book, a contributor for *Publishers Weekly* felt that the book's allusions to the literary world of London will probably "be lost on American readers," but went on to observe that "this memoir reveals an otherwise hidden world." *Newsweek* contributor Susan H. Greenberg had higher praise for the book, calling it "irresistible," as well as "probing, intelligent and funny." Likewise, a critic for *Kirkus Reviews* called *Ghosting* a "poignant and even-spirited memoir," and deemed Erdal's descriptive passages "rich and gently humorous." *Booklist* contributor Donna Seaman dubbed the work a "mind-blowing story," while for Seaman, Erdal's memoir is both an "exquisitely composed confession" and a "hilarious tale of decadence and duplicity."

BIOGRAPHICAL AND CRITICAL SOURCES:

BOOKS

Erdal, Jennie, *Ghosting: A Double Life,* Canongate Books (Edinburgh, Scotland), 2004, Doubleday (New York, NY), 2005.

PERIODICALS

Booklist, February 15, 2005, Donna Seaman, review of *Ghosting,* p. 1051.
Kirkus Reviews, January 1, 2005, review of *Ghosting,* p. 32.
Library Journal, December 1, 2004, Barbara Hoffert, review of *Ghosting,* p. 92.
Newsweek, April 4, 2005, Susan H. Greenberg, review of *Ghosting,* p. 54.
Publishers Weekly, February 14, 2005, review of *Ghosting,* p. 63.
Time International, November 29, 2004, Donald Morrison, "A Writer's Writer," review of *Ghosting,* p. 72.

ONLINE

Economist Online, http://www.economist.com/ (November 11, 2004), "Tiger Burning Bright," review of *Ghosting.*
Guardian Online, http://books.guardian.co.uk/ (December 18, 2004), Blake Morrison, "Breaking Cover," review of *Ghosting.*
ReadySteadyBook.com, http://www.readysteadybook.com/ (July 5, 2005), Jodie Hamilton, review of *Ghosting.*
San Francisco Chronicle Online, http://www.sfgate.com/ (April 10, 2005), Carlo Wolff, "His Glory Rested on Her Words," review of *Ghosting.*
Telegraph Online, http://www.arts.telegraph.co.uk/ (November 2, 2004), Lloyd Evans, "A Ghostwriter Spills the Beans," review of *Ghosting.*
Times Online, http://www.timesonline.co.uk/ (December 17, 2004), Valerie Grove, "I Wrote Naim Attallah's Every Word."*

*   *   *

ESLICK, Tom

PERSONAL: Married; wife's name Susan; children: two sons. *Education:* Nasson College, Springvale, ME, B.A.; University of New Hampshire, M.A.; Emerson College, M.F.A.

ADDRESSES: Agent—c/o Author Mail, Viking Publicity, Penguin Group, 375 Hudson St., New York, NY 10014. *E-mail*—tomeslick@proctornet.com.

CAREER: Writer, educator, singer and songwriter. Vermont College, Brattleboro, English instructor; Proctor Academy, Andover, NH, current English teacher and former department chair. Trapp Family Lodge, Stowe, VT, house musician; has released several recordings. Rescue squad volunteer.

WRITINGS:

Tracked in the Whites, Write Way Publishing (Aurora CO), 1997.
Snow Kill, Write Way Publishing (Aurora CO), 2000.

Deadly Kin: A White Mountains Mystery, Viking (New York, NY), 2003.

Mountain Peril: A White Mountains Mystery, Viking (New York, NY), 2005.

Also author of song lyrics.

WORK IN PROGRESS: A novel in the "White Mountains Mystery" series.

SIDELIGHTS: Musician, songwriter, teacher, and outdoorsman Tom Eslick is also the author of several novels set in the White Mountains of northern New England, where he resides. Eslick did not take up writing until 1997, shortly after completing a master's degree in creative writing. His debut title, *Tracked in the Whites,* introduces Will Buchanan, a natural history teacher in a private New Hampshire school. In this initial outing, Buchanan takes his students out for the annual hike, but things go wrong from the outset. A prowler frightens the camp, and then a student, the daughter of a famous rock singer, goes missing. Buchanan is the primary suspect in the case, and to prove his innocence, he must set out to find the missing girl and capture the real perpetrator. Reviewing the novel in *Booklist,* John Rowen found it "fresh and accomplished," as well as a "compelling mystery." Rowen also had praise for the "realistic characters" in this first novel.

Eslick stayed in familiar terrain for his second novel, *Snow Kill,* setting the book in a New Hampshire town. He also used his own emergency medical technician (EMT) training for his main character, Chad Duquette, who is still reeling from the death of his wife. But Chad soon has problems worse than grief, as someone is planting evidence that frames him as the prime suspect in a murder investigation. Forced to go on the run to prove his innocence, Chad must battle personal demons as well as a very real nemesis. A *Publishers Weekly* reviewer was largely unimpressed with this second novel, calling it a "so-so whodunit" and "less than a stellar read."

Subsequent books from Eslick have reprised his debut character, Will Buchanan, and continued the "White Mountains Mystery" series. Buchanan is again wrongfully accused in the 2003 *Deadly Kin: A White Mountains Mystery.* This time out one of Buchanan's

students accuses him of rape after he accompanies her to meet her brother along a hiking trail. The two siblings appear to have more than familial affection for one another, and next morning the brother turns up dead. The girl in question, Erin, after making her accusation of rape, subsequently disappears. Now Buchanan must once more set out to prove his own innocence. Reviewers responded to this novel positively. *Library Journal* reviewer Rex Klett praised the clear prose, the description of the setting's natural beauty, "and a deceptively simple plot," while *Booklist* critic Rowen noted that Eslick "sets a breakneck pace and never lets it slacken." A *Kirkus Reviews* critic, while finding the story "ragtag, with shadowy characters," deemed the nature and action scenes "worth the price of admission." A contributor for *Publishers Weekly* complained of "occasional lapses into melodrama," but concluded by noting that mystery fans will "enjoy the excitement" afforded by accompanying Will Buchanan on another trek through the White Mountains.

Eslick's third "Buchanan" novel, *Mountain Peril: A White Mountains Mystery,* appeared in 2005. In this mystery-thriller, Buchanan uncovers body parts along a lonely trail while searching for a missing boy. It appears a serial killer is at work, and two women are already dead. Buchanan, in at the beginning of this case, refuses to leave it to the professionals, and becomes even more involved when his love interest, Laurie, the local police chief, is shot at a holdup. Suspicion for not only the holdup, but also the murders, falls on a local man, Nelson Carpenter, the former lover of one of the dead women. Buchanan thinks otherwise, however, and pursues who he thinks the real perpetrator is. Once again, critical reception for an installment of the "White Mountains Mystery" series was generally positive. *Booklist* contributor Rowen noted that Eslick "sets a suspenseful . . . pace" and includes "plot twists and surprises." A *Kirkus Reviews* critic had a less favorable assessment of the work, noting that "Eslick seems uncomfortable with mystery" and does not develop his characters. However, a *Publishers Weekly* contributor felt that "Eslick knows this rugged terrain . . . and depicts its many perils [well]," while Klett, reviewing the novel for *Library Journal,* praised its "lively, outdoors action."

BIOGRAPHICAL AND CRITICAL SOURCES:

PERIODICALS

Booklist, July, 1997, John Rowen, review of *Tracked in the Whites,* p. 1802; April 1, 2001, John Rowen, review of *Deadly Kin: A White Mountains Mystery,* p. 1449; March 15, 2005, John Rowen, review of *Mountain Peril: A White Mountains Mystery,* p. 1269.

Kirkus Reviews, July 1, 2003, review of *Deadly Kin,* p. 885; February 15, 2005, review of *Mountain Peril,* p. 200.

Library Journal, May 1, 2001, Rex Klett, review of *Deadly Kin,* p. 130; March 1, 2005, Rex E. Klett, review of *Mountain Peril,* p. 71.

MBR Bookwatch, April, 2005, review of *Mountain Peril.*

Publishers Weekly, April 17, 2000, review of *Snow Kill,* p. 55; April 16, 2001, review of *Deadly Kin,* p. 48; August 25, 2003, review of *Deadly Kin,* p. 43; March 7, 2005, review of *Mountain Peril,* p. 53.

ONLINE

AllReaders.com, http://www.allreaders.com/ (July 5, 2005), Harriet Klausner, reviews of *Deadly Kin* and *Mountain Peril.*

Tom Eslick Home Page, http://www.tomeslick.com (July 5, 2005).

Who-dunnit.com, http://www.who-dunnit.com/ (July 5, 2005), "Tom Eslick."*

F

FALLA, Jonathan 1954-
[A pseudonym]

PERSONAL: Born 1954, in Jamaica; married a doctor; children: one son. *Education:* Graduated from Cambridge University; attended University of Southern California film school, 1992; studied nursing in Oxford and London, England, and Aberdeen, Scotland.

ADDRESSES: Home—Fife, Scotland. *Agent*—The Agency, 24 Pottery Lane, Holland Park, London W11 4LZ, England.

CAREER: Certified as a general, pediatric, and tropical nurse; writer and musician. Worked for various international aid agencies in Indonesia, Sudan, Uganda, Burma, and Nepal, 1978-91; part-time nurse, Perth, Scotland. Singer, instrumentalist, and cofounder of Renaissance music quartet Fires of Love. Worked as a writer/producer for radio stations in Scotland and Indonesia.

AWARDS, HONORS: Voted Most Promising Playwright, London Drama Critics, 1983; Fulbright fellowship, 1992; audience jury prize for best film, Reims Festival, and Prix de la Ville de Laon, Laon Festival, both 1992, both for *The Hummingbird Tree*; Scottish PEN award, 2000.

WRITINGS:

Topokana Martyrs' Day (play), produced in London, England, 1983, performed in New York, NY, 1987.

The Hummingbird Tree (screenplay), British Broadcasting Corporation (BBC) Films, 1991.

True Love and Bartholomew: Rebels on the Burmese Border (nonfiction), Cambridge University Press (New York, NY), 1991.

Down the Tubes (play), produced in Edinburgh, Scotland, 1996.

Diriamba! (play), produced in Edinburgh, Scotland, 1997.

Free Rope (play), produced in Edinburgh, Scotland, 1998.

Blue Poppies (novel), 11/9 (Glasgow, Scotland), 2001, Delta Trade Paperbacks (New York, NY), 2003.

Poor Mercy (novel), Polygon, 2005.

Also author of a children's musical and short stories; author of reviews and essays.

Author's work has been translated.

ADAPTATIONS: Topokana Martyrs' Day was adapted as a radio play produced for BBC World Service, 1986.

SIDELIGHTS: Pediatric nurse, musician, and author Jonathan Falla—the name is actually a pseudonym—had already led a remarkable life by the time he was in his thirties. From 1978 until 1991, he visited many troubled countries in Africa and Asia, working in educational publishing and then in health care for various international aid organizations. During this time, he experienced fascinating but troubled cultures in such places as Sudan, Nepal, and Burma, while battling the frustrating limitations of bureaucracy that hindered his efforts to help people, and the chaos born of war and famine. He ultimately left foreign-aid work after becoming disillusioned and because he had gotten married. After winning a Fulbright fellowship, Falla studied film at the University of California. While there, he worked on a screenplay for a movie about 1940s Tibet that would later become the critically acclaimed novel *Blue Poppies*. Before this novel's publication, however, Falla would address the problems of Third World countries in works for the stage and in a nonfiction study about Burmese rebels.

Falla's 1983 play, *Topokana Martyrs' Day,* which was produced in both London and New York City, mocks the inefficient bureaucracy that plagues Western nations' attempts to provide aid to Africa. The comedy features four relief workers trying to help the Tokokana tribe in East Africa. Their efforts are ultimately thwarted by both cultural differences and problems that stem from their European base which, in one pathetically satirical episode, ships the hungry Africans a load of inedible biscuits that are long past their expiration date. While a critic for *Variety,* reviewing the 1985 New York performance of the play, found the production "not funny enough, at least not to an American ear," *New York Times* critic Walter Goodman described Falla's dialogue as "smartly written and delivered." Goodman admitted that Falla does not make the relationships between the white colleagues clear enough to justify some of their emotional reactions on the stage, but the reviewer praised the overall "strength of the writing."

Falla again draws on his personal experience—this time more directly—to write the nonfiction work *True Love and Bartholomew: Rebels on the Burmese Border.* The book, which is part sociological study and part cultural travelogue, concerns a year Falla spent living with the rebel Karen people in Burma, just west of the Thailand border. The Karen have declared their region to be the country of Kawthoolei, though its existence has not been recognized by the international community, and the result has been years of military strife between them and the government. Falla's mission while there was illegal: he was trying to train the Karen people in basic medical skills. Meanwhile, he became intimately familiar with their hardships, including how the Karen men are regularly murdered and their women raped by soldiers. Since the book was published by Cambridge University Press, a publisher best known for its academic titles, some reviewers were confused to find that *True Love and Bartholomew*

is not a work of sociology or anthropology. As *Man* contributor Ananda Rajah concluded, it "is an anthropologically ambiguous contribution to Karen studies." *Journal of Southeast Asian Studies* writer Anthony R. Walker similarly felt that the odd mix of scholarship and personal impressions that imbue the work makes it "difficult to review," yet he declared it "a truly marvellous book; by any measure it is an extraordinarily good read."

In *Blue Poppies* and *Poor Mercy* Falla turns to fiction. *Blue Poppies,* which was originally intended for film, eventually morphed into a novel after the author failed to find financial backing for his screenplay. The story was inspired by Falla's reading about a radio operator named Robert Ford, who lived in Tibet just before the Chinese invasion in 1950. Ford becomes Jamie Wilson in Falla's novel, a Scotsman and World War II veteran who is sent to Tibet to monitor radio transmissions. He finds himself in the nearly medieval conditions of the village of Jyeko, where life has changed little in centuries. Jamie is both astonished by the beauty of Tibet and appalled by some of the conditions there. In particular, he is troubled by how the villagers treat a crippled woman named Puton and Puton's daughter. The villagers have concluded that Puton is bad luck, and have thus ostracized her, but when the monk Khenpo Nima charges Puton to be Jamie's domestic help, an unlikely romance begins to bloom. Soon, however, the Chinese invade, and the Tibetans react in a bloody rebellion during which the Chinese soldiers are killed. Realizing that they will pay dearly for their actions, the villagers flee their home, leaving Puton behind. Reviewers of *Blue Poppies* particularly praised the way in which Falla offers a balanced portrayal of both Tibetans and Chinese; both sides demonstrate acts of cruelty as well as courage and compassion. In addition, the author's detailed and vivid descriptions of Tibet rang true with reviewers. Julia Lovell, writing in the *Times Literary Supplement,* asserted that the book "is neither a paean to Tibetan resistance nor an anti-China polemic," attesting that *"Blue Poppies* is an engaging historical tale, intelligently and imaginatively told."

Although the war-torn and famine-stricken region of Sudan known as Darfur had been much in the news at the time Falla's second novel, *Poor Mercy,* was released in 2005, the author writes about a time years before Darfur made international headlines. Set in 1991, when Falla himself was there, the novel once again addresses the author's concern about the dilemma of international aid to Third World countries. Members of the fictional Action Agency are trying to decide how best to help the people in Darfur. The group's leader, Xavier Hopkins, knows that food shipments could stave off hunger, but it could also hurt the local markets, which would only serve to exacerbate the region's economic problems. Some levity is added to the desperate situation in the form of Mr. Mogga, an optimistic, inspiring, and sometimes comical figure whom London *Guardian* reviewer Michel Faber declared to be "a creation worthy of immortality." Despite some laudable aspects of the story, such as Mogga, Faber felt it is less successful than *Blue Poppies* because the plot is not as well constructed. "*Poor Mercy*," Faber concluded, "is more ambitious and more problematic." But the critic concluded that "what makes this book gripping is its pervasive air of authenticity." A *Times Literary Supplement* writer asserted that "*Poor Mercy* fulfils an important function, preserving a wretched moment in history, giving substance to events that would otherwise soon be forgotten in favour of the next humanitarian crisis."

BIOGRAPHICAL AND CRITICAL SOURCES:

PERIODICALS

Booklist, January 1, 2003, Kevin Canfield, review of *Blue Poppies,* p. 844.
Guardian (London, England), March 26, 2005, Michel Faber, "The Day of the Locust," review of *Poor Mercy,* p. 27; April 1, 2005, Claudia Pugh-Thomas, review of *Poor Mercy.*
Journal of Southeast Asian Studies, September, 1993, Anthony R. Walker, review of *True Love and Bartholomew: Rebels on the Burmese Border,* p. 401.
Man, March, 1994, Ananda Rajah, review of *True Love and Bartholomew,* p. 198.
New York Times, February 23, 1987, Walter Goodman, "The Stage: 'Topokana' at Nat Horne Theatre," p. C15.
Publishers Weekly, April 5, 1991, Genevieve Stuttaford, review of *True Love and Bartholomew,* p. 126; November 25, 2005, review of *Blue Poppies,* p. 40.
Times Literary Supplement, January 4, 2002, Julia Lovel, "Ping-Pong Diplomacy," review of *Blue Poppies,* p. 20.
Variety, February 20, 1985, review of *Topokana Martyrs' Day,* p. 84.

ONLINE

Author Zone, http://www.11-9.co.uk/authorzone/ (July 20, 2005), "Jonathan Falla."

*　　*　　*

FARRIS, Ann 1937-

PERSONAL: Born January 15, 1937, in Vancouver, British Columbia, Canada; daughter of John Lauchlan (a lawyer) and Dorothy Beatrice (a homemaker; maiden name, Colledge) Farris; married Robert Darling (a stage director and designer). *Education:* University of British Columbia, B.A., 1959; Yale University, M.F.A., 1963. *Hobbies and other interests:* Hiking, classical music and opera.

ADDRESSES: Home—132 Broderick St., San Francisco, CA 94117. *Office*—Dyslexia Discovery, P.O. Box 170036, San Francisco, CA 94117. *E-mail*—ann@dyslexiadiscovery.com.

CAREER: Writer. Producer and manager for opera companies and world expositions, 1963-86. Global Art and Business, New York, NY, and Fort Worth, TX, president, 1989-96; Robert Half International, San Francisco, CA, administrator-recruiter, 1997—. Teaches dyslexic students in San Francisco Bay area. Creator of DVD's.

AWARDS, HONORS: Professional Excellence Award, American Society of Training and Development; Alumni Seventy-fifth Anniversary Award, University of British Columbia.

WRITINGS:

The Other Side of Dyslexia, Dyslexia Discovery, 2004.
Dyslexia: Taking Control of Your Confusion (DVD), Dyslexia Discovery, 2004.

SIDELIGHTS: Ann Farris told *CA:* "I learned I was dyslexic when I was director of the Opera-Musical Theatre Program at the National Endowment for the Arts. Most counselors told me there was little I could do. In fact, they said, 'learn to live your disability.' However, I was determined to discover and change within myself whatever was necessary to improve my quality of life. And, I realized that goal.

"My exploration took me on physical, emotional, spiritual, and intellectual paths that were new for me. I discovered that my 'technical' reading skills were in fairly good shape. I sound out words without much difficulty—that skill was taught to me as a child. However, my poor concentration and retention along with physical pain and confusion was making my life miserable.

"I discovered that refined sugar was impacting negatively on my body and my ability to read. Therefore, I made the decision to eliminate it from my diet. I discovered that daily physical exercise as well as Brain Gym exercises are essential to stay grounded and read more easily. I decided to undertake emotional work and found that unexpressed anger and fear had a big impact on my inability to read.

"I focused on learning more about my senses, discovering I have the talent of synesthesia (ability to experience two or more senses simultaneously). However, this talent has the downside of causing confusion which can feel like the dyslexic confusion. Now I know the difference between the two and therefore can control it.

"Still, I was being overwhelmed at times by confusion and discovered that it is an energy/feeling in my body which can be harnessed. I am now in control of my discomfort; it is not in control of me. And, I have greater ability to both concentrate and retain information.

"Currently I am giving workshops for adult dyslexics in San Francisco. The first series of five classes focuses on the basic elements that I found to be essential in my transformation process, including color, diet considerations, physical exercises, mastering synesthetic confusion, grounding, and much more. For those who want to learn more and make changes in their lives, I run an ongoing class. I also offer an introductory class which runs about ninety minutes during which I provide an overview of the above. This class is interactive and usually there is spirited discussion. I have produced a DVD of this introductory class."

BIOGRAPHICAL AND CRITICAL SOURCES:

ONLINE

Ann Farris Home Page, http://www.dyslexiadiscovery. com (May 30, 2005).

*   *   *

FIREBAUGH, Glenn

PERSONAL: Male. *Education:* Grace College (IN), B.A., 1970; Indiana University, Bloomington, M.A., 1974, Ph.D., 1976.

ADDRESSES: Home—306 Lake Road, Centre Hall, PA 16828. *Office*—Pennsylvania State University, Department of Sociology, 206 Oswald Tower, University Park, PA 16802.

CAREER: Writer. Vanderbilt University, Nashville, TN, assistant professor, 1976-82, associate professor, 1982-88, director of graduate studies, 1986-88; Pennsylvania State University, University Park, professor, 1988-2004, sociology department head, 2001-04, liberal arts research professor, 2004—senior scientist in Population Research Institute, 1988—; University of Michigan ISR Summer Institute, visiting faculty, 1992-2001; Harvard University, visiting scholar, 2004-05. National Institute of Mental Health fellow in quantitative methods, 1972-76.

MEMBER: American Sociological Association, Sociological Research Association, Eastern Sociological Association.

AWARDS, HONORS: Alumnus of the Year, Grace College, 1995; Distinction in Social Sciences Award, Pennsylvania State University College of Liberal Arts, 2000; Best Article Prize, Cornell University Center for the Study of Inequality, 2001, for "Empirics of World Income Inequality"; Faculty Scholar Medal for Outstanding Achievement in the Social and Behavioral Sciences, Pennsylvania State University, 2001.

WRITINGS:

Analyzing Repeated Surveys, Sage (Thousand Oaks, CA), 1997.
The New Geography of Global Income Inequality, Harvard University Press (Cambridge, MA), 2003.

Contributor to books, including *Urbanization in the World Economy,* edited by Michael Timberlake, Academic Press (Orlando, FL), 1985; *Research in the Sociology of Work,* Volume 5, edited by Richard L. Simpson and Ida H. Simpson, JAI Press (Greenwich, CT), 1995; and *Studying Aging and Social Change: Conceptual and Methodological Issues,* edited by Melissa Hardy, Sage (Thousand Oaks, CA), 1997. Contributor of articles to scholarly journals, including *American Journal of Sociology, Studies in Comparative International Development, Sociological Methodology, American Sociological Review, Annual Review of Sociology, International Journal of Sociology and Social Policy, Sociological Focus, Journal for the Scientific Study of Religion, Criminology, Sociology and Social Research, Demography, International Studies Quarterly,* and *Social Forces.* Editor, *American Sociological Review,* 1997-99.

*   *   *

FLANDERS, John
See DE KREMER, Raymond Jean Marie

*   *   *

FORMAN, Gayle

PERSONAL: Married Nick Tucker (a librarian); children: Willa.

ADDRESSES: Home—New York, NY. *Agent*—c/o Author Mail, Rodale Press, 33 E. Minor St., Emmaus, PA 18098-0099. *E-mail*—info@gayleforman.com.

CAREER: Freelance journalist and author.

WRITINGS:

You Can't Get There from Here: A Year on the Fringes of a Shrinking World (travel memoir), Rodale Press (Emmaus, PA), 2005.

Contributor of articles to periodicals, including the *New York Times Magazine, Nation, Glamour, Elle, Details, Travel & Leisure, Jane,* and *Budget Travel. Seventeen* magazine, contributing editor.

SIDELIGHTS: A freelance journalist, Gayle Forman and her husband spent 2002 year traveling around the world, and the result of her voyages was the 2005 title *You Can't Get There from Here: A Year on the Fringes of a Shrinking World. Booklist* contributor Margaret Flanagan called the book a catalog of "offbeat locales and colorful experiences," as Forman searches for the "wacky, weird, and wonderful." Forman's travels took her from Africa to Central and East Asia and on to Europe, as she investigated destinations off the usual tourist route and met people who, like Forman views herself, are outsiders to society. For Lorraine Ali, writing in *Newsweek International,* Forman describes "travel through a secret . . . door."

Forman encountered plenty of eccentrics on her journeys: there were the J.R.R. Tolkien fans in the Central Asian republic of Kazakhstan performing Hobbit rituals, hip-hop devotees in Zanzibar, the madam of a sadomasochism parlor in Amsterdam, and many more. Along the way, Forman also doles out travel advice, such as the warning that travelers should be sure to take time away from their travel partners—Forman's own marriage gained stress fractures from the adventure. A reviewer for *Publishers Weekly* described Forman's book as "a richly woven narrative" that focuses on either an individual or a group from each locale. The same reviewer went on to dub Forman's recounted travels as "smart, well-written tales." A critic for *Kirkus Reviews* had a more mixed appraisal of *You Can't Get There from Here,* noting the lack of an overarching theme to connect her vignettes and the occasional slip in fact-checking. As the same contributor concluded, "Forman writes breezily and pleasantly, though some of her set pieces go on too long" and lose their momentum. Alison Hopkins, writing in *Library Journal,* had higher praise, calling Forman's year-long voyage a "fascinating adventure" that in *You Can't Get There from Here* is "packaged in a personal, engrossing description."

BIOGRAPHICAL AND CRITICAL SOURCES:

BOOKS

Forman, Gayle, *You Can't Get There from Here: A Year on the Fringes of a Shrinking World,* Rodale Press (Emmaus, PA), 2005.

PERIODICALS

Booklist, February 15, 2005, Margaret Flanagan, review of *You Can't Get There from Here,* p. 1053.

Kirkus Reviews, January 15, 2005, review of *You Can't Get There from Here,* p. 99.

Library Journal, February 1, 2005, Alison Hopkins, review of *You Can't Get There from Here,* p. 106.

Newsweek International, May 9, 2005, Lorraine Ali, review of *You Can't Get There from Here,* p. 57.

Publishers Weekly, February 7, 2005, review of *You Can't Get There from Here,* p. 50.

ONLINE

Court TV Web site, http://www.courttv.com/ (June 11, 2001), "Chat with Gayle Forman."

Gayle Forman Home Page, http://www.gayleforman.com (July 7, 2005).*

* * *

FOUSE, Gary C. 1945-

PERSONAL: Born July 25, 1945, in Los Angeles, CA; son of Orville K. (a film executive) and Jean C. (a homemaker) Fouse; married Maria del Socorro Fouse (a homemaker), March 22, 1975: children: Gabriella T., David. *Education:* California State University, Los Angeles, B.S., 1970; University of Virginia, M.Ed., 1993. *Politics:* "Independent." *Religion:* Protestant. *Hobbies and other interests:* Languages.

ADDRESSES: Home—25022 Paseo Cipres, Lake Forest, CA 92630. *E-mail*—gfouse@peoplepc.com.

CAREER: Writer. U.S. Customs Agency Service, Los Angeles, CA, special agent, 1970-73; U.S. Department of Justice, Drug Enforcement Agency, special agent, 1973-95; Northern Virginia Community College, Annandale, adjunct lecturer in English as a second language (ESL), 1995-98; University of California, Irvine, adjunct lecturer in ESL, 1998—. Virginia Department of Adult Education, Fairfax County, volunteer teaching assistant, 1992-94. *Military service:* U.S. Army Military Police Corps, 1966-68; specialist fourth class stationed in Germany.

MEMBER: Association for the Study of Nationalities of Eastern Europe and Ex-USSR, Teachers of English to Speakers of Other Languages.

WRITINGS:

The Languages of the Former Soviet Republics: Their History and Development, University Press of America (Lanham, MD), 2000.

The Story of Papiamentu: A Study in Slavery and Language, University Press of America (Lanham, MD), 2002.

Erlangen: An American's History of a German Town, University Press of America (Lanham, MD) 2004.

* * *

FRATTINI, Alberto 1922-

PERSONAL: Born March 29, 1922, in Florence, Italy; married; wife's name, Lea. *Education:* University of Rome, degree in modern languages, 1945, degree in philosophy, 1946.

ADDRESSES: Agent—c/o Author Mail, Instituti Editoriali e Poligrafici Internazionali, via Carducci, 60, 56010, Ghezzano, Italy.

WRITINGS:

EDITOR

Giacomo Leopardi, *Canti,* Scuola (Brescia, Italy), 1960.

(With Pasquale Tuscano) *Poeti italiani del XX secolo,* Scuola (Brescia, Italy), 1974.

Poesie e tragedie di Alessandro Manzoni, Scuola (Brescia, Italy), 1981.

(With Marcella Uffreduzzi) *Poeti a Roma: 1945-1980,* Bonacci (Rome, Italy), 1983.

(With Franco Manescalchi) *Poeti della Toscana,* Forum/Quinta Generazione (Forli, Italy), 1985.

Giacomo Leopardi: il problema delle "fonti" alla radice della sua opera, Coletti (Rome, Italy), 1990.

Le problematiche dell'espressione e della comunicazione in prospettiva duemila, Studium (Rome, Italy), 1990.

Clemente Rebora, *Ritratto, antologìa degli scritti, profilo antològico della crìtica,* M. Boni (Bologna, Italy), 1994.

OTHER

Il problema dell'esistenza in Leopardi (criticism), Gastaldi (Milan, Italy), 1950.

Giorni e sogni, Pagine Nuove (Rome, Italy), 1950.

Leopardi e Rousseau (criticism), Pagine Nuove (Rome, Italy), 1951.

Poeti italiani del novecento (criticism), Accademia (Alcamo, Italy), 1953.

Fioraia bambina, Canzoniere (Rome, Italy), 1953.

Speranza e destino (poems; title means "Hope and Destiny"), Canzoniere (Rome, Italy), 1954.

La poesia della redenzione nel Tommaseo (criticism), Accademia (Alcamo, Italy), 1955.

Il canto XXXIII dell'inferno (criticism), Accademia (Alcamo, Italy), 1955.

Studi sulla poesia italiana del dopoguerra (criticism), Accademia (Alcamo, Italy), 1955.

Studi Leopardiani (criticism), Nistri-Lischi (Pisa, Italy), 1956.

Come acqua alpina (poetry; title means "Like Alpine Water"), Accademia (Alcamo, Italy), 1956.

Critici contemporanei (criticism), Gismondi (Rome, Italy), 1957.

La poesia e il tempo, Hermes (Rome, Italy), 1957.

Critica e fortuna dei "Canti" di G. Leopardi (criticism), Scuola (Brescia, Italy), 1957.

Cultura e pensiero in Leopardi (criticism), Ausonia (Rome, Italy), 1958.

Latomie (poems; title means "State Prisons"), Vallecchi (Florence, Italy), 1958.

Da Tommaseo a Ungaretti, Cappelli (Bologna, Italy), 1959.

Il canto XXVIII del Paradiso (criticism), S.E.I. (Turin, Italy), 1960.

Il canto XXVII del Purgatorio (criticism), Le Monnier (Florence, Italy), 1963.

La giovane poesia italiana, Nistri-Lischi (Pisa, Italy), 1964.

Il neoclassicismo e Ugo Foscolo (criticism), Cappelli (Bologna, Italy), 1965.

Salute nel miraggio (poems; title means "Health in the Mirage"), Storia e Letteratura (Rome, Italy), 1965.

Poeti e critici italiani dell'Otto e del Novecento (criticism), Marzorati (Milan, Italy), 1966.

Poeti italiani tra il primo e secondo Novecento (criticism), IPL (Milan, Italy), 1967.

Poesia nuova in Italia: Tra ermetismo e neoavanguardia (criticism), IPL (Milan, Italy), 1968.

Giacomo Leopardi (criticism), Cappelli (Bologna, Italy), 1969, revised edition, Studium (Rome, Italy), 1986.

Dai crepuscolari ai Novissimi, Marzorati (Milan, Italy), 1969.

Tra il nulla e l'amore (poem; title means "Between Nothingness and Love"), Società Edizioni Nuove (Rome, Italy), 1969.

Scoperta di paesi, IPL (Milan, Italy), 1969.

Studi di poesia e di critica (criticism), Marzorati (Milan, Italy), 1972.

Critica, strutture, stile, IPL (Milan, Italy), 1977.

Caro atomo (poetry; title means "Dear Atom"), Locusta (Venice, Italy), 1977.

Letteratura e scienza in Leopardi (criticism), Marzorati (Milan, Italy), 1978.

Il vento e le gemme (poems; title means "The Wind and the Jewels"), Piazza Navona (Rome, Italy), 1981.

La sfida nel labirinto (poems; title means "The Challenge within the Labyrinth"), Rebellato (Padua, Italy), 1982.

Poesia e regione in Italia, IPL (Milan, Italy), 1983.

Introduzione a Giorgio Vigolo (criticism), Marzorati (Milan, Italy), 1984.

Il sogno della morte (poems; title means "The Dream of Death"), Piovan (Padua, Italy), 1986.

Stupendo enigma (poems), IPL (Milan, Italy), 1988.

Giacomo Leopardi: Una lettura infinita, IPL (Milan, Italy), 1989.

Leopardi e noi, Studium (Rome, Italy), 1990.

Arcana spirale: poesie, 1943-1992, Sciascia (Caltanissetta), 1994.

Leopardi alle soglie dell'Infinito e altri saggi leopardiani, Instituti Editoriali e Poligrafici Internazionali (Pisa, Italy), 1998.

Avventure di Parnaso nell'Italia del Novecento (collected essays), M. Baroni (Viarregio, Italy), 2002.

Contributor of poetry and articles to periodicals, including *Cultura-e-Scuola* and *Riscontri.*

SIDELIGHTS: The works of Italian poet Alberto Frattini incorporate "clear references to metaphysical as well as phenomenological and existentialist elements that unite individuals in a common humanity," according to Pietro Pelosi in a *Dictionary of Literary Biography* essay. The seeming influence of the neorealistic school in works such by Frattini as *Come acqua alpina* and *Latomie* comes more from his avoidance of rococo rhetorical flourishes and overly dramatic language than it does from the ideology behind his poems. In fact, his writings are rooted in feeling and cognition. "The importance of Frattini's poetry," said

Pelosi, "lies precisely in the profoundly felt adherence of thought and sentiment to language; the result is limpid lyrics that exclude experimentalism in order to articulate his dignity and mission, even in verses that denounce the pain of living."

Spirituality has been important to Frattini since he began writing poetry in the mid-1950s. The scion of a prominent Italian family, he began penning verse at age six. His talents, Pelosi noted, were carefully and discreetly nurtured by his parents, both of whom had keen aesthetic and moral beliefs. According to Pelosi, Frattini was also influenced in his early years by his mother's cousin, Ernesto Buonaiuti, "a much-discussed figure in his day and the proponent of a renewed Christianity based on its old roots. Frattini attended many of Buonaiuti's lectures, which dealt with the interrelationship of poetry, thought, and culture." Frattini's own adherence to Christian spirituality in his works comes in part from Buonaiuti's influence, and in part, said Pelosi, from his relationship with his wife Lea, who "belonged to a Catholic cultural milieu and had written her doctoral thesis on Christian inscriptions."

"Like all genuine art," Pelosi added, "Frattini's poetry is the product of its time while transcending it, because his vision of time is an ethical and universal one." In collections such as *Speranza e destino, Come acqua alpina, Salute nel miraggio, Tra il nulla e l'amore, La sfida nel labirinto,* and *Stupendo enigma,* the poet combines a strong anthropocentrism with an equally powerful sense of spirituality. In *Come acqua alpina,* images of internal and external landscapes combine to form a reflection of the writer himself—reminiscent, observed Pelosi, of the medieval "Great Book of Nature," in which scholars hoped to come to a complete understanding of God. In "Anche se non puoi salpare," a poem included in the collection *La sfida nel labirinto,* the poet argues that knowledge often comes with a sense of arrogance, and that true wisdom is gained by accepting the absurd and the ridiculous. Even in *Stupendo enigma,* a collection in which, according to Pelosi, "the forms of daily life fade into more metaphysical reflections," the poet comes closer to God through encounters with the natural world. In general, Frattini sees human experiences and emotions in the natural world as symbols of the soul's instinctive drive toward God as well as "toward the external world and other human beings," Pelosi declared, and this same instinctive drive, brought about through encounters with the natural world, leads to "an act of communion with all of creation."

BIOGRAPHICAL AND CRITICAL SOURCES:

BOOKS

Dictionary of Literary Biography, Volume 128: *Twentieth-Century Italian Poets, Second Series,* Thomson Gale (Detroit, MI), 1993.

PERIODICALS

Fuoco, Volume 2, 1982, Raffaele Pellecchia, "La dificile speranza nella poesia di Alberto Frattini," pp. 16-26.
Humanitas, June, 1990, pp. 281-302.
Silarus, May, 2000, pp. 133-134.
Studium, Volume 70, 1974, Ferruccio Mazzariol, "Recente e ultima poesai di Alberto Frattini," pp. 278-283.*

*   *   *

FREND, W.H.C. 1916-2005
(William Hugh Clifford Frend)

OBITUARY NOTICE— See index for *CA* sketch: Born January 11, 1916, in Shottermill, Surrey, England; died August 1, 2005, in Cambridge, England. Priest, historian, archaeologist, educator, and author. Frend was a noted scholar of the early Christian church and his work is unique in its emphasis on history and archaeology over theology and written texts. After graduating from Keble College, Oxford, in 1937, he earned a doctorate there three years later. Upon joining the British War Office in 1940, he spent World War II working in Intelligence for the Foreign Office, and earned a Gold Cross of Merit with Swords while in North Africa. His time in North Africa and Yugoslavia piqued his interest in those regions as they pertained to early church history. After the war, Frend remained an officer in the Territorial Army through 1967 while also pursuing an academic career. First, however, he spent four years in Germany working for the Foreign Ministry there and editing its documents. Frend then joined the University of Nottingham as a research fellow for a year, moving on to Gonville and Caius College, Cambridge, in 1952. At Cambridge he became a fellow and was university lecturer in divinity from 1956 to 1969. While at Gonville and Caius, he also was university proctor in the late 1950s and dean of divinity from 1972 to 1975. He taught at the University of Glasgow from 1969 to 1984, where he was professor of ecclesiastical history and chair of the department. Despite his appointments in theology posts, however, Frend did not become an ordained priest until 1983. After his ordination, he served as priest-in-charge of the Barnwell Group of Parishes in Peterborough until 1990, after which he was honorary assistant priest for Little Wilbraham. He also edited the journal *Modern Churchman* from 1964 to 1983. Always a pragmatist, Frend wrote books on early church history distinguished by their reliance on hard archaeological evidence. Among his works are *The Donatist Church* (1952; 3rd edition, 1985), *The Early Church* (1965), *The Rise of Christianity* (1983), *The Archaeology of Early Christianity: A History* (1996), and *Orthodoxy, Paganism, and Dissent in Early Christianity: From Dogma to History* (2003).

OBITUARIES AND OTHER SOURCES:

PERIODICALS

Daily Telegraph (London, England), August 11, 2005.
Independent (London, England), August 19, 2005, p. 48.
Times (London, England), August 24, 2005, p. 60.

ONLINE

Church Times Online, http://www.churchtimes.co.uk/ (August 19, 2005).

*   *   *

FREND, William Hugh Clifford
See FREND, W.H.C.

*   *   *

FREY, James 1969-

PERSONAL: Born 1969; married; wife's name, Maya (an advertising executive); children: one daughter. *Education:* Attended Denison University.

ADDRESSES: Home—New York, NY. *Agent*—c/o Author Mail, Penguin Group, c/o Riverhead Books Publicity, 375 Hudson St., New York, NY 10014.

CAREER: Writer. Worked variously as a camp counselor, bouncer, film director, skateboard salesman, picture-framer, film producer, busboy, hotel security guard, and as costumed characters such as Santa Claus and the Easter bunny in department-store promotions.

AWARDS, HONORS: Hermosa Beach Film Festival, best film (director), 1998, and No Dance Film Festival, best director, 1999, both for *Sugar: The Fall of the West.*

WRITINGS:

A Million Little Pieces, N.A. Talese/Doubleday (New York, NY), 2003.
My Friend Leonard, Riverhead Books (New York, NY), 2005.
Kissing a Fool (screenplay), MCA/Universal Pictures, 1998.
Sugar: The Fall of the West (screenplay), Next Generation, 1998.

SIDELIGHTS: James Frey became a public figure in early 2006 when it was revealed that his memoir of addiction and recovery, titled *A Million Little Pieces,* is mostly fictionalized. Frey has more recently published another purported memoir, titled *My Friend Leonard.*

A Million Little Pieces introduces twenty-three-year-old Frey, who has been an alcoholic for ten years and a crack addict for three. He awakens on a plane, not knowing where he has come from or where he is going, covered in a mixture of leaked and expelled bodily fluids, missing four front teeth and bearing a broken nose and a nickel-sized hole through his cheek. He is completely bereft of hope, physically and mentally, worn to his lowest possible point by his multiple and converging addictions. He shortly finds out that his battered state was due to a face-first fall down a fire escape, and that he is on a plane to meet with his parents in Chicago, who plan to immediately put him into rehab in a rural Minnesota facility since identified as Hazelden. The bulk of the book describes in raw detail the exhausting, soul-wrenching work of kicking a half-lifetime's worth of destructive habits and physical addictions. "Frey's lacerating, intimate debut chronicles his recovery from multiple addictions with adrenal rage and sprawling prose," commented a *Kirkus Reviews* critic.

Frey's approach to his recovery immediately puts him at odds with the staff of Hazelden. He refuses to commit to the required twelve-step program, declines to surrender an iota of his life to any higher power, and declares that he will beat his addictions on his own terms and in his own way. He takes full responsibility for the condition he is in and for the person that may emerge after treatment. He refuses to see his addiction as a disease. "What sets *Pieces* apart from other memoirs about twelve-stepping is Frey's resistance to the concept of a higher power," commented a *Publishers Weekly* reviewer.

He also describes the many characters he meets during treatment, including Leonard, an affable mobster; Lily, a heroin-addicted ex-prostitute with whom he falls in love; and a variety of other lost and abandoned people who forge deep friendships in the crucible of treatment that will lead to lives changed by recovery or doomed by addictions that cannot be overcome. "Frey discovers that, aside from being some of the most tormented souls on the planet, these are the nicest people he's ever met; together, they shakily plumb the depths," observed *Spectator* contributor William Leith.

"Starkly honest and mincing no words, Frey bravely faces his struggles head on, and readers will be mesmerized by his account of his ceaseless battle against addiction," commented Kristine Huntley, writing in *Booklist*. "What really separates this title from other rehab memoirs, apart from the author's young age, is his literary prowess," observed *School Library Journal* reviewer Jamie Watson. *Library Journal* contributor Rachel Collins commented that "this raw and intense book reveals a rare author whose approach to memoir writing is as original as his method to getting straight." Jennifer Reese, writing in *Entertainment Weekly*, noted that "All the ferocious energy and will Frey once devoted to self-destruction he turned toward fixing himself. Frey's prose is muscular and tough, ideal for conveying extreme physical anguish and steely determination" to succeed. A *Publishers Weekly* reviewer called the book "a remarkable memoir of addiction and recovery." Louis Bayard, writing on the

Salon.com Web site, stated that "if this bullheaded, lionhearted book doesn't reach the level of masterpiece, it's not for lack of trying. Frey has devised a rolling, pulsing style that really *moves*—an acquired taste, perhaps, but undeniably striking."

In *My Friend Leonard*, Frey resumes his "memoir" as he gains sobriety and leaves treatment. The book begins with him in jail, serving his time for offenses committed while he was in the grip of his multiple addictions. When he is released, he heads to Chicago to see Lily, but learns that she has committed suicide only hours before. Torn with grief, Frey once again finds himself teetering on the edge of the abyss. However, before he can descend, he renews his friendship with avuncular mobster Leonard, who offers him financial support and the occasional simple odd job, usually courier work, which is quite probably illegal. The memoir dwells on Frey's relationship with Leonard and the contradictory elements of his friend's life of crime and stoic dedication to his friends. Leonard teaches Frey that addictive substances are not the answer to any problem, and that enjoying life and its simple pleasures is its own best reward. Though there are still tragedies to endure, with Leonard's support, financial assistance, and genuine affection, Frey manages to maintain the discipline of his recovery and avoid any relapses into addiction.

"Frey's extraordinary relationship with Leonard is alive, a flesh-and-blood bond forged in the agony of rehab and sustained through honesty and trust," commented a writer in *Publishers Weekly*. "As smart as it is heartfelt, this tribute to friendship is a far sunnier book than Frey's debut," remarked *Newsweek* reviewer Malcolm Jones. A *Kirkus Reviews* contributor called the book "a fine, grim tale, full of smarting immediacy, with stylistic tics—repetitions, an aversion to commas, run-ons—that skip close to the irritating but lend a musicality and remind the reader to pay attention."

In 2006 a *Smoking Gun* report claimed that parts of Frey's memoir *A Million Little Pieces* were fabricated. Although Frey did not immediately confirm the allegations, the book's publisher, Doubleday, offered refunds to its direct customers. While talk-show host Oprah Winfrey, who had chosen *A Million Little Pieces* for her popular book club, at first defended the overall message of the memoir as valuable despite any embellishments, evidence soon mounted as to the extent of the fabrications. Doubleday reported that new copies of Frey's memoir would contain a note with an explanation of the controversy and an apology; the note was also posted on the Random House Web site. In addition, Frey's literary manager announced that she would no longer represent the writer. Ultimately, Winfrey apologized to viewers of her talk show, *Oprah*, for initially defending Frey's purported memoir. She then invited the now-notorious writer to appear on her nationally televised program. Under Winfrey's grilling Frey admitted that his memoir was almost wholly fiction and his book was officially removed from the Oprah Book Club. Ironically, sales of *A Million Little Pieces* soared shortly thereafter.

BIOGRAPHICAL AND CRITICAL SOURCES:

BOOKS

Frey, James, *A Million Little Pieces,* N.A. Talese/ Doubleday (New York, NY), 2003.
Frey, James, *My Friend Leonard,* Riverhead Books (New York, NY), 2005.

PERIODICALS

Booklist, April 15, 2003, Kristine Huntley, review of *A Million Little Pieces,* p. 1432.
Entertainment Weekly, April 4, 2003, Karen Valby, "James Frey Does Not Care What You Think about Him (Please Love Him)," p. 60; April 25, 2003, Jennifer Reese, review of *A Million Little Pieces,* p. 152; June 17, 2005, Thom Geier, review of *My Friend Leonard,* p. 86.
Kirkus Reviews, February 1, 2003, review of *A Million Little Pieces,* p. 204; May 1, 2005, review of *My Friend Leonard,* p. 523.

Library Journal, March 1, 2003, Rachel Collins, review of *A Million Little Pieces,* p. 106; April 15, 2005, Dale Raben, review of *My Friend Leonard,* p. 99.
Miami Herald, June 29, 2005, Andy Diaz, "In His Latest Memoir, James Frey Can't Make the Reader Care Whether He's Drunk or Sober," review of *My Friend Leonard.*
New Statesman, May 26, 2003, Julian Keeling, "The Yellow Gloom of Sleepless Nights," review of *A Million Little Pieces,* p. 52.
Newsweek, June 27, 2005, Malcolm Jones, "Friends in Low Places," review of *My Friend Leonard,* p. 65.
People, June 27, 2005, "Great Reads," review of *My Friend Leonard,* p. 47.
Publishers Weekly, February 24, 2003, Charlotte Abbott, "One in a Million," review of *A Million Little Pieces,* p. 17; March 10, 2003, review of *A Million Little Pieces,* p. 67; March 28, 2005, review of *My Friend Leonard,* p. 64.
School Library Journal, August, 2003, Jamie Watson, review of *A Million Little Pieces,* p. 188.
Smoking Gun, January 8, 2006, "The Man Who Conned Oprah."
Spectator, May 24, 2003, William Leith, "Plumbing the Lower Depths," review of *A Million Little Pieces,* p. 40.

ONLINE

CNN.com, http://www.cnn.com/ (January 12, 2006), "Some 'Pieces' Buyers Offered Refund"; "Winfrey Stands behind 'Pieces' Author."
Salon.com, http://www.salon.com/ (April 19, 2003), Louis Bayard, "The Sound Bite and the Fury," profile of James Frey.*

G

GAGE, Eleni N. 1974-

PERSONAL: Born October 8, 1974, in New York, NY; daughter of Nicholas Gage (a writer). *Education:* Harvard College, B.A., 1996.

ADDRESSES: Agent—Andy McNicol, William Morris Agency, 1325 Avenue of the Americas New York, NY 10019. *E-mail*—Eleni_gage@yahoo.com.

CAREER: Worked for magazines *Allure* and *Elle,* New York, NY; *InStyle,* New York, NY, contributing editor; freelance writer, 2001—; *People* magazine, beauty editor, 2004—.

WRITINGS:

North of Ithaka: A Journey Home through a Family's Extraordinary Past (memoir), St. Martin's Press (New York, NY), 2005.

Also contributor to *Travel & Leisure, Real Simple, American Scholar, New York Times,* and other journals.

Author's work has been translated into Dutch and Greek.

SIDELIGHTS: Eleni N. Gage is the author of *North of Ithaka: A Journey Home through a Family's Extraordinary Past.* The book is connected to *Eleni,* a book written by Gage's father, Nicholas Gage, that tells the story of Gage's grandmother and namesake. Gage's grandmother was able to send her children out of war-torn Greece during the late 1940s, but was herself betrayed by neighbors and killed by the Communist insurgents who occupied her village. Nicholas Gage reconstructed his mother's life and death in *Eleni,* and Gage, who eventually rebuilt her Grandmother Eleni's house, chronicles her own effort to reclaim her family history in *North of Ithaka.*

When Gage announced her intention of returning to the village of Lia, the scene of her family's tragedy, her aunts were deeply disturbed and fearful. They even told her she would be eaten by wolves or killed by Albanians. Gage was determined to rebuild the ancestral home, "both a metaphor for and a means by which the family's emotional wounds begin to heal," in the words of *Library Journal* contributor Sheila Kasperek. At the same time, she reconnected with her family's homeland, discovering a Greece rarely seen by tourists. As Gage put it on her Web site, "I spent 10 months going to gypsy weddings, presiding over rooster sacrifices, learning how to cook Dishrag Pie, and combating road rage." In addition to participating in the many religious festivals of the devoutly Orthodox villagers, she also learned about the older Greece that still believes in signs and omens and family curses. Her rebuilding project also brought her into intimate contact with the frustrations of Greek bureaucracy, but she was able to complete the project with the help of neighbors, including some of those Albanians so feared by her aunts. From those neighbors she also heard tales of her grandmother and the terrible events of the past, as well as pointed questions about why she was still unmarried at the ripe old age of twenty-seven.

About Gage's combination of family saga and innocent abroad memoir, a *Kirkus Reviews* writer observed that "her narrative is a curiously lackadaisical mixture of American earnestness and superficiality." A *Publishers Weekly* reviewer found Gage's account "occasionally maudlin, but the scope of her rebuilding effort is Herculean enough to keep readers turning pages to see the finished product for themselves." In a more favorable assessment, *Wall Street Journal* contributor Pia Catton said that "Gage writes of her adventures in pleasantly honest, often amusing, prose. As an earnest 27-year-old, she treats tradition with respect and history with steady realism." Writing in the London *Observer,* Carl Wilkinson added: "Refreshingly, Gage doesn't opt for the obvious city-girl meets village folk humour for long, but mucks in with village life and instead . . . unearths a more interesting saga of immigration, belonging and community."

Gage told *CA:* "As a child, I had no interest in becoming an author; it was what my parents did and therefore inherently unpalatable. I thought it would be more fun to run a bookstore or lingerie shop or to name lipsticks or nail polishes. But in college, I began writing ethnographies for my folklore and mythology classes, and articles for the weekly lifestyle magazine of the *Harvard Crimson.* I enjoyed these experiences so much that I decided to pursue a career in journalism, and moved to New York four days after graduation to begin my first job as an editorial assistant at *Allure* magazine. My writing process involves taking copious notes, writing something heinous and unwieldy, and then whittling it down to more easily digested morsel."

"The most surprising thing I have learned as a writer is that even if you are writing about your own life, sometimes people will read their own experiences in the story. I find that very gratifying when it happens."

"I hope readers will find my books informative, enjoyable, and thought-provoking. But I'll be happy just to have them find the books at all."

BIOGRAPHICAL AND CRITICAL SOURCES:

BOOKS

Gage, Eleni N., *North of Ithaka: A Journey Home through a Family's Extraordinary Past,* St. Martin's Press (New York, NY), 2005.

PERIODICALS

Kirkus Reviews, March 1, 2005, review of *North of Ithaka,* p. 273.
Library Journal, April 1, 2005, Sheila Kasperek, review of *North of Ithaka,* p. 103.
Observer (London, England), July 4, 2004, Carl Wilkinson, review of *North of Ithaka.*
Parade, August 4, 2004, review of *North of Ithaka.*
Publishers Weekly, April 4, 2005, review of *North of Ithaka,* p. 53.
Sunday Times (London, England), July 24, 2005, review of *North of Ithaka.*
Travel & Leisure, May, 2005, Amy Farley, "T&L Reports: Greek Revival."
Wall Street Journal, May 20, 2005, Pia Catton, review of *North of Ithaka,* p. W10.
Washington Times, August 7, 2004, review of *North of Ithaka.*

ONLINE

Eleni Gage Home Page http://elenigage.com (July 7, 2005).

*   *   *

GAINES, James R. 1947-

PERSONAL: Born August 11, 1947, in Dayton, OH; married Leslie Friedman, May 23, 1971 (divorced, 1978); married Pamela Butler, July 19, 1983 (divorced, 1989); married Karen Lipton, February 9, 1992; children: (first marriage) Allison, (third marriage) Nicholas, William, Lillian. *Education:* University of Michigan, B.A., 1970.

ADDRESSES: Home—Paris, France. *Agent*—c/o Author Mail, Fourth Estate, 77-85 Fulham Palace Road, Hammersmith, London W6 8JB, England.

CAREER: Journalist. *Herald,* New York, NY, editor, 1971-72; *Saturday Review,* New York, NY, San Francisco, CA, associate editor, 1972-73; WNET-13, *51st State,* New York, NY, associate editor, 1973-74; *Newsweek,* New York, NY, associate editor, 1974-76; *People,* New York, NY, associate editor, 1977-78, senior editor, 1979-82, assistant managing editor, 1982-86, executive editor, 1986-87; managing editor, 1987-89; *Life,* New York, NY, managing editor and publisher, 1989-92; *Time,* New York, NY, managing editor, 1993-95; Time Inc., New York, NY, corporate editor, 1996-97; *Travel & Leisure,* Boulder, CO, editor-in-chief, 1998.

WRITINGS:

NONFICTION

Wit's End: Days and Nights of the Algonquin Round Table, Harcourt Brace Jovanovich (New York, NY), 1977.

(Editor) *The Lives of the Piano,* Holt, Rinehart and Winston (New York, NY), 1981.

Evening in the Palace of Reason: Bach Meets Frederick the Great in the Age of Enlightenment, Fourth Estate (London, England), 2005.

SIDELIGHTS: James R. Gaines is a former editor at *People, Time,* and *Life,* as well as the author of several nonfiction books. An amateur musician, Gaines published a book on music, *The Lives of the Piano,* in 1981. An earlier work, *Wit's End: Days and Nights of the Algonquin Round Table,* was an experiment in cultural history, dealing with the intellectuals, artists, writers, and comedians who were regulars at New York City's Algonquin Hotel during the early part of the twentieth century. With his 2005 title, *Evening in the Palace of Reason: Bach Meets Frederick the Great in the Age of Enlightenment,* Gaines blends these two strands to present "an absorbing cultural history," according to a reviewer for *Publishers Weekly.*

Evening in the Palace of Reason describes the ten days in 1747 that the baroque composer Johann Sebastian Bach spent at the court of Frederick the Great in Potsdam, Prussia, there to be tested in the art of counterpoint and fugue by the much-younger royal. This well-recorded historical event is one of the few instances in Bach's life to be copiously written down; much of the rest of the composer's life is shrouded in mystery, for he kept no diaries, sent few letters, and was recognized as a great composer only long after his death. Gaines uses this meeting between polar opposites to contrast two worldviews: that of the pious, Lutheran Bach and Frederick, a champion of the Age

of Reason and the Enlightenment. That Bach created one of his masterpieces, *The Musical Offering,* as a result of this testing is, for Gaines, a victory for faith over critical reason. Thus, this personal gamesmanship becomes a metaphor for differing worldviews, and Gaines spends much of his book detailing the lives of both Bach and the Prussian king, in addition to delving into musical technique.

The two men could hardly have been more different from one another. Bach, aged sixty-two at the time of their meeting, was the father of twenty children, a devout Lutheran, and humble composer; Frederick, aged thirty-five, had been abused by his authoritarian father but had also been an avid musician since his youth. A king not afraid to take his people to war, Frederick was enjoying a time of peace in 1747, and his court was the center of Enlightenment culture; Frederick himself was a devotee of French writer Voltaire.

Gaines's work brought differing views from critics. A contributor for *Kirkus Reviews* found it "an ambitious, if not entirely successful, synthesis," as well as "dazzling but somewhat fractured," but also conceded that this history was "composed with a refreshingly non-scholarly flourish." John Leonard, writing in *Harper's,* also was divided in his assessment of *Evening in the Palace of Reason..* Likening Gaines's book to "an Italian opera crossed with a medieval morality play," Leonard took issue with Gaines's negative assessment of the supposed "skeptical excesses of the Age of Reason," calling such a critique "the latest in anti-rationalist, original-sinful yadda yadda." *Time* reviewer Christopher Porterfield also had mixed feelings about the book, noting that "much of the material is dauntingly complex, but Gaines works hard to keep his prose accessible and entertaining—sometimes too hard."

Other reviewers had less-qualified praise for *Evening in the Palace of Reason.* Bich Minh Nguyen, writing in *People,* called it a "moving portrait of genius and human failure," while Scott D. Paulin of *Entertainment Weekly* felt Gaines "maps sweeping cultural history . . . with dazzling virtuosity." *Booklist* critic Gilbert Taylor called the book a "marvelous story" and further commented that it is "clever without being frivolous, and explanatory without being effete." Similarly, Larry Lipkis, writing in *Library Journal,* concluded that Gaines's book was "an enormous pleasure."

BIOGRAPHICAL AND CRITICAL SOURCES:

PERIODICALS

Booklist, March 1, 2005, Gilbert Taylor, review of *Evening in the Palace of Reason: Bach Meets Frederick the Great in the Age of Enlightenment,* p. 1127.
Entertainment Weekly, January 10, 1997, James W. Seymore, Jr., "Gaines and a Loss," p. 5; March 18, 2005, Scott D. Paulin, review of *Evening in the Palace of Reason,* p. 74.
Harper's, April, 2005, John Leonard, review of *Evening in the Palace of Reason,* p. 85.
Kirkus Reviews, January 1, 2005, review of *Evening in the Palace of Reason,* p. 33.
Library Journal, February 1, 2005, Larry Lipkis, review of *Evening in the Palace of Reason,* p. 80.
People, March 28, 2005, Bich Minh Nguyen, review of *Evening in the Palace of Reason,* p. 50.
Publishers Weekly, February 7, 2005, review of *Evening in the Palace of Reason,* p. 53.
Reviewer's Bookwatch, November, 2004, Medb, review of *Evening in the Palace of Reason.*
Spectator, January 8, 2005, Julian Shuckburgh, "King's Gambit Accepted," review of *Evening in the Palace of Reason,* p. 32.
Time, January 8, 1996, Norman Pearlstine, "To Our Readers," p. 16; March 14, 2005, Christopher Porterfield, "Duel at the Tipping Point," review of *Evening in the Palace of Reason,* p. 62.*

*   *   *

GALLOWAY, Gregory 1962(?)-

PERSONAL: Born c. 1962, in Keokuk, IA; married. *Education:* University of Iowa, B.A., 1984, M.A., 1986, Iowa Writers' Workshop, M.F.A., 1989.

ADDRESSES: Home—Hoboken, NJ. *Agent*—c/o Author Mail, Putnam Publicity, Penguin Group, 375 Hudson St., New York, NY 10014.

CAREER: Author. Worked in publishing, marketing, and Internet consulting.

WRITINGS:

As Simple as Snow (novel), Putnam (New York, NY), 2005.

Contributor of poems and short stories to periodicals, including *Iowa Review, McSweeney's,* and *Rush Hour.*

SIDELIGHTS: First-time novelist Gregory Galloway reprised an old form—the whodunit—with his 2005 novel *As Simple as Snow.* Despite its title, Galloway's novel is anything but simple, according to Starr E. Smith in *School Library Journal.* As Smith wrote, "this clever first novel enmeshes its characters in" complexities that become evident only over time. The book's narrator, a high school boy living in a sleepy town, suddenly tunes in to his reality after Anna, the new girl in school, becomes part of the school's Goth clique. Immediately attracted to her, the boy is also mystified; the sophisticated Anna seems to hide bruises and is a devotee of Harry Houdini; a fan of codes and ciphers, she is also a lover of wordplay. Her major hobby, besides reading the works of French poet Rimbaud, is penning fictional obituaries for everybody in town. When Anna goes missing, the boy tries to get to the bottom of her disappearance, sifting through clues both obvious and subtle. Her dress was neatly folded near a hole in the ice, and he wonders if she did not die trying to mimic one of Houdini's escape stunt. Or perhaps it was murder and a teacher at school or her parents were involved. Maybe it was suicide, or maybe Anna is not dead at all.

Despite the wealth of clues, Galloway raises more questions than he answers in *As Simple as Snow,* and this situation frustrated some reviewers. A critic for *Kirkus Reviews,* for example, found the work "engagingly written" but also a "pointless exercise." Allison Lynn, writing in *People,* noted such rifts but went on to conclude, "this strange tale" sticks in the mind. Similarly, Harriet Klausner, writing in *MBR Bookwatch,* observed that Galloway paints a picture of "disenchanted teens, but . . . leaves too much unanswered especially the spooky elements that haunt" the narrator. Mixing media, Galloway addresses these dangling plot threads in his novel via a Web site devoted to the book that is filled with more clues, ciphers, and information about Houdini and the fictinal Anna.

Prudence Peiffer, reviewing *As Simple as Snow* in *Library Journal,* regretted the fact that so much of the book is "open ended," but also praised it as a "promising first novel." Other reviewers found more to like, despite—or because of—the fact that its central mystery remains unsolved at book's end. A contributor for *Publishers Weekly* called it a "quirky, engrossing debut," and a "rich, complex puzzle [that] is the work of a talented author." Michael Cart, reviewing the title in *Booklist,* felt the novel's "ambiguities and unanswered questions, its teasing foreshadowings and forebodings, make" the work memorable. Smith dubbed it "an intriguing debut."

BIOGRAPHICAL AND CRITICAL SOURCES:

PERIODICALS

Booklist, January 1, 2005, Michael Cart, review of *As Simple as Snow,* p. 814.
Kirkus Reviews, January 15, 2005, review of *As Simple as Snow,* p. 71.
Library Journal, February 15, 2005, Prudence Peiffer, review of *As Simple as Snow,* p. 116.
MBR Bookwatch, March, 2005, Harriet Klausner, review of *As Simple as Snow.*
People, May 2, 2005, Allison Lynn, review of *As Simple as Snow,* p. 48.
Publishers Weekly, February 7, 2005, review of *As Simple as Snow,* p. 42.
School Library Journal, May, 2005, Starr E. Smith, review of *As Simple as Snow,* p. 168.
Weehawken Reporter (Hudson County, NJ), May 8, 2005, Caren Lissner, review of *As Simple as Snow.*

ONLINE

As Simple as Snow Web site, http://www.assimpleassnow.com/ (July 7, 2005).
Grade Winner, http://www.gradewinner.com/ (March, 2005), Carolyn Mumick, "Gregory Galloway: The Whodunit May Seem Old Hand, but with His Debut Novel, Gregory Galloway Gives the Form a Twenty-First-Century Spin."*

*   *   *

GANN, Kirby 1968-

PERSONAL: Born 1968.

ADDRESSES: Home—Louisville, KY. *Office*—Sarabande Books, 2234 Dundee Rd., Ste. 200, Louisville, KY 40205; fax: 502-458-4065; Spalding University, Master of Fine Arts in Writing Program, 851 S. 4th St., Louisville, KY 40203. *E-mail*—kgt@kirbygann.net.

CAREER: Writer, editor, educator, and musician. Sarabande Books, Louisville, KY, managing editor; Spalding University, Louisville, teacher in M.F.A. writing program. Musician in band Jakeleg. Former semi-professional soccer player and bookseller.

AWARDS, HONORS: Individual artist fellowship, and two professional assistance awards, all from Kentucky Arts Council.

WRITINGS:

(Editor, with Kristin Herbert) *A Fine Excess: Contemporary Literature at Play* (stories, essays, and poetry), Sarabande Books (Louisville, KY), 2001.
The Barbarian Parade; or, Pursuit of an Un-American Dream (novel), Hill Street Press (Athens, GA), 2003.
Our Napoleon in Rags (novel), Ig (Brooklyn, NY), 2005.

Short stories have appeared in numerous journals, including *Witness, Best of Witness, Crescent Review, American Writing, Louisville Review, Southeast Review,* and *Southern Indiana Review.*

SIDELIGHTS: Editor and writer Kirby Gann is the author of two novels and the coeditor with Kristin Herbert, of a collection of essays, poetry, and fiction stories titled *A Fine Excess: Contemporary Literature at Play.* Gann and Herbert chose the writings for the collection based on writers' "dynamic and inventive choice of language and structure," as noted by *Booklist* contributor Ted Leventhal. The volume features such well-known writers as e.e. cummings and William Gass as well as up-and-coming writers Rick Moody, Mike Newirth, and Connie Voisine. Instead of conventional, realistic writings, the authors chosen for inclusion take unconventional approaches to their craft, contributing stories with no plot or characterization and tales involving truly eccentric characters placed in surreal situations. Leventhal called the book "a worthy collection and refreshing for those tired of popular conventions." While a *Publishers Weekly* contributor commented that "this miscellany will appeal only to the literarily adventurous—a small but discrete market," Stacy Voeller, writing in *Library Journal,* remarked that, "throughout, the descriptive language breathes life into words, giving them dimensions all their own."

In the novel *Our Napoleon in Rags*, Gann tells the story of Haycraft Keebler, a man who suffers from bipolar disorder and hangs out in a bar called the Don Q (a reference to Don Quixote, the idealistic and chivalrous title character of Spanish writer Miguel de Cervantes' novel). Keebler dreams up heartfelt if misguided plans to save the world, such as applying gold spray paint to trash cans. Other characters in the novel are also misfits of society, such as anarchist Romeo Diaz and his ballerina girlfriend, a woman who eventually runs off to become a porn star. A teenage street hustler named Lambret Dellinger becomes the object of Haycraft's affections and ultimately causes disaster and chaos among this community of off-kilter characters. Jim Dwyer, writing in *Library Journal*, explained that "all serve as narrators, and although all are archetypes, they are real and compelling characters." A *Kirkus Reviews* contributor noted that the novel contains "closing fictional moments of the wonderful and significant." In a review for the Louisville, Kentucky, *Courier General*, Frederick Smock remarked that "there are abundant felicities of style that make this an enjoyable—as well as provocative—novel to read."

BIOGRAPHICAL AND CRITICAL SOURCES:

PERIODICALS

Booklist, January 1, 2001, Ted Leventhal, review of *A Fine Excess: Contemporary Literature at Play*, p. 900.

Courier-Journal (Louisville, KY), May 8, 2005, Frederick Smock, review of *Our Napoleon in Rags*.

Kirkus Reviews, February 15, 2005, review of *Our Napoleon in Rags*, p. 190.

Library Journal, December, 2000, Stacy Voeller, review of *A Fine Excess*, p. 131; May 15, 2005, Jim Dwyer, review of *Our Napoleon in Rags*, p. 105.

Publishers Weekly, January 1, 2001, review of *A Fine Excess*, p. 86.

ONLINE

AllReaders.com, http://www.allreaders.com/ (June 25, 2005), James Eugene, review of *Our Napoleon in Rags*.

Kirby Gann Home Page, http://www.kirbygann.net (June 25, 2005).

Sarabande Books Web site, http://www.sarabande books.org/ (June 25, 2005), profile of Kirby Gann.

Spalding University Web site, http://www.spalding.edu/ (June 25, 2005), profile of Kirby Gann.*

*   *   *

GARDNER, Robert 1911-2005

OBITUARY NOTICE—See index for *CA* sketch: Born December 27, 1911, in Arlington, WA; died August 27, 2005, in Corona del Mar, CA. Lawyer, judge, justice of the peace, and author. Gardner was a longtime judge in California who gained an appreciative audience for his frank and witty court opinions. As a young man, he initially wanted to work as a forest ranger, but he followed his mother's advice and instead studied law at the University of Southern California. After earning his law degree in 1935, Gardner was admitted to the Bar of California the following year; he then began a private law practice. His early success as a defender led to his being hired by the Orange County district attorney in 1936, and two years later he was appointed to the bench of the Newport Beach Municipal Court. After serving in the U.S. Navy in the Pacific theater during World War II, Gardner was appointed superior court justice in Orange County, a job he held from 1947 until 1970. Governor Ronald Reagan then named him to the 4th District Court of Appeals in San Bernardino, and he retired from the bench in 1982. The U.S. Department of the Interior then requested that he move to American Samoa to serve as the chief justice in Pago Pago. Gardner held this post for the next three years. From 1985 until his final retirement in 2000, he assisted the Orange County court system by serving as a private judge who presided over out-of-court settlements. While serving as a judge and justice, Gardner was known for his quotable pronouncements, a number of which regularly appeared in the *Santa Clara Law Review* column "A Gallery of Gardner." An avid surfer, Gardner also published the book *The Art of Body Surfing* (1972). His second book, *Bawdy Balboa* (1992), was about his childhood.

OBITUARIES AND OTHER SOURCES:

PERIODICALS

Los Angeles Times, August 30, 2005, p. B11.

ONLINE

Orange County Register Online, http://www.ocregister.
com/ (August 29, 2005).

*   *   *

GEER, Charlie 1970-

PERSONAL: Born 1970, in Charleston, SC. *Education:* College of Charleston, B.A., 1994; University of Florida, M.F.A., 2001. *Hobbies and other interests:* Travel.

ADDRESSES: Office—Department of English, College of Charleston, 66 George St., Charleston, SC 29424. *E-mail*—geerc@cofc.edu.

CAREER: Educator and fiction writer. Worked variously as a circus roustabout, orchard keeper, commercial fisherman, high school teacher, and carpenter; College of Charleston, Charleston, SC, instructor. Visiting instructor at University of Charleston. Assistant editor, *Crazyhorse.*

AWARDS, HONORS: Fellowships from University of Florida and South Carolina Academy of Authors; winner, South Carolina Fiction Project and Piccolo Fiction Open.

WRITINGS:

Outbound: The Curious Secession of Latter-Day Charleston (novel), River City Publishing (Montgomery, AL), 2005.

Contributor to periodicals, including *Tin House, Sun,* and *Bloomsbury* magazine.

SIDELIGHTS: Charlie Geer has given readers a lighthearted social satire with his debut novel, *Outbound: The Curious Secession of Latter-Day Charleston.* In the story, three major festivals take place at the same time on the peninsula where Charleston, South Carolina, is located. The weight of all that humanity causes the peninsula to break off from the mainland and drift out to sea. The locals find themselves trapped on the newly made island together with far too many tourists, yet the U.S. government, the Coast Guard, and the media all seem unconcerned by the situation. Geer pokes fun at several types— pampered artists, tour guides, yacht club members and more—as the characters in his book bicker and complain. He exposes the "elitism, pettiness, racism, greed, and lust" of his characters, indicated a reviewer for the *Charleston City Paper.* Although his characters are not well developed, because "the author's too busy cracking jokes and hammering home his points to flesh out the protagonists," the fast-paced story will keep readers from being too concerned about whether or not the plot makes sense, according to the critic. "If readers enjoy *Outbound* half as much as Geer obviously enjoyed writing it," the critic added, "they're in for a grand ride." A *Kirkus Reviews* contributor stated that the story is "implausible, but a good romp with plenty of characters who ring true."

BIOGRAPHICAL AND CRITICAL SOURCES:

PERIODICALS

Kirkus Reviews, March 1, 2005, review of *Outbound: The Curious Secession of Latter-Day Charleston,* p. 248.

ONLINE

Charleston City Paper Online, http://www.
charlestoncitypaper.com/ (June 9, 2005), review of *Outbound.**

*   *   *

GELSTED, Einar Otto
See GELSTED, Otto

*   *   *

GELSTED, Otto 1888-1968
(Einar Otto Gelsted)

PERSONAL: Born November 4, 1888, in Middelfart, Fyn, Denmark; died December 22, 1968, in Copenhagen, Denmark.

WRITINGS:

Johannes V. Jensen, Gyldendal (Copenhagen, Denmark), 1913.

(With others) *Psalmer,* H.H. Thiele (Copenhagen, Denmark), 1918.

Ekspressionisme (criticism), Nordisk (Copenhagen, Denmark), 1919.

De evige Ting (poems; title means "The Eternal Things"), 1920.

Dansens Almagt (poems), Levin & Munksgaard (Copenhagen, Denmark), 1921.

Enetaler (poems), Levin & Munksgaard (Copenhagen, Denmark), 1922.

Jomfru Gloriant (criticism; title means "Maiden Gloriant"), 1923.

Digte (poems), Levin & Munksgaard (Copenhagen, Denmark), 1924.

Lazarus' Opvækkelse, Sirius (Copenhagen, Denmark), 1924.

Paa flugt, 1925.

Gunnar Gunarsson, P. Haase (Copenhagen, Denmark), 1926.

Rejsen til Astrid (poems; title means "The Journey to Astrid"), 1927.

Enehøje-Digte (poems), Levin & Munksgaard (Copenhagen, Denmark), 1929.

Henimod Klarhed (poems), Levin & Munksgaard (Copenhagen, Denmark), 1932.

Under Uvejret (poems; title means "During the Storm"), Monde (Copenhagen, Denmark), 1934.

Oluf Høst, Naver (Copenhagen, Denmark), 1934.

Danmark-Ruslandi litteraturen, Monde (Copenhagen, Denmark), 1937.

(With others) *Aarets Kunst,* [Copenhagen, Denmark], 1938.

Udvalte digte (poems), Monde (Copenhagen, Denmark), 1938.

(With others) *Casanovas erindringer,* Martin (Copenhagen, Denmark), 1940.

De danske Strande, 1940.

Hymn til Badstuestræde, 1940.

Solemærker (poems), A. Jensen (Copenhagen, Denmark), 1941.

Fyns Land, A. Jensen (Copenhagen, Denmark), 1942.

Hunstner-leksikon, A. Jensen (Copenhagen, Denmark), 1942.

Emigrantdigte (poems; title means "Emigrant Poems"), Athenaeum (Copenhagen, Denmark), 1945.

Flygtningene i Husaby (novel), Athenaeum (Copenhagen, Denmark), 1945.

Arnulf Øverland, Athenaeum (Copenhagen, Denmark), 1946.

Frihedens Aar (poems), Tiden (Copenhagen, Denmark), 1947.

Stå op og tænd lys (poems), Athenaeum (Copenhagen, Denmark), 1948.

Sange under den kold krig (poems), Tiden (Copenhagen, Denmark), 1952.

Døden I badekarret (poems), Thaning & Appel (Copenhagen, Denmark), 1955.

Guder og helte, 1956.

Udvalgte digte, Gyldendal (Copenhagen, Denmark), 1957.

Græsk drama (criticism), Thaning & Appel (Copenhagen, Denmark), 1957.

Den græske tanke, Thaning & Appel (Copenhagen, Denmark), 1958.

Goddag liv! (poems), Sirius (Copenhagen, Denmark), 1958.

Aldrig var dagen så lys (poems), Thaning & Appel (Copenhagen, Denmark), 1959.

Digte fra en solkyst (poems; title means "Poems from a Sunny Coast"), Thaning & Appel (Copenhagen, Denmark), 1961.

Axel Salto, Carit Andersens (Copenhagen, Denmark), 1962.

Hellas i mit hjerte, Gyldendal (Copenhagen, Denmark), 1969.

Poesi og politik: 18 udvalgte digte, Danmarks Kommunistiske Parti (Valby, Denmark), 1982.

Work represented in collections; contributor to books by others, including author of foreword, Hans Christian Andersen, *Alt på sin rette plads: Og andre eventyr,* illustrations by Marlie Brande, A. Jensen (Copenhagen, Denmark), 1942. Translator of works by Homer, Sigmund Freud, Walt Whitman, Bertolt Brecht, and Pablo Neruda into Danish; contributor to periodicals, including *Klingen, Land og Folk, Politiken,* and *Sirius.*

SIDELIGHTS: Otto Gelsted was a Danish writer whose numerous publications included both poetry and criticism. Gelsted fueled his interest in philosophy and the arts during his years as a student, and he began his literary career by writing about modern art. His 1919 publication *Ekspressionisme,* for example, provides analysis of the expressionist movement in pictorial arts. In the ensuing decades, while he succeeded in producing numerous collections of poetry, Gelsted continued—through his various critical writings and his leftist polemics—to serve as an influential figure in Danish culture.

Gelsted's early poetry, including *De evige Ting, Dansens Almagt,* and *Enetaler,* all of which appeared in the early 1920s, indicates his interests in Kantian philosophy, Marxist politics, and Greek poetry. In the 1930s, as Nazism spread across Europe, his poetry came to express a greater degree of fatalism. During this period, Gelsted remained a staunch communist, even though Marxism—particularly as practiced in dictator Josef Stalin's Soviet Union—sometimes seemed at odds with his humanist perspective.

After World War II, Gelsted continued to publish prolifically in his native Denmark. In the 1950s, for instance, he produced the poetry collections *Sange under den kold krig, Døden I badekarret,* and *Goddag liv!,* and in 1961, when he reached age seventy-three, he produced still another verse volume, *Digte fra en solkyst.* After producing that collection, however, Gelsted completed little further work.*

*   *   *

GENTRY, Christine 1954-

PERSONAL: Born 1954, in La Plata, MD. *Education:* University of Florida, B.S.; Master Groomer degree.

ADDRESSES: Home—FL. *Agent*—c/o Author Mail, Poisoned Pen Press, 6962 East First Ave., Ste. 103, Scottsdale, AZ 85251. *E-mail*—Christine@gentrybooks.com.

CAREER: Worked for twenty years as a bookseller and assistant manager for Waldenbooks; founder of Brush Puppies Mobile Pet Grooming; freelance writer, 1979—. Teaches courses on freelance writing and police report writing.

MEMBER: Bloody Pens.

WRITINGS:

When Dogs Run Wild: The Sociology of Feral Dogs and Wildlife, McFarland (Jefferson, NC), 1983.
(With Sally Gibson-Downs) *Encyclopedia of Trekkie Memorabilia: Identification and Value Guide,* Books Americana (Florence, AL), 1988.

(With Sally Gibson-Downs) *Greenburg's Guide to Star Trek Collectibles,* three volumes, Greenburg Publishers (Sykesville, MD), 1992.
(With Sally Gibson-Downs) *Motorcycle Toys: Identification & Values: Antique and Contemporary,* Collector Books (Paducah, KY), 1995.

Contributor to wildlife periodicals.

"ANSEL PHOENIX" MYSTERY SERIES

Mesozoic Murder, Poisoned Pen Press (Scottsdale, AZ), 2003.
Carnosaur Crimes, Poisoned Pen Press (Scottsdale, AZ), 2005.

SIDELIGHTS: Christine Gentry began a career as a mystery writer after many years as a bookseller, dog groomer, and a rather eclectic freelance writer. Her previous books have included guides to Star Trek collectibles and motorcycle toys and a study of the sociology of feral dogs. She has taught classes on magazine writing for interested amateurs, as well as on police-report-writing for law-enforcement professionals. At the same time, her interest in paleontology is the subject of her "Ansel Phoenix" mysteries.

Introduced in *Mesozoic Murder,* Phoenix has a mixture of talents and interests, like her creator. She is an artist and a scientist, drawing on both skills in her job creating pictures of dinosaurs based on fossils and logical deductions from the natural world. She is also half Blackfoot, proud of her Native-American heritage but also sensitive about it due to childhood slights. All these aspects of her character come together when she discovers the grave of a murdered colleague during a fossil-hunting trip. Mistrusting the police for her own reasons, Phoenix begins her own investigation of the crime and soon finds herself caught in a dangerous mystery involving stolen fossils, scientific rivalry, and Native American lore. At the same time, she begins to realize that her own nonprofit fossil-hunting organization, the Pangaea Society, includes some rather unsavory members and quite possibly the murderer. According to a *Publishers Weekly* reviewer, "Gentry's appealing heroine . . . and the intriguing milieu in which she operates should ensure both a warm reception and a speedy encore.

Phoenix reappears in *Carnosaur Crimes.* This time, she is trying to save the Big Toe Natural History Museum following attempts to make off with its prized

Allosaurus tracks. Although the thief was unsuccessful, FBI investigators are threatening to remove the tracks for safekeeping and study at a distant university. At the request of the museum's curator, Dr. Dieselmore, Phoenix agrees to help out in a sting operation designed to catch the mastermind behind the attempted theft. Soon she is drawn into the dangerous world of fossil poaching, a world populated by corrupt antiquities dealers, drug smugglers, and clever but ruthless con artists. A *Kirkus Reviews* contributor felt the results are weighed down by "an overloaded plot [and] prose as desiccated as those dinosaur bones." In a more favorably assessment, a *Publishers Weekly* reviewer wrote: "Though several plot-thickening coincidences strain credulity, the snowballing pace will keep the reader turning the pages until the unexpected finish." *Booklist* reviewer Sue O'Brien added that "plot twists, fast pacing, and vivid descriptions distinguish this second in the series." Similarly, a reviewer for *MBR Bookwatch* concluded that Gentry's "story line hooks the audience from the moment that Dr. Dieselmore calls Ansel and never lets up until the final confrontation."

BIOGRAPHICAL AND CRITICAL SOURCES:

PERIODICALS

Booklist, March 1, 2005, Sue O'Brien, review of *Carnosaur Crimes*, p. 1144.
Kirkus Reviews, March 1, 2005, review of *Carnosaur Crimes*, p. 262.
MBR Bookwatch, April, 2005, review of *Carnosaur Crimes*.
Publishers Weekly, July 28, 2003, review of *Mesozoic Murder*, p. 82; March 21, 2005, review of *Carnosaur Crimes*, p. 39.

ONLINE

Christine Gentry Home Page, http://www.gentrybooks.com (July 7, 2005).
Poisoned Pen Press Web site, http://www.poisonedpenpress.com/ (July 7, 2005), biography of Christine Gentry.*

*   *   *

GEYER, Andrew 1964-

PERSONAL: Born May 9, 1964, in Austin, TX; Son of Frank A. (a rancher) and Judy (an administrative assistant; maiden name, Starr) Geyer; married Christina Kotoske, 1997 (divorced 2002); married second wife, Jay Jay Wiseman (an English instructor); children: Joshua, Caleb. *Ethnicity:* "Caucasian." *Education:* University of Texas, Austin, B.A., 1988; University of South Carolina, M.F.A., 1992; Texas Tech University, Ph.D., 2003. *Politics:* "Independent." *Religion:* Non-denominational Christian. *Hobbies and other interests:* Distance running.

ADDRESSES: Home—506 Resimont Dr., Russellville, AR 72801. *Office*—Arkansas Tech University, Department of English, Witherspoon 151, Russellville, AR 72801. *E-mail*—ageyer64@earthlink.net.

CAREER: Writer and educator. Arkansas Tech University, Russellville, assistant professor of English, 2003—.

AWARDS, HONORS: Book of the Year Award for Best Work of Short Fiction, Silver Medal, *ForWord,* and Spur Award for Best Work of Short Fiction, Western Writers of America, both 2004, both for "Whispers in Dust and Bone."

WRITINGS:

Whispers in Dust and Bone (short stories), Texas Tech University Press (Lubbock, TX), 2003.

Contributor to *New Texas 2001,* edited by Donna Walker-Nixon and James Ward Lee, University of Mary Hardin-Baylor Press (Belton, TX), 2001. Contributor to journals, including *South Dakota Review, Southwestern American Literature, Concho River Review, Salt Fork Review, Chiron Review, Savannah Literary Journal, Georgia Guardian,* and *Analecta.*

SIDELIGHTS: Andrew Geyer told *CA:* "A native Texan, I grew up on a working ranch in Southwest Texas. The experience of growing up on the land—working outdoors with horses and cattle, at the mercy of the elements—has shaped the lens through which I view the world, and made me the writer that I am. It doesn't matter whether I'm setting fiction in Southwest Texas, South Carolina, or South America—that clear, no-nonsense worldview helps me cut to the heart of the matter at hand. Much like writing fiction, there is not much room for fluff or sentimentality trying to make a living at ranching in that semi-desert brush country—the boundary between success and failure is razor-thin."

GIBSON, David 1959-

PERSONAL: Born June 23, 1959, in NJ. *Education:* Furman University, B.A., 1981. *Religion:* Roman Catholic. *Hobbies and other interests:* Life drawing.

ADDRESSES: Home—42 Strong Place, Apt. 4, Brooklyn, NY 11231. *Agent*—Jimmy Vines, The Vines Agency, 648 Broadway, Ste. 901, New York, NY 10012. *E-mail*—dgibson@nyc.rr.com.

CAREER: Writer. Vatican Radio, Vatican City, broadcast journalist, 1986-90; *Bergen Record,* Hackensack, NJ, religion writer, 1990-99; *Star-Ledger of New Jersey,* Newark, NJ, religion writer, 1999-2003; freelance writer, 2003—. Board member, Religion Newswriters Association, 2000—.

AWARDS, HONORS: Named Religion Writer of the Year, Religion Newswriters Association, 1999; named Templeton Religion Reporter of the Year, Religion Newswriters Association, 2000; American Society of Newspaper Editors prize for deadline news reporting by a team, 2001.

WRITINGS:

The Coming Catholic Church: How the Faithful Are Shaping a New American Catholicism, HarperSanFrancisco (San Francisco, CA), 2003.

TELEVISION DOCUMENTARIES

(Writer and producer, with Michael McKinley) *The Mystery of Jesus,* Cable News Network Productions, 2004.
(Writer and producer, with Michael McKinley) *The Two Marys: The Madonna and the Magdelene,* Cable News Network Productions, 2004.

Contributor of articles to periodicals, including *New York Times, Boston, New York Observer, New Jersey Monthly, Commonweal,* and *America.*

*   *   *

GIFFORD, Francis Newton
See GIFFORD, Frank

GIFFORD, Frank 1930-
(Francis Newton Gifford, Frank N. Gifford)

PERSONAL: Born August 16, 1930, in Santa Monica (one source says Bakersfield), CA; son of Weldon and Lola Mae Gifford; married Maxine Ewart, January 13, 1952 (divorced); married Astrid Lindley, 1978 (divorced, 1986); married Kathie Lee Johnson, October 18, 1986; children: (first marriage) three; (third marriage) Cody Newton, Cassidy Erin. *Education:* University of Southern California, received degree.

ADDRESSES: Home—355 Taconic Rd., Greenwich, CT 06830. *E-mail*—info@sportsstarsusa.com.

CAREER: Professional football player and sports commentator. New York Giants (professional football team), New York, NY, defensive back, running back, and flanker, 1952-60, 1962-64. KERO-TV, Bakersfield, CA, sportscaster, 1957; Columbia Broadcasting System (CBS), commentator on NFL pre-game show, 1957-61, sports reporter and host of *Sunday Sports Spectacular,* 1965-71; WCBS-TV, New York, NY, sports reporter, 1961-65; American Broadcasting Companies (ABC), sports reporter on *Wide World of Sports* and color commentator on *Monday Night Football,* 1971-98, New York sportscaster on *Eyewitness News,* c. 1972-73, host of *Monday Night Blast* (*Monday Night Football* pre-game show), 1998.

Has appeared in films, including (as athletic double for Jerry Lewis) *That's My Boy,* Paramount, 1951; (as Stan Pomeroy; and technical consultant) *All American,* 1953; (as himself) *Paramount Pacemaker: Touchdown Highlights,* 1954; (as stuntperson) *Sign of the Pagan,* Universal, 1954; *Darby's Rangers,* Warner Bros., 1958; (as Mount) *Up Periscope,* Warner Bros., 1959; *Turnpike Cop,* 1960; (as himself) *Paper Lion,* United Artists, 1968; (as announcer) *The World's Greatest Athlete,* Buena Vista, 1973; (as himself) *Two-Minute Warning,* Universal, 1976; (as himself) *Viva Knievel!,* Warner Bros., 1977; and (as himself) *Jerry Maguire,* Columbia/Tristar, 1996. Appeared in television pilots, including *Public Enemy* and *Turnpike.* Guest star on television series, including *What's My Line?, Hazel, The Six Million Dollar Man, The San Pedro Beach Bums, Webster, Life Goes On, The Adventures of Pete and Pete, Coach,* and *Spin City.* Has also appeared in numerous television specials. Former chair of sportscasting committee for Special Olympics; board member, New York Society of Multiple Sclerosis; also works on behalf of Association to Benefit Children, New York, NY.

MEMBER: Phi Sigma Kappa.

AWARDS, HONORS: Named All-Pro halfback, 1955-57 and 1959; named National Football League (NFL) Player of the Year, United Press International (UPI) and *Sporting News,* and most valuable player, NFL, all 1956; named most valuable player of NFL Pro Bowl, 1959; named NFL comeback player of the year, UPI, 1962; named sportsman of the year, Catholic Youth Organization, 1964; inducted into National Football Foundation Hall of Fame, 1975; inducted into National Collegiate Athletic Association (NCAA) College Football Hall of Fame, 1976; inducted into Pro Football Hall of Fame, 1977; Emmy Award for Outstanding Sports Personality, Academy of Television Arts and Sciences, 1977; Christopher Award, 1984, for coverage of 1983 International Special Olympics on *Wide World of Sports;* Founders Award, Multiple Sclerosis Society of New York, 1984; Career Achievement Award, NFL Alumni, 1985, for "demonstrating the higher values of football throughout his career, and after"; Lifetime Achievement Award, March of Dimes, 1989; inducted into University of Southern California's Athletic Hall of Fame, 1994; Pete Rozelle Award, 1995; Emmy Award, 1997, for lifetime achievement—sports; number retired by New York Giants, 2000.

WRITINGS:

Frank Gifford's Football Guidebook: Basic Plays and Playing Techniques for Boys, McGraw-Hill (New York, NY), 1965.
NFL-CBS Football Guide 1967, New American Library (New York, NY), 1967.
NFL-AFL Football Guide 1968, New American Library (New York, NY), 1968.
Pro Football Guide for 1970, New American Library (New York, NY), 1970.
(With Charles Mangel) *Gifford on Courage,* M. Evans (New York, NY), 1976.
(With Harry Waters) *The Whole Ten Yards* (memoir), Random House (New York, NY), 1993.

SIDELIGHTS: Frank Gifford first rose to fame as a professional football player for the New York Giants in the 1950s. His career was nearly ended by a severe concussion during the 1960 season, but after taking a year off, Gifford fought his way back in 1962. Finally, he retired for good in 1964. He set several impressive records during his football career: he ran for 9,753 combined yards, while the seventy-eight touchdowns he scored is still a Giants record. His 5,434 yards as receiver was only surpassed in 2003. Even before leaving football, however, Gifford had been providing sports commentary for the National Football League (NFL) pre-game show; and after 1964 he moved into sports journalism full time. For many years, Gifford was best known as one of the hosts of *Monday Night Football.* He joined the program in 1971, during its second season, and remained on the show until 1998, making him the longest-running host in the program's history.

Gifford wrote about his football and post-football experiences in his memoir, *The Whole Ten Yards,* which was published in 1993. The book opens with an "honest and deeply revealing account" of Gifford's itinerant childhood, Steve Gietschier commented in *Sporting News.* Gifford's father worked in the oil fields, and Gifford's family traveled with him throughout the United States. They lived in, by Gifford's count, over forty-seven different towns—and at one time hopped around fifteen different towns in a single year—before they settled in Bakersfield, California. While attending high school there, Gifford fell under the influence of the school's football coach, who groomed him into a star player and set him on the path that would take the athlete to first the University of Southern California and then to the New York Giants. This "easygoing, informative and anecdotal" memoir is "a good, solid sports autobiography," a reviewer concluded in *Publishers Weekly.*

BIOGRAPHICAL AND CRITICAL SOURCES:

BOOKS

Gifford, Frank, and Harry Waters, *The Whole Ten Yards,* Random House (New York, NY), 1993.
St. James Encyclopedia of Popular Culture, St. James Press (Detroit, MI), 2000.

PERIODICALS

Buffalo News, August 31, 1998, Eric Mink, "Gifford Says ABC Fumbled 'MNF' Pre-Game Pass," p. A12.

Daily News (Los Angeles, CA), January 28, 2002, Tom Hoffarth, "Sideways Glance Giff, Sweetness, the Task-Master Coach, and a Couple of Super Joes," p. S3.

People, May 21, 1990, Jeannie Park, "Kathie Lee and Frank Gifford Finally Make It a Threesome," p. 162.

Publishers Weekly, October 4, 1993, review of *The Whole Ten Yards,* p. 62.

Record (Hackensack, NJ), October 19, 2000, Vinny DiTrani, "Gifford's 16 to Be Retired," p. S11.

San Francisco Chronicle, September 18, 1998, Susan Slusser, "'MNF' Fine with Boomer, but 'Blast' Is a Bummer," p. E2.

Saturday Night, December, 1996, Mark Kingwell, "Men's Night Out," p. 111.

Sporting News, November 29, 1993, Steve Gietschier, review of *The Whole Ten Yards,* p. 7.

Star-Ledger (Newark, NJ), February 11, 1999, "Report: Gifford Is Out on 'MNF' Telecasts," p. 62.

ONLINE

ESPN Web site, http://espn.go.com/ (April 19, 2005), Mike Puma, "Gifford Was Star in Backfield, Booth."

HickokSports.com, http://www.hickoksports.com/ (July 21, 2005), "Frank Gifford."

Sports Stars USA Web site, http://www.sportsstarsusa.com/ (July 21, 2005), "Frank Gifford, Pro Football Hall of Famer."*

*   *   *

GIFFORD, Frank N.
See GIFFORD, Frank

*   *   *

GIUDICI, Giovanni 1924-

PERSONAL: Born June 26, 1924, in Le Grazi, La Spezia, Italy; married; children: two sons. *Education:* Attended university in Rome, Italy; earned degree in French literature.

ADDRESSES: Home—Milan, Italy. *Agent*—c/o Author Mail, Arnold Mondadori Editore, via Mondadori, 1, 20090, Seagrate, Milan, Italy.

CAREER: Writer. Olivetti (publishing house), Ivrea, Turin, and Milan, Italy, former copywriter.

AWARDS, HONORS: Viareggio prize, 1969.

WRITINGS:

Fiorì d'improvviso (poems; title means "Sudden Blooming"), Canzoniere (Rome, Italy), 1953.

La stazione di Pisa e altre poesie (title means "The Pisa Railroad Station and Other Poems"), Instituto Statale d'Arte (Urbino, Italy), 1955.

L'intelligenza col nemico (poems; title means "Intelligence with the Enemy"), All'Insegna del Pesce d'Oro (Milan, Italy), 1963.

L'educazione cattolica (1962-1963) (poems; title means "A Catholic Education"), All'Insegna del Pesce d'Oro (Milan, Italy), 1963.

La vita in versi (title means "Life in Verse"), Mondadori (Milan, Italy), 1965, 2nd edition, 1980.

Autobiologia (poems), Mondadori (Milan, Italy), 1965.

(Translator) Sara Lidman, *Cinque diamanti,* Rizzoli (Milan, Italy), 1966.

(Translator, with Giovanni Galtieri) Edmund Wilson, *Saggi letterari, 1920-1950,* Garzanti (Milan, Italy), 1967.

(Translator, with Ljudmila Kortikova) Jurij Tynjanov, *Il problema del linguaggio poetico,* Il Saggiatore (Milan, Italy), 1968, 2nd edition, 1981.

Omaggio a Praga = Hold Praze: cinque poesie e tre prose con una piccola antologia di poeti cèchi del '900 (includes poems and prose in Italian by Giudici and translations of Czech poetry by other authors into Italian), All'Insegna del Pesce d'Oro (Milan, Italy), 1968.

(Translator and author of preface) Jirí Orten, *La cosa chiamata poesia,* edited by Vladimir Mikeš, G. Einaudi (Turin, Italy), 1969.

(Translator, with J. Spendel and G. Venturi) *Poesia Sovietica degli anni sessanta,* Mondadori (Milan, Italy), 1970.

O Beatrice, Mondadori (Milan, Italy), 1972.

Poesie scelte (title means "Selected Poems"), edited by Fernando Bandini, Mondadori (Milan, Italy), 1975.

La letteratura verso Hiroshima e altri scritti, Riuniti (Rome, Italy), 1976.

(Author of text) Gianni Berengo-Gardin, *Tevere* (photography), Dalmine, 1976.

Il male dei creditori, Mondadori (Milan, Italy), 1977, 2nd edition, 1987.

Il ristorante dei morti, Mondadori (Milan, Italy), 1981.

(Translator) *Addio, proibito piangere: e altri versi tradotti (1955-1980),* Einaudi (Turin, Italy), 1982.

(With others) *Design Process,* Olivetti (Turin, Italy), 1983.

Lume dei tuoi misteri, Mondadori (Milan, Italy), 1984.

(Translator and author of introduction) St. Ignatius of Loyola, *Esercizi spirituali,* Mondadori (Milan, Italy), 1984.

La dama non cercata: poetica e letteratura, 1968-1984, Mondadori (Milan, Italy), 1985.

Salutz (1984-1986), Einaudi (Turin, Italy), 1986.

(Translator) Samuel Taylor Coleridge, *La rima del vecchio marinaio; Kubla Khan,* SE Studio Editoriale (Milan, Italy), 1987.

Frau Doktor, Mondadori (Milan, Italy), 1989.

Prove del teatro, Einaudi (Turin, Italy), 1989.

Scarabattole (poems for children), illustrated by Nicoletta Costa, Mondadori (Milan, Italy), 1989, 2nd edition, 1999.

Fortezza (title means "Fortitude"), Mondadori (Milan, Italy), 1990.

Il paradiso: perché mi vinse il lume d'esta stella: satura drammatica, Costa & Nolan (Genoa, Italy), 1991.

Poesie: 1953-1990, two volumes, Garzanti (Milan, Italy), 1991.

Andare in Cina a piedi: racconto sulla poesia, Edizioni (Rome, Italy), 1992.

Quanto spera di campare Giovanni (title means "How Long Does John Want to Live?"), Garzanti (Milan, Italy), 1993.

(With Franco Brovelli and Franco Gallivanone) *Una parabola da comprendere: riflessioni sulla vita del prete nel postconcilio,* Àncora (Milan, Italy), 1994.

Un poeta del golfo, Longanesi (Milan, Italy), 1995.

Empie stelle (1993-1996), Garzanti (Milan, Italy), 1996.

Per forza e per amore: critica e letteratura (1966-1995), Garzanti (Milan, Italy), 1996.

A una casa non sua: nuovi versi tradotti (1955-1995) (poems), Mondadori (Milan, Italy), 1997.

Eresia della sera, Garzanti (Milan, Italy), 1999.

(Translator) Aleksandr Pushkin, *Eugenio Onieghin* (translation of *Eugene Onegin*), Garzanti (Milan, Italy), 1999.

(With Cesare Segre and Alessandro Pancheri) *Le varianti e la storia: il Canzoniere di Francesco Petrarca: lezione Sapegno 1999,* Bollati Boringhieri (Turin, Italy), 1999.

(With Carlo di Alesio, Carlo Ossola, and Rodolfo Zucco) *I versie della vita,* Mondadori (Milan, Italy), 2000.

Author of introduction to books, including *Isabella della Grazia,* by Giancarlo Buzzi, All'Insegna del Pesce d'Oro, 1967; *Tre Racconti,* by Gustave Flaubert, Garzanti, 1974; and *Umberto Saba,* Mondadori, 1976. Contributor to books, including *From Pure Silence to Impure Dialogue: A Survey of Post-war Italian Poetry (1945-1965),* edited and translated by Vittoria Bradshaw, Las Américas, 1971; and *The New Italian Poetry: 1945 to the Present,* edited and translated by Lawrence Smith, University of California Press, 1981. Also contributor to periodicals, including *Communità, Aut Aut, Paragone, Rinascita,* and *Quaderni piacentini.*

SIDELIGHTS: Italian poet, essayist, and translator Giovanni Giudici is known for penning existentialist verses that often deal with the difficulties of living in modern Western society. Initially planning an academic career, after earning a degree in French literature Giudici found work as a copywriter for the publishing house Olivetti, remaining there until his retirement. In his spare time, he wrote poetry and prose, with his first poetry collection, *Fiorì d'improvviso,* being released in 1953. Since then, Giudici has become known as a political and existentialist poet who nonetheless reject the idea that "the social condition is not synonymous to the human condition," as Rosetta Di Pace-Jordan explained in an essay for the *Dictionary of Literary Biography.* Though strongly opposed to Western materialism and capitalism, the poet acknowledges that one cannot extricate him or herself completely from the necessities of life to lead an ideal existence: to be, as philosopher Jean-Paul Sartre once held, completely true to oneself. Rejecting violence in favor of determined but passive resistance to political oppression, Giudici likewise rejects the boundaries placed on him by his Catholic background, while simultaneously realizing that his religious upbringing is a part of who he is. Another dichotomy in his poems is the tension between "a sense of determinism and a desire for action," noted Pace-Jordan.

Rather than leaning on metaphor, generalizations, or symbolism in his poetry, Giudici relies heavily on autobiography, drawing on his own experiences and relationships with family and friends to express himself. One of the best examples of this approach is his collection *La vita in versi.* Here, Giudici attempts to capture and explain the common experience of modern man by using his own life as an example. *Autobiologia,* as the title implies, is also autobiographical. Here is a prime example of the poet's theme that, as Pace-Jordan wrote, "the individual can never be self-sufficient; self-realization needs to be always reciprocal in some way." Furthermore, just as individuals are inextricably tied to human society, they are also tied to nature. Giudici "knows that one cannot change nature through an act of the will," commented Pace-Jordan. "He is also aware that the point at which instincts and actions connect eludes consciousness. This knowledge does not allow him to overestimate freedom or to underestimate the determining forces impinging on the self."

Because Giudici focuses on the ordinary occurrences and situations of everyday life, his verses are not only autobiographical but also take on a documentary air. As Keith Bosley noted in a review of *Poesie scelte* for the *Times Literary Supplement,* "His poems are insistently about ordinary people." Although their subjects are quotidian, the verses are not without lyricism and musicality, as several critics have observed. Spiritualism is also infused in many of his poems, which typically take the form of a "formal, rhetorical prayer," wrote Pace-Jordan. In a *World Literature Today* review of *Empie stelle (1993-1996),* Patricia M. Gathercole further commented: "We need to read Giudici's poetry aloud to appreciate its true worth. There is a haunting beauty about his lines which emanates from his acute attention to sound."

BIOGRAPHICAL AND CRITICAL SOURCES:

BOOKS

Dictionary of Literary Biography, Volume 128: *Twentieth-Century Italian Poets, Second Series,* Thomson Gale (Detroit, MI), 1993.

PERIODICALS

Modern Language Review, April, 1987, Massimo Bacigalupo, review of *La dama non cercata: poetica e letteratura, 1968-1984,* pp. 501-502.
Times Literary Supplement, September 25, 1969, G. Singh, "Exploiting the Subjective," review of *Autobiologia,* p. 1063; July 21, 1972, "Italian Ironies," review of *O Beatrice,* p. 839; October 31, 1975, Keith Bosley, "Melancholy Moments,"

review of *Poesie scelte,* p. 1308; October 4, 1991, Peter Hainsworth, "Montale and After," review of *Poesie: 1953-1990,* p. 32.
World Literature Today, autumn, 1978, Rosetta d. Piclardi, review of *Il male dei creditori,* p. 609; spring, 1982, Thomas G. Bergin, review of *Il ristorante dei morti,* p. 320; winter, 1985, Rosario Ferreri, review of *Lume dei tuoi misteri,* p. 73; summer, 1994, Patricia M. Gathercole, review of *Quanto spera di campare Giovanni,* p. 547; spring, 1997, Patricia M. Gathercole, review of *Empie stelle (1993-1996),* p. 365.*

*   *   *

GOLDSTEIN, Abraham S. 1925-2005
(Abraham Samuel Goldstein)

OBITUARY NOTICE—See index for *CA* sketch: Born July 27, 1925, in New York, NY; died of heart failure, August 20, 2005, in Woodbridge, CT. Lawyer, educator, dean, and author. Goldstein was Sterling Professor of Law and a former dean at Yale University. After serving in the U.S. Army during World War II in demolitions, the military police, and finally intelligence, he attended City College. He earned an economics degree in 1946, and then enrolled at Yale to complete a law degree in 1949. After graduating, he worked as a law clerk for two years and then was a partner for the firm Donohue & Kaufman in Washington, DC. Returning to Yale, he joined the faculty in 1956 and five years later was promoted to professor of law. Goldstein served as dean of the school from 1970 to 1975, and in 1978 was named provost. However, he resigned from the latter post amid allegations that he had spent too much money renovating the university-owned provost's house. He continued to teach at Yale, however, as Sterling Professor, going into semi-retirement in the spring of 2005. Goldstein gained a reputation as a scholar who argued persuasively on such topics as plea bargaining, judicial authority, and the insanity plea. He was the author of several books, including *The Insanity Defense* (1967) and *The Passive Judiciary: Prosecutional Discretion and the Guilty Plea* (1981).

OBITUARIES AND OTHER SOURCES:

PERIODICALS

Los Angeles Times, August 26, 2005, p. B11.

New York Times, August 24, 2005, p. C16.
Washington Post, August 24, 2005, p. B5.

*   *   *

GOLDSTEIN, Abraham Samuel
    See GOLDSTEIN, Abraham S.

*   *   *

GONDRY, Michel 1963-

PERSONAL: Born May 8, 1963, in Versailles, France; children: Paul.

ADDRESSES: Agent—Partizan Ltd., 7 Westbourne Grove Mews, London W11 2UR, England.

CAREER: Music video director in London, England, and Paris, France, 1990—; director of commercials, including for companies Volvo, Smirnoff, Adidas, and Levi's, 1995—. Drummer and video director for band Oui Oui, c. 1980s. Director of films and videos, including *High Head Blues,* Def American Recordings, 1995, *Vingt pétites tours,* 1989, *Björk: Volumen,* 1998, *D.A. F.T.,* 1999, *Massive Attack: Eleven Promos,* 2001, *Human Nature,* 2001, *I've Been Twelve Forever,* 2003, *The Chemical Brothers: Singles 93-03,* 2003, *The Work of Director Michel Gondry,* 2003, and *Master of Space and Time,* 2006. Actor in films, including *D.A.F.T.,* 1999, and *One Day . . . ,* 2001.

MEMBER: D&AD (charity).

AWARDS, HONORS: Golden Lion, Cannes Film Festival, 1995; three silver awards and British Advertisement of the Year award, D&AD, 1995; Silver award, D&AD, 1996; Clio Award Grand Prix, 1996; named European MTV Best Director of 1996; best director of 1997 award, and feature film video of the year award, both Music Video Production Association, both 1998; International Jury Award for best black-and-white film, Cork International Film Festival, 1998, and FICC Prize, Öberhausen International Short Film Festival, 1999, both for *La lettre;* Celebrate New York Award, 2004, and Academy Award for best screenplay (with Pierre Bismuth and Charlie Kaufman), 2005, both for *Eternal Sunshine of the Spotless Mind.*

WRITINGS:

SCREENPLAYS

La lettre (short film; also released as *The Letter*), 1998.
One Day . . . , 2001.
Pecan Pie, 2003.
The Science of Sleep, 2005.

OTHER

(Author of introduction) Charlie Kaufman, *Eternal Sunshine of the Spotless Mind* (screenplay), Newmarket Press (New York, NY), 2004.

SIDELIGHTS: "Michel Gondry," declared critic Todd Pruzan in *Print* magazine, "has done a lot of things." "The French director," Pruzan continued, "is . . . blessed with the hyperactive imagination and attention span of a teenage nerd, dreaming up, designing, and directing some of the past decade's most inventive TV commercials and music videos." Gondry has also solidified his reputation as one of the most innovative film directors of the early twenty-first century through two critically acclaimed movies: *Human Nature,* released in 2001, and the Academy Award-winning *Eternal Sunshine of the Spotless Mind,* released in 2004. Critics agree that Gondry's uniqueness comes from his tendency to approach subjects in a highly individual way. "'Michel is probably one of the last true artists working as a director—he could be compared to [Charlie] Chaplin and the influence he had in the '20s and '30s,' said Georges Bermann, founder of Partizan, Gondry's commercial production company," the *Print* contributor concluded. "'He probably would have belonged to the surrealist group and been one of the leading creative members, along with Duchamp, Ernst, or Bunuel,'" Bermann added, as quoted in *Print.* "'Today, there is no group like that any more, and he's just one-of-a-kind.'"

Considered "a legend for his music-video and advertising work" at the time his first feature film debuted in 2001, according to Jeff Chu in *Time International,* Gondry has been "setting the standard for other French directors who are giving Hollywood a Gallic accent." He was born and raised outside Paris, in the village of Versailles, and attended art school for a time before flunking out. He spent some time as a drummer in a rock band, but first found his métier when he picked up a camera to shoot a video of one of the band's songs. That video was seen by Icelandic pop star Björk, who hired him to direct a video for her in 1993. Soon he was also directing quirky advertisements for television, including a spot for Levi's jeans titled "Drugstore," which was honored with the Golden Lion award at the Cannes Film Festival and has become the most award-winning commercial of all time, according to the *Guinness Book of World Records.* "Many of Gondry's videos, commercials and short films, plus a charming documentary called *I've Been 12 Forever,*" declared Kevin Lally in *Film Journal International,* "are collected on a Palm Pictures disk entitled *The Work of Director Michel Gondry*—one of the best DVDs you can own."

By 2001 commercials and music videos had brought Gondry to the point where he could try his hand at directing his first feature film. The result, *"Human Nature,"* reported Paula Carson stated in *Creative Review,* "stars Patricia Arquette, Tim Robbins and Rhys Ifans in a funny, sometimes tragic look at the interplay between a hirsute woman, a feral young man and a repressed rodent researcher." The script, written by Charlie Kaufman—who also wrote the hit *Being John Malkovich,* "is not about culture and repression," according to James Parker in *American Prospect,* "any more than *Being John Malkovich* was about celebrity and identity." "In the film, Arquette is Lila, a beautiful misfit with full body hair who thinks she looks like an ape and tries to live in the woods," Richard Linnett commented in *Advertising Age.* "Ifans is Puff, a man raised as an ape who already lives in the woods. And Tim Robbins is Nathan, a dweeb scientist who romances Lila, tames Puff and is eventually murdered in the woods."

Nathan and Lila discover Puff in the woods, and Nathan immediately sees in him a subject for experimentation. He attempts to introduce Puff to the accepted values of civilization, values which to Puff make no sense at all. For her part, Lila is attracted to Puff, partly because he offers her a chance for sexual satisfaction and partly because he represents the pure, unsullied Nature she abandoned to live with Nathan. Eventually, Lila and Puff meet and satisfy their mutual urges. The story "has a few more twists after that," Todd McCarthy wrote in *Variety,* "but while the approach remains pranky and the mood buoyant, the idea

begins feeling played out before the finish line is in sight. Partly it's because the theme of civilization existing to repress sexuality, while comically exploitable for a while, has so many more angles than can ever be raised here." Nonetheless, the film demonstrates "truly brilliant direction and inspired acting," Linnett concluded, "especially by Robbins and Ifans."

Gondry's second major film, *Eternal Sunshine of the Spotless Mind,* takes stars Jim Carrey and Kate Winslet through an emotional roller-coaster. Carrey, as the reclusive Joel, and Winslet, as the free-spirit Clementine, become involved in a relationship that ultimately turns sour. Clementine seeks a high-tech solution to the resulting pain: she has her memories of Joel erased by a brainwashing machine. Joel, distraught, seeks the same solution, but he realizes that Clementine is being manipulated by the machine's technicians, and is forced to try to find places to hide his memories of her from the machine's actions. "The story's emotional dynamic is hard to miss, as are its glancing but touching reflections on the centrality of memory in defining one's personality," wrote McCarthy, "and the richness and value of both positive and negative memories in the overall scheme of life." "Gondry figures out how to keep the special effects special," stated Mark Steyn in the *Spectator.* "He shows Joel's memories vanishing around him . . . but because these effects occur within Gondry's overall scheme—a scurfy, hand-held camera roaming a prosaic suburban landscape—they don't overpower the story." "Gondry's virtuosity lifts the film far past science fiction into cinematic efflorescence," concluded Stanley Kauffmann in the *New Republic.* "He shows us, more seductively than other directors have done, how freehand use of film can capture the flashes in our minds that slip between words."

BIOGRAPHICAL AND CRITICAL SOURCES:

PERIODICALS

Advertising Age, April 15, 2002, Richard Linnett, "Adages," review of *Human Nature,* p. 44.
American Prospect, May 6, 2002, James Parker, "Of Mice and Monkeys: The Brilliant, Depthless Nonsense of *Human Nature,*" p. 28.
Campaign, June 21, 2002, "Legends of Commercials Production: Established Directors," p. 4; April 23, 2004, review of *Eternal Sunshine of the Spotless Mind,* p. 10.

Commonweal, April 23, 2004, Rand Richards Cooper, "Scaling the Depths," p. 18.

Creative Review, October, 2001, Paula Carson, "Michel in Dreamland," p. 30.

Entertainment Weekly, April 19, 2002, Owen Gleiberman, review of *Human Nature,* p. 47; February 13, 2004, Neil Drumming, "Director's Cut: Michel Gondry," p. 72.

Film Journal International, April, 2004, Kevin Lally, "Brain Twister," p. 18, and review of *Eternal Sunshine of the Spotless Mind,* p. 99.

Magazine of Fantasy and Science Fiction, August, 2004, Lucius Shepard, "Forget about It," review of *Eternal Sunshine of the Spotless Mind,* p. 123.

New Republic, April 5, 2004, Stanley Kauffmann, review of *Eternal Sunshine of the Spotless Mind,* p. 26.

New Statesman, May 3, 2004, Mark Kermode, review of *Eternal Sunshine of the Spotless Mind,* p. 54.

Newsweek, April 15, 2002, Devin Gordon, "Talk about a Hairy Situation: Probing 'Human Nature,'" p. 56.

Print, September-October, 2004, Todd Pruzan, "Self-Made Maniac," p. 41.

Shoot, May 1, 1998, Millie Takaki, "Michel Gondry Named Director of the Year at the MVPA Awards," p. 7.

Spectator, May 1, 2004, Mark Steyn, "Mental Hygiene," review of *Eternal Sunshine of the Spotless Mind,* p. 50.

Time International, April 26, 2004, Jeff Chu, "Here Comes the Sun," p. 112.

Variety, May 28, 2001, Todd McCarthy, review of *Human Nature,* p. 19; March 15, 2004, Todd McCarthy, "Romantic 'Mind' Games," p. 38.*

*   *   *

GOODAN, Kevin 1969-

PERSONAL: Born 1969, in MT. *Education:* Attended University of Montana; University of Massachusetts, M.F.A.

ADDRESSES: Agent—c/o Author Mail, Alice James Books, 238 Main St., Farmington, ME 04938.

CAREER: Poet. Has lectured about terrorism at various universities; former employee of U.S. Forest Service.

AWARDS, HONORS: L.L. Winship/PEN New England Award, 2005, for *In the Ghost-House Acquainted.*

WRITINGS:

In the Ghost-House Acquainted (poetry) Alice James Books (Farmington, ME), 2004.

Poems have appeared in several publications, including *Ploughshares.*

SIDELIGHTS: Raised on an Indian reservation in Montana, Kevin Goodan is a poet whose first published collection of poems, *In the Ghost-House Acquainted,* focuses on the rural, farming life and the nature, animals, culture, and history associated with this type of life. For example, in the poem "Between Brightness and Weight," Goodan writes about the frost on nearby buildings and landscape. But Goodan's poems do not aim at presenting a mere sentimental image of rural life and nature. "Barn-cleaning," for example, tells of the necessity of and anger felt at having to kill an injured pigeon that falls from the barn rafters. Other poems involve a stillborn foal and a dead llama. Writing on the *Bookslut* Web site, Maria Halovanic commented that this "first collection of poetry . . . looks unflinchingly at the beauty and pain of living." Halovanic went on to praise the author's "sparse vocabulary," adding that "his voice is laconic, even soulful, making use of the same words and subjects as a carpenter makes use of well-worn tools. In the hands of a less-skilled craftsman, such repetition would be tiring." The reviewer also felt that Goodan's best quality as a poet is his ability to "gracefully illustrate . . . complex interactions in an unassuming and yet powerful voice." Comparing Goodan's style to that of poets Robert Frost and David Lee, David Hellman wrote in *Library Journal* that Goodan nevertheless "presents a unique voice." Hellman especially appreciated the poems in the second half of the book, which he claimed "make . . . for exhilarating poetry with vivid lines."

BIOGRAPHICAL AND CRITICAL SOURCES:

PERIODICALS

Library Journal, August, 2004, David Hellman, review of *In the Ghost-House Acquainted,* p. 85.

ONLINE

Bookslut, http://www.bookslut.com/ (June 26, 2005),
    Maria Halovanic, review of *In the Ghost-House
    Acquainted.*
Poems.com, http://www.poems.com/ (June 26, 2005),
    brief profile of Kevin Goodan.

*   *   *

GORDON, Gus 1948-

PERSONAL: Born January 14, 1948, in Waco, TX; son
of Tom (an entrepreneur) and Joy (a homemaker;
maiden name, Rust) Gordon. *Ethnicity:* "Caucasian."
Education: Earned a Ph.D.

ADDRESSES: Home—5415 Ashburg Ct., Tyler, TX
75708. *E-mail*—gaganso@aol.com.

CAREER: Entrepreneur, consultant, and writer.

WRITINGS:

Understanding Financial Statements, South-Western
    Publishing Company (Cincinnati, OH), 1992.
(With Thurmon Williams) *Doing Business in Mexico:
    A Practical Guide,* Best Business Books (New
    York, NY), 2002.

*   *   *

GOTTLIEB, Marvin R. 1939-

PERSONAL: Born September 1, 1939, in Cincinnati,
OH; son of Alex (a business owner) and Ida (a busi-
ness owner; maiden name, Mautner) Gottlieb; married
Gail Zipf, September 1, 1969; children: Aaron. *Ethnic-
ity:* "Caucasian." *Education:* Northwestern University,
B.S.S., 1961; Columbia University Teachers' College,
M.A., 1966, professional diploma, 1967; New York
University, Ph.D., 1972.

ADDRESSES: Home—97 Juniper Hill Rd. NE,
Albuquerque, NM 87122. *Office*—The Communication
Project, Inc., 2601 Wyoming Blvd. NE, Albuquerque,
NM 87112. *E-mail*—marving@comproj.com.

CAREER: Writer. Lehman College, City University of
New York, associate professor of communications; The
Communication Project, Inc., president. Management
development trainer, executive career coach, and
featured speaker at professional seminars and
conferences.

WRITINGS:

Oral Communication, McGraw-Hill (New York, NY),
    1980.
Interview, Longman (New York, NY), 1986.
(With William J. Healy) *Making Deals: The Business
    of Negotiating,* New York Institute of Finance
    (New York, NY), 1990.
(With Lori Conklin) *Managing the Workplace Survi-
    vors: Organizational Downsizing and the Commit-
    ment Gap,* Quorum (Westport, CT), 2003.
*Getting Things Done in Today's Organization: The
    Influencing Executive,* Quorum (Westport, CT),
    1999.
Managing Group Processes, Praeger (Westport, CT),
    2003.

SIDELIGHTS: Marvin R. Gottlieb told *CA:* "Because
I spent much of my life as an academic, writing was
more of a necessity than a choice. Early on, I
discovered that the type of writing required for articles
in my field was not compatible with my style, so I
began writing books. The subject matter I choose is
determined by a combination of personal interest and
content that supports my consulting practice. I like to
base my conclusions on sound research, but in recent
years I find that I trust my own experience more than
I used to. I tend to work from a fairly high-level
outline, and, since I spend a lot of time in front of
audiences, I will dictate large portions of chapters for
later editing. I have written six books up to now, and I
have sworn that each one would be the last. But then,
a couple of years go by and the itch returns."

*   *   *

**GRANT, Maxwell
    See LYNDS, Dennis**

*   *   *

GRANT, Richard 1952-

PERSONAL: Born 1952; married Elizabeth Hand (a
writer).

ADDRESSES: Home—Lincolnville Beach, ME. *Agent*—c/o Author Mail, HarperCollins Publishers, 10 East 53rd St., 7th Fl., New York, NY 10022.

CAREER: Writer. Previously worked as columnist.

AWARDS, HONORS: New England Journalism Award, for best column in a weekly publication; Philip K. Dick Award, for *Through the Heart,* and special citation for best North American paperback novel, both for *Saraband of Lost Time;* Maine Newspaper Award, for best column.

WRITINGS:

NOVELS

Saraband of Lost Time (science fiction), Avon Books (New York, NY), 1985.
Rumors of Spring (science fiction), Bantam Books (New York, NY), 1987.
Views from the Oldest House, Doubleday (New York, NY), 1989.
Through the Heart (science fiction), Bantam Spectra (New York, NY), 1991.
Tex and Molly in the Afterlife (fantasy), Avon Books (New York, NY), 1996.
In the Land of Winter (fantasy), Avon Books (New York, NY), 1997.
Kaspian Lost (science fiction), Spike (New York, NY), 1999.

OTHER

Also contributor of short stories to anthologies, including *Full Spectrum* and *The Ascent of Wonder.* Contributing editor, *Down East.*

WORK IN PROGRESS: Another Green World

SIDELIGHTS: Richard Grant has written several novels, primarily in the science-fiction and fantasy genres. In several of his stories, the author focuses on the fate of the world following a collapse of civilization as we know it; he speculates on the types of technology and institutions that might survive or be adapted for a new society and how they might combine with ancient, pre-industrial technologies. Rather than approaching his subject from a serious, or even a melancholy, viewpoint, he employs humor to address these questions. His first novel, *Saraband of Lost Time,* depicts precisely this sort of amalgam of old and new societies while relating a quest for the ancient power or machine that can rescue the world from its post-collapse situation.

Grant's second novel explores similar themes. *Rumors of Spring* also takes place several centuries after an ecological collapse of modern society. The collapse was the result of a mysterious project that was being conducted in the Carbon Bank Forest. The protagonists of the story go on a crusade of sorts, intent on stopping whoever was responsible for the metamorphosis of the original research from doing more damage.

In *Kaspian Lost* Grant turns his attention to otherworldly phenomena. Fifteen-year-old Kaspian Aaby disappears from summer camp for four days. When he returns, he has memories of an extraordinary adventure involving leprechauns, his dead father, and an angel. Already a troublemaker, Kaspian finds his story sufficiently bizarre for his mother to ship him off to boarding school, where he spends his time trying to keep his experiences from the many adults intent on "helping" him. A reviewer for *Publishers Weekly* noted that "Grant's acute ear for adolescent angst and a plot a step or two left of reality lift this coming-of-age tale a few inches out of the [ordinary]." Margaret A. Smith remarked in *Library Journal* that the book provides "equal amounts of humor and pathos, with events and characters often suggesting Holden Caulfield in a Kurt Vonnegut yarn."

With *In the Land of Winter* Grant creates a modern fairy tale about a single working mother who just happens to be a practicing witch. Pippa Rede soon learns there is a price to pay for witchcraft; she loses custody of her daughter, Winterbelle, and then loses her job and her home. In order to go up against the town's powers that be, she rejects the notion of displaying supposedly normal behavior and instead embraces her skills. Her journey involves a wolf, a wise woman, and a young prince, as well as a measure of personal growth. A contributor to *Publishers Weekly* wrote that "despite patches of self-conscious, coy prose, Grant delivers an entertaining fairy tale." In a review for the *Magazine of Fantasy and Science Fiction,* Michelle West wrote that the author's "phrasing, the tenor of the language, the small but completely apt descriptions, the dance of words across the interior landscape of Pippa's . . . life—they're luminous. They glow." *Library Journal* contributor Michele Leber described the book as "a wonderful, witty feminist fable . . . suffused with the supernatural yet grounded in morality."

Tex and Molly in the Afterlife reveals more of Grant's naturalist leanings. The story follows the adventures of hippies Molly and Tex after they fall down a well and die. Their earthly lives as members of a theater troop interested in raising environmental awareness prove a good foundation for their activities in the afterlife, where they take on a corporation responsible for repopulating the Great North Woods with manmade trees. Molly and Tex encounter various people and creatures during their quest, including elfin children and a tree sprite. A reviewer for *Publishers Weekly* remarked that "the book's whimsical format . . . sometimes leans too far into eccentricity," but also stated that the work "combines the literate but gonzo artistry of Tom Robbins with the obsessive spirituality of dedicated New Agers."

BIOGRAPHICAL AND CRITICAL SOURCES:

BOOKS

St. James Guide to Science-Fiction Writers, fourth edition, St. James Press (Detroit, MI), 1996.

PERIODICALS

Library Journal, October 15, 1997, Michele Leber, review of *In the Land of Winter,* p. 92; July, 1999, Margaret A. Smith, review of *Kaspian Lost,* p. 131.
Magazine of Fantasy and Science Fiction, July, 1998, Michelle West, review of *In the Land of Winter,* p. 45.
Publishers Weekly, August 12, 1996, review of *Tex and Molly in the Afterlife,* p. 64; September 8, 1997, review of *In the Land of Winter,* p. 55; May 24, 1999, review of *Kaspian Lost,* p. 73.*

* * *

GRAY, Kenneth R. 1952-

PERSONAL: Born January 14, 1952; married; wife's name Doris.

ADDRESSES: Agent—c/o Author Mail, Paragon House, 1925 Oakcrest Ave., Ste. 7, St. Paul, MN 55113-2619.

CAREER: Educator, editor, and writer. Florida A & M University, Tallahassee, Eminent Scholar chair professor of international management. Member of board of trustees, University of Bridgeport, Bridgeport, CT.

AWARDS, HONORS: Senior Fulbright scholar to Al Akhawayn University, Morocco.

WRITINGS:

(Editor, with Jude J. Ongong'a) *Bottlenecks to National Identity: Ethnic Co-Operation Towards Nation Building: Proceedings of the Third PWPA Eastern African Regional Conference Held in Mombasa, Kenya, Sept. 15-18, 1988,* Professors World Peace Academy of Kenya (Nairobi, Kenya), 1989.
(Editor, with P.P.W. Achola and B. Wanjala Kerre) *Trends & the Future of University Education in Kenya: Proceedings of the Sixth PWPA Conference, Eastern Region, Held in Nairobi, Kenya, December, 1989,* Professors World Peace Academy of Kenya (Nairobi, Kenya), 1990.
(Editor) *Employment & Education: Strategies & Opportunities for Development: Proceedings of the Seventh PWPA Conference Eastern Region, Held in Nairobi, Kenya, December, 1990,* Professors World Peace Academy of Kenya (Nairobi, Kenya), 1991.
(Editor, with Kivuto Ndeti and others) *The Second Scramble for Africa: A Response & a Critical Analysis of the Challenges Facing Contemporary Sub-Saharan Africa,* Professors World Peace Academy of Kenya (Nairobi, Kenya), 1992.
(With others) *Entrepreneurship in Micro-Enterprises: A Strategic Analysis of Manufacturing Industries in Kenya: Textiles, Woodwork, and Metalwork,* University Press of America (Lanham, MD), 1996.
(With Larry A. Frieder and George W. Clark, Jr.) *Corporate Scandals: The Many Faces of Greed: The Great Heist, Financial Bubbles, and the Absence of Virtue,* Paragon House (St. Paul, MN), 2005.

Member of editorial board of *International Journal on World Peace, Journal of Entrepreneurship and Management,* and *Journal of African Business.*

SIDELIGHTS: Kenneth R. Gray is coauthor with Larry A. Frieder and George W. Clark, Jr., of *Corporate Scandals: The Many Faces of Greed: The Great Heist, Financial Bubbles, and the Absence of Virtue.* The book focuses in part on the headline-grabbing corporate scandals that erupted at the turn of the twenty-first century and involved such corporations as Enron, Tyco, and World-Com. In addition to bringing about legislation focusing on business reforms, these scandals and others impacted millions of investors and workers, as well as U.S. financial markets and the general economy at large. Although the book closely reviews scandals that took place in the early 2000s, the authors also provide a history of corporate wrongdoings dating back to the early eighteenth century. In addition, they explain the various types of corporate crimes, such as fraud and theft, and the government's role in these scandals, from partial responsibility through lax regulations to government efforts to address the problem. The authors also provide recommendations on how to prevent future scenarios with the same potential for corruption.

Harvey Rosenblum, writing in *Business Economics,* felt that one of the book's strong points is the questions the authors ask readers at the end of each chapter, noting: "To answer these questions, the reader must reflect carefully, not just about the content of the chapter, but about the moral and ethical dilemmas posed by the incentive systems of the corporate world and the behaviors it sometimes fosters." As Rosenblum went on to note, "the book challenges us to think about the true complexities of the problem and the difficulties of simultaneously encouraging and regulating greed through the forces of Adam Smith's invisible hand." A *Library Bookwatch* contributor commented that *Corporate Scandals* "should be on the reading list of corporate CEO[s] and mandatory reading for every student in a 'Business Ethics' class."

Gray told *CA:* "I became interested in writing while living in Kenya. I lived there for over ten years. My interest in writing stems from the work I was doing in Africa on economic development. My wife, Doris, who is a journalist by training, and a professor of French, greatly influenced my writing.

"The book that I've written that has had the greatest impact is *Entrepreneurship in Micro-Enterprises: A Strategic Analysis of Manufacturing Industries in Kenya: Textiles, Woodwork, and Metalwork.* This book examines interviews of over three hundred informal business owners in East Africa. The stories are quite revealing with respect to the tenacity of human character."

BIOGRAPHICAL AND CRITICAL SOURCES:

PERIODICALS

Business Economics, January, 2005, Harvey Rosenblum, review of *Corporate Scandals: The Many Faces of Greed: The Great Heist, Financial Bubbles, and the Absence of Virtue,* p. 58.
Library Bookwatch, June, 2005, review of *Corporate Scandals.*

ONLINE

Paragon House Web site, http://www.paragonhouse. com/ (June 27. 2005), brief profile of Kenneth R. Gray.

*   *   *

GREENLAND, Seth

PERSONAL: Born in NY; married; children: one daughter.

ADDRESSES: Home—Cold Spring, NY. *Agent*—c/o Author Mail, Holtzbrinck Publishers, 175 5th Ave., New York, NY 10010.

CAREER: Novelist, playwright, screenwriter, and director. Director of television films, including *The Love Doctor,* MTV.

AWARDS, HONORS: Kennedy Center Fund for New American Plays Award, and American Theatre Critics Association Award, both for *Jungle Rot.*

WRITINGS:

Jungle Rot (play; produced in Chicago, IL, 2004), Dramatists Play Service (New York, NY), 1997.

Jerusalem (two-act play), produced in Cleveland, OH, 2001.

The Bones (novel), Bloomsbury (New York, NY), 2005.

Author of other plays, including *Girls in Movies, Partners in Crime,* and *Red Memories.* Work appears in anthologies, including *The Best American Plays of 1995-1996.* Author of screenplay *Who's the Man?,* and of teleplay *The Love Doctor,* MTV Networks.

WORK IN PROGRESS: An adaptation of *Girls in Movies* for television; a screenplay for Propaganda Films; a screen adaptation of *The Bones* for Columbia Pictures; a novel about a middle-class man who loses his job and must resort to disreputable means to support his family.

SIDELIGHTS: Seth Greenland has spent more than two decades writing scripts for movies and television, authoring plays, and, in 2005, penning a novel portraying the Hollywood scene. In his play *Jungle Rot,* Greenland presents a black comedy involving an assassination plot targeting the prime minister of the Congo and an American embassy worker/CIA agent named John Stillman. The hapless Stillman is not only dealing with orders to help another agent assassinate the prime minister, but he also is coping with his dissatisfied and bitter wife, who is unhappy about her husband's lack of ambition. Thrown into the mix are a Cleveland auto-parts salesman and his wife, who have come to the Congo to search for their daughter and eventually become involved in the assassination attempt. The plan ultimately goes awry when Stillman decides against completing the mission and reveals the plot in front of a group of partygoers, including the prime minister himself.

Matthew Jaster, writing for the *Columbia Chronicle Online,* noted, "Historically, mixing politics and paranoia can lead to a vast array of opinions. Some might find the satire very satisfying, while others might understand the jokes, but fail to see the humor. Seth Greenland's play *Jungle Rot* not only succeeds at bringing these elements together, but also manages to create a memorable cast of characters along the way."

Greenland's two-act play *Jerusalem* focuses on psychiatrist Will Solomon, who, after watching one of his patients commit suicide, suffers a crisis of self-doubt. The play then follows the escapades of Solomon's dysfunctional inlaws, as the psychiatrist and his wife, Meg, go on a trip to visit them. Eventually the couple is joined by Meg's sister and her husband on a trip to Jerusalem as Solomon seeks to learn more about his Jewish heritage. Chris Jones, writing in *Variety,* commented that the "splendid *Jerusalem* should be this journeyman scribe's breakthrough play." Jones went on to remark that *Jerusalem* is "sufficiently wry and quirky to qualify as an accessible and commercial comedy, yet it also conveys enough thematic heft to feel like a theatrical evening of substance."

For his first novel, *The Bones,* Greenland draws on his vast experience writing for film and television and working with comedians. The story focuses on Frank Bones, a relatively successful comedian who desperately wants his own television series, which he tentatively calls *My Life and High Times.* Like a true Hollywood megalomaniac, Bones wants the television show to focus on him and him alone. When Bones asks television comedy writer Lloyd Melnick to help him, Melnick turns him down. Bones retaliates by driving a Humvee into Melnick's living room and then heads for the Mexican border chased by the police. A *Publishers Weekly* contributor noted that, despite the novel's hectic pace, Greenland "slows down enough along the way to expound intelligently on topics ranging from self-knowledge to 'the anxiety of affluence.'" In a review in *Booklist,* Joanne Wilkinson observed that the author "takes readers on an entertaining, behind-the-scenes tour of sitcoms and their socially maladroit, dyspeptic creators."

BIOGRAPHICAL AND CRITICAL SOURCES:

PERIODICALS

Booklist, February 1, 2005, Joanne Wilkinson, review of *The Bones,* p. 941.

Entertainment Weekly, March 4, 2005, Jennifer Reese, review of *The Bones,* p. 78.

Hollywood Reporter, March 16, 2005, Liza Foreman, "Columbia Collects *Bones* for Mamet," p. 4.

Kirkus Reviews, January 15, 2005, review of *The Bones,* p. 72.

Library Journal, February 15, 2005, Bob Lunn, review of *The Bones,* p. 116.

Publishers Weekly, January 31, 2005, review of *The Bones,* p. 49.

School Library Journal, April, 2005, Matthew L. Moffett, review of *The Bones,* p. 161.

Variety, April 26, 1993, Leonard Klady, review of *Who's the Man?,* p. 69; January 30, 1995, Chris Jones, review of *Jungle Rot,* p. 58; April 30, 2001, Chris Jones, review of *Jerusalem* p. 38.

Washington Post Book World, March 27, 2005, Michael Schaub, review of *The Bones,* p. 6.

ONLINE

Columbia Chronicle Online, http://www.ccchronicle. com/ (June 27, 2005), Matthew Jaster, review of *Jungle Rot.*

Doollee.com, http://www.doollee.com/ (June 27, 2005).

Kennedy Center Web site, http://www.kennedy-center. org/ (June 27, 2005), brief profile of Seth Greenland.

WordnBass.com, http://www.wordnbass.com/ (June 27, 2005), interview with Greenland.*

*   *   *

GREGORY, Julie 1969-
(Julie Jo elle Gregory)

PERSONAL: Born May 16, 1969, in Columbus, OH. *Ethnicity:* "Caucasian."

ADDRESSES: Agent—c/o Author Mail, Publicity Director, Bantam Dell Books, 1745 Broadway, New York, NY 10019.

CAREER: Writer.

WRITINGS:

Sickened: The Memoir of a Munchausen by Proxy Childhood, Bantam Books (New York, NY), 2003.

SIDELIGHTS: Julie Gregory told *CA:* "Looking back, I can see that I wrote as a means of escapist survival. All my little notes and letters to people as a kid were like messages stuffed in a bottle and sent off the island where the clan rulers were hostile. I used to see kids in a K-Mart parking lot, swap addresses with them, and then they'd become my pen pals. My exchange with them was usually under a minute—in between the time I jumped out of the car in the parking lot and my mother got out and yelled for me to get my ass over there—and sometimes it took them so much by surprise they'd give me their address before even realizing what I was asking. It didn't matter if they were twelve or twenty-four. Complete strangers would get these letters from me with who knows what contained in those pages because there was no other means for me to say what was going on.

"My first writing cast out and responded to was by *Readers Digest,* I read an article about the bombings in Belfast, Ireland, and I saw this boy my age who had lost his parents and was in an orphanage and couldn't wait to get out of there and join the fighting. I wanted to write back and forth to him. Actually I wanted to be his girlfriend. I was ten then. I got a nice letter back from *Readers Digest,* but they said they couldn't send my letter over to him. That's the first time I grasped how sometimes media would use its subjects with little intent on helping or following up on any of the people it was reporting on. It wasn't that articulate, but of course they could have sent my letter to him; they knew where he was, what orphanage he was in, they read the letter, it was wonderful, they just didn't want to take the time; it wasn't in the direction of any of their goals.

"What influences my work is probably feeling the gulf between reality, between perception and the infinite variables of the outside world's reality and perception. I have the urge to write then and to chasm the distance between the two. When I'm at risk of being grown over by another's distorted or shy-of-the-truth perceptions or beliefs, I write to gain clarity of my own inner landscape. Then when I'm done, a lot of that writing [done for personal reasons] seems to have universal properties that can be applied to lots of situations. This is particularly helpful in good old-fashioned family dysfunction, which is where most of my published work leads from. There tends to usually be one truthful black sheep and the rest of the family is steeped in denial. This can really shake one's sense of reality, especially when sorting out the truth of family members or the past. And dysfunction is the same the world over; far more rampant and horrific than we'd ever want to comprehend.

"I usually hem and haw, procrastinate like crazy, start dreaming words on the page, in perfect text, feel anxious, have a few panic attacks, write on why I'm resisting writing, complain to my partner that I'm not writing on my work, watch a lot of baddd tv while mentally kicking myself for not tapping my god-given talent and just doing it, and then finally, after I've hit rock bottom in that cycle, I just start a thread, it unravels and I have a major portion of writing done in an insanely small amount of time. I wrote *Sickened: The Memoir of a Munchausen by Proxy Childhood,* in about three months and it was close to thirty pages longer before the editing of it. I think I might have started the first chapter on one of those little snack napkins you get on an airline flight with the peanuts. I don't know how other writers are, but I couldn't read a book for almost a year after writing and editing mine. It literally was a self-induced, man-made obsessive-compulsive disorder I gave myself. I must have printed out the manuscript one hundred times and it was 300 pages. I read and re-read the same paragraphs until the words were automatically imprinted and I would read along in my head before my eyes were even caught up with the words. In late edits, I would hear the old way the paragraph read, even though I'd changed it. Then when it was done, I couldn't read a book without editing it as I read along.

"The most surprising thing I have learned as a writer is that I got tired of talking. When I first started writing for a living, I was living pretty isolated—think Nell in a farmhouse on a mid-sized town campus. I didn't have many social skills and I was kind of desperate for a little intellectual interaction—and I certainly wasn't going to get it from the small-town yahoos I lived among. I think I loved to talk about my writing then because it was safe, I wasn't talking with someone face to face, I was doing interviews on the phone or e-mail and it was another medium to writing, one where I wasn't in hiding all the time and feeling like prey when I was out in public. But then I got tired of talking. And I started to see some of the banality of it, that no matter how good an interview you give, it's only as sharp as the reporter. Now, I just like to have entire days where I don't have to talk to anyone. Not even my partner if I'm too saturated or externalized. I use the time to float back to myself. I languish in my own interior world because if I don't, I can't write. You need space to do it, space to feel yourself and even find the threads of what you feel or want to say and if your partner isn't supportive of that, you're going to be fighting against yourself all the time. Stephen King gives the best advice: be willing to find a room with a door. And be willing to close it.

"Some of my favorite writing is my short or unfinished pieces, the stuff that is going to be used for books in the future. I once lived in this abandoned, three-storey pink hurricane house on Key West that perched in the back of an empty parking lot and had a mile of rotting sea grass running along outside. The week I unscrewed the boards that nailed the plywood to the door and started sleeping in the dark and peeing in an igloo cooler, was the week I began to write in my sleep. I saw perfect reams of text lined up and I put my sleepy hand out and could capture enough of the prime words to be able to reconstruct the feeling later, when I was awake. It also was the same week that the traveling carnival set up in that parking lot, right outside my door. So I'd have this peaceful model house interior with all these dreamy candles in tall skinny glass with religious motifs on them (because they were only ninety-nine cents from the grocery store) and then open the door to Motley Crue's "Shout at the Devil" blaring from the tilt-a-whirl twenty feet away. Surreal.

"I hope all sorts of things. That some of my writing will be carried around in a depressive kid's backpack and slipped, dog eared and double-underline inked (complete with exclamation marks) under his pillow at night, as a sort of teenage blankie. My work finds its way into the hands of young cutters and kids with suicidal tendencies due to being lone wolves in families or societies that can't or don't or won't see them and from there, I can lead them to others (people, places, or books) who offer mirroring and understanding. That the reader can realize that it doesn't matter what anybody tells you, or how anyone might try to hold you back in life, or mistreat you; you can get away and start your life where you want it or at least strive to get there. That you don't have to go from here to there, dragging your pain around like an old dying flap of skin, but you can unplug, make a quantum leap, slot into the highest place of your own shine and have that be your new base of self.

"For people that are new to writing and want to try to earn a living at it I offer this: I have no official high school diploma, have been homeless a couple times, have a crummy family and took only one writing class, and yet got accepted into a master's program when I was in my thirties based on my hard work and ambition, then went on to write a book that made its way to twenty countries—and as you know, I wrote part of that book (before it ever sold) when I was living in a miner's shack in Death Valley. You don't have to come from something to be something. If you have a vision as an artist, start from the top, only work backwards if you have to. Do anything you can to keep your inspiration alive and don't let small voices around you in. Most people, especially in small towns, cannot recognize true talent, beauty, or genius. People in general, even people who say they love you, often have little to zero comprehension of what you are really here to do in this life. You do. So tap into that and don't look back."

BIOGRAPHICAL AND CRITICAL SOURCES:

BOOKS

Gregory, Julie, *Sickened: The Memoir of a Munchausen by Proxy Childhood,* Bantam Books (New York, NY), 2003.

*   *   *

GREGORY, Julie Jo elle
See GREGORY, Julie

*   *   *

GRIGGS, Jeff 1971-

PERSONAL: Born 1971.

ADDRESSES: Office—ImprovOlympic, 3541 N. Clark St., Chicago, IL 60657.

CAREER: Actor, educator, and director. ImprovOlympic, Chicago, IL, artistic director. Travels throughout United States teaching and directing improvisation.

WRITINGS:

Guru: My Days with Del Close (nonfiction), Ivan R. Dee (Chicago, IL), 2005.

SIDELIGHTS: Jeff Griggs is the author of *Guru: My Days with Del Close,* a chronicle of the final years in the life of Close, an actor and director who worked at Chicago's famous ImprovOlympic, a training ground for actors learning the art of improvisation. Among the school's most notable alumni are comedians and actors Bill Murray, John Belushi, and Chris Farley. In the book, Griggs—who was a student at the ImprovOlympic—writes about chauffeuring Close around on the weekends and acting as a general assistant in return for free tuition. By the time the two meet, Close is sickly and suffering from emphysema, a lung condition that causes coughing and labored breathing. Initially Close and Griggs engage in a battle of wills and continually antagonize each other, but eventually they form a close a friendship. The book is written in alternating chapters, interspersing Griggs's relationship with Close with a more straightforward biography of Close's life and his career dedicated to training actors. The pair's daily adventures feature episodes in which the two improvised various characters in public; in one case, in a restaurant Close takes on the persona of a nobleman and Griggs his mentally disabled sidekick. "Griggs' prose may be rough, but it is also energetic and heartfelt, honest and utterly riveting," wrote Jack Helbig in *Booklist.* Rosellen Brewer, writing in *Library Journal,* commented that the book "offers insight into the world of improvisational theater." A *Kirkus Reviews* contributor called *Guru* "a wild and fascinating ride," adding that "Griggs's timed and textured prose is anything but improvisational, and each of the short chapters here is a success."

BIOGRAPHICAL AND CRITICAL SOURCES:

BOOKS

Griggs, Jeff, *Guru: My Days with Del Close,* Ivan R. Dee (Chicago, IL), 2005.

PERIODICALS

Booklist, March 1, 2005, Jack Helbig, review of *Guru: My Days with Del Close,* p. 1126.
Kirkus Reviews, January 15, 2005, review of *Guru,* p. 100.
Library Journal, March 15, 2005, Rosellen Brewer, review of *Guru,* p. 87.
MBR Bookwatch, June, 2005, Diane C. Donovan, review of *Guru.**

*   *   *

GRILLO, John 1942-

PERSONAL: Born November 29, 1942, in Watford, Hertfordshire, England.

ADDRESSES: Agent—Michell Braidman Associates, 3rd Ste., 10 Lower John St., London W1F 9EB, England.

CAREER: Actor in plays, including (as Dabble) *Lock up Your Daughters,* (as Billy Bones) *Treasure Island,* (as poet) *Five to a Flat,* (as Ingham) *Little Malcolm and His Struggle against the Eunuchs,* (in various roles) *Beyond the Fringe,* (as Andrei) *The Three Sisters,* (as Clarence) *2 Henry IV,* (as Max) *The Homecoming,* (as Jopplin) *A Shouting in the Streets,* and (as Rusty Charley) *Guys and Dolls,* all Lincoln, England, 1996-67; (as Old Man) *Hello Goodbye Sebastian,* and (as Rasputin) *The Rasputin Show,* both Brighton, England, 1968; (as Verlaine) *Total Eclipse,* Royal Court Theatre, London, England, 1968; (as Glendower) *Henry IV,* and (various roles) *Erogenous Zones,* both Royal Court Theatre, 1969; (as Eddy) *Tango,* (as millionaire) *Cliffwalk,* (as Fawcett) *Oh Everyman, Oh Colonel Fawcett,* and (as Don Pedro) *Much Ado about Nothing,* all Castle Theatre, Farnham, England, 1969-70; (as Peowne) *AC/DC,* Royal Court Theatre, 1970; (as nurse) *Number Three,* Soho Theatre Club, London, 1970; (as reporter and deaf-and-dumb man) *Lulu,* and (as Marx) *Anarchist,* both Royal Court Theatre, 1971; (as thug) *Dynamo,* 1971; (as recorder) *Inquisition,* Soho Theatre Club, 1971; (as Mr. Bickerstaff) *Mr. Bickerstaff's Establishment,* London, 1972; (as Doc) *The Tooth of Crime,* London, 1972; (as Sergeant Kite) *The Recruiting Officer,* Hornchurch, Essex, England, 1972; (as Dr. Rank) *A Doll's House,* Greenwich, England, 1972; (as Poltorne) *The Director of the Opera,* Chichester, England, 1973; (as Gremio) *The Taming of the Shrew,* London, 1974; (as Ashley Withers) *The End of Me Old Cigar,* London, 1975; (as Horatio) *Hamlet,* Piccadilly Theatre, London, 1982; (as Comolet) *Bussy D'Ambois,* Old Vic Theatre, London, 1988; and *Storm/After the Fire/The Ghost Sonata,* Notting Hill, England, 1997.

Actor in films, including (as first man) *Dynamo,* 1972; (as Goodyear) *Scum,* World Northal, 1979; (as bank official) *The Great Riviera Bank Robbery* (also known as *Dirty Money* and *Sewers of Gold*), 1979; (as customs officer) *Firefox,* Warner Bros., 1982; (as interview official) *Brazil,* 1985; (as Jonah) *Ha-Kala* (also known as *The Seventeenth Bride* and *The Bride*), 1985; (as hotel manager) *Blame It on the Bellboy,* Bellboy Films Ltd., 1992; (as Chios Mapmaker) *Christopher Columbus: The Discovery,* Warner Bros., 1992; (as first official) *Orlando,* 1992; (as Mr. Berry) *B & B,* 1992; (as landlord) *Jack and Sarah,* 1995; (as Mr.

West) *FairyTale: A True Story* (also known as *Illumination*), 1997; (as Sir Dinshaw Petit) *Jinnah,* 1998; (as Dr. Legear) *The Affair of the Necklace,* 2001; and (as Nina's father) *Max,* 2002; also appeared in *The F and H Film.*

Actor in television movies, including (as Joseph) *The Lady of the Camellias,* 1976; (as Caroline's husband) *A Christmas Carol,* 1977; (as Oswale) *King Lear,* 1982; (as Bell) *Amy,* 1984; *Afterward,* 1985; (as Barrow) *A Little Princess,* Public Broadcasting Service (PBS), 1986; (as Jake Shapiro) *The Alamut Ambush,* 1986; (as Markos Togas) *Out of the Shadows,* Showtime, 1988; (as Mr. Parker) *Danny, the Champion of the World,* Disney Channel, 1989; (as Cantor) *Shalom Joan Collins,* 1989; (as Joseph Weiss) *Max and Helen,* Turner Network Television (TNT), 1990; (as pathologist) *A Murder of Quality,* PBS, 1991; (as Dr. Bronowski) *Selected Exits,* 1993; (as Dr. Ian Matthews) *Trust,* 1999; and (as Franks) *Shackleton,* 2002. Actor in television miniseries, including (as Mr. Samgrass) *Brideshead Revisited,* PBS, 1981; (as Prime) *Blott on the Landscape,* 1985; (as lawyer) *Paradise Postponed,* 1986; (as Johann Krauss) *Queenie,* American Broadcasting Companies (ABC), 1987; (as Cunningham) *A Perfect Spy,* PBS, 1988; (as Von Behr) *The Man Who Lived at the Ritz,* syndicated, 1988; *The Modern World: Ten Great Writers,* segment "Mann," 1988; *Titmuss Regained,* 1991; and (as Mr. Grimwig) *Oliver Twist,* 1999. Actor in television series, including (as Wilf) *Three Up, Two Down,* British Broadcasting Corporation Channel 1 (BBC-1), 1985-89; (as Jemadah) *Watt on Earth,* beginning 1991; (as Oscar William Leonard "Owly" Johnstone) *Under the Hammer,* began 1993; and (as Mr. Carkdale) *Chalk,* began 1997. Actor in television specials, including (as Judge Teasdale) *Rumpole and the Bubble Reputation,* PBS, 1989; (as man at the gallery) *Mother Love,* PBS, 1990; and (as Barty Pine) *Titmuss Regained,* PBS, 1992. Guest star on television series, including *Chocky, Blackadder II, Rumpole of the Bailey, This Is David Harper, The Darling Buds of May, Boon, Between the Lines, Mike & Angelo, Lovejoy,* and *Cracker.*

WRITINGS:

STAGE PLAYS

Gentlemen I . . . , produced in Cambridge, England, 1963.
It Will Come or I Won't, produced in Dublin, Ireland, 1965.

Hello Goodbye Sebastian, produced in Cambridge, England, 1965.

The Downfall of Jack Throb, produced in London, England, 1967.

The Fall of Samson Morocco, produced in London, England, 1969.

Oh Everyman, Oh Colonel Fawcett, produced in Farnham, Surrey, England, 1969.

Mr. Bickerstaff's Establishment, produced in Glasgow, Scotland, 1969, expanded version produced in London, England, 1972.

Number Three, (produced in London, England, 1970), published in *Short Plays,* Methuen (London, England), 1972.

Blubber, produced in London, England, 1971.

Zonk, produced in London, England, 1971.

Food, produced in London, England, 1971.

Will the King Leave His Tea Pot, produced in London, England, 1971.

George and Moira Entertain a Member of the Opposite Sex to Dinner, produced in London, England, 1971.

The Hammer and the Hacksaw, produced in Edinburgh, Scotland, 1971.

Christmas Box and *Civitas Dei* (double-bill), produced London, England, 1972.

History of a Poor Old Man, produced in London, England, 1972.

Snaps, produced in London, England, 1973.

Crackers, produced in London, England, 1973.

Mr. Ives' Magic Punch and Judy Show, produced in London, England, 1973.

Also author of television play *Nineteen Thirty Nine,* 1973.

SIDELIGHTS: British writer and actor John Grillo began his career as a playwright in the 1960s and wrote several plays over the next ten years. Among his most popular is *Hello Goodbye Sebastian,* about a gravedigger who aspires to a more genteel life. As an actor, Grillo has played a great many parts on stage, and has been cast in numerous roles in films and television productions.

BIOGRAPHICAL AND CRITICAL SOURCES:

BOOKS

Contemporary Dramatists, fifth edition, St. James Press (Detroit, MI), 1993.

PERIODICALS

Sunday Times (London, England), January 19, 1997, John Peter, review of *Storm/After the Fire/The Ghost Sonata,* p. 19.

ONLINE

Internet Movie Database, http://www.imdb.com/ (June 30, 2005), profile of Grillo.*

* * *

GROSS, Michael Joseph

PERSONAL: Male.

ADDRESSES: Home—CA. *Agent*—c/o Author Mail, Bloomsbury Publishing, 175 5th Ave., Ste. 300, New York, NY 10010.

CAREER: Freelance writer.

AWARDS, HONORS: Discovery Award for nonfiction, PEN/New England, 2002.

WRITINGS:

Starstruck: When a Fan Gets Close to Fame (sociology), Bloomsbury (New York, NY), 2005.

Contributor to periodicals, including *New York Times, Boston Globe, Atlantic Monthly, Entertainment Weekly, Elle, Nation,* and *Salon.com.*

SIDELIGHTS: Freelance writer Michael Joseph Gross is the author of *Starstruck: When a Fan Gets Close to Fame,* a semi-memoir, semi-investigation about what makes the legions of movie-stars and musician fans tick. Gross was a fan himself as a teenager—he collected over 4,000 autographs and even managed to meet President Ronald Reagan—so he understands his subject. This personal knowledge allows Gross "to deliver piercing insights into the behavior of the fans he encounters and the stars with whom he crosses paths," Kristine Huntley noted in *Booklist*. Those fans include enthusiasts of singers Michael Jackson and Dolly Parton who Gross met at Neverland and Dollywood, respectively. Gross also interviews people who get paid to be fans, such as professional autograph collectors and entertainment journalists such as Mary Hart, host of *Entertainment Tonight*. On the star side, Gross recounts his relationship with actor Sean Astin (best known as Samwise Gamgee in the *Lord of the Rings* trilogy of films), which is partly a friendship and partly something more professional. Because of this relationship Gross even gets to experience a touch of celebrity himself, when he passes through the gauntlet of fans on the red carpet with Astin before the Screen Actors' Guild awards. Through these anecdotes Gross examines several deep issues in the current American celebrity culture, including "the symbiotic economics of celebrity/fandom [and] the celebrity as saint in a secular religion," as Dave Szatmary noted in *Library Journal*.

BIOGRAPHICAL AND CRITICAL SOURCES:

PERIODICALS

Advocate, May 24, 2005, review of *Starstruck: When a Fan Gets Close to Fame*, p. 82.
Booklist, March 1, 2005, Kristine Huntley, review of *Starstruck*, p. 1117.
Kirkus Reviews, February 1, 2005, review of *Starstruck*, p. 164.
Library Journal, March 15, 2005, Dave Szatmary, review of *Starstruck*, p. 102.
Los Angeles Magazine, May, 2005, Ariel Swartley, review of *Starstruck*, p. 134.
Publishers Weekly, February 21, 2005, review of *Starstruck*, p. 167.*

*   *   *

GUILIANO, Mireille 1946-

PERSONAL: Name is pronounced "*meer*-ray julie-*ah*-no"; born April 14, 1946, in France; naturalized U.S. citizen; married Edward Guiliano (president and CEO of New York Institute of Technology), 1976. *Educa-*

tion: Undergraduate degree from Sorbonne, University of Paris; Institut Supérieur d'Interprétariat et de Traduction, master's degree.

ADDRESSES: Home—New York, NY. *Agent*—c/o Author Mail, Alfred A. Knopf, 1745 Broadway, New York, NY 10019.

CAREER: Businessperson, spokesperson, and writer. House of Champagne Veuve Clicquot, spokesperson; Clicquot, Inc., cofounder, 1984, then president and CEO. Worked as a translator for United Nations. Also works with various groups promoting business opportunities and education for women. Has appeared on television programs, including *Oprah, The Today Show, The Early Show,* and *Dateline*. James Beard Foundation Board, trustee. Member, Committee of 200.

WRITINGS:

French Women Don't Get Fat: The Secret of Eating for Pleasure (nonfiction), Knopf (New York, NY), 2005.

Contributor to periodicals, including *Gourmet, Town & Country,* and *Quarterly Review of Wines*.

French Women Don't Get Fat has been translated into thirty languages, including German, Dutch, Russian, Chinese, Spanish, Finnish, Swedish, Portuguese, Croatian, and Japanese.

ADAPTATIONS: French Women Don't Get Fat: The Secret of Eating for Pleasure was adapted as an audio book, Random House Audio, 2005.

SIDELIGHTS: Mireille Guiliano is a native of France who lives in the United States and has worked for many years in the wine, spirits, and luxury-goods industries. Her book *French Women Don't Get Fat: The Secret of Eating for Pleasure* is a best-selling diet and exercise book based on her experience with French cuisine and lifestyle. Writing on her home page, Guiliano noted that she wrote the book "in response to years of being asked how do you eat and drink what you do, enjoy it so much but never get fat?" The author went on to say, "I wrote it, though, to share and give back: to help people eat for pleasure and not diet. It has been called the ultimate non-diet book, and I like that because diet books don't work. If they did, no one would be fat." The author also added that "unbalanced" diets often "offend my French soul."

French Women Don't Get Fat expresses Guiliano's philosophy on eating and enjoying life sensibly to prevent weight gain, and it is also partly a memoir of the author's life. In the book, she looks back on her own early weight problem; she gained thirty pounds at age nineteen when she came to America as an exchange student and started eating like other Americans. On a visit to her French family physician, Guiliano was guided back to eating in moderation rather than eliminating all high-calorie foods. Guiliano refers to her doctor as "Dr. Miracle" and presents the doctor's advice and philosophy on eating well yet staying trim. Despite the "anti-diet" tone of the book, the author does offer specific steps for losing weight and keeping the pounds off. She first advises readers to keep an inventory of what is eaten for three weeks and then for the next three months to focus on reforming eating habits. Specific weight-loss tricks include an initial weekend of eating only leek broth, adding yogurt to the diet, and drinking more water. Although the author warns against overindulging in high-calorie foods such as bagels and chocolate and high-calorie drinks such as juice and liquor, she maintains that eating these and other foods in controlled portions with planned meals is fine. In addition to including numerous recipes, the author also advocates more walking and other non-gym approaches to exercise.

Writing in the *Weekly Standard*, Rachel DiCarlo noted that "overall it's a fun book with plenty of practical wisdom." A *Tufts University Health & Nutrition Letter* contributor pointed out that almost all of Guiliano's advice has been set forth before but added "somehow, though, the . . . French champagne-company executive communicates all this mostly sensible advice with a certain je ne sais quoi that's the stuff of bestsellers." In a review in *Library Journal*, Florence Scarinci suggested that the book would be "a unique addition to health and nutrition collections." A *Publishers Weekly* contributor remarked that Guiliano's "book . . . is a stirring reminder of the importance of joie de vivre." Mark Knoblauch claimed in *Booklist* that the author presents "a commonsense diet based on both restraint and simple exercise."

BIOGRAPHICAL AND CRITICAL SOURCES:

BOOKS

Guiliano, Mireille, *French Women Don't Get Fat: The Secret of Eating for Pleasure* (nonfiction), Knopf (New York, NY), 2005.

PERIODICALS

Booklist, December 1, 2004, Mark Knoblauch, review of *French Women Don't Get Fat: The Secret of Eating for Pleasure,* p. 626.
Business Week, April 25, 2005, Susan Berfield, "Fat Times for a French Woman; The Skinny on How Diet Author Mireille Guiliano Is Milking Her Newfound Fame," p. 113.
Library Journal, November 1, 2004, Florence Scarinci, review of *French Women Don't Get Fat,* p. 112.
New Statesman, January 17, 2005, Michele Roberts, review of *French Women Don't Get Fat,* p. 53.
Newsweek International, January 24, 2005, Jeffrey Wasserstrom, review of *French Women Don't Get Fat,* p. 57.
People, January 24, 2005, Kim Hubbard and Debbie Seaman, review of *French Women Don't Get Fat,* p. 147.
Publishers Weekly, November 22, 2004, Lynn Andriani, "C'est si bon," interview with Mireille Guiliano, p. 46; November 22, 2004, review of *French Women Don't Get Fat,* p. 46; January 17, 2005, Charlotte Abbott, "Knopf Tries to Keep Up with French Diet," p. 15; February 7, 2005, review of *French Women Don't Get Fat,* p. 35.
Town & Country, February 2005, Chantal M. McLaughlin, review of *French Women Don't Get Fat,* p. 108.
Tufts University Health & Nutrition Letter, May 2005, review of *French Women Don't Get Fat,* p. 6.
Weekly Standard, March 14, 2005, Rachel DiCarlo, review of *French Women Don't Get Fat,* p. 43.

ONLINE

Mireille Guiliano Home Page, http://www.mireille guiliano.com (June 29, 2005).
MostlyFiction.com, http://mostlyfiction.com/ (March 27, 2005), Jan Kraus, review of *French Women Don't Get Fat: The Secret of Eating for Pleasure.*

H

HALL, Alex M. 1942-

PERSONAL: Born December 17, 1942, in Toronto, Ontario, Canada; son of Malcolm M.R. (a radiologist) and Mildred I. (a nurse; maiden name, MacLennan) Hall; married Lia M. Ruttan (a social worker), June 6, 1974; children: Graham, Evan. *Education:* University of Western Ontario, B.Sc., 1964; University of Toronto, M.Sc., 1971. *Politics:* Liberal.

ADDRESSES: Home—P.O. Box 130, Fort Smith, Northwest Territories X0E OP0, Canada. *E-mail*— alex@canoearctic.com.

CAREER: Writer. Canoe Arctic, Inc., Northwest Territories, Canada, president, 1974—.

AWARDS, HONORS: Top 100 books published in Canada designation, *Globe and Mail,* 2003, for *Discovering Eden: A Lifetime of Paddling Arctic Rivers.*

WRITINGS:

Discovering Eden: A Lifetime of Paddling Arctic Rivers, Key Porter Books (Toronto, Ontario, Canada), 2003.

SIDELIGHTS: Alex M. Hall told *CA:* "*Discovering Eden: A Lifetime of Paddling Arctic Rivers* is the story of the Barren Lands and my life there over the past several decades. It's a collection of stories, essays, and commentaries about the largest wilderness left in North America, its animals and the lessons they have taught me, about my experiences on its remote wild rivers as a professional canoeing guide, and my hopes and dreams for the area's future.

"My primary motivation for writing this book was the accelerating mineral exploration and mining activity in the area along with the inevitable roads, power dams, and electrical transmission lines that are bound to follow. If I learned anything about writing in producing *Discovering Eden,* it was that the first draft has to come from the heart. Writing with your head is what it takes to polish that first draft and you'll probably spend much more time and effort in this than in the original creative process. But if a piece wasn't written from the heart to begin with, it will never entertain, move, or inspire the reader."

*   *   *

HALLOWAY SCOTT, Susan
(Miranda Jarrett)

PERSONAL: Female. *Education:* Brown University, B.A. (art history).

ADDRESSES: Office—P.O. Box 1102, Paoli, PA 19301-1145.

CAREER: Writer.

AWARDS, HONORS: Romantic Times award nominations, 1996, for *Sparhawk's Angel,* 2000, for *Starlight,* 2001, for *The Very Daring Duchess; Romantic Times* award, 1999, for *Wishing;* finalist for two Romance Writers of America RITA awards.

WRITINGS:

ROMANCE NOVELS; UNDER PSEUDONYM MIRANDA JARRETT

Gift of the Heart, Harlequin Books (New York, NY), 1996.

The Captain's Bride, Pocket Books (New York, NY), 1997.

Cranberry Point, Pocket Books (New York, NY), 1998.

Star Bright, Sonnet Books (New York, NY), 2000.

The Very Comely Countess ("Napoleonic Wars" series), Sonnet Books (New York, NY), 2001.

The Very Daring Duchess ("Napoleonic Wars" series), Sonnet Books (New York, NY), 2001.

"SPARHAWK" SERIES ROMANCE NOVELS; UNDER PSEUDONYM MIRANDA JARRETT

The Sparhawk Bride, Harlequin Books (New York, NY), 1995.

Sparhawk's Lady, Harlequin Books (New York, NY), 1995.

Sparhawk's Angel, Harlequin Books (New York, NY), 1996.

The Secrets of Catie Hazard, Harlequin Books (New York, NY), 1997.

"FAIRBOURNE" SERIES ROMANCE NOVELS; UNDER PSEUDONYM MIRANDA JARRETT

Wishing, Sonnet Books (New York, NY), 1999.
Moonlight, Sonnet Books (New York, NY), 1999.
Sunrise, Sonnet Books (New York, NY), 2000.

SIDELIGHTS: With a dozen books that have sold over two million copies, as well as numerous awards to her credit, Miranda Jarrett—the pen name of Susan Halloway Scott—has enjoyed considerable success as a writer in the area of historical romance. Her first published works—*Sparhawk's Lady, The Sparhawk Bride,* and *Sparhawk's Angel*—center around a single family in colonial-era America. In *The Secrets of Catie Hazard,* the heroine becomes pregnant by Anthony Sparhawk, a young soldier on his way to England. She marries an innkeeper, but eight years later Sparhawk returns—now as a British soldier fighting the rebel-lious colonials. Kristin Ramsdell in *Library Journal* called the book "a powerful story that transcends its historical setting."

The colonial era—specifically, the year 1721—also provides the setting for *Wishing,* which begins with a sea captain making a promise to the gods. Samson Fairbourne vows that if he finds "a young woman sweet in temper and without vanity, modest and truthful in words and manner, obedient and honorable," he will marry her, and after writing these words on a piece of paper, he seals the promise in an empty rum bottle and throws it in the ocean. In time Polly Bray, desperately struggling to survive after her father's death, finds the bottle and eventually winds up in Fairbourne's arms. Wrote Melanie Duncan in *Booklist,* "Jarrett fashions a winning nautical tale that is sure to appeal to all fans of colonial-era romances."

Moonlight and its sequel *Sunrise* also concern members of the Fairbourne family. In *Sunrise,* widower Daniel Fairbourne rescues Juliette LaCroix from the sea and nurses her back to health. A romance between them grows, but as the amnesiac Juliette gradually recovers the details of her past, the facts of her life seem to preclude any future relationship between the two. According to a reviewer in *Publishers Weekly,* "Jarrett evokes the era with accuracy and draws her protagonists vividly and with charm."

The Napoleonic wars provide the backdrop for *The Very Daring Duchess* and its sequel, *The Very Comely Countess.* In the first installment Edward Ramsden, a dashing officer in the Royal Navy, comes ashore in Naples and visits a gallery featuring pornographic paintings and forged masterpieces. He is quite taken with the proprietress, Francesca Robin, who is half English and half Neapolitan. When the French threaten to invade the Italian city, Edward offers to marry Francesca to ensure her safe passage to England. "Jarrett's sex scenes are steamy and descriptive," noted a reviewer in *Publishers Weekly,* while Kathe Robin, in the *Romantic Times,* concluded that "you can always count on Ms. Jarrett to gift us with something intelligent, new, and vibrant."

BIOGRAPHICAL AND CRITICAL SOURCES:

PERIODICALS

Booklist, January 1, 1999, Melanie Duncan, review of *Wishing,* p. 841.

Library Journal, May 15, 1997, Kristin Ramsdell, review of *The Secrets of Catie Hazard,* p. 66.

Publishers Weekly, December 20, 1999, review of *Sunrise,* p. 62; August 27, 2001, review of *The Very Daring Duchess,* p. 62.

ONLINE

Romance Reader Web site, http://www.theromance reader.com/ (September 16, 2003), Jean Mason, review of *The Very Daring Duchess.*

Romantic Times Web site, http://www.romantictimes. com/ (September 16, 2003), biography of Miranda Jarrett, and Kathe Robin, review of *The Very Daring Duchess.**

*   *   *

HAMANN, Jack 1954-

PERSONAL: Born 1954; married; wife's name Leslie; children: two. *Education:* University of California, Los Angeles, B.A., 1976; University of Oregon School of Law, J.D., 1980.

ADDRESSES: Home—Seattle, WA. *Agent*—c/o Author Mail, Algonquin Books of Chapel Hill, P.O. Box 2225, Chapel Hill, NC 27515-2225. *E-mail*—jackhamann@ comcast.net.

CAREER: Journalist, writer, and producer. Has worked as a network correspondent and television documentary producer; *NewsHour with Jim Lehrer,* Public Broadcasting Service, Seattle bureau chief.

AWARDS, HONORS: Emmy Awards, 1985, 1990, for news feature, 1986, for both sports news and sports special, 1987, for spot news, 1988, for news special, 1990 for both investigative news and news special, and 2000, for documentary; New York Film Festival silver awards, 1984, 1994; Environmental Media award first place, 1992; CableAce award, 1993; Houston Film Festival gold award, 1994; Headliner award first place, 2000; Communicator award, 2000; CINE award, 2001; Silver Chris award, 2002, for *Hot Potatoes;* Barnes & Noble Star of Washington award, 2005.

WRITINGS:

On American Soil: Murder, the Military, and How Justice Became a Casualty of World War II, Algonquin Books of Chapel Hill (Chapel Hill, NC), 2005.

TELEVISION SCRIPTS; DOCUMENTARIES

(And coproducer and correspondent) *Diane Downs: Circle of Abuse,* National Broadcasting Company, Inc. (NBC)/King TV, 1984.

(And coproducer and correspondent) *Mary and Zola: After the Fall,* NBC/King TV, 1985.

(And coproducer and correspondent) *Shelter from the Storm,* NBC/King TV, 1986.

(And coproducer and correspondent) *Discovery Park Graves,* NBC/King TV, 1987.

(And coproducer and correspondent) *The Quake and the Lives It Shook,* NBC/King TV, 1989.

(And coproducer and correspondent) *The Earth Summit,* Cable News Network (CNN), 1992.

(And coproducer and correspondent) *Green Plans,* Public Broadcasting Service (PBS), 1995.

(And coproducer and correspondent) *Peace Frogs,* CNN, 1997.

(And coproducer and correspondent) *The Russia Factor,* CNN, 1999.

(And coproducer and correspondent) *Faith & Fear: The Children of Krishna,* PBS, 2001.

(And coproducer and correspondent) *Hot Potatoes,* PBS, 2001.

Also writes a regular column for *Nature.*

SIDELIGHTS: A journalist who has worked extensively in television, Jack Hamann is the author of *On American Soil: Murder, the Military, and How Justice Became a Casualty of World War II.* The book came about when the author learned of a riot that broke out at Fort Lawton, Washington during World War II. There Italian prisoners of war fought with black U.S. soldiers, leading to numerous injuries and the lynching of Italian soldier Private Guglielmo Olivotto. Although courts-martial of American soldiers were convened, Olivotto's murder was never solved. Commenting on the justice of the court-martial, Hamann told Alex Fryer in an article for the *Seattle Times Pacific Northwest* magazine: "There are some defendants who did not get as severe a penalty as things might have warranted. But there were many others who were nothing but peacekeepers. For the three men charged with murder, none of them was responsible for Olivotto's death, in my view."

On American Soil recounts the prisoner-of-war battle and the ensuing courts-martial, as well as the many individuals involved, including riot participants and the lawyers representing both sides in the trial. The author also explores such issues as race relations within the military, the overall treatment of POWs, and the wide-ranging political implications of the revolt and subsequent trials. A *Kirkus Reviews* contributor noted that the author "cites declassified documents, court transcripts and interviews to show how the segregated Army compromised justice so that black soldiers were pinned to the crime and leaving possible white suspects overlooked." The reviewer added that the author is successful in "adroitly balancing racism and legal questions." Alan Moores, writing in *Booklist,* commented that "it is the crime's historical context . . . that makes the book so relevant now." A reviewer writing in *Publishers Weekly* felt that the author "is best in depicting the men involved and the waste of lives that the episode entailed." Elizabeth Morris wrote in the *Library Journal* that "Hamann's lively narrative and incisive commentary raise the standard for investigational writing."

BIOGRAPHICAL AND CRITICAL SOURCES:

PERIODICALS

Booklist, February 15, 2005, Alan Moores, review of *On American Soil: Murder, the Military, and How Justice Became a Casualty of World War II,* p. 1055.
Kirkus Reviews, February 15, 2005, review of *On American Soil,* p. 212.
Library Journal, March 15, 2005, Elizabeth Morris, review of *On American Soil,* p. 96.
Publishers Weekly, February 7, 2005, review of *On American Soil,* p. 50.

ONLINE

Jack Hamann Home Page, http://www.jackhamann. com (June 29, 2005).
Pacific Northwest (a magazine of the *Seattle Times*), http://seattletimes.nwsource.com/pacificnw/ (June 29, 2005), Alex Fryer, "Jack Hamann Opens the Prison of Our Past," interview with author.*

*   *   *

HAMNER, Linda
(Linda Elin Hamner)

PERSONAL: Married; husband's name Gary.

ADDRESSES: Agent—c/o St. Martin's Griffin, 175 5th Ave., New York, NY 10010. *E-mail*—cleoandtyrone@ yahoo.com

CAREER: Author of television scripts and fiction. Script consultant for Television Corporation of Singapore.

AWARDS, HONORS: Daytime Emmy Award (with others) for outstanding writing team in a drama series, National Television Academy/Academy of Television Arts and Sciences, 1991, and Writers Guild Award, Writers Guild of America, both for *Santa Barbara.*

WRITINGS:

(With L. Virginia Browne) *Letters from Cleo and Tyrone: A Feline Perspective on Love, Life, and Litter,* illustrated by Steve Feldman, St. Martin's Griffin (New York, NY), 2000.

Writer for television series, including *Another World,* National Broadcasting Company (NBC), *General Hospital,* American Broadcasting Company (ABC), *Guiding Light,* Columbia Broadcasting System (CBS), *Santa Barbara,* NBC, and *Texas,* NBC.

WORK IN PROGRESS: With L. Virginia Browne, an original online serial for Warner Bros.

SIDELIGHTS: Linda Hamner and L. Virginia Browne appear as themselves in their joint novel *Letters from Cleo and Tyrone: A Feline Perspective on Love, Life, and Litter.* However, the two women are far offscreen in the story, whose protagonists are their cats: Cleo the Divine, who lives with Hamner, and Tyrone the Great, owned by Browne. In the epistolary tale, the correspondents are the cats, who discuss everything from their mutual attraction to the art of regurgitating hairballs.

The book's initial premise is not so different from that of the popular 1920s and 1930s "archy and mehitabel" series by Don Marquis, in which the cockroach archy types notes for the cat mehitabel on Marquis's manual typewriter, and the names appear in lowercase because the correspondents could not use the shift key on the machine. However, *Letters from Cleo and Tyrone* involves a technological component that roots it firmly in its time: the two correspond via e-mail. Furthermore, their amorous dialogue and subversive attitudes toward their "mommies" (roundly criticized by both) identify Cleo and Tyrone as denizens of the post-1960s generation, worlds away from the less-ironic sensibilities of Marquis's time.

While a reviewer in *Publishers Weekly* noted that the authors "wring from [their premise] some moments of wicked, if painfully obvious, humor," a commentator in *Kirkus Reviews* was more positive, calling *Letters from Cleo and Tyrone* an "amusing first novel and takeoff on the old archy and mehitabel series." Sally Rosenthal wrote in *Cats* magazine that "while reading it, I laughed so long my cats came into my room, wondering what was so funny."

BIOGRAPHICAL AND CRITICAL SOURCES:

PERIODICALS

Cats, May, 2001, Sally Rosenthal, review of *Letters from Cleo and Tyrone: A Feline Perspective on Love, Life, and Litter,* p. 62.
Kirkus Review, September 15, 2000, review of *Letters from Cleo and Tyrone.*
Publishers Weekly, October 16, 2000, review of *Letters from Cleo and Tyrone,* p. 51.

ONLINE

Cleo and Tyrone Home Page, http://www.cleoand tyrone.com/ (September 16, 2003).*

*   *   *

HAMNER, Linda Elin
    See HAMNER, Linda

*   *   *

HARDING, John Wesley
    See STACE, Wesley

HAYDER, Mo 1962(?)-

PERSONAL: Born c. 1962, in England; partner of Keith Quinn; children: Lotte-Genevieve. *Education:* American University (Washington, DC), M.A.; Bath Spa University, M.A.

ADDRESSES: Home—Bath, England. *Agent*—Gregory & Company Authors' Agents, 3 Barb Mews, Hammersmith, London W6 7PA, England.

CAREER: Novelist and educator. University of Bath, Bath, England, creative-writing teacher. Previously worked as a barmaid, security guard, filmmaker, hostess in a Tokyo club, educational administrator, and teacher of English as a foreign language in Asia.

AWARDS, HONORS: W.H. Smith Thumping Good Read award, 2002, for *The Treatment.*

WRITINGS:

FICTION

Birdman, Doubleday (New York, NY), 1999.
The Treatment, Doubleday (New York, NY), 2002.
Tokyo, Bantam (London, England), 2004, published as *The Devil of Nanking,* Grove Press (New York, NY), 2005.

Also author of the novel *The Creature,* 2006.

WORK IN PROGRESS: A novel.

SIDELIGHTS: Mo Hayder is the author of dark, disturbing, and violent thrillers. Her debut novel, *Birdman,* which became an international bestseller, is set in Greenwich, England, and tells the story of Detective Inspector Jack Caffrey and his search for a serial killer of five women. The murderer's modus operandi includes a mangled corpse with a bird sewn inside of it. As he searches for the killer, the glum Caffrey must deal with his own personal problems, including new competition at the office, a failing relationship with his girlfriend, and a pedophile neighbor, Ivan Penderecki, who may have murdered Caffrey's brother when he and Caffrey were children. Because of the precision with which the birds have been sewn into the women's bodies, Caffrey believes that the perpetrator has some surgical skills and, as a result, he focuses on workers at a nearby hospital. When his prime suspect commits suicide and the murders continue, Caffrey must reevaluate the case and take it in a new direction.

Jane Jorgenson, writing in *Library Journal,* noted that the detective's "search is at times gruesome but always compelling." A *Publishers Weekly* contributor wrote that the author "is impressively successful in appealing to a broad, multigenre fan base (mystery/police procedural, thriller, horror)," and added that Hayder "displays a good working knowledge of forensics and English police procedures, and *Birdman*'s plot has more twists than a surgeon's knot."

Detective Caffrey returns in *The Treatment.* This time the beleaguered, insomniac policeman is on the trail of a murdering pedophile who has run off into the wooded Brockwell Park with a beaten and naked boy. As Caffrey investigates, he becomes immersed in the world of sexual deviancy and crimes, including the case of Tracey Lamb, who appeared in films that depicted her brother molesting children. Caffrey soon discovers that there may be a link between the current perpetrator and next-door neighbor Penderecki. (Caffrey still lives in his boyhood home). Along with the main story, the author includes several ongoing stories concerning potential suspects in the case and their various misdeeds.

In a review of *The Treatment* in *Publishers Weekly,* a contributor wrote that "Hayder handles procedural detail . . . , dialogue . . . and volatile subject matter with powerful dexterity, crafting another deliciously chilling thriller." Emily Melton, writing in *Booklist,* compared the novel to *Birdman,* calling it "another story that is equally intense, disturbing, and violent." Melton also called the book "a complex, emotional, and thoroughly riveting read." In his review for *Trashotron.com,* Kleffel commented that "it's certainly one of the most terrorizing novels to come down the pike in a long, long time." Joseph Egan commented in *Library Journal* that "Hayder successfully weaves together a complex plot and continues the strong development of Caffrey begun in her debut novel."

In *The Devil of Nanking,* published in England as *Tokyo,* Hayder tells the story of Grey Hutchins, an Englishwoman who was raped and is still suffering

from the trauma. Hutchins, who has become obsessed with the Japanese atrocities committed in the city of Nanking in the late 1930s, goes to Tokyo to find a Chinese professor who supposedly has some film of the Nanking massacre, which occurred when the Japanese invaded China. The Chinese scholar refuses to show the film to Hutchins, who decides to stay in Japan and pursue her quest while working as a hostess in "The Club." She meets a crippled, violent, and very old Japanese criminal who supposedly has a secret elixir that keeps him alive. Eventually the professor offers to give Hutchins the film in exchange for a dose of this elixir. As the novel unfolds, readers follow two story lines: the professor in 1930s Nanking; and Hutchins's search, the latter which leads her to discover her own personal connection to the atrocities committed in Nanking.

Writing in *MBR Bookwatch,* Harriet Klausner noted that the author's "skill lies in the way the subplots deftly intermingle without disturbing each other yet connect through events and people." In a review in *Booklist,* Frank Sennett commented that, "although the narrative . . . takes a while to pick up steam, it ends up delivering a potent punch." A *Kirkus Reviews* contributor called the book "a superb third thriller" and also noted that the novel is "even more haunting than it is shocking as the author urgently addresses basic, agonizing existential issues." Beth Lindsay, writing in *Library Journal,* pointed out that "Hayder's novel moves beyond the mystery and suspense angles into larger issues of history, memory, and power."

BIOGRAPHICAL AND CRITICAL SOURCES:

PERIODICALS

Booklist, October 15, 2001, Emily Melton, review of *The Treatment,* p. 356; February 15, 2005, Frank Sennett, review of *The Devil of Nanking,* p. 1064.

Entertainment Weekly, April 15, 2005, Jennifer Reese, review of *The Devil of Nanking,* p. 86.

Guardian (London, England), May 8, 2004, Chris Petit, review of *Tokyo.*

Kirkus Reviews, November 1, 2001, review of *The Treatment,* p. 1506; February 15, 2005, review of *The Devil of Nanking,* p. 191.

Library Journal, September 15, 1999, Jane Jorgenson, review of *Birdman,* p. 112; November 1, 2001, Joseph Egan, review of *The Treatment,* p. 132; April 1, 2005, Beth Lindsay, review of *The Devil of Nanking,* p. 86.

MBR Bookwatch, March, 2005, Harriet Klausner, review of *The Devil of Nanking.*

People, March 11, 2002, Laura Italiano, review of *The Treatment,* p. 49.

Publishers Weekly, October 4, 1999, review of *Birdman,* p. 59; October 29, 2001, Adam Dunn, "PW Talks with Mo Hayder," p. 35; October 29, 2001, review of *The Treatment,* p. 34; January 31, 2005, review of *The Devil of Nanking,* p. 48; May 30, 2005, Wendy Smith, "Kafka's Chick," p. 24.

ONLINE

AllReaders.com, http://www.allreaders.com/ (June 29, 2005), review of *Birdman.*

Deadly Pleasures.com, http://www.deadlypleasures. com/ (April 29, 2001), Russ Isabella, review of *The Treatment.*

Mo Hayder Home Page, http://www.mohayder.net (June 29, 2005).

Mystery Reader, http://www.themysteryreader.com/ (June 29, 2005), Thea Davis, review of *The Treatment.*

ReviewingtheEvidence.com, http://reviewingthe evidence.com/ (April, 2004), Denise Wels Pickles, review of *Tokyo.*

Trashotron.com, http://trashotron.com/ (February 2, 2002), Rick Kleffel, review of *Birdman;* (March 3, 2002) Rick Kleffel, review of *The Treatment.**

*   *   *

HEIKEL, Karin Alice
   See VALA, Katri

*   *   *

HENDRICKS, Judith Ryan 1947(?)-

PERSONAL: Born c. 1947, in San José, CA; married; husband's name, Geoff. *Education:* Attended Furman University; graduated from Georgia State University.

ADDRESSES: Home—Santa Fe, NM. *Agent*—c/o Author Mail, William Morrow and Company, 10 E. 53rd St., 7th Fl., New York, NY 10022. *E-mail*—contact@judithhendricks.com.

CAREER: Writer. Has worked variously as a journalist, copywriter, computer instructor, travel agent, and waitress; McGraw Street Bakery, Seattle, WA, baker.

WRITINGS:

Bread Alone (novel), William Morrow (New York, NY), 2001.

Isabel's Daughter (novel), William Morrow (New York, NY), 2003.

The Baker's Apprentice (novel; sequel to *Bread Alone*), William Morrow (New York, NY), 2005.

Contributor of nonfiction to *San Francisco Chronicle, Tiny Lights, A Journal of Personal Essay, Grand Gourmet* (Italy), and London *Sunday Express.* Short fiction has appeared in *Women's Weekly* and in anthology *American Girls about Town.*

WORK IN PROGRESS: A novel about a female voiceover specialist.

SIDELIGHTS: Judith Ryan Hendricks has worked a variety of jobs, but when she found work at the McGraw Street Bakery in Seattle, she developed a love for all things having to do with baking bread. The experience heavily influenced her and became the inspiration for her first novel, *Bread Alone.* In this book she tells the story of thirty-year-old Wynter Morrison, whose husband throws her out in favor of a younger woman. Wynter, who finds herself stripped of her previous life in Los Angeles, is left with very little work experience, a single good friend named Mac who lives in Seattle, and alimony payments. Moving north to live near Mac, she takes a job in a Seattle bakery. Hendricks follows Wynter through her period of recovery and her growth into a self-sufficient woman, all the while mining her own experience working in a bakery and including recipes along the way. A contributor to *Publishers Weekly* wrote that "Hendricks creates a compelling narrator whose wry, bemused and ultimately wise voice hooks the reader." Neal Wyatt, writing for *Booklist,* commented that the story is "fun to read and meaningful to remember—no small feat at all." In a review for *Library Journal,* Robin Nesbitt stated that this "engaging first novel will appeal to fans of a good story and intriguing characters."

In *Isabel's Daughter,* Hendricks tells the story of Avery Jones, a young woman who was deposited at an orphanage as an infant and who remains bitter toward the mother who abandoned her. At age thirteen, Avery runs away from the orphanage, landing in a small town in New Mexico. She is taken in by an older woman, Cassie, and starts a new life. When Cassie passes away, Avery runs once more, afraid the truth about her past will be revealed. She eventually finds herself in Santa Fe, where a painting provides clues to the identity of her long-lost mother. In a review for *School Library Journal*, Molly Connally remarked that "while the story is somewhat fantastic, the characters . . . are well drawn and the dialogue is true to life." A contributor for *Publishers Weekly* called the book "heartfelt if predictable," and Karen Holt stated in *Booklist* that "Hendricks writes so convincingly and with such appealing characters that nothing about the book feels tired."

The Baker's Apprentice is a sequel to *Bread Alone*. In this volume, Wynter Morrison gets the opportunity to help Mac. Unlike Wynter, Mac is not anxious for her to return the favor, despite the fact that they are now in a romantic relationship. However, Wynter has by now become something of a force to be reckoned with, and Hendrick illustrates just how far she has come. A contributor for *Kirkus Reviews* commented on the lack of plot, while Neal Wyatt, writing for *Booklist,* found that the book illustrats "heartfelt and committed love, sense of community, and pervasive kindness via fabulously cool and competent heroes." A reviewer for *Publishers Weekly* concluded that Hendricks's effort is a "warm and savory if somewhat predictable sequel to her debut novel."

Critics have noted that Hendricks's novels contain underlying themes of rebirth and reinvention, their focus on characters forced to radically remake their lives. In an interview with Tatyana Mishel for the *Seattle Post-Intelligencer,* the author remarked: "I believe we all reinvent ourselves, and everything we do in life brings us right to where we need to be. All these jobs that I had that I came to hate . . . now I find uses for a lot of this information."

BIOGRAPHICAL AND CRITICAL SOURCES:

PERIODICALS

Booklist, June 1, 2001, Neal Wyatt, review of *Bread Alone*, p. 1840; June 1, 2003, Karen Holt, review of *Isabel's Daughter,* p. 1742; November 15, 2004, Neal Wyatt, review of *The Baker's Apprentice,* p. 561.

Kirkus Reviews, December 1, 2004, review of *The Baker's Apprentice*, p. 1107.

Library Journal, July, 2001, Robin Nesbitt, review of *Bread Alone*, p. 123; February 1, 2005, Robin Nesbitt, review of *The Baker's Apprentice*, p. 68.

Pages, March-April, 2005, Beth A. Fhaner, "The Queen Street Bakery Revisited," review of *The Baker's Apprentice*.

Publishers Weekly, June 25, 2001, review of *Bread Alone*, p. 47; June 2, 2003, review of *Isabel's Daughter*, p. 36; March 21, 2005, review of *The Baker's Apprentice,* p. 37.

School Library Journal, September, 2003, Molly Connally, review of *Isabel's Daughter*, p. 240.

Seattle Post-Intelligencer, April 15, 2005, Tatyana Mishel, "Hendricks Rolls out a Delicious Sequel in 'Baker's Apprentice.'"

ONLINE

AllReaders.com, http://www.allreaders.com/ (August 31, 2005), review of *Bread Alone*.

BookBrowse.com, http://www.bookbrowse.com/ (August 31, 2005), "Judith Ryan Hendricks."

BookReporter.com, http://www.bookreporter.com/ (August 31, 2005), Terry Miller Shannon, review of *The Baker's Apprentice*.

Judith Ryan Hendricks Home Page, http://www.judith hendricks.com (August 31, 2005).

MyShelf.com, http://www.myshelf.com/ (August 31, 2005), review of *The Baker's Apprentice*.

Round Table Reviews Online, http://www.roundtable reviews.com/ (August 31, 2005), Tracy Farnsworth, review of *The Baker's Apprentice.**

*   *   *

HENRY, Anne
See WALL, Judith Henry

*   *   *

HILL, Polly
See HUMPHREYS, Mary Eglantyne Hill

*   *   *

HONEY, Patrick James
See HONEY, P.J.

HONEY, P.J. 1922-2005
(Patrick James Honey)

OBITUARY NOTICE— See index for *CA* sketch: Born December 16, 1922, in Navan, County Meath, Ireland; died August 17, 2005. Educator and author. Honey was a world-renowned authority on Vietnam who taught for many years at the University of London. His first exposure to the Southeast Asian country came while he was serving with the Royal Navy during World War II. He served in Europe but also in the Far East, where he was a lieutenant under General Douglas Gracey stationed in Saigon. After returning home following the war, he graduated from University College London in 1949. As the cold war heated up, interest in Southeast Asia grew, and Honey was enlisted to take an intensive course in Vietnamese at the School of Oriental and African Studies at the University of London. He then traveled to French Indochina (later renamed Vietnam) just as the conflict between the French colonial government and Ho Chi Minh's forces was becoming intense. Fearing capture by Vietnamese nationalists, he fled to Hanoi and was able to conduct his research there for a time. Returning to London, he became a lecturer in Vietnamese and helped establish Vietnamese studies as a bachelor's degree program. Honey was regarded as an authority on Vietnam and his advice was often sought by government officials. He published numerous books about Southeast Asia and Vietnam, including *Politics in South and South East Asia* (1963) and *Genesis of a Tragedy: The Historical Background to the Vietnam War* (1968), as well as translating *Voyage to Tonking in the Year At-hoi* (1976). Becoming a reader in Vietnamese studies in 1965, Honey tried to remain involved in the country, though war prevented him from traveling there, and he was active in briefing officials during the "boat people" crisis following the 1975 fall of Saigon. He also worked with the British Broadcasting Corporation's Vietnamese Service for many years. Honey's last years at the University of London, from 1982 to 1985, were spent as head of the Department of South-East Asia.

OBITUARIES AND OTHER SOURCES:

PERIODICALS

Times (London, England), September 14, 2005, p. 54.

HOPWOOD, Keith 1946-

PERSONAL: Born 1946. *Education:* Earned an M.A.

*ADDRESSES: Office—*Department of Classics, University of Wales, Lampeter, Ceredigion SA48 7ED, Wales. *Agent—* *E-mail—*sn022@lamp.ac.uk.

CAREER: Writer and educator. University of Wales, Lampeter, lecturer in ancient history.

MEMBER: Comité d'Études Pré-Ottomanes et Ottomanes (assistant secretary).

WRITINGS:

Scripta Hierosolymitana XXV, [Jerusalem, Israel], 1994.
(Compiler) *Ancient Greece and Rome: A Bibliographical Guide,* Manchester University Press (New York, NY), 1995.
The Reign of Nero: A Companion to the Penguin Translation, Bristol Classical Press (Bristol, England), 1996.
(Editor and contributor) *Organised Crime in Antiquity,* Duckworth/Classical Press of Wales (London, England), 1998.

Contributor to books, including *Patronage in Ancient Society,* edited by Andrew Wallace-Hadrill, Routledge (London, England), 1989; *CIEPO, VII Sempozyumu Bildirileri,* edited by J.-L. Bacque-Grammont and others, [Ankara, Turkey], 1994; and *Acta Viennensia Ottomanica: Akten des 13. CIEPO-Symposiums (Comité International des Études Pré-Ottomanes et Ottomanes) vom 21. bis 25. September 1998 in Wien,* edited by M. Köhbach, G. Procházka-Eisl, and C. Römer, [Vienna, Austria], 1999.

SIDELIGHTS: A professor at the University of Wales in Lampeter, Keith Hopwood has been interested in Asia Minor, including the histories of the Ottoman, Byzantine, and Roman Empires. His published work in the area includes *Organised Crime in Antiquity,* which he edited and to which he contributed. Offering insights into the differences between ancient and modern concepts about crime, the book's "major conclusion," according to Denis Saddington in *Scholia*

Review, is that "organized crime flourishes best in a society where there is a large gap between the rich and the poor." James Davidson commented in the *Times Literary Supplement* that the book is unique in "the way that ancient outlawry is treated as a large geopolitical question." Saddington concluded, "What we have is a valuable collection of essays which, besides discussing crime, throw an interesting light on aspects of 'the state' in early Athens and Rome and various rural and urban situations at the end of the Roman Empire."

As a bibliographer, Hopwood has organized resources for academic and general audiences, compiling more than 8,000 citations to English-language books, book chapters, conference proceedings, and journal articles written between 1800 and 2000 in his *Ancient Greece and Rome: A Bibliographical Guide.* Reviewing the guide in a *Choice* article, B. Juhl asserted that "librarians and students are sure to find this bibliography extremely useful for projects ranging from World Civ papers to doctoral research."

BIOGRAPHICAL AND CRITICAL SOURCES:

PERIODICALS

Choice, March, 1996, B. Juhl, review of *Ancient Greece and Rome: A Bibliographical Guide,* pp. 1096, 1098.

Scholia Reviews, September, 2000, Denis Saddington, review of *Organised Crime in Antiquity,* p. 9.

Times Literary Supplement, April 28, 2000, James Davidson, "The Plunder Club," review of *Organised Crime in Antiquity,* pp. 4-6.

ONLINE

University of Wales, Lampeter, Web site, http://www. lamp.ac.uk/ (February 15, 2006).*

*   *   *

HORNUNG, Eva Katerina
See SALLIS, Eva

*   *   *

HORSFALL, Melissa
See HORSFALL, Missy

HORSFALL, Missy
(Melissa Horsfall)

PERSONAL: Married; husband a pastor; children: three.

ADDRESSES: Agent—c/o Author Mail, WaterBrook Press, 1745 Broadway, New York, NY 10014.

CAREER: Writer. Speaker at seminars.

WRITINGS:

(With Susan Stevens) *Double Honor* (Christian novel), WaterBrook Press (Colorado Springs, CO), 2002.

SIDELIGHTS: Missy Horsfall is coauthor, with Susan Stevens, of *Double Honor,* the story of the failing marriage of Mallory and Jake Carlisle. Mallory, an illustrator, is commissioned to work on a children's book about sexual abuse. The assignment refreshes her own memories, which she has suppressed for so long, but enables her to understand that her marriage is suffering because of her childhood trauma.

The authors write of the pain of living within a dysfunctional family and the faith that Mallory draws upon to help her heal and cope. "This is a book with a ministry casually woven through a wonderful work of fiction," commented Bev Huston for *Romantic Times Book Club* online. A *Publishers Weekly* contributor felt that "adult survivors of childhood sexual abuse will appreciate this story of Christian faith and emotional healing."

Romance Reader's Connection reviewer Tracy Farnsworth called the novel a "touching story." Farnsworth also interviewed the authors for the site. Horsfall said that both she and Stevens "have seen first hand the devastating results of child sexual abuse in the lives of those we have counseled, Susan through her pastoral ministry, and I in my role as pastor's wife. We have seen God take the worst of circumstances and use them in the most astounding ways to change lives. We desire this book to be a powerful tale of God's love and want our readers to know that there is hope, there is healing, and it is found in God."

BIOGRAPHICAL AND CRITICAL SOURCES:

PERIODICALS

Publishers Weekly, February 25, 2002, review of *Double Honor,* p. 39.

ONLINE

Romance Reader's Connection, http://www.the romancereadersconnection.com/ (June 7, 2005), Tracy Farnsworth, review of *Double Honor* and interview with Horsfall and Stevens.
Romantic Times Book Club, http://www.romantictimes. com/ (June 7, 2005), Bev Huston, review of *Double Honor.**

* * *

HOUSDEN, Maria

PERSONAL: Born in Traverse City, MI; married first husband, Claude (divorced); married Roger Housden; children: Hannah (deceased), three other children.

ADDRESSES: Home—Fair Haven, NJ. *Agent*—c/o Author Mail, Harmony Books, 1745 Broadway, New York, NY 10019. *E-mail*—hannahsgift@juno.com.

CAREER: Writer. Lecturer and bereavement support group leader. Kimberly Fund, member of board of directors, 1995-99; Grief in Action (international grief support group), founder.

WRITINGS:

Hannah's Gift: Lessons from a Life Fully Lived, Bantam Books (New York, NY), 2002.
Unraveled: The True Story of a Woman Who Dared to Become a Different Kind of Mother, Harmony Books (New York, NY), 2004.

Hannah's Gift has been translated into fifteen languages.

SIDELIGHTS: Maria Housden writes honestly about some of the saddest and yet most revealing experiences in her life. Her first book, *Hannah's Gift: Lessons from a Life Fully Lived,* chronicles the last year of her daughter Hannah's life after she was diagnosed with cancer at the age of three. Housden shares the joys and the hardships of watching her child fight to live, as well as her ultimate acceptance and bravery in the face of her death. Although Housden, as the parent, attempted to be strong for her daughter and talked to her about the meaning behind what was happening to her, it was often Housden herself who learned lessons from her child, such as the importance of honesty and that it was all right to ask for the things that she wanted. A contributor to *Kirkus Reviews* remarked that the book is "unsentimental for the most part," adding that "this portrait of a short, joyous life can be comforting to anyone who has lost a child." In a review for *Publishers Weekly,* a contributor wrote that Housden's book provides "a lyrical, heartbreaking and heartwarming account of her three-year-old daughter's illness and death," while *Booklist* contributor David Pitt stated that "the reader who does not shed a tear while reading it is not human."

In the wake of her daughter's death, Housden decided to divorce her then-husband, Claude. She also allowed him to have primary custody of their remaining children, believing that she would be a better mother if given a certain amount of distance. Housden had met and fallen in love with Roger Housden, with whom she felt happy for the first time since before Hannah's death. Eventually, they married, and the couple moved across the country, with Housden visiting with her children on weekends. In *Unraveled: The True Story of a Woman Who Dared to Become a Different Kind of Mother* Housden explains her decisions and their consequences. In *Kirkus Reviews,* a contributor found fault with Housden's apparent rationalization of an extra-marital relationship as acceptable if it is motivated by love, stating that "her blasé acceptance of adultery, together with the suggestion that her affair was the transformative event that allowed her to discover her true self, rankles." However, a reviewer for *Publishers Weekly* found that "Housden's poignant, raw book has no easy answers for life's difficult moments, but her bravery will soothe those enduring similar trials."

Housden continues to work to enhance the quality of life for patients with fatal illnesses. She lectures frequently across the country, and has led bereavement support groups. In addition, she has taken several groups of women into Death Valley for spiritual, meditative journeys. On her home page, Housden stated, "Since Hannah's death, a stillness that she opened in me has become the foundation for a new life; a life that I sense had been living in me all along. . . . I no longer let my fears hold me back. I now know that there is a death more painful than the one that took Hannah's body from this world; a soul suffocated by fear leaves too many joys unlived."

Housden told *CA:* "From the age of twelve, I wanted to write a book, but it was my daughter Hannah's death from cancer at the age of three that became the catalyst for me as a writer. I believe that to write is to surrender to the truth in yourself at that moment, and the craft of writing involves the distillation of memory or inspiration to its essence. Poetry, with its fierce and direct use of language, inspires this perspective in my work.

"Writing has opened me to a new way of being in the world, for to write is to see, to see is to remember, and to remember is to arrive again in each moment as if for the first time. The Book of Psalms in the Bible is perhaps my favorite book, not only because its beauty has stood the test of time, but because it speaks to a mystery that, while I cannot see it or fully understand it, always challenges, comforts, and inspires me."

BIOGRAPHICAL AND CRITICAL SOURCES:

BOOKS

Housden, Maria, *Hannah's Gift: Lessons from a Life Fully Lived,* Bantam Books (New York, NY), 2002.
Housden, Maria, *Unraveled: The True Story of a Woman Who Dared to Become a Different Kind of Mother,* Harmony Books (New York, NY), 2004.

PERIODICALS

Booklist, January 1, 2002, David Pitt, review of *Hannah's Gift,* p. 783.
Bookseller, July 26, 2002, review of *Hannah's Gift,* p. 31; September 6, 2002, review of *Hannah's Gift,* p. 10.
Kirkus Reviews, December 15, 2001, review of *Hannah's Gift,* p. 1738; March 15, 2005, review of *Unraveled,* p. 335.
Library Journal, May 1, 2005, Kay Hogan Smith, "Mama's Got a New Bag," review of *Unraveled,* p. 104.
Publishers Weekly, November 26, 2001, "The Nearly and Dearly Departed," review of *Hannah's Gift,* p. 54; April 18, 2005, review of *Unraveled,* p. 52.

ONLINE

Hannah's Gift Web site, http://www.hannahsgift.com/ (August 30, 2005).

*   *   *

HOWARD, Cheryl
    See CREW, Cheryl Howard

*   *   *

HULSE, Lloyd K. 1928-

PERSONAL: Born May 26, 1928, in La Grande, OR; son of Hugh Clifton (a farmer and rancher) and Edna (Scott) Hulse; married Maria Reyes (a homemaker and translator), 1960; children: Stephen, Laura, Bernadette, Michele, José, María Ines, Francisco, Rodrigo. *Education:* Mexico City College (now University of the Americas), M.A., 1952; University of Cincinnati, Ph.D., 1973. *Politics:* Democrat. *Religion:* Roman Catholic.

ADDRESSES: Home—2133 S.W. Taylor's Ferry Rd., Portland, OR 97219. *E-mail*—nomequejo@gmail.net.

CAREER: Writer. U.S.-Mexican campaign against hoof-and-mouth disease, Mexico, livestock inspector, 1949-50; Peerless Pump Company, Los Angeles, CA, sales engineer and translator, 1952-55; Johnston Pump Company, Pasadena, CA, assistant export and regional sales manager, Central America and the Caribbean, 1955-61; Tracto-Motor, Ltd., administrator, Bogotá, Colombia, 1961-62; high-school Spanish teacher, Monrovia, CA, and La Grande, OR, 1957-64; Eastern Oregon College, Spanish instructor, 1963; University of Cincinnati, Spanish instructor, 1969-71; Indiana State University, assistant professor of foreign languages and lab director, 1971-72; Lewis and Clark College, Portland, OR, assistant professor of Spanish, 1964-69, began as associate professor, became full professor of Spanish, 1973-91, emeritus. Freightliner Corporation, Portland, OR, Spanish translator, 1992-94; SunSounds, Tucson, AZ, volunteer Spanish reader, 2002.

WRITINGS:

Tres caminos hacia el sur (nonfiction), University Press of America (Lanham, MD), 2000, translation by the author published as *Three Roads South,* University Press of America (Lanham, MD), 2002.

Contributor of articles to periodicals, including *Selecta, Revista Interamericana, Káñina, Occitan-Catalan Studies, Chasqui,* and *Journal of Lewis and Clark College.*

WORK IN PROGRESS: French translation of his English-language memoir *The Right Place,* written by Hulse's father, Hugh Clifton.

SIDELIGHTS: Lloyd K. Hulse told *CA:* "I was first drawn to writing by the example of my father's diaries, which he kept for extended periods over the years, and also by his constant reading. I remember keeping diaries of my own starting in my childhood, plus one attempt to start a novel inspired by the lore of Spanish California—which was also the reason for my beginning to study Spanish on my own when I was in the seventh grade. This later exercised a profound influence on what I later read and wrote.

"Another early influence was the example of my father's work on his manuscript, based on the journal he kept during his participation as an American soldier in the First World War in France. His manuscript was posthumously published one year after his death in 1969 under the title *The Right Place.* The book has been praised by many people, and now has been reprinted; however, it was published and sold without a copyright. For years I have wanted to set this right. My current project is to translate my father's excellent story into French, and eventually see it published in this language with a proper copyright. First, I thought of having it done, but I decided two years ago, after the publication of *Three Roads South,* my own translation of my original *Tres caminos hacia el sur,* to translate my father's book myself, while seeking the advice, review, and suggestions of educated native French speakers. I have already translated more than half of the book, an activity, which, together with constantly reading French stories and novels and comparing translations from English to French (and vice versa), has helped me to activate the language I began to study in Mexico City even before I had totally mastered Spanish.

"After translating my father's book, I plan to organize and synthesize my diaries in order to write my memoirs. As for the writing process, and my advice for aspiring writers, you should write about what you know and what you feel, or what you must express—an idea or an argument that will bring you recognition. Secondly, good writing requires much writing practice, also much reading and talking. I recall one writer having said that you can't just 'want to be a writer,' rather, you have to 'want to write,' and then you have to write a lot to become proficient at it. Then, after writing you must revise. As for publishing, I, myself, cannot consider what I am going to write just to get published. I have to write it first, then worry about getting published."

*   *   *

HUMPHREYS, Mary Eglantyne Hill 1914-2005 (Polly Hill)

OBITUARY NOTICE— See index for *CA* sketch: Born June 10, 1914, in Cambridge, England; died August 21, 2005, in Isleham, Cambridgeshire, England. Economist, social anthropologist, and author. Humphreys combined her knowledge of economics with anthropology to demonstrate that African people were perfectly capable of engaging in modern economic practices without the intrusion of European colonialists. The member of a famous family that included her uncle, economist John Maynard Keynes, and her Nobel Prize-winning physiologist father, A.V. Hill, Humphreys earned a B.A. in economics from Newnham College, Cambridge, in 1936. She worked on unemployment studies for a year for the Fabian Society and was a civil servant from 1940 until 1951.

Her work in Africa began in 1951, when she joined the *West Africa* weekly as a journalist. After two years, she left the periodical to work as a research fellow for the University of Ghana. There she conducted her landmark studies on local cocoa farmers. Humphreys proved that, contrary to what Europeans believed, Africans were not a backward people and in fact were creating a thoroughly modern farming economy in Ghana without the knowledge of the colonial government. Humphreys's *The Migrant Cocoa Farmers of Southern Ghana* (1963) changed the way economists and scholars thought about native Africans. Humphreys was at the forefront of economic anthropology, a field she helped create, and developed her own research methods for her studies. Because of this, she unfortunately received little academic recognition for her work and never had a teaching appointment. After leaving Africa, she was a fellow at Clare Hall, Cambridge from 1965 to 1981, and was Leverhulme emeritus fellow from 1981 to 1982, as well as Smuts Reader in Commonwealth Studies at Cambridge from 1973 to 1979. Among her other books, which were written under her maiden name, Polly Hill, are *Through the Dark Wood* (1945), *Hidden Trade in Hausaland* (1969), *Population, Prosperity, and Poverty: Rural Kano, 1900 and 1970* (1977), and *Development Economics on Trial: The Anthropological Case for a Prosecution* (1986). She also edited the correspondence collection *Lydia and Maynard* (1989), and her last book was *Who Were the Fen People?* (1993).

OBITUARIES AND OTHER SOURCES:

PERIODICALS

Guardian (London, England), August 26, 2005, p. 31.
Independent (London, England), August 25, 2005, p. 33.

*   *   *

HUNT, Swanee 1950-
(Swanee G. Hunt)

PERSONAL: Born May 1, 1950, in Dallas, TX; daughter of H.L. Hunt; married Charles Alexander Ansbacher (a symphony conductor); children: three. *Education:* Texas Christian University, B.A., 1972;

Ball State University, M.A., 1976; Iliff School of Theology, M.A., 1977, Ph.D., 1986; Webster University, Ph.D., 1994.

ADDRESSES: Office—Women and Public Policy Program, John F. Kennedy School of Government 79 John F. Kennedy St., Cambridge, MA 02138. *E-mail*—swanee_hunt@harvard.edu.

CAREER: Educator, writer, and composer. Hunt Alternatives Fund, president, 1981; Karis Community, cofounder and member, 1980-83; Capital Heights Presbyterian Church, minister of pastoral care, 1983; Community Mental Health Commission, vice-chair, 1983-87; member of Governor's Policy Academy on Families and Children at Risk, 1989-90; Colorado Coordinating Council on Housing and the Homeless, chair, 1989-92; U.S. ambassador to Austria, 1993-97; Harvard University, Cambridge, MA, director of Women and Public Policy Program at the Kennedy School of Government, 1997—. Founder and chair of Inclusive Security: Women Waging Peace, an initiative of Hunt Alternatives Fund. Composer of the *The Witness Cantata,* 1989. Has spoken at numerous conferences and meetings and has appeared on various radio and television programs.

MEMBER: Council on Foreign Relations, Women's Foundation (cofounder and member of board of directors), Mayor's Human Capital Agenda Council (chair, 1992-93), Denver Initiative Children and Families (cochair), United Nations Commission on Refugees, International Crisis Group, International Alert.

AWARDS, HONORS: Mental Health Association of Colorado award, 1984, 1994; National Mental Health Association award, 1985; Caring Connection award, KUSA-TV award, International Women's Forum award, and United Methodist Church award, all 1989; Martin Luther King, Jr., Humanitarian award, University of Colorado, and National Conference for Community and Justice award, both 1992; Mile High award, United Way, 1993; American Heritage award, Anti-Defamation League, 1995; Cordon Bleu du Saint Esprit Peace award, 1996; Humanitarian Lifetime Service award, Denver Holocaust Awareness, Together for Peace award, three Austrian government decorations, and Ambassador award, The Conflict Center, all 1997; Institute for International Education award, 1998.

WRITINGS:

This Was Not Our War: Bosnian Women Reclaiming the Peace, foreword by William Jefferson Clinton, Duke University Press (Durham, NC), 2004.

Articles have appeared in numerous publications, including *Foreign Affairs, Foreign Policy,* and the *International Herald Tribune, Chicago Tribune, Boston Globe,* and *Denver Post.* Author of syndicated column for Scripps Howard.

SIDELIGHTS: Swanee Hunt is the author of *This Was Not Our War: Bosnian Women Reclaiming the Peace.* Based on Hunt's diplomatic and humanitarian work in the Bosnian region, as well as numerous interviews she conducted as a diplomat there, the book provides the testimony of twenty-six women who experienced the turmoil in Bosnia. A strong advocate for women having a bigger role in government and policymaking decisions, Hunt once pointed out to Thane Petersen during an interview in *Business Week Online,* "When I was the ambassador [to Austria], Bosnia was right next door, and there was a terrible refugee flood into Austria. What I noticed quickly was that the 60 people who were sent up from Croatia and Bosnia for the [peace] negotiations were all men—even though there were more women Ph.D.s per capita in the former Yugoslavia than in any country in Europe. It made me wonder why the warriors involved wanted to make sure there were no women." Through the women's voices in her book, readers gain an alternative perspective on the region and what happened there during the war and violence of the 1990s. The women come from various ethnic and religion backgrounds and include Serbs, Croats, Muslims, and Roman Catholics. In a review in the *Boston Herald,* Rob Mitchell noted that the stories "make a compelling case for the inclusion of women at the world's decision-making tables." Mitchell added, "It was not their war, but Hunt insists that is precisely why they should shape the peace." As a *Publishers Weekly* contributor noted, "Hunt succeeds in capturing, organizing and analyzing the complexities inherent in conversations with twenty-six very different people during and after an abhorrent war."

BIOGRAPHICAL AND CRITICAL SOURCES:

PERIODICALS

Boston Herald, January 30, 2005, Rob Mitchell, review of *This Was Not Our War: Bosnian Women Reclaiming the Peace.*

Business Week Online, April 15, 2003, Thane Peterson, "What If Women Ran the World?"
Europe, December, 1995, Robert J. Guttman, "The 'Multifaceted' Ambassador," p. 16.
New Republic, August 8, 1994, Thomas Omestad, "Green with Envoy: Are U.S. Ambassadorships for Sale?," p. 20.
Publishers Weekly, December 6, 2005, review of *This Was Not Our War,* p. 53.

ONLINE

Council on Foreign Relations Web site, http://www.cfr.org/ (April 14, 2005), "Bosnian Women Reclaiming the Peace."
Harvard University Women and Public Policy Program Web site, http://www.ksg.harvard.edu/wappp/ (June 30, 2005), brief biography of author.
Swanee Hunt Home Page, http://www.swaneehunt.com (June 30, 2005).
Women Waging Peace, http://www.womenwagingpeace.net/ (June 30 2005), brief biography of author.*

*   *   *

HUNT, Swanee G.
  See HUNT, Swanee

*   *   *

HUSHER, Helen 1951-

PERSONAL: Born 1951, in Spring House, PA. *Education:* Boston University, B.A., 1980, M.A., 1981; attended Pratt Institute, Brooklyn, NY.

ADDRESSES: Home—Montpelier, VT. *Office*—Sustainable Agriculture Research and Education—Northeast Region, University of Vermont, Hills Bldg., Burlington, VT 05405-0082; fax: 802-656-4656. *E-mail*—helen.husher@uvm.edu.

CAREER: Publications manager and writer. University of Vermont, Burlington, communications specialist for Sustainable Agriculture Research and Education, Northeast Region.

WRITINGS:

NONFICTION

Off the Leash: Subversive Journeys around Vermont, Countryman Press (Woodstock, VT), 1999.

A View from Vermont: Everyday Life in America, Globe Pequot Press (Guilford, CT), 2004.

Conversations with a Prince: A Year of Riding at East Hill Farm, Lyon's Press (Guilford, CT), 2005.

Articles and stories have appeared in numerous publications, including *Boston Phoenix, Vermont Life, Vermont,* and *Seven Days.*

SIDELIGHTS: Helen Husher is the author of nonfiction books focusing on Vermont and her life in northeast New England. In *Off the Leash: Subversive Journeys around Vermont* Husher focuses on places and areas in Vermont that the author finds particularly appealing. Not a typical travel book in that Husher largely ignores tips and information on lodging, restaurants, and typical tourist attractions, *Off the Leash* instead presents an insider's look at the state, from obscure historical facts and incidents to places like the Donohue Sea Caves and the author's hometown of Randolph. In a review in *Booklist,* Alice Joyce noted that "Husher seems to appreciate settings with a more subtle, perhaps even more profound, resonance." Alison Hopkins, writing in *Library Journal,* called the book "a cross between travel essays and tourist guide," while a *Publishers Weekly* contributor noted that "her tour is . . . [bound] to stir up curiosity not only about Vermont but also about all the places lost in the daze of hotels and gift shops."

A View from Vermont: Everyday Life in America is a collection of essays in which Husher takes a look at her home state's culture and people with an emphasis on life in rural towns. In chapters such as "How to Dress like a Vermonter," "Edge of the Clearing," and "Sounds of Winter," Husher provides a loving tribute to the state where she lives. Noting that "the collection also amounts to a meditation on Yankee temperament," a *Publishers Weekly* contributor also wrote that "a gentle wit and uniquely philosophical approach to the everyday distinguish Husher's best writing."

While attending a horse show, Husher decided to return to the horseback-riding she had enjoyed as a child. She recounts her experiences in *Conversations with a Prince: A Year of Riding at East Hill Farm.* Prince, her training horse at her riding school, helps her learn not only about riding techniques but also offers her insights into horses themselves and leads Husher to recall her favorite horse during her youth. The author also ruminates on the relationship between horses and women riders and on theories about why horse riding seems to have such a broad-based appeal for women, such as the idea that it gives them a sense of power. Husher also provides her own thoughts on this topic, stressing that there is a communication between animal and rider that women enjoy. A *Kirkus Reviews* contributor called the book "a graceful and leisurely memoir" and also noted that the author "is extraordinarily perceptive, and her observations . . . are nuanced and thoughtful without drifting into sentimentality." Patsy E. Gray, writing in *Library Journal,* commented: "Not for horse lovers only, Husher's tome will be enjoyed by anyone with a passion for a particular activity."

BIOGRAPHICAL AND CRITICAL SOURCES:

BOOKS

Husher, Helen, *Conversations with a Prince: A Year of Riding at East Hill Farm,* Lyon's Press (Guilford, CT), 2005.

PERIODICALS

Booklist, September 1, 1999, Alice Joyce, review *Off the Leash: Subversive Journeys around Vermont,* p. 65.

Kirkus Reviews, February 15, 2005, review of *Conversations with a Prince: A Year of Riding at East Hill Farm,* p. 212.

Library Journal, September 1, 1999, Alison Hopkins, review *Off the Leash,* p. 222; June 1, 2005, Patsy E. Gray, review of *Conversations with a Prince,* p. 162.

Publishers Weekly, July 26, 1999, review of *Off the Leash,* p. 72; February 23, 2004, review of *A View from Vermont: Everyday Life in America,* p. 63.

ONLINE

Boston University Web site, http://www.bu.edu/ (July 1, 2005), brief profile of author.

J

JACKSON, Buzzy

PERSONAL: Female. *Education:* University of California, Berkeley, Ph.D.

ADDRESSES: Home—Berkeley, CA. *Agent*—c/o Author Mail, W.W. Norton and Company, Inc., 500 5th Ave., New York, NY 10110.

CAREER: Writer.

WRITINGS:

A Bad Woman Feeling Good: Blues and the Women Who Sing Them, W.W. Norton (New York, NY), 2005.

SIDELIGHTS: Buzzy Jackson turned her doctoral thesis from the University of California, Berkeley, into the 2005 title, *A Bad Woman Feeling Good: Blues and the Women Who Sing Them.* Jackson provides biographical information on blues singers from Bessie Smith to Etta James, Aretha Franklin, and Janis Joplin, among a host of other female blues greats. Jackson uses her biographical sketches to make the point that these female blues singers have furthered the cause of feminism, working to make women across America feel free to be themselves. Writing in *Booklist,* June Sawyers noted that this debut title gives full voice to the notion that female blues singers "refused to follow the rules about how women should behave in society," Reviewers were generally positive in their assessment of Jackson's work. A critic for *Kirkus Reviews* found her book "well-researched," and "an enthusiastic, patently feminist history." A contributor for *Publishers*

Weekly had higher praise for Jackson's work, calling it a "thoughtful, fluent book." Similarly, *Library Journal* contributor Bill Walker called the book an "excellent introduction to pioneering women blues singers," although he complained that Jackson "stretches credibility" by her inclusion of singers such as Madonna into the blues category.

BIOGRAPHICAL AND CRITICAL SOURCES:

PERIODICALS

Booklist, February 1, 2005, June Sawyers, review of *A Bad Woman Feeling Good: Blues and the Women Who Sing Them,* p. 936.
Kirkus Reviews, December 1, 2004, review of *A Bad Woman Feeling Good,* p. 1132.
Library Journal, January 1, 2005, Bill Walker, review of *A Bad Woman Feeling Good,* p. 115.
Publishers Weekly, December 13, 2004, review of *A Bad Woman Feeling Good,* p. 58.

ONLINE

W.W. Norton Web site, http://www.wwnorton.com/ (May 28, 2005).*

*   *   *

JACKSON, Lorna M. 1956-

PERSONAL: Born January 11, 1956, in Vancouver, British Columbia, Canada; daughter of Rex (an appraiser) and Edith (a bookseller; maiden name, Bryer) Jackson; married Tom Henry (a writer and editor);

children: Lily Kate Henry. *Education:* University of Victoria, B.A., 1990, M.A., 1993.

ADDRESSES: Home—4753 Rocky Point Rd., Victoria, British Columbia V9C 4E9, Canada. *Office*—University of Victoria, Department of Writing, P.O. Box 11700, STN CSC Victoria, British Columbia V8W 2Y2, Canada. *Agent*—Anne McDermid, Anne McDermid and Associates, 92 Willcocks St., Toronto, Ontario M53 1C8, Canada. *E-mail*—ljackson@finearts.uvic.ca.

CAREER: Writer. Vancouver, British Columbia, Canada, musician, 1978-86; University of Victoria, lecturer and assistant professor, 1995—.

WRITINGS:

Dressing for Hope (short stories), Goose Lane Editions (Fredericton, New Brunswick, Canada), 1995.
A Game to Play on the Tracks (novel), Porcupine's Quill (Erin, Ontario, Canada), 2003.

Malahat Review, editorial board member.

WORK IN PROGRESS: Cold-Cocked: On Hockey, a nonfiction book, expected 2005; *Flirt: The Interviews,* a work of creative nonfiction, expected 2005.

SIDELIGHTS: Lorna M. Jackson told *CA:* "In early writing, my work was influenced by the music I was playing and the life I was leading traveling through British Columbia as a saloon singer. More recently, in fiction and nonfiction, I continue to explore the generative and creative aftermath of grief and the roles of art, sport, and landscape in how we endure often difficult lives. I live in Metchosin, British Columbia, a small rural community. We raise sheep and chickens and garden well enough to fill our freezer. This life, too—its strong nouns and active verbs—feeds my writing."

*   *   *

JARDINE, Quintin 1946-

PERSONAL: Born 1946, in Lanarkshire, Scotland; married; wife's name Kate (died, 1997); married; second wife's name, Eileen; children: (first marriage) two; two stepchildren.

ADDRESSES: Home—Gullane, Scotland; Catalonia, Spain. *Agent*—Bell Lomax Agency, James House, 1 Babmaes St., London SW1Y 6HF, England.

CAREER: Novelist. Formerly worked as a journalist, media and public relations consultant, and government information officer.

WRITINGS:

"ROBERT SKINNER" NOVEL SERIES

Skinner's Trail, Headline (London, England), 1993, St. Martin's Press (New York, NY), 1996.
Skinner's Rules, Headline (London, England), 1993, St. Martin's Press (New York, NY), 1994.
Skinner's Festival, Headline (London, England), 1994, St. Martin's Press (New York, NY), 1995.
Skinner's Round, St. Martin's Press (New York, NY), 1995.
Skinner's Ordeal, Headline (London, England), 1996.
Skinner's Mission, Headline (London, England), 1997.
Skinner's Ghost, Headline (London, England), 1998.
Murmuring the Judges, Headline (London, England), 1999.
Gallery Whispers, Headline (London, England), 1999.
Thursday Legends, Headline (London, England), 2000.
Autographs in the Rain, Headline (London, England), 2001.
Head Shot, Headline (London, England), 2002.
Fallen Gods, Headline (London, England), 2003.
Stay of Execution, Headline (London, England), 2004.
Lethal Intent, Headline (London, England), 2005.

"OZ BLACKSTONE" NOVEL SERIES

Blackstone's Pursuits, Headline (London, England), 1996.
A Coffin for Two, Headline (London, England), 1997.
Wearing Purple, Headline (London, England), 1998.
Screen Savers, Headline (London, England), 2000.
On Honeymoon with Death, Headline (London, England), 2001.
Poisoned Cherries, Headline (London, England), 2002.
Unnatural Justice, Headline (London, England), 2003.
Alarm Call, Headline (London, England), 2004.

ADAPTATIONS: Author's books have been adapted as audiobooks.

WORK IN PROGRESS: More books in the "Oz Blackstone" and "Robert Skinner" series and a humorous novel.

SIDELIGHTS: Quintin Jardine is a successful crime novelist who turns out approximately two novels a year per his publishing contract. He did not begin writing novels until he was in his mid-forties on a dare from his wife when he boasted that he could write a better story after reading a novelization of a British Broadcasting Company (BBC) television mystery series. Jardine proved he is more than capable. He has become a best-selling author in Scotland and is gaining popularity elsewhere with his two series of detective novels, which focus on two distinct and disparate characters.

In his series of novels featuring Bob Skinner, deputy chief constable of Edinburgh, Scotland, Jardine has created a character billed as the "toughest cop" in Great Britain. In *Skinner's Rules,* the constable is on the trail of a killer and soon finds that what he initially thinks is a straight-forward murder case turns out to be a complicated series of murders involving a disparate group of people, from an advocate lawyer to a cleaning lady to a homeless drunk. Skinner eventually discovers that the murders may involve a conspiracy with wide-ranging political consequences. Writing in *Booklist,* Emily Melton called the book "a rollercoaster ride of a story that's gripping from beginning to end." A *Publishers Weekly* contributor wrote that "solid plotting (including surprises) and short, snappy chapters that tell the story through action and dialogue."

Skinner's Festival finds the Scottish cop tracking down a militant group whose bombing of the Edinburgh Arts Festival is part of a political agenda fostered by an international group of terrorists. As Skinner investigates the case, the bombings continue. Skinner's daughter also falls for a mysterious man and is eventually kidnapped, along with Skinner's wife, by the terrorists. A *Publishers Weekly* contributor noted that "Jardine offers spectacularly effective action scenes, and Skinner, while sometimes too hard-boiled to swallow, is an admirable hero." In her review in *Booklist,* Melton wrote that Jardine "writes a nearly flawless police procedural . . . but his real forte is the way he gets into the minds and hearts of his characters."

Skinner is celebrating the birth of his son in *Skinner's Trail* when a local Laundromat tycoon is murdered. Skinner soon learns that the businessman had many shady dealings, and the list of suspects mounts. *Booklist* contributor Melton called the book "another winner from this very talented writer" and also noted that the book is "chock-full of high-octane action." *Skinner's Trail* features the case of a millionaire found dead in his golf club's Jacuzzi with a slit throat. The plot involves golf, witches, and moguls in what Melton called "another winning entry in an outstanding police procedural series."

Thursday Legends takes it title from a weekly football game Skinner plays with some of his other over-the-hill athlete friends. When the naked and mutilated body of a fellow detective and football player is found, the murder turns out only to be the first that will involve the group of players. With the help of detective Andy Martin, Skinner sets out to solve the case. A *Publishers Weekly* contributor commented that "this gritty, fast-paced mystery will pin even the most squeamish readers to the page."

Autographs in the Rain finds Skinner's wide authority within the police department being questioned. Further complicating Skinner's life is the fact that a famous local movie star who once was Skinner's lover has returned to town only to be shot at. Furthermore, Skinner's secretary is the primary suspect in the murder of her uncle, and another case involves a local trout business. A *Kirkus Reviews* contributor noted that the author "excels at coordinating the multiple crimes crucial to a police procedural and setting his coppers against the clock."

In *Fallen Gods* Skinner once again must deal with multiple problems, which include an arson case at the Royal Scottish Academy, the discovery of his brother's body many years after the man went missing, and the murder charge his wife faces in America. "Luckily, there's nothing Skinner . . . can't sort out, including adultery, dysfunctional family histories, corrupt politicians, and digital photography," wrote a *Kirkus Reviews* contributor.

Pope John XXV's visit to Edinburgh is the driving plot device in *Stay of Execution.* This time Skinner must deal with a group of terrorists intent on assassinating the visiting dignitary. Although Skinner knows there is a plot against the pontiff, he must race against the clock to uncover the details of the plan in order to save the pope. Once again, Jardine includes several subplots involving seemingly unrelated murders and the possibility that Skinner's wife may leave him. A *Kirkus Reviews* contributor called the novel "a deft, entertaining police procedural in the patented Jardine manner, with a full complement of sexy, savvy, busy cops."

Jardine's "Oz Blackstone" crime series focuses on a character much different from Skinner. Oz is a hapless private detective living in London whose good looks and charm lead him to Hollywood stardom. In *On Honeymoon with Death* Oz has married Primavera "Prim" Phillips after the death of his first wife. His movie career and a lottery win allow him to move to a villa in Spain, where Oz discovers a body at the bottom of his swimming pool. Oz finds that he is once again drawn into detective work and a case involving white slave trafficking and more murders. A *Publishers Weekly* contributor noted that the author "offers plenty of foul language, treachery and carnal intrigue" in this offering.

Poisoned Cherries finds Oz haunting Detective Skinner's home turf of Edinburgh, where a movie is being filmed. Dealing with the fact that his wife has left him and his girlfriend is pregnant, Oz nevertheless becomes involved in the investigation of another former girlfriend's lover when the girlfriend, Suzie, becomes the prime suspect in the case, which soon involves other murders. Rex Klett, writing in the *Library Journal,* noted that Jardine does a good job of combining the plot's "procedural and intrigue" components.

Oz is finally monogamous and married to Suzie in *Unnatural Justice.* The plot revolves around a hostile takeover of Suzie's company that becomes dangerously personal when a bomb is sent to the company offices. As a *Kirkus Reviews* contributor noted, "the pace is brisk, sure enough, but Oz's enthusiastic vigilantism will be offensive to some." *Alarm Call* finds Oz still devoted to Suzie but willing to help ex-wife Prim, who is battling for money as well as for custody of her child from her con-artist husband, Paul. While Oz and Prim track Paul to the United States, Oz must deal with his wife Suzie's suspicions that Oz is cheating on her. "Blackstone shows new depth this time, using brains rather than brawn to solve the puzzle in this altogether more nuanced thriller," noted a reviewer writing in *Kirkus Reviews.*

Jardine told *CA:* "A long time ago, my father planted the idea in my mind that I could be a writer. It's one of my great regrets that he didn't live to see it happen.

"Nothing and nobody influences my work. My writing process: no synopsis; I switch on and let it all escape from my head. My most surprising discovery: how perceptive my readers are, and also how friendly, in the United States as well as the United Kingdom and Canada. And I don't have a favourite book. Would you rank your children from one to twenty-four?"

BIOGRAPHICAL AND CRITICAL SOURCES:

PERIODICALS

Booklist, May 15, 1994, Emily Melton, review of *Skinner's Rules,* p. 1667; April 1, 1995, Emily Melton, review of *Skinner's Festival,* p. 1380; April 29, 1996, Emily Melton, review of *Skinner's Trail,* p. 1424; December 1, 1996, Emily Melton, review of *Skinner's Round,* p. 642.

Bookseller, May 16, 2003, Benedicte Page, "Big Bob Heads South: Quintin Jardine Is Poised to Be the Next Big Export in Scottish Crime," p. 27.

Edinburgh Evening News, July 8, 2004, "Prolific Writer Who Proves That Crime Does Pay."

Kirkus Reviews, September 1, 2001, review of *Autographs in the Rain,* p. 1249; July 15, 2003, review of *Poisoned Cherries,* p. 939; September 1, 2003, review of *Fallen Gods,* p. 1103; February 1, 2004, review of *Unnatural Justice,* p. 111; October 1, 2004, review of *Stay of Execution,* p. 941; February 15, 2005, review of *Alarm Call,* p. 201.

Library Journal, September 1, 2003, Rex Klett, review of *Poisoned Cherries,* p. 214; March 1, 2005, Rex Klett, review of *Alarm Call,* p. 71.

Publishers Weekly, May 9, 1994, review of *Skinner's Rules,* p. 65; March 13, 1995, review of *Skinner's Festival,* p. 63; April 15, 1996, review of *Skinner's Trail,* p. 55; August 6, 2001, review of *Thursday Legends,* p. 67; November 12, 2001, review of *Murmuring the Judges,* p. 40; April 15, 2002, review of *On Honeymoon with Death,* p. 45; March 15, 2004, review of *Unnatural Justice,* p. 59.

ONLINE

Quintin Jardine Home Page, http://www.quintin jardine.com (July 1, 2005).

Scotland on Sunday, http://scotlandonsunday.scotsman. com/ (February 29, 2004), Aidan Smith, "Murder He Wrote for a Capital Cop," profile of author.

Scotsman Online, http://news.scotsman.com/ (February 26, 2004), Struan Mackenzie, "Top Crime Author Is Write On."

*　　*　　*

JARRETT, Miranda
See HALLOWAY SCOTT, Susan

*　　*　　*

JENNINGS, Peter 1938-2005
(Peter Charles Archibald Ewart Jennings)

OBITUARY NOTICE— See index for *CA* sketch: Born July 29, 1938, in Toronto, Ontario, Canada; died of lung cancer, August 7, 2005, in New York, NY. Journalist, broadcaster, reporter, and author. Jennings was a highly respected news broadcaster best known for his work as anchor for the American Broadcasting Company's (ABC) *World News Tonight.* The son of Canadian news anchor Charles Jennings, Peter was enamored with journalism and broadcasting at a young age. When he was nine years old he hosted the children's Canadian radio program *Peter's People.* He did not do well in school, however, and he dropped out in the tenth grade. He worked as a bank teller for a couple of years before serving as host of the television dance party *Club Thirteen* in 1957. Jennings continued to work in Canadian television and radio as a reporter and interviewer before hosting the programs *Let's Face It* and *Time Out.* During the early 1960s he was host and coproducer of the late-night television show *Vue* and was a reporter and coanchor on *CTV National News.* It was in this last job that Jennings was noticed by ABC executives, who invited him to join their company. Jennings became a fixture at ABC for the next forty-one years. He was given an anchor job almost immediately for *Peter Jennings with the News,* but his two years there showed that the young reporter was still too inexperienced to lead a major news program. He was then made a roving correspondent for several years, and from 1969 to 1974 was head of the Middle East bureau in Beirut, Lebanon. In this roll, Jennings covered such events as the Six-Day War and the 1972 terrorist attacks against Israeli athletes at the

Munich Olympics. Promoted to chief correspondent in 1975, he was based in London for three years and, in 1978, given the foreign-desk anchoring job on *World News Tonight.* With more experience behind him, Jennings excelled, and when Frank Reynolds passed away in 1983, Jennings was given Reynolds's job as anchor and chief editor. Jennings gained a reputation for his improvisational skills; he was cool and collected while covering such terrible disasters as the 1986 space shuttle *Challenger* explosion and, more recently, the September 11, 2001, terrorist attacks. When Jennings faced his own lung cancer, he did so with his famous resolve and dignity; unfortunately, he passed away not long after his diagnosis. Honored with numerous journalism and broadcasting awards, including several Emmy awards, Oversea Press Club awards, and, in 2004, the Edward R. Murrow award for best documentary for his *The Kennedy Assassination—Beyond Conspiracy,* Jennings was coauthor of such books as *The Pope in Britain: Pope John Paul II British Visit, 1982* (1982) and *In Search of America* (2002).

OBITUARIES AND OTHER SOURCES:

PERIODICALS

Chicago Tribune, August 8, 2005, section 1, p. 1.
Los Angeles Times, August 8, 2005, pp. A1, A15.
New York Times, August 9, 2005, p. C21.
Times (London, England), August 9, 2005, p. 48.

*　　*　　*

JENNINGS, Peter Charles Archibald Ewart
See JENNINGS, Peter

*　　*　　*

JOHNSON, John H. 1918-2005
(John Harold Johnson)

OBITUARY NOTICE— See index for *CA* sketch: Born January 19, 1918, in Arkansas City, AR; died of heart failure, August 8, 2005, in Chicago, IL. Publisher, businessperson, and author. Johnson was the founder of Johnson Publishing, which produced the magazines *Jet* and *Ebony,* the first such publications aimed at the

African-American market. Coming from humble beginnings, he got his start as a high school graduate at the insurance company Supreme Life, a black-owned business in Chicago. One of his jobs there was to collect magazine and newspaper clippings. This inspired his idea to begin a African-American version of *Reader's Digest* that he called *Negro Digest* and, later, *Black World*. Through creative marketing, persistence, and the help of friends and family, he managed to boost circulation up to fifty thousand subscribers. The publication eventually folded in 1976. By then, however, Johnson was already succeeding with other magazines. After attending the University of Chicago and Northwestern University in the late 1930s, he founded Johnson Publishing in 1942. He started the publication of *Ebony* three years later. The idea of creating a mainstream, middle-class, African-American-oriented publication was highly original, and Johnson found an eager audience. He then added *Jet* to his publications list in 1951, and by 2004 their combined circulations totaled more than 2.5 million. He also started a magazine for young readers, *Ebony, Jr.* Johnson added other business interests to his company over the years, including Fashion Fair Cosmetics, which was established in 1973, and for a time he owned several radio stations as well. *Ebony* and *Jet* typically focused on delivering positive messages about the black community, though controversial issues were also addressed, especially during the civil rights movement. As the magazines moved into the mainstream, however, they were sometimes criticized for avoiding controversy. Nonetheless, Johnson remained firm in his efforts to include mostly upbeat stories in the periodicals. In 2002 he turned over the chief executive officer position to his daughter, Linda, but remained publisher and chair of the company until his death. Johnson wrote about his life story in *Succeeding against the Odds* (1989) and was also the coauthor of a children's book titled *Every Wall a Ladder* (1996). For his many contributions to society, business, and journalism, Johnson received numerous honors over his lifetime, including the Columbia Journalism Award and induction into the Black Press Hall of Fame; in 1996 he was given the Presidential Medal of Freedom.

OBITUARIES AND OTHER SOURCES:

BOOKS

Johnson, John H., and Lerone Bennett, Jr., *Succeeding against the Odds*, Warner Books (New York, NY), 1989.

PERIODICALS

Chicago Tribune, August 9, 2005, section 1, pp. 1, 12.
Los Angeles Times, August 9, 2005, p. B10.
New York Times, August 9, 2005, p. C22.
Times (London, England), August 15, 2005, p. 44.
Washington Post, August 9, 2005, pp. A1, A4.

*   *   *

JOHNSON, John Harold
   See JOHNSON, John H.

*   *   *

JOHNSON, Susan 1939-
   (Jill Barkin)

PERSONAL: Born June 7, 1939, in Hibbing, MN; married Pat MacKay, 1957 (marriage ended); married Craig Johnson, 1966; children: (first marriage) two; (second marriage) one. *Education:* University of Minnesota, B.A., 1960, M.A., 1969.

ADDRESSES: Home—North Branch, MN. *Agent*—Author Mail, Penguin Group, c/o Berkley Publicity, 375 Hudson St., New York, NY 10014. *E-mail*—info@susanjohnsonauthor.com.

CAREER: Writer. Formerly worked as an art historian.

WRITINGS:

ROMANCE NOVELS

The Play, Fawcett (New York, NY), 1987.
To Please a Lady, Fawcett (New York, NY), 1999.
Tempting, Kensington (New York, NY), 2001.
Seduction in Mind, Bantam (New York, NY), 2001.
Again and Again, Brava (New York, NY), 2002.
Force of Nature, Brava (New York, NY), 2003.
Pure Silk, Brava (New York, NY), 2004.

Also author of series book *Outlaw,* 1993. Contributor to anthologies *Fascinated,* Kensington (New York, NY), 2000; *Taken by Surprise,* Brava (New York, NY),

2003; *Twin Peaks,* Berkley Sensation (New York, NY), 2005; *Captivated; Naughty, Naughty; Rough around the Edges; Strangers in the Night; Not Just for Tonight,* and *American Beauty.*

"RUSSIAN" ROMANCE SERIES

Seized by Love, Playboy Press (New York, NY), 1979.
Love Storm, Playboy Press (New York, NY), 1981.
Sweet Love Survive, Berkeley (New York, NY), 1985.
Golden Paradise, Harlequin (Toronto, Ontario, Canada), 1990.

"BRADDOCK BLACK" ROMANCE SERIES

Blaze, Berkeley (New York, NY), 1986.
Silver Flame, Berkeley (New York, NY), 1988.

Also author of series books titled *Forbidden, Pure Sin,* and *Brazen.*

"ST. JOHN/DURAS" ROMANCE SERIES

Sinful, Doubleday (New York, NY), 1992.
Wicked, Bantam (New York, NY), 1996.
Taboo, Bantam (New York, NY), 1997.
A Touch of Sin, Bantam (New York, NY), 1999.
Legendary Lover, Bantam (New York, NY), 2000.
Temporary Mistress, Bantam (New York, NY), 2000.

"HOT CONTEMPORARIES" ROMANCE SERIES

Blonde Heat, Bantam (New York, NY), 2002.
Hot Pink, Berkeley Books (New York, NY), 2003.
Hot Streak (previously published under pseudonym Jill Barkin), Bantam (New York, NY), 2004.
Hot Legs, Berkeley Books (New York, NY), 2004.
Hot Spot, Berkley Sensation (New York, NY), 2005.

WORK IN PROGRESS: An historical novel set in England in 1788.

SIDELIGHTS: Susan Johnson is an historical romance writer known for the accuracy of her period pieces and her wit. "Her fictional style, which has steadily developed since her first novel, *Seized by Love,* is an interesting combination of Regency romance, erotica, and 'glitz and glamour,'" noted a contributor to *Twentieth-Century Romance & Historical Writers.* "The fantasy she constructs is reinforced by her use of multiple points of view—the hero, heroine, or even a minor character, an onlooker—which draw the reader into the story."

One of Johnson's series romances is the nineteenth-century historical "St. John/Duras" series. In *Sinful,* the first book in the series, Chelsea, the daughter of the English earl of Dumfries, defies her arranged marriage by bedding Sinjin St. John, the duke of Seth. Chelsea becomes pregnant and Sinjin is imprisoned, only to escape with the help of an American Indian. New adventures lead to Sinjin's captivity in Tunis with Chelsea coming to the rescue. A *Publishers Weekly* contributor noted, "Johnson . . . uses her fertile imagination to blend a strong heroine, unbridled sex, and a modicum of history into unadulterated fun." In *Wicked,* Johnson introduces the reader to Serena Blythe, a governess who is on her way to Italy to study painting when she loses all her possessions in a ship hijacking. She eventually stows away on the ship of Beau St. Jules, whose father is Sinjin St. John, and the two soon fall in love. Noting the novel's strong sexual content, a *Publishers Weekly* contributor commented that "it's not for the prudish but Johnson fans will love it."

The story in *Taboo* takes place following the French Revolution and features a torrid love affair between Russian Countess Teo Korsakova and French General André Duras, the latter who is based on the historical figure of General André Massena. A *Publishers Weekly* contributor noted that "there's plenty of solid history to cool down the pages—complete with lengthy footnotes." The son of this love affair is the protagonist in Johnson's *A Touch of Sin.* Although a confirmed bachelor and rake, Pasha Duras falls for Lady Trixi Grosvenor, whose young son is the object of murderous intents by relatives who want his inheritance. But Pasha comes to the rescue. The historical framework for this novel includes the Greek War of Independence in the early nineteenth century. A *Booklist* contributor called the novel "a fast tale of lust, love, and greed that exemplifies the tried-and-true spirit of romance fiction." *Legendary Lover* features a Victorian romance between an English marquis and a progressive and independent French woman. "Here, as usual, readers get their money's worth from Johnson's erotic-escapade novels," wrote a *Publishers Weekly* contributor.

To Please a Lady, a non-series offering by Johnson, tells the story of a love affair between the teenage rascal named Robbie Carrie—who first appeared in Johnson's earlier novel, aptly named *Outlaw*—and a widow named Roxanne, who is in her thirties. When Roxanne is forced to succumb to the lecherous intentions of a duke, Robbie comes to the rescue. A *Publishers Weekly* contributor noted that the author "rewards readers with a slew of footnotes detailing the historic setting."

Johnson tells the story of Princess Christina in her novel *Tempting*. Unhappily married to a cheating husband, Christina nevertheless tries to remain true to her marriage and is successful until she encounters Maxwell Falconer, an American who has become the marquis of Vale. Kristin Ramsdell, writing in *Library Journal,* commented that "Johnson is an acclaimed author of highly sensual romances . . . and her fans will be waiting for this one." *Seduction in Mind* focuses on the love affair between the Viscount Ranelagh and Alexandra Ionides, a model he first saw in a painting. Writing in *Booklist,* a reviewer noted that "Johnson knows exactly what her devoted readers desire, and she delivers it with her usual flair."

In *Again and Again,* the author recounts the story of Caroline Morrow, a former noblewoman through marriage who has fallen on hard times and is now forced to work as a governess. Her fortunes seem about to turn when she meets her former lover, Lord Simon Blair. *Booklist* contributor Mary K. Chelton wrote that the author "has written an extremely arousing erotic romance." *Hot Pink* takes place in present day and features the love affair between graphic designer Chloe Chisholm and handsome Rocco Vinelli. Once again writing in *Booklist,* Chelton commented that the author "overcomes a silly premise . . . to present an entertainingly conveyed tale rich in lovingly described sex scenes."

BIOGRAPHICAL AND CRITICAL SOURCES:

BOOKS

Twentieth-Century Romance & Historical Writers, 3rd edition, St. James Press (Detroit, MI), 1994.

PERIODICALS

Booklist, February 15, 1999, Grace Lee and David Pitt, review of *A Touch of Sin,* p. 1047; July, 2001, John Charles, review of *Seduction in Mind,* p. 1990;

May 1, 2002, Mary K. Chelton, review of *Again and Again,* p. 1512; July, 2003, Mary K. Chelton, review of *Hot Pink,* p. 1874.

Library Journal, February 15, 2001, Kristin Ramsdell, review of *Tempting,* p. 153.

Publishers Weekly, June 29, 1993, review of *Sinful,* p. 52; October 4, 1993, review of *Outlaw,* p. 70; November 25, 1996, review of *Wicked,* p. 70; September 29, 1997, review of *Taboo,* p. 86; February 1, 1999, review of *A Touch of Sin,* p. 82; August 20, 1999, review of *To Please a Lady,* p. 81; April 10, 2000, review of *Legendary Lover,* p. 79; October 2, 2000, review of *Fascinated,* p. 59; February 19, 2001, review of *Tempting,* p. 71; June 4, 2001, review of *Seduction in Mind,* p. 63; April 29, 2002, review of *Again and Again,* p. 45.

ONLINE

Bookbug on the Web, http://www.geocities.com/ Athens/Forum/8078/author-johnson.html/ (July 1, 2005), Mary T. Knibbe, Sr., "An Interview with Susan Johnson."

Susan Johnson Home Page, http://www.susanjohnson author.com (July 1, 2005).*

*   *   *

JOHNSTON, Dorothy 1948-

PERSONAL: Born 1948, in Geelong, Victoria, Australia; children: one son, one daughter. *Education:* Attended University of Melbourne.

ADDRESSES: Agent—c/o Jenny Darling, Jenny Darling and Associates, P.O. Box 413, Toorak, Victoria 3142, Australia. *E-mail*—Dorothy@webone.com.au.

CAREER: Writer and educator. Taught English; former researcher in education.

AWARDS, HONORS: Australian Capital Territory Book of the Year joint winner, 2001, for *The Trojan Dog.*

WRITINGS:

FICTION

Tunnel Vision, Hale & Iremonger (Sydney, New South Wales, Australia), 1984.

Ruth, Hale & Iremonger (Sydney, New South Wales, Australia), 1986.

Maralinga, My Love (novel), McPhee Gribble/Penguin (Fitzroy, Victoria, Australia), 1988.

One for the Master, Wakefield Press (Kent Town, South Australia, Australia), 1997.

The Trojan Dog, Wakefield Press (Kent Town, South Australia, Australia), 2000 Dunne/St. Martin's Minotaur (New York, NY), 2005.

The White Tower (sequel to *The Trojan Dog*), Wakefield Press (Kent Town, South Australia, Australia), 2003.

The House at Number 10, Wakefield Press (Kent Town, South Australia, Australia), 2005.

Short stories have appeared in numerous anthologies, including *Canberra Tales,* Penguin, 1988; *Amnesty,* William Heinemann Australia, 1993; *Mother Love,* Random House Australia, 1996; and *Below the Waterline,* HarperCollins, 1999.

OTHER

Essays have appeared in *Australian Book Review, Australian Humanities Review, HEAT 13 (Series 1),* and *HEAT 1 (Series 2).*

SIDELIGHTS: Dorothy Johnston is recognized for her literary fiction and is also a crime novelist. As noted on the *AustLit* Web site, the author "often makes explicit links between the realms of the public and the private." For example, in *One for the Master,* Johnston writes about the woolen mill that existed in her hometown of Geelong, Victoria, Australia. Covering nearly five decades beginning in 1950, the story focuses on Helen Sullivan. As noted by Ivor Indyk in the *Sydney Morning Herald* and reprinted on Johnston's home page, Sullivan's "own life has been determined by her relation to the mill." Written in the first person through Sullivan's eyes, the reader is given her social and political perspectives involving both the personal, such as weddings and funerals, and the

public happenings, such as political strikes and floods. Indyk called the book "a quiet novel, courageous in its modesty, and in its own loyalty to the past."

The author long thought of writing a crime novel before producing her first in the genre in 2000. *The Trojan Dog* tells the story of Sandra Mahoney, who has returned to the work force after being a stay-at-home mom. Her job in the Australian Labor Relations Service Department Industries Branch ends up casting Sandra in the middle of intrigue when her boss is suspected of embezzling money via computer fraud. Mahoney tries to stay loyal to her boss and prove her innocence even though her coworkers have treated her badly and fully expect her to wind up taking the fall for a crime she did not commit. Writing in *MBR Bookwatch,* Harriet Klausner noted that the book "is a terrific Australian amateur sleuth starring a delightful protagonist, a fabulous support cast who makes the office seem real, and a fantastic look at Canberra." A *Publishers Weekly* contributor commented that "Johnston's literary, character-driven crime debut explores white-collar corruption as well as a modern woman's personal transformation." A *Kirkus Reviews* contributor noted that the character of Mahoney "narrates her tale with cool precision" and noted that the author "has created a tense but droll psychological thriller about office dynamics."

Johnston followed up her crime debut with a sequel titled *The White Tower,* which is about a young man who is devoted to an interactive computer game. Mahoney investigates what appears to be his suicide, scripted to look like a chilling execution in the game.

Johnston told *CA:* "One of the most delightful things about being a writer is realizing the power of the written word to travel across continents, and across time as well. In the 1980s I wrote a novel about the British atomic bomb tests at Maralinga in South Australia, and I'm still receiving letters from members of the Nuclear Veterans' Association. Recently, I had the experience of walking into a New York bookstore and seeing *The Trojan Dog* on the counter, and discovering how much the bookshop owner had enjoyed it. As for writing crime—it is the most fun anyone can have this side of legal.

"I am a morning person and write best after I've just woken up. When I taught full-time I used to get up at five in the morning so I could write before I went to work. These days, luckily, I don't have to do that."

"One of the most important influences on my writing is the Australian-born novelist Christina Stead, and meeting her in Melbourne in the 1970s was a great inspiration for me. My favourite book is the one that I'm about to write. The joys and pitfalls are all still ahead of me."

BIOGRAPHICAL AND CRITICAL SOURCES:

PERIODICALS

Kirkus Reviews, January 15, 2005, review of *The Trojan Dog,* p. 86.
MBR Bookwatch, March, 2005, Harriet Klausner, review of *The Trojan Dog.*
Publishers Weekly, February 28, 2005, review of *The Trojan Dog,* p.46.

ONLINE

AllReaders.com, http://www.allreaders.com/ (March, 2005), Harriet Klausner, review of *The Trojan Dog.*
AustLit, http://www.austlit.edu.au/ (July 1, 2005), biography of author.
Dorothy Johnston Home Page, http://members.iinet. net.au/~dorothy1 (July 5, 2005), *Sydney Morning Herald,* Ivor Indyk, review of *One for the Master.*

*   *   *

JONES, Tayari 1970-

PERSONAL: Born 1970, in Atlanta, GA. *Education:* Spelman College, B.A. (magna cum laude), 1991; University of Iowa, M.A., 1994; Arizona State University. M.F.A., 2000.

ADDRESSES: Office—Department of English, University of Illinois at Urbana-Champaign, 608 South Wright St., Urbana, IL 61801. *E-mail*—info@ tayarijones.com.

CAREER: Educator and writer. University of Iowa, graduate instructor, 1992-94; Prairie View A&M University, faculty member, 1994-97; Arizona State University, graduate instructor, 1999-2000; East Ten-nessee State University, Geier writer-in-residence, 2003-04; University of Illinois, Urbana-Champaign, assistant professor of English, 2004—. Cultural Services Department, City of Tempe, AZ, public arts assistant, 2001.

AWARDS, HONORS: Martindale Foundation Award for Fiction, 2000; Zora Neale Hurston/Richard Wright Foundation Award, 2000; Voices of Our Nation Arts Foundation scholarship, 2001; Ledig House International Writers Colony fellowship, LEF Foundation Award for African-American and Native-American Writers, Gerald Freund fellowship, MacDowell Colony in Peterborough, Jakobson fellow, Wesleyan Summer Writing Conference, and artist fellowship, Arizona Commission on the Arts, all 2002; professional development grant, Arizona Commission on the Arts, Fletcher Pratt fellowship, Bread Loaf Writers Conference and Chateau de Lavigny International Writers Colony fellowship, all 2003; Legacy Award in the Category of Debut Fiction, Zora Neale Hurston/ Richard Wright Foundation, for *Leaving Atlanta;* College of Liberal Arts and Sciences alumni leader, Arizona State University, Walter E. Dankin fellowship, Sewanee Writers Conference, and GE Fund residency, Corporation of Yaddo, all 2004.

WRITINGS:

FICTION

Leaving Atlanta, Warner Books (New York, NY), 2002.
The Untelling, Warner Books (New York, NY), 2005.

Contributor to short stories in periodicals and journals, including *Sou'wester, Crab Orchard Review, 64, Figdust, HealthQuest,* and *Catalyst,* and in anthologies, including *Am I the Last Virgin?,* edited by Tara Roberts, Simon & Schuster, 1997; *Gumbo,* edited by Marita Golden, Doubleday, 2002; *Proverbs for the People,* edited by TaRessa Stovall, Kensington Press, 2003; and *New Stories from the South: The Year's Best 2004,* Algonquin Books, 2004. Creative nonfiction and literary criticism have appeared in *Father Songs,* edited by Gloria Wade Gayles, Beacon Press, 1997; *Letters of Intent,* edited by Meg Daly, Free Press, 1999; and *Langston Hughes Review.*

ADAPTATIONS: Leaving Atlanta was adapted as an audiobook by Recorded Books (Prince Frederick, MD), 2003.

SIDELIGHTS: Tayari Jones is a novelist and short-story writer whose fiction often focuses on the urban south, where she grew up. In her critically acclaimed first book, *Leaving Atlanta,* Jones sets the scene in Atlanta during the 1979-81 period when a number of real-life African-American children were murdered, many of them near the author's home as a child. "This novel is my way of documenting a particular moment in history," Jones noted on her home page. "It is a love letter to my generation and also an effort to remember my own childhood. To remind myself and my readers what it was like to be eleven and at the mercy of the world. And despite the obvious darkness of the time period, I also wanted to remember all that is sweet about girlhood, to recall all the moments that make a person smile and feel optimistic."

In the novel, Jones tells the story of three inner-city children who go to the same elementary school and the effects that the murders in Atlanta have on them. Tasha struggles to fit in with the popular crowd at school. When another boy, who also does not fit in, expresses interest in her, Tasha seeks approval from the popular kids by announcing in front of her classmates that she wishes the killer would kill him, too. When the boy fails to show up for class, Tasha begins to fret that perhaps her words are more powerful than she thought. Rodney is bright but shy and, unlike Tasha, does not even try to fit in. His grades begin to fail and when his father comes and whips him in front of his classmates, Rodney is set on a confrontational path with someone who may be the killer. Octavia is also a misfit who is made fun of for being poor and extremely black in skin color. As the murders continue, Ocatavia's father, who has had little to do with Octavia and lives in suburban South Carolina with his new family, calls to see if Octavia wants to come stay with him and escape the dangerous Atlanta area where she lives. Octavia, who excels in school, knows it is a good opportunity, but debates leaving her mother behind even as a friend goes missing.

In a review of *Leaving Atlanta* on the *Mostly Fiction* Web site, Kam White noted that "throughout the book, there is little mention of any details of the actual murders that took place. Instead, we are allowed to explore the emotional relationships among the children and the effects that the disappearances of their friends have on them and the community." Melissa Morgan, writing on the *Bookreporter.com,* commented that the author "effortlessly infuses each of the three children in her novel with their own unique voice . . . and through doing so creates the mood of an entire city." A *Publishers Weekly* contributor noted that the author's "strongly grounded tale hums with the rhythms of schoolyard life and proves Jones to be a powerful storyteller." VeTalle Fusilier, writing in the *Black Issues Book Review,* commented that "this first novel by Jones is a work of great promise." Vanessa Bush wrote in *Booklist,* that "Jones is as skillful at evoking the fear and anxiety of that horrendous summer as she is at recalling coming-of-age concerns."

In her second novel, *The Untelling,* Jones tells the story of Aria Jackson, who, along with her mother, survived a terrible car accident that killed her father and baby sister. Psychologically scarred from the ordeal, Aria is struggling fifteen years later to make her life whole and find love while her mother has fallen apart and become a crack addict. Aria is unable to tell her boyfriend or other friends about this past experience, which eventually leads her to deeper feelings of guilt despite the altruistic work she does as a literacy instructor in Atlanta's inner city. Furthermore, her secret tragedy also threatens any hope for happiness that she may have as it keeps others from fully understanding who she is and why. Vanessa Bush, writing in *Booklist,* noted that the author "offers a delicate portrait of a young woman's emotional fragility." In a review in *Library Journal,* Maureen Neville called the book a "bittersweet second novel." *Black Issues Book Review* contributor Nicole Shaw commented that the novel "will stir readers to evaluate the misfortunes of their own lives, and be resolved to the fact that life is what it is." As a *Publishers Weekly* reviewer wrote, "the first-person narration is convincing and genuine, and Jones handles her material with sensitivity and sympathy."

BIOGRAPHICAL AND CRITICAL SOURCES:

PERIODICALS

Black Issues Book Review, July-August, 2002, VeTalle Fusilie, review of *Leaving Atlanta,* p. 38; March-April, 2005, Nicole Shaw, review of *The Untelling,* p. 51.

Booklist, August, 2002, Vanessa Bush, review of *Leaving Atlanta,* p. 1920; March 15, 2005, review of *The Untelling,* p. 1265.

Essence, April, 2005, "A Novelist to Watch," p. 100.

Kirkus Reviews, January 15, 2002, review of *Leaving Atlanta,* p. 830; January 15, 2005, review of *The Untelling,* p. 75.

Library Journal, September 1, 2002, Roger A. Berger, review of *Leaving Atlanta,* p. 214; March 15, 2005, Maureen Neville, review of *The Untelling,* p. 72.

Publishers Weekly, June 17, 2002, review of *Leaving Atlanta,* p. 38; February 28, 2005, review of *The Untelling,* p. 40.

ONLINE

AllReaders.com, http://www.allreaders.com/ (July 5, 2005), Harriet Klausner, review of *Leaving Atlanta.*

Bookreporter.com, http://www.bookreporter.com/ (July 5, 2005), Melissa Morgan, review of *Leaving Atlanta.*

English Department University of Illinois at Urbana-Champaign Web site, http://www.english.uiuc.edu/ (July 5, 2005), profile of author.

Mostly Fiction, http://mostlyfiction.com/ (February 10, 2003), Kam White, review of *Leaving Atlanta.*

Spellman University Web site, http://www.spelman.edu/ (July 5, 2005), "Interview with Tayari Jones."

Tayari Jones Home Page, http://www.tayarijones.com (July 5, 2005).

*   *   *

JOZSA, Frank P., Jr. 1941-

PERSONAL: Born September 12, 1941, in Terre Haute, IN. *Education:* Indiana State University, B.S., 1963, M.S., 1972; Butler University, M.B.A., 1971; Georgia State University, Ph.D., 1977.

ADDRESSES: Home—1062 Woodlake Lane, Fort Mill, SC 29708.

CAREER: Writer. Fort Motor Company, Dearborn, MI, buyer, 1968-69; Indiana National Bank, Indianapolis, profit planning analyst, 1969-71; ITT Educational Service, Indianapolis, budget analyst, 1971; University of Maryland, instructor of economics and business, 1975-76; Clemson University, SC, instructor of economics, 1976-77; Kennesaw College, GA, assistant professor of economics, 1977-78; Bethune-Cookman College, Daytona Beach, FL, assistant professor of economics, 1978-80; Embry-Riddle Aeronautical University, Dayton Beach, FL, assistant professor of management and finance, 1980-84; Allentown College, Allentown, PA, assistant professor of economics, 1984-91; Pfeiffer University, Misenheimer and Charlotte, NC, associate professor of economics and business, 1991—.

WRITINGS:

(With John J. Guthrie, Jr.) *Relocating Teams and Expanding Leagues in Professional Sports: How the Major Leagues Respond to Market Conditions,* Quorum Books (Westport, CT), 1999.

American Sports Empire: How the Leagues Breed Success, Praeger (Westport, CT), 2003.

Sports Capitalism: The Foreign Business of American Professional Leagues, Ashgate (Burlington, VT), 2004.

Contributor of articles to periodicals, including *Carolina Journal, Healthcare Journal, Athletic Business, Business Journal, Organizational Development Journal, Florida Runner,* and *American Statistical Association Proceedings.* Also contributor of book reviews to *Wall Street Review of Books.*

K

KALB, Bernard 1922-

PERSONAL: Born February 4, 1922, in New York, NY; married; wife's name Phyllis; children: four. *Education:* City College of New York, B.S.S., 1951; Harvard University, M.A., 1953.

ADDRESSES: Agent—Harry Walker Agency, 355 Lexington Ave., 21st Fl., New York, NY 10017.

CAREER: New York Times, New York, NY, reporter, 1946-60; Columbia Broadcasting System (CBS), Moscow correspondent, 1960-63, diplomatic affairs correspondent, 1963-80, anchor of *CBS Morning News,* 1970-72; National Broadcasting Company (NBC), chief diplomatic affairs correspondent, 1980-85; U.S. Department of State, Washington, DC, assistant secretary of state for public affairs, 1985-86; Cable News Network, panelist on *Reliable Sources,* 1988-2001; Freedom Forum, moderator of international panels on state of the media, 1997—member of U.S. delegation to Anti-Incitement Committee (part of the Mideast peace process), beginning 1998. DuPont-Columbia awards committee, juror; Hamilton College, Clinton, NY, visiting professor. Appeared as himself in film *Dave,* 1993. *Military service:* Served in U.S. Army for two years.

AWARDS, HONORS: Senior fellow, Columbia University Freedom Forum Media Studies Center, 1991-92; Council on Foreign Relations fellowship; Overseas Press Club award for *Viet Cong* (television documentary); Weintal Prize for lifetime achievement, Georgetown University Institute for the Study of Diplomacy, 2005.

WRITINGS:

(With brother, Marvin L. Kalb) *Kissinger,* Little, Brown (Boston, MA), 1974.
(With Marvin L. Kalb) *The Last Ambassador,* Little, Brown (Boston, MA), 1981.

Wrote and produced *Viet Cong* (documentary film). Contributor to periodicals, including *New York Times Magazine, Esquire, Smithsonian,* and *Newsweek.*

SIDELIGHTS: Bernard Kalb began his journalism career as a *New York Times* reporter covering the events that eventually led the United States into the Vietnam War. Kalb was a foreign correspondent based in Indonesia, Hong Kong, Paris, and Saigon until 1985, when he returned stateside to take a position with the Reagan administration as assistant secretary of state for public affairs under George Shultz. He remained only until the following year, when he quit over what he saw as a "disinformation campaign" undertaken by the administration to mislead Libya's Muammar Gaddafi as to the intentions of the United States toward his country. Kalb claimed that the government created untrue stories to the effect that Gaddafi was planning terrorist activities that justified retaliation. Kalb, who had spent years as correspondent for major networks, said that "you face a choice, as an American, as a spokesman, as a journalist, whether to allow oneself to be absorbed in the ranks of silence, whether to vanish into unopposed acquiescence or to enter a modest dissent. Faith in the word of America is the pulse beat of our democracy."

Kalb's world view is based on his first-hand observations of history gained while working as a journalist beginning in the 1950s. He covered President Richard

Nixon's trip to China in 1972 and was part of the U.S. delegation that accompanied President Reagan to Geneva, Switzerland, in 1985, for a summit with Soviet leader Mikhail Gorbachev. After leaving his government post, Kalb served on the panel of *Reliable Sources,* a program that studied the media and its accuracy and service to readers, listeners, and viewers. He also moderated Freedom Forum panels worldwide, and has participated in meetings and documentaries on issues that include global conflicts, human rights, and the environment as well as the state of the media. He was a correspondent for a Public Broadcasting Service (PBS) documentary on India and traveled to Brazil for a television documentary on the Earth Summit. Other destinations included Budapest, Hungary, for the International Media Fund seminar on government-press relations and Istanbul, Turkey, for a meeting of the World Business Council.

With his brother, Marvin L. Kalb, Kalb authored *Kissinger,* a study of President Nixon's secretary of state. *The Last Ambassador* is a novel set against the background of the fall of Saigon in 1975. Kalb produced the award-winning documentary *Viet Cong,* which is based on his years covering the Vietnam conflict. He continues to lecture and comment on the state of the media, including its coverage of the Iraqi conflict. *Florida Times Union* reporter Jessie-Lynne Kerr, covering a 2003 address in Jacksonville, Florida, recorded Kalb noting that when the bombs began falling on Baghdad, he was visiting Hanoi in Vietnam: "I was caught up in the echoes of a war that still haunts America. There was a spooky feeling to it. I wondered if the B-52s that were bombing Baghdad were the same ones that bombed Hanoi a generation and a half ago."

BIOGRAPHICAL AND CRITICAL SOURCES:

PERIODICALS

Florida Times Union, April 3, 2003, Jessie-Lynne Kerr, "Media Critic Kalb Says War Coverage Scooped," p. B4.
New Republic, December 30, 1981, Morton Kondracke, review of *The Last Ambassador,* p. 40.
New York Times, August 28, 1981, Edwin McDowell, review of *The Last Ambassador,* p. 21; September 25, 1981, Richard F. Shepard, review of *The Last Ambassador,* p. C23.

New York Times Book Review, January 1, 1984, Alan Cheuse, review of *The Last Ambassador,* pp. 14-15.
Publishers Weekly, July 24, 1981, Barbara A. Bannon, review of *The Last Ambassador,* p. 142.
Time, October 20, 1986, John S. DeMott, "Bernard Kalb's 'Modest Dissent': The State Department Spokesman Quits over Disinformation," p. 40.
Washington Monthly, September, 1981, Michael Hiestand, review of *The Last Ambassador,* pp. 58-59.

ONLINE

Hamilton University Web site, http://www.hamilton. edu/ (July 2, 2005).
Harry Walker Agency Web site, http://www.harry walker.com/ (July 2, 2005).
National Debate Online, http://www.thenationaldebate. com/ (July 2, 2005).*

*   *   *

KALLOSS, Stephanie

PERSONAL: Born in Lincoln, WA; daughter of Greg and Dorie Kallos.

ADDRESSES: Home—Seattle, WA. *Agent*—c/o Author Mail, Grove, 841 Broadway, New York, NY 10003.

CAREER: Writer. Previously worked as an actor and teacher.

WRITINGS:

Broken for You (fiction), Grove Press (New York, NY), 2004.

SIDELIGHTS: Stephanie Kalloss is an actress turned novelist who impressed many critics with her first novel *Broken for You.* The story centers around two women living with loss. The first, Margaret, has lived in virtual isolation in a Seattle mansion since the death of her son and her divorce from her husband. In her seventies, Margaret discovers she has a brain tumor and decides that she must do something different with her life as the end is apparently near. She opens her mansion to borders, among them Wanda, a maniacally organized stage manager who was abandoned by her parents and is in town looking for a recent boyfriend who did the same. The novel essentially follows Margaret and Wanda as they interact with each other and come to terms with the ghosts of their respective pasts. Bronwyn Miller, in a review for *Bookreporter. com,* noted that as the book is "told in alternating chapters that illuminate the characters as they are now, we also are privy to their back-stories of how they came to be 'broken.' With such insight into these people, *Broken for You* ends up being a life-affirming read rather than a depressing one." Writing in *Booklist,* Jennifer Baker commented, "Well-crafted plotting and crackling wit make this debut novel . . . a delight to read and a memory to savor." Jenn B. Stidham wrote in *Library Journal* that the author "has given us a compelling, richly layered story," and a *Publishers Weekly* contributor commented, "Though it takes a while to get started, this haunting and memorable debut is . . . peopled by lovably imperfect and eccentric characters."

BIOGRAPHICAL AND CRITICAL SOURCES:

PERIODICALS

Booklist, August, 2004, Jennifer Baker, review of *Broken for You,* p. 1900.
Kirkus Reviews, July 15, 2004, review of *Broken for You,* p. 650.
Library Journal, August, 2004, Jenn B. Stidham, review of *Broken for You,* p. 68.
Publishers Weekly, July 12, 2004, review of *Broken for You,* p. 41.

ONLINE

Bookreporter.com, http://www.bookreporter.com/ (May 30, 2005), Bronwyn Miller, review of *Broken for You.**

*   *   *

KAMHOLZ, Edward J. 1946-

PERSONAL: Born August 6, 1946, in Portland, OR; son of Marvin (a newspaper owner and publisher) and Amy (a teacher; maiden name, Hughes) Kamholz; children: Mark. *Education:* University of Oregon, B.S.

(business management), 1968; University of Portland, M.B.A., 1974; Foothill College, A.A. (graphic design), 2001. *Hobbies and other interests:* Hiking, fly-fishing, nature, visual arts, reading, storytelling, writing.

ADDRESSES: Home—1 Sorrel Lane, San Carlos, CA 94070. *E-mail*—ekamholz@comcast.net.

CAREER: Writer. International Telephone and Telegraph, Chicago, IL, marketing manager, 1976-80; Plantronics, Inc., Santa Cruz, CA, marketing manager, 1981-84; Cushman Electronics, San Jose, CA, director of marketing and sales, 1984-85; The Horizon Company, Menlo Park, CA, marketing consultant, 1986-2000; Designs by Design, San Carlos, CA, graphic designer, 2001—.

AWARDS, HONORS: 2004 Book Award, Bay Area Independent Publishers Association, for *The Oregon-American Lumber Company: Ain't No More.*

WRITINGS:

(With Jim Blain and Gregory Kamholz) *The Oregon-American Lumber Company: Ain't No More,* Stanford University Press (Stanford, CA), 2003.

Contributor to *Business Age.*

WORK IN PROGRESS: Pacific Northwest and Northwest Oregon history.

SIDELIGHTS: Edward J. Kamholz told *CA:* "I go where the materials lead me. I'm never quite sure of the destination until I arrive. I also edit my own work, endlessly. I wrote *The Oregon-American Lumber Company: Ain't No More* because the mechanical marvels of a steam-powered, stump-to-the-boxer lumbering operation were at my doorstep, bestowing me with a rich source of childhood memories. The sheer magnitude and depth of the former company president's correspondence files told of the social, economic, political, industry, and strategic issues underlying the company's existence from a single point of view and inspired me to write the company's story."

KANE, Stephanie

PERSONAL: Born in Brooklyn, NY. *Education:* Attended University of Colorado; graduated from law school.

ADDRESSES: Home—CO. *Agent*—c/o Author Mail, Scibner, 1230 Avenue of the Americas, New York, NY 10020.

CAREER: Briefly owned and ran a karate studio in Boulder, CO; attorney, first in banking law, then in criminal defense.

AWARDS, HONORS: Colorado Authors League Award, 2005, for *Seeds of Doubt.*

WRITINGS:

SUSPENSE NOVELS

Blind Spot, Bantam Books (New York, NY), 2000.
Quiet Time, Bantam Books (New York, NY), 2001.
Extreme Indifference, Scribner (New York, NY), 2003.
Seeds of Doubt, Scribner (New York, NY), 2004.

WORK IN PROGRESS: Sequel to *Seeds of Doubt.*

SIDELIGHTS: Stephanie Kane was born and raised in Brooklyn, New York, but migrated west for college, attending the University of Colorado, where she majored in Italian language and literature. After graduation, she briefly owned and operated a karate studio, and earned a second-degree black belt. She went on to attend law school, and to work at a prestigious Denver firm that specialized in banking law where she was eventually awarded a partnership. Shortly following this achievement, she went on vacation in Turkey, where she climbed Mount Ararat. Something about the trip and her level of achievement gave her a new perspective on her life, and when she returned home she quit her job and began to take classes with an eye toward applying to medical school. Though her test scores were good, she failed to gain acceptance to any of the schools she applied to, and instead returned to the law. This time, however, she was hired by a criminal defense firm, and was thrilled to be working in a courtroom. The new position served as inspiration when Kane began to write her legal suspense thrillers.

Kane's first novel, *Blind Spot,* introduces readers to criminal defense attorney Jackie Flowers, a Denver lawyer with a unique handicap to overcome: she's dyslexic. In an interview for *LD.org,* Kane explained why she chose this particular difficulty for her character. "I knew I wanted to write about a female lawyer—but I didn't want her to be me. To do that, I decided to give her both a challenge and an advantage that I never had as an attorney, thinking that this would keep me on the straight and narrow, and I wouldn't backslide into writing about myself." Kane determined that dyslexia would be a difficult thing to face as an attorney, since the job requires so much reading and research. Conversely, she gave her heroine the ability to think swiftly on her feet, which would give her the impression of strength in the courtroom along with minimizing the need for her to refer to written notes during a trial. A contributor for *Publishers Weekly* remarked that "Kane . . . can certainly weave a captivating yarn." Roland A. Soler and Phyllis A. Roestenberg, writing for *Florida Bar Journal,* stated that "Kane proves herself by delivering a creative work of fiction that is entertaining and suspenseful but also realistic."

Several books continue the "Jackie Flowers" series, including *Extreme Indifference* and *Seeds of Doubt.* In *Extreme Indifference* college freshman Amy Lynch manages to escape a mountain cabin in Colorado where she has been held captive, only to die of pneumonia she catches while wandering naked in the snow. Jackie Flowers finds herself defending U.S. District Judge Glenn Ballard, the owner of the cabin. A contributor for *Kirkus Reviews* remarked that the novel offers "sturdy intrigue in and out of court with an especially sharp eye for the riptides of power running just beneath the legal quiddities." *Seeds of Doubt* finds Jackie defending Rachel Boyd, a convicted murderer who has just finished a thirty-year prison sentence, only to be accused of killing again a mere days after her release. A *Publishers Weekly* reviewer commented that "Kane deserves to join the ranks of the big-time legal-thriller eagles."

BIOGRAPHICAL AND CRITICAL SOURCES:

PERIODICALS

Booklist, September 15, 2004, Jenny McLarin, review of *Seeds of Doubt,* p. 212.

Florida Bar Journal, December, 2000, Roland A. Soler and Phyllis A. Roestenberg, review of *Blind Spot,* p. 65.

Kirkus Reviews, September 1, 2003, review of *Extreme Indifference,* p. 1103; September 15, 2004, review of *Seeds of Doubt,* p. 883.

Publishers Weekly, September 11, 2000, review of *Blind Spot,* p. 74; October 13, 2003, review of *Extreme Indifference,* p. 57; September 27, 2004, review of *Seeds of Doubt,* p. 36.

ONLINE

LD.org, http://www.ld.org/ (August 31, 2005), "Stephanie Kane."

Stephanie Kane Home Page, http://www.writerkane. com (August 31, 2005).

Trashotron.com, http://www.trashotron.com/ (August 31, 2005), "Stephanie Kane."*

*   *   *

KARET, Evelyn

PERSONAL: Female. *Education:* Columbia University, Barnard College, B.A.; Wellesley College, M.A.; Harvard University, Radcliffe Institute, certificate in arts administration; Columbia University, M.Phil., Ph.D.

ADDRESSES: Agent—c/o Publicity Director, American Philosophical Society, 104 S. 5th St., Philadelphia, PA 19106.

CAREER: Art historian and writer. Clark University, Worcester, MA, associate professor in art history. Worcester Art Museum, Worcester, MA, member of the corporation; Higgins Armory Museum, trustee and chairperson; Worcester Community School for the Performing Arts, trustee; Worcester Heritage Preservation Society, trustee and chairperson.

MEMBER: Art Watch International, International Congress for Medieval Studies, International Center for Medieval Art, National Coalition of Independent Scholars, College Art Association of America, Renaissance Society of America, Medieval Academy of America, Sixteenth Century Society, Italian Art Society, Drawings Society, Italian Academy for Advanced Study, Harvard University Center for Literary and Cultural Studies.

WRITINGS:

The Drawings of Stefano da Verona and His Circle and the Origins of Collecting in Italy: A Catalogue Raisonné, American Philosophical Society (Philadelphia, PA), 2002.

Contributor of articles to periodicals, including *Arte Lombarda* and *Atti e memorie della academia di scienza e lettere di Verona.*

Author's work has been translated into Italian.

WORK IN PROGRESS: The International Gothic Style in Europe (1375-1445); and *Antonio II Badile (1424-c. 1507) Album of Drawings.*

*   *   *

KARGMAN, Jill 1974-

PERSONAL: Born 1974, in New York, NY.

ADDRESSES: Home—New York, NY. *Agent*—c/o Author Mail, Broadway Books, 1745 Broadway, New York, NY 10019.

CAREER: Writer.

WRITINGS:

NOVELS

(With Carrie Karasyov) *The Right Address,* Broadway Books (New York, NY), 2004.

(With Carrie Karasyov) *Wolves in Chic Clothing,* Broadway Books (New York, NY), 2005.

Also author, with Carrie Karasyov, of screenplay *Bittersweet 16.* Coauthor and coproducer, with Karasyov, of film *Intern;* coadaptor, with Karasyov, of *Auntie*

Claus, for Nickelodeon. Writer of programs for MTV. Contributor to periodicals, including *Vogue, Harper's Bazaar, Interview,* and *Elle.* Author of weekly column "Eye Spy" for *Salon.com.*

WORK IN PROGRESS: Two film projects; adapting the screenplay *Bittersweet 16* into a novel.

SIDELIGHTS: Jill Kargman and frequent collaborator Carrie Karasyov were both raised on New York City's prestigious Upper East Side. Their insight into life in that exclusive world inform their novels *The Right Address* and *Wolves in Chic Clothing.* Karasyov and Kargman attended the same private schools and, after graduation, worked together on some screenplays. In *The Right Address* they present a comic tale of Melanie Korn, a social-climbing airline stewardess who marries an elderly billionaire whose fortune was made in the funeral business. Though her marriage brings her all the trappings of the upper-crust life, Melanie finds acceptance into high society elusive, despite her best efforts to win the approval of the old-money set. Melanie seeks advice from one of her servants on how to handle herself, as she goes to the right charity balls, lunches and gossips at the most fashionable spots, and spends lavishly on shopping sprees. The plot is "predictable," according to *People* reviewer Allison Lynn, and the dialogue sometimes "awkward. . . . Yet even with these flaws, it's impossible to resist the charms of this modern Manhattan fairy tale."

In an interview for the Random House Web site, the authors remarked: "There are several buildings in Manhattan that are considered the most elusive and prestigious addresses in New York City. The New York newspapers are constantly covering these buildings, and discussing the rituals and decisions made by the co-op boards in these various buildings—it's a topic we found fascinating. Having grown up in Manhattan, we were particularly interested in how the denizens of co-ops interact with each other, and basically how they don't interact with each other." In relating the lives of several families within the neighborhood, they hoped to describe "how different people's lives can be, even though they are being led only a few floors apart."

BIOGRAPHICAL AND CRITICAL SOURCES:

PERIODICALS

Library Journal, April 1, 2004, review of *The Right Address,* p. 124.

People, May 17, 2004, Allison Lynn, review of *The Right Address,* p. 50.

Publishers Weekly, April 5, 2004, review of *The Right Address,* p. 41.

Town & Country, June, 2004, Chantal M. McLaughlin, review of *The Right Address,* p. 60.

ONLINE

Random House Web site, www.randomhouse.com/ (October 29, 2004), interview with Carrie Karasyov and Jill Kargman.

* * *

KARNAZES, Dean 1962-

PERSONAL: Born 1962; married Julie Abbott (a dentist), 1988; children: two. *Education:* Holds two graduate degrees, including an M.B.A.

ADDRESSES: Home—San Francisco, CA. *Agent*—c/o Author Mail, Penguin Group, 375 Hudson St., New York, NY 10014. *E-mail*—info@ultramarathonman. com.

CAREER: Athlete, businessperson, and public speaker. Ultra marathoner; EnergyWell Natural Foods, president. Also helps develop running footwear and apparel and raises money for charity. Previous jobs included working as a sales executive for GlaxoSmithKline. Has appeared on television programs, including *60 Minutes* and *David Letterman Show. Member, American Ultrarunning Team.*

MEMBER: All American Trail Running Association.

AWARDS, HONORS: Winner of numerous marathons and ultra marathons, including Inaugural South Pole Marathon, Running Division; Ultra Division champion (six times), Saturn Relay; Western States 100-Mile Endurance Run Silver Buckle (nine times); Outdoor World Championships, 2000; Arabian Stallion Award, Angels Crest 100-Mile Endurance Run, 2003. Top Ten Runners of the Year 2003, *Ultrarunning* magazine; Ultrarunner of the Year 2004, *Competitor* magazine; *Outside* Magazine Top Ten Ultimate Athletes, 2004.

WRITINGS:

Ultra Marathon Man: Confessions of an All-Night Runner, J.P. Tarcher/Penguin (New York, NY), 2005.

SIDELIGHTS: Dean Karnazes, recognized as one of the world's greatest endurance athletes, has accomplished such feats as running the equivalent of ten marathons, or 262 miles, without stopping. In an article in the *Mississippi Business Journal,* Jim Laird quoted Karnazes as saying: "I run because long after my footprints fade away, maybe I will have inspired a few to reject the easy path, hit the trails, put one foot in front of the other, and come to the same conclusion I did: I run because it always takes me where I want to go."

Karnazes, whose ultimate goal is to run 300 miles nonstop, details his ultra-athletic life in his book *Ultra Marathon Man: Confessions of an All-Night Runner.* "When I wrote the book, I thought, just tell your stories, tell it like it is, try and tell them how you feel when you do these things, why you do it as best as you can, tell them some of the funny things that happen," Karnazes told Lynn Andriani in an interview for *Publishers Weekly.* "Be truthful, and if it appeals to people, it does, if it doesn't, it doesn't."

In his autobiography, the author recounts that he was not a devoted athlete in high school; in fact he quit the cross-country running team after only one season. As described by Karnazes, his life was headed on a routine path after he graduated with an M.B.A., got married, and held a job as a salesman with a pharmaceutical company. But, he writes, he was getting bored and felt he was stuck in a routine. Then, after a thirtieth-birthday-party bash during which he had a drink at a bar, he decided on a whim to run from San Francisco to Half Moon Bay, a distance of thirty miles. Karnazes writes that the run invigorated his mind and body and convinced him that the running life was for him.

Karnazes details in his autobiography many of the races he has run, such as competing in the Badwater 135-mile ultra marathon through Death Valley in the middle of summer, noting that it was so hot that he had to run on the white lines on the road or the soles of his shoes would melt. He also writes about the extreme conditions he faced while running a marathon in the snow in Antarctica (other competitors wore snowshoes) and numerous other tests of ultra endurance. The author ruminates on why he runs such demanding distances and says that part of the reason may have to do with the death of his sister at the age of eighteen in a car accident: running long distances requires one to essentially shut down one's thinking process. He also notes that he likes having goals to reach and that he may have an obsessive-compulsive nature.

A *Kirkus Reviews* contributor described the book as "charming and surprisingly quirky, providing the perfect escapist fantasy for couch potatoes and weekend warriors alike." A *Publishers Weekly* reviewer commented that the author's "masochism is a reader's pleasure, and Karnazes's book is intriguing." Bill Syken noted in *Sports Illustrated* that the book is "fascinating" and "an engaging memoir."

BIOGRAPHICAL AND CRITICAL SOURCES:

BOOKS

Karnazes, Dean, *Ultra Marathon Man: Confessions of an All-Night Runner,* J.P. Tarcher/Penguin (New York, NY), 2005.

PERIODICALS

Esquire, March, 2005, Brendan Vaughan, "The Indefatigable Man," interview with Karnazes, p. 116; April, 2005, Tyler Cabo, "Dean's Diet: Eating Advice from This Guy, Who Knows from Power Food," p. 116.

Kirkus Reviews, January 15, 2005, review of *Ultra Marathon Man: Confessions of an All-Night Runner,* p. 101.

Mississippi Business Journal, April 11, 2005, Jim Laird, "Learning Valuable Lessons a Mile at a Time," profile of Karnazes, p. A5.

Outside, January, 2004, Ben Hewitt, "Bodywork and Destinations Special: Fit to the Core Balanced Beings."

People, March 21, 2005, "Ultramarathon Man: Think Your Husband's Obsessed with Working Out? Meet Dean Karnazes, 42, One of an Elite Group of Runners Who Compete in Ultramarathons—Races of 100 Miles or More—Just for Fun," p. 62.

Publishers Weekly, January 3, 2005, review of *Ultra Marathon Man,* p. 43; January 3, 2005, Lynn Andriani, "When a Marathon Is Just a Warm-Up," interview with Karnazes, p. 44.

Runner's World, October, 2004, "Kiehl's Badwater Ultramarathon," p. 96; February, 2005, Ben Hewitt, "300: The 300-Mile Man," p. 56.

SFWeekly, January 14, 2004, Lessley Anderson, "Ultra Marathon Man: Even among Long-Distance Runners, S.F.'s Dean Karnazes Is a Phenom."

Sports Illustrated, March 14, 2005, Bill Syken, review of *Ultra Marathon Man,* p. A14.

Time, February 28, 2005, Bill Saporito, "Born to Run—For 300 Miles: In the Realm of the Ultramarathon, 100 Miles Is Routine," p. 61.

ONLINE

Dean Karnazes Home Page, http://www.ultramarathon man.com (July 6, 2005).*

*   *   *

KEEFE, Patrick Radden 1976-
(Patrick S. Radden Keefe)

PERSONAL: Born 1976. *Education:* Yale University Law School, J.D., 2005.

ADDRESSES: Office—World Policy Institute, New School University, 66 5th Ave., 9th Fl., New York, NY 10011. *E-mail*—Patrick.keefe@yale.edu.

CAREER: Attorney. Project leader for World Policy Institute.

AWARDS, HONORS: Marshall scholar; Dorothy and Lewis B. Cullman Center for Scholars and Writers fellow, New York Public Library, 2003.

WRITINGS:

Chatter: Dispatches from the Secret World of Global Eavesdropping, Random House (New York, NY), 2005.

Contributor to periodicals, including *New York Review of Books, Yale Journal of Constitutional Law, Slate, Boston Globe, New York Times,* and *Legal Affairs.* Book reviewer, *New York Review of Books.*

ADAPTATIONS: Chatter was adapted to audiocassette, Books on Tape, 2005.

SIDELIGHTS: In the aftermath of the September 11, 2001, terrorist attacks against the United States, a familiar watchword appeared in the American vernacular: "chatter." Prior to a number of terrorist attacks throughout the world, and particularly before the 9/11 attacks, intelligence sources detected increased amounts of chatter: communication among and between foreign groups and individuals. Greater levels of communication thereby correlated with a greater possibility of more attacks. Even as the public dreaded news of increased chatter, they often did not know exactly what the chatter was about, how it was identified and gathered, and what governments did with information derived from it. In *Chatter: Dispatches from the Secret World of Global Eavesdropping* Patrick Radden Keefe works to "demystify a very mysterious subject," that of electronic espionage and large-scale communications monitoring, noted William Grimes in the *San Diego Union-Tribune.*

Published while Keefe was still a student at the Yale University Law School, *Chatter* is a careful examination of the techniques and uses of signals intelligence, or SIGINT, as a means of gathering information on terrorists, criminals, and a variety of other enemies of the state. Keefe "explores the nature and context of communications interception, drawing together strands of history, investigative reporting and riveting anecdotes," commented a reviewer on the Milton Academy Web site. "The result is part detective story, part travel-writing, part essay on paranoia and secrecy in a digital age."

In his book, Keefe describes Menwith Hill, a surreal-looking high-technology surveillance base nestled in the countryside of North Yorkshire, England, that is the "largest eavesdropping base on Earth and America's ear on the world," related James Bamford in the *Washington Post Book World.* Keefe relates how he was consistently stymied in his attempts to get information directly from the organizations involved with signals intelligence. His requests for access to the

U.S. National Security Agency (NSA), for example, were met with complete silence; no one in the NSA would even acknowledge him. Keefe had to winnow the story out of available public resources, including news reports, patent filings, and even informal chats with SIGINT workers in local bars.

Keefe also explores other instances in which the desire for useful intelligence conflicts with the potential to cross into wholesale invasions of privacy, such was in the case of the ominous Echelon system. Echelon, a collaborative effort between the United States, Great Britain, and a number of other ally countries, had the ability to intercept millions of electronic communications per hour, but the secrecy in which it operated meant that the general public had little knowledge of its existence, and no outside agencies or individuals were able to report on Echelon's activities. "Echelon clearly threatened individual privacy and raised questions around how much secrecy democratic governments should be able to maintain in the name of national security," observed a writer on the Yale University Law School Web site. Similarly, the U.S. government's aborted Total Information Awareness program, promising the ability to monitor nearly every aspect of Americans' lives through massive linkages among private and government databases, was criticized as being almost Orwellian in its potential to impose Big Brother-like scrutiny on ordinary citizens. "A suspicious Congress strangled the program in its cradle," Grimes reported.

"In the end, Keefe argues that the vital debate over where to draw that line should not be left just to intelligence officials and Congress," commented Bamford. "The public, he insists, must educate itself as best it can and weigh in on the decision" as to what constitutes enough surveillance to reasonably ensure public safety and an unacceptable level of intrusion into the lives of everyday citizens, Bamford added. "Keefe's book will reach readers interested in intelligence as well as those worried by it," concluded *Booklist* reviewer Gilbert Taylor.

"Provocative, sometimes funny, and alarming without being alarmist, *Chatter* is a journey through a bizarre and shadowy world with vast implications for our security as well as our privacy," stated a contributor to the Milton Academy Web site. "Keefe writes, crisply and entertainingly, as an interested private citizen rather than an expert," Grimes commented. He "does

a wonderful job" of exploring the world of electronic surveillance and eavesdropping, Bamford added.

BIOGRAPHICAL AND CRITICAL SOURCES:

PERIODICALS

Booklist, February 1, 2005, Gilbert Taylor, review of *Chatter: Dispatches from the Secret World of Global Eavesdropping,* p. 923.
Kirkus Reviews, December 15, 2004, review of *Chatter,* p. 1183.
Library Journal, February 1, 2005, Harry Charles, review of *Chatter,* p. 101.
San Diego Union-Tribune, April 10, 2005, William Grimes, "*Chatter* Is a Decent Attempt to Demystify the Murky World of Electronic Espionage."
Washington Post Book World, February 20, 2005, James Bamford, ". . . We're Watching Them," review of *Chatter,* p. T05.

ONLINE

Milton Academy Web site, http://www.milton.edu/ (August 30, 2005), "Patrick Radden Keefe '94 Sparks National Praise, Intrigue with *Chatter,* an Exposé of Modern Espionage."
Yale University Law School Web site, http://www.law.yale.edu/ (March 18, 2005), "Patrick Keefe '05 Investigates SigInt in *Chatter.**

*   *   *

KEEFE, Patrick S. Radden
    See KEEFE, Patrick Radden

*   *   *

KEHOE, Elisabeth

PERSONAL: Female. *Education:* University of London, doctoral degree.

ADDRESSES: Agent—c/o Author Mail, Atlantic Monthly Press, 841 Broadway, New York, NY 10003.

CAREER: Writer and historian.

WRITINGS:

The Titled Americans: Three American Sisters and the British Aristocratic World into Which They Married, Atlantic Monthly Press (New York, NY), 2004.

SIDELIGHTS: Historian Elisabeth Kehoe recounts the lives of the Jerome sisters in her first book, *The Titled Americans: Three American Sisters and the British Aristocratic World into Which They Married.* Jennie Churchill, Clara Frewen, and Leonie Leslie all came to England and married into the British upper class, and Jennie's eldest son, Winston Churchill, would later guide England through World War II. Although Jennie has been written about extensively, the other sisters and their lives are less well known. Kehoe details the close bond the sisters maintained with each other throughout their lives, as well as discussing their aristocratic lifestyles, their troubled marriages, and their extramarital affairs. "Kehoe's readable book . . . perfectly captures the decadence of the sisters' privileged world in its historical context of a British Empire just past its peak," wrote a *Publishers Weekly* contributor. Writing on the *Bookpage* Web site, Anne Bartlett called the biography "a beguiling chronicle of a long-gone world." Noting that "the author has done an impressive amount of research," *Spectator* contributor Hugh Massingberd also stated, "I am happy to say that I derived a measure of enjoyment from Kehoe's book, which is well stocked with diverting material." Mary Ellen Quinn, writing in *Booklist,* commented that the author's "combination of meticulous research, good storytelling, and glimpses into the lifestyles of the rich . . . and famous circa 1900 will satisfy a range of readers." In a review for *Library Journal,* Gail Benjafield deemed the book "a remarkable achievement and a real treat."

BIOGRAPHICAL AND CRITICAL SOURCES:

PERIODICALS

Booklist, November 1, 2004, Mary Ellen Quinn, review of *The Titled Americans: Three American Sisters and the British Aristocratic World into Which They Married,* p. 456.
Kirkus Reviews, September 1, 2004, review of *The Titled Americans,* p. 849.

Library Journal, December 1, 2004, Gail Benjafield, review of *The Titled Americans,* p. 136.
Publishers Weekly, September 13, 2004, review of *The Titled Americans,* p. 65.
Spectator (London, England), November 13, 2004, Hugh Massingberd, review of *The Titled Americans,* p. 59.

ONLINE

Bookpage.com, http://www.bookpage.com/ (May 30, 2005), Anne Bartlett, review of *The Titled Americans.**

*   *   *

KELLER, Julia

PERSONAL: Born in Huntington, WV. *Education:* Marshall University, B.A., M.A.; Ohio State, Ph.D., 1995.

ADDRESSES: Home—Chicago, IL. *Office*—Chicago Tribune, 435 N. Michigan Ave., Chicago, IL 60611. *E-mail*—JIkeller@tribune.com.

CAREER: Journalist. Reporting intern for syndicated columnist Jack Anderson in Washington, DC; worked for *Ashland Daily Independent,* Ashland, KY; *Columbus Dispatch,* Columbus, OH, reporter, 1981-98; *Chicago Tribune,* Chicago, IL, reporter, 1998—.

AWARDS, HONORS: Nieman fellow, Harvard University, 1998; Pulitzer Prize, 2005, for feature writing.

SIDELIGHTS: Long-time journalist Julia Keller, who interned with famous syndicated columnist Jack Anderson, won the 2005 Pulitzer Prize for feature writing for her exhaustive account in the *Chicago Tribune* of a ten-second tornado that ripped through the town of Utica, Illinois, which is southwest of Chicago. According to the Pulitzer Prize Web site, Keller was honored "for her gripping, meticulously reconstructed account." Interestingly, Keller actually did not want to cover the story. "I fought it viciously, I thought it was a terrible idea," Keller told *Editor & Publisher* contributor Jennifer Saba. "The metro staff did a great job covering the tornado as it happened." Her editors insisted, believing that Keller was the right kind of reporter to get the inside story and further details of the events, including the long-term effects the catastrophe had on the townspeople's psyche. As a result, Keller started visiting Utica on a weekly basis, interviewing those who witnessed the tornado and its aftermath. Keller's three-part report took her seven months to put together as she had to win the trust of the townspeople, who had grown tired of all the media attention, and conduct numerous interviews. The resulting story focuses on the townspeople before, during, and after the twister hit and destroyed a local bar. Keller's story made the front page of the *Chicago Tribune* in several installments. "It was a beautifully reported and beautifully written piece," Keller's editor Tim Bannon told Saba.

BIOGRAPHICAL AND CRITICAL SOURCES:

PERIODICALS

Editor & Publisher, May 1, 2005, "Pulitzers: No Twisting the Truth in Illinois."

ONLINE

Ohio State University Web site, http://www.osu.edu/ (June 22, 2005), "Three Ohio State Alums Take Pulitzer Honors."

Pulitzer Prize Web site, http://www.pulitzer.org/ (June 22, 2005).*

*   *   *

KELLY, Mij

PERSONAL: Born in Edinburgh, Scotland; children: two. *Education:* Attended York University and Stirling University.

ADDRESSES: Home—Yorkshire, England. *Agent*—c/o PFD, Drury House, 34-43 Russell St., London WC2B 5HA, England. *E-mail*—mijinyork@dsl.pipex.com.

CAREER: Writer, editor, and journalist.

AWARDS, HONORS: Kathleen Fidler Award, 1993, for *48 Hours with Franklin;* White Ravens selection, International Youth Library, 2002, for *William and the Night Train.*

WRITINGS:

FOR CHILDREN

48 Hours with Franklin (novel), Blackie (London, England), 1993.
Franklin Falls Apart, Dutton (London, England), 1995.
I Hate Everyone, illustrated by Ruth Palmer, David Bennett Books (St. Albans, England), 2000.
William and the Night Train, illustrated by Alison Jay, Hodder Headline (London, England), 2000, Farrar, Straus, Giroux (New York, NY), 2001.
One More Sheep, illustrated by Russell Ayto, Hodder Headline (London, England), 2004.
Sweet Pea and Boogaloo, Hodder (London, England), 2004.
Where's My Darling Daughter?, illustrated by Katharine McEwen, Oxford University Press (Oxford, England), 2005.
Potty Thieves, Hodder (London, England), 2006.

OTHER

(Editor with Tim Edensor) *Moving Worlds,* Polygon (Edinburgh, Scotland), 1989.

SIDELIGHTS: At age five British children's-book author Mij Kelly knew writing was her destiny; as Kelly explained on her home page, her grandma predicted it would be so. The author of picture books such as *William and the Night Train, One More Sheep,* and *Where's My Darling Daughter?,* Kelly spins her simple stories in verse because, as she explained, "writing in rhyme makes it much easier to control the rhythm and therefore the way the story ultimately sounds. It doesn't matter whether it's a teacher, parent or older sibling who's going to be doing the reading, you want them to read with expression—you want them to declaim your story like an orator." In her review of *One More Sheep* for the London *Guardian*, Julia Eccleshare wrote that "Kelly's rhyming text has terrific panache."

Illustrated by Alison Jay and released in both Kelly's native England and the United States, *William and the Night Train* centers around a young boy who, like so many children, has difficulty falling asleep. Using subtle imagery, Kelly portrays sleep as a midnight locomotive, its passengers boarding as they close their eyes, then traveling through the nighttime toward Tomorrow. William's family joins many other people as well as a diverse group of animals, boarding the train in Jay's illustrations. Although the young boy is eager for tomorrow to come, he is too excited to fall asleep on the train, and his restlessness disrupts his sleepy fellow passengers and postpones the train's departure. Ultimately, his mother finally convinces him that shutting his eyes will allow tomorrow to come. "This is the kind of book that children and adults will pore over together" commented Connie Fletcher in a *Booklist* review, while a *Publishers Weekly* critic praised Jay's "soothing illustrations, bathed in muted earth tones," and added that "Kelly's poetic text unspools in a seamless strand, twining scrumptious rhymes . . . with nimble worldplay."

BIOGRAPHICAL AND CRITICAL SOURCES:

PERIODICALS

Booklist, February 15, 2001, Connie Fletcher, review of *William and the Night Train*, p. 1135.
Bulletin of the Center for Children's Books, June, 2001, review of *William and the Night Train*, p. 376.
Guardian (London, England), July 10, 2004, Julia Eccleshare, review of *One More Sheep*.
New Statesman and Society, August 18, 1989, Nancee Oku Bright, "Moving Worlds: Personal Recollections of 21 Immigrants to Edinburgh," p. 29.
Publishers Weekly, December 18, 2000, review of *William and the Night Train*, p. 77.
School Librarian, February, 1994, review of *48 Hours with Franklin*, p. 21; May, 1996, review of *Franklin Falls Apart*, p. 62.
School Library Journal, March, 2001, Rosalyn Pierini, review of *William and the Night Train*, p. 213.
Teacher Librarian, December, 2001, review of *William and the Night Train*, p. 12; February, 2002, review of *William and the Night Train*, p. 50.
Today's Parent, August, 2005, Stephanie Simpson McLellan, review of *One More Sheep*, p. 26.

ONLINE

Mij Kelly Home Page, http://www.mijinyork.dsl.pipex.com (November 6, 2005).
PFD Web site, http://www.pfd.co.uk/ (November 6, 2005), "Mij Kelly."*

*   *   *

KENNEDY, Michelle

PERSONAL: Born in Baltimore, MD; married; husband's name John; children: five. *Education:* Attended American University.

ADDRESSES: Agent—Ami Greko, Penguin Group, c/o Viking Publicity, 375 Hudson St., New York, NY 10014. *E-mail*—misha@mishakennedy.com

CAREER: Writer, journalist, and columnist. *Green Bay News-Chronicle*, Green Bay, WI, reporter and humor columnist. Worked variously as a waitress, bartender, farmer, sled-dog musher, bread-baker, nursing assistant, U.S. Senate page, restaurant owner, and as a tour guide for Ben and Jerry's ice cream company.

AWARDS, HONORS: Pushcart Prize nomination, for work in *Brain, Child* magazine; Reader's Choice Award, *Elle* magazine, and Borders Original Voices selection, both 2005, both for *Without a Net*.

WRITINGS:

It Worked for Me—1,001 Real-Life Pregnancy Tips, Barron's Educational Series (Hauppauge, NY), 2004.
Without a Net: Middle Class and Homeless in America: My Story, Viking (New York, NY), 2005.

Contributor to periodicals, including *Family Circle, New York Times, Christian Science Monitor, Brain, Child, Milwaukee Journal Sentinel, Green Bay Press Gazette, Fox Cities Newspaper*, and *Herald of Randolph*, and to online publications *Mothers Movement* and *Salon.com*. Author of syndicated column "Life Happens."

"LAST STRAW STRATEGIES" SERIES

Crying, Barron's (Hauppauge, NY), 2003.
Eating, Barron's (Hauppauge, NY), 2003.
Sleeping, Barron's (Hauppauge, NY), 2003.
Tantrums, Barron's (Hauppauge, NY), 2003.
Jealousy, Barron's (Happauge, NY), 2004.
Manners, Barron's (Hauppauge, NY), 2004.
Staying Dry: 99 Tips to Bring You Back from the End of Your Rope, Barron's (Hauppauge, NY), 2004.
Letting Go: Giving up Those Bottles, Blankies, Pacifiers, and So On, Barron's Educational Series (Hauppauge, NY), 2004.

SIDELIGHTS: Journalist, columnist, and book author Michelle Kennedy, once a college student with a bright future and then a suburban homemaker, never expected that she would one day find herself and her three children living in their car along the beaches of the coast of Maine, homeless and struggling just to survive. In *Without a Net: Middle Class and Homeless in America: My Story* Kennedy describes her deteriorating family situation and the missteps and the bad judgment that led her to live the reality of a worst-case scenario.

"What began as an experiment in voluntary simplicity and a move to the far north of Maine, quickly became a nightmare for me and three of my children," Kennedy stated in an article published on the *Mothers Movement* Web site. Seemingly on a whim, Kennedy's then-husband, Tom, decided to move the family from suburban Maryland to a primitive cabin—little more than a shack—in northern Maine. Determined to make the best of the situation and support her husband, Kennedy went along with the plan despite the hardships. She started a sled dog team and worked in husky rescue, eventually learning to enjoy a simpler life. However, increasing irresponsibility on her husband's part began to erode the family's cohesion. Kennedy earned money as a bartender in a local club, while her husband became less and less interested in making a living, finally deciding that he did not want a job at all. The final blow came when their three-year-old daughter was attacked and mauled by one of the sled dogs while Kennedy was at work; her husband was supposed to have been supervising the children at the time. When Tom chose to keep the dogs, a decision Kennedy perceived as favoring the animals over the children, she packed her three kids and their belongings into her Subaru station wagon and left.

Over the next three months, Kennedy and her children had no other home but their car. They slept parked in campgrounds and along the beach, subsisting on ramen noodles, showering at truck stops, and doing their best to look like tourists rather than homeless people. Kennedy worked as a waitress but was not able to put together enough money for an apartment, and child-care costs drained her meager earnings. Often, her children slept in the car while she worked, helpful cooks keeping a watchful eye on the Subaru through the kitchen windows. Eventually, she was able to put aside enough to rent a small apartment and rise above her diminished circumstances.

"Many of the details about the family's day-to-day survival are compelling, but it's hard to muster much sympathy for Kennedy," commented Jennifer Gonnerman in *Mother Jones,* noting that the author did have parents that she could have called for assistance, but declined to do so. She was also tragically unaware of social assistance programs that could have helped her out of her desperate situation. A *Publishers Weekly* critic observed that Kennedy's articulateness, intelligence, and resourcefulness left little doubt that she would overcome her troubles. However, the same critic observed that "once readers learn the details, the story of Kennedy's downfall goes from being unlikely to horribly plausible." The "vivid account of her months of homelessness makes a lively read," remarked *Entertainment Weekly* contributor Jennifer Reese. "Kennedy's perseverance in saving money and finally finding a home for her family is impressive," Gonnerman stated.

Kennedy is also the author of parenting guides known as the "Last Straw Strategies" series. As the mother of five children herself, she has seen firsthand how strategies and recommendations offered by child-care experts are sometimes ineffective. In the "Last Straw Strategies" books, Kennedy offers practical, time-tested solutions to a variety of child-rearing dilemmas.

Among these parenting guides is *Letting Go: Giving up Those Bottles, Blankies, Pacifiers, and So On,* which provides advice for parents who seek to help their children end their attachments to blankets, bottles, toys, and other unneeded objects that provide security or comfort. Kennedy suggests allowing children an appropriate degree of freedom and autonomy to show them that independence does not require support from blankets or bottles. Other guides include *Jealousy,* which offers almost a hundred tips on handling strained relations between children and their siblings; and *Sleeping,* which describes sleep habits of babies and young children, plus includes strategies for parents to use when toddlers and preschool children resist clocking out at bedtime. *Tantrums* provides harried parents useful solutions to end tantrums and help children gain control over their anger. Kennedy also examines more sophisticated child-raising issues in *Manners,* which suggests that teaching children manners and social interaction skills should begin no later than age eighteen months. Techniques are presented to teach children to share, to control temper outbursts, and to avoid fighting.

Kennedy told *CA:* "I have always been interested in writing. When I was in high school I wrote a lot in a journal as well as a lot of really bad poetry that I thought was brilliant. I also had visions of being a rock star and tried hard to put my bad poetry to music. As I got older, I wanted to write professionally, but didn't know how—or even what to write about. Having quit college, I lacked a lot of basic structure and style information. The Internet helped me greatly and after a while I learned how to write columns and articles, which eventually led to my first position at a local daily newspaper.

"My children certainly influence my work, probably more than anything else. But I am influenced by all sorts of things—people I meet, situations I find myself in. There isn't any one author who has influenced me. I love all sorts of writing—from literary fiction to more niche genre novels. I have always loved nonfiction and can find myself just as engrossed in a how-to book as the latest bestseller.

"The hardest thing for me is actually putting my hands on the keyboard and typing. I am a huge procrastinator. One of my favorite quotes is from author David Rakoff who said, 'I hate writing, but I love having written.' That's how I feel a lot of the time. Mostly though, I have to find that beginning scene and it has to ring true. If I can't put myself in the scene, then I can't write it. It's a lot like watching a movie in your head and then just writing it down.

"The most surprising thing for me is that some people are bent on hating what you write. I haven't had many negative reviews, but the few I've had have been vehement. When I don't like a book, I just set it aside and move on—but there are some people who really need you to know how much they hate what you've written. I was quite shocked by that.

"Some books just stay with me and I can't seem to shake them. Gary Paulsen's *Winterdance* was like that for me. I must have read it six or seven times before I finally said enough. But of all the books I've read, I think *East of Eden* by John Steinbeck is probably my favorite. It just grabbed me and wouldn't let go—it's rare that I'm so engrossed in a story and awed by the writing all at the same time.

"My biggest hope is that people will come away from a book like *Without a Net* a little less judgmental. We are such a judgmental society. Everyone claims to have the moral high ground and if I've learned anything in my life it's that people make mistakes and we just have to let them move on from those mistakes. Further, we have to let them make them. Life throws amazingly difficult choices our way. Sometimes we don't recognize the impact those choices will have until it's too late to do anything about them. But we all have the right to make those choices and we have to acknowledge everyone else's right to do the same."

BIOGRAPHICAL AND CRITICAL SOURCES:

PERIODICALS

Booklist, January 1, 2005, Deborah Donovan, review of *Without a Net: Middle Class and Homeless in America: My Story,* p. 790.

Entertainment Weekly, February 25, 2005, Jennifer Reese, review of *Without a Net,* p. 107.

Kirkus Reviews, December 15, 2004, review of *Without a Net,* p. 1183.

Milwaukee Journal-Sentinel, February 5, 2005, Laura Velicer, "Life in Car Shows Homelessness Can Happen to Anyone," review of *Without a Net.*

Mother Jones, March-April, 2005, Jennifer Gonnerman, review of *Without a Net,* p. 84.

New York Times, February 27, 2005, Sarah Wildman, "Mobile Home," review of *Without a Net.*

Publishers Weekly, October 18, 2004, review of *Without a Net,* p. 54.

San Diego Union-Tribune, February 27, 2005, Jane Clifford, "Lost in America," review of *Without a Net.*

ONLINE

Michelle Kennedy Home Page, http://www.misha kennedy.com (August 18, 2005).

Mothers Movement Online, http://www.mothers movement.org/ (September 15, 2005), Michelle Kennedy, "The Face of Homelessness."

*   *   *

KERR, Peter 1940-

PERSONAL: Born 1940, in Lossiemouth, Morayshire, Scotland; married; children: two boys.

ADDRESSES: Home—East Lothian, Scotland. *Agent*—c/o Tina Betts, Andrew Mann Ltd., 1 Old Compton St., London W1D 5JA, England. *E-mail*—peter@peter-kerr.co.uk.

CAREER: Writer and musician. Worked in British civil service, and as a farmer, a record producer, and a jazz musician, including as clarinetist/leader of Scottish jazz band Clyde Valley Stompers. Appeared as member of band in film *It's All Happening.* Produced bagpipe version of "Amazing Grace" with Royal Scots Dragoon Guards.

AWARDS, HONORS: Bronze award winner, American Book of the Year Awards, 2002, for *Snowball Oranges.*

WRITINGS:

NONFICTION

Snowball Oranges: One Mallorcan Winter, Summersdale (Chichester, West Sussex, England), 2000, published as *Snowball Oranges: A Winter's Tale on a Spanish Isle,* Lyons Press (Guilford, CT), 2002.
Mañana, Mañana: One Mallorcan Summer, Summersdale (Chichester, West Sussex, England), 2001, Lyons Press (Guilford, CT), 2003.
Thistle Soup: A Ladleful of Scottish Life, Lyons Press (Guilford, CT), 2004.
Viva Mallorca!: One Mallorcan Autumn, Lyons Press (Guilford, CT), 2005.

Also author of *A Basketful of Snowflakes, One Mallorcan Spring,* published in England, 2005.

SIDELIGHTS: After a career in music and farming in Scotland, Peter Kerr and his family moved from Scotland to the Spanish island of Mallorca and bought an orange farm in disrepair. Their family's experience trying to make a success of the effort led Kerr to write his first travel memoir, *Snowball Oranges: One Mallorcan Winter.* Published in the United States as *Snowball Oranges: A Winter's Tale on a Spanish Isle,* the book recounts the Kerr family's trials as they cope with bad and unusual weather—such as snow on their oranges in the usually mild Mallorcan winter—overflowing cesspits, pets leftover from the farm's previous owner, and numerous other mini-catastrophes. In a review in *Geographical,* Caroline Magnay noted that Kerr describes the locals "with warmth and a touch of humour" and added that he "paints an appealing picture of Mallorca." Danise Hoover, writing in *Booklist,* commented that "Readers will relish Kerr's . . . insights into one couple's bold transplanting of their lives." *Library Journal* contributor Olga B. Wise wrote that the author "manages to give us a lively spin on the difficulties and successes he and his family experience."

In *Mañana, Mañana: One Mallorcan Summer* Kerr continues the story of his family's life on the Spanish island and focuses on their first spring and summer there. Although they no longer have to face winter, the family's problems continue, including a misunderstanding with the local police, a run-in with a wild pig, and the author's difficulty with the local dialect. In a review in *Geographical,* Caroline Magnay commented that "Kerr's relaxed prose paints a colourful portrait of the daily struggles." Justin Doherty, writing in *M2 Best Books,* felt that the book "is in a class of its own," noting that the author focuses "his story firmly on the characters and their personalities." Doherty added that Kerr "has a great talent for creating endearing, funny and oftentimes touching characters that warm and elevate the book." A *Publishers Weekly* contributor noted that the author "evokes a spirit of place that will appeal to both armchair travelers and vacationers who'd like to know the best eating establishments on the island."

Viva Mallorca!: One Mallorcan Autumn continues the family's Mallorcan saga as the author writes humorously about the death of a pet canary, the swarming mosquitoes, and the local eccentrics, including some constant visitors who keep stopping in uninvited. The author also writes about the local cuisines and his older son's dilemma on whether or not to move back to Scotland. Noting that the author "interjects informative historical and geographical facts" about their new home and the people who live there, *Library Journal* contributor Richard Dickey also called the book "a quick and uplifting read." Kerr is also the author of *Thistle Soup: A Ladleful of Scottish Life,* which focuses on family life in rural Scotland.

BIOGRAPHICAL AND CRITICAL SOURCES:

BOOKS

Kerr, Peter, *Snowball Oranges: A Winter's Tale on a Spanish Isle,* Lyons Press (Guilford, CT), 2002.
Kerr, Peter, *Mañana, Mañana: One Mallorcan Summer,* Lyons Press (Guilford, CT), 2003.
Kerr, Peter, *Thistle Soup: A Ladleful of Scottish Life,* Lyons Press (Guilford, CT), 2004.
Kerr, Peter, *Viva Mallorca!: One Mallorcan Autumn,* Lyons Press (Guilford, CT), 2005.

PERIODICALS

Booklist, July, 2002, Danise Hoover, review of *Snowball Oranges: A Winter's Tale on a Spanish Isle,* p. 1819; August, 2003, Danise Hoover, *Mañana, Mañana: One Mallorcan Summer,* p. 1938.
Geographical, October, 2000, Caroline Magnay, review of *Snowball Oranges: One Mallorcan Winter,* p. 94; August, 2001, Caroline Magnay, review of *Mañana, Mañana,* p. 83.
Kirkus Reviews, February 15, 2005, review of *Viva Mallorca!: One Mallorcan Autumn,* p. 213.
Library Journal, August, 2002, Olga B. Wise, review of *Snowball Oranges,* p. 125; August, 2003, Herbert E. Shapiro, review of *Mañana, Mañana,* p. 113; April 15, 2005, Richard Dickey, review of *Viva Mallorca!,* p. 109.
M2 Best Books, February 14, 2002, Justin Doherty, review of *Mañana, Mañana.*
Publishers Weekly, June 2, 2003, review of *Mañana, Mañana,* p. 44.

ONLINE

Peter Kerr Home Page, http://www.peter-kerr.co.uk (July 7, 2005).

KIRK, Heather 1949-

PERSONAL: Born October 17, 1949, in London, Ontario, Canada; daughter of Jack Willsie (a civil engineer) and Gwendolyn Lundy (a homemaker; maiden name Pearson) Kirk; married John Ernest Winzer (a engineering professor), 1984. *Education:* Dalhousie University, B.A., 1973; University of Toronto, M.A., 1975; York University, M.A., 1989. *Hobbies and other interests:* Long-distance swimming, dog walking.

ADDRESSES: Home—155 Owen St., Barrie, Ontario L4M 3H8, Canada. *E-mail*—shall-be@rogers.com.

CAREER: Writer, teacher, and editor. Freelance writer and editor; University of Alberta, Edmonton, Alberta, Canada, lecturer, 1975-77; University of Warsaw, Warsaw, Poland, instructor, 1977-79; Grande Prairie R. College, Grande Prairie, Alberta, instructor, 1980-84; Georgian College, Barrie, Ontario, Canada, part-time instructor, 1990-2005.

MEMBER: Canadian Society of Authors, Illustrators, and Performers; Writers' Union of Canada.

AWARDS, HONORS: Second prize, L.F. Brannan Memorial Essay Competition, 1987, for *Negative Capability;* Frank E. Thomas Award, 1988, for nonfiction prose in *Cross-Canada Writers'* magazine; nonfiction prize, *Grain,* 1999; finalist, Writers' Union of Canada Writing for Children Competition, 2000.

WRITINGS:

Warsaw Spring, Napoleon Pub. (Toronto, Ontario, Canada), 2001.
A Drop of Rain (sequel to *Warsaw Spring*), Napoleon Publishing (Toronto, Ontario, Canada), 2004.
Wacousta (based on the novel by John Richardson), Winding Trail Press (Embrun, Ontario, Canada), 2005.

Contributor to periodicals, including *Canadian Literature 84, Grain, Beaver, Bookbird, Books in Canada, Canadian Author, Canadian Children's Literature, Canadian Review of Materials, Canadian Women's Studies, Contemporary Verse II, Cross-Canada Writers', Literary Review of Canada, Poetry*

Toronto, *Quill & Quire, Scrivener, Wascana Review,* and *Western People.* Author of radio scripts for Canadian stations, including Canadian Broadcasting Corporation.

WORK IN PROGRESS: A novel for young adults; a humorous grammar book; a junior biography, *Mazo de la Roche: Rich and Famous Writer,* for XYZ Publishing, 2006.

SIDELIGHTS: Heather Kirk once commented: "I wrote the novels *Warsaw Spring* and *A Drop of Rain* because I admire modern Poland. The Polish solidarity uprising was one of the greatest passive-resistance movements of the twentieth century, if not the greatest!

"I rewrote the classic Canadian novel *Wacousta,* by John Richardson, because I am fascinated with the early history of Canada. *Wacousta* illuminates the early conflicts between aboriginals and Europeans, and it is fair to both sides."

BIOGRAPHICAL AND CRITICAL SOURCES:

PERIODICALS

Books in Canada, April, 2003, Clara Thomas, review of *Warsaw Spring.*
Midwastern Book Review, October, 2004, review of *A Drop of Rain.*
Resource Links, October 2, 2004, Margaret Mackey, review of *A Drop of Rain.*

ONLINE

Canadian Society of Children's Authors, Illustrators, and Performers Web site, http://www.canscaip.org/ (November 6, 2005), "Heather Kirk."
Writers Union of Canada Web site, http://www.writers union.ca/ (November 6, 2005), "Heather Kirk."

*   *   *

KIRWAN, Larry 1957(?)-

PERSONAL: Born c. 1957, in County Wexford, Ireland; immigrated to United States c. 1970s; married; wife a choreographer; children: two boys.

ADDRESSES: Home—New York, NY. *Agent*—c/o Author Mail, Thunder's Mouth Press, 1400 65th St., Ste. 250, Emeryville, CA 94608. *E-mail*—blk47@aol. com.

CAREER: Musician, playwright, and writer. Cofounder, guitarist and lead vocalist for band Black 47; recordings (with Black 47) include: *Home of the Brave/Live in London,* 1989; *Black 47,* 1992; *Black 47 EP,* 1993; *Fire of Freedom,* 1993; *Home of the Brave,* 1994; *Green Suede Shoes,* 1996; *Live in New York City,* 1999; *Ten Bloody Years,* 1999; *Trouble in the Land,* 2000; *On Fire,* 2001; *New York Town,* 2004; and *Elvis Murphy's Green Suede Shoes,* 2005. Recorded solo album *Kilroy Was Here,* and children's album, *Keltic Kids,* Pirate Moon Records, 1998.

WRITINGS:

Liverpool Fantasy (fiction; adapted from author's play of the same name), Thunder's Mouth Press (New York, NY), 2003.
Green Suede Shoes: An Irish-American Odyssey (memoir), Thunder's Mouth Press (New York, NY), 2005.

Also author of plays *Liverpool Fantasy* (produced in Liverpool, England) and *Poetry of Stone,* published in *Mad Angels.*

WORK IN PROGRESS: A musical, tentatively titled *Transport,* based on a book by Thomas Keneally about women convicts being deported from Ireland to Australia; *Rockin' the Bronx,* a novel set in the early 1980s Bronx.

SIDELIGHTS: Larry Kirwan is an accomplished musician whose band Black 47 has recorded numerous albums. Born in Ireland but now living in New York City, Kirwan is also the author of several plays, a novel, and a memoir. Kirwan's novel *Liverpool Fantasy*—based on his play of the same title—is an alternative history based on the idea that the rock band the Beatles never became famous because John Lennon quit the band in 1962. John goes on to lead an embittered life of self-doubt and unemployment; George Harrison becomes a Jesuit priest and is wracked with doubts concerning his faith in God and

Man; Ringo Starr drums occasionally with the band Gerry and the Pacemakers and is the only one who remains close to John; while Paul McCartney goes on to have a successful career as a Las Vegas lounge-act star under the name Paul Montana and specializes in singing standards. All the band's members' lives appear to be failures because of unhappy marriages and other bad relationships. Then, when Paul's career seems to be on the downside, he decides to hold a Beatles reunion to play for Princess Di. The novel is set in 1987, as a fascist group called the National Front is on the verge of taking over England, and to further complicate matters, one of the group's leaders is John's son Julian Lennon.

In a review of *Liverpool Fantasy* in the *South Florida Sun-Sentinel,* John Dolen wrote that "Kirwan's edgy storytelling is by turns meticulous, raw, bawdy and heart-rending." Dolen also wrote, "This history is so real, that by the end of this novel, you may have nearly forgotten the other." A *Kirkus Reviews* contributor felt that the novel is not entirely successful, but noted that it contains "moments of real vision, pathos and poetry." Writing for the *San Francisco Chronicle Online,* Steven H. Silver commented: "Kirwan is strongest when he is providing a character study of his four main characters." Silver also felt that "Kirwan does a good job of getting into the heads of people who feel that they may have missed their best chance and now have a chance to revisit it."

In his memoir *Green Suede Shoes: An Irish-American Odyssey* Kirwan takes the reader from his birth in County Wexford, Ireland, where he grew up in a loving Catholic family, to his move to the United States in the 1970s and his ensuing career as a musician and writer. In New York he meets an assortment of Irish expatriates, such as the writers Frank and Malachy McCourt, and eventually starts the band Black 47, which becomes a cult band in the Bronx and goes on to produce several critically acclaimed albums. Referring to the narrative in *Green Suede Shoes* as "lively," a *Kirkus Reviews* contributor also noted that, "describing his youth, he relies on vivid, memorable language and frequently irreverent images, as he does throughout."

Kirwan told *CA:* "I liked story-telling, having grown up in a culture that valued this tradition. I always seemed to have this need or desire to create—whether in song-writing, playwrighting or writing novels. Hem-ingway was an inspiration as are Yeats and Joyce. Henry Miller too, though for different reasons.

"Being on the road with Black 47, I tend to take any spare moment I can for writing. I'm never guaranteed a full day to luxuriate in the task, so must grab what spare time I can. The most surprising things I have discovered as a writer are my abject limitations, first and foremost, and the sheer thrill of creating something that wasn't there before I set down to work on it."

BIOGRAPHICAL AND CRITICAL SOURCES:

BOOKS

Kirwan, Larry, *Green Suede Shoes: An Irish-American Odyssey,* Thunder's Mouth Press (New York, NY), 2005.

PERIODICALS

Billboard, June 6, 1998, Moira McCormick, review of recording *Keltic Kids,* p. 75.
Entertainment Weekly, March 19, 1993, Greg Sandow, "Black and Tan and Green All Over," discusses Black 47, p. 60.
Guitar Player, May, 1993, Jas Obrecht, "Black 47: No Sham Rock," p. 16.
Kirkus Reviews, April 15, 2003, review of *Liverpool Fantasy,* p. 560; January 15, 2005, review of *Green Suede Shoes: An Irish-American Odyssey,* p. 102.
Publishers Weekly, May 26, 2003, review of *Liverpool Fantasy,* p. 49.
South Florida Sun-Sentinel, July 17, 2003, John Dolen, review of *Liverpool Fantasy.*

ONLINE

Black 47 Band Web site, http://www.black47.com/ (July 8, 2005).
Celebrity Café Online, http://www.thecelebritycafe. com/ (July 8, 2005), Dominick A. Miserandino, "Black 47—Larry Kirwan," interview with author.
Celtic Café, http://www.celticcafe.com/ (July 8, 2005), C.P. Warner, "An Overview, Plus Questions and Answers with Larry Kirwan."

RootsWorld.com, http://www.rootsworld.com/ (July 8, 2005), "Bill Nevins Talks with Black 47's Larry Kirwan about Politics, Beer, and Sex."

San Francisco Chronicle Online, http://www.sfsite. com/ (July 8, 2005), Steven H. Silver, review of *Liverpool Fantasy.*

*   *   *

KLASS, Philip J. 1919-2005
(Philip Julian Klass)

OBITUARY NOTICE— See index for *CA* sketch: Born November 8, 1919, in Des Moines, IA; died of prostate cancer, August 9, 2005, in Cocoa, FL. Electronics engineer, journalist, and author. A well-known aviation journalist credited with coining the term "avionics," Klass was also famous for debunking stories about Unidentified Flying Objects (UFO's). After graduating from Iowa State University with a degree in engineering in 1941, he worked for General Electric for eleven years. Klass then joined the staff at *Aviation Week & Space Technology,* where he was senior avionics editor until his 1986 retirement (he remained a contributing editor there until 2002). At the magazine, he specialized in writing about the electronic aspects of aviation, as well as on surveillance and communications satellites, arms control, missile defense systems, and lasers. Originally, a main avocation of his was U.S. Civil War history, and he enjoyed building animated battle displays for the National Park Service. This hobby was eclipsed, however, when he became interested in UFOs in the mid-1960s. He started investigating claims about UFO sightings, but repeatedly discovered that such stories could be explained away as actual sightings of meteors, weather balloons, airplanes, satellites, or other normal occurrences and objects. Klass was a founder of the Scientific Investigation of Claims of the Paranormal, started the *Skeptics UFO Newsletter,* and published several books about UFOs over the years. Among these are *UFO—Identified* (1968), *UFOs Explained* (1974), and *Bringing UFOs down to Earth* (1997). At one point, he even offered a ten thousand dollar reward to anyone who could offer proof of the existence of UFOs, but the prize was never won. For his work as a science writer, Klass earned numerous awards of his own, including four writing awards from the Aviation/Space Writers Association, the Professional Achievement in Engineering award from Iowa State University in 1988, the Lauren D. Lyman award in 1989, and the 1998 aerospace journalist award from the Royal Aeronautical Society. In 1999 a meteor that was originally discovered in 1983 was named in his honor.

OBITUARIES AND OTHER SOURCES:

PERIODICALS

Chicago Tribune, August 14, 2005, section 4, p. 7.
New York Times, August 12, 2005, p. A17.
Times (London, England), September 12, 2005, p. 58.
Washington Post, August 11, 2005, p. B5.

*   *   *

KLASS, Philip Julian
See KLASS, Philip J.

*   *   *

KLEIN, Ursula

PERSONAL: Female. *Education:* Free University of Berlin, M.A., 1979; University of Konstanz, Ph.D., 1993.

ADDRESSES: Agent—c/o Author Mail, The MIT Press, 55 Hayward St., Cambridge, MA 02142-1493.

CAREER: Writer. Teacher of chemistry, biology, and philosophy, 1980-88; Research Center for the History and Philosophy of Science, Berlin, Germany, postdoctoral fellow, 1993-95; Max Planck Institute for the History of Science, Berlin, Germany, research scholar, 1995-97, director in independent research group, 1998—; Harvard University, Cambridge, MA, visiting research scholar, 1996-98; Dibner Institute for the History of Science and Technology, Massachusetts Institute for Technology, Cambridge, MA, resident senior fellow, 1997-98. Member of *Ambix* editorial board.

MEMBER: Federation of European Chemical Societies.

WRITINGS:

Verbindung und Affinität: Die Grundlegung der neu-zetilichen Chemie an der Wende vom 17. zum 18. Jahrhundert, Birkhäuser (Boston, MA), 1994.

(Editor and contributor) *Tools and Modes of Representation in the Library Sciences,* Kluwer Academic Publishers (Boston, MA), 2001.

Experiments, Models, Paper Tools: Cultures of Organic Chemistry in the Nineteenth Century, Stanford University Press (Stanford, CA), 2003.

Contributor to periodicals, including *Science in Context, Philosophia Naturalis, NTM: Internationale Zeitschrift für Geschichte und Ethik der Naturwissenschaften, Technik und Medizin, Foundations in Chemistry, Studies in History and Philosophy of Science, Studies in History and Philosophy of Biological and Biomedical Sciences, Sixteenth-Century Essays and Studies, Storia della scienza,* and *Perspectives on Science.* Contributor to books, including *Die Entwicklung unserer Atom-und Moleküvorstellungen,* edited by Peter C. Hägele and Axel Schunk, Universitätsverlag Ulm (Ulm, Germany), 1994; *Dilettanten und Wissenschaft: Zur Geschichte und Aktualität eines wechselvollen Verhältnisses,* edited by Elizabeth Strauß, Rodopi (Amsterdam, Holland), 1996; *Experimental Essays—Versuche zum Experiment,* edited by Michael Heidelberger and Friedrich Steinle, Nomos Verlagsgesellschaft (Baden-Baden, Germany), 1998; *Models as Mediators,* edited by Mary S. Morgan and Margaret C. Morrison, Cambridge University Press (Cambridge, MA), 1999; *Ars Mutandi: Issues in Philosophy and History of Chemistry,* edited by Nikos Psarros and Kostas Gavroglu, Leipziger Universitätsverlag (Leipzig, Germany), 1999; and *Observation and Experiment in the Natural and Social Sciences,* edited by Maria Carla Galavotti, Kluwer (Dordrecht, Netherlands), 2003.

BIOGRAPHICAL AND CRITICAL SOURCES:

PERIODICALS

Canadian Journal of History, April, 2004, Trevor H. Levere, review of *Experiments, Models, Paper Tools: Cultures of Organic Chemistry in the Nineteenth Century,* p. 214.

Chemistry and Industry, October 20, 2003, William Brock, review of *Experiments, Models, Paper Tools,* p. 25.

*   *   *

KONNER, Melvin J. 1946-
(Melvin Joel Konner)

PERSONAL: Born August 30, 1946, in Brooklyn, NY; married; children: one daughter. *Education:* Brooklyn College, City University of New York, graduated 1966; Harvard University, Ph.D., 1973; postdoctoral work at Laboratory of Neuroendocrine Regulation, Massachusetts Institute of Technology; Harvard Medical School, M.D., 1985.

ADDRESSES: Office—106 Geosciences Building, Emory University, Atlanta, GA 30322. *E-mail*—antmk@emory.edu.

CAREER: Harvard University, Cambridge, MA, professor of anthropology, late 1970s; Emory University, Atlanta, GA, Samuel Candler Dobbs professor of anthropology, associate professor of psychiatry and neurology, and department chair. Culture of Toys project, cochair.

AWARDS, HONORS: Fellowships from Center for Advanced Study in the Behavioral Sciences, Guggenheim Foundation, Social Science Research Council, and Foundations Fund for Research in Psychiatry; research grants from National Science Foundation and National Institutes of Mental Health.

WRITINGS:

The Tangled Wing: Biological Constraints on the Human Spirit, Holt (New York, NY), 1982, revised edition, Times Books (New York, NY), 2002.

Becoming a Doctor: A Journey of Initiation in Medical School, Viking (New York, NY), 1987.

(With S. Boyd Eaton and Marjorie Shostak) *The Paleolithic Prescription: A Program of Diet and Exercise and a Design for Living,* Harper (New York, NY), 1988.

Why the Reckless Survive: And Other Secrets of Human Nature, Viking (New York, NY), 1990.

Childhood (companion book to the Public Broadcasting Service television series), Little, Brown (Boston, MA), 1991.

Dear America: A Concerned Doctor Wants You to Know the Truth about Health Reform, Addison-Wesley (Reading, MA), 1993.

Medicine at the Crossroads: The Crisis in Health Care (companion to the Public Broadcasting Service television series), Pantheon (New York, NY), 1993.

The Nature of Our Nature: Instinct and Passion in the Human Spirit, W.H. Freeman (New York, NY), 2000.

Unsettled: An Anthropology of the Jews, Viking (New York, NY), 2003.

Contributor to periodicals, including *New York Times, American Prospect,* and *Atlanta Journal-Constitution.*

SIDELIGHTS: Anthropologist Melvin J. Konner spent two years studying infant development among the bushmen of Africa before teaching at and earning his medical degree from Harvard University. He then became department chair at Emory University and the author of a number of volumes that benefit from his training and knowledge across disciplines.

Konner's first book, *The Tangled Wing: Biological Constraints on the Human Spirit,* draws on research in the fields of human biology, genetics, psychology, and ethnography in studying human behavior. Meredith F. Small reviewed the revised second edition for *Natural History,* noting that "Konner moves easily from chapters on such general topics as human sociality, adaptation, ingenuity, brain development, genes, and culture to those focused on particular aspects of human emotion and desire."

Becoming a Doctor: A Journey of Initiation in Medical School focuses on third-year clinical rotations. Based on Konner's own experiences, it is written for a general audience. Konner is honest in his descriptions of the treatment of medical students, as well as of patients, by indifferent staff and the rare instances of true compassion, competence, and decency. "The result is a thoughtful insider's account of how young men and women with innocent hearts and the best of intentions gradually adopt values and behaviors that render

them less and less able to truly care for their patients," noted Tom Ferguson in *Medical Self-Care.* Ferguson added that "Konner is not a naive critic out to belittle every aspect of modern medicine. His portraits of the rare good doctors he encounters radiate from the page like a powerful beacon of hope." *Journal of the American Medical Association* reviewer Walter M. Swentko called the book "outstanding" and said that Konner "artistically paints procedures, conditions, and anatomy-physiology with beautiful descriptive phrases." Konner describes a woman's labor as being "like an earthquake inside her body" and cardiopulmonary resuscitation as "squeezing death out of the chest seventy times a minute." Swentko said that "the book is richly endowed with such metaphors and numerous aphorisms."

The Paleolithic Prescription: A Program of Diet and Exercise and a Design for Living is based on assumptions about man's early ancestors gained in part by studying contemporary hunter-gatherer cultures. Konner and coauthors S. Boyd Eaton and Marjorie Shostak note the differences in the fat content of meat hunted and eaten by early man and the high-fat levels found in modern animals bred for food. They demonstrate how the time and energy expended in the quest for food offset the caloric content and how the hunter-gatherers did not exhibit the conditions of aging that we assume to be unavoidable. Their book includes healthy recipes and suggestions for dietary and lifestyle changes.

Konner has become an outspoken advocate for a single-payer health care system, about which he has testified before the U.S. Senate. He has addressed health care in *Dear America: A Concerned Doctor Wants You to Know the Truth about Health Reform* and *Medicine at the Crossroads: The Crisis in Health Care,* the latter a companion to a Public Broadcasting Service television series. The latter volume is a series of chapters on a variety of topics, including the history of medicine, contemporary medicine, drug use, genetics, psychiatry, AIDS, and the aged and dying. *Commonweal* reviewer Madeline Marget called it "a thoughtful survey" and said that Konner "honors both scientific achievement and spiritual life, and sees social progress—especially if it learns from and includes tradition—as the basis for the prevention and cure of suffering."

Konner was a practicing Orthodox Jew until age seventeen and he returned to his faith after the birth of his daughter. Then he traveled to Israel, studied, and wrote *Unsettled: An Anthropology of the Jews,* a history that begins in the prebiblical period. He takes the approach of an anthropologist in that he makes comparisons between ancient and contemporary times. Jonathan Rosen noted in the *New York Times Book Review* that "Konner is perfectly comfortable segueing from a discussion of Jews who arrived in China 1,000 years ago to an interview with a Brooklyn woman who moved to Alaska, repeating an ancient pattern in which new communities are pioneered by a handful of settlers."

The volume includes the writings of Holocaust survivors, as well as works from great Hebrew poets, leading *Washington Post* contributor Stuart Schoffman to comment that it "seems much more an anthology than an anthropology of Jews, with an emphasis on literature no less than on social behavior." It also addresses Jewish ritual, dietary laws, resistance to fascism, and the modern state of Israel. Konner lists Jewish achievers by percentage, claiming that approximately .2 percent of the world's population have garnered 155 Nobel Prizes. He offers his own theory about Jewish intellectual achievement, saying that "the mainstream of Jewish thought went through rabbinical academies, where the best minds gathered, competed, were nurtured, and were married off in every generation, creating a kind of cult of the intellect. With the opening of European secular thought to Jews, these outsiders' contribution was way out of proportion to their numbers." A *Kirkus Reviews* contributor concluded that "rich in learning and observation, *Unsettled* ought to inspire discussion, perhaps even controversy at points. A splendid treatise that will inform readers of whatever background."

BIOGRAPHICAL AND CRITICAL SOURCES:

BOOKS

Konner, Melvin J., *Becoming a Doctor: A Journey of Initiation in Medical School,* Viking (New York, NY), 1987.
Konner, Melvin J., *Unsettled: An Anthropology of the Jews,* Viking (New York, NY), 2003.

PERIODICALS

Austin American-Statesman, May 30, 1999, interview with Konner, p. J2.

Commonweal, October 22, 1993, Madeline Marget, review of *Medicine at the Crossroads: The Crisis in Health Care,* p. 28.
Journal of the American Medical Association, August 18, 1989, Walter M. Swentko, review of *Becoming a Doctor: A Journey of Initiation in Medical School,* p. 959; January 26, 1994, Keith Whittaker, review of *Medicine at the Crossroads,* p. 322.
Kirkus Reviews, July 15, 2003, review of *Unsettled: An Anthropology of the Jews,* p. 953.
Medical Self-Care, March-April, 1989, Tom Ferguson, review of *Becoming a Doctor,* p. 59; November-December, 1989, Melanie Scheller, review of *The Paleolithic Prescription: A Program of Diet and Exercise and a Design for Living,* p. 39.
Natural History, June, 2002, Meredith F. Small, review of *The Tangled Wing: Biological Constraints on the Human Spirit,* p. 76.
New York Times Book Review, December 14, 2003, Jonathan Rosen, review of *Unsettled,* p. 26.
Publishers Weekly, June 1, 1990, review of *Why the Reckless Survive: And Other Secrets of Human Nature,* p. 52; September 1, 2003, review of *Unsettled,* p. 80.
U.S. News and World Report, January 14, 1991, Alvin P. Sanoff, interview with Konner, p. 53.
Washington Post, October 26, 2003, Stuart Schoffman, review of *Unsettled,* p. T7.

ONLINE

Emory University Web ite, http://www.emory.edu/ (July 3, 2005), Konner profile.*

*   *   *

KONNER, Melvin Joel
See KONNER, Melvin J.

*   *   *

KORGEN, Kathleen Odell 1967-

PERSONAL: Born October 11, 1967, in Olean, NY; daughter of Walter Tomkins (a political-science professor) and Patricia (a mathematics professor; maiden name, McIntyre) Odell; married Jeffry Korgen (a lay ecclesiastical minister), August 5, 1995; children: Julie

Ellen, Jessica Elizabeth. *Ethnicity:* "Irish-English." *Education:* College of the Holy Cross, B.A., 1989; Boston College, Ph.D., 1997. *Politics:* Democrat. *Religion:* Roman Catholic.

ADDRESSES: Home—319 Powell Ave., Newburgh, NY 12550. *Office*—William Patterson University, Department of Sociology, Wayne, NJ 07470. *E-mail*—korgenk@wpunj.edu.

CAREER: Writer. Drury College, Springfield, MO, assistant professor, 1998; William Patterson University, Wayne, NJ, assistant professor, 1998-2003, associate professor, 2003—. Jesuit Volunteer Corps, Portland, ME, 1989-90.

MEMBER: American Sociological Association, Association of American Colleges and Universities, Society for the Study of Social Problems, Eastern Sociological Society.

WRITINGS:

From Black to Biracial: Transforming Racial Identity, Praeger (Westport, CT), 1998.
Crossing the Racial Divide: Close Friendships Between Black and White Americans, Praeger (Westport, CT), 2002.

Contributor to periodicals, including *Teaching Sociology, American Sociologist, Social Insight, CyberPsychology and Behavior, College Student Journal, Innovative Higher Education,* and *Contemporary Sociology.* Contributor to books, including *Perspectives: Criminal Justice,* edited by Alejandro del Carmen, CourseWise Publishing (Madison, WI), 1999; *Perspectives: Race and Crime,* edited by Robert L. Bing, III, and del Carmen, CourseWise Publishing, 1999; *Racial and Ethnic Relations in America,* edited by Carl L. Bankston, III, with others, Salem Press (Pasadena, CA), 2000; and *The Quality of Contact: African Americans and Whites on College Campuses,* edited by Robert Moore, University Press of America (Lanham, MD), 2002.

WORK IN PROGRESS: How Sociology Can Save Democracy, a book with Howard Lune, to be published by Prentice-Hall.

SIDELIGHTS: Kathleen Odell Korgen told *CA:* "I've always been attracted to sociology because of its unique capability to help citizens become informed and effective members of their society. My work, ranging from issues of race to civic engagement, has always centered around issues of social justice. In order to change society and make it more just, we first have to understand how it operates. Sociology provides us with the tools to do just that. As a professor and a writer, I get to share this knowledge with many others. I am very fortunate!"

BIOGRAPHICAL AND CRITICAL SOURCES:

PERIODICALS

American Journal of Sociology, May, 1999, Michelle D. Byng, review of *From Black to Biracial: Transforming Racial Identity,* p. 1867.
Journal of Ethnic and Migration Studies, April, 1999, Kevin Mumford, review of *From Black to Biracial,* p. 357.

*   *   *

KOŠ, Erih 1913-

PERSONAL: Born April 15, 1913, in Sarajevo, Yugoslavia. *Education:* Belgrade Faculty of Law, graduated 1935.

ADDRESSES: Agent—c/o Author Mail, Srpska knjizevna zadruga, Srpskih vladara 19/I, YU-11000 Belgrade, Serbia.

CAREER: Lawyer, 1935-41; Cultural Committee of Government of the Federal People's Republic of Yugoslavia, president; Yugoslavian Ministry for Culture and Education, diplomat; Yugoslavian National Museum, assistant director; Yugoslav League for Peace, Independence and Equality of Peoples, secretary general, 1964-69; *Contemporary* (magazine), founder and first editor. *Military service:* Fought with the Serbian partisans during World War II.

MEMBER: Association of Writers of Serbia, PEN Club of Serbia (past president), Serbian Academy of Sciences and Arts.

AWARDS, HONORS: Yugoslav Writers Association award, 1958, for *Big Poppy;* Belgrade October award, 1964, for *Prvo lice jednine;* NIN award, 1968, for *Mreze;* Seventh of July Award, for life accomplishments; lifetime achievement award, Zlatni Beocug, 2003.

WRITINGS:

Tri hronike (stories; title means "Three Chronicles"), 1949.

Zapisi o mladim ljudima (stories; title means "Notes on Young People"), 1950.

Vreme: ratno (stories; title means "Time: War"), Novo Pokolenje (Belgrade, Yugoslavia), 1952.

Veliki Mak (novel), 1956, translation by Lovett F. Edwards published as *The Strange Story of the Great Whale, also Known as Big Mac,* Harcourt (New York, NY), 1962.

Il tifo (novel), Matica Srpska (Belgrade, Yugoslavia), 1958.

Kao vuci, Nolit (Belgrade, Yugoslavia), 1958.

Novosadski pokolj (novel; title means "Slaughter at Novi Sad"), Rad (Belgrade, Yugoslavia), 1961.

Vrapci Van Pea (novel), Nolit (Belgrade, Yugoslavia), 1962.

Prvo lice jednine (stories; title means "First Person Singular"), Veselin Maslesa (Sarajevo, Yugoslavia), 1963.

Names (novel; originally published in Serbo-Croatian), 1964, translation by Lovett F. Edwards, Harcourt (New York, NY), 1966.

Mreze (novel; title means "Nets"), Matica Srpska (Novi Sad, Yugoslavia), 1967.

Satire, 1968.

Mesano drustvo, 1969.

Eis, 1970.

Zasto da ne? (essays; title means "Why Not?"), Nolit (Belgrade, Yugoslavia), 1971.

Dosije Hrabak (novel; title means "Hrabak File"), Prosveta (Belgrade, Yugoslavia), 1971.

Cve'ce i bodlje, 1972.

Na autobuskoj stanici (stories; title means "At the Bus Stop"), Prosveta (Belgrade, Yugoslavia), 1974.

Rasskazy, 1974.

Sneg i led, [Belgrade, Yugoslavia], 1977.

U potrazi za mesijom (novel; title means "Searching for Messiah"), 1978.

Short Story and Story Telling, 1980.

Izlet u Paragvaj (stories; title means "Journey to Paraguay"), Prosveta (Belgrade, Yugoslavia), 1983.

Stories from Bosnia, 1984.

Satira i satiricari (essays; title means "Satire and Satirists"), Prosveta (Belgrade, Yugoslavia), 1985.

Samforova smrt (novel; title means "Death of Samfor"), [Belgrade, Yugoslavia], 1986.

Pisac govora (novel; title means "Talks with Writers"), Svjetost (Sarajevo, Yugoslavia), 1989.

Odlomci se'canja pisci (title means "Fragments and Memories"), Prosveta (Belgrade, Yugoslavia), Volume one, 1990, Volume two, 1996.

Uzgredne zabeleske (essays; title means "Side Notes"), Svjetlost (Sarajevo, Yugoslavia), 1990.

Izmedu redova (essays; title means "Between the Lines"), Prosveta (Belgrade, Yugoslavia), 1994.

Ku'ca 25a (novel; title means "House No. 25a") Srpska Knjizevna Zadruga (Belgrade, Yugoslavia), 1994.

Nove i stare bosanske price, BIGZ (Belgrade, Yugoslavia), 1996.

Poverljivi izvestaj: o upotrebi i svetskom dejstvu koka-kole: spijunsko-satiricna farsa, Srpska Knjizevna Zadruga (Belgrade, Yugoslavia), 1997.

Also author of other works published in Serbian, including *Fire* (stories), 1947; *The Best Years* (stories), 1955; *As Wolves* (stories), 1958; and *That Strange Writers' Craft* (essays), 1965. Translator of works from German and English to Serbo-Croatian.

SIDELIGHTS: Erih Koš held several positions with the Yugoslav government. He then became a journalist and a prolific writer of essays, articles, stories, and novels, many of which have been translated and published internationally, including several in English.

BIOGRAPHICAL AND CRITICAL SOURCES:

ONLINE

Serbian Academy of Sciences and Arts Web site, http://www.sanu.ac.yu/ (July 3, 2005).*

*   *   *

KOSTOVA, Elizabeth 1965(?)-

PERSONAL: Born c. 1965; married; husband's name Georgi (a computer scientist). *Education:* Yale University, degree; University of Michigan, M.F.A., 2004.

ADDRESSES: Agent—c/o Author Mail, Little, Brown and Company, 1271 Avenue of the Americas, New York, NY 10020.

CAREER: Writer. Has worked recording folk music in Bulgaria, mowing lawns, as a business writing teacher, and as a freelance magazine writer.

AWARDS, HONORS: Hopwood Award for novel-in-progress, for *The Historian.*

WRITINGS:

The Historian (novel), Little, Brown (New York, NY), 2005.

The Historian have been translated into twenty-eight languages.

ADAPTATIONS: The Historian was optioned for film by Sony Pictures, and has been adopted for audiocassette.

WORK IN PROGRESS: A second novel.

SIDELIGHTS: The idea at the center of Elizabeth Kostova's lengthy debut novel, *The Historian,* is that the legendary, dreaded Count Dracula still walks among mortals. The Dracula of Kostova's world, however, does not resemble the urbane but deadly charmer characterized by Bela Lugosi in film, nor does he share the wanton violence and feral characteristics of more recent vampires. Instead, Kostova's Dracula is himself an historian: He is an archivist, a dusty academic, a scholar more at home with crumbling books and historical documents than waiflike victims and flapping bats. *The Historian* "is a tale of such fiendish complication that while writing it, Kostova kept a chart on her wall tracing the narratives," noted Malcolm Jones in *Newsweek.* "But it is a testament to her skill that, as you're reading, the book never feels complicated," Jones added. This Dracula has nothing to do with the version put forth by Stoker; Kostova's character is based on Vlad Tepes, also known as Vlad the Impaler, the sadistic prince of Wallachia who refined slow torture to its pinnacle using the blunt point of a stake in the ground.

The novel and its labyrinthine plot, occult conspiracies, and international academic mysteries have garnered comparisons to Dan Brown's *The Da Vinci Code,* but Kostova started the novel eight years before Brown's book was published. The idea for *The Historian* occurred to Kostova more than a decade ago, while she was hiking through the Appalachian mountains with her husband. What if a father was telling stories about Dracula to his daughter, she thought, and what if Dracula himself was there to listen in on them?

The story begins when the novel's unnamed narrator, who is sixteen years old in 1972, finds an unusual book and a mysterious packet of letters in her father Paul's library in Amsterdam. The book is blank, except for an ominous center spread depicting a dragon holding a banner emblazoned with the word "Drakulya." The letters, alarming in themselves, are dated 1930 and addressed to "My dear and unfortunate successor." Initially hesitant to provide any information, Paul eventually relates a complicated tale of encounters with ancient evil. The book, Paul tells his daughter, mysteriously appeared on his desk when he was a graduate student and inspired him to undertake some research on the historical Dracula—a word that, in Romanian, means "Dragon." When Paul mentions the book to his professor, Bartholomew Rossi, he learns that Rossi also received a copy of the unusual tome. Rossi's research, however, convinced him that the historical Dracula was still alive. A few days later, Rossi disappeared from his blood-spattered office, and despite the unreality of the situation, Paul was convinced that his mentor was in the hands of Dracula and in deadly danger. Searching for the man, Paul encountered Helen Rossi, who said she was the professor's unknown daughter, but who bore the first name of the narrator's mother. Helen joined Paul on his unsuccessful search. A few days after telling his daughter this story, Paul also disappears, allegedly called away on business, but leaving a note imploring his daughter to start carrying garlic in her pockets and wearing a crucifix.

Kostova weaves together a sophisticated interconnected storyline that spansthe 1930s, 1950s, and 1970s, as the narrator searches for her father, Paul searches for Rossi, and Rossi makes his own investigation into relationships between the mysterious book, its recipients, and the uncanny truth about Tepes. Some reviewers have been critical of the novel's slow pace. "The characters wander from dusty old archive to archive, their pockets stuffed full of garlic, perusing crumbling volumes, analyzing creepy Balkan folk songs, and debriefing sage Eastern European elders who hoard ancestral secrets," commented Jennifer Reese in *Entertainment Weekly.* "Eventually, even the most patient reader may begin to tire of all this talking and touring."

Numerous other critics, however, found considerably more to like about Kostova's novel. "The writing is excellent, and the pace is brisk, although it sags a bit in the middle," noted Patricia Altner in *Library Journal.* "Blending history and myth, Kostova has fashioned a version so fresh that when a stake is finally driven through a heart, it inspires the tragic shock of something happening for the very first time," Jones remarked. *Salon.com* reviewer Laura Miller commented on the book's settings and atmosphere, stating that "Kostova has a genius for evoking places without making you wade through paragraphs of description."

Kostova has "done something quite extraordinary," concluded June Sawyers in a review for the *San Francisco Chronicle.* "She has refashioned the vampire myth into a compelling contemporary novel, a late-night page-turner that will be sure to make you lose some precious hours of sleep. It is a sprawling piece of work, the kind of novel that supposedly doesn't get published anymore."

BIOGRAPHICAL AND CRITICAL SOURCES:

PERIODICALS

Bookseller, July 16, 2004, review of *The Historian,* p. 29.
Denver Post, June 12, 2005, Brian Richard Boylan, "A Thrill Ride through History," review of *The Historian.*
Entertainment Weekly, May 27, 2005, Karen Valby, "Creature Feature: Elizabeth Kostova Kicks off a Season of Must-Reads with Her Chilling New Dracula Thriller *The Historian,*" p. 103; June 24, 2005, Jennifer Reese, "Neck at Night: Is Elizabeth Kostova's Vampire Thriller, *The Historian* a Book You Can Sink Your Teeth Into?," p. 166.
Guardian (London, England), July 18, 2005, Gary Younge, "Bigger than Dan Brown," profile of Elizabeth Kostova.

Houston Chronicle, July 15, 2005, Michael D. Clark," Creepy Secrets: Inventive, Best-Selling Page-Turner Lives up to the Hype," review of *The Historian.*
Library Journal, June 15, 2005, Patricia Altner, review of *The Historian,* p. 58.
Miami Herald, June 26, 2005, Connie Ogle, "Stake Out: With Scholarly Intrigue and Globetrotting Adventure, Intriguing Novel Delves Deep into the Myth of Dracula," review of *The Historian.*
Newsweek, June 13, 2005, Malcolm Jones, "A High-Stakes Debut, Elizabeth Kostova's Dracula Novel Drew an Unheard-of $2 Million Advance. Now for the Twist: It Was Worth It," review of *The Historian,* p. 74.
New York Daily News, June 12, 2005, Sherryl Connelly, "Vlad Chic: Sprawling Vampire History-Mystery Set to Spike *Da Vinci Code* Sales," review of *The Historian.*
New York Times, June 13, 2005, Janet Maslin, "Scholarship Trumps the Stake in Pursuit of Dracula," review of *The Historian.*
People, July 4, 2005, Jonathan Durbin, review of *The Historian,* p. 44.
Publishers Weekly, April 11, 2005, review of *The Historian,* p. 31; April 11, 2005, Anne Sanow, "Vivifying the Undead," interview with Elizabeth Kostova.
San Francisco Chronicle, June 12, 2005, June Sawyers, "Dracula Dead? Not Exactly . . . ," review of *The Historian.*
San Jose Mercury News, June 19, 2005, Charles Matthews, "Putting the Bite On," review of *The Historian.*
Seattle Times, July 15, 2005, Deloris Tarzan Ament, "*The Historian*; Elegant Vampire Story Gets in Your Blood."
Time, June 20, 2005, Lev Grossman, review of *The Historian,* p. 70.
Times (London, England), July 16, 2005, Saffron Burrows, "The Tooth Is out There."

ONLINE

CollectedMiscellany.com, http://www.collected miscellany.com/ (July 8, 2005), review of *The Historian.*
January Online, http://www.januarymagazine.com/ (August 19, 2005), Tony Buschbaum, "Sucker Punch," review of *The Historian.*
Salon.com, http://www.salon.com/ (June 6, 2005), Laura Miller, review of *The Historian.**

KREITMAN, Esther 1891-1954
(Hinde Esther Singer Kreitman)

PERSONAL: Name sometimes transliterated Ester Kreytman; born 1891, in Bilgoray, Poland; died 1954, in London, England; married; children: Maurice Carr.

CAREER: Writer.

WRITINGS:

FICTION

Der sheydim-tants, Warsaw, Poland, 1936, translated from the Yiddish as *Deborah,* W. & G. Foyle (London, England), 1946, translated by Maurice Carr, introduction by Clive Sinclair, St. Martin's Press (New York, NY), 1983, with introduction by Ilan Stavans, afterword by Anita Norich, Feminist Press at the City University of New York (New York, NY), 2004.

Briliantn (title means "Diamond"), [London, England], 1944.

Yihus, dertseylungen un skitsn, Narod Press (London, England), 1950.

SIDELIGHTS: Esther Kreitman, the elder sister of well-known writer Isaac Bashevis Singer, wrote novels in Yiddish. In *Prooftexts: A Journal of Jewish Literary History,* Dafna Clifford commented that the author "was a talented Yiddish writer with a unique voice. Her work is notable for its richly idiomatic Polish Yiddish and for her illumination of unusual corners of Jewish life." Noting that Kreitman deserved more recognition for her portrayal of Hasidic communities, Clifford went on to comment: "She wrote about power, its abuse, and those systematically excluded from taking an active part in the narrative of their own lives. She gave moving and powerful expression to the need for the recognition of the dignity of women, while maintaining a strong emotional attachment to the society she criticized so feelingly."

Kreitman's first novel was the autobiographical *Der sheydim-tants,* published in 1936 in Yiddish. The book was translated into English as *Deborah,* in 1946 with several new editions being published over the years, including one in 2004. The title character Deborah, whose early life greatly reflects Kreitman's, is bright like her older brothers, but as a woman she is op-

pressed by Hassidic society. Deborah wants an education and freedom; she also temporarily becomes interested in socialism. After a traditional marriage is arranged for Deborah by her unyielding parents, she finds herself in a foreign land with a man she does not love. Writing in *Booklist,* Margaret Flanagan noted that the book "resonates with the often bitter truths of a unique time and culture," and went on to call the novel "an important contribution to . . . feminist Yiddish literature." In a review for *Library Journal,* Molly Abramowitz pointed out the author's daring as a woman writer in a male-dominated culture, noting: "The protagonist's feminine view of the Polish shtetls . . . puts a modern twist on a scene long dominated by men." Kreitman died in London in 1954.

BIOGRAPHICAL AND CRITICAL SOURCES:

PERIODICALS

Booklist, August, 2004, Margaret Flanagan, review of *Deborah,* p. 1899.

Kirkus Reviews, June 15, 2004, review of *Deborah,* p. 553.

Library Journal, August, 2004, Molly Abramowitz, review of *Deborah,* p. 68.

Prooftexts: A Journal of Jewish Literary History, fall, 2003, Dafna Clifford, "From Diamond Cutters to Dog Races: Antwerp and London in the Work of Esther Kreitman," p. 320.

ONLINE

Ester Kreytman Web site, http://www.ugr.es/~aramos/kreytman/index.html (June 1, 2005).*

*   *   *

KREITMAN, Hinde Esther Singer
See KREITMAN, Esther

*   *   *

KUGIYA, Hugo

PERSONAL: Children: a daughter.

ADDRESSES: Home—Brooklyn, NY. *Office*—Newsday, 235 Pinelawn Rd., Melville, NY 11747-4250.

CAREER: Journalist. *Newsday,* Melville, NY, national correspondent. Formerly worked for *Seattle Post-Intelligencer.*

AWARDS, HONORS: Publisher's Award, *Newsday,* 2001, for article on the sinking of the *Arctic Rose.*

WRITINGS:

58 Degrees North: The Mysterious Sinking of the Arctic Rose (nonfiction), Bloomsbury (New York, NY), 2005.

Articles have appeared in *Pacific* magazine.

SIDELIGHTS: In his first book, *58 Degrees North: The Mysterious Sinking of the Arctic Rose,* journalist Hugo Kugiya writes about an incident he first covered for a series of articles in *Newsday.* The industrial fishing boat the *Arctic Rose* and its entire crew of fifteen disappeared in the treacherous Bering Sea one April morning in 2001. The resultant search discovered the sunken boat but recovered only one crewmember's body. After an extensive and expensive two-year investigation, the Coast Guard decided the accident resulted primarily from inexperience and human error and may also have been contributed to by bad boat design and a laxness in maintenance. In his book, Kugiya profiles all the crew members, most of whom were young and came from varied backgrounds, including Mexican immigrants, reformed drug users, and born-again Christians. He also discusses the hazardous life of those who work the high seas in the American fishing industry, pointing out that these fishermen have a fifteen-times higher chance of dying on the job than those who work in such dangerous professions as fighting crime or fires. The author also details the search and investigation. A *Kirkus Reviews* contributor noted that the author had produced "solid investigative journalism, though of no comfort to anyone contemplating a tour aboard a factory ship." Edwin B. Burgess, writing in *Library Journal,* called the book "an intriguing look into one of the most dangerous occupations in America." Noting that the book "isn't flawlessly executed," a *Publishers Weekly* contributor nevertheless commented that "the portraits of the doomed fishermen . . . grip and fascinate."

BIOGRAPHICAL AND CRITICAL SOURCES:

PERIODICALS

Kirkus Reviews, January 15, 2005, review of *58 Degrees North: The Mysterious Sinking of the Arctic Rose,* p. 103.
Library Journal, March 1, 2005, Edwin B. Burgess, review of *58 Degrees North,* p. 98.
Publishers Weekly, February 14, 2005, review of *58 Degrees North,* p. 63.*

L

LAFFERTY, Perry 1917-2005
(Perry Francis Lafferty)

OBITUARY NOTICE— See index for *CA* sketch: Born October 3, 1917, in Davenport, IA; died of prostate cancer, August 25, 2005, in Century City, CA. Television producer, director, and author. Lafferty was a former television executive at the Columbia Broadcasting System (CBS) and the National Broadcasting Company (NBC) who was credited with bringing such award-winning programs as *MASH, All in the Family,* and *The Mary Tyler Moore Show* to audiences. He was also a gifted pianist who went on to earn a music certificate at Yale University in 1938. He then worked in radio in New York City before World War II. With America's entry into the war, he enlisted in the U.S. Army Air Forces, where he produced radio shows for the troops. After the war, Lafferty entered television work by becoming a producer and director for such shows as *Studio One, Twilight Zone, Rawhide,* and *The Danny Kaye Show.* The quality of these shows led him to be hired by CBS as vice president of programs. It was here that Lafferty became well known. Unafraid of producing ground-breaking series, his other credits included *Hawaii Five-O, The Bill Cosby Show, Sonny and Cher,* and *The Bob Newhart Show.* He left CBS in 1976, joining NBC in 1979 as senior vice president of movies, miniseries, and special projects. Here, he continued to produce cutting-edge movies, such as 1985's *An Early Frost,* a drama about AIDS that was broadcast when the epidemic was first gaining national attention. He worked at NBC through the early 1980s before retiring. Lafferty then embarked on a career as a mystery novelist. Among his books are *Birdies Sing and Everything* (1964), *How to Lose Your Fear of Flying* (1980), and *Jablonski of L.A.* (1991).

OBITUARIES AND OTHER SOURCES:

PERIODICALS

Los Angeles Times, September 9, 2005, p. B8.
New York Times, September 18, 2005, p. A33.
Variety, September 12, 2005, p. 81.

*   *   *

LAFFERTY, Perry Francis
See LAFFERTY, Perry

*   *   *

LAFFEY, Marcus
See CONLON, Edward

*   *   *

LARSEN, Darl 1963-

PERSONAL: Born 1963, in Bakersfield, CA; son of a college professor and consulting geologist (father), and middle-school teacher (mother); married; wife an elementary-school teacher; children: Keir, Emrys, Brynmor, Eamonn, Dathyl, Ransom, Cuchulainn. *Education:* University of California, Santa Barbara, B.A., 1990; Brigham Young University, M.A., 1993; Northern Illinois University, Ph.D., 2000. *Religion:* Church of Jesus Christ of Latter-Day Saints (Mormon).

ADDRESSES: Office—Brigham Young University, Department of Theatre and Media Arts, D-581 HFAC, Provo, UT 84602. *E-mail*—darl_larsen@byu.edu.

CAREER: Writer. Brigham Young University, Provo, UT, associate professor of theatre, 1998—.

WRITINGS:

Monty Python, Shakespeare, and English Renaissance Drama, McFarland (Jefferson, NC), 2003.

ADAPTATIONS: Larsen's short story "The Snell Show" was adapted for film by Andrew Black, 2003.

*   *   *

LAUER, Betty 1926-

PERSONAL: Born Bertel Weissberger, 1926; daughter of Oskar and Ilona Weissberger; married Lawrence Lauer (deceased); children: two sons. *Education:* Earned a master's degree.

ADDRESSES: Home—Wilder, NH. *Agent*—c/o Author Mail, Smith & Kraus Publishers, P.O. Box 127, Lyme, NH 03768.

CAREER: Writer and educator. Queens College, New York, NY, formerly taught German literature. Has also taught German at the high-school level.

WRITINGS:

Hiding in Plain Sight: The Incredible True Story of a German-Jewish Teenager's Struggle to Survive in Nazi-Occupied Poland, Smith & Kraus (Hanover, NH), 2004.

SIDELIGHTS: Betty Lauer—born Bertel Weissberger—waited nearly six decades to write her memoir of growing up as a Jew during World War II; her book is titled *Hiding in Plain Sight: The Incredible True Story of a German-Jewish Teenager's Struggle to Survive in Nazi-Occupied Poland.* The author's father was deported from Germany in 1938. While he was in America trying to arrange for the rest of his family to follow, Bertel, her mother, and sister were gathered up, together with thousands of other Jews, and sent to Poland, where they lived in a Jewish ghetto under strict control by the local authorities. After the German occupation of Poland, it became apparent that Jews were being liquidated. After her sister, Eva, was taken by authorities, Bertel and her mother acquired fake papers certifying them as Polish Christians. In her memoir, the author recounts her continuous struggle to keep her and her mother's real identities a secret. The two traveled to Warsaw and fought in an uprising, got deported to a camp, eventually began their search for Eva, and then moved to America. "Even if you think you've read enough about the Holocaust, start this extraordinary eyewitness account, and you won't quit till you're finished," wrote a *Publishers Weekly* contributor. A reviewer for the *Wisconsin Bookwatch* called the memoir "a testament to the enduring human spirit," while in *Library Journal,* Elizabeth Morris commented that "the book is distinguished by a wealth of careful personal detail." Writing on the *Enter Stage Right* Web site, Steven Martinovich noted that, "as talented as a writer as Lauer is, there are likely no words capable of communicating her experiences." "Yet," the reviewer went on to comment, "*Hiding in Plain Sight* reminds us that there is good as well as evil in the world and that the human spirit is capable of unimagined strength."

BIOGRAPHICAL AND CRITICAL SOURCES:

BOOKS

Lauer, Betty, *Hiding in Plain Sight: The Incredible True Story of a German-Jewish Teenager's Struggle to Survive in Nazi-Occupied Poland,* Smith & Kraus (Hanover, NH), 2004.

PERIODICALS

Library Journal, September 15, 2004, Elizabeth Morris, review of *Hiding in Plain Sight: The Incredible True Story of a German-Jewish Teenager's Struggle to Survive in Nazi-Occupied Poland,* p. 65.

Publishers Weekly, July 5, 2004, review of *Hiding in Plain Sight,* p. 44.

Valley News (White River Junction, VT), April 2, 2005, Dan Mackie, "Author of Holocaust Memoir Counts Herself among the Lucky,"
Wisconsin Bookwatch, August, 2004, review of *Hiding in Plain Sight.*

ONLINE

Enter Stage Right, http://www.enterstageright.com/ (July 19, 2004), Steven Martinovich, review of *Hiding in Plain Sight.**

*   *   *

LAWSON, Michael 1948-

PERSONAL: Born 1948.

ADDRESSES: Agent—c/o Author Mail, Doubleday, 1745 Broadway, New York, NY 10019.

CAREER: Writer. Formerly worked with U.S. Navy as senior civilian executive contractor in Seattle, WA.

WRITINGS:

The Inside Ring (fiction), Doubleday (New York, NY), 2005.

ADAPTATIONS: The Inside Ring was adapted as an audiobook.

WORK IN PROGRESS: Another thriller, tentatively titled *Miss July.*

SIDELIGHTS: In his first novel, *The Inside Ring,* Michael Lawson presents a thriller about an assassination attempt on the president of the United States. Unlike other assassination thrillers, *The Inside Ring* opens with the assassination attempt gone wrong. The sniper-assassin misses the president, but kills a secret service agent and a reporter. The supposed perpetrator commits suicide a few days later, leaving behind a note admitting to the attempt. There is more going on, however: the director of Homeland Security had received an early tip that the assassination attempt was going to take place, but when he passed the information on to the head of the Secret Service, that man seemingly ignored the threat. Joe Demarco, a troubleshooting, tough lawyer who works as a "fixer" for the U.S. Speaker of the House, is asked by the Homeland Security director to look into the failed attempt, which may involve members of the Secret Service itself. "Thus begins a series of compelling incidents, enlivened by just the right touch of menace and mystery," wrote Ronnie H. Terpening in the *Library Journal.* A *Publishers Weekly* contributor called Lawson's first novel "high-level entertainment from a writer who could soon rise to the top of the thriller heap." In a review on *Bookreporter.com* Joe Hartlaub commented that the first-time author "comes right out of the gate with a confident work containing intriguing characters working their way through a complex but navigable plot." Hartlaub also noted that "DeMarco is an interesting character," and added that "Lawson, given the nature of DeMarco's work and his position, will have a broad canvas to work from in future novels."

BIOGRAPHICAL AND CRITICAL SOURCES:

PERIODICALS

Booklist, March 1, 2005, David Pitt, review of *The Inside Ring,* p. 1147.
Library Journal, May 15, 2005, Ronnie H. Terpening, review of *The Inside Ring,* p. 106.
Publishers Weekly, June 21, 2004, John F. Baker, "A Winning First Sentence," p. 12; March 21, 2005, review of *The Inside Ring,* p. 36.

ONLINE

Bookbrowse.com, http://www.bookbrowse.com/ (July 19, 2005), brief biography of author.
Bookreporter.com, http://www.bookreporter.com/ (July 10, 2005), Joe Hartlaub, review of *The Inside Ring.**

*   *   *

LE, Chap T. 1948-

PERSONAL: Born August 1, 1948, in Binh-Dinh, Vietnam; married Minh-Ha T. Nguyen; children: Mina N., Jenna N. *Ethnicity:* "Asian." *Education:* California State University, Fresno, B.A. and B.S., 1970, M.A., 1971; University of New Mexico, Ph.D., 1978.

ADDRESSES: Home—5913 Fairfax Ave., Edina, MN 55424. *Office*—University of Minnesota, Division of Biostatistics, MMC 303, 420 Delaware St. SE, Minneapolis, MN 55455. *E-mail*—chap@biostat.umn. edu.

CAREER: Writer. University of Hue, Vietnam, instructor, 1971-75; University of Minnesota, Minneapolis, professor, 1978—. University of Minnesota Cancer Center, director of biostatistics.

AWARDS, HONORS: Distinguished teaching professorship, University of Minnesota, 2001.

WRITINGS:

Fundamentals of Biostatistical Inference, Dekker (New York, NY), 1992.
(With James R. Boen) *Health and Numbers: Basic Biostatistical Methods,* Wiley (New York, NY), 1995.
Applied Survival Analysis, Wiley (New York, NY), 1997.
Applied Categorical Data Analysis, Wiley (New York, NY), 1998.
Health and Numbers: A Problem-Based Introduction to Biostatistics, Wiley (New York), 2001.
Introductory Biostatistics, Wiley (New York, NY), 2003.

Contributor of numerous articles to professional journals.

WORK IN PROGRESS: Research in survival analysis and statistical methods for cancer research.

*   *   *

LEE, Elisa T. 1939-

PERSONAL: Born May 1, 1939, in Yungsing, China; immigrated to United States; became naturalized citizen; daughter of Chi-Lan (a politician) and Hwei-chi Lee (a homemaker) Tan; married Samuel Lee (a professor), August 21, 1965; children Vivian S., Jennifer S. *Ethnicity:* "Chinese." *Education:* National Taiwan University, B.A., 1961; University of California, Berkeley, M.A., 1964; New York University, Ph.D., 1973. *Hobbies and other interests:* Cooking, watching old movies.

ADDRESSES: Home—1812 Valley Ridge, Norman, OK 73072. *Office*—University of Oklahoma Health Science Center, 801 NE 13th St., Oklahoma City, OK 73104. *E-mail*—elisa-lee@ouhsc.edu.

CAREER: Writer. Bell Laboratories, Murray Hill, NJ, associate member of technical staff, 1965-71; M.D. Anderson Cancer Center, Houston, TX, operations research analyst, 1971-75; University of Oklahoma, Oklahoma City, professor, 1975—. U.S. Food and Drug Administration, member of arthritis and over-the-counter advisory committee; National Institutes of Health, member of EDC1 Study Section.

MEMBER: American Statistical Association (fellow, 1996), National Advisory Council on Minority Health and Health Disparities.

AWARDS, HONORS: Founders Day Award for outstanding scholarship, New York University, 1974; Regents Award for superior teaching, University of Oklahoma, 1983; George Lynn Cross research professorship, University of Oklahoma, 1990.

WRITINGS:

Statistical Methods for Survival Data Analysis, Lifetime Learning Publications (Belmont, CA), 1980, 3rd edition (with John Wenyu Wang), John Wiley (New York, NY), 2003.

Contributor of articles to books and professional journals.

WORK IN PROGRESS: Cardiovascular disease in American Indians; health-related research, training, and community outreach for American Indians; clinical trials to prevent heart disease among Native Americans with diabetes.

SIDELIGHTS: Elisa T. Lee told *CA:* "When I started to work on the first edition of *Statistical Methods for Survival Data Analysis,* the subject area was very popular because it was extremely useful in cancer and other health-related research. However, there were only a few books on the subject and most of them were not written for non-statisticians. The publisher and I decided that an easy-to-read book with less theory and more applications would be helpful to many researchers in the health field. I have kept the same style in the second and third editions. Many readers have told me that they have benefited from the book and really enjoy the application-oriented style. It has been a good experience."

*   *   *

LENDE, Heather 1959-

PERSONAL: Born 1959; married; husband's name, Chip; children: five. *Hobbies and other interests:* Coaching the high school cross-country running team; volunteering on local radio station KHNS, running, cycling, hiking, snowshoeing, boating.

ADDRESSES: Home—Haines, AK. *Office*—Pyramid Island Press, P.O. Box 936, Haines, AK 99827. *E-mail*—heather@heatherlende.com.

CAREER: Chilkat Valley News, Haines, AK, obituary writer; *Anchorage Daily News,* Anchorage, AK, columnist. Member of Haines public school board, public library board, and hospice board.

MEMBER: Klondike Trail of '98 Road Relay (women's running team), Lady Gu-Divas.

AWARDS, HONORS: Suzan Nightingale McKay Best Columnist Award, Alaska Press Club, 2002; Citizen of the Year, Haines Chamber of Commerce, 2004.

WRITINGS:

If You Lived Here, I'd Know Your Name: News from Small-Town Alaska, Algonquin Books of Chapel Hill (Chapel Hill, NC), 2005.

Also contributor to *Christian Science Monitor* and National Public Radio's *Morning Edition.*

SIDELIGHTS: As an active volunteer in her local school and library, Heather Lende is a familiar figure in the small town of Haines, Alaska. As an obituary writer for the local newspaper, a columnist for the *Anchorage Daily News,* and a frequent commentator on National Public Radio, she is also a chronicler conveying something of the lives and outlooks of her neighbors to a wider audience. Lende has drawn on this background in *If You Lived Here, I'd Know Your Name: News from Small-Town Alaska,* "an autobiographical love letter to this isolated community," according to *Entertainment Weekly* reviewer Gilbert Cruz. Each chapter is centered around a particular obituary, and one of the book's themes is the closeness of death from mud slides, small-plane crashes, and the sea that provides a living to many of the town's residents. Each obituary is also a celebration of a life, and Lende provides a colorful picture of the town's residents, from the aging hippie who launches many civic drives to the high school principal who doubles as a Roy Orbison impersonator and the Presbyterian minister who sports a number of elaborate tattoos. She also brings out larger points, such as the deeply personal nature of local issues and the dangers and pleasures of living so close to nature. After reading the book, "the reader has a good idea of what it's like to live among the varied citizens . . . of Haines, in the shadow of a glacier," concluded *Booklist* contributor Rebecca Maksel.

Lende told *CA:* "I began writing because I found myself full of stories at the dinner table every night that seemed worth sharing beyond my friends and family. I also live in a remarkable Alaskan town, full of interesting people and surrounded by spectafular wilderness. I think it is important to write about small towns and real people—life and death and families—as well as the value of time spent outdoors in wild places. My columns and commentaries are short by design and deadline driven. The book was fun because I had more time and more words to work with.

"When I do my columns I procrastinate at my desk most of the day, then make myself finish a passable draft before going to bed around ten. Then I toss and turn and wake up about three a.m. and get busy, rewriting, tuning, cutting, and sometimes starting all over again. By nine a.m. I figure I'll be fired, that I have nothing to say that is worth printing in a newspaper, and panic sets in. I have until noon to finish it. That is when I do my best work. I have never missed a deadline, and the only week I didn't write a column was the time I was run over by a truck and almost died. I wrote the next one from the hospital. I'm proud of that.

"While I live in a remote place without much feedback or contact with other writers and the literary or media world, I read all the time—newspapers online as well as magazines, novels, poems and nonfiction. Favorites include Anne LaMott, Ellen Gilchrist, Ivan Doig, John Erving, E.B. White, Larry McMurtry, Calvin Trillin, Frank Rich, Maureen Dowd, Anna Quindlen, Annie Dillard, P.D. James, James Lee Burke, Jane Kenyon, Billy Collins, Mary Oliver, Tom McGuane, and fellow Alaskan John Straley. I also listen to *A Prairie Home Companion* each week and a lot of country music, which I suspect colors my writing.

"The most surprising thing I've learned as a writer is that no matter what I write about, if there is a pet in the story—a dog, cat, bunny, or even a chicken, everyone loves it even if it is not very good.

"I hope that when someone puts down something I have written they feel like they've just read a letter from an old friend in Alaska."

BIOGRAPHICAL AND CRITICAL SOURCES:

PERIODICALS

Booklist, March 15, 2005, Rebecca Maksel, review of *If You Lived Here, I'd Know Your Name: News from Small-Town Alaska,* p. 1261.

Entertainment Weekly, May 27, 2005, Gilbert Cruz, review of *If You Lived Here, I'd Know Your Name,* p. 149.

Kirkus Reviews, March 1, 2005, review of *If You Lived Here, I'd Know Your Name,* p. 275.

Library Journal, April 1, 2005, Melissa Stearns, review of *If You Lived Here, I'd Know Your Name,* p. 116; April 15, 2005, Rebecca Miller, "Heather Lende: Q&A," p. 108.

People, June 13, 2005, review of *If You Lived Here, I'd Know Your Name,* p. 52.

Publishers Weekly, April 18, 2005, review of *If You Lived Here, I'd Know Your Name,* p. 54.

USA Today, May 26, 2005, Bob Minzesheimer, review of *If You Lived Here, I'd Know Your Name,* p. D6.

ONLINE

Heather Lende Home Page, http://heatherlende.com (July 11, 2005).

*   *   *

LEVITHAN, David 1972-

PERSONAL: Born 1972, in Short Hills, NJ. *Education:* Brown University, B.A., 1994. *Hobbies and other interests:* Photography.

ADDRESSES: Office—Scholastic, 557 Broadway, New York, NY 10012-3999. *E-mail*—david@davidlevithan. com.

CAREER: Writer; Scholastic, New York, NY, editorial director of Push imprint. New School University Graduate School of Creative Writing, New York, NY, professor of children's and teen literature.

WRITINGS:

(Editor) *You Are Here, This Is Now: The Best Young Writers and Artists in America: A Push Anthology,* Scholastic (New York, NY), 2002.

Boy Meets Boy, Knopf (New York, NY), 2003.

The Realm of Possibility, Random House (New York, NY), 2004.

Are We There Yet?, Knopf (New York, NY), 2005.

Marly's Ghost: A Remix of Charles Dickens' A Christmas Carol, illustrated by Brian Selznick, Dial (New York, NY), 2005.

(Editor, with Ann M. Martin) *Friends: Stories about New Friends, Old Friends, and Unexpectedly True Friends,* Scholastic (New York, NY), 2005.

(Editor) *When We Are, What We See: A Push Anthology,* Scholastic (New York, NY), 2005.

(With Rachel Cohn) *Nick and Norah's Infinite Playlist,* Knopf (New York, NY), 2006.

(Editor, with Billy Merrell) *The Full Spectrum: A New Generation of Writing about Gay, Lesbian, Bisexual, Transgender, Questioning, and Other Identities,* Knopf (New York, NY), 2006.

Wide Awake, Knopf (New York, NY), 2006.

Contributor to anthologies, including *Everything Man for Himself,* edited by Nancy Mercato; *Sixteen,* edited by Megan McCafferty, Three Rivers Press, 2004, and *What a Song Can Do,* edited by Jennifer Armstrong, Knopf, 2004.

MEDIA TIE-INS

The Mummy: A Junior Novelization (based on the motion picture by Stephen Sommers), Scholastic (New York, NY), 1999.

(With Anne Downey and James Preller) *The Mummy: Movie Scrapbook,* Scholastic (New York, NY), 1999.

101 Ways to Get away with Anything! (based on the television series *Malcolm in the Middle*), Scholastic (New York, NY), 2001.

101 Ways to Stop Being Bored (based on the television series *Malcolm in the Middle*), Scholastic (New York, NY), 2003.

Charlie's Angels: Full Throttle (based on the motion picture by John August), Aladdin (New York, NY), 2003.

The Perfect Score (based on the motion picture by Mark Hyman and Jon Zack), Simon Spotlight (New York, NY), 2004.

Also author of a novelization of the movie *Ten Things I Hate about You* and spin-off books based on the movie *The Sixth Sense.*

WORK IN PROGRESS: More novels.

SIDELIGHTS: David Levithan has written several novels for teens and young adults, as well as novelizations of movies and television-show tie-ins. Several of his novels actually began as short stories written as Valentine's Day gifts for friends, a tradition he began many years ago; his novels *Boy Meets Boy, The Realm of Possibility,* and *Are We There Yet?* all got their start this way. Along with his work as a writer, Levithan works as editorial director and executive editor at Scholastic, where his responsibilities include editing the entire Push imprint. A line focusing on new voices and new authors in young adult literature, Push led to Levithan's editorship of the anthology *You Are Here, This Is Now: The Best Young Writers and Artists in America: A Push Anthology,* which was the first book-length work to feature his name on its cover.

Levithan's first original novel, *Boy Meets Boy,* is set in a utopian high school where all students are tolerated, regardless of their sexual preference. At this high school, the football quarterback is also a drag queen, and narrator Paul is in the middle of a tricky romance. He has just broken up with Kyle and is beginning a new relationship with Noah, but Noah suspects Paul of being unfaithful, and Paul has to prove his feelings for Noah. According to Michael Rosen in the London *Guardian,* Levithan has "written a book that cunningly superimposes some previously unwritten-about feelings and behaviour on to a thoroughly familiar frame." Rosen went on to compare *Boy Meets Boy* to the popular teen romances set in the fictional Sweet Valley High, and television shows such as *Saved by the Bell* and concluded that the novel "is intimate, feel-good, and quick-fire." Michael Cart, writing in *Booklist,* considered *Boy Meets Boy* to be "the first upbeat gay novel for teens," while Johanna Lewis pointed out in *School Library Journal* that "Levithan's prophecy of a hate-free world in which everyone loves without persecution makes this a provocative and important read." *Lambda* reviewer Nancy Garden saw the book less as prophetic than as an achievable goal: "We are treated to a glimpse of what life can and should be for GLBT kids, and what, in some enlightened parts of the country, it to a large extent already is."

The Realm of Possibility, Levithan's second novel, is a series of linked poems, taking the perspectives of twenty students from the same high school to create a communal picture of what their lives are like. The perspectives of a wide variety of teens, from the outsiders to the most popular, give details about friendship, relationships, and changes that happen during high school. The book begins with a poem by Daniel and wraps up with a poem by his boyfriend, Jed. Though initially, the poems seem to stand alone, connections can be drawn among them to form a narrative. Miranda Doyle, writing in *School Library Journal,* called *The Realm of Possibility* an "enchanting collection of linked poems that delve deep and go far beyond the original stereotypes." John Green, a contributor to *Booklist,* considered the book a "hugely ambitious novel in verse," noting that while some teen readers will be frustrated by the structure, "the distinct voices and plethora of poetic styles make for interesting reading."

The relationship between two brothers is the focus of Levithan's *Are We There Yet?* Seventeen-year-old Elijah and his older brother, Danny, an advertising executive, are tricked into taking a trip to Italy together by their parents. While their parents feel it will be good for the brothers to bond, Elijah and Danny believe they are so different that they share little common ground. When Elijah falls for a college dropout named Julia, it seems like true love, but Julia is interested in Danny as well. The story alternates point of view from Elijah to Danny, so that each brother's experience is fleshed out. Calling the novel "insightful and gently humorous," *School Library Journal* reviewer Susan Riley commented that Levithan "gets better and better with each book." A *Kirkus Reviews* contributor wrote that the author "works his magic creating two real and round narrators in a series of poetic vignettes."

When asked by an interviewer on the Barnes & Noble Web site to give his advice for writers waiting to be discovered, Levithan commented: "Don't write to be published. Write because it's something you want (or have) to write."

BIOGRAPHICAL AND CRITICAL SOURCES:

PERIODICALS

Booklist, August, 2003, Michael Cart, review of *Boy Meets Boy,* p. 1980; January 1, 2004, review of *Boy Meets Boy,* p. 779; September 1, 2004, John Green, review of *The Realm of Possibility,* p. 108.

Guardian (London, England), April 15, 2005, Michael Rosen, review of *Boy Meets Boy.*

Horn Book, January-February, 2004, Roger Sutton, review of *Boy Meets Boy,* p. 83.

Kirkus Reviews, August 15, 2003, review of *Boy Meets Boy,* p. 1075; July 15, 2004, review of *The Realm of Possibility,* p. 689; July 1, 2005, review of *Are We There Yet?,* p. 738.

Lambda Book Report, March-April, 2004, Nancy Garden, "Brave New World," p. 32.

Publishers Weekly, October 6, 2003, review of *Boy Meets Boy,* p. 85; April 11, 2005, John F. Baker, "YA Stars Combine on Novel," p. 16; July 11, 2005, audiobook review of *Boy Meets Boy,* p. 97.

School Librarian, summer, 2005, Gerry McSourley, review of *Boy Meets Boy,* p. 103.

School Library Journal, September, 2003, Johanna Lewis, review of *Boy Meets Boy,* p. 216; June, 2004, Angela M. Boccuzzi, review of *The Perfect Score,* p. 145; September, 2004, Miranda Doyle, review of *The Realm of Possibility,* p. 211; April, 2005, review of *The Realm of Possibility,* p. S72; July, 2005, Susan Riley, review of *Are We There Yet?,* p. 105.

Voice of Youth Advocates, April, 2005, Nancy Zachary, review of *The Realm of Possibility,* p. 14.

ONLINE

Barnes & Noble Web site, http://www.bn.com/ (December 20, 2005), interview with Levithan.

David Levithan Home Page, http://www.davidlevithan. com (November 30, 2005).

Teen Reads.com, http://www.teenreads.com/ (November 30, 2005), "David Levithan."

*   *   *

LEWIS, William Henry 1967-

PERSONAL: Born 1967.

ADDRESSES: Home—New Providence Island, Bahamas. *Office*—College of the Bahamas, P.O. Box N-4912, Nassau, Bahamas.

CAREER: Writer and educator. College of the Bahamas, Nassau, writing and literature teacher.

AWARDS, HONORS: Sonja H. Stone Fiction Competition winner, 1995, for manuscript *In the Arms of Our Elders.*

WRITINGS:

FICTION

In the Arms of Our Elders, Carolina Wren Press (Durham, NC), 1994.

I Got Somebody in Staunton: Stories, Amistad (New York, NY), 2005.

Fiction has appeared in journals and anthologies, including *Best American Short Stories 1996* and *New Letters,* 2000.

SIDELIGHTS: William Henry Lewis is the author of two short-story collections. In his second collection, *I Got Somebody in Staunton: Stories,* the author presents ten tales about a diverse range of characters and situations. In one story, a fourteen-year-old boy who lives in a culture of violence sees his father for the first time walking the streets of his hometown in Tennessee. In the title story, a black college teacher is on his way to Staunton to visit an uncle when he picks up a white woman who has flirted with him at a restaurant. He agrees to drive her to Staunton and the couple makes a rest stop where four thuggish-looking white men begin to talk with the woman. As he watches, the professor recalls the days when black men were lynched for being with white women, considers the continued racial divide, and wonders if this is a situation in which he will have to either make a stand or run. A *Kirkus Reviews* contributor called the title story "a masterpiece of nuance" and noted that the collection contains "evocative stories with a potent kick." Writing in the *Los Angeles Times,* Susan Salter Reynolds called the tales "beautifully written and carefully crafted," while in a review for the *Boston Globe,* Renee Graham commented that the author "reveals the sharp edges, as well as the stubborn grace, of African-American lives." Graham went on to write: "Moving but unsentimental, these are stories of hard-won wisdom, potent intelligence, and compassion for the cadence of everyday life, establishing Lewis as a writer to be appreciated and admired." Vanessa Bush, writing in *Booklist,* felt that the author's stories are presented "with an easy style and sharp character portraits." A *Publishers Weekly* contributor called the book "a thoughtful, appealing collection deeply concerned with the pride and pain of African-American heritage."

BIOGRAPHICAL AND CRITICAL SOURCES:

PERIODICALS

Booklist, February 1, 2005, Vanessa Bush, review of *I Got Somebody in Staunton: Stories,* p. 937.
Boston Globe, April 4, 2005, Renee Graham, review of *I Got Somebody in Staunton,* p. B10.
Entertainment Weekly, April 1, 2005, Brian Palmer, review of *I Got Somebody in Staunton,* p. 73.
Kirkus Reviews, January 1, 2005, review of *I Got Somebody in Staunton,* p. 12.
Los Angeles Times, May 8, 2005, Susan Salter Reynolds, review of *I Got Somebody in Staunton,* p. R11.

New York Times Book Review, April 10, 2005, Lizzie Skurnick, review of *I Got Somebody in Staunton,* p. 23.
Publishers Weekly, February 28, 2005, review of *I Got Somebody in Staunton,* p. 40.

ONLINE

Carolina Wren Press Web site, http://carolinawrenpress. org/ (June 3, 2005).
Ploughshares Online, http://www.pshares.org/ (June 3, 2005).*

*   *   *

LIGHTFOOT, Gordon 1938-
(Gordon Meredith Lightfoot)

PERSONAL: Born November 17, 1938, in Orilla, Ontario, Canada; son of Gordon Meredith and Jessie Vick (Trill) Lightfoot; married second wife, Elizabeth Moon; children: (first marriage) Fred, Ingrid; (second marriage) Eric, Miles. *Education:* Attended Westlake College of Music.

ADDRESSES: Office—1365 Yonge St., No. 207, Toronto, Ontario M4T 2P7, Canada.

CAREER: Songwriter, singer, and guitarist. Has also appeared in movies, including *Harry Tracy, Desperado,* 1982, and *Tears Are Not Enough,* 1985, and in television shows, including the series *The Country and Western Show,* beginning 1963, the movie *One Hundred Years Young,* 1967, and episodes of *The Midnight Special,* 1974-77, *Saturday Night Live,* 1976, *Hotel,* 1988, and *Life and Times,* 1996.

AWARDS, HONORS: Canadian Juno Awards for top folk singer, 1965, 1966, 1968, 1969, 1973, 1974, 1975, 1976, 1977, for top male vocalist, 1967, 1970, 1971, 1972, 1974, and for composer of the year, 1972, 1976; Canadian Medal of Service, 1970; songwriting awards, American Society of Composers, Authors and Publishers, 1971, 1974, 1976, 1977; named to Order of Canada, 1970, elevated to Companion, 2003; pop record of the year award, Music Operators of America, 1974, for "Sundown"; Vanier Award, Canadian

Jaycees, 1977; named Canadian male recording artist of the 1970s, 1980; inducted into Juno Hall of Fame, 1986; Governor General's Performing Arts Award; honored by Martin Guitar Company with its D-18GL Gordon Lightfoot Limited Edition Signature model, 2001; inaugural member, Canadian Folk Music Walk of Fame, 2003, inducted into Canadian Railway Hall of Fame, with special award for composing "Canadian Railway Trilogy"; inducted into Canadian Songwriter Hall of Fame, 2003; inducted into Canadian Music Industry Hall of Fame, 2005; named to Order of Ontario.

WRITINGS:

AUTHOR OF LYRICS; RECORDINGS

Two Tones at the Village Corner, Canatal Records, 1962.

The Canadian Talent Library, Canadian Talent Library, 1964.

Lightfoot, United Artists, 1966.

Way I Feel, United Artists, 1967.

Did She Mention My Name, United Artists, 1968.

Back Here on Earth, United Artists, 1968.

Early Lightfoot, United Artists, 1969.

Sunday Concert, United Artists, 1969.

The Ballad of Yarmouth Castle, United Artists, 1969.

If You Could Read My Mind (originally released as *Sit down Young Strangers*), Reprise, 1970.

Summer Side of Life, Reprise, 1971.

Classic Lightfoot, United Artists, 1971.

The Gordon Lightfoot Story, United Artists, 1971.

Don Quixote, Reprise, 1972.

Old Dan's Records, Reprise, 1972.

Sundown, Reprise, 1973.

The Very Best of Gordon Lightfoot, United Artists, 1974.

The Very Best of Gordon Lightfoot, Volume II, United Artists, 1975.

A Lightfoot Collection: Best of Gordon Lightfoot Volume III, United Artists, 1975.

Cold on Shoulder, Reprise, 1975.

Gord's Gold, Reprise, 1975.

Early Morning Rain, Sunset, 1976.

Summertime Dream, Reprise, 1976.

Fantastic Gordon Lightfoot, two albums, K-Tel Records, 1977.

Endless Wire, Warner Bros., 1978.

The First Time Ever I Saw Your Face, Pickwick Records, 1979.

Dream Street Rose, Warner Bros., 1980.

The Best of Gordon Lightfoot, EMI-Manhattan, 1980.

The Gordon Lightfoot Collection, Warner Bros., 1981.

The Best of Gordon Lightfoot, Warner Bros., 1981.

Shadows, Warner Bros., 1982.

The Best of Anne Murray and Gordon Lightfoot (eight-album boxed set), Capitol Records/Reader's Digest, 1982.

Salute, Warner Bros., 1983.

Songbook, EMI America Records, 1985.

East of Midnight, Warner Bros., 1986.

Over 60 Minutes with . . . Lightfoot, Capitol Records, 1987.

Gord's Gold, Volume II, Warner Bros., 1989.

Early Morning Rain, EMI-USA, 1990.

Best of Gordon Lightfoot, Curb/WEA, 1991.

The Original Lightfoot: The United Artists Years, United Artists, 1992.

The United Artists Collection (contains four 1960s United Artists studio albums), EMI Records, 1993.

Waiting for You, Warner Bros., 1993.

Thirty-six All-Time Favorites, three CDs, Time/Life, 1993.

A Painter Passing Through, Warner Bros., 1998.

Gordon Lightfoot Songbook 1962-1998 (four-CD boxed set), Rhino, 1999.

Complete Greatest Hits, Rhino, 2002.

(Songwriter) *Beautiful: A Tribute to Gorden Lightfoot,* Northern-Blues Music/Borealis Recording, 2003.

Harmony, Linus Entertainment, 2004.

Many albums have been rerecorded with slight alterations; composer of numerous songs for other artists, including Peter, Paul & Mary, Judy Collins, and Johnny Cash. Poetic selections from Lightfoot's songs are collected in *I Wish You Good Spaces,* Blue Mountain Arts, 1977.

ADAPTATIONS: The lyrics of Lightfoot's song "The Pony Man" were adapted into a children's book of the same name, Harper's Magazine Press, 1972. Lightfoot's songs have been featured in movies, including *One Hundred Years Young* (television movie), 1967; *Hail, Hero!,* 1969; *Paperback Hero* (also known as *Le coq du village*), 1973; *Lighthead,* 2002; and *The Brown Bunny,* 2003.

SIDELIGHTS: Gordon Lightfoot has been called an unpretentious singer and songwriter, but despite his simple arrangements, his evocative ballads have made him one of the most popular and enduring folk singers of the late twentieth century, while one of Lightfoot's best-known songs is "The Wreck of the Edmund Fitzgerald," about a maritime disaster on Lake Superior in 1975, he has also sung of Canadian history and culture in many other songs. "His evocative lyrics sweep you across the land with painterly observations," *Chatelaine* contributor Peter Goddard commented in a review of *Waiting for You,* an album that is particularly rich with Canadian lore.

Lightfoot is known, too, for the hundreds of songs he has written both solo and with other artists. "I've always enjoyed writing, because I like getting on the roll of knowing it was going someplace, beginning to ending," he told Rod Harmon for the *Knight Ridder/ Tribune News Service.* Lightfoot added, "I like exploring the various vowels, the A, E, I, O, U. You gotta use 'em all. That way, you get some variety in your rhyme schemes. Because I still believe that songs have to rhyme or they're not songs."

Lightfoot has continued to write new songs and tour, although he was forced to take several months off after he suffered an abdominal aneurysm in 2002 that left him in a coma for more than a month and which kept him confined to a hospital bed for three months. In April of 2003, he granted his first post-illness interview, announcing his plans to release another album, the vocal and guitar tracks for which had been recorded before his illness, and return to touring. During that year, his lifetime of work was acknowledged by a number of hall of fame inductions and with a tribute album recorded by a number of singers and groups, including Bruce Cockburn, Cowboy Junkies, Tragically Hip, Maria Muldaur, and Blackie and the Rodeo Kings. The album, *Beautiful: A Tribute to Gorden Lightfoot,* was the joint project of two independent Canadian labels, Northern-Blues Music of Ottawa and Borealis Recording of Toronto. Colin Linden contributed to the project as guitarist and producer. Larry LeBlanc noted in *Billboard* that, "despite Lightfoot's repertoire of more than 100 songs spread across some 19 albums, Linden says it was often difficult to match artists to song. 'Gordon casts such a big shadow,' he explains. 'It's hard for another singer/songwriter to do something that wouldn't pale in comparison.'" Lightfoot favors the Martin guitar, and in 2001, the company honored him with a limited edition D-18GL, only sixty of which were manufactured.

Early in 2004, the post-production work on *Harmony* was completed, and Lightfoot also shot a music video for his new single, "Inspiration Lady." Before the release of *Harmony,* a number of the tracks were made available through iTunes. In May, the album was released, Lightfoot's twentieth of original material. Mike Regenstreif wrote in *Sing Out!* that "Lightfoot's voice sounds frailer than it did years ago. But it still communicates both the implicit and explicit emotional content of his songs. *Harmony* marks a welcome return, and return to form by a musical legend." Lightfoot's first performance since his illness was in his hometown of Orilla, and he returned to the concert stage in November of 2004 in Hamilton, Ontario.

Lightfoot continued playing for his fans in 2005, and in April he began his first concert tour since 2002. Randy Lewis reported on a stop in Cerritos, California in the *Los Angeles Times,* noting that although Lightfoot is only a few years older than fellow Canadians Joni Mitchell and Neil Young, whose careers also began in the 1960s and fully developed in the 1970s, he "always seemed more the elder statesman. That's less because of his age than an artistic sensibility that mines the permanence of the land beneath him and the history behind him." Lewis said of *Harmony* that "it is musically and lyrically in keeping with his [Lightfoot's] '60s and '70s work."

BIOGRAPHICAL AND CRITICAL SOURCES:

BOOKS

Contemporary Musicians, Volume 3, Thomson Gale (Detroit, MI), 1990.

PERIODICALS

Billboard, September 6, 2003, Larry Leblanc, "Folk Vet Lightfoot Praises 'Beatiful' Tribute," p. 52.
Chatelaine, April, 1993, Peter Goddard, review of *Waiting for You,* p. 18.
Knight Ridder/Tribune News Service, March 21, 2001, Rod Harmon, interview with Lightfoot, p. K3234.
Los Angeles Times, April 25, 2005, Randy Lewis, "Pop Music Review; Spring Is Back in Lightfoot's Step," p. E2.
Sing Out!, fall, 2004, Mike Regenstreif, review of *Harmony,* p. 150.

ONLINE

Gordon Lightfoot Home Page, http://www.lightfoot.ca (July 6, 2005).

Internet Movie Database, http://www.imdb.com/ (July 6, 2005), "Gordon Lightfoot."*

*   *   *

LIGHTFOOT, Gordon Meredith
  See LIGHTFOOT, Gordon

*   *   *

LINDSAY, Nicola

PERSONAL: Female. *Education:* Studied at Italian Institute, Dublin, Ireland, and Irish Writers' Centre.

ADDRESSES: Home—County Kildare, Ireland. *Agent*—c/o Author Mail, Poolbeg Press, 123 Baldoyle Industrial Estate, Baldoyle, Dublin 13, Ireland. *E-mail*—nlindsay@nicolalindsay.ie.

CAREER: Writer, poet, actor, and broadcaster. Formerly worked as a nurse, flautist, and model; actor in numerous films, including *Zardoz, The American, The Ambassador,* and *The General.* Has also appeared on Irish soap operas, including *Glenroe* and *Fair City,* and has been featured in fashion program *Off the Rails.* Performs personal monologues and works in broadcasting.

MEMBER: PEN, Irish Writers Union, Irish Actors Equity.

AWARDS, HONORS: Yvonne O'Connor Perpetual Trophy for Poetry; Gerard Manly Hopkins Annual International School Award; Dunlavin Festival of the Arts award; Drogheda Creative-Writing Groups award; Capricorn International Authors Guild award; Jonathan Swift Poetry Competition award.

WRITINGS:

FICTION, EXCEPT AS NOTED

Batty Cat, Kestrel Books (Wicklow, Ireland), 1998.
A Place for Unicorns, Kestrel Books (Wicklow, Ireland), 1999.

Lines of Thought (poetry), Kestrel Books (Wicklow, Ireland), 1999.
Diving through Clouds, Poolbeg (Dublin, Ireland), 2001.
Eden Fading, Poolbeg (Dublin, Ireland), 2003.
Tumbling Jude, Poolbeg (Dublin, Ireland), 2004.
Butterfly, Poolbeg (Dublin, Ireland), 2005.

Writings have appeared in anthologies and periodicals published in England and Ireland. Creator of *Selected Poems* (audio recording).

SIDELIGHTS: Nicola Lindsay began her career as a nurse, a model, and a flautist, and then went on to become an actor and broadcaster before turning her talents to poetry and fiction. In her novel *Diving through Clouds,* Lindsay tells the story of Kate, who has died from cancer and finds herself caught in limbo watching the lives of her loved ones, including her unloving husband, her daughter, and her best friend. Because she is dead, Kate can also read peoples' minds and discovers that her husband and best friend were having an affair. In addition, she follows the life of her grandson and has an opportunity to intervene in way to help the boy and his mother. Aided by an exuberantly upbeat angel named Thomas who loves jazz, Kate eventually turns from being a mischievous onlooker and prankster to putting her life in the proper perspective, including her own affair with a gardener—so Kate can move on to the next level of existence. Before she leaves for good, Kate wants to achieve her goal of bringing about the return home of her daughter Celia, who fled her controlling father years earlier. Noting that the novel requires "a major suspension of disbelief," a *Kirkus Reviews* contributor commented that "lively dialogue and an affecting portrayal of a boy who desperately needs grandmotherly guidance . . . make a peculiar contrast with the appallingly realistic portrait of passive, self-deprecating Kate's marriage." June Sawyers, writing in *Booklist,* called the book "touching, humorous, and ultimately sweet," and noted that it is "a lovely, enjoyable read."

Lindsay told *CA:* "I first became interested in writing at school but never for one moment considered the possibility of it as a career. Only when I was in my early fifties and at a low point in my life did I start writing seriously. At first, it was only poetry and then I progressed to short stories, monologues, reviews and, finally, novels.

"Although I read a wide range of authors, particularly the contemporary American, English, Indian and African writers, I try not to let any of them influence my work as I have always wanted to develop my own style and voice. When I am working on a novel, I try to write five days a week from ten in the morning to five or six in the evening with a brief break in the middle of the day to re-establish my circulation. I never play music and need complete peace and quiet, which is easily achieved as my study looks out onto the garden and cows grazing in the fields beyond. I regularly go back and read what I have just written out loud and find this especially important to see if the dialogue rings true or not.

One of the most surprising things I have learned as a writer is that my characters and the plot quite often develop in a way I have not planned.

"I think my favourite book I have written is the most recent, *Butterfly.* Possibly because it has only just been published and like the most recently born child, it occupies my mind a lot. Also, there is quite a lot of myself in the main character, Hebe Sayer, which came out in surprising ways.

"I hope that anyone reading my books will enjoy the story, will want to know what happens next, will want to engage with the characters, and will want to rush out and buy one of the other novels of mine that they haven't yet read! I never try to preach or put over a message. I am trying to write in a way that will, hopefully, strike a chord with the reader, be thought-provoking as well as enjoyable. I also do my best to craft each book better than the last, and hope that this is apparent to the discerning reader."

BIOGRAPHICAL AND CRITICAL SOURCES:

PERIODICALS

Booklist, March 1, 2005, June Sawyers, review of *Diving through Clouds,* p. 1142.
Kirkus Reviews, January 1, 2005, review of *Diving through Clouds,* p. 12.

ONLINE

Nicola Lindsay Home Page, http://www.nicola-lindsay.ie (June 3, 2005).

LITTLE, Benilde 1958-
(Benilde Elease Little)

PERSONAL: Born 1958, in Newark, NJ; daughter of a nurse and a General Motors employee; married; husband's name, Clifford (a stockbroker); children: a daughter and a son. *Education:* Howard University. B.A., c. 1980; graduate study at Northwestern University.

ADDRESSES: Agent—c/o Author Mail, Free Press, 1230 Avenue of the Americas, New York, NY 10020.

CAREER: Journalist and novelist. Worked at *Newark Star-Ledger; People* magazine, journalist for five years; *Essence* magazine, entertainment editor. Reporter for *Cleveland Plain Dealer.*

WRITINGS:

Good Hair (novel), Simon & Schuster (New York, NY), 1996.
The Itch (novel), Simon & Schuster (New York, NY), 1998.
Acting Out (novel), Free Press (New York, NY), 2003.
Who Does She Think She Is? (novel), Free Press (New York, NY), 2005.

Contributor to periodicals, including *In-Style* and *Allure.* Contributing editor at *Heart and Soul.*

ADAPTATIONS: Good Hair and *The Itch* were adapted for film.

SIDELIGHTS: Benilde Little is a journalist turned novelist whose first novel, *Good Hair,* received critical praise and became a best seller. The book is about a middle-class, African-American woman named Alice Lee who is working as a reporter in New York City when she falls in love with a rich and successful surgeon named Jack Russworm. The only problem, in Alice's eyes, is that Jack is an upper-class African American who she perceives as someone with little understanding or caring about the plight of many poorer blacks. As a result, she perceives him as haughty and cold in some ways. The relationship develops further problems, including a wayward sexual liaison, until Alice reevaluates her outlook on both life and the man she loves. A *Publishers Weekly* contributor noted that Little "shows a discerning eye for class divisions among socially mobile blacks and an astute insight into the damaged psyches that can result." The reviewer went on to call the novel "a compelling read." In *Essence* a contributor noted that the author "offers a searing look at the ways in which class and upbringing prejudice our responses to one another."

In *The Itch* Little focuses on the privileged Abra, who attended an Ivy League school and never had the problem of worrying about money. She also seemingly has a loving and successful husband. Abra's close friends come from similar backgrounds and somewhat similar fairy-tale lives. As the novel progresses, however, each begin to confront the downside of the American Dream, including lost love and the search for a deeper meaning to life. After Abra discovers that her husband is cheating on her, she moves with her friend Natasha, a filmmaker, to Hollywood, where she must cope with the single life and dating. Another friend of Abra's, Cullen Dixon, leaves her safe marriage for a lesbian relationship. A *Publishers Weekly* contributor reviewed the novel and noted that "What distinguishes Little among commercial novelists is her honest ambivalence toward her characters' conspicuous consumption; their glitz comes at a spiritual price." Lillian Lewis, writing in *Booklist,* called the novel "a winning tale" and "a good African American novel."

Little once again writes about a good life taking a detour in *Acting Out.* Ina finds herself alone after her husband leaves her for a model after more than decade of marriage. Ina decides she needs time to think and look after herself so she leaves her three children with her parents. After a series of affairs and soul searching, she encounters her ex-husband's girlfriend, which sets Ina in a new direction of reconciliation and a heightened awareness of what really matters in life. "A familiar women's fiction premise . . . is well served by Little's . . . feisty, conversational style and her memorable depiction of black upper-class life," wrote a *Publishers Weekly* contributor. Angela Bronner, writing in *Black Issues Book Review,* commented that Little "tells an engaging contemporary tale in all its colors, nuances and shades." As an *Ebony* contributor noted, "Once again she has created characters that are real and memorable, despite their flaws."

Who Does She Think She Is? finds the beautiful and well-to-do Aisha Branch planning her wedding to an extremely rich white man. Aisha's wedding plans go awry, however, when she meets a successful, older, and wealthy black man. Intertwined with Aisha's story is the story of Aisha's mother, Camille, and her grandmother, Geneva. Camille is in her forties and undergoing a sexual reawakening, while Geneva's story is one of an outwardly respectable black woman who ends up alienating her family by deciding to live a life on the road with a jazz musician. A *Kirkus Reviews* contributor noted that "it's a rare novel that depicts older women as real people capable of change, which makes Little's portrayal of Camille and Geneva as admirable as it is entertaining." Karen Fauls-Traynor, writing in *Library Journal,* called the effort a "fast-paced novel" and "entertaining." A *Publishers Weekly* contributor commented that "Little strikes a nice balance between heartfelt intergenerational saga and sexy love story."

BIOGRAPHICAL AND CRITICAL SOURCES:

BOOKS

Phelps, Shirelle, editor, *Contemporary Black Biography,* Volume 21, Thomson Gale (Detroit, MI), 1999.

PERIODICALS

Black Issues Book Review, January-February, 2003, Angela Bronner, review of *Acting Out,* p. 30.
Booklist, October 15, 1996, Mary Carroll, review of *Good Hair,* p. 405; April, 1998, Lillian Lewis, review of *The Itch,* p. 1278; December 15, 2002, Lillian Lewis, review of *Acting Out,* p. 733.
Detroit Free Press, January 28, 2003, Marta Salij, review of *Acting Out.*
Ebony, March, 2003, review of *Acting Out,* p. 22.
Entertainment Weekly, October 18, 1996, Vanessa V. Friedman, review of *Good Hair,* p. 75; June 26, 1998, Lori L. Tharp, review of *The Itch,* p. 120.
Essence, September, 1996, review of *Good Hair,* p. 100; June, 2005, review of *Who Does She Think She Is?,* p. 107.
Jet, August 10, 1998, "Acclaimed Author Benilde Little Feted at 'Tea for Ladies Only!' in L.A.," p. 38.
Kirkus Reviews, November 1, 2002, review of *Acting Out,* p. 1557; February 15, 2005, review of *Who Does She Think She Is?,* p. 193.

Library Journal, November 1, 2002, Ann Burns, review of *Acting Out,* p. 111; January, 2003, Beth Gibbs, review of *Acting Out,* p. 156; April 1, 2005, Karen Fauls-Traynor, review of *Who Does She Think She Is?,* p. 86.

People, February 10, 1997, review of *Good Hair,* p. 37; June 6, 2005, review of *Who Does She Think She Is?,* p. 49.

Publishers Weekly, August 26, 1996, review of *Good Hair,* p. 76; May 11, 1998, review of *The Itch,* p. 49; November 25, 2002, review of *Acting Out,* p. 42; April 11, 2005, review of *Who Does She Think She Is?,* p. 34.

ONLINE

Benilde Little Home Page, http://www.benildelittle. com (July 11, 2005).*

*   *   *

LITTLE, Benilde Elease
    See LITTLE, Benilde

*   *   *

LONG, Kate 1965(?)-

PERSONAL: Born c. 1965; married; husband a government worker; children: two.

ADDRESSES: Home—Shropshire, England. *Agent*—c/o Author Mail, Picador, 175 5th Ave., New York, NY 10010.

CAREER: Writer and educator. High school English teacher, c. 1991-2004.

WRITINGS:

FICTION

The Bad Mother's Handbook (novel), Picador (London, England), 2004.
Swallowing Grandma (novel), Picador (London, England), 2005.

SIDELIGHTS: Kate Long retired from teaching high school after her first novel, *The Bad Mother's Handbook,* became a best seller in England. The novel focuses on several women in the same British family struggling to better themselves and make ends meet, with the individual characters narrating their own stories. In an interview with Stephen Moss for the London *Guardian,* the author explained her choice of characters: "I couldn't think of any female writers who were writing about this kind of grey class that's just out of the working class and is clinging by its fingertips to middleclassness. All the novels I read that I thought were going to be about my kind of life—about women juggling lots of things—were actually about women with fantastic jobs, in London, with nannies. There didn't seem to be anything at all for me, reflecting my kinds of concerns."

In the novel, the character of Karen is upset that her seventeen-year-old daughter Charlotte has become pregnant. Karen's concern is that her daughter is following in her own footsteps: she had Charlotte when she was sixteen and knows firsthand how such an early pregnancy can be a barrier to a better life and, in Charlotte's case, college. Karen's mother, Nan, is sick and declining rapidly when Karen learns she is adopted. She sets out to find her birth mother, thinking that possibly this may put her in touch with a better, middle-class existence. In a review of *The Bad Mother's Handbook* in *Booklist,* Joanne Wilkinson called the novel "charming, [and] funny" and commended the author for her "her saucy humor and resourceful characters." As a *Publishers Weekly* reviewer noted, "Long tells the story . . . through shifting first-person sections . . . moving wittily and gracefully toward an ending that's happily realistic." Long is also the author of *Swallowing Grandma,* about a teenage girl and the aging grandmother who is the girl's only parent.

BIOGRAPHICAL AND CRITICAL SOURCES:

PERIODICALS

Booklist, March 1, 2005, Joanne Wilkinson, review of *The Bad Mother's Handbook,* p. 1138.
Guardian (London, England), March 31, 2004, Stephen Moss, "G2: Portrait: The Tesco Triumph," p. 8.

Kirkus Reviews, January 1, 2005, review of *The Bad Mother's Handbook,* p. 13.

Library Journal, March 15, 2005, Amy Brozio-Andrews, review of *The Bad Mother's Handbook,* p. 73.

Publishers Weekly, March 28, 2005, review of *The Bad Mother's Handbook,* p. 56.*

*   *   *

LORIE, James Hirsch 1922-2005

OBITUARY NOTICE— See index for *CA* sketch: Born February 23, 1922, in Kansas City, MO; died of pancreatic cancer, August 6, 2005, in Chicago, IL. Lorie was a longtime business professor at the University of Chicago. He created a stock-price database and helped to make the Chicago business school a national leader. A graduate of Cornell University, where he earned a B.A. in 1942 and an M.A. in 1945, he went on to complete his Ph.D. at the University of Chicago in 1947. That year, he joined the faculty as an assistant professor, and remained there for the rest of his academic career. Rising to the position of professor of business administration by 1956, he was also the graduate school's associate dean in the late 1950s, director of research in the early 1960s, and founding director of the Center for Research in Security Prices from 1960 to 1975. He retired in 1992 as Eli B. and Harriet B. Williams professor emeritus. During his time as associate dean, Lorie was credited with attracting several Nobel Prize winners to teach at the university. As director of the research center, he headed the arduous task of recording the history of stock prices from 1926 until 1960. This valuable information formed indispensable groundwork for further economic research that, among other things, led to the establishment of index funds. Lorie wrote, cowrote, or edited several books in his field, including *Causes of Annual Fluctuations in the Production of Livestock and Livestock Products* (1947), *The Stock Market: Theories and Evidence* (1973), and *A Half-Century of Returns on Stocks and Bonds* (1977).

OBITUARIES AND OTHER SOURCES:

PERIODICALS

Chicago Tribune, August 11, 2005, section 3, p. 9.

ONLINE

University of Chicago Chronicle Online, http://chronicle.uchicago.edu/ (October 6, 2005).

*   *   *

LOUIS, Laura Glen

PERSONAL: Born in Macau S.A.R. (Special Administrative Region), China; immigrated to United States; married; children: one son.

ADDRESSES: Agent—c/o Author Mail, Harcourt, 6277 Sea Harbor Dr., Orlando, FL 32887.

CAREER: Writer.

AWARDS, HONORS: Katherine Anne Porter Prize, 1990, for short story "Verge."

WRITINGS:

Talking in the Dark: Stories, Harcourt (New York, NY), 2001.

Work represented in anthologies, including *Best American Short Stories,* 1994 and 1997.

WORK IN PROGRESS: A novel.

SIDELIGHTS: Laura Glen Louis was born in China and immigrated to the United States from Hong Kong as a child. Many of the characters in the eight stories of her first collection, *Talking in the Dark: Stories,* are also Chinese American. The stories are about love and loss and vulnerability, and several feature middle-aged men who leave their wives for younger women. The title story features a woman who seeks comfort from her married doctor when her husband abandons her. The story "Fur," which is about a man whose dead wife's mink coat is taken by a gold-digging young woman, was chosen for inclusion in the 1994 edition of *Best American Short Stories.* Other stories include a tale about a woman who allows herself to be seduced by her daughter's boyfriend, a couple who lose their baby to crib death, and a young tennis player who becomes the object of an older man's obsession.

Reviewing *Talking in the Dark,* Will Blythe wrote in the *New York Times Book Review* that Louis's "prose aims for a kind of poetic intensity. The best stories here keep the rhetoric fierce and astringent." *Boston Review* critic Randall Curb described the book as "a debut collection of lean, sinewy prose and tightly compressed emotional implications, all related to matters of the heart."

BIOGRAPHICAL AND CRITICAL SOURCES:

PERIODICALS

Boston Review, April-May, 2001, Randall Curb, review of *Talking in the Dark: Stories.*

Kirkus Reviews, February 1, 2001, review of *Talking in the Dark,* p. 133.

Library Journal, January 1, 2001, Debbie Bogenschutz, review of *Talking in the Dark,* p. 160.

New York Times Book Review, July 15, 2001, Will Blythe, review of *Talking in the Dark.*

Publishers Weekly, February 19, 2001, review of *Talking in the Dark,* p. 67.

Washington Post Book World, April 8, 2001, Elizabeth Roca, review of *Talking in the Dark,* p. T13.*

*   *   *

LYNDS, Dennis 1924-2005

(William Arden, Nick Carter, Michael Collins, John Crowe, Carl Dekker, Maxwell Grant, Mark Sadler)

OBITUARY NOTICE— See index for *CA* sketch: Born January 15, 1924, in St. Louis, MO; died of septic shock due to bowel necrosis and multiple organ failure, August 19, 2005, in San Francisco, CA. Author. Lynds was an award-winning mystery novelist who was particularly well known for his "Dan Fortune" series written under the pen name Michael Collins. After distinguished service in the U.S. Army infantry during World War II (where he earned such medals as the Purple Heart and Bronze Star), he studied chemistry at Hofstra University. He completed his bachelor's degree there in 1949, and went on to finish a second degree in journalism from Syracuse University in 1951. Lynds combined these two disciplines by working as an editor for a variety of science magazines during the 1950s and 1960s, including *Chemical Week, Chemical Engineering Progress,* and *Chemical Equipment.* His first novel, *Combat Soldier* (1962), was based on his war experiences; during the 1960s, he also wrote for such television series as *The Man from U.N.C.L.E.* and *Alfred Hitchcock Presents.* By the mid-1960s Lynds was producing a steady stream of mystery and detective novels under various pseudonyms. His work was often compared to that of his friend Kenneth Miller, who wrote as Ross Macdonald, and he was credited with lending his heroes a realistic, emotional hue. Over the years, he won a number of awards for his fiction, including an Edgar Allan Poe Award in 1968 and a Special Award from the Mystery Writers of America the next year. In 1988 he also received a lifetime achievement award from the Private Eye Writers of America, and in 2003 he was presented with the Marlowe Award from the Southern California chapter of the Mystery Writers of America for his body of work. Lynds wrote over eighty novels and hundreds of short stories and was still writing at the time of his death. Lynds was also a mentor to his fellow writers, offering encouragement to aspiring novelists at the Santa Barbara Writers Conference and working with the Authors Guild on issues regarding copyright protection.

OBITUARIES AND OTHER SOURCES:

PERIODICALS

Chicago Tribune, August 26, 2005, section 3, p. 9.

Los Angeles Times, August 25, 2005, p. B10.

New York Times, August 24, 2005, p. C16.

Washington Post, August 25, 2005, p. B6.

M

MAGEE, Jeffrey 1961-

PERSONAL: Born 1961. *Education:* Oberlin College, B.M., 1983; University of California, Berkeley, M.A., 1986; University of Michigan, Ph.D., 1992.

ADDRESSES: Office—School of Music, Indiana University, 107 S. Indiana Ave., Bloomington, IN 47405-7000. *E-mail*—jmagee@indiana.edu.

CAREER: Educator and writer. Indiana University, associate professor of musicology. Executive editor of "Music of the United States of America" (series of scholarly recorded editions), for National Endowment for the Humanities.

WRITINGS:

(With Richard Crawford) *Jazz Standards on Record, 1900-1942: A Core Repertory,* Center for Black Music Research, Columbia College Chicago (Chicago, IL), 1992.
The Uncrowned King of Swing: Fletcher Henderson and Big Band Jazz, Oxford University Press (New York, NY), 2005.

Author's writings on music have appeared in numerous periodicals and anthologies, including *American Music, Lenox Avenue, International Dictionary of Black Composers, Musical Quarterly, The Cambridge History of American Music,* and *Journal of the American Musicological Society.*

SIDELIGHTS: Jeffrey Magee studies and teaches American music with a special focus on jazz, ragtime, and popular songs. He is also the author of *The Uncrowned King of Swing: Fletcher Henderson and Big Band Jazz.* Considered the first comprehensive biography of the musician, the book chronicles Henderson's life from Atlanta to New York, where he became a big band leader, as well as a talented composer and arranger. Henderson provided songs and arrangements to many of the Swing Era's biggest stars, including Benny Goodman and the Dorsey Brothers. In addition to chronicling Henderson's life and career, Magee provides analyses of many of Henderson's musical scores.

Writing in the *Los Angeles Times,* Don Heckman pointed out that the author provides a valuable insight into "Henderson's identity as both a creative facilitator of other musicians' efforts and the frustrated composer-arranger of music that was a foundational element in the Swing Era." In a review in the *Boston Globe,* Renee Graham commented, "Magee is less concerned with personal minutiae than his subject's progression as a musician. This may leave those in search of a more straightforward Henderson biography wanting, but creates room for an engrossing history of jazz's evolution between the world wars." A *Publishers Weekly* contributor called the book "more a 'portrait of a musical collaboration' than a biography," and wrote that it serves as "a welcome addition to the study of swing." Dave Szatmary commented in the *Library Journal* that the author "does an excellent job of placing his subject in the context of uncertain social changes in the African American community."

BIOGRAPHICAL AND CRITICAL SOURCES:

PERIODICALS

Boston Globe, January 12, 2005, Renee Graham, review of *The Uncrowned King of Swing: Fletcher Henderson and Big Band Jazz,* p. C6.

Library Journal, January 1, 2005, Dave Szatmary, review of *The Uncrowned King of Swing,* p. 115.

Los Angeles Times, March 27, 2005, Don Heckman, review of *The Uncrowned King of Swing,* p. E39.

Publishers Weekly, December 6, 2004, review of *The Uncrowned King of Swing,* p. 52.

ONLINE

Indiana University Media Relations Web site, http://newsinfo.iu.edu/ (June 3, 2005), biographical information on author.*

* * *

MAHBUBANI, Kishore 1948-

PERSONAL: Born October 24, 1948, in Singapore; son of Mohandas and Janki (Devki) Mahbubani; Married Anne King Markey, March 30, 1985; children: three. *Education:* University of Singapore, B.A. (honors), 1971; Dalhousie University, M.A., 1976. *Hobbies and other interests:* Tennis, reading.

ADDRESSES: Office—National University of Singapore, Lee Kuan Yew School of Public Policy, 29 Heng Mui Keng Terrace, Singapore 119620. *E-mail*—sppdean@nus.edu.sg.

CAREER: Civil servant, ambassador, and writer. Ministry of Foreign Affairs, Singapore, administrator, 1971-73; Singapore Embassy, Phnom Penh, Kampuchea, charge d'affaires, 1973-74; Singapore High Commission, Kuala Lumpur, counselor, 1976-79; Ministry of Foreign Affairs, deputy director, 1980-82; Singapore Embassy, Washington, DC, deputy chief of mission, 1982-84; Singapore Permanent Mission to the United Nations, New York, NY, permanent representative, 1984-89, deputy secretary, 1998-2004; Singapore Foreign Ministry, permanent secretary, 1993-98; United Nations Security Council, president,

2001-02; Lee Kuan Yew School of Public Policy, National University of Singapore, dean 2004—. Fellow at Center for International Affairs, Harvard University, 1991-92. Served in advisory capacities to numerous organizations, including International Peace Academy, Institute of International Education, United Nations Association of the United States of America, Young Presidents' Organization, Global Strategy Group, and International Center for Ethics, Justice, and Public Life at Brandeis University.

AWARDS, HONORS: President's Scholarship, 1967; honorary doctorate, Dalhousie University, 1995; Public Administration Medal (Gold), Singapore Government, 1998; Foreign Policy Association Medal, 2004.

WRITINGS:

Can Asians Think?, Times Books International (Singapore), 1996, published as *Can Asians Think?; Understanding the Divide between East and West,* Steerforth Press (South Royalton, VT), 2002.

Beyond the Age of Innocence: A Worldly View of America, Public Affairs (New York, NY), 2005.

Has written numerous articles for professional journals, including *Foreign Affairs, National Interest,* the *New York Times* and the *Wall Street Journal.*

SIDELIGHTS: A long-time Singapore diplomat who spent many years working throughout the world, including the United States, Kishore Mahbubani is the author of the controversial book, *Can Asians Think?; Understanding the Divide between East and West.* In this collection of essays, the author explores the history of Asian societies over the past few centuries in the context of a future world dominated by Asian economies. Central to Mahbubani's thesis is the question of how well Asian societies can integrate themselves into the modern world while maintaining their historical roots and traditions. In an interview for *Salon.com* the author explained to Suzy Hansen: "In the year 1000 the most successful, the most flourishing and the most dynamic societies in the world were Asian. Europe was still struggling out of the Middle Ages and North America hadn't been discovered. One thousand years later you get the exact reverse of that: the most dynamic and flourishing societies are in North

America, Europe is one tier below and Asia is far behind. And my question is why? How did societies that were once at the leading edge of global civilization lose an entire millennium?"

The first edition of *Can Asians Think?* was written and published in 1996, while Asia was experiencing a new era of economic success. In his essays, Mahbubani argues that this success will ultimately lead Asian countries such as Japan and China to become the world's economic leaders while Western nations will experience a steady decline in influence and power. Mahbubani also discusses his belief that this decline will be due largely to Western arrogance and hubris reflected by an insistence that capitalism and democracy are the only ways to conduct a successful society and establish an economically advanced nation. In a review in *Time*, Joshua Cooper Ramo commented that "Mahbubani writes with a diplomat's charm, gleefully untangling political knots into simple threads." Lucian W. Pye, writing in *Foreign Affairs*, called the author "an exceptionally lively and provocative polemicist."

In *Beyond the Age of Innocence: A Worldly View of America* the author analyzes what he sees as a weakening of prestige and power in America's global influence largely due to how other countries view the United States. According to the author, these negative views are based on far more than any single U.S. presidential administration. While the United States has done more than any other country to help the world, it has also failed in many areas, causing harm through unfulfilled promises and mixed messages. A *Publishers Weekly* contributor called the book a "lucid analysis of America's diminishing prestige," and Brendan Driscoll, writing in *Booklist,* noted that the author's "obligatory discussion of the U.S. and Islam is eclipsed by his astute analysis of Chinese-American relations." In a review in *Newsweek International,* Max Boot noted that Mahbubani is only one of a recent spate of authors "castigating American policymakers," but added that the author "delivers one of the more gentle indictments, with a more-in-sorrow-than-in-anger tone."

BIOGRAPHICAL AND CRITICAL SOURCES:

PERIODICALS

Booklist, March 1, 2005, Brendan Driscoll, review of *Beyond the Age of Innocence: A Worldly View of America*, p. 1119.

Foreign Affairs, May, 1999, Lucian W. Pye, review of *Can Asians Think?*, p. 150.
Fortune, November 26, 2001, "Kishore Mahbubani: U.N. Ambassador, Singapore" (interview), p. 106.
Kirkus Reviews, January 15, 2005, review of *Beyond the Age of Innocence*, p. 104.
Newsweek International, April 11, 2005, Max Boot, review of *Beyond the Age of Innocence*, p. 97.
Publishers Weekly, January 24, 2005, review of *Beyond the Age of Innocence*, p. 231.
Time, July 12, 1999, Joshua Cooper Ramo, review of *Can Asians Think?*, p. 40.

ONLINE

Carnegie Council on Ethics and International Affairs, http://www.carnegiecouncil.org/ (January 24, 2004), edited transcript of remarks given by author at "Books for Breakfast" meeting.
Global Policy Forum Online, http://www.globalpolicy.org/ (July 12, 2005), profile of author.
Kishore Mahbubani Home Page, http://www.mahbubani.net (July 12, 2005).
National University of Singapore Web site, http://usp1.scholars.nus.edu.sg/ (July 12, 2005), faculty profile of author.
Salon.com, http://salon.com/ (March 25, 2002), Suzy Hansen, "'Can Asians Think?'*

*   *   *

MAHON, Annette

PERSONAL: Born in Hilo, HI. *Education:* Master's degree. *Hobbies and other interests:* Quilting.

ADDRESSES: Home—Paradise Valley, AZ. *Agent*—c/o Author Mail, Avalon Books, 160 Madison Ave., 5th Fl., New York, NY 10016. *E-mail*—Annette@annettemahon.com; annettemahon@aol.com.

CAREER: Writer. Formerly worked in public and university libraries; worked for a Veteran's Administration Hospital Library for one year. Host of library cable television show, *The Children's Room,* in Fort Wayne, IN.

MEMBER: Romance Writers of America, Mystery Writers of America, Sisters in Crime, Novelists, Inc.

WRITINGS:

ROMANCE NOVELS

Above the Rainbow, Avalon Books (New York, NY), 1995.
Lei of Love, Avalon Books (New York, NY), 1996.
Maui Rose, Avalon Books (New York, NY), 1996.
Chase Your Dreams, Avalon Books (New York, NY), 1997.
Just Friends, Avalon Books (New York, NY), 1998.
The Secret Admirer, Avalon Books (New York, NY), 2001.
The Secret Wedding, Avalon Books (New York, NY), 2002.
The Secret Santa, Avalon Books (New York, NY), 2003.
The Secret Beau, Avalon Books (New York, NY), 2004.
The Secret Wish, Avalon Books (New York, NY), 2006.

MYSTERIES

A Phantom Death, Avalon Books (New York, NY), 2000.
An Ominous Death, Five Star Press (Waterville, ME), 2006.

OTHER

Author's articles have appeared in *Mystery Readers Journal* and *TCI Bulletin,* for Thimble Collectors International.

SIDELIGHTS: Annette Mahon spent many years as a librarian before turning her attention to writing romance and mystery books full time. In her romances, Mahon is noted for her Hawaiian settings and multicultural lovers, and in many instances, she involves her romantic leads in unsolved mysteries. In *Just Friends,* for example, Kimo Ahuna becomes involved with Ilima Lyman while trying to find out who caused the hit-and-run accident that put Ilima's brother in a coma. *Lei of Love,* pairs Dana Long with Brian Veira, a police detective looking for Dana's missing father.

An avid quilter, Mahon has also put her avocation into her books, such as her romance novel *Chase Your Dreams,* which features Pamela Perreira, who owns a successful quilt shop and falls in love with a triathlete. Mahon wrote a prequel to this book titled *Above the Rainbow.*

In *The Secret Wedding,* the author tells the story of a Hawaiian resort's wedding coordinator, Luana, who develops a relationship with Jake Lawrence, who has asked her to arrange a wedding for a secret celebrity couple. Mahon writes of the romance between Kim Ascencion and her high school classmate Greg Yamamoto in her novel *The Secret Beau.* Greg, a nerd in high school, now is a handsome and successful veterinarian. The starting point for their relationship is when Kim invites Greg to pretend to be her boyfriend for a wedding she is attending. Kristin Ramsdell, writing in *Library Journal,* noted that the author "does a masterly job of putting a Hawaiian twist on an old theme."

BIOGRAPHICAL AND CRITICAL SOURCES:

PERIODICALS

Booklist, September 15, 2000, Nina Davis, reviews of *Maui Rose, Lei of Love, Just Friends, Chase Your Dreams,* and *Above the Rainbow,* p. 224; September 15, 2002, John Charles and Shelley Mosley, review of *The Secret Wedding,* p. 219.
Library Journal, August, 2004, Kristin Ramsdell, review of *The Secret Beau,* p. 56.

ONLINE

Annette Mahon Home Page, http://www.annettemahon.com (June 6, 2005).*

*   *   *

MANCHETTE, Jean-Patrick 1942-1995
(J.P. Bastid, J.P. Manchette)

PERSONAL: Born in Marseille, France, 1942; died of lung cancer, 1995, in Paris, France. *Hobbies and other interests:* Played jazz saxophone.

WRITINGS:

(As J.P. Manchette) *Nada* (novel), Gallimard (Paris, France), 1972.
(With Michel Martens) *Les tours d'angoisse* (novel), Gallimard (Paris, France), 1974.

(As J.P. Bastid; with R. Koch) *Le passeur basque* (novel), Presses de la Cité (Paris, France), 1975.

(As J.P. Bastid; with Michel Martens) *Le tapir* (novel), J.C. Lattès (Paris, France), 1976.

(As J.P. Manchette) *Que d'os!* (novel), Gallimard (Paris, France, 1976.

Petit bleu de la côte ouest (novel), 1976, translated by Donald Nicholson-Smith as *Three to Kill,* City Lights (San Francisco, CA), 2002.

Fatale (novel), Gallimard (Paris, France), 1977.

(With Michel Martens) *F.O.O.D.* (novel), J.C. Lattès (Paris, France), 1977.

Mélanie White, illustrated by Serge Clerc, Hachette (Paris, France), 1979.

(With others) *Cache ta joie, ou, Le théâtre provoqué par le rock* (nonfiction), Comédie de Saint-Etienne (Saint-Etienne, France), 1979.

La position du tireur couché (novel), 1981, translated by James Brook as *The Prone Gunman,* City Lights (San Francisco, CA), 2002.

La princesse du sang (novel), Rivages (Paris, France), 1996.

Chroniques (literary criticism), Rivages (Paris, France), 1996.

Spécial manchette, Rivages (Paris, France), 1997.

Les yeux de la momie: chroniques de cinéma (nonfiction), Rivages (Paris, France), 1997.

Also translator of works by others, including Ross Thomas, Alan Moore, and Donald E. Westlake; reviewer of films.

SCREENPLAYS

La peur et l'amour (also released as *Torment*), 1966.

Une femme aux abois (also released as *The Slave*), 1967.

Le Socrate (also released as *Socrates*), 1968.

Ras le bol (also released as *Fed Up*), 1972.

Folle à tuer (also released as *Mad Enough to Kill*), 1975.

L'agression (also released as *Act of Aggression*), 1975.

L'ordinateur des pompes funèbres (also released as *The Probability Factor* and *The Undertaker Parlor Computer*), 1976.

La guerre des polices (also released as *The Police War*), 1979.

Trois hommes à abattre (also released as *Three Men to Destroy* and *Three Men to Kill*), 1980.

Les maîtres du temps (also released as (video) *Time Masters*), 1982.

Légitime violence, 1982.

La Crime (also released as *Cover Up*), 1983.

Polar, 1984.

Also writer for television series, including *Les globe-trotters,* 1966; "Une dernière fois Catherine," in *Série noire,* 1984. Author of miniseries *Le tiroir secret,* 1986, and for television movie *Noces de plomb.*

ADAPTATIONS: Novels adapted as films include: *Nada,* filmed as *The Nada Gang,* 1974; *Que d'os!,* filmed as *Pour la peau d'un flic* (also released as *For a Cop's Hide* and *Whirlpool*), 1981; and *La position du tireur couché,* filmed as *Le Choc* (also released as *Contract in Blood* and *Shock*), 1982.

SIDELIGHTS: Jean-Patrick Manchette was an amateur jazz saxophonist, political activist, and film and screen writer who wrote nearly a dozen noir novels, primarily during the 1970s. He was one of the leading contributors to the "polar" genre that incorporated politics and culture into crime and mystery novels. All of Manchette's 1970s novels are set in France. Jon B. Hassel, who reviewed *La princesse du sang* in the *French Review,* noted that they "all had in common . . . the fact that the style in which they were written was as important as what they were about." Manchette published no novels during the 1980s, remained in ill health following his diagnosis with a pancreatic tumor in 1989 and died of lung cancer in 1995. His final novel, *La princesse du sang,* remained unfinished at the time of his death and was published posthumously. Set in 1956, it incorporates the revolution and invasion of Hungary and the Algerian war, though most of the plot unfolds in Cuba. Hassel wrote that "arms dealers, French and American secret services, and the actual historical events influence all the characters, in a world of manipulation in which it is difficult to know who is manipulated and who manipulates."

Manchette's leftist politics are evident in his writings. As James Sallis wrote in the *Boston Globe,* "Manchette consistently skewered capitalist society and indicted the media for their emphasis on spectacle. He saw the world as a giant marketplace in which gangs of thugs—be they leftists, terrorist, or socially approved thugs like police and politicians—compete relentlessly, and in which tiny groups of alienated individuals go on trying to cling to the flotsam of their lives."

Two of Manchette's novels were translated and published in English in 2002. In *Three to Kill,* originally published in French in 1976, middle-aged Georges Gerfaut is being hunted by two killers, Carlo and Bastien, who were sent by a Mr. Taylor. Georges uses this opportunity to leave what is becoming for him a boringly comfortable bourgeois life. "The theme of paranoid man-on-the-run is a staple of B-thrillers, but the author shows such superb elan in handling the material that it almost seems as if he's the first to craft it," wrote a *Publishers Weekly* reviewer. "Writing with economy, deadpan irony, and an eye for the devastating detail," commented a *Kirkus Reviews* critic, "Manchette spins pulp fiction into literature."

Nation contributor Hillary Frey reviewed both *Three to Kill* and *The Prone Gunman,* saying that they "are full of nasty, sadistic violence, leavened just enough by irony and black humor to be tolerable." Frey added that Manchette's style is "plain. . . . It's French. Like Camus . . . he writes a cool and lean prose; each sentence exists only to advance from disaster to disaster, or to relay some painful moment from the past." Several other critics noticed the author's minimalist style, too, in *The Prone Gunman.* For example, Katy Munger commented in the *Washington Post Book World* that "the writing style is so very stark that it comes off as jarring at times, even for noir." Marilyn Stasio said in the *New York Times Book Review* that "there's not a superfluous word or overdone effect."

The Prone Gunman is the story of Martin Terrier, a hired assassin who continues in his lucrative line of work in order to amass the fortune he feels he must have before he can approach the wealthy woman he has loved since childhood. Martin is planning one last big job that he feels will enable him to approach his love, but she has already moved on to a bigger catch. When he tries to abandon his plan, the people who hired him make him their next target. Munger concluded in her review of the book that the novel "is noir at its darkest. It is a tale of betrayal and violence that transports you to a world far from the madding crowd. By the time it's done, you just might be glad to return to your own world once again."

BIOGRAPHICAL AND CRITICAL SOURCES:

PERIODICALS

Boston Globe, September 29, 2002, James Sallis, "Masterworks of Murder Most French Manchette Consistently Skewered Capitalist Society," p. D9.

Chicago Tribune, April 14, 2002, Dick Adler, review of *Three to Kill,* p. 2.
French Review, December, 1998, Jon B. Hassel, review of *La princesse du sang,* pp. 366-367.
Kirkus Reviews, February 1, 2002, review of *Three to Kill,* p. 146.
Nation, March 15, 2004, Hillary Frey, reviews of *Three to Kill* and *The Prone Gunman,* p. 30.
New York Times Book Review, November 17, 2002, Marilyn Stasio, review of *The Prone Gunman,* p. 54.
Publishers Weekly, February 18, 2002, review of *Three to Kill,* p. 79.
Washington Post Book World, December 1, 2002, Katy Munger, review of *The Prone Gunman,* p. T13.*

*   *   *

MANCHETTE, J.P.
  See MANCHETTE, Jean-Patrick

*   *   *

MANCINI, Federico 1927-1999
(Giuseppe Federico Mancini)

PERSONAL: Born December 23, 1927, in Perugia, Italy; died July 21, 1999; son of Ettore and Fulvia Lina (Valigi) Mancini; married Vittoria Ghigi, 1956; children: two. *Education:* Attended University of Bologna, University of Bordeaux, University of Paris, and University of Chicago.

CAREER: University of Urbino, Urbino, Italy, lecturer, 1956; University of Bologna, Bologna, Italy, lecturer, 1962, professor of labor law, 1965-79, professor of comparative law, 1982; University of Rome, Rome, Italy, professor of political science, 1979-82; European Court of Justice, Luxembourg, Belgium, advocate general, 1982-88, judge, 1988-99, president of 6th chamber, 1990-93. Visiting professor at University of North Carolina, Johns Hopkins University, Baltimore, MD, 1957-76, and Harvard University, 1965, 1990; University of New South Wales, adjunct professor, 1997. Member of Consiglio Superiore della Magistratura, 1976-81.

AWARDS, HONORS: Honorary doctorate, University of Cordoba, 1984; honorary bencher, King's Inns

(Dublin, Ireland), 1995; named patron of European Law Centre; honorary degree from University of New South Wales, 1996; G. Frederico Mancini Prize in European law named in his honor at Harvard University and University of New South Wales, 1997.

WRITINGS:

Costituzione e movimento operaio (nonfiction), Il Mulino (Bologna, Italy), 1976.
(With others) *Lo Statuto dei lavoratori, un bilancio politico: nuove prospettive del diritto del lavoro e democrazia industriale* (nonfiction), De Donato (Bari, Italy), 1977.
Terroristi e riformisti (nonfiction), Il Mulino (Bologna, Italy), 1981.
La circulación de los trabajadores por cuenta ajena en la jurisprudencia comunitaria (nonfiction), University of Granada [Grenada], 1990.
Democracy and Constitutionalism in the European Union: Collected Essays, Hart Publishing (Portland, OR), 2000.

SIDELIGHTS: Federico Mancini was first a professor, then an advocate general and judge with the European Court of Justice. He wrote several volumes on labor law, legislation, and other issues important to the European community. In honor of his seventieth birthday, the festschrift *Scritti in onore di Giuseppe Federico Mancini* was published. The two volumes of essays, totaling more than 1,800 pages, are written in five languages by professors and specialists in labor and European Community law, including past and present members of the Court of Justice and the Court of First Instance. The tribute was prepared by the law faculty of the University of Bologna. A press release announcing the presentation of the volumes to Mancini noted that the work forms part of an ancient university tradition according to which this rare distinction is reserved to the most eminent professors and bears witness to the widespread and deep influence of Judge Mancini's teaching in both Italian university circles and on the European state."

BIOGRAPHICAL AND CRITICAL SOURCES:

BOOKS

Scritti in onore di Giuseppe Federico Mancini, two volumes, A. Giuffrè (Milan, Italy), 1998.

PERIODICALS

Political Studies, March, 2001, Frank Vibert, review of *Democracy and Constitutionalism in the European Union: Collected Essays,* p. 174.
Times Literary Supplement, February 8, 2002, Terry Bishop, review of *Democracy and Constitutionalism in the European Union,* p. 28.

ONLINE

University of New South Wales Web site, http://www.arts.unsw.edu/ (June 11, 2005), Federico Mancini, "The Italians in Europe" (undelivered lecture).*

*   *   *

**MANCINI, Giuseppe Federico
See MANCINI, Federico**

*   *   *

**MARSHALL, Donald S. 1919-2005
(Donald Stanley Marshall)**

OBITUARY NOTICE—See index for *CA* sketch: Born September 10, 1919, in Danvers, MA; died of kidney failure, August 28, 2005, in Alexandria, VA. Army officer, anthropologist, and author. Marshall was a retired army colonel who also studied Polynesian cultures and later went on to become an authority on war and civil defense as well as a museum publications editor and research director. Marshall was working as a photography studio manager when the United States entered World War II. After enlisting in the army, he was stationed in Panama for a time, and it was here that his interest in indigenous peoples was sparked. After the war, he studied anthropology at Harvard University, earning a B.A. in 1950, M.A. in 1951, and Ph.D. in 1956. During much of the 1950s, he worked for the Peabody Museum as a researcher stationed in Polynesia, where he gained particular knowledge of the Mangaia people inhabiting the Cook Islands. This research would lead to two books: *Ra'ivavae: An Expedition to the Most Fascinating and Mysterious Island in Polynesia* (1961) and the coauthored *A Dictionary of Some Tuamotuan Dialects of the Polynesian Language* (1964). In 1959 Marshall founded the research and publishing firm Far Lands House, which specialized in anthropology. At the time, he was an officer in the U.S. Army Reserve, and when war in Vietnam began to escalate he returned to active duty in 1963. He also worked on the General Staff in Washington, DC, and was an assistant for Vietnam for the Office of the Assistant Secretary of Defense, among other duties. During the early 1970s, Marshall, who had risen to the rank of colonel, became an expert on military defense and was deputy director of the Pentagon's Strategic Arms Limitations Treaty (SALT) task force. His last three years of active duty, before retiring in 1976, were spent as a special assistant for policy to the assistant secretary of defense. Among his military medals, he earned the Bronze Star, Legion of Merit with Oak Leaf Cluster, and the Army Commendation Medal. After leaving the military, Marshall continued to work on civil defense as executive director of the Military Conflict Institute. Next, he spent the 1980s collecting and organizing papers for the Vietnam Project at the University of California at Berkeley. From 1990 until 2000, he served as director of publications and research covering the area of Oceania for the Peabody Essex Museum in Salem, Massachusetts; he also edited the periodical *Neptune*. In addition to his authored works, Marshall was editor of the books *Songs and Tales of the Sea Kings* (1957) and *Human Sexual Behavior: Variations across the Ethnographic Spectrum* (1971), the latter co-edited with Robert C. Suggs. At the time of his death he was editing a book about hieroglyphics.

OBITUARIES AND OTHER SOURCES:

PERIODICALS

Washington Post, September 7, 2005, p. B6.

*   *   *

MARSHALL, Donald Stanley
  See MARSHALL, Donald S.

*   *   *

MARSHALL, Sybil Mary 1913-2005
  (Sybil Mary Edwards Marshall)

OBITUARY NOTICE—See index for *CA* sketch: Born November 26, 1913, in Ramsey, Huntingdon, England; died August 29, 2005. Educator and author. Marshall

was a highly innovative educator of young children whose books and teachings were credited with helping to liberalize the English school system during the 1960s. She began work as a village school teacher at the age of nineteen. Although she had received very little formal training for the job, she became a highly inspiring and innovative teacher who fostered great creativity in her students. Her talents recognized, Marshall was made head teacher of Kingston Country Primary School in Cambridgeshire, where she taught for eighteen years. After enrolling in college in 1960, she attended New Hall, Cambridge, where she earned a bachelor's degree in 1962 and a master's degree in 1967. Her first book, *An Experiment in Education* (1963), drew on her early teaching experience and encouraged educators to be more creative in the classroom. From 1962 to 1967 Marshall was a lecturer in primary education at Sheffield University, and from 1967 to 1976 she was a reader in the field for Sussex University, where she was head of the primary education department. Meanwhile, she published several books about primary-school teaching, including *Adventure in Creative Education* (1968) and *Creative Writing* (1974). She also served as an advisor for the British children's television program *Picture Box* for twenty-three years. In addition to her works concerning creativity in education, Marshall was a noted folklorist, winning the Angel Prize for her *Everyman's Book of English Folk Tales* (1981). She also wrote a number of books about her life and family, including *Fenland Chronicle* (1963), *Once upon a Village* (1979), and *The Silver New Nothing: Edwardian Children in the Fen* (1987). In more recent years, Marshall wrote novels with strongly autobiographical roots, including *A Nest of Magpies* (1993), *Sharp through the Hawthorn* (1994), *Strip the Willow* (1996), and *Ring the Bell Backwards* (2000).

OBITUARIES AND OTHER SOURCES:

PERIODICALS

Daily Telegraph (London, England), October 3, 2005.
Guardian (London, England), August 31, 2005, p. 20.
Independent (London, England), September 5, 2005, p. 50.
Times (London, England), September 28, 2005, p. 66.

*   *   *

MARSHALL, Sybil Mary Edwards
  See MARSHALL, Sybil Mary

MARTIN, Bradley K.

PERSONAL: Male. *Education:* Princeton University; studied law at Emory University.

ADDRESSES: Office—Bloomberg News, Yusen Bldg., 2-3-2 Marunouchi, Chiyoda-ku, Tokyo 100-0005 Japan. *E-mail*—eastgate@mozart.inet.co.th.

CAREER: Journalist. Peace Corps volunteer in Thailand; *Charlotte Observer,* reporter; *Baltimore Sun,* Baltimore, MD, bureau chief in Tokyo, New Delhi and Beijing; *Asian Wall Street Journal, Newsweek, Asia Times,* and *Asian Financial Intelligence,* Tokyo bureau chief; *Asia Times,* Bangkok, Thailand, deputy executive editor, and cofounding managing editor of *Asia Times Online*; *Bloomberg Markets* magazine, senior writer. East-West Center, Honolulu, HI, journalist-in-residence, then POSCO visiting fellow; Tuck School of Business, Dartmouth College, Distinguished journalist-in-residence; E.W. Scripps School of Journalism, Ohio University, Athens, Scripps Howard visiting professional; Manship School of Mass Communication, Lousiana State University, Manship chair.

AWARDS, HONORS: Fulbright fellowships in Japan and Korea; Stanford professional journalism fellowship.

WRITINGS:

Under the Loving Care of the Fatherly Leader: North Korea and the Kim Dynasty, Thomas Dunne Books (New York, NY), 2004.
Intruding on the Hermit: Glimpses of North Korea, East-West Center, 1993.

Contributor to *The Kwangju Uprising: Eyewitness Press Accounts of Korea's Tiananmen,* edited by Henry Scott-Stokes and Le Jai Eui. Contributor to newpapers, including *Los Angeles Times, San Francisco Chronicle, Baltimore Sun,* and *Dallas Morning News.* Author of column "Pyongyang Watch," *Asian Times.*

SIDELIGHTS: Bradley K. Martin is a veteran foreign correspondent and an expert on Asia, particularly North and South Korea. In his book *Under the Loving*

Care of the Fatherly Leader: North Korea and the Kim Dynasty Martin focuses on the world's only communist "dynasty" that of North Korea's Kim family and reining leader Kim Jong-Il. The author delves into the country's political and economic history dating back seventy years and discusses in depth Kim Jong-Il's father Kim Il-Sung, who was known as the "Great Leader." In an interview with Jamie Glazov for *FrontPageMag.com,* Martin noted: "I was fascinated from the moment I set foot in Pyongyang on my first visit there in 1979. North Korean society was so different from what I or any other American was used to—the regimentation, the true-believer gazes from people proclaiming their adoration of the Beloved and Respected Great Leader."

Although the Kim family lives in notorious secrecy from the Western press, Martin provides new insights into North Korea's ruling elite and, in the process, the lives of the North Koreans. In a review of *Under the Loving Care of the Fatherly Leader* for *Kirkus Reviews,* a contributor felt that "Martin goes on too long, but offers much good information along the way about a decidedly strange and dangerous land." John F. Riddick, writing in the *Library Journal,* called the book a "massive study" and added that "the discerning reader can gain much from this work." In a review in *Booklist,* Jay Freeman commented that "Martin eloquently illustrates in this important book . . . [that] the control of the Kim dynasty may well be tenuous." Christian Caryl wrote in *Newsweek International* that the book is "a scrupulously detailed, intimate portrait of the Kims."

BIOGRAPHICAL AND CRITICAL SOURCES:

PERIODICALS

Booklist, September 15, 2004, Jay Freeman, review of *Under the Loving Care of the Fatherly Leader: North Korea and the Kim Dynasty,* p. 183.
Kirkus Reviews, July 15, 2004, review of *Under the Loving Care of the Fatherly Leader,* p. 675.
Korea Herald, May 16, 2005, "U.S. Nuclear Negotiator Reading Book on North Korean Leaders," p. 3.
Library Journal, September 15, 2004, John F. Riddick, review of *Under the Loving Care of the Fatherly Leader,* p. 70.
Los Angeles Times Book Review, October 17, 2004, Warren I. Cohen, review of *Under the Loving Care of the Fatherly Leader.*

Newsweek International, April 11, 2005, Christian Caryl, review of *Under the Loving Care of the Fatherly Leader,* p. 97.

New York Review of Books, February 10, 2005, Nicholas Kristof, review of *Under the Loving Care of the Fatherly Leader,* p. B8.

Washington Times, February 13, 2005, Doug Bandow, review of *Under the Loving Care of the Fatherly Leader,* pp. 25-27.

ONLINE

A Times Online, http://www.atimes.com/ (June 12, 2005), Yoel Sano, review of *Under the Loving Care of the Fatherly Leader.*

FrontPageMag.com, http://frontpagemag.com/ (April 5, 2005), Jamie Glazov, "North Korea's Death Chambers," interview with author.

Louisiana State University School of Communication Web site, http://www.manship.lsu.edu/ (June 4, 2005), information on author's career.

*   *   *

MARTIN, Troy W. 1953-
(Troy Wayne Martin)

PERSONAL: Born March 15, 1953, in Seminole, TX; son of Troy Sibbley Martin and Lavalta Ruth (Floyd) Martin; married Sheryl Mae Couch, June 23, 1974; children: Andrea Valen, Amie Danae. *Education:* Southern Nazarene University, B.A. (summa cum laude), 1974, M.A. (summa cum laude), 1978; Nazarene Theological Seminary, M.Div. (magna cum laude), 1980; University of Chicago, Ph.D., 1990.

ADDRESSES: Home—513 Cleveland Ave., Bourbonnais, IL 60914-2229. *Office*—Saint Xavier University, 3700 W. 103rd St., Chicago, IL 60655. *E-mail*—martin@sxu.edu.

CAREER: First Church of the Nazarene, Atchison, KS, pastor, 1979-81; Church of the Nazarene, Lemont, IL, associate pastor, 1982-88; Olivet Nazarene University, Kankakee, IL, assistant professor, 1988-91; Saint Xavier University, Chicago, IL, assistant professor, 1991-94, associate professor, 1994-2001, professor of religious studies, 2001—.

MEMBER: Society of Biblical Literature, American Academy of Religion, Wesleyan Theological Society, Chicago Society for Biblical Research.

AWARDS, HONORS: Baker Book House Distinguished Achievement Award, 1974; Biblical Languages Award, American Bible Society, 1980; Lilly grant, 1991; teaching incentive grants, 1993, 1992, CEP research grants, 1995 and 1997, Excellence in Scholarship awards, 1996, 1999, 2000, 2001, 2002, CEP development grants, 1998, 2000, and 2001, CEP faculty research initiative grants, 1998, 2000, 2001, 2002, Dean's summer stipend for scholarly Development, 1999, 2001, 2002, Dean's fund for scholarly development, 2000, CEP collaborative research grants, 2000, 2001, and School of Arts and Sciences Teacher/ Scholar Award, 2000, all from Saint Xavier University; Deutscher Akademischer Austausch Dienst scholarship, 1998.

WRITINGS:

Metaphor and Composition in First Peter, Scholars Press (Atlanta, GA), 1992.

By Philosophy and Empty Deceit: Colossians as Response to a Cynic Critique, Sheffield Academic Press (Sheffield, England), 1996.

(With Avis Clendenen) *Forgiveness: Finding Freedom through Reconciliation,* Crossroad (New York, NY), 2002.

Contributor to books, including *Judgment Day at the White House: A Critical Declaration Exploring Moral Issues and the Political Use and Abuse of Religion,* edited by Gabriel Fackre, William B. Eerdmans (Grand Rapids, MI), 1999; *Antiquity and Humanity: Essays on Ancient Religion and Philosophy Presented to Hans Dieter Betz on His Seventieth Birthday,* edited by Adela Yarbro Collins and Margaret M. Mitchell, J.C.B. Mohr/Paul Siebeck, 2001; *Paul and Pathos,* edited by Thomas H. Olbricht and Jerry L. Sumney, Society of Biblical Literature (Atlanta, GA), 2001; and *The Galatians Debate,* edited by Mark D. Nanos, Hendrickson (Peabody, MA), 2002. Contributor to journals, including *Olivet Theological Journal, Pneuma and Praxis, Herald of Holiness, Wesleyan Theological Journal, Journal of Biblical Literature, Biblical Research, Novum Testamentum, Illustrated Bible Life, New Testament Studies, Expository Times, Journal for the Study of the New Testament,* and *Hermes: Zeitschrift für die klassische Philologie.*

SIDELIGHTS: A religion professor at Saint Xavier University who teaches subjects that include the Reformation, medieval history, and theology, Troy W. Martin has also authored or contributed to several books. His first publication, *Metaphor and Composition in First Peter,* is based on his doctoral dissertation. In his analysis of the New Testament book, Martin explains it was actually an epistle and that the main metaphor running through I Peter is that of the diaspora. While reviewers of the book found Martin's scholarship impeccable, some felt that his conclusions are not entirely convincing. For example, in a review for the *Catholic Biblical Quarterly,* Peter H. Davids called *Metaphor and Composition in First Peter* a "'must read' for those involved in research on I Peter," but also noted that the author "cannot do an exegesis of the Epistle thorough enough to lay doubts completely to rest." *Journal of Biblical Literature* contributor J. Ramsey Michaels similarly commented that while Martin's arguments for the diaspora metaphor achieve "mixed success," "many of the points he makes are worthy of consideration entirely apart from the merits of his major thesis."

In *By Philosophy and Empty Deceit: Colossians as Response to a Cynic Critique* Martin attempts to explain what lies behind another New Testament book. Most scholars view Colossians as Paul's response to an outside religious group attacking the Christian practices of the faithful in Collosae. Martin, according to Barry S. Crawford in the *Catholic Biblical Quarterly,* takes a "radically different view," however, arguing that the critics of the Colossians were actually Cynics. To support his argument, the scholar relies on text from the original Greek to analyze the language of Colossians in ways that have not been done before. Although Crawford noted that the translation on which Martin relies, "if not completely idiosyncratic, differs sharply from the standard English versions," the critic concluded, "It would be hard to find a study whose author is more deeply immersed in the details of Colossians' vocabulary or the intricacies of its puzzling syntactical constructions. For this reason alone, no one interested in the problem of identifying the Colossian opponents can afford to overlook this book."

More recently, Martin collaborated with fellow Saint Xavier University professor Avis Clendenen to write *Forgiveness: Finding Freedom through Reconciliation,* which readdresses the Christian concept of forgiveness in the Bible. It is the authors' contention that forgive-ness, in the Christian sense, is not a one-sided exercise; rather, reconciliation can only be achieved when two sides come together. However, Martin and Clendenen also recognize that sometimes direct interaction can be dangerous; in this case, they explain that God's help may be enlisted for help in forgiving others. As Stephen A. Schmidt reported in a *Religious Education* review, "the book ends with helpful, creative insights about the 'transferal' of ultimate forgiveness responsibility to God, followed by an engaging discussion of Purgatory." Schmidt concluded that all readers "will benefit from a serious reading of this carefully argued, well-written, and theologically profound explanation of this seminal doctrine in the Christian tradition."

BIOGRAPHICAL AND CRITICAL SOURCES:

PERIODICALS

Catholic Biblical Quarterly, July, 1993, Peter H. Davids, review of *Metaphor and Composition in First Peter,* pp. 594-595; April, 1997, Barry S. Crawford, review of *By Philosophy and Empty Deceit: Colossians as Response to a Cynic Critique,* pp. 386-387.

Journal of Biblical Literature, summer, 1993, J. Ramsey Michaels, review of *Metaphor and Composition in First Peter,* pp. 358-360; fall, 1998, F. Gerald Downing, review of *By Philosophy and Empty Deceit,* pp. 542-544.

Library Journal, March 15, 2002, Pam Matthews, review of *Forgiveness: Finding Freedom through Reconciliation,* p. 97.

Religious Education, winter, 2003, Stephen A. Schmidt, review of *Forgiveness.*

Religious Studies Review, July, 1993, Casimir Bernas, review of *Metaphor and Composition in First Peter,* p. 265; January, 1997, Ronald F. Hock, review of *By Philosophy and Empty Deceit,* p. 74.

ONLINE

Saint Xavier University Web site, http://www.sxu.edu/ (June 3, 2005), information on the works of Troy W. Martin.*

*   *   *

MARTIN, Troy Wayne
See MARTIN, Troy W.

MASTERS, Priscilla 1952-

PERSONAL: Born April 21, 1952, in Halifax, Yorkshire, England; adoptive father an orthopedic surgeon; adoptive mother an elementary and high school teacher; married; husband a doctor; children: two sons. *Education:* Studied nursing at Queen Elizabeth II Hospital, Birmingham, England. *Hobbies and other interests:* Playing piano and harp, antiques, ornithology, long country walks, visiting places of cultural and architectural interest.

ADDRESSES: Agent—c/o Author Mail, Allison & Busby, Ashwell Grange, Gardiners Lane, Ashwell, Hertforshire SG7 5NA, England.

CAREER: Writer. Also works as a nurse. Public speaker on the topic of crime writing.

WRITINGS:

MYSTERY NOVELS; "JOANNA PIERCY" SERIES

Winding up the Serpent, Macmillan (London, England), 1992.
A Wreath from My Sister, Macmillan (London, England), 1995.
Catch the Fallen Sparrow, Macmillan (London, England), 1996.
And None Shall Sleep, Macmillan (London, England), 1997.
Scaring Crows, Macmillan (London, England), 1999.
Embroidering Shrouds, Macmillan (London, England), 2001.

Also author of *Endangering Innocents,* Allison & Busby (Ashwell, Hertfordshire, England).

OTHER

Mr. Bateman's Garden (juvenile), 1987.
Night Visit (mystery novel), Macmillan (London, England), 1998.
A Fatal Cut (mystery novel), Macmillan (London, England), 2000.
Disturbing Ground (mystery novel), Allison & Busby (Ashwell, Hertfordshire, England), 2002.

ADAPTATIONS: The novel *A Fatal Cut* was recorded as an audio book, released by Recorded Books, 2000.

BIOGRAPHICAL AND CRITICAL SOURCES:

PERIODICALS

British Medical Journal, July 27, 2002, Trisha Greenhalgh, review of *Disturbing Ground,* p. 226.
Publishers Weekly, September 30, 3003, review of *Embroidering Shrouds,* p. 55.

ONLINE

Joanna Piercy Web site, http://www.joannapiercy.com (July 14, 2003).
Tangled Web, http://www.twbooks.co.uk/ (May 18, 2000).*

*   *   *

MASTRO, Jim 1953-

PERSONAL: Born 1953; married; wife's name Lisa; children: one son. *Education:* San Diego State University, B.S.; University of New Hampshire, M.A.

ADDRESSES: Home—NH. *Office*—MastroMedia, 12 Cherokee St., Dover, NH 03820. *E-mail*—info@ mastromedia.com.

CAREER: Writer and photographer. MastroMedia, Dover, NH, photographer and writer. Photography has appeared in *Omni, Discover, International Wildlife,* and *Geo.* Worked in Antarctica, 1982-96, including for ITT Antarctic Services and as manager of U.S. scientific diving program for National Science Foundation's Office of Polar Programs for five years.

WRITINGS:

Antarctica: A Year at the Bottom of the World, Little, Brown (Boston, MA), 2002.
(With Norbert Wu) *Antarctic Ice,* photographs by Wu, Holt (New York, NY), 2003.

(With Norbert Wu) *Under Antarctic Ice: The Photographs of Norbert Wu,* photographs by Wu, University of California Press (Berkeley, CA), 2004.

Contributor to periodicals, including *International Wildlife* and *Skin Diver.*

SIDELIGHTS: Jim Mastro is a freelance writer and photographer who spent nearly fifteen years working in Antarctica, including time as a diver on a scientific research project. "There were many times when I saw underwater landscapes that had never before been seen by a human being," Mastro explained on *Antarctica Online.* "Those were the times when I felt like a true explorer." Referring to his experience in Antarctica, the author also noted: "My entire perception of the planet we live on has been irrevocably altered." Since returning from Antarctica, Mastro has authored or coauthored several books focusing on the frozen land. In *Antarctica: A Year at the Bottom of the World,* for example, he writes about his experiences diving in the Antarctica waters and also includes numerous photographs both of the landscape and the animals he encounters.

Mastro has also collaborated with noted undersea photographer Norbert Wu on two books about the area. In *Antarctic Ice,* Mastro and Wu focus on the brief Antarctic summer, highlighting the life and landscape both below the water and on shore. In addition to Wu's photographs, the text provides explanations about Antarctic life with a focus on the Weddell seal, Orca whale, and Adelie and Emperor penguins. He discusses how their surrounding habitat helps these creatures survive. A *Kirkus Reviews* contributor noted that the book is "well-written, smooth, and interesting," and Cristina Macrinici noted in *Childhood Education* that the "book makes for a fascinating read."

In *Under Antarctic Ice: The Photographs of Norbert Wu* Mastro provides most of the text explaining the region's animal and plant life, including the introductory chapter about the area's natural history, while Wu provides the photographs and notes about his pictures. Betty Galbraith, writing in *Library Journal,* noted that "Mastro tries to condense complex scientific information to an understandable level" but felt that difficulties remain for those not familiar with some scientific terminology. As *Booklist* contributor Nancy Bent

noted, "Mastro's text artfully summarizes Antarctic ecology for the lay reader." Writing in *Geographical,* Octavia Lamb called the book a "scintillating tome," labeled the author's introduction "informative and evocative," and added that Mastro's text "manages to convey the struggle of diving . . . in the perishing cold and the beauty of the sublime wonderland." Writing in the *American Scientist,* David Schoonmaker noted that the "photographs and captions offer peeks into places few of us will ever be privileged enough to visit." *Natural History* contributor Laurence A. Marschall, wrote that "Wu's photographs, along with Mastro's background text, provide access for the armchair traveler."

BIOGRAPHICAL AND CRITICAL SOURCES:

PERIODICALS

American Scientist, January-February, 2005, David Schoonmaker, review of *Under Antarctic Ice: The Photographs of Norbert Wu,* p. 77.
Booklist, December 1, 2003, Carolyn Phelan, review of *Antarctic Ice,* p. 679; October 15, 2004, Nancy Bent, review of *Under Antarctic Ice: The Photographs of Norbert Wu,* p. 375.
Childhood Education, fall, 2004, Cristina Macrinici, review of *Antarctic Ice,* p. 48.
Choice, April, 2005, P.E. Lutz, review of *Under Antarctic Ice,* p. 1426.
Geographical, March, 2005, Octavia Lamb, review of *Under Antarctic Ice,* p. 82.
Kirkus Reviews, October 15, 2003, review of *Antarctic Ice,* p. 1273.
Library Journal, September 1, 2004, Betty Galbraith, review of *Under Antarctic Ice,* p. 183.
Natural History, December, 2004, Laurence A. Marschall, review of *Under Antarctic Ice,* p. 54.
Publishers Weekly, December 15, 2003, review of *Antarctic Ice,* p. 72.
School Library Journal, November, 2003, Margaret Bush, review of *Antarctic Ice,* p. 128; October, 2004, review of *Antarctic Ice,* p. S23.
Science News, November 13, 2004, review of *Under Antarctic Ice,* p. 319.

ONLINE

Antarctica Online, http://www.antarcticaonline.com/ (June 6, 2005), author home page.*

MATLINS, Antoinette L.
(Antoinette Leonard Matlins)

PERSONAL: Daughter of Antonio C. Bonanno (a gemologist and writer).

ADDRESSES: Agent—c/o Author Mail, GemStone Press, P.O. Box 237, Woodstock, VT 05091.

CAREER: Gemologist, writer, lecturer, and consumer advocate.

MEMBER: Accredited Gemologists Association.

AWARDS, HONORS: Antonio C. Bonanno Award for Excellence in Gemology, Accredited Gemologists Association, 2005.

WRITINGS:

(With Antonio C. Bonanno) *The Complete Guide to Buying Gems: How to Buy Diamonds and Colored Gemstones with Confidence and Knowledge,* Crown (New York, NY), 1984, 2nd edition published as *Jewelry and Gems: The Buying Guide; How to Buy Diamonds, Pearls, Precious, and Other Popular Gems with Confidence and Knowledge,* GemStone Press (South Woodstock, VT), 1987, 5th edition published as *Jewelry and Gems, the Buying Guide: How to Buy Diamonds, Pearls, Colored Gemstones, Gold, and Jewelry with Confidence and Knowledge,* 2001.

(With Antonio C. Bonanno) *Gem Identification Made Easy: A Hands-on Guide to More Confident Buying and Selling,* GemStone Press (South Woodstock, VT), 1989, 2nd edition, 2002.

(With Antonio C. Bonanno and Jane Crystal) *Engagement and Wedding Rings: The Definitive Buying Guide for People in Love,* GemStone Press (South Woodstock, VT), 1990, 3rd edition, 2003.

The Pearl Book: The Definitive Buying Guide; How to Select, Buy, Care For, and Enjoy Pearls, GemStone Press (Woodstock, VT), 1996, 3rd edition, 2002.

Diamonds: The Antoinette Matlins Buying Guide; How to Select, Buy, Care For, and Enjoy Diamonds with Confidence and Knowledge, GemStone Press (Woodstock, VT), 2001.

Colored Gemstones: The Antoinette Matlins Buying Guide: How to Select, Buy, Care For, and Enjoy Sapphires, Emeralds, Rubies, and Other Colored Gems with Confidence and Knowledge, GemStone Press (Woodstock, VT), 2001.

(With Jill Newman) *Jewelry and Gems at Auction: The Definitive Guide to Buying and Selling at the Auction House and on Internet Auction Sites,* GemStone Press (Woodstock, VT), 2002.

Editor of *National Jeweler.* Contributor to books by others, including *Encyclopedia of Investments,* 2nd edition, Warren, Gorham & Lamont (Boston, MA), 1990.

SIDELIGHTS: Gemologist Antoinette L. Matlins learned her craft from her father, Antonio C. Bonanno, founder of the Accredited Gemologists Association and, for forty years, president of the National Gem Appraising Laboratory and director of the Columbia School of Gemology in Silver Spring, Maryland. As a consumer advocate, Matlins has appeared frequently on television and radio shows to educate the public about precious gems and jewelry and raise buyers' awareness of fraud. She also acts as an agent for clients who seek unusual or rare gems and jewelry.

For many years Matlins was an editor for *National Jeweler* magazine. In 1984 her first book was published, *The Complete Guide to Buying Gems: How to Buy Diamonds and Colored Gemstones with Confidence and Knowledge,* which she cowrote with her father. The second edition was published as *Jewelry and Gems: The Buying Guide; How to Buy Diamonds, Pearls, Precious, and Other Popular Gems with Confidence and Knowledge.* By the fifth edition, more small title changes had taken place, and it was published as *Jewelry and Gems, the Buying Guide: How to Buy Diamonds, Pearls, Colored Gemstones, Gold, and Jewelry with Confidence and Knowledge.*

Each edition of Matlins' guide has become the standard for consumers, offering advice on choosing a jeweler, appraiser, and insurer and providing the most recent information on fraudulent practices and values. The book also describes settings and metals and includes charts and diagrams that demonstrate various cuts and how to identify flaws. It also gives advice on selecting less-expensive alternatives that share the color and characteristics of more-expensive gems. In a review of the first edition, Anne E. Prentice, a contributor for *American Reference Books Annual,* noted that "a gemstone chart giving gem family, popular name, color(s), retail cost per carat, brilliance, wearability, and availability of the better-known gems provides a useful quick reference tool."

Matlins and Bonanno worked together again to write *Gem Identification Made Easy: A Hands-on Guide to More Confident Buying and Selling.* The gemologists offer advise on setting up a lab and the lighting and tools necessary to accurately determine the authenticity of gems. The book includes information on identifying blemishes and techniques used to enhance antique and estate jewelry and gems. For their next volume, *Engagement and Wedding Rings: The Definitive Buying Guide for People in Love,* the father and daughter collaborated with fashion writer Jane Crystal. The book explains everything there is to know about choosing a diamond ring, or one of the many colored gems that have become popular for engagement rings. As in previous books, consumers can find advice on quality, price, and how to detect fraudulent merchandise.

In *The Pearl Book: The Definitive Buying Guide; How to Select, Buy, Care For, and Enjoy Pearls* Matlins not only writes about evaluating, buying, and wearing pearls but also notes the history of the pearl in curing disease and depression. Powdered pearls continue to be used medicinally and as a beauty enhancer in contemporary Asia. A chapter on quality explains that unlike diamonds, which can be evaluated based on universally accepted standards, pearls are judged subjectively. *Lapidary Journal* contributor Anna M. Miller noted the author's "thorough research, vivid writing style, ability to distinguish between necessary and superficial information, and a unique talent to combine these elements into a book that is valuable to the gemologist, interesting to the jeweler, and an asset to the jewelry appraiser."

Matlins concentrates on a single stone in *Diamonds: The Antoinette Matlins Buying Guide; How to Select, Buy, Care For, and Enjoy Diamonds with Confidence and Knowledge* and covers a range of colored gems in *Colored Gemstones: The Antoinette Matlins Buying Guide; How to Select, Buy, Care For, and Enjoy Sapphires, Emeralds, Rubies, and Other Colored Gems with Confidence and Knowledge.* Stephen Allan Patrick noted in *Library Journal* that both books "include

extensive appendixes that cover the information needed for investing and purchasing gems of all types."

Jewelry and Gems at Auction: The Definitive Guide to Buying and Selling at the Auction House and on Internet Auction Sites explains terms unfamiliar to the novice who wishes to buy through auctions or online. The second half of the book includes much of the information regarding quality and value available in previous books by Matlins, but as *Booklist* critic Barbara Jacobs observed, "given the current auction fever, it makes dollars and cents to cool down by reading her very practical recommendations."

BIOGRAPHICAL AND CRITICAL SOURCES:

PERIODICALS

American Reference Books Annual, Volume 16, 1985, Ann E. Prentice, review of *The Complete Guide to Buying Gems: How to Buy Diamonds and Colored Gemstones with Confidence and Knowledge,* p. 607.

Booklist, November 15, 1983, review of *The Complete Guide to Buying Gems,* p. 461; October 1, 1990, Sue-Ellen Beauregard, review of *Gem Identification Made Easy: A Hands-on Guide to More Confident Buying and Selling,* p. 236; October 15, 2002, Barbara Jacobs, review of *Jewelry and Gems at Auction: The Definitive Guide to Buying and Selling at the Auction House and on Internet Auction Sites,* p. 375.

Jewelers Circular Keystone, July, 1988, Steven C. Hofer, review of *Jewelry and Gems: The Buying Guide; How to Buy Diamonds, Pearls, Precious, and Other Popular Gems with Confidence and Knowledge,* p. 222; July, 2005, Gary Roskin, "AGA Awards Jobbins and Matlins," p. 54.

Lapidary Journal, April, 1990, review of *Gem Identification Made Easy,* p. 223; November, 1990, Jane Culp Zeitner, review of *Engagement and Wedding Rings: The Definitive Buying Guide for People in Love,* p. 108; January, 1994, June Culp Zeitner, review of *Jewelry and Gems,* p. 137; June, 1997, Anna M. Miller, review of *The Pearl Book: The Definitive Buying Guide; How to Select, Buy, Care For, and Enjoy Pearls,* p. 115.

Library Journal, May 15, 1984, Marian S. Setterberg, review of *The Complete Guide to Buying Gems,* p. 977; September 1, 1990, Stephen Allan Patrick, review of *Gem Identification Made Easy,* p. 220; May 1, 1994, Therese D. Baker, review of *Jewelry and Gems,* p. 100; March 15, 1997, Stephen Allan Patrick, review of *The Pearl Book,* p. 59; February 15, 2002, Stephen Allan Patrick, reviews of *Diamonds: The Antoinette Matlins Buying Guide; How to Select, Buy, Care For, and Enjoy Diamonds with Confidence and Knowledge* and *Colored Gemstones: The Antoinette Matlins Buying Guide; How to Select, Buy, Care For, and Enjoy Sapphires, Emeralds, Rubies, and Other Colored Gems with Confidence and Knowledge,* p. 140.

Los Angeles Times Book Review, March 11, 1984, Charles Solomon, review of *The Complete Guide to Buying Gems,* p. 6.

MBR Bookwatch, March, 2005, Diane C. Donovan, review of *Jewelry and Gems at Auction.*

National Jeweler, May 1, 2003, Barbara Green, "Book Smarts: Offer Bridal Buying Guides to Customers," review of *Engagement and Wedding Rings,* p. 28.

New Technical Books, September, 1990, Patricia Ann Sarles, review of *Gem Identification Made Easy,* pp. 1407-1408.

ONLINE

GemStone Press Web site, http://gemstonepress.com/ (September 18, 2005), profile of Antoinette L. Matlins.*

*   *   *

MATLINS, Antoinette Leonard
    See MATLINS, Antoinette L.

*   *   *

MATTSON, Gary A. 1947-
    (Gary Armes Mattson)

PERSONAL: Born November 3, 1947, in New York, NY; married Elosia Robinson (a librarian), May 11, 1976. *Education:* State University of New York, Albany, B.A., 1969; City University of New York, John Jay College of Criminal Justice, M.P.A., 1976; University of Rhode Island, M.C.P., 1978; University of Delaware, Ph.D., 1986.

ADDRESSES: Office—Northern Kentucky University, 535A Old Science Bldg., Highland Heights, KY 41099. *E-mail*—mattsong1@nku.edu.

CAREER: Educator and administrator. NAC commission, State of New York, senior administrator, 1970-73; Fulton County Regional Planning, OH, director, 1976-78; U.S. Department of the Interior, New England grants administrator, 1979; New Mexico State University, Las Cruces, assistant professor of government; University of Texas, San Antonio, assistant professor and coordinator of public administration program, 1984-87; University of Florida, Gainsville, associate professor and director of Center for Local Government, 1987-92; Kansas State University, Manhattan, associate professor and coordinator of graduate program in environmental studies, 1992-2000; Iowa State University, Iowa City, associate professor and director of graduate education and college architecture, 2000-04; Northern Kentucky University, Highland Heights, director of public administration, 2004—. Kansas Tax and Budget Commission, senior policy advisor, 1995-97. *Military service:* U.S. Army, 1969-71; served in 301st Logistical Support Group.

MEMBER: American Society for Public Administration, American Political Science Association, Urban Affairs Association, American Institute of Certified Planners (charter member).

AWARDS, HONORS: Silver pin for public service, American Society for Public Administration, 1997.

WRITINGS:

Municipal Services, Economic Revitalization, and Small Cities in an Era of Retrenchment, Institute of Urban and Regional Research, University of Iowa (Oakdale, IA), 1983.

Perspectives on Small City Planning and Policy Making, Ginn Press (Lexington, MA), 1986.

Towns of Purpose: Community Vitality among Iowa's Rural County Seat Towns, Iowa State University (Ames, IA), 2003.

WORK IN PROGRESS: Book on the revitalization of small-town main streets.

MATTSON, Gary Armes
    See MATTSON, Gary A.

*   *   *

McCARTY, Clifford 1929-2005

OBITUARY NOTICE— See index for *CA* sketch: Born June 13, 1929, in Los Angeles, CA; died of emphysema, August 13, 2005, in Topanga, CA. Book seller and author. McCarty was a former bookstore owner who became well known for his books about film music and movie stars. A 1952 graduate of California State College, he worked as a salesman and taxi driver before establishing the Boulevard Bookshop in Los Angeles in 1958. The business remained successful for many years before closing in 1980. A cofounder of the Society for the Preservation of Film Music, which was later renamed the Film Music Society, he was the editor of the organization's journal, *Cue Sheet,* from 1984 to 1987. McCarty was the author or coauthor of several books, including *Film Composers in America: A Checklist of Their Work* (1953; second edition, 2000), *Bogey: The Films of Humphrey Bogart* (1965), *The Films of Errol Flynn* (1969), and the edited *Film Music 1* (1989).

OBITUARIES AND OTHER SOURCES:

PERIODICALS

Daily Variety, September 19, 2005, p. 28.
Los Angeles Times, August 25, 2005, p. B11.

*   *   *

McCLELLAND, Ted 1967-
    (Ted R. McClelland)

PERSONAL: Born January 14, 1967, in Lansing, MI; son of Robert (an economist) and Gail (a social worker; maiden name, Allen) Kleine. *Ethnicity:* "Scotch-Irish, English, Jewish." *Education:* Attended University of Michigan, 1985-87; Michigan State University, B.A., 1989. *Politics:* Democrat. *Religion:* Presbyterian. *Hobbies and other interests:* Running, horseplaying.

ADDRESSES: Home—7726 N. Eastlake Terrace, Ste. 3, Chicago, IL 60626. *E-mail*—tedsgarage@ameritech. net.

CAREER: Writer. *Lansing State Journal,* Lansing, MI, reporter, 1989-90; *Chicago Reader,* Chicago, IL, staff writer, 2001-05.

MEMBER: National Writers Union.

WRITINGS:

Horseplayers: Life at the Track, Chicago Review Press (Chicago, IL), 2005.

SIDELIGHTS: Ted McClelland told *CA:* "Originally, writing and gambling were separate passions of mine. I wrote, not very successfully, in the mornings, and played horses, not very successfully, in the afternoons. Only when I combined the two did I find a way to make them both pay. Simply wanting to be a writer isn't enough to make you a writer. You have to find a subject you love."

*   *   *

McCLELLAND, Ted R.
    See McCLELLAND, Ted

*   *   *

McCOMISKEY, Bruce 1963-

PERSONAL: Born November 13, 1963, in Newton, MA; son of Thomas (a theologian) and Eleanor (Carp) McComiskey; married Cynthia Ryan (a professor), June 14, 1994; children: Celia, Lena. *Education:* Illinois State University, B.S., 1987, M.A., 1988; Purdue University, Ph.D., 1994.

ADDRESSES: Home—1856 Glendmere Dr., Birmingham, AL 35216. *Office*—University of Alabama, Department of English, 1530 3rd Ave. S., Birmingham, AL 35294. *E-mail*—mccomisk@uab.edu.

CAREER: Writer. East Carolina University, Greenville, NC, assistant professor, 1994-98; University of Alabama, Birmingham, assistant professor, 1998-2001, associate professor, 2001—.

MEMBER: Modern Language Association, Rhetoric Society of America, National Council of Teachers of English, National Council on Writing Program Administrators, Conference on College Composition and Communication, Phi Beta Delta, Phi Kappa Phi.

AWARDS, HONORS: James L. Kinneavy Award, 1997, for best article in *JAC: A Journal of Composition Theory.*

WRITINGS:

Teaching Composition as a Social Process, Utah State University Press (Logan, UT), 2000.
Gorgias and the New Sophistic Rhetoric, Southern Illinois University Press (Carbondale, IL), 2002.
(Editor, with Cynthia Ryan) *City Comp: Identities, Spaces, Practices,* State University of New York Press (Albany, NY), 2003.

Contributor to periodicals, including *JAC: A Journal of Composition Theory, Composition Chronicle, Teaching English in the Two-Year College, Rhetoric Review, Rhetoric Society Quarterly, Composition Forum, Business Communication Quarterly,* and *North Carolina English Teacher.* Contributor to books, including *Reforming College Composition: Writing the Wrongs,* edited by Ray Wallace, Alan Jackson, and Susan Lewis, Greenwood Press (Westport, CT), 2000. Contributor of poetry to *Chameleon, Druid's Cave, Inky Trails, Ripples, Ryerson Almanac, Songs for all Seasons,* and *Voices in Poetics.*

WORK IN PROGRESS: English Studies: An Introduction to the Discipline(s).

SIDELIGHTS: Bruce McComiskey told *CA:* "I write every day. No exceptions. Every day."

*   *   *

McDONALD, Ian 1960-

PERSONAL: Born 1960, in Manchester, England; immigrated to Northern Ireland, 1965; married; wife's name Patricia.

ADDRESSES: Agent—Extreme Production, 1 Church View, Hollywood, County Down BT18 9DP, Northern Ireland. *E-mail*—ianmc@extremeproduction.com.

CAREER: Network of East-West Women, Washington, DC, executive director, 1994-95; International Museum of Women, San Francisco, CA, former program director; U.S. Holocaust Memorial Museum, Washington DC, former media relations director; Taube Foundation for Jewish Life and Culture, Jewish Heritage Initiative in Poland, San Francisco, CA, former director. Mills College, Oakland, CA, visiting scholar; board member, San Francisco Jewish Film Festival.

AWARDS, HONORS: Philip K. Dick Award for best original SF paperback; Theodore Sturgeon Memorial Award for best short science fiction, 2001, for *Tendeléo's Story.*

WRITINGS:

SCIENCE FICTION

Desolation Road, Bantam (New York, NY), 1988.
Empire Dreams, Bantam (New York, NY), 1988.
Out on Blue Six, Bantam (New York, NY), 1989.
The Broken Land, Bantam (New York, NY), 1992.
Terminal Café, Bantam (New York, NY), 1994.
Evolution's Shore, Bantam (New York, NY), 1995.
Ares Express, Earthlight (New York, NY), 2001.
River of Gods, Simon & Schuster (New York, NY), 2004.

Also contributor of novella *Tendeléo's Story,* to *Futures: Four Novellas,* edited by Peter Crowther, Warner Books, NY, 2001. Contributing editor, *Lilith.*

SIDELIGHTS: Ian McDonald has earned a reputation for using unusual settings and characters in his science-fiction novels. As he told Rick Kleffel in an online interview for the *Trashotron Agony Column,* "It's no novelty—science-fictionally speaking—for the mothership to land on the White House Lawn. It is if it's Uhuru Park in Nairobi—or Ormeau Park in Belfast. And that to me makes it automatically more interesting. For the same reason that I tend to use female characters because, in our male-oriented society, a woman has always the longer and more challenging narrative journey to go on, Third World locations have a more interesting leap to make."

McDonald introduces one of his best-known creations, the Chaga, in the 1990 novella *Toward Kilimanjaro*. The Chaga is an alien ecosystem that begins seeding the southern hemisphere of Earth despite all of humanity's efforts to stop it. It decimates or transforms the landscape, depending on one's perspective. McDonald expanded this work into a full-length novel, *Evolution's Shore*, which describes the journey of Irish reporter Gaby McAslin to explore a mysterious meteor crash on Mt. Kilimanjaro. Soon McAslin encounters the strange and frightening phenomenon of the Chaga, but also the curiously benevolent ways in which it transforms the humans who come in contact with it. In another novella, the award-winning *Tendeléo's Story*, McDonald tells the story from the perspective of an African woman. When the Chaga takes over her village, Tendeléo flees to Kenya's capital, Nairobi, but soon that too is abandoned to the alien vegetation. She flees again, this time to England, where the authorities discover that she is carrying the infection, and she begins to discover the new powers this "disease" gives her. For *Science Fiction Chronicle* contributor Don D'Ammassa, the result is a story that "is tragic and hopeful at the same time, and packs a great deal of good writing, sharp commentary, and fine characterization."

A similar transformative strangeness appears in another McDonald novel, but the effect is darker. *River of Gods* is set in mid-twenty-first-century India, or, rather, Bharat, one of a fractured India's successor states. Here the Aeais, who are advanced artificial intelligences, battle the neighboring state of Awadh for the dwindling waters of the Ganges. The story is told from the viewpoint of ten different characters, from gangsters to computer-generation actors, who have come to Bharat's capital for various reasons on the centennial of India's independence. Together, they illustrate the curious ways in which technology transforms a culture but also leaves much of it intact. *Chronicle* contributor Don D'Ammassa called it a "major new work" from a science-fiction novelist "who is at his best one of the most thought provoking and original authors working in the genre."

BIOGRAPHICAL AND CRITICAL SOURCES:

BOOKS

St. James Guide to Science Fiction Writers, fourth edition, St. James Press (Detroit, MI), 1996.

PERIODICALS

Chronicle (Radford, England), October, 2004, Don D'Ammassa, review of *River of Gods,* p. 26.
Fantasy & Science Fiction (Hoboken, NJ), May, 2002, James Sallis, review of *Futures: Four Novellas,* p. 32.
New Scientist, September 18, 2004, Elizabeth Sourbut, "Drowning the Future," p. 47.
Science Fiction Chronicle, February, 2001, Don D'Ammassa, review of *Tendeléo's Story,* p. 43; June, 2002, Don D'Ammassa, review of *Ares Express,* p. 33.

ONLINE

SFSite, http://www.sfsite.com/ (July 12, 2005), biography of Ian McDonald.
Trashotron Agony Column, http://trashotron.com/ agony/ (August 23, 2004), Rick Kleffel, "From the *River of Gods* to the Department of Social Services," interview with Ian McDonald.*

*   *   *

McEVEDY, Colin 1930-2005
(Colin Peter McEvedy)

OBITUARY NOTICE— See index for *CA* sketch: Born June 6, 1930, in Salford, Lancashire, England; died of myelofibrosis, August 1, 2005, in London, England. Psychiatrist, historian, demographer, and author. Although his vocation was that of a hospital psychiatrist, McEvedy spent his spare time as an historical demographer and author of historical atlases. Earning a B.A. from Magdalen College, Oxford, in 1948, his education continued with a B.M. and B.Ch. in 1955. He then went to work at Guy's Hospital for a year before joining the Royal Air Force in 1956. His military service was largely spent testing the effects of oxygen deprivation on pilots at the Royal Aircraft Establishment. McEvedy then was hired by Maudsley Hospital, where he received training in psychiatry. Earning a diploma in psychology from London University in 1963, he then went to Middlesex Hospital while completing a D.M. in 1970 at Oxford; his doctoral thesis was on the subject of hysteria. From 1972 until he retired in 1995, McEvedy was a consulting psychiatrist at both St. Bernard's Hospital in Southall, England, and Ealing Hospital. All through his years as a student and professional psychiatrist, McEvedy was engrossed by history. However, he had no desire to become an academic because he felt university life would constrain his choice of research and writing subjects. He was fascinated in particular by demographics: changes in population and civilization's growth over the millennia. This led to his publication of numerous historical atlases. Among these are *The Penguin Atlas of Ancient History* (1967), *Atlas of African History* (1980), and *The Penguin Historical Atlas of the Pacific* (1998). McEvedy's work was based on existing research and publications, though his conclusions at times were considered quite original, such as his assertion that historians tend to exaggerate population numbers in ancient cities.

OBITUARIES AND OTHER SOURCES:

PERIODICALS

Independent (London, England), August 30, 2005, p. 30.
Times (London, England), August 13, 2005, p. 66.

*   *   *

McEVEDY, Colin Peter
   See McEVEDY, Colin

*   *   *

McFAUL, Thomas R. 1941-

PERSONAL: Born October 27, 1941, in Rockford, IL; son of Carson E. (a barber) and Dorothy (a factory worker; maiden name Thalaker) McFaul; married, wife's name Shirley (deceased, 2002); married April 19, 2003; wife's name Sally; children: Kim McFaul Chiappetta, Bradley F. *Ethnicity:* "Euro-American." *Education:* Northern Illinois University, B.A. (sociology), 1964; Pacific School of Religion, Berkeley, CA, M.Div. (first in class); Boston University, Ph.D., 1972; North Central College, Naperville, IL, B.A. (Spanish), 1998; College of DuPage, Glen Ellyn, IL, certificate in travel and tourism, 1998. *Religion:* Protestant. *Hobbies and other interests:* Aerobic fitness, music, film, art, travel, humor.

ADDRESSES: Home—4 Ridge Ct., Bolingbrook, IL 60440. *Office*—College of DuPage, 425 Fawell Blvd., Glen Ellyn, IL 60137. *E-mail*—tsmcfaul@aol.com.

CAREER: Writer. Notre Dame College, Manchester, NH, instructor and sociology department chair, 1970-72; Mount Union College, Alliance, OH, assistant professor, 1972-74; University of Houston, Clear Lake, TX, assistant professor, 1974-76, associate professor, 1976-81, professor, 1981-82, acting dean, 1980-81, director of programs in human sciences, 1978-82; University of Baltimore, professor, 1982-85, dean of Yale Gordon College of Liberal Arts, 1982-84, assistant provost, 1984-85; George Williams College, Downers Grove, IL, professor and senior vice president for academic and student affairs, 1985-86; North Central College, Naperville, IL, professor of ethics and religious studies, 1986-2003, director of graduate programs, 1986-95, coordinator of cultural events, 1995-2003, acting dean, 1998-99, professor emeritus, 2003—; College of DuPage, Glen Ellyn, IL, professor of philosophy and religious studies, 2004—.

MEMBER: Pi Gamma Mu (lifetime member).

AWARDS, HONORS: Danforth Foundation fellowship, 1967-68; Piper Professor Award for teaching excellence, University of Houston, 1976; Dissinger Award for teaching, North Central College, 1999.

WRITINGS:

(Editor) *The Future of Global Economic Disparities,* Joint Strategy and Action Committee (New York, NY), 1985.
(Editor) *The Future of Global Nuclearization,* Joint Strategy and Action Committee (New York, NY), 1985.
Transformation Ethics: Developing the Christian Moral Imagination, University Press of America (Lanham, MD), 2003.

Contributor to *Handbook of Futures Research,* edited by Jib Fowles, Greenwood Press (Westport, CT), 1978. Contributor of articles to periodicals, including *Journal of Religion, Journal for the Scientific Study of Religion, Religion in Life, Teaching Sociology, Sociology and Social Research, Planning for Higher*

Education, Case Currents, Liberal Education, Christian Century, Visions, and Religious News/Trends. Also contributor of book reviews to periodicals, including Choice, Sociological Analysis, Religious Studies Review, and Visions.

WORK IN PROGRESS: Peace, Prosperity, and Justice in the Emerging Global Village.

SIDELIGHTS: Thomas R. McFaul told CA: "My primary motivation for writing is to express the truth. My influences are persons who have a similar passion—from all walks of life and perspectives. My writing process involves daily discipline and continuous learning for personal and professional growth. My inspirations come from the great thinkers in the Eastern and Western traditions."

*   *   *

MEAD-FERRO, Muffy 1960-

PERSONAL: Born 1960, in Jackson Hole, WY; married Michael Ferro (second husband); children: Belle, Joe.

ADDRESSES: Home—Salt Lake City, UT. Agent—c/o Author Mail, Da Capo Press, 11 Cambridge Center, Cambridge, MA 02142.

CAREER: Writer. Has worked as an advertising copywriter and creative director.

WRITINGS:

NONFICTION

Confessions of a Slacker Mom, Da Capo Lifelong Books (Cambridge, MA), 2004.
Confessions of a Slacker Wife, Da Capo Lifelong Books (Cambridge, MA), 2005.

SIDELIGHTS: Muffy Mead-Ferro decided not to forego her career in advertising when she began having kids, but she also consciously chose not to follow other working moms in trying to overachieve in the

home as well as at work. This philosophy led her to write her first book, Confessions of a Slacker Mom, in which she describes how she decided to lessen her time devoted to housework and the kids while striving to find time for herself. "A lot of women call it selfish unless you're constantly putting your kids' needs first," the author noted to Peg Tyre in a Newsweek article posted on MSNBC.com. "But I think that's just bogus." Mead-Ferro is not the only one who thinks so; in an article about the author and other "slacker" moms, University of Michigan professor Susan Douglas told USA Today Web site contributor Kim Painter: "There is something like an incipient mother's movement out there," Douglas adding that "Mothers are really saying that they have had it with these standards of perfection."

In the book, Mead-Ferro uses her own experiences and a good deal of humour to describe her life as a slacker mom. She discusses everything from dealing with overachieving moms like the one who wanted to memorialize her child's first meal of peas in a scrapbook to her old-fashioned spanking of her kids. In a review of Confessions of a Slacker Mom, in Library Journal, Mirela Roncevic called the author "quirky and unpretentiously honest." Describing the book as being about a mom who "has decided to opt out of the super-mom race," Jennifer Huget, writing in the Washington Post, noted that "Mead-Ferro might sound callous were it not for her wicked sense of humor."

Mead-Ferro furthers her ruminations on her family duties as she sees them in Confessions of a Slacker Wife. The author once again uses humor to address the issue of society's emphasis on having a "perfect" life and on the burden women face to see that perfection come to fruition. As in her previous book, she discusses chores but also a host of other societal demands, including the psychological ones stressed by magazine publishers who present an idealized version of reality for women to try and achieve. The ten essays also include a look at dirty houses, the idea of having breast implants, and the possibility of her and her husband sleeping in separate beds. In addition, she talks about growing up on a ranch in Wyoming and her mother's less-than-meticulous approach to housework. A Publishers Weekly contributor felt that Mead-Ferro meets the "terrific" standards set by her previous book and called Confessions of a Slacker Wife "a refreshing complement to the hundreds of titles out there that explain how to do it all perfectly."

Mead-Ferro told *CA:* "I had wonderful childhood. My first book, *Confessions of a Slacker Mom,* was not so much a criticism of modern parenting as it was a love letter to my own mother, who died several years before the book was published. I'm so grateful to her and to my father for raising me to be self-sufficient and to think for myself. I only hope I can be the kind of parent they each were.

"*Confessions of a Slacker Wife* was written in response to the surprise (and dismay) I feel about the emphasis my generation of women places on certain 'wifely' things—cleaning, decorating, competitive entertaining. It seems odd that my generation of women, the most educated so far, the one with the most professional experience yet, apparently cares more about these things than our mothers and grandmothers ever did.

"I try to write with humor; however, because I personally have fallen prey to all of the social foibles I write about, I also enjoy laughing at myself."

BIOGRAPHICAL AND CRITICAL SOURCES:

BOOKS

Mead-Ferro, Muffy, *Confessions of a Slacker Mom,* Da Capo Lifelong Books (Cambridge, MA), 2004.
Mead-Ferro, Muffy, *Confessions of a Slacker Wife,* Da Capo Lifelong Books (Cambridge, MA), 2005.

PERIODICALS

Kirkus Reviews, February 15, 2005, review of *Confessions of a Slacker Wife,* p. 215.
Library Journal, April 15, 2004, Mirela Roncevic, review of *Confessions of a Slacker Mom,* p. 110.
Publishers Weekly, February 21, 2005, review of *Confessions of a Slacker Wife,* p. 168.
Washington Post, May 11, 2004, Jennifer Huget, "Here Comes Slacker Mom," p. HE01.

ONLINE

MSNBC.com, http://www.msnbc.com/ (February 13, 2005), Peg Tyre, "Meet the Slacker Mom."

USA Today Online, http://www.hyper-parenting.com/usatoday2.htm/ (May 4, 2004), Kim Painter, "Moms Swing from Super to 'Slacker'."

*   *   *

MEHIGAN, Joshua 1969-

PERSONAL: Born 1969, in Johnstown, NY. *Education:* Purchase College, B.A., 1991; Sarah Lawrence College, M.F.A., 1994.

ADDRESSES: Home—151 14th St., Apt. 1, Brooklyn, NY 11215. *E-mail*—jmehigan@earthlink.net.

CAREER: Editor, educator, and poet. Sarah Lawrence College, Bronxville, NY, teaching assistant, 1994; Bronx Community College, Bronx, NY, adjunct lecturer in the English Department, 2003; University of Southern Maine, Portland, visiting writer, 2006; *Poets & Writers Online,* editor; *Society of Underground Poets* (syndicated radio program), poetry book reviewer. Worked previously as jobs, including teaching English at a Manhattan Beach yeshiva, delivering food, serving as managing editor of *Fire Island News,* and working in marketing at Cambridge University Press. Tennessee Williams Scholar, Sewanee Writers' Conference, 2000, and scholar, West Chester University Poetry Conference, 1996-2005.

AWARDS, HONORS: Hollis Summers Poetry Prize, 2004; Dogwood Poetry Prize, 2004, for the poem "Promenade"; Pushcart Prize, 2005; Walter E. Dakin fellow, Sewanee Writers' Conference, 2005; finalist, *Los Angeles Times* Book Prize.

WRITINGS:

Confusing Weather (chapbook), Black Cat Press (West Chester, PA), 1998.
The Optimist: Poems, Ohio University Press (Athens, OH), 2004.

Poems have appeared in numerous periodicals, including *New York Times, Ploughshares, Poetry, Verse, New Criterion, Pequod, Formalist, Chattahoochee Review,*

Sewanee Review, Dogwood, and *Illinois Review,* and in online collections, including *Poetry Daily, Verse Daily, Ploughshares Authors & Articles,* and *Poem Tree.* Poems and translations have appeared in anthologies, including *Phoenix Rising,* edited by Sonny Williams, Textos Books (Cincinnati, OH), 2004; *Pushcart Prize XXX: Best of the Small Presses,* edited by Bill Henderson, Pushcart, 2005; *The Zoo Anthology of Younger Poets,* edited by David Yezzi, Zoo Press, 2005; and *Poetry in Performance 33,* edited by Barry Wallenstein, City College of New York (New York, NY), 2005.

WORK IN PROGRESS: An untitled poetry manuscript and a verse translation of Arthur Rimbaud's poems.

SIDELIGHTS: Joshua Mehigan told John Freeman Gill in the *New York Times* that he had declared that he was going to give up writing when, an hour later, he learned he had won the Hollis Summers Poetry Prize. The prize included the publication of his book *The Optimist: Poems.* Another 1,000-dollar prize and growing recognition soon followed. "I think we're going to hear a lot about Joshua Mehigan," David Yezzi, director of the Unterberg Poetry Center, told Gill in the *New York Times.* "Josh is an extraordinary musician in language, with a very distinctive sound and rhythm and pitch." Mehigan writes realistic poems—from such everyday events as an old man walking in his apartment or an umbrella vendor watching people pass by on the streets—that sometimes incorporate life-changing events, such as a woman battling cancer. Writing on the *Valparaiso Poetry Review* online, D.A. Jeremy Telman commented: "Such realism, tinged with wary humor, characterizes many of Mehigan's poems, which describe events with such clarity, one is convinced that Mehigan himself has experienced them." Telman noted that the author's "technique is varied and irreproachable," adding that "Mehigan writes so well, he invites one to simply take pleasure in the reading, and he takes pains not to highlight his poems' intricacy and formal virtuosity." Telman also wrote that "Mehigan's first full-length poetry collection, *The Optimist,* not only repays re-reading, but requires it." In a review in *Poetry,* D.H. Tracy called the book "a work of some poise and finish, by turns delicate and robust, making balanced use of the imposing and receptive facets of intelligence."

BIOGRAPHICAL AND CRITICAL SOURCES:

PERIODICALS

ForeWord, November-December, 2005, Peter Skinner, "Seventh Annual Look at ForeWord's Big Ten Picks."
Hartford Courant, April 24, 2005, John Freeman, review of *The Optimist: Poems.*
Hudson Review, summer, 2005, Davis Mason, review of *The Optimist.*
Mid-American Review, spring, 2005, Jeannie Kidera, review of *The Optimist,* pp. 201-202.
Midwest Book Review, July, 2005, Michael Dustin, review of *The Optimist.*
New York Sun, November 3, 2004, Adam Kirsch, review of *The Optimist.*
New York Times, April 17, 2005, John Freeman Gill, "Finding the Verse in Adversity," profile of author.
Poetry, June, 2005, D.H. Tracy, review of *The Optimist,* p. 255.
Star Democrat, March 4, 2005, John Goodspeed, review of *The Optimist.*
Valparaiso Poetry Review, spring-summer, 2005, D.A. Jeremy Telman, review of *The Optimist.*

ONLINE

Joshua Mehigan Home Page, http://www.joshua mehigan.net (July 16, 2005).

* * *

MILLER, Arthur I.

PERSONAL: Male. *Education:* City College of New York, B.S.; Massachusetts Institute of Technology, Ph.D.

ADDRESSES: Home—London, England *Office*—Department of Science and Technology Studies, University College London, Gower St., London WC1E 6BT, England. *E-mail*—ucrhaim@ucl.ac.uk.

CAREER: Educator and writer. University College London, London, England, professor; Ettore Majorana Centre for Scientific Culture, Erice, Sicily, director of School of International History of Physics. Visiting professor at École Pratique des Hautes Études, Paris, France, 1977.

MEMBER: American Physical Society (fellow; vice chairman, Division of History of Physics, 1983-84, chairman 1984-85), Académie Internationale d'Histoire des Sciences (corresponding fellow).

AWARDS, HONORS: Fellowships and grants from John Simon Guggenheim Memorial Foundation, American Philosophical Society, American Council of Learned Societies, National Endowment for the Humanities, National Science Foundation, Centre National de la Recherche Scientifique, and Fritz Thyssen stiftung.

WRITINGS:

Albert Einstein's Special Theory of Relativity: Emergence (1905) and Early Interpretation, 1905-1911, Addison-Wesley (Reading, MA), 1981, reprinted, Springer (New York, NY), 1998.
Imagery in Scientific Thought: Creating Twentieth-Century Physics, Birkhäuser (Boston, MA), 1984.
Frontiers of Physics, 1900-1911: Selected Essays with an Original Prologue and Postscript, Birkhäuser (Boston, MA), 1986.
(Editor) *Sixty-two Years of Uncertainty: Historical, Philosophical, and Physical Inquiries into the Foundations of Quantum Mechanics,* Plenum Press (New York, NY), 1990.
(Editor and contributor) *Early Quantum Electrodynamics: A Source Book,* translations from the German by Walter Grant, Cambridge University Press (New York, NY), 1994.
Insights of Genius: Imagery and Creativity in Science and Art, Copernicus (New York, NY), 1996.
Einstein, Picasso: Space, Time, and Beauty That Causes Havoc, Basic Books (New York, NY), 2001.
Empire of the Stars: Obsession, Friendship, and Betrayal in the Quest for Black Holes, Houghton Mifflin (Boston, MA), 2005.

American Journal of Physics, former associate editor.

SIDELIGHTS: Arthur I. Miller specializes in the history and philosophy of science with an emphasis on nineteenth-and twentieth-century science and technology, cognitive science, and scientific creativity. He is the author of several books on these topics, both for a scientific audience and for the interested general public. Intended for a scientific audience, *Early Quantum Electrodynamics: A Source Book,* which Miller edited, presents eleven papers on renormalization theory that are considered classics in the physics community. The book includes a frame-setting essay by Miller.

Miller has also written extensively about the relationship between art and science. His book *Insights of Genius: Imagery and Creativity in Science and Art* explores the idea that visual imagery played a vitally important role in the development of modern science. Although much of the book focuses on topics in the philosophy of science, such as scientific realism, it also explores the work of artists such as Cezanne and Pablo Picasso as they relate to developments in science. "Miller's understanding of the quantum and relativistic revolutions is impressive," wrote Christopher D. Green in *Isis.* Green went on to note that the author "presents an engaging account of the personalities, cognitive styles, and internal political struggles that underlay the transformation from a Newtonian worldview to the twentieth-century view."

In *Einstein, Picasso: Space, Time, and Beauty That Causes Havoc* the author discusses the revolutions in science and art brought about by Albert Einstein and Picasso, respectively. Although the artist and the scientist never met, Miller sets forth the theory that both were influenced by a paper on non-Euclidean geometry written by Henri Poincare. In his treatise, Poincare discussed the theory that artists and physicists could capture dimensions of time and space beyond those that are known in physical life. Miller theorizes that science and art, in the hands of Einstein and Picasso, merged in the realm of ideas and profoundly affected the normal worldview. In the course of his discussion, Miller examines the lives, friends, colleagues, and lovers who also influenced Einstein and Picasso; he includes both scientific diagrams and art by Picasso and other artists. Reviewing *Einstein, Picasso* in the *Library Journal,* Martin R. Kalfatovic noted that "Miller creates a compelling argument for the confluence of aesthetics and science." A *Publishers Weekly* contributor called the book an "eloquent and wide-ranging interdisciplinary history of ideas." Martin H. Levinson, writing in *Etc.: A Review of General Semantics,* stated that "Miller reveals the humanity and intellectuality of Einstein and Picasso through alternating chapters." Levinson also commented that the author's "lucid writing style makes

Einstein, Picasso a particularly entertaining and informative read."

Empire of the Stars: Obsession, Friendship, and Betrayal in the Quest for Black Holes focuses on the development of the theory that black holes exist in space and the scientific infighting that occurred over whether or not the theory was in fact true. The first to propose the existence of black holes was a twenty-year-old Cambridge student of physics in 1935 named Subrahmanyan Chandrasekhar, known as Chandra. A graduate-student prodigy, Chandra underwent ridicule even from his own mentor, Sir Arthur Eddington. Miller recounts Chandra's battle to prove he was right and he also discusses the progress of astrophysics from the 1930s forward, including portraits of famed physicists Edward Teller, J. Robert Oppenheimer, and Niels Bohr. Noting that the book emphasizes complex science, a *Kirkus Reviews* contributor went on to comment: "The rewards for the diligent, however, are many and profound." Another reviewer, writing in *Publishers Weekly,* said that "astronomy buffs and readers fascinated by the history of science will find this a compelling read."

BIOGRAPHICAL AND CRITICAL SOURCES:

PERIODICALS

Etc.: A Review of General Semantics, winter, 2002, Martin H. Levinson, review of *Einstein, Picasso: Space, Time, and the Beauty That Causes Havoc,* p. 462.

Isis, December, 2003, Christopher D. Green, review of *Insights of Genius: Imagery and Creativity in Science and Art,* p. 748.

Kirkus Reviews, February 15, 2005, review of *Empire of the Stars: Obsession, Friendship, and Betrayal in the Quest for Black Holes,* p. 216.

Library Journal, June 1, 2001, Martin R. Kalfatovic, review of *Einstein, Picasso,* p. 154; December 1, 2004, Barbara Hoffert, review of *Empire of the Stars,* p. 92; April 1, 2005, Margaret F. Dominy, review of *Empire of the Stars,* p. 121.

Publishers Weekly, March 12, 2001, review of *Einstein, Picasso,* p. 71; March 14, 2005, review of *Empire of the Stars,* p. 57.

Science, September 9, 1994, Katherine Livingston, review of *Early Quantum Electrodynamics: A Source Book,* p. 1605.

ONLINE

University College London Web site, http://www.ucl.ac.uk/ (July 16, 2005), biographical information on author.

*   *   *

MITTELBACH, Margaret

PERSONAL: Female

ADDRESSES: Home—Brooklyn, NY. *Agent*—c/o Author Mail, Villard Books, 1745 Broadway, New York, NY 10019.

CAREER: Writer and naturalist.

WRITINGS:

(With Michael Crewdson) *Wild New York: A Guide to the Wildlife, Wild Places & Natural Phenomena of New York City,* Crown (New York, NY), 1997.
(With Michael Crewdson) *Carnivorous Nights: On the Trail of the Tasmanian Tiger,* artwork by Alexis Rockman, Villard Books (New York, NY), 2005.

Author has written extensively about the natural world for numerous publications, including *New York Newsday.*

SIDELIGHTS: For Sidelights, see CREWDSON, Michael.

BIOGRAPHICAL AND CRITICAL SOURCES:

PERIODICALS

Kirkus Reviews, February 15, 2005, review of *Carnivorous Nights: On the Trail of the Tasmanian Tiger,* p. 217.

Library Journal, April 1, 2005, Edell M. Schaefer, review of *Carnivorous Nights,* p. 121.

Publishers Weekly, March 14, 2005, review of *Carnivorous Nights,* p. 60.

Science News, May 14, 2005, review of *Carnivorous Nights,* p. 319.*

*   *   *

MOAVENI, Azadeh 1976-

PERSONAL: Born 1976, in Palo Alto, CA. *Education:* University of California, Santa Cruz; also attended American University (Cairo, Egypt).

ADDRESSES: Home—Beirut, Lebanon. *Agent*—c/o Kasey Pfaff, Perseus Books, 250 W. 57th St., Ste. 1321, New York, NY 10107.

CAREER: Journalist. Middle-East correspondent for *Time* magazine; covered the war in Iraq for *Los Angeles Times.*

WRITINGS:

Lipstick Jihad: A Memoir of Growing up Iranian in America and American in Iran, Public Affairs (New York, NY), 2005.

WORK IN PROGRESS: Cowriting the memoirs of Iranian Nobel Peace Prize winner Shirin Ebadi.

SIDELIGHTS: Azadeh Moaveni is an Iranian American who grew up in California and went on to become a journalist. She visited relatives in Iran in the late 1990s and then moved there in 2000 as a correspondent for *Time* magazine. In her book, *Lipstick Jihad: A Memoir of Growing up Iranian in America and American in Iran,* Moaveni writes both about her time in Iran and about growing up in America, where she felt caught between two cultures. Moaveni's memoir describes how, in many ways, she is a typical California girl growing up in America and enthralled with its popular culture. Nevertheless, she is still trained in and practices some of the traditional Iranian ways, such as serving tea to her elders. Although Moaveni writes about her personal journey to reconcile her two cultural heritages once she moves to Iran, she also focuses on the country she dreamed of as a young girl

but found to be very different from her imagination once she arrived there. In the book she discusses the country's varied culture, its politics, and its long-standing combative relationship with the United States.

"The author's account of trying, on the one hand, to be a foreign reporter under a theocratic regime, and, on the other, a normal young woman with a career and family and her own apartment, is beautifully nuanced, complex, and illuminating," according to a *Kirkus Reviews* contributer. Maria C. Bagshaw, writing in the *Library Journal,* called the book "a charming and informative memoir." A *Publishers Weekly* contributor was equally enthusiastic, commenting: "Although she reports on the overall tumult and repression felt by Iranians between the 1999 prodemocracy student demonstrations and the 2002 'Axis of Evil' declaration, the . . . dominant story is more intimate." In addition, *Entertainment Weekly* contributor Gilbert Cruz noted that the author "shines a fascinating light on a nation at odds with itself."

BIOGRAPHICAL AND CRITICAL SOURCES:

BOOKS

Moaveni, Azadeh, *Lipstick Jihad: A Memoir of Growing up Iranian in America and American in Iran,* Public Affairs (New York, NY), 2005.

PERIODICALS

Booklist, February 15, 2005, John Green, review of *Lipstick Jihad,* p. 1040.
Curve, June, 2005, Rachel Llewellyn, review of *Lipstick Jihad,* p. 80.
Entertainment Weekly, March 25, 2005, Gilbert Cruz, review of *Lipstick Jihad,* p. 78.
Houston Chronicle, April 8, 2005, Rachel Graves, review of *Lipstick Jihad.*
Kirkus Reviews, January 15, 2005, review of *Lipstick Jihad,* p. 106.
Library Journal, February 15, 2005, Maria C. Bagshaw, review of *Lipstick Jihad,* p. 140.
Mother Jones, March 9, 2005, Michal Lumsden, "Lipstick Jihad: An Interview with Azadeh Moaveni."
Publishers Weekly, January 17, 2005, review of *Lipstick Jihad,* p. 42.

ONLINE

Impression Web sites, http://impressions-ba.com/ (July 16, 2005), Rebecca L. Weber, "Culture Clash—Azadeh Moaveni."

Lipstick Jihad, http://www.lipstickjihad.com/ (July 16, 2005), includes brief profile of author.

MuslimWakeUp.com, http://www.muslimwakeup.com/ (March 1, 2005), Bibi Eng, "Not Your Mullah's Iran: An Interview with Azadeh Moaveni."*

* * *

MOORE, Lisa 1964-
(Lisa Lynne Moore)

PERSONAL: Born 1964, in St. John's, Newfoundland, Canada; married; children: Eva, Cotheo. *Education:* Nova Scotia College of Art and Design, B.A.; attended Memorial University.

ADDRESSES: Home—St. John's, Newfoundland, Canada. *Agent*—c/o Author Mail, House of Anansi Press, 110 Spadina Ave., Ste. 801, Toronto, Ontario M5V 2K4, Canada.

CAREER: Writer. *Globe and Mail,* Toronto, Ontario, Canada, bi-weekly columnist. Also writes for radio and television. Worked numerous full-and part-time jobs in the arts and has taught continuing education at Memorial University.

Has also worked with the Choices for Youth organization and appeared as herself in the Canadian television documentary, *Hard Rock & Water,* 2005.

AWARDS, HONORS: Canadian Authors' Association Prize for short fiction, for *Open: Stories;* first prize, Writers' Alliance of Newfoundland award; Labrador awards, including 2002, for short story "Contra," Arts and Letters Award, Province of Newfoundland, for "Contra."

WRITINGS:

Degrees of Nakedness: Stories, Mercury Press (Stratford, Ontario, Canada), 1995.

Open: Stories, Anansi (Toronto, Ontario, Canada), 2002.

Short stories have appeared in numerous Canadian literary journals, including *Prism, Event, Canadian Fiction, Tickleace,* and the *New Quarterly.* Work has also appeared in anthologies, including *Extremities: Stories from the Burning Rock, Coming Attractions,* and *The Journey Prize Stories,* selected by Elizabeth Hay, Lisa Moore, and Michael Redhill, McClelland & Stewart, 2004.

Open has been translated into French.

SIDELIGHTS: Lisa Moore trained as an artist, but she is also the author of short-story collections. Most of Moore's stories take place in her birthplace and home, St. John's, Newfoundland, Canada. In her first collection, *Degrees of Nakedness: Stories,* published in 1995, each story features a female narrator dealing with life's various problems, such as family upheavals and infidelity. Each narrator is unique, from a tough woman who wants to kill her husband's mistress to an absent-minded artist. Reviewing *Degrees of Nakedness* in *Herizons,* Kerry Ryan noted that in the stories the author "captur[es] . . . raw, intense images—of sex, motherhood and complex family relationships—against a variety of backdrops." Ryan went on to comment that "each story is brightly coloured by intense emotion and vivid, wonderful language," and called the book "a lovely collection by an extraordinarily fine writer."

Like her previous collection, the tales in *Open: Stories* take place mostly in St. John's but are "also connected to the larger world thematically and geographically," as noted by Elizabeth Ruth in the Toronto *Globe & Mail.* For the most part, Moore focuses on the vagaries of the female-male relationship in a world of moral ambiguities and explores how much control people have over determining the course of their lives. "If a reader can see both sides of a question then the important thing is not the answer but the question," Moore told Ruth. The author went on to note, "I like the idea of making it impossible to know the right answer or at least to bring people to the understanding that often there aren't right answers."

Writing in *Herizons,* Sara Cassidy called *Open* "deliriously rich, visceral and sexy," and noted that the stories are "tenuously balanced on spare dialogue and packed with startling, sensuous images." "They're also dreamy, if mercifully free of the sentimentality, implausibility and self-consciousness," the critic added. Brian Bethune, writing in *Maclean's,* stated that "Moore's talent is staggering, her images arresting, her dialogue, particularly between men and women, needle-to-the-eye sharp." A *Globe & Mail* contributor noted that the author's "writing is often daring" and commented that Moore uses "narrative as a beautiful necklace of moments strung together."

BIOGRAPHICAL AND CRITICAL SOURCES:

PERIODICALS

Globe & Mail (Toronto, Ontario, Canada), May 11, 2002, review of *Open: Stories;* May 11, 2002, Elizabeth Ruth, "Interview: Hot from the Rock"; October 12, 2002, Sandra Martin, "Voice from the World of the Senses," interview with author, p. 1; December 28, 2002, Shelagh Rogers, review of *Open,* p. 1; November 6, 2004, Fiona Foster, review of *The Journey Prize Stories,* p. D12.

Herizons, summer, 2003, Sara Cassidy, review of *Open,* p. 33; winter, 2005, Kerry Ryan, review of *Degrees of Nakedness: Stories,* p. 36.

Maclean's, July 1, 2002, Brian Bethune, review of *Open,* p. 84.

This, March-April, 2002, Alana Wilcox, "Lisa Moore Opens Up," p. 41.

ONLINE

Anansi Press Web site, http://www.anansi.ca/ (July 16, 2005), brief profile of author.

Banff Centre Web site, http://www.banffcentre.ca/ (July 16, 2005), brief profile of author.

St. Thomas University Web site, http://www.stthomasu.ca/ (July 16, 2005), brief profile of author.*

*   *   *

MOORE, Lisa Lynne
    See MOORE, Lisa

*   *   *

MORÉAS, Jean
    See PAPADIAMANTOPOULOS, Johannes

MORGENSTERN, Joe 1932-
    (Joseph Morgenstern)

PERSONAL: Born October 3, 1932, in New York, NY; son of Mark E. and Mollie (Fisch) Morgenstern; married Rosetta Jacobs (an actor under name Piper Laurie), January 21, 1962 (divorced, April, 1981); children: Anna. *Education:* Lehigh University, B.A. (magna cum laude), 1953.

ADDRESSES: Home—Santa Monica, CA. *Office*—Wall Street Journal, P.O. Box 1946, Santa Monica, CA 90406-1946.

CAREER: Movie critic and writer. *New York Times,* New York, NY, news clerk and later a foreign correspondent; *New York Herald Tribune,* New York, NY, theatre and movie critic; *Newsweek,* New York, NY, movie critic, 1965-72; *L.A. Herald Examiner,* Los Angeles, CA, columnist, 1982-87; *Wall Street Journal,* California Bureau, Santa Monica, film critic, 1995—. Also reviews for CNBC. Guest cohost on television show *Siskel & Ebert at the Movies,* 1999.

MEMBER: National Society of Film Critics (founding member), New York Film Critics Circle, Phi Beta Kappa.

AWARDS, HONORS: Pulitzer Prize, 2005, for film criticism.

WRITINGS:

World Champion (fiction), Simon & Schuster (New York, NY), 1968.

Saul Bass: A Life in Film and Design, Stoddart (England), 1997.

Writer for television, including episodes "The Sonata for a Solo Organ" and "Corporate Veil" for *Law & Order,* 1991-92, and television movie *The Boy in the Plastic Bubble,* 1976. Contributor to numerous periodicals, including the *New Yorker, New York Times Magazine, Los Angeles Times Magazine, Playboy, Gentleman's Quarterly,* and *Columbia Journalism Review.*

SIDELIGHTS: Joe Morgenstern has been a film critic for more than four decades and has also written for television. In 2005 he received the Pulitzer Prize for his film reviews published in the *Wall Street Journal*. Among the articles submitted for the award were his reviews of the movies *The Passion of the Christ, Fahrenheit 9/11, The Motorcycle Diaries, Sideways, Eternal Sunshine of the Spotless Mind,* and the animated feature *The Incredibles.* According to the announcement of the award on the Pulitzer Prize Web site, Morgenstern won "for his reviews that elucidated the strengths and weaknesses of film with rare insight, authority and wit." In an article on the *Business Wire, Wall Street Journal* editorial page editor Paul A. Gigot was quoted as saying that Morgenstern is an "impassioned lover of movies who is endowed with a superb critical ability—all of which he manages to transmit into radiant prose."

Morgenstern began his career as a news clerk but worked his way up to a job as a foreign correspondent covering Switzerland and France for the *New York Times.* He soon turned to writing criticism full time, covering both films and the theater for the *New York Herald Tribune.* Before joining the *Wall Street Journal* in 1995, Morgenstern worked as a film critic for *Newsweek* and then as a columnist for the *L.A. Herald Examiner.* Although primarily a columnist and movie critic throughout his career, Morgenstern has written episodes for the television show *Law & Order* and penned the screenplay for the 1970s television movie *The Boy in the Plastic Bubble.*

BIOGRAPHICAL AND CRITICAL SOURCES:

PERIODICALS

Hollywood Reporter, April 5, 2005, "*Journal, Times* Win Two Pulitzers," p. 8.
Wall Street Journal, April 5, 2005, "*Journal* Wins Pulitzers for Beat Reporting, Criticism," p. A2.

ONLINE

Internet Movie Database, http://www.imdb.com/ (July 17, 2005).
KCRW Radio Web site, http://www.kcrw.com/ (July 17, 2005), brief biography of author.

Opinion Journal Online (*Wall Street Journal* editorial page), http://www.opinionjournal.com/ (July 17, 2005), brief biography of author.
Pulitzer Prize Web site, http://www.pulitzer.org/ (July 17, 2005).*

* * *

MORGENSTERN, Joseph
See MORGENSTERN, Joe

* * *

MORRISSEY, Jake
(J.P. Morrissey)

PERSONAL: Male.

ADDRESSES: *Agent*—c/o Author Mail, William Morrow & Company, 10 E. 53rd St., 7th Fl., New York, NY 10022.

CAREER: Editor, writer, and publisher. Formerly worked at United Media; Scribner, New York, NY, former senior editor; Harmony Books, New York, NY, former executive editor; former comics publisher; Riverhead Books, New York, NY, executive editor, 2004—.

WRITINGS:

(Editor) *The J. Pretension Catalog: Owner's Manual H2SO4: A Very Tasteful Parody,* Andrews McMeel (Kansas City, MO), 1997.
(As J.P. Morrissey) *A Weekend at Blenheim* (fiction), St. Martin's Press (New York, NY), 2003.
The Genius in the Design: Bernini, Borromini, and the Rivalry That Transformed Rome, William Morrow (New York, NY), 2005.

Writings have appeared in numerous periodicals, including *Washington Post, Chicago Tribune,* and *San Francisco Chronicle.*

SIDELIGHTS: Jake Morrissey has written about architecture for numerous periodicals and is also the author of a novel, a parody, and a book of nonfiction.

In his novel *A Weekend at Blenheim,* Morrissey tells the story of American John Vanbrugh, who, in 1905, is asked by the duchess of Marlborough, Consuelo Vanderbilt, to remodel part of Blenheim Palace. The duchess chooses Vanbrugh, partially because an earlier renovator had the exact same name. As he works on the remodeling job, Vanbrugh discovers in the walls a hidden, cryptic message involving murder and a love triangle. A sketchbook of nudes also surfaces, to the consternation of some who would prefer that it remain lost. As the mystery advances, the reader becomes aware of parallels between the past and present, not only in the renovator's name but also in the relationship between the current duke and duchess. The period novel also includes such historic characters as artist John Singer Sargent, who is searching for his missing sketchbook, and Winston Churchill.

A *Kirkus Reviews* contributor called *A Weekend at Blenheim* a "coldly stylish debut." Another reviewer, writing in *Publishers Weekly,* felt the novel is "generally suspenseful and entertaining." Rex E. Klett commented in the *Library Journal* that the author's "incredible knowledge of period, place, and events" make the "mystery a special treat."

In *The Genius in the Design: Bernini, Borromini, and the Rivalry That Transformed Rome* Morrissey delves into the heated rivalry between two seventeenth-century Italian artists. Bernini, who has connections and knows how to gain favor, is named over Borromini as chief architect at St. Peter's in Rome, even though Borromini is chief assistant to the former director who has died. The two work together for a while and virtually create the baroque style of architecture as they progress on various projects. Borromini eventually leaves because of their rivalry, which is fueled by the fact that much of Borromini's work is being credited to Bernini. After years of struggling to find commissions—partly because of his insistence on total autonomy in his work—Borromini commits suicide while Bernini goes on to become perhaps the best-known Italian artist of the period.

In a review of *The Genius in the Design, Booklist* contributor Bryce Christensen called the book "a highly successful double biography." While a *Publishers Weekly* contributor felt that the work is "sometimes plodding but often entertaining," a *Kirkus Reviews* critic commented that the author should be given "credit for not just gleaning cogent commentary from

previous volumes on the output of his two subjects but for enhancing it." The reviewer added, "His handling of these personalities and their divergent careers brings . . . [fresh] passion" to the story.

BIOGRAPHICAL AND CRITICAL SOURCES:

PERIODICALS

Booklist, January 1, 2002, review of *A Weekend at Blenheim,* p. 819; February 1, 2005, Bryce Christensen, review of *The Genius in the Design: Bernini, Borromini, and the Rivalry That Transformed Rome,* p. 928.
Kirkus Reviews, December 1, 2001, review of *A Weekend at Blenheim,* p. 1649; December 15, 2004, review of *The Genius in the Design,* p. 1188.
Library Journal, March 1, 2002, Rex E. Klett, review of *A Weekend at Blenheim,* p. 142.
Publishers Weekly, February 11, 2002, review of *A Weekend at Blenheim,* p. 165; August 23, 2004, "Morrissey Named Editor at Riverhead," p. 7; February 21, 2005, review of *The Genius in the Design,* p. 172.*

*   *   *

MORRISSEY, J.P.
See MORRISSEY, Jake

*   *   *

MULLER, Marcia 1944-

PERSONAL: Born September 28, 1944, in Detroit, MI; daughter of Henry J. (a marketing executive) and Kathryn (Minke) Muller; married Frederick T. Gilson, Jr. (in sales), August 12, 1967 (divorced, 1981); married Bill Pronzini (a novelist), 1992. *Education:* University of Michigan, B.A. (English), 1966, M.A. (journalism), 1971.

ADDRESSES: Agent—Molly Friedrich, Aaron M. Priest Literary Agency Inc., 708 3rd Ave., 23rd Fl., New York, NY 10017-4103.

CAREER: Sunset magazine, Menlo Park, CA, merchandising supervisor, 1967-69; University of Michigan Institute for Social Research, Ann Arbor, field

Marcia Muller, 1995

interviewer in San Francisco Bay area, 1971-73; freelance writer and novelist, 1973—; Invisible Ink, San Francisco, partner (with Julie Smith), 1979-83.

AWARDS, HONORS: American Mystery Award, 1989, for *The Shape of Dread;* Private Eye Writers of America Shamus award, 1991; Private Eye Writers of America Life Achievement award, 1993; Anthony Boucher awards, 1994, for *Wolf in the Shadows,* and 1996, for *The McCone Files; Romantic Times* Lifetime Achievement in Suspense Award, 1999; Spur Award nomination, Western Writers of America, for short story "Time of the Wolves"; Grand Master Award, Mystery Writers of America, 2005.

WRITINGS:

CRIME NOVELS; "SHARON MCCONE" SERIES

Edwin of the Iron Shoes, McKay (New York, NY), 1977.

Ask the Cards a Question, St. Martin's (New York, NY), 1982.

The Cheshire Cat's Eye, St. Martin's (New York, NY), 1983.

Games to Keep the Dark Away, St. Martin's (New York, NY), 1984.

Leave a Message for Willie, St. Martin's (New York, NY), 1984.

(With husband, Bill Pronzini) *Double,* St. Martin's (New York, NY), 1984.

There's Nothing to Be Afraid Of, St. Martin's (New York, NY), 1985.

Eye of the Storm, Mysterious Press (New York, NY), 1988.

The Shape of Dread, Mysterious Press (New York, NY), 1989.

There's Something in a Sunday, Mysterious Press (New York, NY), 1989.

Trophies and Dead Things, Mysterious Press (New York, NY), 1990.

Where Echoes Live, Mysterious Press (New York, NY), 1991.

Pennies on a Dead Woman's Eyes, Mysterious Press (New York, NY), 1992.

Wolf in the Shadows, Mysterious Press (New York, NY), 1993.

Till the Butchers Cut Him Down, Mysterious Press (New York, NY), 1994.

A Wild and Lonely Place, Mysterious Press (New York, NY), 1995.

The McCone Files: The Complete Sharon McCone Stories, Crippen & Landru (Norfolk, VA), 1995.

The Broken Promise Land, Mysterious Press (New York, NY), 1996.

Both Ends of the Night, Mysterious Press (New York, NY), 1997.

While Other People Sleep, Mysterious Press (New York, NY), 1998.

(With Bill Pronzini) *Duo* (stories), Five Star (Unity, ME), 1998.

A Walk through the Fire, Mysterious Press (New York, NY), 1999.

Listen to the Silence, Mysterious Press (New York, NY), 2000.

McCone and Friends (stories), Crippen & Landau (Norfolk, VA), 2000.

Season of Sharing: A Sharon McCone and "Nameless Detective" Story, Crippen & Landru (Norfolk, VA), 2001.

Dead Midnight, Mysterious Press (New York, NY), 2002.

The Dangerous Hour, Mysterious Press (New York, NY), 2004.

Vanishing Point, Mysterious Press (New York, NY), 2006.

CRIME NOVELS; "ELENA OLIVEREZ" SERIES

The Tree of Death, Walker & Company (New York, NY), 1983.

The Legend of the Slain Soldiers, Walker & Company (New York, NY), 1985.

(With Bill Pronzini) *Beyond the Grave,* Walker & Company (New York, NY), 1986.

CRIME NOVELS; "JOANNA STARK" SERIES

The Cavalier in White, St. Martin's (New York, NY), 1986.

There Hangs the Knife, St. Martin's (New York, NY), 1988.

Dark Star, St. Martin's (New York, NY), 1989.

"SOLEDAD COUNTY" SERIES

Point Deception, Mysterious Press (New York, NY), 2001.

Cyanide Wells, Mysterious Press (New York, NY), 2003.

Cape Perdido, Mysterious Press (New York, NY), 2005.

OTHER CRIME NOVELS

(With Bill Pronzini) *The Lighthouse: A Novel of Terror,* St. Martin's (New York, NY), 1987.

ANTHOLOGIES; EDITOR WITH BILL PRONZINI

The Web She Weaves: An Anthology of Mystery and Suspense Stories by Women, Morrow (New York, NY), 1983.

Child's Play: An Anthology of Mystery and Suspense Stories, Macmillan (New York, NY), 1984.

Witches' Brew: Horror and Supernatural Stories by Women, Macmillan (New York, NY), 1984.

Chapter and Hearse: Suspense Stories about the World of Books, Morrow (New York, NY), 1985.

Dark Lessons: Crime and Detection on Campus, Macmillan (New York, NY), 1985.

Kill or Cure: Suspense Stories about the World of Medicine, Macmillan (New York, NY), 1985.

She Won the West: An Anthology of Western and Frontier Stories by Women, Morrow (New York, NY), 1985.

The Wickedest Show on Earth: A Carnival of Circus Suspense, Arbor House (New York, NY), 1985.

The Deadly Arts: A Collection of Artful Suspense, Arbor House (New York, NY), 1985.

1,001 Midnights: The Aficionado's Guide to Mystery and Detective Fiction, Arbor House (New York, NY), 1986.

(Also with Martin H. Greenberg) *Lady on the Case,* Bonanza (New York, NY), 1988.

Detective Duos, Oxford University Press (New York, NY), 1997.

CRIME SHORT STORIES

Deceptions, Mystery Scene Press, 1991.

The Wall (novella; originally published in *Criminal Intent I*), Dark Harvest, 1993.

OTHER

(Author of preface) *Hard-Boiled Dames: A Brass-Knuckled Anthology of the Toughest Women from the Classic Pulps,* St. Martin's (New York, NY), 1986.

Time of the Wolves: Western Stories (includes short story "Time of the Wolves"), Five Star (Waterville, ME), 2003.

Manuscript collection is held at the Popular Culture Library, Bowling Green State University, Bowling Green, OH.

SIDELIGHTS: Novelist Marcia Muller has been instrumental in creating an audience for private eye fiction that features a female protagonist. "When Marcia Muller introduced Sharon McCone in 1977 [in *Edwin of the Iron Shoes*], the author created the first contemporary female hard-boiled private investigator to feature in a series of American crime fiction novels," wrote Adrian Muller in the *St. James Guide to Crime and Mystery Writers.* Sharon McCone, Muller's favorite heroine, is an ace San Francisco legal investigator who differs from some of her more hard-boiled counterparts in that she is more apt to use her wits than her gun. The author once explained that in creating McCone, her aim was "to use the classical puzzle form of the mystery to introduce a contemporary female sleuth, a figure with surprisingly few counterparts in the world of detective fiction." Not only did Muller achieve this personal goal, she also helped pave the way for other women writers who were using female sleuths in their work. Few authors have had more success in the genre than Muller herself, however—McCone has been featured in more than twenty novels, as well as two collections of short stories.

Muller began writing fiction at the age of twelve, but her career as a successful author emerged slowly. In a *Booklist* interview, she recalled: "I took a creative writing course in college, and the instructor told me I would never be a writer because I had nothing to say." Taking the advice to heart, she earned an advanced degree in journalism. Only after moving to San Francisco—and discovering the novels of fellow University of Michigan graduate Ross Macdonald—did she determine to give fiction writing another try. Even after she created Sharon McCone, she still faced some obstacles. "Following *Edwin of the Iron Shoes,* publishers felt that female protagonists held little appeal for readers of crime fiction," Adrien Muller noted, "and it wasn't until 1982 that McCone reappeared in *Ask the Cards a Question.*" In a *Booklist* review, Connie Fletcher stated that *Ask the Cards a Question* is a "perfectly plotted follow-up to Muller's first novel." *Publishers Weekly* critic Barbara A. Bannon also praised the book, commenting that "fans . . . won't be disappointed with this." The "Sharon McCone" series—and Muller's career—were finally launched, and soon McCone had a growing fan base of both male and female readers.

McCone's one-time small investigation operation has grown over the course of more than twenty novels. In titles such as *Listen to the Silence,* she learns she has much to discover about her own past, while in *Dead Midnight,* McCone has to learn to let the past go as she grieves over her brother's suicide. The former book showed "good pacing as Sharon's past is slowly revealed," according to Barbara Perkins in *School Library Journal.* Katherine Fitch, reviewing the book for the same journal, noted that beyond Muller's usual adult audience, "Teens will be fascinated by Sharon's search for her roots." In *Dead Midnight* McCone struggles to deal with her brother's death while investigating another young man's suspicious suicide.

"Subplots and Sharon's introspection add a counterbalance of maturity, intelligence, and emotion to the well-plotted story," wrote Michelle Foyt of the novel in *Library Journal,* while a *Publishers Weekly* critic called *Dead Midnight* "Muller's best yet." *Dead Midnight* marked the twenty-fifth anniversary of McCone's first published investigation, and Marilyn Stasio of the *New York Times Book Review* commented, "this San Francisco private detective has never stopped growing." Christine W. Randall, writing for Charleston, South Carolina's *Post and Courier,* noted that Muller "has managed to keep her heroine fresh and entertaining in the more than twenty novels since" McCone's first appearance.

McCone's growth as a character has been reflected by the growth of her agency as well. *The Dangerous Hour* deals with a threat to McCone Investigations at a time when the agency's future looks golden. When one of McCone's operatives is accused of credit-card theft, McCone delves into the case, and finds out that someone may be out to shut her down by framing her employees. The book is marked by "smooth prose, a diverting plot, and diverse characters," according to *Library Journal* reviewer Rex E. Klett. As a *Publishers Weekly* contributor wrote, "Muller has a knack for painting a full picture of McCone's life without getting too cutesy," while Judith Evans, in the *St. Louis Post-Dispatch,* commented that the novel contains a "fast-moving story, its well-developed characters, and a plot that veers from the expected."

Muller has been praised for both the realistic depiction of her heroine and for giving readers vivid descriptions of the series' Bay area locales. "San Francisco is a place that lends itself to description," Muller mused in an interview with *Time Warner Bookmark Online.* "It's the city of many small enclaves; each with distinctive flavor. When I write about it, the city becomes a secondary character in the novel." Fletcher noted the presence of "San Francisco atmosphere, fast action, and Muller's usual witty dialogue," in her *Booklist* review of *Leave a Message for Willie,* the fifth "Sharon McCone" mystery. In a review of *There's Something in a Sunday* for the *Los Angeles Times Book Review,* Charles Champlin maintained that, "as before, Muller's strength is in her characters—McCone is likable and believable—and her ability to convey places and atmospheres." In a review of *The Dangerous Hour,* the twenty-third book in the series, Stephanie Zvirin of *Booklist* noted that Muller provides "a solid slice of a San Francisco community and a protagonist with character."

Adrian Muller commented in the *St. James Guide to Crime and Mystery Writers.* that it is "the supporting characters that make these novels stand out from many other crime fiction series. Not only do many of the secondary characters continue to reappear, so do many of the minor characters; newly introduced or hovering in the background, they occasionally play larger parts in the books. Once established they rarely disappear without a given reason. The effect is that each new McCone novel is like coming back to a cast of well-loved characters. . . . Throughout the novels McCone's character is constantly evolving, both personally and professionally."

Muller's other female detectives are Elena Oliverez and Joanna Stark. Oliverez is an Hispanic curator in an American-Mexican arts museum. She has been featured in three of Muller's novels, beginning with *The Tree of Death,* in which Elena must prove that she had nothing to do with the murder of her boss. The novel is "a tale with an appealing and unusual setting, some well drawn characters and a heroine one wouldn't mind meeting again," according to Bannon's *Publishers Weekly* review.

Muller has edited many short-story anthologies with her husband, writer Bill Pronzini, including *The Web She Weaves: An Anthology of Mystery and Suspense Stories by Women* and *Kill or Cure: Suspense Stories about the World of Medicine.* In *Publishers Weekly,* Bannon critiqued *The Web She Weaves* as an "eminently entertaining and worthwhile collection." "Pronzini and Muller have unearthed some genuine gems," Margaret Cannon wrote of *Kill or Cure* for the Toronto *Globe and Mail.* "There are no turkeys in the collection."

Muller has also collaborated with Pronzini to produce a number of novels. Theirs is a very productive partnership, as both also critique each others' independent novels before the works are mailed to the publisher. Their collaborative novel, *The Lighthouse: A Novel of Terror,* a tale of yuppies and murder in a small town on the Oregon coast, "combines both authors' strengths . . . and avoids their weaknesses" in a setting that is "excellent," according to Cannon in her Toronto *Globe and Mail* review. Adrian Muller suggested that *Double,* another Muller-Pronzini collaboration, is "noteworthy for the fact that the point of view alternates from chapter to chapter between Muller's Sharon McCone and Pronzini's series character, the 'Nameless' detective."

It was Pronzini's success writing a stand-alone novel that encouraged Muller to try writing crime novels outside of her series fiction. "My husband had experimented with the so-called stand-alone novel, and it gave him a tremendous amount of freedom," Muller told an interviewer for *Publishers Weekly.* However, leaving McCone mader her nervous. In a column for the *New York Times,* Muller wrote, "I had misgivings. Could I convincingly write such characters? They were so unlike McCone and her associates, so unlike me. And it had been such a long time since I'd lived within the mind and soul of anyone other than her." Despite these hesitations, Muller forged ahead, creating the fictional Soledad County in her first stand-alone novel, *Point Deception.* Deputy Sheriff Rhoda Swift sees a woman pulled over on the side of a coastal road in fictional Soledad County, California. Unable to stop and help, Swift is filled with guilt when the woman is later discovered to have been murdered. With the aid of New York writer Guy Newberry, Swift takes on the case, connecting the woman's murder with several past murders. "Muller is in peak condition with this story," wrote *Booklist* contributor Barbara Bibel. Ruth H. Miller, writing for *Library Journal,* commented on the three narrators used in the book—Swift, Newberry, and the murder victim, noting that "Muller moves smoothly from the voice of the murdered woman to Rhoda and Guy." According to a *Publishers Weekly* contributor, "You can taste the fog and smell the seaweed along [the] Highway in . . . Muller's Soledad County." Comparing Rhoda Swift to Sharon McCone, Muller told the interviewer at *Publishers Weekly,* "I think that Rhoda is more vulnerable certainly than Sharon McCone. While she's very professional, she's basically a wounded person." Writing for the Cleveland, Ohio *Plain Dealer,* Les Roberts considered *Point Deception* "a shining example of why Muller is one of the most highly respected writers in her field."

Cyanide Wells, another stand-alone mystery, also features the Soledad County setting. This time, Matt Lindstrom, who is suspected to have killed his wife, Gwen, discovers that she was never actually murdered. He travels from his home in British Columbia to the town of Cyanide Wells, California, to try to make sense of her disappearance, only to find out that she has now disappeared again. Matt finds himself teamed up with Carly McGuire, a newspaper publisher and Gwen's partner, with whom she had a child, to track down both Gwen and Gwen and Carly's daughter. What Matt and Carly discover leads them to understand just how deep Gwen's deceptions have been.

"The relationship between these two prickly characters . . . is the most intriguing aspect" of the novel, wrote GraceAnne A. DeCandido in her review for *Booklist*. Calling the book a "brisk, tidy number," a *Kirkus Reviews* felt that *Cyanide Wells* features "Muller's best plotting in years." According to *Plain Dealer* contributor Les Roberts, "Muller has for twenty-five years been one of the world's premier mystery writers," and *Cyanide Wells* "illustrated why." Muller's third stand-alone novel set in Soledad County features a conflict between big business and environmentalists; when two environmentalists disappear, four members of the Cape Perdido community band together to solve the mystery. According to Stephanie Zvirin in *Booklist,* Muller's "carefully measured plot revelations . . . prove more than enough to keep both longtime fans and newcomers spellbound."

Along with her stand-alone crime novels, Muller has also written a collection of Western stories titled *Time of the Wolves*. The titular short story was nominated for a Spur Award by the Western Writers of America. "As with any of my departures from the McCone series, I wanted to experiment with something new and stretch my abilities as a writer," Muller explained to an interviewer for *Bookreporter.com*. A *Publishers Weekly* critic commended the collection, noting that Muller's fans will "enjoy this example of Muller's versatility." McCone makes an appearance in two of the short stories in the collection, and some of the stories are collaborations between Muller and Pronzini.

Muller explained in an essay for the *St. James Guide to Crime and Mystery Writers*: "In my detective fiction I am attempting to explore various problems of contemporary American society through the eyes of women who become involved in situations which compel them to seek the solutions to various crimes. In the cases of amateur detectives Elena Oliverez and Joanna Stark, these circumstances are more or less thrust upon them, and the women have a strong personal stake in seeing the perpetrators of the crimes brought to justice. Private investigator Sharon McCone's involvement is professional, but more often than not she becomes deeply involved with her clients and/or crimes' victims. . . . While not a superwoman, when forced to confront extraordinary situations, she reaches beyond her normal capabilities and grows and changes accordingly."

In a *Booklist* interview, Muller admitted that Sharon McCone was at first "an alter ego: taller, thinner,

braver, etc. But over the years, we've become a whole lot alike. We share the same political views, the same outlook on the world, the same outlook on people. . . . I think that I am trying to work something out through her." In another interview for *Time Warner Bookmark Online,* the writer admitted: "My greatest fear is that Sharon McCone will show up on my doorstep with her .357 [magnum] and get even for all the dreadful experiences I've put her through!"

AUTOBIOGRAPHICAL ESSAY: Marcia Muller contributed the following autobiographical essay to *CA:*

One of a fiction writer's obligations to his or her readers is to create a scene that they can enter, visualize, and to some degree become part of. I'll attempt to do that for you now, as a way of beginning to explain who I am and how I came to have a career as a crime writer.

Imagine a small, cluttered office in the English department at the University of Michigan. The building is institutional, fifties style; the furnishings are metal, Spartan. A thin, nervous nineteen-year-old English major perches on the edge of a chair, across the desk from a big, bearded visiting professor of creative writing, the author of two published literary novels, who looks somewhat depressed by her presence.

The young woman clears her throat and finally speaks. "Why did you give me only a C in the class? Does it mean you don't think I have what it takes to be a writer?"

Now the professor looks weary. He picks up a sheaf of manuscript pages, scans them, and drops them on the desk. "In my opinion, you will never be a writer," he tells her. "You have nothing to say."

As the woman leaves the building, literary aspirations dashed to pieces, she thinks that the gray skies over Ann Arbor, Michigan, have never looked gloomier.

Yes, that young woman was me. And some forty years later I sit here at my computer, living testimony that one shouldn't always pay attention to the opinions of a supposed expert.

Contrary to what the professor said, I'd always believed I had a great deal to say and the ability to learn how to say it. As a child I wrote pamphlet-size

With her siblings, 1946: (clockwise) Carol, Lois, and Henry, holding Marcia.

stories about my cocker spaniel, one per season: "Bally Hoo in the Spring," "Bally Hoo in the Summer," "Bally Hoo in the Fall," "Bally Hoo in the Winter." Granted, the titles could have used some work, but they did say something about the animal and my childhood fantasies.

Next I wrote a pamphlet explaining why I felt compelled to chronicle the dog's adventures, and at age twelve, in a long summer's effort, I typed and illustrated a 144-page saga, "The Dogs of Willowhill," about said cocker spaniel and her friends who were, in reality, my stuffed animals. I was revising it to turn it into a mystery story about the time I discovered I was more interested in boys than in the printed word.

My parents—Henry J. Muller, an oil company executive, and Kathryn S. Muller, a homemaker—were amused by, and tolerant of, my fledgling literary endeavors. (Much more amused and tolerant than they were of my interest in boys.) In fact, my father was a great storyteller—although upon adult reflection, I realize that his stories bore a suspicious resemblance to the cartoons I liked to watch—and he always kept us amused. Both of my parents prized education, and thus the house in a suburb of Detroit, Michigan, where my two sisters, my brother, and I grew up was full of books. Our library contained a set of the classics,

hundreds of volumes of contemporary novels, plays, and poetry, as well as a complete set of the *Encyclopedia Britannica*. Children's books—both new and passed down from my three older siblings—filled a huge cabinet in my bedroom. I read my way through such classics as *The Wind in the Willows* and *The Wizard of Oz,* as well as all the girls' mysteries.

My favorite of the latter was the "Judy Bolton" series by Margaret Sutton. Unlike the books in the "Nancy Drew" series, they were authored by a single person, rather than a syndicate, and were much more adult in content and style. Judy was in many ways the inspiration for my long-running series detective, Sharon McCone: independent, somewhat hotheaded, compassionate, and socially aware. In dipping into one of the Sutton books a few years ago, I noted that she even had, as McCone does, a boyfriend who flew an airplane. Judy not only detected, but grew and changed: she graduated from high school, began a career, got married, had a foster daughter. As a young girl who already idolized writers, I would have been thrilled to know that one day I would meet Margaret Sutton, and that she would request a signed copy of *Edwin of the Iron Shoes* (1977), my first novel. What better validation for a new writer than to have a childhood hero read her fledgling effort?

My reading tastes were about to expand, though: when I was around thirteen my mother presented me with a copy of *Gone with the Wind* and told me I was ready for adult fiction. From then on the library became my refuge from a somewhat lonely childhood.

I was the youngest child and a change-of-life baby, conceived on a frosty December night in 1943, and I often felt like an outsider within my own family. Everyone else had been born in New Jersey (except for my mother, who was born in Germany), and they had moved to Michigan only a year before my birth. By the time I started school, my oldest sister, Lois, had already graduated from high school; my brother, Henry, Jr. (to whom, when he was fourteen, my mother delegated the dubious pleasure of delivering me to kindergarten for my first day), left for college when I was in fourth grade. Even my sister Carol, seven years older, to whom I was closest, was married before I started high school. And when they were all present . . . well, it was like having two sets of parents and one young aunt. Two sets of parents and one young aunt who didn't hesitate to tell me what to do at every opportunity. Possibly this is why, to this day, I have a strong and sometimes unreasonable resistance to authority figures—a trait that I've passed along to many of my fictional characters.

It didn't help that I was shy and, because our home was located in an area populated by older families, unused to children of my own age. As the years passed and I became more socialized, I had a few close friends, but I was always more comfortable in my own company. Today I picture myself as that weird kid people always saw walking home from school alone, muttering to herself. Little did others know that I was actually talking to a large and colorful cast of imaginary playmates.

A lonely childhood is no fun, but it shapes a person so she is able to live inside her own head, creating worlds that have not existed and never will exist. It causes the imagination to twist and turn in ways that it would not, were her time spent in close companionship with others. And it teaches self-reliance. The imaginary playmates that peopled my mind were always strong, independent, and daring, and in them I see the roots of the characters I write about today. In my own loneliness, I see the roots of Sharon McCone, who also felt an outsider in her family.

It was, however, a long road from the creative writing professor's untidy office to the office where, now, those characters are brought to life.

My solution to the professor's judgment of my literary abilities was to study journalism. Even though I might not have anything to say fictionally, I reasoned, I could at least report on activities and activists in the real world. While taking as many undergraduate courses in journalism as my schedule would permit, I became a campus correspondent for *Mademoiselle* magazine, and in 1966 was one of twelve finalists in *Vogue* magazine's annual Prix de Paris writing contest. After receiving my highly useless B.A. in English literature, I entered the university's graduate journalism program.

During the course of my study, however, a disturbing tendency surfaced: I began to fictionalize my nonfiction pieces. Sometimes I'd be interviewing a subject

"My father and me at the University of Michigan in 1964. He was a great storyteller."

and think, "Why am I asking questions of this boring person? I could make up so many more fascinating answers." This was not a tendency that endeared me to my professors or the editors for whom I attempted to freelance.

After my first year of graduate school, I gave up journalism, married a naval officer, Fred Gilson, whom I had dated as an undergraduate, and moved to California. The state immediately fascinated me: magnificent and varied topography; diversity of ethnic groups; rich history. I took a job in the merchandising department of *Sunset* magazine—"The Magazine of Western Living"—and became immersed in the culture of my new home. Two years later, my husband was deployed to the Philippines, and I accompanied him there and on a trip through Hong Kong, Macao, Taiwan, and Japan. In the Philippines we lived off-base in Cavite City, a navy town across the bay from Manila, and there and in the capital city I came into contact with members of a wealthy Chinese family to whom a friend had referred me; U.S. Embassy officials; art dealers; the ordinary shopkeepers and citizens of the navy town; a madam who ran a "resort" with an uncommonly good restaurant, who used to send me food during my husband's frequent sojourns in Vietnam. More eye-opening sights for a still-naive young woman from the American Midwest. More inspiration for the books and stories I didn't yet know I would write.

*

By the time my husband was discharged from the navy and we returned to Ann Arbor—he to study toward an M.B.A. and I to finish my M.A. in journalism—the marriage was crumbling. We'd married, as did so many couples in those days, because it seemed time to do so, but for us it proved to be the wrong time. After receiving my M.A. in 1971, I moved alone to San Francisco, where I supported myself on my small savings and my earnings as a temporary office worker. Since most of the temp jobs required a certain mastery of the typewriter that I didn't possess, these earnings were not large, and I found myself with a great deal of free time on my hands. To fill it, I turned to my old love—reading. And, more specifically, to reading the crime novel.

When I first came back to San Francisco, a friend had loaned me a Ross Macdonald novel, *The Far Side of the Dollar,* to take with me on a long bus ride. Macdonald's vivid depictions of the California scene and his complex plot structures fascinated me. I read all of his books I could find, and was soon making weekly trips to the library to raid the mystery section for books by other authors. Voraciously, I read everything— American, British, foreign translations; cozies, hardboiled, suspense, police procedurals; good, bad, and indifferent. But the one type I kept coming back to was the American private-eye novel. There was something about these independent heroes working the mean streets to right wrongs that appealed to my sense of adventure and justice. The streets around my Mission district apartment certainly were mean, and I was very wary on them, not being a particularly brave person. But perhaps I could create an alter ego who would walk them unafraid. . . .

Private detective Sharon McCone, now in her twenty-eighth year of sleuthing, was about to be born.

It was, however, a birth not without difficulties. In early 1972, I reconciled with my husband, and a year later we moved to the distant East Bay suburb of

Walnut Creek, where we bought a house that was to be under constant construction and remodeling for four years. Money was short, and once again I took on temporary office jobs that later would provide characters and background for my fiction. Construction companies, plumbing suppliers, freight forwarding agents, engineers, small business consultants—all would play a part in McCone's and other series characters' future cases. I had begun a manuscript for what I thought would be the first Sharon McCone novel while living in San Francisco. Now, far from my friends and the pleasant distractions of the city, I began to flesh out the character and her surroundings.

Sharon McCone: Sharon, for my college roommate; McCone, for John McCone, former head of the CIA. (An in joke that was not caught until years later when Mr. McCone's niece read one of the books and contacted me; I was relieved to learn that her uncle was amused.)

Sharon's surroundings: poverty law firm All Souls Legal Cooperative, a name that more or less popped into my mind after I met members of a Los Angeles group, the Bar Sinisters, at a University of California conference for women in the legal profession. True to form, I was at the conference to do research for a freelance article, but ended up with fictional fodder instead.

My first effort at a novel, *The Ph. Parameter,* was dreadful, centering around right-wing conspiracies and improbable situations that triggered phobias, and set mainly in Los Angeles, about which I knew very little. The manuscript was deemed unsalable by every agent and unpublishable by every editor who bothered to read it, and I have to admit they were right. A few years ago, in preparation for writing framing stories for a collection of Sharon McCone short stories—one about her first, unsolved case for the law co-op, the other about the solution to that case that she arrives at on the day the co-op is dissolved—I was forced to reread the opening chapter of *Ph.* It was a humbling experience, except for one fact: Sharon McCone's narrative voice is true, even in that embryonic effort. The novel will never see publication, however; it resides in a box that is swathed in duct tape, with a note attached saying "To be burned in the event of my death."

Fortunately, when the negative comments on *Ph.* started pouring in, I'd already begun my second manuscript. And I'd also learned of a workshop in mystery writing that was being conducted by the University of California Extension in Berkeley.

Jean Backus, the workshop leader, was a wonderful teacher. Although she had published only four books—three spy novels as David Montross and a romance under her own name—and a handful of short stories, she had the gift of being able to look at a manuscript, analyze its flaws, and recommend ways to correct them. In fact, a firm rule of the workshop was that one wasn't allowed to make a criticism without backing it up with a concrete, positive suggestion. The workshop hadn't attracted enough of a signup to make it profitable for UC, so a small group of us met at Jean's house in the Berkeley hills. It was there that my first published novel, *Edwin of the Iron Shoes,* was conceived.

Jean began by giving us an assignment: write a biography of your main character. In the course of doing so, I committed to paper details about Sharon Mc-Cone that had been only hazy notions before. Sharon's family is loosely based on the family of a friend, and their stories became her stories; similarly, many of my family stories and those of other friends made their way into the McCone family history. Sharon attended UC Berkeley because it was the West Coast campus most nearly like the University of Michigan; we shared common experiences during our college years. The Mission district apartment where she lived bore a suspicious resemblance to the one in which I had devoured so many mysteries. All Souls Legal Cooperative occupied the big, brown Victorian in the Bernal Heights district that in reality was occupied by a college classmate and her husband.

Out of the simple facts of the biography came more intimate details: Sharon had often felt an outsider in her own family; she was something of a loner, craving her personal space, but needing others as well; she had bad luck with men. She also had qualities that I wished I possessed, the most important of which were courage and independence.

I'm often asked why I chose to give Sharon an Indian background (she is originally described as being one-eighth Shoshone, a throwback to her great-grandmother). In the beginning this was a descriptive device. Because the McCone novels are written in the first person, I needed to find a way to make the readers aware of what she looked like without using the hackneyed device of having her look in a mirror and describe herself. Everyone has some conception of how Native Americans look (although, as I've found out, it's usually at one extreme or the other, from Cher to the squaws in old western movies). Later, Sharon's Indian background would play a more crucial role in the series, but that's getting way ahead of Jean Backus's writers workshop.

The second assignment Jean gave us was more specific: develop the plot for a short story based on a painting on her living room wall. I looked at it and thought, "Cheap souvenir from Florence." (Later I found out it was a Russian icon of some value.) With the cheap Florentine painting firmly in mind, I sat down and in the course of a week plotted not a short story, but a novel.

The plot I had devised was loosely based upon an enclave of antique shops in San Francisco and the murder victim was one of their owners. (The woman later displayed the book prominently in her shop window, advertising her status as having been fictionally done in.) Unfortunately, the story was also quite skimpy, and as the writing progressed I was forced to improvise, adding characters, scenes, and plot twists, and constantly revising—a free-form method that I use to this day. When I finally presented the draft to Jean Backus, she returned it with twelve handwritten pages of criticism: unbelievable ending; faulty pacing; words repeated ad nauseum. Humbled, I began to rewrite, consulting frequently with Jean. One of our favorite shared stories came out of that period.

I was at the point of revising the ending, and had discussed several alternatives with Jean, none of which was totally satisfying, when a load of dirt for a raised-bed vegetable garden was delivered to my home. I decided to take a break and was shoveling the dirt into the bed when the proper ending to my story occurred to me. I rushed into the house, called Jean, and forever after she delighted in telling people what I had been doing when I had my brainstorm. Unfortunately, like me, Jean possessed the urge to make a story more interesting, and she referred to my outdoor activity as "shoveling shit."

While I was attending the workshop, I'd finished a second manuscript, *Ask the Cards a Question* (1982), and as I wrote *Edwin,* I began to send it out. I had heard that an editor at David McKay Company, Michele Slung, was actively seeking mystery novels. I knew of Michele, from an anthology of short stories featuring women sleuths she had edited, and, from the books she'd suggested in her bibliography, I felt my writing might interest her. So the second manuscript went off to her and was promptly returned with an encouraging note saying that while the plot wasn't strong enough, she liked the McCone character and would be interested in seeing something else featuring her. I was nearly finished with the final draft of *Edwin,* and I wrote back the same day, saying, "I just happen to have. . . " Several months later the manuscript became one of that rare breed, accepted for publication by the first editor who saw it.

Every writer remembers the circumstances of a first sale—where they were, what they were doing when the call came—and I'm no exception, particularly because the circumstances leading up to it had been peculiar and stressful. Michele Slung had written in August to say she wanted to buy the book, but was going on a three-week trip to Europe and would have to finalize things when she returned. Three weeks stretched out to five, six, seven; the agent she had recommended to me to hated the character and returned my manuscript. I didn't know what to do: Query, and maybe kill the sale? Remain silent, and maybe be forgotten? Finally I sent off a brief letter.

Two days later I was paying bills after collecting my meager earnings from a temp job when the phone rang. Michele, calling from New York. She was going to buy the book. That was it—a brief phone call, and my life changed forever.

I celebrated by attending a writers group meeting that I had scheduled (Jean Backus was no longer interested in giving workshops, so several of us had begun holding meetings at each other's homes). Because I had called first to explain why I would be late, the others had time to prepare, and when I walked in I found them all on the floor, bowing as one would to Mecca.

*

Many people have asked me why I chose to write crime novels rather than mainstream fiction. There's the obvious answer, one I've given many times and

heard other mystery novelists assert: The detective story imposes order upon a chaotic world. Terrible things may happen, people may die, but in the end there is an explanation as to why these events occurred and justice is meted out. Unlike in real life, both the reader and the writer are presented with answers and closure.

But for me there's a more personal reason for writing the crime novel, one that, strangely enough, I'd never articulated until the mid-1990s, when I heard myself telling it to a radio talk-show host.

I became a mystery writer because it was a way to exorcize old demons. During my childhood and young adulthood I experienced a series of troubling events: my dentist shot and killed his wife and child; a favorite high school teacher (and mother of a friend) was brutally murdered by her husband; a friend's father was killed when the airliner on which he was flying was exploded in midair by a bomb; a college friend who lived in the next dorm room committed suicide; a college acquaintance was murdered—a killing that has never been solved. I naturally gravitated to crime writing as a way of making sense of these seemingly random events.

The path a professional fiction writer follows is more often than not a rocky one, full of pitfalls. During the four years following *Edwin*'s publication, I revised *Ask the Cards a Question* and wrote two other novels featuring Sharon McCone, as well as two collaborative mysteries with my friend Susan Dunlap, who had been in the workshop with me and who would go on to have a successful career as a mystery writer herself. Neither of those two sold. Years later Sue's and my joint efforts were cannibalized by both of us: we divided up the characters and used them in our own work. A phone call would come from Sue: "Have you used Sylvia Bluefoot yet?" Me: "No." Sue: "Well, then she's mine." Me: "Okay, I'll take E.J. I've got just the place for him."

But that was much later, and the years between 1977 and 1981 were gloomy ones. I moved from a good agent to a bad one, began different sorts of novels and abandoned them. Tried short stories that were met with rejection. The only positive move was back to San Francisco in 1977; living in the city inspired and energized me. I also got to know two other budding mystery writers with a need for support of their writing habits: Julie Smith and Margaret Lucke.

"Bill and me at the 1984 Bouchercon, where he was guest of honor."

Together the three of us formed Invisible Ink, an "editorial services" firm, which by loose definition meant that we would do anything with the printed word that someone was willing to pay us for—editing, ghostwriting, whatever. Assignments came in through whatever contacts we had, and it soon became apparent that Margaret Lucke got the normal, corporate jobs; Julie Smith got the classy, interesting jobs; and I got the weird ones: the grandmother who was writing up her sexual odyssey through Europe for her grandchildren; the black man who was penning a long treatise on why he preferred white women; the airline pilot who could make even his perilous past in the Middle East sound boring, and who would call from Madrid or Paris to ask me to go over to his apartment and water his plants. Why, I wondered repeatedly, did I attract such people?

Yes, those were gloomy years personally as well as professionally. Once again my marriage was crumbling, as we embarked on yet another mammoth home remodeling project. Something, I knew, had to change.

Enter Bill Pronzini.

At that time, Bill was regional vice president of the northern California chapter of Mystery Writers of America, and responsible for chairing their monthly meetings. I had refused to attend these meetings until after my first novel was scheduled to be published, because I was in awe of "real writers" and afraid of not fitting in. My first encounter with Bill was not promising: he introduced me to the assembled group as the author of *Edgar of the Iron Shoes*—a slip that made some people laugh and others mutter, "Well, she must think highly of her work, naming the book after the Edgar award!" Bill, who gave generously of his time to aspiring writers—as others had done for him—made up for the slip in 1981, however, when he offered to read my unpublished manuscripts. During a subsequent trip to New York City for the Mystery Writers of America Edgar Week, he introduced me to his then-editor at St. Martin's Press, Thomas Dunne. And a few months later, at the same time that my marriage finally ended, Tom bought *Ask the Cards a Question*.

Two things are notable about that visit to New York: first, despite four years of resistance to meeting face-to-face with editors, I had sold my novel within two months of meeting Tom Dunne. And second, another editor Bill had introduced me to was Sara Ann Freed, who would eventually become my editor and friend for twenty-one years.

Ask the Cards a Question had roughly the same plot structure as *Edwin*, as did my third book, 1983's *The Cheshire Cat's Eye*—not a great title, but neither I nor anyone at St. Martin's could come up with a viable alternative. The formula went this way: someone is killed; Sharon is on the case; someone else is killed by the same villain; Sharon tracks him down and solves the case. In my anxiety over plotting I had abandoned my free-form style and devised elaborate charts, showing where each character was at every time, in the hope of preventing such glitches as the murderer talking to McCone while he was supposed to be doing someone in. When it came time to start my fourth McCone, *Games to Keep the Dark Away*, Bill suggested I might want to try another plot structure and explained a few alternatives. I plunged into the book without deciding which one I would use, allowing the characters to simply take over as I had with *Edwin*. And the plot charts went into the trash basket.

St. Martin's Press operated on volume publishing principles with mysteries: they didn't pay much or print very many copies, but with those copies going mainly to libraries, they made money on every title. It was not such a happy situation for authors, however, and it soon became apparent that I needed an additional source of income. Invisible Ink wasn't getting many jobs in those days, so I began thinking about trying other forms of fiction.

Why not write romances? my new agent—an associate of Bill's agent at Curtis Brown Ltd.—suggested. God knows I tried. Proposals flew out of my typewriter, all conforming to the tip sheets the romance lines passed out to prospective authors. Proposals flew out of the editors' offices and back into my mailbox; the concepts and characters weren't believable, they claimed. I agreed. My heart wasn't in it, and to be convincing to the reader the author has to believe in the work. Short stories weren't a viable option either. Although Bill had bought the first McCone short, "Merrill-Go-Round," for an anthology he was editing, and encouraged me to write my first western story, "Sweet Cactus Wine," for another, the proceeds from such projects wouldn't keep my cats in food.

Finally I decided to try a second mystery series. On a trip to New York, I ran the idea by Sara Ann Freed, who at the time was an editor at Walker & Company. Sara Ann had taken the trouble to look up and read *Edwin* after we met the year before, and had rejected *The Cheshire Cat's Eye* (which I had been sending out simultaneously with *Ask the Cards a Question*) with positive comment. The series I first proposed to her was to be based in the art world and feature a sleuth, Joanna Stark, who was a partner in a security firm that dealt exclusively with galleries and museums. As we talked, however, I could see Sara Ann's eyes glazing over, so I quickly switched to a subject that had come up in conversation with a friend who was a fundraiser for a Mexican museum in San Francisco.

How about a series with a Latina sleuth? I asked. Sara Ann perked up some. A woman who was a curator with a Mexican museum whose boss is killed, I added. A murder that any number of people had cause to commit? Where would the series be set? Sara Ann asked. Not San Francisco. I already had a series set there. Well, how about Santa Barbara? I asked. I liked the town, had visited there a number of times, and had a friend there who would assist in the research. As it turned out, it was one of Sara Ann's favorite California cities. The deal for the Elena Oliverez series was finalized a week later.

There were only three Oliverez novels—*The Tree of Death* (1983), *The Legend of the Slain Soldiers* (1985), and *Beyond the Grave* (1986), the last which was coauthored with Bill. I never really connected with the protagonist the way I did with Sharon McCone. The problem wasn't her ethnic background; I had a fairly

good sense of the Hispanic community from a former job with a Small Business Administration contractor, a basic grasp of the language, and besides, Elena Oliverez was a second-generation American. But she was also an amateur sleuth and I had to contrive ways for her to stumble onto crimes. *Beyond the Grave* (considered by many to be Bill's and my best collaboration), was a saga that spanned more than a hundred years and paired Elena with Bill's 1890s private detective, John Quincannon; it was also a departure from what I considered a so-so series, and the prospect of going back to routine amateur-sleuth novels made me decide to retire Elena.

*

Around the time I was writing the first Oliverez novel, Bill came up with an idea for an anthology that fit perfectly into the great upsurge in popularity of female mystery writers: classic stories all by women, past and present, titled *The Web She Weaves* (1983). He had edited a number of anthologies previously, and now I learned the process from him. The dozen anthologies we edited together were a wonderful way of getting old stories back into print and showcasing new writers, as well as a steady source of income.

Then there was the project we first called "a labor of love": *1,001 Midnights*. It consisted of 1,001 short reviews of crime novels and short-story collections throughout the history of the genre, some written by us and others that we commissioned. The title *1,001 Nightmares* would have been more suitable; the project and some of the reviewers quickly became unmanageable, and the publisher, Arbor House, became uncooperative and disinterested. By the time the manuscript was finally delivered in 1985, we needed a long rest.

When I look back on the years between 1983 and 1986, I see a blur of manuscripts being typed, seemingly by someone else's hands; manuscripts going off in the mail; copyedited manuscripts and page proofs returning; finished books arriving. The sheer volume of the work should have been overwhelming, but I was energized, in love with being a writer, honing my skills and learning the business of publishing. And when Bill and I began collaborating, those new skills were put to the test.

Our first joint work was a short story, "Cave of Ice," which was published in *Boys' Life* magazine in 1986.

It was inspired by a vacation visit to an ice cave in southern Idaho, and we had to mesh styles, writing from the viewpoint of a teenaged boy. The experience, once I got over my tendency to write a teenager as if he were eight and not very bright, was a positive one. Next we talked to Tom Dunne about doing a collaborative "Nameless Detective" (who is the protagonist of Bill's mystery series) and Sharon McCone novel. The result was *Double,* which we wrote in alternating sections and published in 1984.

Double was written easily. Bill and I approach fiction the same way—as driven by character, rather than plot. And we were each working with a character whom we knew intimately and who got on well with the other's. An amusing sidelight: once the draft was done and we were taking a drive to the seashore to celebrate, it occurred to Bill that one of the three murders had absolutely no motivation or credible killer. Back to the drawing board. Write and learn.

What I learned in those busy years is that there are possibly four certainties about being a successful author, which I often pass on to aspiring writers, hoping it won't make them flee to some more stable profession. 1) It's a difficult business, and to succeed you need talent, drive, and luck. Probably the most important of these is luck. 2) If you're going to become a writer, you need to sit down and write every day, not just talk about it. If you write as little as only a single page a day, you'll have a draft of a novel inside of a year. 3) You should never be content with mimicking market trends. Don't study and imitate what's currently popular. Do your own, original work. 4) To stay in the game, you need to grow and change as a writer.

As it turned out, in 1986 luck played a great role in my ability to stay in the game. Bill and I had just moved from San Francisco to the country town of Sonoma, thinking a change of pace would recharge us. At first this didn't seem too likely. We were working on the final draft of our third book-length collaboration, a suspense novel called *The Lighthouse* (1987), and nothing was going the way we wanted it to. The plot wouldn't mesh, and our hero insisted on being a total jerk. Disagreements ensued amid the unpacked boxes in our cottage with the white picket fence (really, it had one!). I would look at the boxes and think, "Thank God we haven't opened them yet!" Eventually we forged agreements, our hero decided to be likeable, and the manuscript went off to St. Martin's.

Days later I received a call from Sara Ann Freed who had recently moved from Walker & Company to the Mysterious Press, asking me if I would bring the "Mc-Cone" series there.

The move to Mysterious Press energized me. It was a relatively new publishing house with a small list, and Sara Ann was an excellent editor. She said they wanted me to do the "McCone" books at greater length and in more depth than previously, and I was happy to oblige. It was agreed that I'd write one McCone per year and, since I had only two more "Joanna Stark" novels under contract to St. Martin's, I looked forward to the time when I'd have only one deadline a year.

The "Stark" books—the art security firm series that I'd originally described to Sara Ann and later sold to Tom Dunne—had evolved into a trilogy because of the personal story line that connected them. Joanna Stark was a woman with a dark past that had been revealed to me only as I wrote the first entry in the series, 1986's *The Cavalier in White.* It became more apparent as I began the second, *There Hangs the Knife,* that this story line would run throughout the books, and once it was resolved, the series would have to end. Stark was a darker and more complex character than either Elena Oliverez or Sharon McCone, but as I interspersed the writing of *There Hangs the Knife* and *Dark Star* with my first two "McCones" for Mysterious Press, a strange transference took place between Joanna and Sharon.

McCone developed a darker side; her personal demons, which she'd previously denied or held in check, emerged. Gradually I was beginning to dig deep beneath the surface of a character who at the beginning had been what one reviewer referred to as "something of a cheerleader." And what I found was a seriousness and complexity that had been there all along but never developed. In my 1989 novel *The Shape of Dread,* McCone's demons are unleashed full force, when she almost kills a man in cold blood. In *Trophies and Dead Things* she feels alienated not only from her family, but from her friends and associates, who have witnessed first hand the violent tendencies she struggles to keep under control.

McCone has always been my best friend, and a reflection of me, although no one would ever have referred to me as "something of a cheerleader." When we set out on our mutual journey we were both wide-eyed, in love with what we were doing. But as the years went on, we grew world-wise and cynical; while I possessed no violent tendencies of my own, I could very well imagine hers. Our careers seemed to parallel one another's, McCone responding to the tough realities she encountered as a private investigator, and me responding to the tough realities of the publishing industry. True, I have never stumbled across any dead bodies, but along the way I've seen plenty of carnage of a different sort.

Conglomerates and bottom-liners taking over independent houses. Authors' long-standing careers wrecked because sales weren't substantial enough to suit the cost accountants. Books no longer being referred to as books, but as "products" or "units." Editors summarily dismissed because the books they acquired weren't automatic best sellers. The emphasis on money, always on money. I myself felt safe at Mysterious Press because it was a small company—eventually an imprint of Warner Books, who had early on given them financial backing—and unusually loyal to its authors. But change was happening everywhere, and if bad things are visited upon your friends, they can someday visit you.

What do you do in such a situation? It's out of your control, so you write. And you acquire a new agent.

I've long felt that different agents are appropriate for different stages in a writer's career. The agent I worked with from 1982 to 1989 was good at negotiating standard contracts, but did little to improve my advances or persuade my publishers to actively promote my books. This was at the height of women writers' popularity—a time when books by and about contemporary women, and particularly the female private eye novel—were in great demand. I'd been watching my contemporaries' careers thrive, while mine was standing still. A friend, Marilyn Wallace, who had recently gone to the Aaron M. Priest Literary Agency, recommended Molly Friedrich as the solution to my problems. But I balked at approaching Molly, who was known as an extremely high-powered agent.

In the summer of 1989, Bill and I were among the guests at a writers' conference at Dominican College in nearby San Rafael, California. Marilyn and Molly were there, too, and at the opening get-together, Mari-

lyn introduced us, saying pointedly, "You two need to talk." The conversation took place the next day, the two of us sitting on a wooded hillside. Molly turned out to be a warm, lively woman, not the least bit intimidating, and sympathetic to my predicament (although she would later remark on my former "extremely passive" approach to my career), and she agreed to look at my two most recent books. Two weeks later I had a new agent who would actively work for my best interests—more proof that face-to-face meetings can change one's life.

Meanwhile, the editorial relationship with Sara Ann Freed was working out splendidly. She could put into words what I could not: the problems of a book, its strengths and weaknesses. We developed a method of working together that she called "reading each other's minds." When something in a manuscript didn't work for her, she'd point out what and why; almost immediately I'd come up with an alternative. It was much the way Bill and I looked at each other's work, which we exchanged and edited: make the author step back and take an objective look at something he or she may be too close to.

Sara Ann frequently commented that she didn't have to do as much to my manuscripts as to most authors' because they came in already edited. Bill and I have always exchanged work in progress when we feel we have pages that are ready to show and, while initially I hadn't felt experienced enough to criticize his work, he now relies on my input as much as I rely on his. When either of us is at an impasse—a plot or character problem, difficulty with the pacing—we run it by the other and invariably a solution occurs. Once, when I was finishing *Wolf in the Shadows* (1994) I came to him with two scenarios for the ending. He considered and said, "Neither's right. You know what's best and most logical, but you don't want to do it." Yes, I did, but I'd balked at it because it was more violent than my typical resolutions.

Until 1990, I hadn't received much promotional backing for my books. Prior to publication of *Trophies and Dead Things,* that changed. Mysterious brought me to Chicago for the American Library Association meeting and, at a dinner the night before my signing, I was introduced to Larry Kirshbaum, then CEO of Warner Books, the parent company that had recently purchased Mysterious Press. Again, it was one of those happy occasions where luck—or perhaps coincidence—played a huge role.

Larry had read the advance copy of *Trophies,* and told me he especially liked it because it looked back at the Vietnam War era. He added that he and a friend had once done a nonfiction collaborative account of the campus unrest, titled *Is the Library Burning?* I said, "Your friend must be Roger Rapaport." "How did you know?" Larry asked. "I went to college with him," I said. "We were in journalism classes together." "Well then," Larry said, "you also went to college with *me.*"

Not only had Larry and I attended the same university, we'd graduated the same year and had lived only two blocks apart, although in a student population of some 40,000 our paths had never crossed. The connection was strong, however, and Larry became one of the staunchest supporters of my career.

When *Trophies and Dead Things* was published, a full page ad appeared in the *New York Times.* And then I found out about the other side of being an author: the book tour.

In the 1980s and 1990s book signings and tours were all the rage. I'd never been on one, but I'd done numerous signings and appearances at such events as Bouchercon, the annual world mystery convention. For *Trophies,* I embarked on a coast-to-coast tour, lugging too much baggage and spending too much down time in hotels and airports; having flights cancelled and escorts not show up; greeting small turnouts because booksellers had not troubled to publicize the event; talking to reporters who misquoted me and talk show hosts who hadn't read the book. But sales were improved, Mysterious told me.

As the craze for author appearances heated up, Bill and I were often asked to participate in events. A mystery weekend in Colorado sponsored by Rue Morgue Bookshop in Boulder, which involved a train ride from Denver to Glenwood Springs, produced memorable moments: one when an actor was "murdered" at the station upon arrival, and the train porter, who hadn't been alerted to what was going on, nearly had a heart attack; the other when I "unmasked" the villain as Bill. Over the years we traveled to England on the *Queen Elizabeth II* for a London Bouchercon, and to Caribbean ports on a mystery game cruise. After the Caribbean, we—no fans of cruises—decided we'd take our vacations on our own, even though we'd have to pay for them.

*

By 1991, the town of Sonoma had changed and become tourist-ridden, and Bill and I decided to look for a new home in a quieter location with more room to accommodate two offices and our growing collection of more than 20,000 books. The house we found was in Petaluma, forty miles north of San Francisco where, when it was a country town, Bill had grown up. He'd always subscribed to the theory that you can't go home again, at least not permanently; but the town had grown to a small city and become a lively mecca for artists and writers, and when he saw the big house for sale on a hillside backed up by open space, he quickly changed his mind. It was and is was perfect for two writers. The locations of Bill's office, on the ground floor, and my office, on the third floor at the opposite end of the house, preclude the interruptions ("How do you spell acquaintance?" "What's another word for indelible?") that we'd inflicted upon each other in our old Sonoma house, where our offices were right across the hall.

In the spring of 1992, we decided that it was time to make our commitment to each other permanent. We drove to Carson City, Nevada, and got married—a step that Sharon McCone would take with her longtime love, Hy Ripinsky, thirteen years later. Inspiration is everywhere, even in one's own nuptials.

There have been several redefining points in the "McCone" series. With *The Shape of Dread,* the books began taking on a darker tone. And in the 1991 novel *Where Echoes Live* McCone's personal life took a surprising turn. The mysterious Hy Ripinsky was not meant to be a long-running character; I intended him as a suspect who would later fade into the background and disappear. But as I was writing the scenes between him and McCone, I sensed a chemistry that needed to be explored. Ripinsky and McCone virtually insisted on becoming involved. One thing I've done from the very first is to allow my characters have their own way, and the result is almost always positive.

Wolf in the Shadows is one of the darker and more complex books in the series. Ripinsky vanishes and McCone must locate him while contending with assorted individuals from his unrevealed past, including one who wants to kill him. The ending is a particularly violent one for her; while she had killed in self-defense before, in *Ask the Cards a Question,* my description of the killing and its after effects on her was sketchy and somewhat amateurish. In *Wolf,* she faces her choice to take a man's life to save someone she loves straight out—and follows through with cool professionalism.

The Mysterious Mystery Tour, 1993: (left to right) Sara Ann Freed, Peter Lovesey, Patricia Keim, James Crumley, Paco Taibo, Susan Richman, K.K. Beck, Jack O'Connell, and Marcia Muller.

Wolf in the Shadows is the novel I was promoting when I went along on the Mysterious Mystery Tour. The brainchild of my new publicist at Mysterious, Susan Richman, that tour was something unheard of in the mystery world, but Susan is an energetic woman of vision who isn't the least bit afraid to try something new. On a chilly October morning in Omaha, Nebraska, a shivering group boarded a minibus to travel the Midwest: Susan and another publicist, Patricia Keim; Sara Ann Freed; authors K.K. Beck, James Crumley, Peter Lovesey, Jack O'Connell, Paco Ignacio Taibo III, and yours truly.

It might be said we were an ill assorted group. K.K. Beck wrote humorous amateur sleuth novels; James Crumley's books featured a hard-drinking, drug-using private eye; Peter Lovesey wrote in the classic British tradition; Jack O'Connell's novels depicted a hip, edgy world; and Paco Taibo chronicled the adventures of a Mexico City investigator. It may be that our differences

were what made the tour so enjoyable; as we went by bus and plane from Omaha to Des Moines, Iowa, to Madison and Milwaukee, Wisconsin, and finally to Chicago, we found common ground and enjoyed each other's company. The bus tour has never been repeated; it couldn't be, Susan Richman claims, because how would we replicate such a group?

The year 1994 was a major one for me: *Wolf in the Shadows* was nominated for the Mystery Writers of America Edgar award for best novel and, while it didn't win, it was the recipient of the Anthony Boucher award for best novel at Bouchercon in Seattle, Washington, where I was also guest of honor. It was a busy year as well: I was working on *A Wild And Lonely Place,* more of a thriller than my previous books; compiling a short story collection, *The McCone Files,* for a small press; and researching the music business for McCone's next adventure, 1996's *The Broken Promise Land.*

Research has always been one of the most enjoyable parts of writing. I'm a demon researcher. In college, I would go to the library for specific information, take a stack of films to the microfilm machine, and emerge hours later, red-eyed from having gotten off on interesting—but irrelevant—tangents. Had the Internet existed then, I probably wouldn't have emerged at all.

I conduct four different kinds of research: from written sources, conversations with experts, Internet searches, and on-site visits to locations I'm planning to use. The last, by far, is my favorite. Being in a place, photographing it, and making tape-recorded notes can provide unexpected insights or ideas—and is also a perfect excuse for a vacation. Since Bill and I both set the majority of our novels in California, we've had to divide the state between us; one of us may use a certain locale, and the other will return to it years later to describe it in its current state. A walk with friends near the California-Mexico border resulted in *Wolf in the Shadows* after one of them suggested I should write about the problems there. Later, a border patrol officer, who saw me walking on an isolated and dangerous mesa and almost arrested me, allowed me to interview him after I explained who I was and what I was doing there. A stay with friends in a depressed former steel-making town in Pennsylvania prompted me to set part of 1994's *Till the Butchers Cut Him Down* in a similar locale. A trip to the Caribbean and an article about offshore betting inspired *A Wild and Lonely Place*. A vacation on the island of Kauai spawned my 1999 novel *A Walk through the Fire*.

Sometimes a research trip is undertaken for fact checking, to flesh out descriptions I've already written from photographs or distant knowledge of a place. The most frustrating and amusing of these was when Bill and I journeyed to the desert community of Borrego Springs, California, and found the town to be nothing like the posh resort we'd described in *Double*. However, we'd posited a gypsum mine in the hills near there and went looking for a suitable location for our fictional creation; as we drove, a collection of buildings appeared in the distance, and we found a gypsum mine situated at the exact place we'd imagined.

The most fascinating and challenging research task I've taken on was in 1996, when I began flying lessons. I'd made Hy Ripinsky a pilot, for no special reason except my first husband had been a pilot and flying had always interested me. Of course, I didn't

"At the controls of the Cessna 150—my most challenging research project," 1996.

think at the time that Sharon and Hy would ever be together—or that once McCone was exposed to flying, her nature would demand that she become a pilot herself. A writer friend in San Francisco who was a pilot helped me with some of the technical aspects, but quickly became embarrassed because I kept getting things wrong (while acknowledging his help in print); he flew up to Petaluma to have lunch with me at the airport, and by the time I got there he had all but signed me up for lessons with an instructor.

After several lessons, Peggy Bakker, the instructor, didn't know what to make of me. I'd explained that I was researching, but the fact didn't really sink in with her, because most of her students were intent on getting their licenses. A dedicated instructor, she bought a couple of my books and read them. Before our next lesson, she said to me, "I've figured out why we're not making progress. There are three people in our two-seater plane—you, me, and Sharon McCone." She was right; I was too concerned with getting the facts and the feel of flying down for fictional purposes to concentrate on becoming a good pilot. I was writing *Both Ends of the Night* (1997) by the seat of my pants, one step ahead of what McCone needed to know. I admire Peggy for sticking with me and checking the facts in a number of my subsequent manuscripts; she's proved a good friend and flying companion—so long as it's her steady hand on the controls.

Speaking of control—actually lack thereof—the "Sharon McCone" series has been optioned for film and television over the years, beginning in 1984. People at events always ask me about film possibilities; in this visually oriented society having a movie made of one's work seems to be held in higher regard than the work itself. None of these options was ever exercised; although the most recent almost resulted in a TV movie, the deal fell apart in the casting stage. The attention span in Hollywood is very short, and people—in this case, CBS television—lose interest in a project as soon as they confront adversity. I'm of two minds about McCone never making it onto film: it would have been interesting and lucrative, but had it been done badly, it would have had an adverse effect on my work and possibly on my readership.

I did have one excellent experience with film. In 1993 I was contacted by a documentary filmmaker, Pamela Beere Briggs, who was interested in doing a film about the upsurge in popularity of contemporary women mystery writers. Over the next seven years, Pamela and her husband, Bill McDonald, did taped interviews and filmed scenes with Sue Grafton, Sara Paretsky, and me. Seven years seems an inordinate amount of time for one fifty-three-minute documentary, but funding for the arts was—and is—in short supply in this country, and Pamela and Bill had to cobble together grants in order to keep going. We joke about the fact that when I first met them they weren't married; by the time the film was screened, they were married and their daughter, Natalie, was mature enough to attend the premier.

*

By 1999 I had written eleven "Sharon McCone" novels back to back. I was getting burnt out on the series, and both Bill and Sara Ann Freed noticed it. The year before, Sara Ann had approached me about doing what is known in the trade as a "stand-alone" or nonseries novel. The rationale behind this request was that in the past few years several series writers had written stand-

Muller (left) on the set of Women of Mystery, *with producer Pamela Beere Briggs: "The Victorian in the background was the model for character Sharon McCone's All Souls Legal Cooperative," 1997.*

alones that had resulted in a marked jump in their sales figures. I turned the idea down because I had a particularly compelling idea for the next installment—2000's *Listen to the Silence*—in which McCone finds out she is adopted and searches for her birth parents—but I had none for a nonseries novel. The next year, Sara Ann again approached me, and this time I did have an idea.

Bill and I had bought a small house on the Mendocino County coast, and I was driving home from there with a friend, several days before I was due to have a conference with Sara Ann in New York, when my car broke down on the coast highway. No one stopped to help us. Regular motorists and the highway patrol zoomed by. Finally, hours later, a sheriff's deputy arrived and radioed the dispatcher to contact Triple-A for a tow truck. After the incident I couldn't get my mind off how vulnerable my friend and I had been while stranded, and an image appeared in my mind: a young woman, much more vulnerable than we, standing beside her car while no one stopped. It would make a perfect opening for a novel, I thought. Sara Ann agreed, and I began working on my 2001 novel, *Point Deception.*

The story was originally to be set in Mendocino County. It involves a mass murder in a canyon similar to the one containing two creepy, deserted houses that Bill and I had discovered near our well house. I soon realized, however, that an actual location wouldn't do; I was saying negative and unfounded things about the county sheriff's department who, when they loitered in our driveway to catch speeders on a blind curve on the coast highway, also checked on the security of our house. A new county, Soledad, had to be created and sandwiched between Mendocino and Humboldt. This was probably the high point of power in my life—altering the California coastline to suit my purposes.

When *Point Deception* was published, critics proclaimed that I had begun a new series—featuring Rhoda Swift, the sheriff's deputy heroine—while patently ignoring the fact that the book had had another, and equal, male protagonist. This got my back up; I had no intention of starting another series. I decided that in subsequent "Soledad County" books, Swift would make only cameo appearances. The county would become the main connective tissue. I interspersed two other "Soledad County" novels with McCone novels—*Cyanide Wells* and *Cape Perdido*—before concluding from reader response that what people really wanted was Sharon McCone.

The year 2003 was a sad one: my friend and editor, Sara Ann Freed, died in June. I finished the next "Sharon McCone" novel, *The Dangerous Hour,* numbly, saddened by the knowledge that she would never read it. The relationship that had proven so inspiring over the years had come to an end.

I wish Sara Ann had been alive in April of 2005, when I received the Grand Master Award from the Mystery Writers of America. It was both thrilling and humbling to have my name added to a list that began fifty years earlier with Dame Agatha Christie. The award belongs, not solely to me, but to Sara Ann and Bill and all the other good people who offered aid and comfort along the way.

In September of 2005, Bill and I were given lifetime achievement awards at the yearly fan convention for our respective bodies of work. The presenter assured

Marcia Muller in an editing session with Bill Pronzini, 2002: "One of us must have made a hilarious typo!"

us, however, that the fans who voted for us didn't want us to stop writing. And we have no intention of doing so.

An interviewer recently asked me if there had been a defining moment in my career. Something that had made me feel I'd really accomplished what I set out to do. Certainly the honors I've received, particularly the Mystery Writers of America Grand Master Award. But more than those . . . well, I'll create another scene for you.

Imagine the old San Francisco Public Library, a magnificent edifice with wide marble steps sweeping up to the card catalog room. Picture a twenty-something version of me, walking up those steps to the mystery shelves, where she fingers the place where a book of her own might one day sit. Then, burdened by as many volumes as she can check out for the week, she goes to the card catalog, opens the last "M" drawer, and fingers the place where one day a card of her own might be filed.

Fast forward some twenty-five years. A fifty-something version of me walks up those same steps. While the cameras of the documentary film crew roll, she goes to the mystery shelves and takes down one of her own books. Then she goes to the card catalogue, opens the last "M" drawer, and the camera zooms in on the card listing her latest title.

That's about as defining a moment as there is.

BIOGRAPHICAL AND CRITICAL SOURCES:

BOOKS

St. James Guide to Crime and Mystery Writers, fourth edition, St. James Press (Detroit, MI), 1996.

PERIODICALS

Booklist, August, 1982, p. 1510; January 15, 1984, p. 718; October 1, 1984, p. 192; April 15, 1999, Emily Melton, review of *A Walk through the Fire,* p. 1483; May 1, 2000, Barbara Bibel, "The *Booklist* Interview: Marcia Muller," p. 1596; May 1, 2001, Barbara Bibel, review of *Point Deception,* p. 1638; February 15, 2002, Candace Smith, review of *Point Deception,* p. 1039; May 1, 2003, GraceAnne A. DeCandido, review of *Cyanide Wells,* p. 1550; May 1, 2004, Stephanie Zvirin, review of *The Dangerous Hour,* p. 1514; May 1, 2005, Stephanie Zvirin, review of *Cape Perdido,* p. 1532.
Globe and Mail (Toronto, Ontario, Canada), December 7, 1985; April 11, 1987.
Kirkus Reviews, May 1, 2002, review of *Dead Midnight,* p. 621; June 1, 2003, review of *Cyanide Wells,* p. 782; April 15, 2004, review of *The Dangerous Hour,* p. 365.
Kliatt, May, 2002, Nola Theiss, review of *Point Deception,* p. 52; March, 2005, review of *The Dangerous Hour,* p. 51.
Library Journal, October 1, 1977; October 1, 1983, p. 1890; October 1, 1984, p. 1865; May 15, 2001, Ruth H. Miller, review of *Point Deception,* p. 167; June 1, 2002, Michelle Foyt, review of *Dead Midnight,* p. 201; June 15, 2003, Michelle Foyt, review of *Cyanide Wells,* p. 106; June 1, 2004, Rex

E. Klett, review of *The Dangerous Hour,* p. 106; June 1, 2005, Michelle Foyt, review of *Cape Perdido,* p. 107.
Los Angeles Times, August 14, 1985; June 6, 1986.
Los Angeles Times Book Review, October 10, 1982, p. 7; February 12, 1989, p. 6.
New York Times, August 13, 2001, Marcia Muller, "Novelist's Life Is Altered by a Confident Alter Ego: Writers on Writing," p. E1
New York Times Book Review, November 7, 1982, p. 39; October 6, 1985; March 12, 1989, p. 24; December 24, 1989, p. 23; November 4, 1990, p. 30; August 19, 2001, review of *Point Deception,* p. 14; July 7, 2002, Marilyn Stasio, review of *Dead Midnight,* p. 16.
Plain Dealer (Cleveland, OH), July 8, 2001, Les Roberts, "Pacific Coast Plays Role in Murder Tale," p. 10I; July 20, 2003, Les Roberts, "Marcia Muller Turns Suspense into Fine Art," p. J9.
Post and Courier (Charleston, SC), August 18, 2002, Christine W. Randall, "Muller's Heroine's Investigation Hits Too Close to Home," p. 3.
Publishers Weekly, April 30, 1982, p. 48; December 24, 1982, p. 49; September 9, 1983, p. 51; September 23, 1983, p. 63; April 27, 1998, review of *While Other People Sleep,* p. 48; November 16, 1998, review of *Duo,* p. 58; June 25, 2001, review of *Point Deception,* p. 53, and interview with Muller, p. 54; June 3, 2002, review of *Dead Midnight,* p. 67; June 2, 2003, review of *Cyanide Wells,* p. 37; June 7, 2004, review of *The Dangerous Hour,* p. 35; June 27, 2005, review of *Cape Perdido,* p. 45.
St. Louis Post-Dispatch, August 4, 2004, Judith Evans, "Muller, Jance, and Reichs Provide New Thrills," p. E03.
School Library Journal, April 1, 2001, Barbara Perkins, review of *Listen to the Silence,* p. 155; May, 2001, Katherine Fitch, review of *Listen to the Silence,* p. 176.
USA Today, July 27, 1987.
Washington Times, August 8, 2001, Judith Kreiner, review of *Point Deception,* p. 8.

ONLINE

Bookreporter.com, http://www.bookreporter.com/ (January 24, 2006), interview with Muller.
Marcia Muller Home Page, http://www.marciamuller. com (January 24, 2006).
Time Warner Bookmark Online, http://www.tw bookmark.com/ (December 2, 2000), interview with Muller.

N

NAAM, Ramez

PERSONAL: Born in Egypt. *Education:* University of Illinois, degree in computer science.

ADDRESSES: Home—Seattle, WA. *Agent*—Ted Weinstein Literary Management, 35 Stillman St., Ste. 203, San Francisco, CA 94107. *E-mail*—author@ morethanhuman.org.

CAREER: Microsoft Corp., Redmond, WA, computer engineer. Apex NanoTechnologies, founder and head. Nano Business Alliance, member of advisory board, 2002—.

MEMBER: World Future Society, World Transhumanist AssociationExtropy Institute.

WRITINGS:

More than Human: Embracing the Promise of Biological Enhancement (nonfiction), Broadway Books (New York, NY), 2005.

SIDELIGHTS: Computer technologist Ramez Naam, who helped develop two popular software components for Microsoft Corp.—Internet Explorer, a Web browser, and Outlook, an e-mail program—looks at uses of biotechnology in *More than Human: Embracing the Promise of Biological Enhancement.* In this book he examines research that aims to improve human life with gene therapy, cloning, and even electronic implants. Much has already been done, he notes, and he sees the future as holding infinite potential. Scientists have manipulated genes to create mice that are stronger and smarter than ordinary rodents, and Naam theorizes that similar projects are possible with humans. Electrodes, he relates, have restored lost hearing in thousands of people and also have been used to treat Parkinson's disease, and other uses include restoring sight and helping paralyzed people manipulate robotic limbs. In keeping with his subtitle, he makes a case that humanity should embrace rather than fear biotechnological advances. He has remarked that fear has surrounded many scientific and medical breakthroughs.

In an interview for *BookBrowse.com,* he said, "When Jenner first introduced the smallpox vaccine, he was denounced as playing god and as dabbling in things too dangerous for mortal men." He added, "My greatest goal with *More than Human* is to educate people on how these technologies work and what they can and can't do." Naam related that these enhancements will "bring many goods and some ills. Society will have to wrestle with the problems these technologies cause and find solutions. But the alternative—to prohibit these technologies—just isn't viable." Speaking with James M. Pethokoukis for *U.S. News & World Report,* he mentioned that biotech experiments have met with criticism from both liberals and conservatives, "so I thought I would write a counterpoint—a book that educated readers on the underlying science, so they're better able to make judgments for themselves . . . and articulated some of the benefits to both individuals and society—some of the reasons we would actually want this stuff." These reasons, he said, include to "make us smarter, extend our lives, help us understand the world we live in better."

Some reviewers thought he had done so effectively. Naam's book brings "vividly to life" a world where seemingly far-fetched technologies are routinely available, observed Arlene Weintraub in *Business Week*. He provides "a fascinating tour of biotech experiments that could someday bring benefits we would barely recognize as medical," she continued, summing up his work as "provocative—and edifying." A *Kirkus Reviews* critic commented that Naam offers "a logical and structured explanation of bioengineering projects" in "an intriguing presentation." A *Publishers Weekly* contributor called the book "an excellent and comprehensive survey," and concluded: "Naam is persuasive that many of these advances are going to happen no matter what, and . . . they offer hope for our well-being."

BIOGRAPHICAL AND CRITICAL SOURCES:

PERIODICALS

Booklist, February 15, 2005, Gilbert Taylor, review of *More than Human: Embracing the Promise of Biological Enhancement,* p. 1045.

Business Week, April 4, 2005, Arlene Weintraub, "Biotech's Fountain of Youth," p. 22.

Kirkus Reviews, January 1, 2005, review of *More than Human,* p. 39.

Publishers Weekly, February 7, 2005, review of *More than Human,* p. 54.

U.S. News & World Report, July 23, 2003, James M. Pethokoukis, "A Brain Thinks about Its Future."

ONLINE

BookBrowse.com, http://www.bookbrowse.com/ (July 12, 2005), interview with Naam.

Life Enhancement Web site, http://www.life-enhancement.com/ (July 12, 2005), interview with Naam.

More than Human Web site, http://www.morethanhuman.org/ (July 12, 2005).

NuSapiens, http://www.nusapiens.blogspot.com/ (March 11, 2005), interview with Naam.*

*   *   *

NARBY, Jeremy

PERSONAL: Male. *Education:* Attended University of Canterbury; Stanford University, Ph.D.

ADDRESSES: Home—Switzerland. *Agent*—Moulton Agency, 441 Ulloa St., San Francisco, CA 94127.

CAREER: Writer.

WRITINGS:

NONFICTION

The Cosmic Serpent: DNA and the Origins of Knowledge, Jeremy P. Tarcher/Putnam (New York, NY), 1998.

(Editor with Francis Huxley) *Shamans through Time: 500 Years on the Path to Knowledge,* Jeremy P. Tarcher/Putnam (New York, NY), 2001.

Intelligence in Nature: An Inquiry into Knowledge, Jeremy P. Tarcher/Putnam (New York, NY), 2005.

SIDELIGHTS: Jeremy Narby has done extensive research and writing on the practices and beliefs of shamans: those people held to be mystical sages and healers by many cultures, including the indigenous peoples of South America. He became interested in the topic while visiting that continent's upper Amazon river region. He learned about the native people's use of plants in medicine, and was told the information about the plants' healing properties came from the plants' spirits, which revealed this to the shamans. Narby was skeptical, but while drinking a plant brew during a shamanic ceremony, he had a vision of twin serpents, which to him symbolized DNA. This led to his first book, *The Cosmic Serpent: DNA and the Origins of Knowledge,* in which he maintains that DNA has a mind of its own. Writing as a "very thoughtful, curious outsider," related John Petersen in *Whole Earth,* Narby makes "a plausible argument that DNA is alive and intelligent and that humans are but specially designed vehicles for its/their proliferation." A *Publishers Weekly* reviewer found Narby's conclusions unconvincing, but did allow that the author "provides an intriguing detective story, wondrous visions and a wealth of fascinating information."

Narby followed this work by editing, with Francis Huxley, *Shamans through Time: 500 Years on the Path to Knowledge.* This book collects more than sixty previously published pieces on shamanism, some heretofore unavailable in English, from diverse sources ranging from the writings of sixteenth-and seventeenth-century missionaries to the works of modern-day psychologists and anthropologists, including such famous names as Claude Levi-Strauss and Franz Boas. It also includes introductory commentaries on the preconceived ideas each writer brought to his or her discussion of shamanism. Several critics deemed the book a valuable addition to scholarship. It provides "an eye-opening experience," commented Julia Glynn in *Booklist,* while *Kliatt* reviewer Edna Boardman remarked that it "will fill a gap in many collections" thanks to the editors' "considerable resourcefulness." A *Publishers Weekly* contributor called it an "excellent volume," concluding, "This first sweeping study of shamanism is sure to become a classic."

In *Intelligence in Nature: An Inquiry into Knowledge* Narby begins with the belief, derived from his experiences with shamans, that plants and animals have a degree of human-like intelligence, and he surveys scientists who have done research on the intellectual capabilities of non-human life. The scientists provide examples of problem-solving, communication, and acute perceptiveness exhibited by various creatures, including birds, butterflies, and bacteria. "None of these accounts is exactly new to readers of *Science* or *Nature,* but they're nicely summarized here, along with descriptions of nervous systems and extensive endnotes," remarked a *Kirkus Reviews* critic. A *Publishers Weekly* reviewer noted that some scientists may not like Narby's fusion of mysticism with scientific inquiry, but said the author's "well-researched and engagingly presented account of the 'braininess' of even literally brainless creatures raises fascinating questions about the boundaries between man and nature."

BIOGRAPHICAL AND CRITICAL SOURCES:

PERIODICALS

Booklist, April 15, 2001, Julia Glynn, review of *Shamans through Time: 500 Years on the Path to Knowledge,* p. 1513.
Kirkus Reviews, January 1, 2005, review of *Intelligence in Nature: An Inquiry into Knowledge,* p. 64.
Kliatt, March, 2005, Edna Boardman, review of *Shamans through Time,* p. 37.
Library Journal, April 15, 2001, John Burch, review of *Shamans through Time,* p. 116.

Publishers Weekly, February 23, 1998, review of *The Cosmic Serpent: DNA and the Origins of Knowledge,* p. 245; March 26, 2001, review of *Shamans through Time,* p. 82; January 24, 2005, review of *Intelligence in Nature,* p. 229.
Whole Earth, spring, 2002, John Petersen, review of *The Cosmic Serpent,* p. 84.*

* * *

NETTLES, Darryl Glenn 1960-

PERSONAL: Born October 31, 1960, in Buffalo, NY; son of Henry L. and Julie W. Nettles; married Pamela Claybaker (a teacher), June 7, 2003; children: Juila M., Alan R. H. *Ethnicity:* "African American." *Education:* State University of New York, Buffalo, B.F.A. (magna cum laude), 1983; University of Illinois, Urbana-Champaign, M.M., 1987, D.M.A., 1995. *Politics:* "Independent." *Religion:* Christian.

ADDRESSES: Home—543 Annex Ave., Nashville, TN 37209. *Office*—Tennessee State University, Department of Music, 3500 John A. Merritt Blvd., Nashville, TN 37209. *E-mail*—dnettles@tnstate.edu.

CAREER: Writer. Central Lakes College, Brainerd, MN, director of music department, 1992-95, coordinator of humanities/fine arts division, 1994-95; Tennessee State University, Nashville, coordinator of vocal/choral studies, 1995—.

WRITINGS:

African-American Concert Singers before 1950, McFarland (Jefferson, NC), 2003.

BIOGRAPHICAL AND CRITICAL SOURCES:

PERIODICALS

Black Issues Book Review, May-June, 2003, Angela Dodson, review of *African-American Concert Singers Before 1950,* p. 55.

NICHOLS, Thomas M. 1960-

PERSONAL: Born December 7, 1960, in Holyoke, MA. Education: Boston University, B.A., 1983; Columbia University, M.A., 1985; Georgetown University, Ph.D., 1988. Religion: Greek Orthodox.

ADDRESSES: Office—U.S. Naval War College, Strategy and Policy Department, Newport, RI 02841. E-mail—nicholst@nwc.navy.mil.

CAREER: Writer. U.S. Senate, Washington, DC, legislative aide, 1990-91; Dartmouth College, Dartmouth, NH, professor, 1989-97; Naval War College, Newport, RI, professor, 1997—.

WRITINGS:

The Sacred Cause: Civil-Military Conflict over Soviet National Security, 1917-1992, Cornell University Press (Ithaca, NY), 1993.
The Russian Presidency: Society and Politics in the Second Russian Republic, St. Martin's Press (New York, NY), 1999.
Winning the World: Lessons for America's Future from the Cold War, Praeger (Westport, CT), 2003.

Also author of The Current Soviet Debate on National Security: A Survey of Possible Outcomes, Center for Strategic and International Studies (Washington, DC), 1988, and The Logic of Russian Presidentialism: Institutions and Democracy in Postcommunism, University of Pittsburgh Press (Pittsburgh, PA), 1998.

*   *   *

NICHOLSON, Joy 1966-

PERSONAL: Born 1966, in WI; married. Education: Attended Otis-Parsons Art Institute and Santa Monica College.

ADDRESSES: Home—Silver Lake, CA. Agent—c/o Author Mail, St. Martin's Press, 175 5th Ave., New York, NY 10010.

CAREER: Writer and activist. One Dog at a Time (animal rescue placement group), CA, manager and activist. Has also worked variously as a waiter, dog groomer, bartender, personal assistant, and in sales.

WRITINGS:

The Tribes of Palos Verdes (novel), St. Martin's Press (New York, NY), 1997.
The Road to Esmeralda (novel), St. Martin's Press (New York, NY), 2005.

Also contributor to One Little Ball literary 'zine.

ADAPTATIONS: The Tribes of Palos Verdes was adapted for a feature film.

SIDELIGHTS: Although Joy Nicholson was raised primarily in the wealthy Southern California community of Palos Verdes, she could not rely on her parents and was on her own at the age of seventeen. Though she dropped out of high school, Nicholson briefly attended college. As a young adult, she did not believe she would live past age thirty. Those tumultuous teenage years influenced her first novel, The Tribes of Palos Verdes.

The Tribes of Palos Verdes began as a short story that was published in a zine called One Little Ball. The story, which is primarily about Nicholson's brother who committed suicide, was expanded into a novel with the help of a literary agent. Because Nicholson had to learn the writing process as she went along, the novel went through heavy edits.

Writing in the Los Angeles Times, Susan Salter Reynolds commended the way Nicholson draws her protagonist, Medina. Reynolds calls the character "a female Holden Caulfield, noble and honest." A critic writing in Publishers Weekly also spoke well of the way Nicholson depicted Medina and Medina's relationship with her twin brother, Jim. The critic wrote, "the book's most moving passages describe the twins' love for each other and for the beach they share."

After the success of The Tribes of Palos Verdes, Nicholson drove to Mexico with her husband and lived on a beach in Yucatán. Her unexpected experiences there led her to write her second book, a thriller titled *The Road to Esmeralda*. Written in the third person, the novel follows the travels and relationship of struggling novelist Nick Sperry and his girlfriend, Sarah Gustafsson. The couple leaves their home in Los Angeles to travel on an extended vacation to Mexico to escape other Americans. There, they stay at a shady resort run by Karl Von Tollman. Though the couple learns much about themselves, each other, and their relationship, they also encounter corruption and interesting personalities.

A *Publishers Weekly* contributor found the book to be imperfect, stating that "though chiaroscuro of dark doings juxtaposed against the white heat of the jungle makes for an atmospheric read, the flat ending falls a bit short of the novel's promise." However, in a *Los Angeles Times Book Review* appraisal, Jonathan Kirsch remarked that Nicholson "writes like a house on fire, and she conjures up the tortured inner lives of her characters as well as the exotic landscape and folkways of the Yucatán, all so rich and strange, with lush virtuosity."

Nicholson told *CA:* "I think it's also important to point out that I'm a self taught writer—one doesn't need an expensive degree, or even a degree at all, to be a writer—I always try to tell kids that. A huge influence on my life/writing has been the author Peter Singer, and especially his seminal book *Animal Liberation*. I see writing (and all artistic pursuit) as more of a 'concentrated hobby' than a career for myself."

BIOGRAPHICAL AND CRITICAL SOURCES:

PERIODICALS

Kirkus Reviews, March 1, 2005, review of *The Road to Esmeralda,* p. 254.
LA Weekly, June 3-9, 2005, Gendy Alimurung, "Under the Yucatan Sun."
Los Angeles Times, October 17, 1997, Susan Salter Reynolds, "Fear, Loathing, and Adolescent Wisdom in Palos Verdes," p. E8.
Los Angeles Times Book Review, June 5, 2005, Jonathan Kirsch, "West Words; A Paradise That's More of a Paradox," p. R2.
Nation, September 7, 1998, Mindy Pennybacker, review of *The Tribes of Palos Verdes,* p. 38.

Publishers Weekly, September 8, 1997, review of *The Tribes of Palos Verdes,* p. 59; April 25, 2005, review of *The Road to Esmeralda,* p. 37.

ONLINE

Beatrice.com, http://www.beatrice.com/ (July 3, 2005), Ron Hagen, interview with Nicholson.

*   *   *

NIELDS, Nerissa 1967-

PERSONAL: Born 1967, in New York, NY; married David Jones (a musician and teacher; divorced); married Tom Duffy (a writer), 2005. *Education:* Yale University, B.A.

ADDRESSES: Home—Northampton, MA. *Agent*—Ginger Knowlton, Curtis Brown Ltd., 10 Astor Place, New York, NY 10003. *E-mail*—NFNields@aol.com.

CAREER: Singer, songwriter, and writer. The Nields (musical group), performer beginning 1991; musician performing with sister, Katryna Nields, beginning 1998; writing workshop leader. Vocalist on recordings (with The Nields), including *66 Hoxsey Street,* 1992; *Live at the Iron Horse Music Hall,* 1993; *Bob on the Ceiling,* 1994; *Abigail,* 1995; *Gotta Get over Greta,* 1996; *Mousse,* 1998; *Play,* 1998; *If You Lived Here, You'd Be Home Now,* 2000; and *Live from Northampton,* 2001. Vocalist on recordings with sister, Katryna Nields, including *Love and China,* 2001; *This Town Is Wrong,* 2004; and *Songs for Amelia* (for children), 2004.

WRITINGS:

Plastic Angel (novel; included CD of song "This Town Is Wrong" and "Glow-in-the-Dark Plastic Angel"), Orchard Books (New York, NY), 2005.

WORK IN PROGRESS: The Big Idea, a novel; *How to Be an Adult,* a memoir and self-help book.

SIDELIGHTS: A singer and songwriter, as well as one of the founding members of the musical group The Nields, Nerissa Nields has toured North America, had her music recorded on several major labels, and developed a following among folk-music fans in her native New England. In addition to continuing to perform as a musician, often in a duo with sister Katryna Nields—the two first appeared together in 1998 at Lilith Fair—Nields has broadened her creative horizons through her writing. In addition to launching into the field of children's literature with the novel *Plastic Angel,* she also conducts writing retreats and a workshop she calls "Writing It up in the Garden" from her home in western Massachusetts.

Released with a CD recording of two songs performed by the Nields, *Plastic Angel* was described as a "well-written and appealing story" by a *Kirkus Reviews* contributor. The novel focuses on two thirteen-year-old girls, their struggle with conformity in their upscale suburban community, and their ability to cope with family conflicts. It is through the eyes of Randi Rankin, the down-to-earth daughter of an indulgent musician, that readers meet Angela "Gellie" Riddle, Randi's best friend. A beautiful and talented model/actress, Gellie finds herself in a constant battle with her overbearing stage mother, who wants to dominate her daughter's life and career. Together Gellie and Randi decide to start a band, Plastic Angel. True to form, Gellie's mother rejects the idea, trying everything within her power to get her daughter to withdraw from the band. Gellie is then faced with a serious decision when she lands her first big acting role in a commercial film at the same time the band is scheduled to play its debut gig.

Plastic Angel "moves along well," noted the *Kirkus Reviews* contributor, "touching issues of family dissent and emerging individuality," while in *School Library Journal* Diane P. Tuccillo praised the two teen protagonists as "likeable" and cited "Randi's witty and perceptive point of view." *Booklist* contributor Debbie Carton also praised the "considerable charm" of Nields' teen characters, adding that the "pull between acceptance and self-expression" that these girls deal with in *Plastic Angel* "will resonate strongly with young teens."

BIOGRAPHICAL AND CRITICAL SOURCES:

PERIODICALS

Booklist, August, 2005, Debbie Carton, review of *Plastic Angel,* p. 2016.

Kirkus Reviews, May 15, 2005, review of *Plastic Angel,* p. 594.

People, January 26, 2004, Ralph Novak, review of *This Town Is Wrong: Nerissa and Katryna Nields,* p. 36.

School Library Journal, September, 2005, Diane P. Tuccillo, review of *Plastic Angel,* p. 209.

Sing Out, summer, 2002, review of *Love and China,* p. 130; spring, 2004, Daniele Dreilinger, review of *This Town Is Wrong,* p. 139.

ONLINE

Nerissa Nields Home Page, http://www.nerissanields.com (November 6, 2005).

Nields Web site, http://www.nields.com/ (November 6, 2005).

* * *

NORAC, Carl 1960-

PERSONAL: Born 1960, in Mons, Belgium; son of a writer and puppet-theatre owner and an actress; children: Else.

ADDRESSES: Home—269, rue de la Source, 45160 Olivet, France. *E-mail*—carlnorac@wanadoo.fr.

CAREER: Children's book author and poet. Has also worked as a French teacher, television scriptwriter, and journalist. Hans Christian Andersen Ambassador, 2005.

AWARDS, HONORS: Literary prize, c. 1978; recipient of several other awards.

WRITINGS:

Le lion fanfaron, Casterman, 1991.

Romulus et Rémi, une fable à l'opéra, Pastel (Paris, France), 1994.

Dimanche aux Hespérides (poems), Editions de la Différence (Paris, France), 1994.

La semaine de Monsieur Gris, Altiora, 1994.

Coeur de singe, illustrated by Jean Claud Hubert, Pastel (Paris, France), 1995.

La candeur (poems), Editions de la Différence (Paris, France), 1996.

Les mots doux, illustrated by Claude K. Dubois, Pastel (Paris, France), 1996, translated as *I Love You So Much,* Random House (New York, NY), 1998.

Un loup dans la nuit bleue, illustrated by Louis Joos, Pastel (Paris, France), 1996.

Nemo et le volcan, illustrated by Louis Joos, Pastel (Paris, France), 1996.

Beau comme au cinéma, illustrated by Louis Joos, Pastel (Paris, France), 1997.

L'île aux câlins, illustrated by Claude K. Dubois, Pastel (Paris, France), 1998.

L'espoir Pélican, illustrated by Louis Joos, Pastel (Paris, France), 1998.

Le sourire de Kiawak, illustrated by Louis Joos, Pastel (Paris, France), 1998.

La grande ourse, illustrated by Kitty Crowther, Pastel (Paris, France), 1999.

La carnival des animaux, Thèatre royal de la Monnaie, 1999.

Bonjour mon petit coeur, illustrated by Claude K. Dubois, Pastel (Paris, France), 1999, translated as *Hello, Sweetie Pie,* Random House (New York, NY), 2000.

Marine et Louisa, illustrated by Claude K. Dubois, Pastel (Paris, France), 2000.

Le rêve de l'ours, illustrated by Louis Joos, Pastel (Paris, France), 2000.

Le message de la baleine, illustrated by Jean-Luc Englebert, Pastel (Paris, France), 2000.

La petite souris d'Halloween, illustrated by Stibane, Pastel (Paris, France), 2000.

Le père Noël m'a écrit, illustrated by Kitty Crowther, Pastel (Paris, France), 2001.

Un Bisou, c'est trop court, illustrated by Claude K. Dubois, Pastel (Paris, France), 2001.

Le dernier voyage de Saint-Exupéry, Renaissance du livre, 2001.

Luli et le sorcier, illustrated by Dominiqu Mwankumi, Archimède, 2001.

Je veux un bisou!, illustrated by Claude K. Dubois, Pastel (Paris, France), 2001.

Je suis un amour, illustrated by Claude K. Dubois, Pastel (Paris, France), 2001.

Donne-moi un ours!, illustrated by Emile Jadoul, Pastel (Paris, France), 2001.

Zeppo, illustrated by Peter Elliott, Pastel (Paris, France), 2002.

Une visite chez la sorcière, illustrated by Sophie, Pastel (Paris, France), 2002.

Tu m'aimes ou tu m'aimes pas?, illustrated by Claude K. Dubois, Pastel (Paris, France), 2002.

Pierrot d'amour, illustrated by Jean-Luc Englebert, Pastel (Paris, France), 2002.

Lettres du géant à l'enfante qui passé et autres poèmes, Labor (Brussels, Belgium), 2002.

Un secret pour grandir, illustrated by Carll Cneut, Pastel (Paris, France), 2003.

Tu es si gentil, mon ours, illustrated by Anne Isa le Touzé, Pastel (Paris, France), 2003.

Métrpolitaines: tentative de photographier avec le language, métro de Paris, hiver 1999-2000, Escampette (Paris, France), 2003.

Tout près de maman, illustrated by Catherin Pineur, Pastel (Paris, France), 2004.

Mon papa est un géant, illustrated by Ingrid Godon, Bayard Jeunesse (Paris, France), 2004, translated as *My Daddy Is a Giant,* Clarion Books (New York, NY), 2005.

I Love to Cuddle, illustrated by Claude K. Dubois, Dell Dragonfly Books (New York, NY), 2002.

Le petit sorcier de la pluie, illustrated by Anne-Cat de Boel, Pastel (Paris, France), 2004.

Coeur de papier, illustrated by Carll Cneut, Pastel (Paris, France), 2004.

Akli, prince du désert, illustrated by Anne-Cat de Boel, Pastel (Paris, France), 2004.

Angakkeg: la légende de l'oiseau, illustrated by Louis Joos, Pastel (Paris, France), 2004.

Le géant de la grande tour, Sarbacane, 2005.

Mon meilleur ami du monde, illustrated by Claude K. Dubois, Pastel (Paris, France), 2005.

Norac's works have been translated into eighteen languages.

SIDELIGHTS: Belgian-born author and poet Carl Norac discovered his passion for the arts at a young age, while writing poetry and acting out performances with his friends and family. Beginning his career as a children's book author in the mid-1990s, his books quickly gained popularity and are now read all over the world. Several of Norac's works have been translated into English, among them *My Daddy Is a Giant* as well as *I Love You So Much,* and *I Love to Cuddle,* both of which feature a young hamster named Lola. Brought to life in pencil drawings by illustrator Claude K. Dubois, Lola experiences the same emotions as a loving child; she serves as an "affectionate" protagonist in *I Love to Cuddle,* which a *Publishers Weekly* dubbed a "winsome" book that "trumpets an uplifting and timeless theme."

Norac explores a child's love and admiration for his father in *My Daddy Is a Giant,* illustrated by Ingrid

Godon. From the small child's close-to-the-ground perspective, his father is like a towering giant whose shoulders reach as high as the clouds and whose sneezes can blow back the tides of the seas. The story's simple text expresses "the child's belief that Daddy possesses extraordinary powers," noted a *Publishers Weekly* reviewer, adding that "Children may enjoy this story's gentle humor best from the warmth of Daddy's lap." Amy Lilien-Harper, writing in *School Library Journal,* stated that Godon's "slightly simplistic drawings depict the loving bond between father and son perfectly, bringing the relationship and text to life."

BIOGRAPHICAL AND CRITICAL SOURCES:

PERIODICALS

Bookbird (annual), 1999, review of *L'espoir Pelican,* p. 62.
Booklist, April 1, 2000, Ilene Cooper, review of *Hello, Sweetie Pie,* p. 1470.
Horn Book, May-June, 2005, Joanna Rudge Long, review of *My Daddy Is a Giant,* p. 311.
Kirkus Reviews, May 15, 2005, review of *My Daddy Is a Giant,* p. 594
Publishers Weekly, January 5, 1998, review of *I Love You So Much,* p. 66; December 21, 1998, review of *I Love to Cuddle,* p. 66; July 31, 2000, review of *Hello, Sweetie Pie,* p. 97; January 14, 2002, review of *I Love You So Much,* p. 63; December 2, 2002, review of *I Love You So Much,* p. 54; December 16, 2002, review of *I Love to Cuddle,* p. 70; August 25, 2003, review of *Hello, Sweetie Pie,* p. 67; December 15, 2003, review of *I Love to Cuddle,* p. 75; June 6, 2005, review of *My Daddy Is a Giant,* p. 63.
Reviewer's Bookwatch, May, 2005, Lynne Marie Pisano, review of *My Daddy Is a Giant.*
School Library Journal, February, 1998, Jacke Kechtkopf, review of *I Love You So Much,* p. 89; March, 1999, Marcia Hupp, review of *I Love to Cuddle,* p. 183; August, 2000, Sally R. Dow, review of *Hello, Sweetie Pie,* p. 162; May, 2005, Amy Lilien-Harper, review of *My Daddy Is a Giant,* p. 94.

ONLINE

École des Loisirs Web site, http://www.ecoledesloisirs.fr/ (November 6, 2005), "Carl Norac."
Hans Christian Andersen Ambassadors 2005 Web site, http://www.hca2005.com/ (November 6, 2005), "Carl Norac."

Ricochet-Jeunes Web site, http://www.ricochet-jeunes.org/ (November 6, 2005), "Carl Norac."*

                    *   *   *

NORTON, Melissa

PERSONAL: Married.

ADDRESSES: Agent—c/o Author Mail, Chandler House Press, Tatnuck Bookseller, 335 Chandler St., Worcester, MA 01602.

CAREER: Retired math and computer-science teacher.

WRITINGS:

Just the Two of Us: A Cycling Journey across America, Chandler House Press (Worcester, MA), 2001.

SIDELIGHTS: Melissa Norton is a mother and grandmother who crossed the country by bicycle with her husband when they were in their fifties. Norton wrote an account of their journey, *Just the Two of Us: A Cycling Journey across America,* in which she documents their sixty-three-day adventure across 4,611 miles, which began in Astoria, Oregon, and ended in Bar Harbor, Maine. She comments on the inns in which they stayed and restaurants where they ate, as well as the people they met and some of the difficulties they faced, including crossing mountainous terrain. In this book, which is written as a journal, she offers tips on embarking on such a trip and how it affected the personal relationship between Norton and her husband. *Library Journal* contributor John McCormick felt that "the book has the potential to appeal to both the bicyclist and the armchair traveler."

BIOGRAPHICAL AND CRITICAL SOURCES:

BOOKS

Norton, Melissa, *Just the Two of Us: A Cycling Journey across America,* Chandler House Press (Worcester, MA), 2001.

PERIODICALS

Library Journal, March 15, 2002, John McCormick, review of *Just the Two of Us: A Cycling Journey across America,* p. 100.*

O

OCHSNER, Gina 1970-

PERSONAL: Born 1970; married; children: four. *Education:* Graduated from George Fox University; attended graduate school at Iowa State University; attended University of Oregon.

ADDRESSES: Home—Keizer, OR. *Agent*—c/o Author Mail, Houghton Mifflin Company, Trade Division, Adult Editorial, 222 Berkeley St., 8th Fl., Boston, MA 02116-3764.

CAREER: Writer. George Fox University, Newberg, OR, part-time instructor. Also worked at a Brazilian Café, Ames, IA.

AWARDS, HONORS: Flannery O'Connor Award for Short Fiction and Publication, 2002, H.L. Davis Award for Fiction, Oregon Books Awards, 2002, Pacific Northwest Booksellers Association Book Award for short stories, 2003, *Austin Chronicle Top Ten Pick,* all for *The Necessary Grace to Fall: Stories*; Raymond Carver Award, Humboldt State; Katherine Ann Porter Award; Chelsea Award for Short Fiction.

WRITINGS:

SHORT STORY COLLECTIONS

The Necessary Grace to Fall: Stories, University of Georgia Press (Athens, GA), 2002.
People I Wanted to Be, Mariner/Houghton Mifflin (Boston, MA), 2005.

Also contributor to *Prairie Schooner, Mid-American Review, New Yorker, Kenyon Review,* and *Nimrod.* Contributor to *Best American Nonrequired Reading.*

SIDELIGHTS: While raising a family and teaching part time at her alma mater in Oregon, Gina Ochsner has published short stories in periodicals as well as in two collections. Her first collection, *The Necessary Grace to Fall,* features eleven tales set in various locales. Many of the stories feature characters that are dead or are bothered by death. For example, the title story "The Necessary Grace to Fall," focuses on a man named Howard who works as an insurance investigator. Howard becomes obsessive over the case of a female policyholder who dies by drowning. His interest is piqued in part because the woman lived near him as a child, and his investigation eventually uncovers problems in his marriage. In the *Virginia Quarterly Review,* a reviewer called the book a "clever collection of haunting, desolate stories."

Ochsner's second collection, *People I Wanted to Be,* was called "offbeat" and "affecting" by a critic writing in *Publishers Weekly.* "Ochsner knows that vindication and inspiration often come from unlikely places," The critic also wrote, "and she can capture this contradiction gorgeously in a gesture." Each story in this collection features a character who is aware of a major fault in himself or herself and would like to be without it or learn how to handle it. The characters take chances, though they nearly always fail. Death and the dead also remain important themes, and many fantastical elements are also present.

Ochsner has traveled around Eastern Europe and Russia, and she has set many of the stories from *People*

I Wanted to Be in these locales. For example, "From the Fourth Row" focuses on a character named Jiri and the unusual events taking place at his worksite in Prague. A Czech is also at the center of "Signs and Markings." The story features a Czech street worker who is in an unfulfilling relationship with a nurse; it also explores the effects of occupation on the country.

Ochsner's work often focuses on the cold winters experienced in extreme northern climates and the effect on those who live there. Her story "A Blessing" revolves around Nikolai and Vera, a couple who used to live in Siberia but now reside in Oregon. Another story in which the cold plays a role is "Articles of Faith." In this tale, a Finnish husband and his Russian wife are trying to conceive. Outside in the frozen yard, their miscarried or dead children exist in ghost form. Gillian Engberg, writing in *Booklist,* wrote that "Ochsner's flawed, wholly sympathetic characters miraculously stumble into small moments, shaped with a delicious sense of the absurd, which connect them to a world that's magical, merciful, and infinite."

BIOGRAPHICAL AND CRITICAL SOURCES:

PERIODICALS

Booklist, March 15, 2005, Gillian Engberg, review of *People I Wanted to Be,* p. 1266.
Kirkus Reviews, March 1, 2005, review of *People I Wanted to Be,* p. 254.
Oregonian, February 13, 2005, Jeff Baker, "Comb That Wet Dog, Gina," author profile.
Publishers Weekly, April 4, 2005, review of *People I Wanted to Be,* p. 42.
Virginia Quarterly Review, autumn, 2002, review of *The Necessary Grace to Fall: Stories,* p. 128.

ONLINE

Diagram, http://www.thediagram.com/ (June 29, 2005), biography of Gina Ochsner.
Houghton Mifflin Books Web site, http://www.houghtonmifflinbooks.com/ (June 29, 2005), biography of and interview with Gina Ochsner.
Writers on the Edge Web site, http://www.writersontheedge.org/ (February 15, 2003), biography of Gina Oschner.*

OLIVER, Anna Cypra 1969(?)-

PERSONAL: Born c. 1969; daughter of Lewis Weinberger; married (divorced). *Education:* University of Minnesota, M.F.A.

ADDRESSES: Agent—c/o Author Mail, Houghton Mifflin Company, Trade Division, Adult Editorial, 8th Fl., 222 Berkeley St., Boston, MA 02116-3764.

CAREER: Writer.

AWARDS, HONORS: New York Foundation of the Arts fellowship.

WRITINGS:

Assembling My Father: A Daughter's Detective Story, Houghton Mifflin (Boston, MA), 2005.

SIDELIGHTS: Anna Cypra Oliver is the author of *Assembling My Father: A Daughter's Detective Story,* a book about the author's deceased father, her own life, and her journey to discover more about her parent. As the reader learns, Oliver's father, Lewis Weinberger, committed suicide in a primitive cabin outside of Taos, New Mexico, in 1974, when Oliver was only five years old and living in Colorado with her mother and stepfather. For years, Oliver knew little about her father other than the fact that he had been trained as an architect and was highly intelligent. She became interested in finding out more about him after finding some papers in a trunk and experiencing a low period in her life epitomized by the loss of her Christian faith. In 1995, Oliver set out to piece together the puzzle that was her father's life. She had her father's old journal to help her begin her quest and was soon talking with his friends and family members. What she discoverd is both good and bad. Although highly intelligent, her father was also heavily into drugs, including possibly smuggling and selling them. But she also learned from old friends who respected him that her father, who was from an intellectual Jewish family, was a good friend with a quick wit. The book also reveals much about Oliver's own life and struggles, including her strained relationship with her stepfather and her own marriage, which ends in divorce.

To tell her story, Oliver employs old photographs, pages from her father's journal, newspaper clippings, and e-mails. A *Kirkus Reviews* contributor noted, "Oliver's structure is part scrapbook, part narrative, part mosaic, part meta-memoir." The reviewer also called the book "an emotional demonstration that Humpty Dumpty can be put together again." Writing in *Booklist,* Donna Seaman commented, "Oliver depicts the '60s as a time of wrenching change and toxic self-medication, and reveals the inextricable pull of genetics." Valeda Dent wrote in the *Library Journal* that the author's "emotionally challenging, eye-opening quest yields a well-structured, vivid picture of countercultural life in the 1960s and 1970s," where a *Publishers Weekly* contributor commented: "Oliver's memorial to her elusive dad—and the way researching and writing it changes her own identity—is unforgettable."

BIOGRAPHICAL AND CRITICAL SOURCES:

BOOKS

Oliver, Anna Cypra, *Assembling My Father: A Daughter's Detective Story,* Houghton Mifflin (Boston, MA), 2005.

PERIODICALS

Albuquerque Journal, September 5, 2004, David Steinberg, review of *Assembling My Father: A Daughter's Detective Story.*
Booklist, August, 2004, Donna Seaman, review of *Assembling My Father,* p. 1882.
Boston Globe, September 19, 2004, Kate Bolick, review of *Assembling My Father.*
Entertainment Weekly, August 6, 2004, Emily Mead, review of *Assembling My Father,* p. 87.
Kirkus Reviews, June 15, 2004, review of *Assembling My Father,* p. 569.
Library Journal, September 1, 2004, Valeda Dent, review of *Assembling My Father,* p. 162.
Publishers Weekly, June 7, 2004, review of *Assembling My Father,* p. 41.*

*   *   *

OLNEY, Buster

PERSONAL: Male.

ADDRESSES: Office—ESPN Magazine, 19 E. 34th St., New York, NY 10016.

CAREER: Journalist. Entertainment & Sports Network (ESPN), senior writer, 2003—. Previously worked as a sports writer for *New York Times.*

WRITINGS:

The Last Night of the Yankee Dynasty: The Game, the Team, and the Cost of Greatness, Ecco (New York, NY), 2004.

SIDELIGHTS: Buster Olney is a sports journalist who formerly worked at the *New York Times,* where one of his beats was the New York Yankees. In his book, *The Last Night of the Yankee Dynasty: The Game, the Team, and the Cost of Greatness,* Olney focuses on the 2001 Yankee team, which was in line that year to win back-to-back championships, only to lose in the seventh game of the World Series to the Arizona Diamondbacks. Olney takes that game as the focal point to explore the team, its players, its coaches, and management, including the team's vociferous and hands-on owner, George Steinbrenner. "I wanted to write it for the more general baseball audience, maybe in the same way that I wrote for the *New York Times,*" Olney told Alex Belth in an online interview for the *Bronx Banter* Web site. "I always felt that I could slip in enough stuff that would appeal to baseball nerds like myself, but I wanted to write it for people who like characters. I wanted to write about the people."

Olney details each inning of the fateful seventh—and deciding—World Series game. However, in the process he takes time to digress and talk about how the team was put together and to explore the entire year and its successes and disappointments. He also profiles the team's players, revealing both their on-and-off-field personalities. In a review of *The Last Night of the Yankee Dynasty* for *Library Journal,* Jim Burns called the book "an excellent work of sports writing." Burns also wrote that readers will "begin to care about them far beyond their performance in this one crucial game." Alan Moores declared in *Booklist* that Olney "delivers a winning valedictory to the five years he covered the team." A *Kirkus Reviews* contributor felt that "Olney provides crisp profiles of players" and called the effort "both subtle and opinionated, a densely layered portrait of the Yankees' late-20th-century dynasty." Writing in *Publishers Weekly,* a reviewer felt that "both Yankees fans and Yankee haters will find this one interesting."

BIOGRAPHICAL AND CRITICAL SOURCES:

PERIODICALS

Booklist, September 1, 2004, Alan Moores, review of *The Last Night of the Yankee Dynasty: The Game, the Team, and the Cost of Greatness,* p. 50.

Kirkus Reviews, August 1, 2004, review of *The Last Night of the Yankee Dynasty,* p. 730.

Library Journal, September 15, 2004, Jim Burns, review of *The Last Night of the Yankee Dynasty,* p. 64.

Publishers Weekly, July 5, 2004, review of *The Last Night of the Yankee Dynasty,* p. 43.

ONLINE

Baseball Musings, http://www.baseballmusings.com/ (May 29, 2003), "Exodus from the *Times.*"

Bronx Banter, http://www.all-baseball.com/ bronxbanter/ (September 1, 2004), Alex Belth, interview with Olney.*

*   *   *

OLSON, James C. 1917-2005
(James Clifton Olson)

OBITUARY NOTICE— See index for *CA* sketch: Born January 23, 1917, in Bradgate, IA; died August 17, 2005, in Kansas City, MO. College administrator, historian, educator, and author. Olson was president emeritus at the University of Missouri. He completed a B.A. at Morningside College in 1938 and a Ph.D. at the University of Nebraska in 1942, just before America entered World War II. During the war, he served in the U.S. Army Air Forces as an historical officer, attaining the rank of first lieutenant. Afterward, he began his academic career at the University of Nebraska; he became Martin professor of history in 1962, and served as dean and vice-chancellor of graduate studies and research in the late 1960s. Olson then joined the University of Missouri at Kansas City faculty as chancellor from 1968 to 1976. That year, he was selected as interim president of the University of Missouri system, and he became president the next year, ultimately retiring from the post in 1984. In ad-

dition to his academic career, Olson was active in his local community, serving on the chamber of commerce, as president of the Civic Council of Greater Kansas City, on a variety of company boards, and as cofounder of the Business-Higher Education Forum. For such accomplishments, he was presented with the Centurion leadership award. As an historian, Olson was active in such groups as the Organization of American Historians. He was a former president of the American Association for State and Local History and he was editor of *Nebraska History* from 1946 to 1956. In addition, Olson was the author or coauthor of several books, including *History of Nebraska* (1955; 3rd edition, 1997), *Red Cloud and the Sioux Problem* (1965), and *Stuart Symington: A Life* (2003).

OBITUARIES AND OTHER SOURCES:

PERIODICALS

St. Louis Post-Dispatch, August 24, 2005, p. B4.

ONLINE

Columbia Daily Tribune Online, http://www.showme news.com/ (August 20, 2005).

University of Missouri News Releases Web site, http:// www.umsystem.edu/news/releases/ (August 18, 2005).

*   *   *

OLSON, James Clifton
See OLSON, James C.

*   *   *

OVASON, David

PERSONAL: Male. Education: Has attended graduate school.

ADDRESSES: Agent—c/o Author Mail, HarperCollins Publishers, 10 East 53rd St., 7th Fl., New York, NY 10022.

CAREER: Teacher of astrology.

WRITINGS:

The Secrets of Nostradamus: The Medieval Code of the Master Revealed in the Age of Computer Science, Century (London, England), 1997, published as *The Nostradamus Code,* Arrow (London, England), 1998, published as *The Secrets of Nostradamus: A Radical New Interpretation of the Master's Prophecies,* HarperCollins (New York, NY), 2001.

(Editor) Mark Hedsel, *The Zelator: A Modern Initiate Explores the Ancient Mysteries,* Century (London, England), 1998.

The Book of the Eclipse: The Hidden Influences of Eclipses, Arrow (London, England), 1999.

The Secret Zodiacs of Washington, DC: Was the City of Stars Planned by Masons?, Century (London, England), 1999, published as *The Secret Architecture of Our Nation's Capital: The Masons and the Building of Washington, DC,* HarperCollins (New York, NY), 2000.

Nostradamus: Prophecies for America, HarperCollins (New York, NY), 2001.

The Two Children: A Study of the Two Jesus Children in Literature and Art, Century (London, England), 2001.

The Secret Symbols of the Dollar Bill, HarperCollins (New York, NY), 2004.

SIDELIGHTS: David Ovason is a scholar of the life and prophecies of sixteenth-century French mystic Michel Nostradamus, as well as an expert on arcane symbolism. His *The Secrets of Nostradamus: The Medieval Code of the Master Revealed in the Age of Computer Science*—published in America as *The Secrets of Nostradamus: A Radical New Interpretation of the Master's Prophecies*—interprets the language of Nostradamus, which is sometimes known as the Green Language. A number of experts on the famous prognosticator, including Ovason, claim that Nostradamus predicted most of the great events of history, including the 1666 London fire, the great plague, the royal lineage of England, the French Revolution, and a number of geological events, such as earthquakes. It is said that he foresaw the rise to power of German chancellor Adolf Hitler, the Spanish Civil War, and the sightings of Unidentified Flying Objects (UFOs). Ovason asserts that the coded predictions are so complex that they can be understood only after the fact.

In *The Secret Zodiacs of Washington, DC: Was the City of Stars Planned by Masons?,* published in America as *The Secret Architecture of Our Nation's Capital: The Masons and the Building of Washington, DC,* Ovason explains that most of the architects who designed the significant structures in Washington were Freemasons who incorporated their symbolism into their designs. They included James Hoban, who designed the White House. Many of America's founding fathers were Masons, including Benjamin Franklin, as were several later presidents, such as James A. Garfield and James K. Polk. A *Publishers Weekly* reviewer noted that "when President George Washington laid the cornerstone of the Capitol building in 1793, he wore a Masonic apron adorned with occult Masonic symbols and an image of the zodiac." Ovason writes that the designs of French engineer Pierre-Charles L'Enfant and planners Andrew Ellicott and James McMillan, all of whom were reportedly Masons, included Masonic symbolism in the buildings of the Federal Reserve, Library of Congress, and other Washington landmarks. He also notes the importance of the astrological sign of Virgo to the Masons and claims that the triangle formed by the Capitol, White House, and Washington Monument represents the stars of the constellation.

Writing about *The Secret Architecture of Our Nation's Capital,* a *Kirkus Reviews* contributor called the volume "essential for experts or, shall we say, believers. For casual readers, a curiosity." Margaret Flanagan admitted in *Booklist* that the volume "does include some fascinating information about both the builders and the buildings of the nation's capital." A reviewer for the *Grand Lodge of British Columbia and Yukon Online* provided a commentary from the Masonic perspective, saying that Ovason became a Freemason after publishing this volume, but added that the author "is an astrologer by trade and inclination, and his perspective is strongly influenced by his own beliefs. This leads him to conclusions about Freemasonry and Freemasons that are not contained within the rituals and teachings of Freemasonry. Unfortunately, a number of his unsubstantiated claims can be used by those who do wish to condemn Freemasonry."

In a work that bears some similarities to his study of Washington architecture, Ovason's *The Secret Symbols of the Dollar Bill* studies the details of the dollar bill, including what the author points to as Masonic symbols, such as the one-eyed pyramid and the frequency of the number thirteen. "So if you've ever wondered what The Great Seal represents or the true significance of what the eagle carries in its claws, then this is the book for you," commented Ivan Schneider in *Bank Systems & Technology.*

Ovason's *Nostradamus: Prophecies for America* was published following the terrorist attacks of September 11, 2001. In it he examines a quatrain he feels predicted the attack. Ovason was not the only one who looked to Nostradamus for answers. The number of online searches of the prophet's name increased dramatically following the tragedy. In this volume, Ovason notes the number of positive predictions that have come to pass and foresees a hopeful future for the United States.

In *The Two Children: A Study of the Two Jesus Children in Literature and Art* Ovason revisits the idea, reflected in the gospels of Matthew and Luke, that there were two children conceived by Jesus, an idea that has never been supported by the official church, but which as been documented by such sects as the Gnostics. It has also been preserved in the ancient Hebrew, Aramaic, Greek, and Coptic writings that have been discovered in modern times at sites in Egypt and near the Dead Sea.

BIOGRAPHICAL AND CRITICAL SOURCES:

PERIODICALS

Bank Systems & Technology, February, 2004, Ivan Schneider, review of *The Secret Symbols of the Dollar Bill,* p. 50.

Booklist, July, 2000, Margaret Flanagan, review of *The Secret Architecture of Our Nation's Capital: The Masons and the Building of Washington, DC,* p. 1990.

Kirkus Reviews, June 15, 2000, review of *The Secret Architecture of Our Nation's Capital,* pp. 863-864; December 1, 2000, review of *The Secrets of Nostradamus: A Radical New Interpretation of the Master's Prophecies,* p. 1664.

Library Journal, June 1, 2000, Eric Linderman, review of *The Secret Architecture of Our Nation's Capital,* p. 122.

Money, May, 2004, David Futrelle, review of *The Secret Symbols of the Dollar Bill,* p. 39.

Publishers Weekly, December 6, 1999, review of *The Zelator: A Modern Initiate Explores the Ancient Mysteries,* p. 64; June 5, 2000, review of *The Secret Architecture of Our Nation's Capital,* p. 84; December, 2000, review of *The Secrets of Nostradamus,* p. 75; September 24, 2001, Charlotte Abbott, review of *The Secrets of Nostradamus,* p. 13.

Wall Street Journal, July 25, 2000, Bill Kauffman, review of *The Secret Architecture of Our Nation's Capital,* p. A20.

ONLINE

Astrology.about.com, http://astrology.about.com/ (July 11, 2005), review of *Nostradamus: Prophecies for America.*

David Ovason Home Page, http://www.davidovason.com (July 11, 2005).

Grand Lodge of British Columbia and Yukon, http://freemasonry.bcy.ca/ (July 11, 2005), review of *The Secret Zodiacs of Washington, DC: Was the City of Stars Planned by Masons?*

HarperCollins Web site, http://www.harpercollins.com/ (July 11, 2005), profile of Ovason.*

P

PANARELLO, Melissa 1985-
(Melissa P.)

PERSONAL: Born December 3, 1985, in Catania, Sicily, Italy.

ADDRESSES: Agent—c/o Author Mail, Grove Press, 841 Broadway, New York, NY 10003.

CAREER: Writer.

WRITINGS:

(As Melissa P.) *Cento colpi di spazzola prima di andare a dormire* (fiction), Fazi (Rome, Italy), 2003, translation by Lawrence Venuti published as *100 Strokes of the Brush before Bed,* Black Cat (New York, NY), 2004.

Author's writing has been translated into twenty-four languages.

ADAPTATIONS: 100 Strokes of the Brush before Bed was optioned for film.

WORK IN PROGRESS: A novel titled *The Smell of Your Breath.*

SIDELIGHTS: Melissa Panarello is a young Italian writer whose first book, *100 Strokes of the Brush before Bed,* is a sexually explicit, fictionalized memoir that became a best seller in Italy. The book has also raised controversy largely because the author was only eighteen years old when the book was published. In an interview with Carrie Hill Wilner on the *Nerve.com* Web site, the author noted, "It's an autobiographical novel written in the form of the diary of Melissa P., my alter ego, recounting this series of sort of degrading sexual experiences she has through the age of sixteen. And well, teenagers having and talking about extreme sexual experiences will always cause controversy."

Written in the form of a diary, the novel focuses on fifteen-year-old Melissa's search for love, which leads her to a series of varied sexual encounters, including sadomasochism. For the most part, she does not have good relationships with her sexual partners and finds friendship with other social outsiders, including a transvestite and a lesbian. Although Melissa understands that her sexual obsessions are not healthy, she finds it difficult to stop and rationalizes her love affairs as part of growing up and learning about life. Although Melissa feels the pain of knowing her lovers ultimately care little for her as a person, she also is proud that she can seduce people so easily. To help calm herself at nights and come to terms with her sexual lifestyle, she counts out one hundred strokes of the brush through her hair before she goes to bed. At one point in the book, Melissa's mother tells her a fable that is designed to help her deal with many sexual experiences and the people she encounters. In a *Nerve.com* interview Panarello noted: "I definitely think the lesson of that fable is relevant to the book, and to my experience. It's not incidental."

"The movement between fable and teenage confession—all that loneliness, angst and longing—makes for an odd tension in a story that otherwise might be considered conventional erotica, full of cliché and tease, stiletto-heeled lovers and spankers," wrote Lenora Todera in the *New York Times.* "One day she's hard-core, the next Cinderella." Several reviewers, including Todera, noted that the novel reveals the author's immaturity and contains clichés often associated with young writers. Dale Raben, writing in the *Library Journal,* commented that the seemingly contrived language could "be the fault of the book's translation, as a Romance language would make all the metaphors sound less cheesy." However, a *Kirkus Reviews* contributor called the novel a "staggeringly assured debut," and in a review for *People,* Kyle Smith dubbed the book "upscale erotica" and "plenty sultry." A *Publishers Weekly* contributor wrote that "Melissa tells herself no fairy tales—and therein lies the odd, potent purity of these pages."

BIOGRAPHICAL AND CRITICAL SOURCES:

BOOKS

P., Melissa, *100 Strokes of the Brush before Bed,* translation by Lawrence Venuti, Black Cat (New York, NY), 2004.

PERIODICALS

China Daily, December 25, 2003, "Teenager Takes Italy by Storm, with Her Lust Tale."

Guardian (London, England), August 22, 2004, Sophie Arie, "I Regret Nothing, Says Italy's Porn Teen" (interview).

Kirkus Reviews, August 1, 2004, review of *100 Strokes of the Brush before Bed,* p. 709.

Library Journal, August, 2004, Dale Raben, review of *100 Strokes of the Brush before Bed,* p. 69.

New York Times, November 7, 2004, Lenora Todaro, review of *100 Strokes of the Brush before Bed.*

People, November 1, 2004, Kyle Smith, review of *100 Strokes of the Brush before Bed,* p. 49.

Publishers Weekly, September 20, 2004, review of *100 Strokes of the Brush before Bed,* p. 45.

Telegraph (London, England), Jane Shilling, review of *100 Strokes of the Brush before Bed.*

ONLINE

Best of Sicily Web site, http://www.bestofsicily.com/ (June 20, 2005), Maria Luisa Romano, review of *100 Strokes of the Brush before Bed.*

Melissa P. Home Page, http://www.melissap.org (June 20, 2005).

Nerve.com, http://www.nerve.com/ (June 20, 2005), interview with author.*

*   *   *

PAPADIAMANTOPOULOS, Johannes 1856-1910
(Jean Moréas, Yannis Papadiamantopoulos)

PERSONAL: Given name also spelled Iohannes or Yiannis; born April 15, 1856, in Athens, Greece; immigrated to France, c. 1879; naturalized French citizen, 1909; died of hemiplegia, March 31, 1910, in Saint-Mandé, France. *Education:* Studied law in Bonn and Heidelberg, Germany.

CAREER: Poet and author. Cofounder, *Symboliste* (literary magazine), 1886.

AWARDS, HONORS: Named officer, French Legion of Honor, c. 1909.

WRITINGS:

Trygones kai echidnai (poetry; title means "Doves and Vipers"), [Greece], 1878.

Les syrtes (poetry), [France], 1884, revised edition published as *Les syrtes (1883-1884),* L. Vanier (Paris, France), 1892.

Les cantilènes: funèrailles, interlude, assonances, cantilènes, le pur concept, histoires merveillueuses (poetry), L. Vanier (Paris, France), 1886.

(With Paul Adam) *Le thé chez Miranda* (title means "Tea at Miranda's Home"), Tresse et Stock (Paris, France), 1886.

(With Paul Adam) *Les demoiselles Goubert: moeurs de Paris,* Tresse et Stock (Paris, France), 1886.

Le pèlerin passioné (poetry), L. Vanier (Paris, France), 1891, revised edition published as *Le pèlerin passioné: édition refondue compreant plusieurs poèmes nouveaux,* 1893.

Autant en emporte le vent (1886-1887), L. Vanier (Paris, France), 1893.

Ériphyle: poème suivi de quatre sylves, Bibliotèque artistique et littéraire (Paris, France), 1894.

Poésies, 1886-1896: le pèlerin passionné. Énone au clair visage et Sylves. Eriphyle et Sylves nouvelles (omnibus), Bibliotèque artistique et littéraire (Paris, France), 1898, published as *Poèmes et sylves, 1886-1896. Le pèlerin passioné. Énone au clair visage. Eriphyle, Sylves* (omnibus), Société du Mercure de France (Paris, France), 1907.

(Translator) *L'histoire de Jean de Paris, roi de France,* Bibliotèque artistique et littéraire (Paris, France), 1899.

Le voyage de Grèce, Editions de la Plume (Paris, France), 1902.

Feuillets, Editions de la Plume (Paris, France), 1902.

Iphigénie: tragedie en cinq actes (five-act play), Mercure de France (Paris, France), 1904.

Contes de la vielle France (short stories; title means "Tales of Old France"), Mercure de France (Paris, France), 1904.

Les stances: Les six livres complet (poetry; title means "The Stances: The Complete Six Books"; also see below), Editions de la Plume (Paris, France), 1905, twenty-fifth edition, Société du Mercure de France (Paris, France), 1929.

Paysages et sentiments, E. Sansot (Paris, France), 1906.

Premières poésies, 1883-1886 (poetry); title means "First Poems"), Mercure de France (Paris, France), 1907.

Esquisses et souvenirs (poetry), Mercure de France (Paris, France), 1908.

Variations sur la vie et les livres (title means "Variations on Life and Books"), Mercure de France (Paris, France), 1910.

Sur Lamartine, [Paris, France], 1910.

Le septème livre des stances (poetry; title means "The Seventh Book of Stances"), F. Bernouard (Paris, France), 1920.

Trois nouveaux contes de la vielle France (short stories; title means "Three New Tales of Old France"), Émile-Paul (Paris, France), 1921.

Le VIIIe livre des "Stances" (poetry; title means "The Eighth Book of 'Stances'"), Éditions de la Douce France (Paris, France), 1922.

Oeuvres de Jean Moréas (collected poetry), two volumes, Mercure de France (Paris, France), 1923–1926.

Trois contes d'amour (short stories; title means "Three Tales of Love"), H. Jonquieres (Paris, France), 1924.

Oeuvres en prose: morceaux choisis (title means "Works in Prose: Choice Morsels"), Librairie Valois (Paris, France), 1927.

Cent soixante-treize lettres de Jean Moréas à Raymond de la Tailhède et à divers correspondants (correspondence), Lettres Modernes (Paris, France), 1968.

Also author, as Johannes Papadiamantopoulos, of *Tourterelles et viperes,* 1872. Contributor of articles to periodicals, including *Figaro littéraire.* English translations of Moréas's poems have been published in anthologies, including *Contemporary French Poetry, The Poets of Modern France,* and *French Symbolist Poetry.*

SIDELIGHTS: Poet Johannes Papadiamantopoulos, best known by his adoptive name Jean Moréas, was a founder of the French symbolist movement but later abandoned this school in order to pursue more classical forms of poetry. The son of the attorney general of the Greek supreme court of appeals, his family had a noble lineage, which afforded him a quality education. He was put into the care of a French governess, who instilled in the young boy a love for French literature. By the time he was ten, Papadiamantopoulos had resolved to become a French poet, but his father had other plans. Sent to law school in Germany, Papadiamantopoulos was supposed to become an attorney like his father, but by this time he was already writing poems in French. Although his first verse collection, *Trygones kai echidnai,* was mostly in Greek (though it did contain four poems in French), the rest of his works would be in French. Leaving law school behind, he adopted the name of Moréas, traveled Europe for a time, and soon settled in Paris, where he became a frequenter of the city's cafés.

Thoroughly enjoying the culture of France, Moréas read his poems at local cafés, discussed literary theory with fellow intellectuals and poets such as Paul Verlaine and Laurent Tailhède, and read the works of the Middle Ages and Renaissance at the national library. Moréas, as it happened, arrived in France while the country was still feeling the aftershocks of the 1870 Franco-Prussian War, in which France lost the regions of Alsace and Lorraine to Germany. The political upheaval had an effect on the arts, causing painters and writers to reject traditional schools of thought. With regard to poetry, there was a reaction against the rigid forms practiced by the Parnassians. Younger poets began writing instead in free verse. Moréas became central to this movement, which was first called decadism (also called decadentism) but which evolved into symbolism. "The period was idealist in its general temper but anarchist in the detail of its aspirations and its attempt to realize the formulae it proposed," explained John Davis Butler in his book *Jean Moréas: A Critique of His Poetry and Philosophy.*

Moréas's early verse collection *Les syrtes* "was considered [symbolism's] classic representation," according to Butler. A collection of reveries, laments, love poems, and remembrances, the book was nevertheless regarded by the poet to be an immature work. Still, Butler commented that it "contains many pieces that are not only readable but thoroughly enjoyable and rewarding." Already regarded as the leader of the Symbolist movement in France, Moréas was invited by the editors of the magazine *Figaro littéraire* to provide a definitive statement of purpose for Symbolism. The result was the article "Manifeste du symbolisme," which was published in 1886. Many scholars also credit the poet with changing the name from decadentism to symbolism, as Moréas felt the former was too derogatory a name.

Les syrtes was soon followed by *Les cantilènes: funérailles, interlude, assonances, cantilènes, le pur concept, histoires merveillueuses.* Though many, according to Butler, now consider this collection inferior to *Les syrtes,* the critic commented that "Moréas skillfully recaptures a sense of spontaneity and the folk-feeling in some of the adaptations from the Middle Ages, and some of the *Cantilènes* are delightful."

When the poetry collection *Le pèlerin passioné* was published in 1891, it prompted Moréas's contemporaries to once again acknowledge him as the leader of the symbolist poets; a banquet was even held in his honor. By the time this work's second edition came out in 1893, however, Moréas was already abandoning symbolism for a new literary movement that would be called the école Romane (the Roman school). Butler noted that there were already hints of the poet's defection from symbolism in *Le pèlerin passioné,* which he felt "in one sense [was] a reaction against Symbolism" in its return in some ways to more classical concerns.

Although Moréas was passionate about his adoptive country, he was also beginning to return to his Greek roots, and searching for a way of fusing the two countries' literary heritages. As Butler stated, the poet's intention was "to create a poetry in French that above all, respects and manifests its racial-national qualities and its Greco-Latin traditions." But, explained Butler, "This shift in content . . . is not as consciously conceived or as much emphasized as it is Moréas' concern with language, the prime matter of poetry. Moréas is plainly abashed and dismayed at the negative influence upon the French language of foreign literatures and their trends toward excessive mystery, willful obscurity, and vagueness of expression. Now Symbolism, successor to Decadentism, was the chief and most recent offender in this verbal license that many considered so deleterious to the language. The more Moréas became oriented toward the classicism of the literary heritage of his native land, the more it became necessary for him to repudiate the abuses of the movement."

With the École Romane, Moréas, and other poets who followed his example, such as Raymond de la Tailhède and Ernest Raynaud, began to return to more classical forms, respecting rhyme schemes and rhythms in their verses once again. This is plainly seen in his next major collection, which is considered by many critics to be his eight-volume masterpiece, *Les stances: Les six livres complet.* Butler reported that, at the time the first six volumes were published in 1905, the collection was praised by Moréas's contemporaries. Reviews at the time contained "a plethora of unstinted, frequently almost reverent and ecstatic praise of Moréas and his *Stances.*" Multiple themes are found in *Les stances,* observed Butler, demonstrating a "manifestation of the poet's ennui, metaphysical in quality, the aspect of drama and tragedy inherent in the work and in the life it reveals, the classical humanism and the philosophy of the poet shown through the poems, the workings of nature in the poetry and its poetic process in general." Although the critic duly noted that the thematic concerns of *Les stances* do not explore new territory, they demonstrate a marvelous "purity of expression."

Les stances represents the final significant step in the poet's evolution, a process Butler found to be "as beautiful as some of Moréas' poetic creations." Butler elaborated that the poet's literary works illustrate his constant search to improve his writing and attain an ideal: "It is interesting to confirm that in his evolution, Moréas did not stop with any one stage in which he found success. We have seen that he published successfully in several veins, his works being hailed as types, of the style of the Decadents, the Symbolists, and of the Roman group. Moréas did not settle in any one of these possible havens of achievement because he sensed in each, that he had not gained what he was seeking. He was seeking relentlessly, as if driven by a Socratic daemon, the form of art that best complemented his temperament. His linguistic search for a purity and perfection of form was interestingly enough paralleled by a quest for purity and perfection of morality and philosophy, a spiritual order in his own life. He found, fairly late in life, the artistic and moral-philosophical representation he sought."

BIOGRAPHICAL AND CRITICAL SOURCES:

BOOKS

Butler, John Davis, *Jean Moréas: A Critique of His Poetry and Philosophy,* Mouton (Paris, France), 1967.
de Gourmont, Jean, *Jean Moréas,* E. Sansot (Paris, France), 1905.
Twentieth-Century Literary Criticism, Volume 18, Thomson Gale (Detroit, MI), 1985.

PERIODICALS

French Review, March, 1998, Richard Shryock, "Reaction within Symbolism: The École Romane," pp. 577-584.

ONLINE

Jean Moréas Web site, http://www.bmlisieux.com/litterature/ (July 21, 2005).*

*   *   *

PAPADIAMANTOPOULOS, Yannis
See PAPADIAMANTOPOULOS, Johannes

*   *   *

PARLAND, Henry 1908-1930

PERSONAL: Born July 29, 1908, in Vyborg, Russia; immigrated to Finland, 1912; died of scarlet fever, November 10, 1930, in Kaunas, Lithuania; son of Oswald (an engineer) and Ida Parland. *Education:* Studied law at University of Helsinki, 1927.

CAREER: Writer and poet. Worked as a secretary at Swedish consulate in Kaunas, Lithuania, 1929-30.

WRITINGS:

Idealrealisation (poetry), [Sweden], 1928.
Hamlet sade det vackrare: samlade dikter, edited by father, Oscar Parland, Gargantua (Göteborg, Sweden), 1963.
Samlad prosa, Wahlström & Widstrand (Stockholm, Sweden), 1966.
Sönder (novel fragment; title means "Apart"), Författarförlaget (Malmö, Sweden), 1966.
Den stora dagenefter (title means "The Great Hangover"), Wahlström & Widstrand (Stockholm, Sweden), 1966.
Säginteannat (title means "So Much for That"), Söderström (Helsingfors, Sweden), 1970.

Also contributor to periodicals, including *Quosego.*

SIDELIGHTS: Although Henry Parland lived only to age twenty-two and had just one published book to his credit upon his death in 1930, he remains known as a voice of modern Scandinavian prose. The eldest of three brothers who were all writers, Parland was born in Vyborg, Russia, to parents with a distant English heritage. Although the family moved to Finland in 1912 to escape the Russian Revolution, the young Parland spoke German at home and wrote in Swedish.

Parland studied law at the University of Helsinki in 1927; a year later he made his literary debut in the magazine *Quosego* as the youngest member of the modernist literary group. As a *Kirjasto* online biographer described it, Parland "was in the beginning more interested in fiction," but a meeting with poet Gunnar Björling encouraged the young writer to explore verse as a literary form. The result of Björling's influence was *Idealrealisation,* a first collection of poems that the *Kirjasto* contributor cited as "a youthfully cynical visit to the jazz age."

In 1929 Parland moved to Lithuania, where a relative got him a job at the Swedish consulate. He began work on his first novel, *Sönder,* but was felled by scarlet fever in November of 1930. Parland's work was not forgotten, however; in 1932 some of his previously unpublished work, including excerpts from *Sönder,* was released.

BIOGRAPHICAL AND CRITICAL SOURCES:

PERIODICALS

Ord och Bild, Volume 73, issue 6, 1964, Peter Curman, "Lite svalkande likgiltichet," pp. 479-484; Volume 75, issue 4, 1966, Henry Parland, "Vad gör det för skillnad," pp. 331-335.

Scandinavian Studies, summer, 2000, George C. Schoolfield, "Krapula: Henry Parland och roman-projektet Sönder," p. 238.

ONLINE

Kirjasto Online, http://www.kirjasto.sci.fi/ (January 30, 2001), biography of Henry Parland.*

*   *   *

PEACOCK, Sheila 1964-

PERSONAL: Born January 4, 1964, in Vancouver, British Columbia, Canada; daughter of Robert L. (a teacher and administrator) and Donna (a homemaker and volunteer) Peacock.

ADDRESSES: Agent—c/o Author Mail, Douglas & McIntyre, 2323 Quebec St., Ste. 201, Vancouver, British Columbia V5T 4S7, Canada.

CAREER: Writer. Canadian Broadcasting Corporation, radio and television producer.

WRITINGS:

Great Canadian Cookies, Bars, and Squares, Douglas & McIntyre (Vancouver, British Columbia, Canada), 2002.
(Editor) Flavours of Vancouver: Dishes from around the World, Douglas & McIntyre (Vancouver, British Columbia, Canada), 2005.

*   *   *

PECKA
    See VALA, Katri

PÉROL, Jean 1932-

PERSONAL: Born 1932, in Lyon, France. Education: Studied in Lyon, France.

ADDRESSES: Home—Paris and Ardèche, France. Agent—c/o Author Mail, Éditions de la Différence, 47, rue de la Villette, 75019 Paris, France.

CAREER: Poet, essayist, novelist, and educator. Has taught in Japan; worked variously for Nouvelle Revue Française, Lettres Françaises, and Magazine Littéraire.

AWARDS, HONORS: Prix Mallarmé, 1988, for Asile exil; Prix du Meilleur Roman, 1998, for Un été mémorable.

WRITINGS:

POETRY

Sang et raisons d'une présence, P. Seghers (Paris, France), 1953.
Le coeur de l'olivier, A. Henneuse (Lyon, France), 1957.
Le feu du gel, A. Henneuse (Lyon, France), 1959.
L'atelier, Guy Chambelland (Goudargues, France), 1961.
Treize poèmes de l'amour-fou, Kota Printing Company (Tokyo, Japan), 1962.
D'un pay lointain (prose poems), Shichôsha (Tokyo, Japan), 1965.
Le point vélique . . . , Guy Chambelland (Goudargues, France), 1966.
Le coeur véhément, Gallimard (Paris, France), 1968.
Ruptures, Gallimard (Paris, France), 1970.
Maintenant les soleils, Gallimard (Paris, France), 1972.
Morale provisoire, Gallimard (Paris, France), 1978.
Histoire contemporaine, Gallimard (Paris, France), 1982.
Asile exil, Éditions de la Différence (Paris, France), 1987.
Pouvoir de l'ombre, Éditions de la Différence (Paris, France), 1989.
Ruines-mères, Cherche midi (Paris, France), 1998.

OTHER

Tokyo (travel), Champ Vallon (Seyssel, France)/Presses Universitaires de France (Paris, France), 1986.

Imaï: Peintures (art criticism), Éditions de la Différence (Paris, France), 1990.

La Nouvelle-Orléans (travel), Champ Vallon (Seyssel, France), 1992.

Regards d'encre: écrivains japonais, 1966-1986 (criticism), Éditions de la Différence (Paris, France), 1995.

Un été mémorable (novel), Gallimard (Paris, France), 1998.

Also contributor to periodicals, including *Nouvelle Revue Française.*

SIDELIGHTS: With more than a dozen books of verse to his credit, Jean Pérol is best known as a modern French poet, although he has also published a novel, travel books, and literary criticism. Over the decades, he has written poems in a wide variety of styles and that range in tone from playful to serious. Among Pérol's enthusiasts is a *Times Literary Supplement* reviewer who remarked on the "altogether admirable energy" evident in such early verse collections as *Ruptures* and *Maintenant les soleils.* A decade later, writing about the pieces contained in Pérol's *Histoire contemporaine,* Mortimer Guiney remarked in *French Review,* that "'Powerful' is the word that keeps coming to mind in reading, rereading, these short texts which vary, in form, from simple paragraphs in highly poetic prose to actual sonnets written in alexandrins. It seems every poetic device is under the control of this amazing man." Guiney concluded that "Pérol is a great poet."

The experience of living and teaching in Japan for twenty years has influenced Pérol's writings as well. In addition to writing about modern Japanese literature in *Regards d'encre: écrivains japonais, 1966-1986* and about the country's capital in *Tokyo,* Pérol composed some poems about his life in Japan employing the Japanese haiku form in his 1998 collection *Ruines-mères.* In a *French Review* article, Marie-Noëlle Little described the Japan-inspired poems as "certainly the most unexpected and new where form is conerned."

BIOGRAPHICAL AND CRITICAL SOURCES:

PERIODICALS

French Review, February, 1984, Mortimer Guiney, review of *Histoire contemporaine,* p. 416; May,

2000, Marie-Noëlle Little, review of *Un été mémorable* and *Ruines-mères,* pp. 1261-1263.

Times Literary Supplement, January 19, 1973, review of *Maintenant les soleils,* p. 69.

ONLINE

La Difference, http://www.ladifference.fr/ (June 8, 2005), "Jean Pérol."*

*   *   *

PERRY, Michael 1964-

PERSONAL: Born 1964; married. *Education:* University of Wisconsin—Eau Clare, B.S., 1987.

ADDRESSES: Agent—c/o Author Mail, Perennial/HarperCollins, 10 E. 53rd St., 7th Fl., New York, NY 10022. *E-mail*—mike@sneezingcow.com.

CAREER: Writer, essayist, musician, registered nurse, emergency medical technician, and volunteer firefighter. Has worked as a cowboy in Wyoming, heavy-machinery operator, truck driver, humorist, proofreader, physical therapy aide, surgeon's assistant, actor in commercials, country music roadie, operator for a suicide hotline, and character actor.

WRITINGS:

Handbook for Freelance Writing, NTC Business Books (Lincolnwood, IL), 1998.

Population: 485: Meeting Your Neighbors One Siren at a Time (biography), HarperCollins (New York, NY), 2002.

Off Main Street: Barnstormers, Prophets, and Gatemouth's Gator (travel essays), Perennial (New York, NY), 2005.

Contributor to periodicals, including *Esquire, Newsweek, Utne Reader, Cowboy, Outside, Men's Health, Salon.com, New York Times Magazine,* and *Backpacker.*

WORK IN PROGRESS: A new nonfiction book.

SIDELIGHTS: Multifaceted author Michael Perry boasts a resume that includes a varied litany of jobs, travels, and experiences that serve as the foundation of his career as a freelance writer. In addition to having a degree in nursing, he is a licensed cycle racer and has worked as a character actor. While on the job as a cowboy in Wyoming, he "learned how to run a cutting torch and a cutting horse; how to nearly avoid a charging bull, which, frankly, isn't good enough; and how to ride like a real cowboy (never grab the saddle horn)," according to a biography posted on his home page. Perry has been a roadie for country music singers and an operator for a suicide hotline.

As an emergency medical technician and volunteer firefighter in New Auburn, Wisconsin, Perry was "the first volunteer fireman in village history to miss the monthly meeting because of a poetry reading," according to the author's home page biography. It was this same volunteer fire department that provided the background for Perry's collection of essays, *Population: 485: Meeting Your Neighbors One Siren at a Time.* "Part portrait of a place, part rescue manual, part rumination on life and death, *Population: 485* is a beautiful meditation on the things that matter," commented Mary Ann Gwinn in the *Seattle Times.* Perry grew up in New Auburn, left, and returned twelve years later. "A ticklish business, returning to a place where folks know you so well," Gwinn observed. "He is never quite clear about what prompted his return—perhaps it was the prospect of no distractions." Serving on the local fire-and-rescue squad provided an easy point of entry back into New Auburn life; it also seemed like a family affair, with his mother, sister, and brothers also members of the unit. Applying his nursing experience, Perry started the long process of becoming reacquainted with his hometown, meeting his neighbors at their points of highest distress, but also understanding them at their most human. He tells the story of his brother Jed, who responds to a car accident and finds his young wife dead in the wreckage; he describes the tricks of the trade in saving lives and rescuing the trapped and injured; he profiles his fellow firefighters, including a man known as the Beagle, who cannot buy gas in town because the sole station is staffed by his two ex-wives. The shadow of death is always present, and the fragile borderline between life and death remains uppermost in Perry's mind. But all the while, Perry possesses "the long view gained by staying in a single spot, the accretion of history, character, and memory that shores up the soul," Gwinn remarked. "So many things make more sense when you know the ghosts that walk your home ground."

"Tragic at times, funny at others, Perry's memoir will appeal to anyone curious about small-town life," noted *Booklist* reviewer Kristine Huntley. *Population: 485* exists "in the best tradition of books that pay quiet homage to community service, place, and the men and women who live there," remarked a *Kirkus Reviews* contributor.

With *Off Main Street: Barnstormers, Prophets, and Gatemouth's Gator* Perry offers another collection of "word portraits of unique people he's met," commented a *Kirkus Reviews* contributor. Truckers, country singers, blues musicians, traveling butchers, and other unique characters populate the book's pages. Throughout the essays, small towns and the people who live in them are highlighted. Perry "has a real talent for mining quirky humor from even the most mundane situations, and humor isn't his only strength," commented the *Kirkus Reviews* critic, who also noted Perry's ability to tell a poignant and emotionally powerful story.

Perry told *CA:* "When people ask me for the secret to surviving as a freelance writer, I usually tell them I discovered that secret years ago while cleaning calf pens on my father's farm. That is, you just keep shoveling until you've got a pile so big, SOMEONE has to notice. A childhood spent slinging manure—the metaphorical basis for a writing career.

"Although I write prose, as a reader I always return to the poets. Dylan Thomas, Sharon Olds, Lucille Clifton, James Wright, Rita Dove, Mark Doty, Bruce Taylor . . . a quiet hour spent reading poetry completely revivifies my respect and hunger for the rhythm and taste of language well chosen."

BIOGRAPHICAL AND CRITICAL SOURCES:

PERIODICALS

Booklist, October 15, 2002, Kristine Huntley, review of *Population: 485: Meeting Your Neighbors One Siren at a Time,* p. 368; February 15, 2005, Rebecca Maksel, review of *Off Main Street: Barnstormers, Prophets, and Gatemouth's Gator,* p. 1057.

Eau Claire Leader-Telegram, April 28, 2005, Ann Barsness, profile of Michael Perry.

Kirkus Reviews, July 15, 2002, review of *Population: 485,* p. 1014; January 15, 2005, review of *Off Main Street,* p. 108.

Library Journal, February 15, 2005, Joyce Sparrow, review of *Off Main Street,* p. 130.

Milwaukee Journal Sentinel, October 19, 2002, Meg Jones, "In Tragedy, Writer Finds Community," review of *Population: 485.*

New York Times Book Review, September 7, 2003, Alida Becker, review of *Population: 485,* p. 24.

Publishers Weekly, July 15, 2002, review of *Population: 485,* p. 62; January 17, 2005, review of *Off Main Street,* p. 41.

Seattle Times, October 3, 2002, Mary Ann Gwinn, review of *Population: 485.*

Tribune Books (Chicago, IL), December 15, 2002, review of *Population: 485,* p. 1.

ONLINE

Michael Perry Home Page, http://www.sneezingcow. com (July 9, 2005).

University of Wisconsin-Eau Claire Web site, http:// www.uwec.edu/ (July 9, 2005), author profile.

*   *   *

PETRUCCI, Paul 1954-

PERSONAL: Born March 13, 1954, in Montclair, NJ; married; children: Sophia. *Education:* Attended University of Maryland and University of Washington, Seattle. *Hobbies and other interests:* Chess, sports, travel, architecture, history.

ADDRESSES: Agent—c/o Author Mail, Booklocker. com, Inc., P.O. Box 2399, Bangor, ME 04402-2399. *E-mail*—paul@paulpetrucci.com.

CAREER: Business process analyst in the information technology field.

WRITINGS:

Prodigal Logic: A Ray Gabriel Floating Home Mystery (novel), Booklocker (Bangor, ME), 2002.

WORK IN PROGRESS: Floating Homely, the second mystery novel in the "Ray Gabriel Floating Home Mystery" series.

SIDELIGHTS: Paul Petrucci told *CA:* "I work in information technology as a business process analyst. I've spent some time in the field of artificial intelligence, which actually gave me the original idea for the *Prodigal Logic: A Ray Gabriel Floating Home Mystery* plot. I was working with expert systems which are programs that attempt to imitate the decision-making rules and heuristics of an expert. I was reading Sherlock Holmes and wondered if I could put his expertise into a computer. Then the thought came: what if a person tried using Sherlock's knowledge in a real investigation; then what if he had to grow it quickly and it kept making mistakes; then what if it started giving the right answer but the protagonist didn't want to hear the right answer. So the idea for the book actually grew out of my day job.

"Living in the Northwest, there is beauty everywhere. For fun I love to ski and bike. I live on a floating home, so we have access to water sports, especially kayaking. I love to read, I love raising my daughter. My wife and I both love to watch movies and to give breakfast parties—before parenthood it used to be dinner parties.

"Umberto Eco gave me something to aspire to: a literary mystery novel that had both Gothic overtones and psychological suspense. Arturo Perez-Reverte is of the same mold, if more accessible; his books have wonderful characters and intricate plots. Stephen Greenleaf was one of my instructors at the University of Washington program. His books, along with those of the other two authors, offered the message that it's okay not to dummy down your plot, to trust your readers and not insult their intelligence.

"There is a difference in feeling between a first draft and subsequent drafts. When writing a first draft, I let everything go and try to have my fingers keep pace with my thoughts. I have found that I listen to words as I write them—I am more auditory than visual—and when the words sound right, I feel like laughing, even if the material isn't necessarily funny. Even if my first draft strays from its intended path, it's usually not frustrating. The frustration comes in subsequent drafts, when the words-per-minute radio slows to a snail's pace. Editing takes a clear head and patience, so frustration is a natural result if it's not working.

"I love the process of creating names, for both characters and book titles. For characters who are known primarily by their first names, the names have to stand alone while subtly saying something about them. My two female leads are Zelda and Miriam, and from the names I think you can determine which is the good girl and which is the naughty one. The two priests are Zebediah and Aquilinio; again, they are very different. One's name is meant to denote someone with a fire-and-brimstone view of religion; the other has very defined physical features that are reflected in the name. For characters who are known by both first and last names, it's also necessary that the sounds flow trippingly off the tongue. My antagonist Julius Dexter's name is meant to connote imperiousness and sinister left-handedness. I like the name Ray Gabriel for my protagonist because it flows and because it's composed of two angels.

"I've been told by more than one person that *Prodigal Logic* doesn't have a 'mystery novel' feel to it. There's no death in the title, or any other sinister word. The reason that I stayed with it is because I like the sound of the two words together, and because I think the phrase very subtly spells out the two competing subjects: religion/philosophy versus computers, or feeling/ethics versus logic. I connect the word 'prodigal' with religion because of the parable of the prodigal son. But even using its formal meaning of 'squandered,' the title works for the book.

"Because I tend to hear the characters speak instead of visualizing scenes, I hear the sound of the words more clearly than I picture the setting. I do that even when describing scenery, which makes that part of writing very difficult to me. Maybe I should have been a poet. When it works for me, it is like hearing good music—so one important goal is self-serving: to hear that music play in my head. It's also important to me to entertain while giving information. I want my books to be thought-provoking and touch on important ideas, but they must be wrapped in a pleasing package so that they'll be read. If they're not read, the messages don't get delivered. I don't want to end up talking to myself."

BIOGRAPHICAL AND CRITICAL SOURCES:

PERIODICALS

Library Journal, August, 2002, Rex Klett, review of *Prodigal Logic: A Ray Gabriel Floating Home Mystery*, p. 150.

ONLINE

BookBrowser.com, http://www.bookbrowser.com/ (August 7, 2002), Phillip Tomasso, III, review of *Prodigal Logic: A Ray Gabriel Floating Home Mystery*.

Electronic Book Reviews, http://www.electronicbookreviews.com/ (July 18, 2002), Cheryl McCann, review of *Prodigal Logic*.

Over My Dead Body! Online, http://overmydeadbody.com/ (December 10, 2002), Karen Meek, review of *Prodigal Logic*.

Paul Petrucci Home Page, http://www.paulpetrucci.com (March 19, 2003).

Spiral Nature Web site, http://www.spiralnature.com/ (August 28, 2002), George Dobbs, review of *Prodigal Logic*.

Suite 101.com, http://www.suite101.com/ (July 18, 2002), Lorie Ham, "Interview with New Mystery Author Paul Petrucci."

* * *

PHAM, Quang X. 1965(?)-

PERSONAL: Born c. 1965; son of Pham Van Hoa (a fighter pilot) and Nguyen Thi Niem; immigrated to United States, 1975; naturalized U.S. citizen, 1984; married, wife's name Shannon. *Education:* Graduated from University of California, Los Angeles; attended University of California, Irvine, c. 1999.

ADDRESSES: Home—CA. *Agent*—c/o Author Mail, Ballantine Books, 1745 Broadway, New York, NY 10019. *E-mail*—author@gxpham.com.

CAREER: Businessperson, entrepreneur, motivational speaker, and writer. AstraMerck (pharmaceutical company), sales representative, 1994-c. 98; Genentech (pharmaceutical company), sales representative, 1998-99; MyDrugRep.com (pharmaceutical marketing company), founder, chief executive officer, and president, c. 2000; QTC Medical Services (medical disability company), vice president and general manager; Lathian Systems (pharmaceutical solutions company), founder and chief executive officer. Has appeared as a guest on television and radio networks. *Military service:* U.S. Marines, c. 1988-95, helicopter pilot in Gulf War, 1991, in Operation Desert Shield, in Operation Desert Storm, and in Somalia; became captain. Marine Reserves, 1997—; became major.

WRITINGS:

A Sense of Duty: My Father, My American Journey (memoir), Ballantine Books (New York, NY), 2005.

Also contributor to *Wall Street Journal, Los Angeles Times, Boston Globe, Houston Chronicle, Orange County Register,* and *Washington Times.*

SIDELIGHTS: In Quang X. Pham's memoir *A Sense of Duty: My Father, My American Journey* the author offers his point of view on the Vietnam War and his immigrant experience in the United States. Pham describes his early life in Vietnam, where his father was a South Vietnamese military hero, his immigration to the United States, and his own experience in the U.S. military. Writing in *Sea Power,* David M. Munns commented that *A Sense of Duty* "is a truly arresting memoir. . . . The emotions infused in Pham's character are expressed in unapologetic terms, filled with controversial insight into his life and the conflict that divided Vietnam, and, in many ways, America."

Pham was born during the Vietnam War and his father, Pham Van Hoa, served as an officer and pilot in the South Vietnamese Air Force which worked in support of the U.S. military. While Pham was still a small child, his father moved Pham, Pham's mother, and Pham's three sisters to the United States. Though Pham's father intended to join them, he was imprisoned by the communists following the war and held in re-education camps for twelve years. One part of *A Sense of Duty* focuses on Pham's complex relationship with his father. Raised without the man's physical presence, Pham was nonetheless greatly influenced by the idea of the elder Pham.

In the book, Pham does not idealize his experiences as a refugee in the United States. He describes what it felt like to grow up in Los Angeles, the struggles his family went through, and how long it took to assimilate. After earning his undergraduate degree, Pham joined the U.S. Marine Corps and became an officer and a pilot like his father. He describes his time in the service as less than ideal; Pham experienced racism because of his ethnic identity.

Throughout the text of *A Sense of Duty,* Pham comments on the state of American politics, the Vietnamese Communists who won the war, anti-war supporters in the United States, and the media. Writing in *Marine Corps Gazette,* Robert R. Darron wrote, "This is a bittersweet book. It is a worthwhile read because it describes Americans from many angles. We must realize that others don't see us in the same rosy light that we perceive ourselves."

BIOGRAPHICAL AND CRITICAL SOURCES:

BOOKS

Pham, Quang X., *A Sense of Duty: My Father, My American Journey,* Ballantine Books (New York, NY), 2005.

PERIODICALS

Journal Record (Oklahoma City, OK), March 28, 2000, "No Hoop, but Net Is Crucial," author profile, p. 1.
Kirkus Reviews, March 1, 2005, review of *A Sense of Duty,* p. 280.
Los Angeles Times, June 30, 1999, Michael Luo, "El Toro, 1943-1999; Memories; For Pham, Base Is Also 'Vietanamese Ellis Island'," p. 4.
Marine Corps Gazette, June, 2005, Robert R. Darron, "From Vietnam to America," p. 69.
Pharmaceutical Executive, November, 2000, Andra Brichacek, "Starting from Scratch with Quang X. Pham," p. 102.
Publishers Weekly, March 14, 2005, review of *A Sense of Duty,* p. 60.
San Francisco Chronicle, June 5, 2005, John Koopman, "Warrior Dad Left a Legacy of Values," p. B6.
Sea Power, June, 2005, David W. Munns, "*Sense of Duty* Tells of Life as a Refugee and Marine," p. 64.

ONLINE

A Sense of Duty Web site, http://www.asenseofduty. com/ (June 29, 2005).

Random House Web site, http://www.randomhouse. com/ (June 29, 2005), biography of Quang X. Pham.*

* * *

PHELPS, Elizabeth Stuart 1844-1911
(Mary Adams, Mrs. Herbert Ward Dickinson, Elizabeth Stuart Phelps Ward)

PERSONAL: Born Mary Gray Phelps; August 31, 1844, in Boston, MA; died January 28, 1911, in Newton, MA; took mother's name, 1852; daughter of Elizabeth Stuart Phelps (an author); married Herbert Dickinson Ward (a journalist), 1888 (separated). *Education:* Attended Abbot Academy and Mrs. Edwards' School for Young Ladies, Andover, MA.

CAREER: Author. Also worked as a Sunday school teacher.

WRITINGS:

NOVELS

The Gates Ajar, Fields Osgood (Boston, MA), 1868.
Hedged In, Fields Osgood (Boston, MA), 1870.
The Silent Partner, Osgood (Boston, MA), 1871.
The Story of Avis, Osgood (Boston, MA), 1877.
Friends: A Duet, Houghton Mifflin (Boston, MA), 1881.
Dr. Zay, Houghton Mifflin (Boston, MA), 1882.
Beyond the Gates, Houghton Mifflin (Boston, MA), 1883.
Burglars in Paradise, Houghton Mifflin (Boston, MA), 1886.
The Madonna of the Tubs, Houghton Mifflin (Boston, MA), 1887.
The Gates Between, Houghton Mifflin (Boston, MA), 1887.
A Singular Life, Houghton Mifflin (Boston, MA), 1895.
(Under pseudonym Mary Adams) *Confessions of a Wife,* Century (New York, NY), 1902.
Trixy, Houghton Mifflin (Boston, MA), 1904.
Though Life Us Do Part, Houghton Mifflin (Boston, MA), 1908.
Walled In, Harper (New York, NY), 1909.

FOR CHILDREN

Ellen's Idol, Massachusetts Sabbath School Society (Boston, MA), 1864.
Up Hill; or, Life in the Factory, Hoyt (Boston, MA), 1865.
Mercy Gliddon's Work, Hoyt (Boston, MA), 1866.
Gypsy Breynton, Graves & Young (Boston, MA), 1866.
Gypsy's Cousin Joy, Graves & Young (Boston, MA), 1866.
Gypsy's Sowing and Reaping, Graves & Young (Boston, MA), 1866.
Tiny, Massachusetts Sabbath School Society (Boston, MA), 1866.
Tiny's Sunday Nights, Massachusetts Sabbath School Society (Boston, MA), 1867.
Gypsy's Year at the Golden Crescent, Graves & Young (Boston, MA), 1868.
I Don't Know How, Massachusetts Sabbath School Society (Boston, MA), 1868.
The Trotty Book, Fields Osgood (Boston, MA), 1870, published as *That Dreadful Boy Trotty: What He Did and What He Said,* Ward Lock (London, England), 1877.
Trotty's Wedding Tour, and Story-Book, Osgood (Boston, MA), 1877.
My Cousin and I, Sunday School Union (Boston, MA), 1879.
Jack the Fisherman, Houghton Mifflin (Boston, MA), 1887.

SHORT STORIES

Men, Women, and Ghosts (includes "The Tenth of January"), Fields Osgood (Boston, MA), 1869.
Sealed Orders, Houghton Osgood (Boston, MA), 1879.
An Old Maid's Paradise, Houghton Osgood (Boston, MA), 1879.
Fourteen to One, Houghton Mifflin (Boston, MA), 1891.
The Oath of Allegiance and Other Stories, Houghton Mifflin (Boston, MA), 1909.
The Empty House and Other Stories, Houghton Mifflin (Boston, MA), 1910, published as *A Deserted House and Other Stories,* Constable (London, England), 1911.

OTHER

What to Wear?, Osgood (Boston, MA), 1873.
Poetic Studies, Osgood (Boston, MA), 1875.

Songs of the Silent World and Other Poems, Houghton Mifflin (Boston, MA), 1884.

A Gracious Life: A Eulogy on Mrs. Charlotte A. Johnson, privately printed (Boston, MA), 1888.

Austin Phelps: A Memoir, Scribner (New York, NY), 1891.

Chapters from a Life (autobiography), Houghton Mifflin (Boston, MA), 1896.

Within the Gates (play), Houghton Mifflin (Boston, MA), 1901.

A Plea for the Helpless, American Humane Society (New York, NY), 1901.

Vivisection and Legislation in Massachusetts, American Anti-Vivisection Society (Philadelphia, PA), 1902.

Contributor of stories and articles to periodicals, including *Atlantic Monthly, Century, Harper's, Independent, Ladies' Home Journal,* and *Woman's Journal.*

Phelps's manuscripts are maintained at the Andover Historical Society, Andover, MA; the Houghton Library, Harvard University; and the Beinecke Library, Yale University.

SIDELIGHTS: Elizabeth Stuart Phelps was a professional writer, an advocate of workers' rights and of women's right to work who wrote prolifically on a variety of topics and created many strong, progressive female characters. In her many novels—particularly those written early in her career—Phelps created heroines who brought a new voice to fiction, speaking actively for women as a class and presenting a critique of those social institutions that placed limits on women's development. A good example of her heroines' point of view can be seen in the author's 1871 pro-labor novel *The Silent Partner,* in which the heroine gives this reason for rejecting her suitor: "The fact is . . . that I have no time to think of love and marriage. . . . That is a business, a trade, by itself to women. I have too much else to do."

Born Mary Gray Phelps in 1844, Phelps was the daughter of a popular writer, Elizabeth Stuart Phelps, and took her mother's name when she was eight years old and her mother died. Phelps was already publishing short fiction in periodicals during her teens. Approaching writing as a full-time profession, she produced fifty-six volumes of fiction, poetry, and other

work before her death in 1911. She also wrote more than 150 short stories, including "The Tenth of January," a portrayal of a crippled factory girl who is trapped during the collapse of the Pemberton Mill. Praised by such contemporaries as Thomas Wentworth Higginson and John Greenleaf Whittier, "The Tenth of January" reflects its author's concern over the social conditions that render women powerless. The experiences of her own mother affected Phelps's writing as well; she based her most well-known work, 1877's *The Story of Avis,* on her mother's struggle to write while fulfilling the traditional role of wife and mother. Avis, a promising artist whose career is stifled by marriage and motherhood, portrays the impossibility of artistic fulfillment for married women.

Surprisingly, given her views of marriage, Phelps married Herbert Dickinson Ward—a man seventeen years her junior—when she was forty-four. The marriage proved to be an unhappy one, and they spent much of their time apart. Despite the aftereffects of a physical breakdown following *The Story of Avis,* Phelps continued to support herself, and later, her husband, through her writing. She also became increasingly active in the antivivisection movement, using her ability as a writer to advance that cause as she had also advanced the cause of women and the poor. As she would write in her 1896 autobiography, *Chapter from a Life,* Phelps was "proud . . . that I have always been a working woman, and always had to be."

BIOGRAPHICAL AND CRITICAL SOURCES:

BOOKS

Bennett, Mary Angela, *Elizabeth Stuart Phelps,* University of Pennsylvania Press (Philadelphia, PA), 1939.

Douglas, Ann, *The Feminization of American Culture,* Knopf (New York, NY), 1977.

Kelly, Lori Duin, *The Life and Works of Elizabeth Stuart Phelps, Victorian Feminist Writer,* Whitston (New York, NY), 1983.

Kessler, Carol Farley, *Elizabeth Stuart Phelps,* G.K. Hall (Boston, MA), 1982.*

*   *   *

PHELPS WARD, Elizabeth Stuart
See PHELPS, Elizabeth Stuart

PHILP, Tom 1962(?)-

PERSONAL: Born c. 1962; son of Nell Farr; married Lisa Lapin (a college assistant vice chancellor); children: Max, Charlotte. *Education:* Northwestern University, Medill School of Journalism, B.S.J., 1983.

ADDRESSES: Home—Carmichael, CA. *Office*— Sacramento Bee, 2100 Q. St., Sacramento, CA 95816. *E-mail*—tphilp@sacbee.com.

CAREER: Writer, journalist, and editorial writer. *San Jose Mercury News,* journalist, 1983-92; *Sacramento Bee,* reporter and staff writer, 1992-97, associate editor and editorial board member, 1997—.

AWARDS, HONORS: Best of the West first-place award for deadline writing, 1992; American Association of University Professors prize, 1994; California Newspaper Publishers Association Better Newspapers first-place award for editorial comment, 2000; Harold Gilliam Award for Excellence in Environmental Reporting, Bay Institute of San Francisco, 2001; Walker Stone Award, Scripps Howard Foundation, Sigma Delta Chi Award, and National Headliner Award for Editorial Writing, all 2004, all for editorials on questionable spending in California water districts; Pulitzer Prize for Editorial Writing, 2005, for editorials on reclaiming California's Hetch Hetchy Valley.

SIDELIGHTS: California-based journalist Tom Philp is a Pulitzer Prize-winning editorial writer for the *Sacramento Bee.* A winner of numerous other awards, Philp has been a journalist since graduating from Northwestern University's prestigious Medill School of Journalism in 1983. As an associate editor and member of the editorial board of the *Sacramento Bee,* Philp writes editorials, columns, and articles for the paper's Sunday Forum section. He concentrates on topics such as agriculture, forestry, energy use, regional planning, health care, and telecommunications. Of great concern to Philp are issues related to water use and conservation in California. "I've loved water issues ever since I got out of Medill and got a job at the *San Jose Mercury News* when Silicon Valley was just starting it's growth," Philp commented in a profile by Belinda Lichty Clarke on the Medill School of Journalism Web site. "Living in California, water and water supplies are constantly at issue and you've

got a long history, science and politics all playing a role." Among many other pieces, these concerns prompted a multiple-award-winning series on corruption, poor business practices, and questionable spending in a number of California's water districts.

Philp's interest in water issues led him to journalism's top award. His Pulitzer Prize-winning editorials focus on the possibility of restoring the Hetch Hetchy reservoir, created from flooding the Hetch Hetchy Valley in the early 1920s. Intended as a water supply source for San Francisco, the reservoir has often been superfluous, as other sources sufficiently supply San Francisco's water needs. Conservationists have suggested the draining of the reservoir and the restoration of the valley, but until Philp's well-received editorials, the notion was routinely dismissed. Philp's work, based in large part on an environmental modeling program developed at the University of California, Davis and on the work of graduate student Sarah Null, outlines scientific evidence that draining the reservoir and restoring the valley would not adversely affect water supplies. Instead, doing so would recover a piece of California's natural history directly connected to Yosemite National Park, and also create the benefits of another recreational area and source of natural resources. The water supply in Hetch Hetchy would be held in other reservoirs downstream.

As a result of his editorials, tangible steps have been taken to analyze the possibility of restoring Hetch Hetchy. The California State Assembly contacted the governor's office, asking for further action on the issue, and Governor Arnold Schwarzenegger responded with the intent to pursue a "full-scale study of the feasibility of the restoration."

In response to his Pulitzer win, Philp remarked to Keli Senkevich in *California Aggie:* "It's a responsibility I have to live up to with every editorial I write. Everything I say has to sound worthy of this honor."

BIOGRAPHICAL AND CRITICAL SOURCES:

PERIODICALS

California Aggie, June 8, 2005, Keli Senkevich, "Pulitzer-Winning Editor Tom Philp Credits UC Davis Research for Award; Computer Model

Demonstrates Possibility of Restoring Hetch Hetchy"; Keli Senkevich, "Question & Answer with Pulitzer Prize Winner Tom Philp; *SacBee* Editor Wins Prize with Help of UCD Study on Hetch Hetchy."

Editor & Publisher, May 1, 2005, Graham Webster, "Pulitzers: At the *Bee,* More Hell-Raising Ahead."

Quill, June-July, 2004, "Award Winner: Editorial Writing," p. 46.

Sacramento Bee, April 5, 2005, Sam Stanton, "*Bee*'s Philp Wins Editorial-Writing Pulitzer."

ONLINE

McClatchy Company Web site, http://www.mcclatchy. com/ (July 9, 2005), profile of Tom Philp.

Medill School of Journalism Web site, http://www. medill.northwestern.edu/ (July 9, 2005), Belinda Lichty Clarke, "Medill Alum Tom Philp Wins 2005 Pulitzer for Editorial Writing."

Pulitzer Prizes Web site, http://www.pulitzer.org/ (July 9, 2005), biography of Tom Philp.*

*   *   *

P., Melissa
  See PANARELLO, Melissa

*   *   *

POSNER, Donald 1931-2005

OBITUARY NOTICE—See index for *CA* sketch: Born August 30, 1931, in New York, NY; died of esophageal cancer, August 13, 2005, in New York, NY. Art historian, educator, and author. Posner was a fine arts professor at New York University's Institute of Fine Arts. He specialized in Italian and French art of the Baroque period. After serving in the Air Force during the Korean War as a radar specialist, he completed a B.A. at Queens College in 1956. He went to Harvard University for his M.A. the next year, and graduated with a Ph.D. from New York University in 1962. While studying at New York University, he came under the influence of Baroque expert Walter Friedlaender, and this inspired him to specialize in seventeenth-and eighteenth-century art. Posner decided to remain at

New York University after he graduated and he joined the faculty as an instructor. He eventually became Ailsa Mellon Bruce Professor of Fine Arts in 1975, as well as deputy director of the Institute of Fine Arts from 1983 until his 2002 retirement. In addition to his work at the institute, he was the author of several well-received studies, including *Annibale Carracci: A Study in the Reform of Italian Painting around 1590* (1972) and *Antoine Watteau* (1984).

OBITUARIES AND OTHER SOURCES:

PERIODICALS

Grand Rapids Press (Grand Rapids, MI), September 4, 2005, p. B7.

New York Times, August 28, 2005, p. A21.

*   *   *

POSTMA, Obe 1868-1963

PERSONAL: Born March 29, 1868, in Cornwerd, Friesland, Netherlands; died June 26, 1963, in Leeuwarden, Netherlands. *Education:* University of Amsterdam, Ph.D., 1895.

CAREER: University of Gröningen, Gröningen, Netherlands, teacher of mathematics and physics, c. 1900-40.

AWARDS, HONORS: Gysbert Japicx prize, 1947, for "It sil bistaen"; Rely Jorritsma prize, 1954, for "Fan de Fjouwer eleminten."

WRITINGS:

Lets over uitstraling en opslorping (poems), J.B. Wolters (Gröningen, Netherlands), 1895.

Fryske lân en Fryske libben (poems), A.J. Osinga (Snits, Netherlands), 1918.

De friesche kleihoeve: bijdrage tot de geschiedenis van den cultuurgrond, vooral in Friesland en Gröningen, met veertien kaarten, [Leeuwarden, Netherlands], 1934.

Over het ontstaan der oudste Friesche geslachtsnamen (nonfiction), Van Gorcum (Assen, Netherlands), 1941.

Samle fersen (poems), two volumes, Brandenburgh (Snits, Netherlands), 1949.

Eigen kar (poems), Laverman (Drachten, Netherlands), 1949.

It fryske doarp as tsjerklike en wraldske ienheit foar 1795 (history), Brandenburgh (Snits, Netherlands), 1953.

Fan wjerklank en bisinnen, Laverman (Drachten, Netherlands), 1957.

(Translator) *Twofold: Ten Poems of Emily Dickinson in Frisian Translation* (poetry in English and Frisian), Friese Pres Boekerij (Leeuwarden, Netherlands), 1982.

What the Poet Must Know: An Anthology, translated by Anthony Paul and Jabik Veenbaas, Tresoar (Ljouwert, Netherlands), 2004.

Also translator of works by others.

SIDELIGHTS: Obe Postma is generally considered the greatest poet to write in the Frisian language. Born in 1868 in Friesland, a northern region of the Netherlands, Postma published his collections of poetry between the years 1918 and 1957. He was especially known for his ability to depict the simplicity of rural Frisian life, often adding philosophical and cosmic elements to his verses. That ability earned him praise from critics, as well as several literary awards, including the Gysbert Japicx prize in 1947 and the Rely Jorritsma prize in 1954. In addition to writing poetry, Postma translated the work of other poets, including Rainer Maria Rilke and American poet Emily Dickinson, the latter with whom Postma felt a kinship. Despite his love for poetry and literature, Postma nearly chose another path in life. After growing up in the seaside village of Cornwerd, he studied physics and mathematics at the University of Amsterdam. Under the tutelage of professor and Nobel Prize winner J.D. Van der Waals, Postma earned his doctorate in 1895 and quickly became a respected figure in the scientific community. During this period, he worked with some of the most important Dutch scientists of the day. However, a scientific life proved too confining for Postma, and he yearned for the life of a poet and philosopher. He returned to his Frisian homeland and became a teacher at the University of Gröningen, where he continued to teach for forty years.

Postma began to write poetry sometime around 1900, and his first volume of poems, *Fryske lân en Fryske libben,* appeared in 1918. Postma's verse was not overly aesthetic and rarely rhymed. Instead, he concentrated on the small details of life, depicting them in a straightforward way. For example, in the poem "What the Poet Must Know," Postma wrote, "Oh, the joy of harvesting, stacking the spacious loft with the world's wealth!" In another poem, "Al myn libbens freugden," he expanded on the theme: "All the delights of my life are in the flowering cherry with a single yellow leaf that is trembling, / In the clouds from the south pushing up across the sky," The poem continues: "It is the light-glimmer of the water in the gully, the opulent smell of the dungheap in the springtime, / The singsong cry of the brent geese on the flats."

Jabik Veenbaas, who translated much of Postma's poetry into Dutch, commented on the appeal of the author's work in a biographical sketch for the Frysk Letterkundich Museum Web site. "Postma wrote, soberly and simply, about the Frisian landscape he loved—the meadows, the little villages, life in and around the farm," Veenbaas said. "He was the poet who witnessed and recorded the experiences of the Frisian people, and placed those experiences within a broader context, that of the all-embracing soul."

Postma, who continued to publish through the remainder of his life, died in 1963 in Leeuwarden, Netherlands. In 1949 a large number of his poems were collected and published in the two-volume *Samle fersen.* Postma's influence has since expanded outside the Netherlands; in 1997 a selection of his poems was published in Dutch translation, and the work proved so popular that a German translation appeared a year later. In 2004 the first English-language collection of his poems was published. Henry J. Baron, reviewing *What the Poet Must Know: An Anthology* in *World Literature Today,* wrote of the collection that "to read much of Postma's poetry, not unlike Robert Frost's, is to be led back by the poet to the time of one's childhood, when visions are fresh and senses acute. It is to rediscover the people and places and sounds and smells that stimulated and enriched our young years and, whose memories having been reawakened in later years, upon recollection enrich us even more."

BIOGRAPHICAL AND CRITICAL SOURCES:

PERIODICALS

Nowele, Volumes 28-29, 1996, Phitti Beruker, "Die Bedeutung Nordfrieslands," pp. 19-37.

World Literature Today, January-April, 2005, Henry J. Baron, review of *What the Poet Must Know: An Anthology,* p. 102.

ONLINE

Frysk Letterkundich Museum en Dokumintaasjesintrum, http://www.museum.com/jb/museum? id=13666/ (March 15, 2001), "The Poetry of Obe Postma, Poet of Friesland," and Jabik Veenbaas, "Obe Postma."*

*   *   *

POUNCEY, Peter R. 1938(?)-

PERSONAL: Born c. 1938, in Tsingtao, China; son of English parents; immigrated to United States, c. 1960s; married. *Education:* Attended Oxford University.

ADDRESSES: Agent—c/o Author Mail, Random House, 1745 Broadway, New York, NY 10019.

CAREER: Writer, educator, classicist, and college administrator. Amherst College, Amherst, MA, president, 1984-94, and professor, then professor emeritus. Taught at Fordham University; Columbia University, New York, NY, former professor and dean.

MEMBER: Society of Senior Scholars at Columbia University.

WRITINGS:

The Necessities of War: A Study of Thucydides' Pessimism, Columbia University Press (New York, NY), 1980.
Rules for Old Men Waiting (novel), Random House (New York, NY), 2005.

SIDELIGHTS: Author, educator, and college administrator Peter R. Pouncey is a classical scholar, a former dean of Columbia College, and president emeritus of Amherst College. A career academic, Pouncey served as the sixteenth president of Amherst. Born in China and raised in England, his education at English board-ing schools and at Oxford University consisted of training in Greek and Latin classics. While at Columbia, he specialized in classical historiography, and as dean helped see the school through a socially and politically tumultuous period in the mid-1970s.

In Pouncey's novel, *Rules for Old Men Waiting,* the outer life of rapidly aging and terminally ill historian Robert MacIver mirrors the inner ruin that he has become. The once-elegant house in which he lives is falling rapidly into disrepair, and the heating system does not work when a Cape Cod winter chills the air. Recently widowed, MacIver finds his loneliness, anger, and sorrow competing with the effects of the illness that ravages him from the inside—a sickness he treats with nothing more than good music and fine liquor. MacIver, expatriate Scotsman and once a noted rugby player, is indeed an old man waiting—in his case, waiting to die.

MacIver comes to consciously realize his dire circumstances when he is nearly injured by collapsing timbers on his front porch, and the incident jolts him back to awareness. He knows his final days are upon him, but he resolves to live them with dignity and self-respect. To do so, he formulates a set of rules for himself, including engaging in such commonplace but easily ignored activities as bathing regularly, keeping warm, eating regular meals, reading, and listening to music. Prime among his rules is the dictum to work every morning, and to tell his story through to the end. To do so, he starts a novel about loyalty, action, and revenge in the deadly, muddy trenches of World War I. The novel-within-a-novel he writes becomes a conduit for reflecting on his own experiences in World War II, and a stage for his feelings about his dead son, killed in Vietnam. The characters include "the brutal sergeant Braddis, who sharpens his nails with his bayonet; the genial Lt. Dodds, who has an unexpected tough side; Pvt. Tim Callum, an artist (sensitive, naturally), and down-to-earth Pvt. Charles Alston," noted Susan Hall-Balduf in the *Detroit Free Press.* "All are from central casting, but their originality is not important. They must be alive to MacIver, and they must have an interesting story he can tell."

As the story of the World War I soldiers takes greater prominence in his life, MacIver considers the meaning of the characters and the issues of morality, life, and death they represent. Through it all, his acute grief at the loss of his dearly loved wife remains undiminished, but his control of his life is unshaken, and he enters his final days on his own terms. "This easy marriage of sorrow and good sense is part of what makes the old Scot such a fine companion; so, too, does it define the beauty of the tough-minded novel that delivers him," commented Gail Caldwell in the *Boston Globe.* "Although mortality is its central theme, this gracefully written novel is never depressing," observed Joanne Wilkinson in *Booklist.* Instead, she remarked, it is "a beautiful testament to one man's resilient spirit." Thane Tierney, writing for *Bookpage.com,* commented that "the bittersweet juxtaposition of love and loss, of a life fiercely lived that is now slinking away, makes for a deeply moving, elegantly told story."

Pouncey "limns characters with such grace that to read this novel is to understand not just MacIver's loves, joys and losses but our own as well," observed reviewer Joe Heim in *People.* A *Publishers Weekly* critic commented that *Rules for Old Men Waiting,* written over a period of more than twenty years, "is proof that sometimes greatness comes slowly and in small packages."

BIOGRAPHICAL AND CRITICAL SOURCES:

PERIODICALS

Booklist, March 15, 2005, Joanne Wilkinson, review of *Rules for Old Men Waiting,* p. 1266.

Boston Globe, April 24, 2005, Gail Caldwell, "Tracing the Poignant Arc of a Long, Resilient Life."

Detroit Free Press, April 10, 2005, Susan Hall-Balduf, "*Rules for Old Men* Stalls but Gets There," review of *Rules for Old Men Waiting.*

Library Journal, December 1, 2004, Barbara Hoffert, review of *Rules for Old Men Waiting,* p. 88.

New York Review of Books, June 9, 2005, W.S. Merwin, review of *Rules for Old Men Waiting,* p. 46.

People, May 16, 2005, Joe Heim, review of *Rules for Old Men Waiting,* p. 59.

Philadelphia Inquirer, May 15, 2005, Susan Balée, "An Old Warrior Muses in His Winter," review of *Rules for Old Men Waiting.*

Publishers Weekly, January 24, 2005, Judith Rosen, "Never too Late," profile of Pouncey, p. 116; March 21, 2005, review of *Rules for Old Men Waiting,* p. 37.

Times (London, England), May 1, 2005, Peter Parker, review of *Rules for Old Men Waiting.*

USA Today, April 27, 2005, Bob Minzesheimer, "Multilayered *Rules for Old Men* Worth Waiting For."

ONLINE

Amherst College Web site, http://www.amherst.edu/ (April 25, 2005), Paul Statt, "Peter Pouncey, President Emeritus of Amherst College, Is Author of *Rules for Old Men Waiting.*"

Bookpage.com, http://www.bookpage.com/ (July 9, 2005), Thane Tierney, "Living in Life's Twilight," review of *Rules for Old Men Waiting.*

Mostly Fiction.com, http://www.mostlyfiction.com/ (June 12, 2005), Bill Robinson, review of *Rules for Old Men Waiting.* *

* * *

POWNING, Beth 1949-

PERSONAL: Born 1949, in Putnam, CT; married Peter Powning (an artist); children: Tate (deceased), Jake. *Education:* Sarah Lawrence College, B.A., 1972.

ADDRESSES: Home—Sussex, New Brunswick, Canada. *Agent*—Jackie Kaiser, Westwood Creative Artists, 94 Harbord St., Toronto, Ontario M5S 1GS, Canada. *E-mail*—beth@powning.com.

CAREER: Writer and photographer. Residencies at Leighton Artist Colony, Banff Centre for the Arts, Banff, Alberta, Canada, 1992, 2001, 2005.

AWARDS, HONORS: Canada Council short-term grant, 1982; solo exhibition grant, New Brunswick Department of Tourism, Recreation, and Heritage, 1991; grants from New Brunswick Department of Municipalities, Culture, and Housing, 1992, 1996; New England Booksellers Association's Discovery Award, 1996, for *Home: Chronicle of a North Country Life;* Canada Council grant for professional writers, 1999; creation grant, New Brunswick Arts Board, 2005.

WRITINGS:

(Photographer) Robert Osborne, *Roses for Canadian Gardens,* Key Porter Books (Toronto, Ontario,

Canada), 1991, revised edition published as *Hardy Roses: A Practical Guide to Varieties and Techniques,* 2001.

(Photographer) Robert Osborne, *Hardy Trees and Shrubs: A Guide to Disease-Resistant Varieties for the North* (nonfiction), Key Porter Books (Toronto, Ontario, Canada), 1994.

(And photographer) *Home: Chronicle of a North Country Life* (memoir), Stewart, Tabori & Chang (New York, NY), 1996.

Seeds of Another Summer: Finding the Spirit of Home in Nature (memoir), Penguin Books Canada (Toronto, Ontario, Canada), 1996.

Shadow Child: An Apprenticeship in Love and Loss (memoir), Carroll & Graf (New York, NY), 1999.

The Hatbox Letters (novel), Knopf Canada (Toronto, Ontario, Canada), 2004, St. Martin's Press (New York, NY), 2005.

Edge Seasons (memoir), Knopf Canada (Toronto, Ontario, Canada), 2005.

Contributor of essays to anthologies, including *Northern Wild: Best Contemporary Canadian Nature Writing,* edited by David R. Boyd, 2001; *When the Wild Comes Leaping Up: Personal Encounters with Nature,* edited by David Suzuki, 2002; and *The Sea's Voice,* edited by Harry Thurston, Nimbus Publishing, 2005. Contributor of articles to periodicals, including *Atlantic Books Today, Atlantic Insight, Camera Canada, Canadian Fiction, Cinema Canada, Prism International, Quarry,* and *Waves.*

SIDELIGHTS: Beth Powning has received praise from several critics for her ability to evoke a setting and demonstrate how places affect the people who live in them. She has written about her life on a farm in Canada, where she and her husband, Peter Powning, moved as young adults in the 1970s, and her first novel deals with a woman who, like herself, grew up in Connecticut but now lives in rural Canada. Her works often intermingle personal stories with observations of nature. *Home: Chronicle of a North Country Life,* for example, describes the Pownings' farm and the surrounding countryside, how they came to move there, and the effect it has had on their lives. Powning displays "an extraordinary understanding and sense of place," remarked a *Publishers Weekly* reviewer, who called the author's writing style "lyrical." Similarly, *Booklist* contributor Alice Joyce thought Powning's prose "poetic" and "compelling," and noted that it is complemented by her color photography.

Another memoir, *Shadow Child: An Apprenticeship in Love and Loss,* portrays the grief she felt at the stillbirth of her first son, Tate, and her attempts to have another child (a second son, Jake, was born several years later). When she became pregnant with Tate, Powning was not entirely sure she wanted to have a child, as she believed motherhood would interfere with her career aspirations. She also was somewhat resentful of her husband's success as an artist, while her efforts to become a writer were less fruitful. Eventually, she entered therapy to work through her sadness at the loss of Tate and her guilty feelings over both her ambivalence about having children and a skiing accident during her pregnancy. In addition to exploring these issues, the book also discusses the evolution of her relationship with Peter and the role that the natural world has played in their lives. "Powning skillfully chronicles her personal metamorphosis" in a "superbly written book," reported Annette Haines in *Library Journal.* A *Publishers Weekly* critic commented that *Shadow Child* is no "ordinary therapeutic memoir," as Powning explores mourning and recovery in "finely wrought prose." Vanessa Bush, writing in *Booklist,* also praised the book's quality, saying Powning is "stirringly self-aware."

The Hatbox Letters, Powning's first novel, is also a story of a woman coming to terms with loss. Kate Harding has been widowed for a year; her children are grown and gone, and she feels isolated in her country home in Canada. A relationship with another man begins unpromisingly, but Kate finally finds some comfort and a sense of life's continuity by going through hatboxes of letters her sister found in their grandparents' house in Connecticut. To Kate, "nostalgia is good for cleansing the soul," Harriet Klausner observed in *MBR Bookwatch.* As in her other works, Powning offers distinct portraits of her settings, leading *Booklist* commentator Joanne Wilkinson to praise the author's "real affinity for crafting delicate descriptions of the natural world," although Wilkinson felt the tale has a "glacial pace," although it is "thoughtful." In much the same vein, a *Kirkus Reviews* contributor related that Powning "has a delicate and lyrical touch, but the story advances by the minutest increments." In Klausner's opinion, however, the novel "is a fabulous character study that showcases a delightful protagonist." The character of Kate, Klausner added, "makes the story line work."

BIOGRAPHICAL AND CRITICAL SOURCES:

BOOKS

Powning, Beth, *Home: Chronicle of a North Country Life,* Stewart, Tabori & Chang (New York, NY) 1996.

Powning, Beth, *Seeds of Another Summer: Finding the Spirit of Home in Nature,* Penguin Books Canada (Toronto, Ontario, Canada), 1996.

Powning, Beth, *Shadow Child: An Apprenticeship in Love and Loss,* Carroll & Graf (New York, NY) 1999.

Powning, Beth, *Edge Seasons,* Knopf Canada (Toronto, Ontario, Canada), 2005.

PERIODICALS

Booklist, July, 1996, Alice Joyce, review of *Home: Chronicle of a North Country Life,* p. 1796; February 15, 2000, Vanessa Bush, review of *Shadow Child: An Apprenticeship in Love and Loss,* p. 1055; February 15, 2005, Joanne Wilkinson, review of *The Hatbox Letters,* p. 1062.

Kirkus Reviews, January 15, 2005, review of *The Hatbox Letters,* p. 79.

Library Journal, December, 1999, Annette Haines, review of *Shadow Child,* p. 163.

MBR Bookwatch, March, 2005, Harriett Klausner, review of *The Hatbox Letters.*

National Post, April 10, 1999, Tasneem Jamal, review of *Shadow Child,* p. 11.

Publishers Weekly, May 13, 1996, review of *Home,* p. 61; January 3, 2000, review of *Shadow Child,* p. 66.

ONLINE

Beth Powning Home Page, http://www.powning.com (June 14, 2005).

*   *   *

PRAHALAD, C.K. 1941-
(Coimbatore Krishnarao Prahalad)

PERSONAL: Born 1941; son of a Madras judge and Sanskrit scholar; married; wife's name Gayatri; children. *Education:* University of Madras, B.Sc., 1960; Indian Institute of Management, M.B.A.; Harvard University, D.B.A., 1975.

ADDRESSES: Office—Stephen M. Ross School of Business, University of Michigan, 701 Tappan St., Ann Arbor, MI 48109-1234.

CAREER: Businessperson, consultant, educator, and writer. University of Michigan Ross School of Business, Ann Arbor, Harvey C. Fruehauf professor of business administration and professor of corporate strategy and international business; PRAJA (media technology firm), San Diego, CA, cofounder and chairman; The Next Practice, San Diego, cofounder and CEO. Held various jobs, including working for Union Carbide factory in India.

AWARDS, HONORS: McKinsey Prize for year's best *Harvard Business Review* article, three times, including 1998, for "The End of Corporate Imperialism"; best paper awards from *Sloan Management Review, Strategic Management Journal,* and *Research and Technology Management.*

WRITINGS:

(Editor, with William J. Abernathy and Alan Sheldon) *The Management of Health Care,* Ballinger (Cambridge, MA), 1974.

(With John Byron Silvers) *Financial Management of Health Institutions,* Spectrum Publications (Flushing, NY), 1974.

(With M.K. Raju) *The Emerging Multinationals: Indian Enterprise in the ASEAN Region,* M.K. Raju Consultants (Madras, India), 1980.

(With Yves L. Doz) *The Multinational Mission: Balancing Local Demands and Global Vision,* Free Press (New York, NY), 1987.

(With Gary Hamel) *Competing for the Future,* Harvard Business School Press (Boston, MA), 1994.

(With Venkat Ramaswamy) *The Future of Competition: Co-Creating Unique Value with Customers,* Harvard Business School Press (Boston, MA), 2004.

The Fortune at the Bottom of the Pyramid, Wharton School Publishing (Upper Saddle River, NJ), 2005.

Contributor of articles to numerous periodicals, including *Harvard Business Review, Management Today, Strategic Management Journal,* and *Strategy and Leadership.*

Author's works have been translated into fourteen languages.

SIDELIGHTS: C.K. Prahalad is recognized internationally as a top business consultant whose expertise includes corporate strategy and the role of top management in diversified multinational corporations. He is also the founder of a company that focuses on new ways to use Web content on various devices and a business consulting company. In addition to his business duties and academic teaching and research, Prahalad is the author or coauthor of several books focusing on core business competency and global strategy, among other business issues. In an article about Prahalad's business philosophy, a contributor to *Thinkers* noted that Prahalad is "regarded as one of the most influential thinkers on strategy in the US. His work stems from a deep concern with the ability of large organisations to maintain their competitive vitality when faced with international competition and changing business environments. Many of his ideas on competitive analysis argue against the supremacy of traditional strategic thinking."

Prahalad's 1987 book, *The Multinational Mission: Balancing Local Demands and Global Vision,* which he coauthored with Yves L. Doz, discusses global business management and focuses on issues facing multinational corporations, such as global integration and local responsiveness. Prahalad also teams up with Gary Hamel to write *Competing for the Future,* a top-selling business book in 1994. In the book, the authors coin the term "core competence," which a *Thinkers* contributor described as "an ability which transcends products and markets, and it results when an organisation learns to harmonise multiple technologies, learning and relationships across levels and functions." The book largely focuses on business strategies and creating markets through a variety of approaches, including using "corporate imagination." A contributor to the *Economist* noted that "this tome was regarded as perhaps the best business book of the 1990s."

In *The Future of Competition: Co-Creating Unique Value with Customers,* Prahalad and coauthor Venkat Ramaswamy discuss the challenges facing companies that must determine how to deliver value to customers who now are spread across the globe. They also discuss how businesses must operate in a business climate of ubiquitous connectivity through the

convergence of modern technology. In an interview for *New Zealand Marketing,* Prahalad noted: "Today there is convergence of a wide variety of industries and technologies: between pharmaceuticals, personal care and fashion, information technology, retailing and banking, and increasingly now even telecoms. So the fundamental change is the convergence of technologies. Today it's not at all clear what is a phone, a digital camera and a computer. They're all rolled into one. Not only is this happening in digital industries but in food, in personal care products and in the automotive industry. This is new." In the interview Prahalad touched on the issue of "value" as discussed in his book, noting: "We are moving to a new form of value creation, when value is not created by the firm and exchanged with customer, but rather when value is co-created by the consumers and the company."

In a review of *The Future of Competition* for *Training* magazine, Skip Corsini noted that "the authors . . . ask business leaders to create new value by doing something unthinkable for most: put themselves in the positions of their customers. I am not sure how new this concept is, but I think it's a good idea from almost any angle." A *Research-Technology Management* contributor commented, "The authors . . . explore the new skills managers will need to learn to compete effectively in this new space, from learning how to experience their business as customers do, to flexibly and rapidly reconfiguring resources on demand, to managing experience quality."

Prahalad turns his attention to the issue of poverty and how it can help be resolved through business in *The Fortune at the Bottom of the Pyramid.* In the book, the author notes: "If we stop thinking of the poor as victims or as a burden and start recognizing them as resilient and creative entrepreneurs and value-conscious consumers, a whole new world of opportunity will open up." The author points out that billions of people live on less than two dollars a day and cannot afford many of the standard products produced by companies. His theory is that companies are missing out on a large market by not creating affordable products for this underserved population. Writing in the *Washington Post,* David Ignatius commented that "what makes Prahalad's book a revelation is that he includes case studies of companies that are serving this 'Bottom of the Pyramid' market. These success stories begin with a recognition that poor people are like everyone else—they just have less money." In his case studies, for example, Prahalad points out that marketing smaller portions of things, such as single-serving packets of shampoo, has proven to be profitable for established companies. Another company has garnered low-income customers by marketing low-interest loans to buy the company's appliances.

"Prahalad's book is mind-blowing because it makes you think about markets in a different way," wrote Ignatius in his review of *The Fortune at the Bottom of the Pyramid.* Stephen Overell, writing in the *Financial Times,* noted that the author "looks to nothing less than a solution for world poverty." As Overell continued, "Prahalad has compiled an array of insightful, detailed material about selling profitably to the developing world. This is where the achievement of his book lies. It takes verve and chutzpah to make a 'win-win' on this scale not sound far-fetched." A contributor to the *Economist* called *The Fortune at the Bottom of the Pyramid* "a controversial new management book that seems destined to be read not just in boardrooms but also in government offices."

BIOGRAPHICAL AND CRITICAL SOURCES:

BOOKS

Prahalad, C.K., *The Fortune at the Bottom of the Pyramid,* Wharton School Publishing (Upper Saddle River, NJ), 2005.

PERIODICALS

Asia Africa Intelligence Wire, June 27, 2003, "C.K. Prahalad Address at Wipro Forum"; October 9, 2004, review of *The Fortune at the Bottom of the Pyramid.*

Business Wire, June 19, 2000, "Guru of Business Strategy, Dr. C.K. Prahalad, Moves into Day-to-Day Role with Converging Media Technology Firm, PRAJA," p. 2822.

Crain's Detroit Business, August 30, 2004, Katie Merx, "UM's C.K. Prahalad Argues in His New Book that the Poorest People Could Be the World's Next Big Growth Market while Helping Themselves Rise from Poverty" (interview with author), p. 1; September 6, 2004, Mary Kramer,

"Immigrant Entrepreneurs Lead New Wave," p. 9; September 13, 2004, DeAnna Belger, "Prahalad to Deliver U-M Lecture," p. 4.

Economist, August 21, 2004, review of *The Fortune at the Bottom of the Pyramid,* p. 54.

eWeek, December 1, 2003, review of *The Future of Competition: Co-Creating Unique Value with Customers.*

Fast Company, August, 2001, Jennifer Reingold, "Can C.K. Prahalad Pass the Test?," p. 108.

Financial Times, August 26, 2004, Stephen Overell, review of *The Fortune at the Bottom of the Pyramid,* p. 10.

Management Today, January, 1998, Rhymer Rigby, "An Audience with C.K. Prahalad," p. 58.

New Zealand Marketing, February, 2004, "C.K. Prahalad on Co-Creating the Future" (interview with author), p. 18.

Research-Technology Management, May-June, 2004, review of *The Future of Competition,* p. 62.

Thinkers, April, 2002, review of *Competing for the Future.*

Training, August, 2004, Skip Corsini, review of *The Future of Competition,* p. 68.

Washington Post, July 6, 2005, David Ignatius, review of *The Fortune at the Bottom of the Pyramid,* p. A17.

ONLINE

CIO.com, http://www.cio.com/ (December 15, 2000-January 1, 2001), interview with author.

Dance with Shadows Web site, http://www.dancewithshadows.com/ (August 19, 2005), review of *The Future of Competition.*

Next Practice Web site, http://www.thenextpractice.com/ (August 19, 2005), contains brief biography of author.

University of Michigan Ross School of Business Web site, http://www.bus.umich.edu/ (August 19, 2005), brief biography of author.*

*　　*　　*

PRAHALAD, Coimbatore Krishnarao
See PRAHALAD, C.K.

PREWITT, J. Everett

PERSONAL: Children: two. *Education:* Lincoln University, B.A., Cleveland State University, M.S. *Hobbies and other interests:* Tennis, backgammon, billiards, working out, reading.

ADDRESSES: Home—Cleveland, OH. *Office*—2775 S. Moreland Blvd., Cleveland, OH 44120. *E-mail*—prewitt@eprewitt.com.

CAREER: Writer, novelist, public speaker, and educator. Northland Research Corporation (real estate appraisal and consulting service), president, 1982—; Myers University, trustee emeritus. *Military service:* U.S. Army, became officer, 1967, served in Vietnam as commander of a supply company.

MEMBER: Cleveland Association of Real Estate Brokers (former president), Cleveland Area Board of Realtors (former president).

AWARDS, HONORS: First Prize for Best Fiction, Los Angeles Black Book Expo, 2005, for *Snake Walkers*; Distinguished Alumni Award, Cleveland State University; Distinguished Alumni Citation, Lincoln University; Realtor of the Year Award, Cleveland Area Board of Realtors; Award for Civic Service, Citizen's League of Greater Cleveland.

WRITINGS:

Snake Walkers (novel), Northland Publishing Company (Cleveland, OH), 2005.

Author of nonfiction work, *Urban Residential Real Estate Market Analysis.*

SIDELIGHTS: As an infantry officer in Vietnam, J. Everett Prewitt experienced first hand the conflicts brought on by racism. "For the young black men who served in Vietnam, especially those I met from the south, it was the first time some had served on equal terms with their white counterparts," Prewitt stated in an essay on his home page. "Sometimes the experience was good and sometimes it created friction," he observed, but one result was almost universal: "If the black kids thought that whites were in some way superior to them before the war, they didn't think so afterwards."

This realistic approach to race and racism lies at the heart of *Snake Walkers,* Prewitt's debut novel, in which he explores issues of race, racism, and unaccountable hatred, but also growth and transformation. Twelve-year-old Anthony Andrew is told to stay out of the woods near Pine Bluff, but his curiosity overwhelms him and he starts exploring the supposedly haunted forests. While there, he witnesses a profoundly traumatic event: the lynching and beating of a young black man by members of the Klan. Though Anthony manages to escape unharmed, the event remains with him throughout his life, though he never tells anyone what he saw and tries his best to suppress the horrible memory.

As an adult in the socially troubled 'sixties, Anthony lands a job as the first black reporter at the *Arkansas Sun,* a paper notorious for espousing racist positions. Assigned to write on the unsolved abandonment of Evesville, a small Arkansas town, and the disappearance of fourteen white men there, Anthony's early experience returns to haunt him. As he conducts his research, however, he encounters a pair of black families, the Williamses and the Coulters, both dignified and strong. More disturbing is the possibility that the two close-knit families may have some responsibility for the disappearances. The Williams family, located in Cleveland, Ohio, seems to know more about the disappearances than they let on. Despite their reticence, Anthony finds the family members to be charming, intelligent, and gracious. As his own relationship with the family blossoms, he feels tremendous conflict; if they are guilty of a crime, was it justified? Was it a crime at all? What is more important to him?: Kowing that justice has been meted out to the deserving, or uncovering a story that could propel his journalistic career forward? And will his budding relationship with college history professor Carla Monroe help or hinder his investigation?

Prewitt "writes with a great mastery of plot and characters, capturing the attention of readers right from the riveting opening to the pounding climax, with the pace never slackening in between," stated a reviewer for *BookWire.com.* "Prewitt clearly writes from wisdom and know-how, which will cause readers to sacrifice a few hours of sleep to read a few more chapters before bedtime," remarked a critic on the *Midwest Book Review* online. "Prewitt has done an excellent job of maintaining the suspenseful plot and providing the reader with characters they can truly care about," commented Kathleen Youmans on the *Fore-Word Reviews* Web site.

Prewitt told *CA:* "When I left Vietnam, I felt compelled to write, but knew I had no experience in writing so I shelved the thought. My intention was to write about the strong, black men and women I had met and/or grew up with during my life. I also wanted to write about the unwritten stories of the South—stories I had heard when growing up about the battles and the outcomes which were not as one-sided as people might think. After taking a creative writing course at Cleveland State, I began to learn the art and was encouraged by the initial response to my work. Thus began the journey.

"My influences came from my family. Both my mother and father were strong, dignified, quiet but fiercely proud and accomplished people. My uncles, aunts, sister and cousins were the same. A lot of the characters in my story are based on them. Authors that influenced me were Earnest Gaines and John Oliver Killens because of their unique perspectives in writing about the black experience.

"Since this was my first book, my writing process was fairly haphazard. I knew the story I wanted to tell, so I just started writing. When I would hit that 'writer's block,' I would either read a novel of an author I admired, or read a book on how to write. I often found that if I did some writing in the evening right before bed, questions that arose would be answered in the morning. I did create a family tree for the family in *Snake Walkers* and did a profile for each of the main characters. I even cut out pictures of people I thought looked like my characters and pasted them on the wall over the computer so they could talk to me at their leisure.

"I've learned that a good writer's group is invaluable and that a big ego is not.

"I would hope that any reader would learn that a close, caring and proud family of parents, siblings, aunts, uncles and cousins is extremely important in overcoming obstacles. I would hope that younger black kids would obtain a better sense of history and benefit from the lessons learned by Anthony and Raymond in my book *Snake Walkers.*"

BIOGRAPHICAL AND CRITICAL SOURCES:

ONLINE

BookWire, http://www.bookwire.com/ (May 18, 2005), review of *Snake Walkers.*

ForeWord Reviews, http://www.forewordreviews.com/ (July 9, 2005), Kathleen Youmans, review of *Snake Walkers.*

J. Everett Prewitt Home Page, http://www.eprewitt.com (July 9, 2005).

Midwest Book Review, http://www.midwestbookreview.com/ (June, 2005), "Emanuel's Bookshelf," review of *Snake Walkers.*

PRWeb, http://www.prweb.com/ (July 9, 2005), biography of J. Everett Prewitt.

Q

QUADAGNO, Jill S.
(Jill Sobel Quadagno)

PERSONAL: Female. *Education:* Pennsylvania State University, B.A., 1964; University of California Berkeley, M.A., 1966; University of Kansas, Ph.D., 1976.

ADDRESSES: Home—250 Rosehill Dr. N., Tallahassee, FL 32312. *Office*—Florida State University, Department of Sociology, Pepper Institute on Aging and Public Policy, 526 Bellamy Bldg., Tallahassee, FL 32306-2270. *E-mail*—jquadagn@coss. fsu.edu.

CAREER: Writer, sociologist, researcher, and educator. University of Kansas, Manhattan, assistant professor, 1977-81, associate professor, 1981-85, professor of Sociology, 1985-87; Florida State University, Tallahassee, Mildred and Claude Pepper eminent scholar in social gerontology and professor of sociology, 1987—. Harvard University, National Science Foundation visiting professorship for women, 1988. President's Bi-Partisan Commission on Entitlement and Tax Reform, senior policy advisor, 1994.

MEMBER: American Sociological Association (vice president, 1993, president, 1997-98), Sociology Honor Society, Social Science Honor Society, Sociological Research Association, National Academy of Social Insurance, Gerontological Society (member, behavior and social sciences public policy committee, 1987-90, member, Student Awards Committee, 1998, member, Research Task Force, 2001-02); Robert Wood Johnson Foundation (member, national advisory committee, Scholars in Health Policy Research Program, 1997-2002, member, site selection committee, 2001-02), Phi Beta Kappa.

AWARDS, HONORS: Predoctoral fellow, National Institute of Mental Health, 1965-66; predoctoral fellow, Midwest Council for Social Research in Aging, 1974-76; Carroll D. Clark Award for Outstanding Scholarship, University of Kansas, 1976; postdoctoral fellow, Cambridge Group for the History of Population and Social Structure, Cambridge University, 1979; National Needs postdoctoral fellow, National Science Foundation, 1979-80; elected to Kansas Women's Hall of Fame, 1984; Mary Ingraham Bunting Institute fellowship, Radcliffe College, 1987-88 (declined); University Teaching Award, Florida State University, 1992; appointed fellow, Gerontological Society of America, 1992; Congressional fellowship, American Sociological Association, 1994; John Simon Guggenheim Memorial fellowship, 1994-95; American Council of Learned Societies fellowship, 1994-95; Distinguished Scholar Award, American Sociological Association Section on Aging, 1994; C. Wright Mills Award finalist, Society for the Study of Social Problems, 1995, and Outstanding Book on the Subject of Human Rights recognition, Gustavos Meyers Center for the Study of Human Rights in North America, 1996, both for *The Color of Welfare*; invited fellow, Center for Advanced Studies in the Behavioral Sciences, Stanford University, 2000; Alumni Distinguished Achievement Award, University of Kansas, College of Liberal Arts and Sciences, 2001-02; Sociology Graduate Student Union Award for contribution to graduate education, 2004; grants from Robert Wood Johnson Foundation, 2000-04, 2001-02, National

Institute on Aging, 2001-03, Florida Agency for Health Care Administration, 2001-02, 2003, Florida Department of Elder Affairs, 2002, Agency for Health Care Administration, 2002-04, Florida State University Cornerstone Program, 2002-04.

WRITINGS:

Aging, the Individual, and Society: Readings in Social Gerontology, St. Martin's Press (New York, NY), 1980.

Aging in Early Industrial Society: Work, Family, and Social Policy in Nineteenth-Century England, Academic Press (New York, NY), 1982.

(Editor, with Warren A. Peterson) *Social Bonds in Later Life: Aging and Interdependence,* Sage Publications (Beverly Hills, CA), 1985.

(With Stuart A. Queen and Robert W. Habenstein) *The Family in Various Cultures,* Harper & Row (New York, NY), 1985.

The Transformation of Old-Age Security: Class and Politics in the American Welfare State, University of Chicago Press (Chicago, IL), 1988.

(Editor, with John Myles) *States, Labor Markets, and the Future of Old-Age Policy,* Temple University Press (Philadelphia, PA), 1991.

The Color of Welfare: How Racism Undermined the War on Poverty, Oxford University Press (New York, NY), 1994.

(Compiler, with Debra Street) *Aging for the Twenty-First Century: Readings in Social Gerontology,* St. Martin's Press (New York, NY), 1995.

(Editor, with Marie E. Cowart) *From Nursing Homes to Home Care,* Haworth Press (New York, NY), 1996.

(With Melissa A. Hardy and Lawrence Hazelrigg) *Ending a Career in the Auto Industry: Thirty and Out,* Plenum Press (New York, NY), 1996.

Aging and the Life Course: An Introduction to Social Gerontology, McGraw-Hill College (Boston, MA), 1999, 3rd edition, 2005.

One Nation, Uninsured: Why the U.S. Has No National Health Insurance, Oxford University Press (New York, NY), 2005.

Contributor to journals and periodicals, including *European Sociological Review, Journal of Health Politics, Policy and Law, Journal of Health and Social Behavior, Journal of Policy History, Sociological Perspectives, Gerontologist,* and *Social Problems.*

Contributor to books, including *Ethnic Families in America,* edited by Charles H. Mindel and Robert W. Habenstein, Elsevier Scientific Publishing (New York, NY), 1976; *Old Age in a Bureaucratic Society: The Elderly, the Experts, and the State in American History,* edited by David Van Tassel and Peter Stearns, Greenwood Press (Westport, CT), 1986; *The Politics of Social Policy in the United States,* edited by Ann Orloff, Margaret Weir, and Theda Skocpol, Princeton University Press (Princeton, NJ), 1988; *States, Labor Markets, and the Future of Old-Age Policy,* Temple University Press (Philadelphia, PA), 1991; *Handbook of Aging and the Social Sciences,* edited by Robert Binstock and Linda George, Academic Press (New York, NY), 1995, new edition, 2001; *The Privatization of Social Policy? Occupational Welfare and the Welfare State in America, Scandinavia, and Japan,* edited by Michael Shalev, Macmillan (New York, NY), 1996; *Handbook of Theories of Aging,* edited by V. Bengtson and K. Warner Schaie, Springer Publishing (New York, NY), 1999; *Handbook of Social Policy,* edited by James Midgley, Sage Publications (Thousand Oaks, CA), 2000; *Restructuring Work and the Life Course,* edited by Victor Marshall and others, University of Toronto Press (Toronto, Ontario, Canada), 2001; *The New Deal and Beyond: Social Welfare in the South since 1930,* edited by Elna Green, University of Georgia Press (Athens, GA), 2003; and *Cambridge Handbook of Age and Aging,* edited by Malcolm Johnson, Cambridge University Press (New York, NY), in press. Member of editorial board of University Press of Kansas, 1984-87, *Political Power and Social Theory,* 1991—, *Journal of Applied Gerontology,* 1991-95, *Journal of Gender, Culture, and Health,* 1994-96, *American Sociologist,* 1997-2004, *Journal of Health Politics, Policy, and Law,* 2000—, and *American Sociological Review,* 2005—. Associate editor for periodicals, including *Contemporary Sociology,* 1984-86, *Sociological Perspectives,* 1985-90, *Journal of Aging Studies,* 1986—, *Sociological Quarterly,* 1986-89, *Gerontologist,* 1987-91, *American Sociological Review,* 1989-91, and *Contemporary Sociology,* 1992-94.

SIDELIGHTS: An expert on subjects such as aging, the welfare state in America, and the plight of the country's poorest and most vulnerable citizens, prolific author, educator, and sociologist Jill S. Quadagno writes on topics related to social gerontology, racism, and the lack of national health insurance in the United States. Her research interests cover subjects such as the sociology of aging, medical sociology, political sociology, and comparative historical sociology.

Contributor to many books and periodicals, Quadagno teaches at the Pepper Institute on Aging and Public Policy at Florida State University.

The Transformation of Old-Age Security: Class and Politics in the American Welfare State provides an account of federal old-age benefits from the post-Civil War era to 1972. In addition, "a sense of history permeates this sociological study of the welfare state's late emergence in America," observed Edward D. Berkowitz in *Business History Review*. "In effect, Jill Quadagno adds history to the list of sociological variables." By doing so, she seeks to offer greater insight into how the relationships between sociological variables change over the years, and how the nature of the variables themselves can be altered to accommodate new situations. She points out three underlying causes for the dynamics of the welfare state in America, Berkowitz noted: the late unionization of workers in factories and on assembly lines; the effects of initiatives in the private sector; and the coexistence of two powerful economic formations: the American South, with its cotton production, and the northern states, with their industry. Berkowitz concluded that "business historians who want to find out what the historical sociologists have to offer in social welfare history should start here with one of the field's best practitioners."

States, Labor Markets, and the Future of Old-Age Policy, edited by Quadagno and John Myles, examines in depth the means whereby countries develop old-age policies. The authors also explore the pressures on old-age and retirement programs imposed by aging workers, early retirements, and increased public expenditures. The essays cover policies in Canada, Great Britain, Poland, and a number of European countries. The book is an "excellent review of each country's economic, social, and political processes that forge old-age policy," commented Mary K. Schneider in *Labor Studies Journal*. It is "a major contribution in the study of social policy and stands as a model for the analysis of other public policy decisions," Schneider concluded.

In *The Color of Welfare: How Racism Undermined the War on Poverty,* Quadagno "posits that racial inequality and conflict has impeded the development of America's welfare state," commented Edwin Amenta in *Social Forces*. As the United States strays further away from a national health-care system or a national

employment program, it also falls further behind other capitalist democracies in social support and spending. For Quadagno, racism helps explain what she views as a regressive social policy. She suggests that "social spending systems are systems of stratification that create or reinforce social cleavages," Amenta noted. Not solely a statement of social problems, Quadagno's book also offers practical suggestions for reviving functional concepts of welfare and adapting them to current social and economic realities, added Dorothy Roberts in the *Yale Law Review*. The work offers hope that "in today's insecure economy, people of all backgrounds can again find ways to demand that our government help protect us all," commented Ann Withorn in the *Women's Review of Books*.

One Nation, Uninsured: Why the U.S. Has No National Health Insurance addresses the failures of attempts at national health care reform in the United States. Quadagno clearly "explains why such reform has failed, despite apparent popular support," noted Alan Moores in *Booklist*. "Every one of the Western industrialized powers guarantees its citizens comprehensive coverage for essential health care—except the United States," commented a *Kirkus Reviews* critic. Quadagno "ably explores the logic behind this appalling fact." She examines how amortization and risk-analysis models, diverse and complex underwriting plans, and the high cost of health care have helped create a situation in which forty-five million Americans may lack basic health-care coverage. Quadagno argues that those with vested interests in health coverage, such as the insurance industry, the small business lobby, and the American Medical Association, have failed to properly make a case for reform to individuals and legislators. Insurance companies have, in fact, strongly resisted any move toward national health care. Among Quadagno's solutions to the problem are creation of a federal stop-loss program designed to help businesses and individuals cover catastrophic health-care losses not accommodated by insurance. The *Kirkus Reviews* critic called *One Nation, Uninsured* a "strongly argued account" that provides useful information to anyone who wants to urge change in a "medical system that willfully excludes so many who so need it."

BIOGRAPHICAL AND CRITICAL SOURCES:

PERIODICALS

American Journal of Sociology, January, 1998, Angela M. O'Rand, review of *Ending a Career in the Auto Industry: Thirty and Out,* p. 1122.

Booklist, September 1, 1994, Mary Carroll, review of *The Color of Welfare: How Racism Undermined the War on Poverty,* p. 9; March 15, 2005, Alan Moores, review of *One Nation, Uninsured: Why the U.S. Has No National Health Insurance,* p. 1250.

Business History Review, spring, 1989, Edward D. Berkowitz, review of *The Transformation of Old-Age Security: Class and Politics in the American Welfare State,* p. 211.

Industrial and Labor Relations Review, October, 1992, Annika E. Sunden, review of *States, Labor Markets, and the Future of Old-Age Policy,* pp. 208-209; January, 1998, Robert Hutchens, review of *Ending a Career in the Auto Industry,* p. 329.

Journal of Urban History, January, 1998, Michael B. Katz, review of *The Color of Welfare,* p. 244.

Kirkus Reviews, February 15, 2005, review of *One Nation, Uninsured,* p. 218.

Labor Studies Journal, winter, 1994, Mary K. Schneider, review of *States, Labor Markets, and the Future of Old-Age Policy,* p. 80.

Social Forces, September, 1996, Edwin Amenta, review of *The Color of Welfare,* p. 371.

Women's Review of Books, March, 1995, Ann Withorn, review of *The Color of Welfare,* p. 23.

Yale Law Journal, April, 1996, Dorothy E. Roberts, review of *The Color of Welfare,* pp. 1563-1602.

*   *   *

QUADAGNO, Jill Sobel
See QUADAGNO, Jill S.

*   *   *

QUEEN, William

PERSONAL: Male.

ADDRESSES: Agent—c/o Author Mail, Random House, 1745 Broadway, New York, NY 10019.

CAREER: Writer, federal agent, and undercover operative. U.S. Department of the Treasury, Bureau of Alcohol, Tobacco, and Firearms, special agent. *Military service:* U.S. Army, served in Vietnam; received Silver Star.

AWARDS, HONORS: Medal of Valor, Federal Bar Association, 2001; Director's Award, U.S. Department of Justice; Robert Faulkner Memorial Outstanding Investigation Award, International Outlaw Motorcycle Gang Investigator Association; Distinguished Service Award, U.S. Bureau of Alcohol, Tobacco, and Firearms, for undercover work.

WRITINGS:

Under and Alone: The True Story of the Undercover Agent Who Infiltrated America's Most Violent Outlaw Motorcycle Gang, Random House (New York, NY), 2005.

SIDELIGHTS: William Queen is a former member of the U.S. Special Forces and a career law-enforcement officer who spent twenty years as a special agent with the U.S. Bureau of Alcohol, Tobacco, and Firearms. The recipient of numerous awards and decorations for his service, Queen specialized in deep and dangerous undercover work. In *Under and Alone: The True Story of the Undercover Agent Who Infiltrated America's Most Violent Outlaw Motorcycle Gang* Queen recounts his work in infiltrating the Mongols motorcycle gang, a notoriously dangerous and unpredictable group that was given a wide berth, even by the Hell's Angels. The gang trafficked in drugs, stolen motorcycles, and illegal weapons to make their money, and a good time with gangmembers was to be had through random violent attacks, stabbings, or unprovoked murder.

Posing as biker Billy St. John, Queen became a full-fledged member of the Mongols' Southern California chapter. During his two-year stint, he rose through the hierarchy of the gang to become treasurer and finally vice president of the San Fernando Valley chapter. At first suspected of being a cop, Queen had to prove himself through participation in a number of dangerous situations. Though he was able to avoid most of the illegal and harrowing membership rites, such as proving loyalty by stabbing a Mongol enemy, Queen's personal demeanor and ferocity earned him the gang's trust and, eventually, the infamous patch that identified him as a true Mongol brother.

In order to gain evidence of illegal activities, Queen would often wear a recording device, even though it would likely mean his death if it was discovered. He had to stand by while illegal activities were conducted, and do what he could to avert murders, assaults, and the abuse and degradation of women involved with the gang. The psychological stress of living the Mongol lifestyle was compounded by the necessity of playing the role of outlaw biker in confrontations with police, never able to identify himself as a fellow law-enforcement officer. While some undercover officers could hope to summon backup when needed, Queen was truly alone, and his outing as a cop would have likely resulted in his brutal murder.

Despite the stresses, Queen came to know the other members of the gang, and he developed deep, if profoundly conflicted, relationships with many of them, genuinely viewing them as friends. When the woman who raised Queen died, his Mongol brothers consoled him, while his friends in law enforcement didn't even mention it. He felt the camaraderie that can only be developed by those who experience, and survive, a dangerous situation together. Still, Queen never lost sight of his ultimate goal: to gather evidence that would lead to the biggest bust in the history of motorcycle gangs.

"The rough language, constant drinking, and violence may put off some readers but are a natural part of this story," noted John R. Vallely in *Library Journal.* "Queen steers clear of melodrama and captures both sides of his double life," commented a *Publishers Weekly* contributor. "Ratcheted up by foreknowledge that Queen would eventually betray the Mongols . . . the narrative is unstoppable," remarked *Booklist* reviewer Gilbert Taylor. "Queen is a natural storyteller and explainer," stated a critic in *Kirkus Reviews,* the critic commenting that the book describes a "dark and twisted world, fully realized." The gang members are "so three-dimensionally drawn," noted Gregory Kirschling in *Entertainment Weekly,* that "it's not so surprising to learn he [Queen] sometimes loved his fellow Mongols like brothers."

BIOGRAPHICAL AND CRITICAL SOURCES:

PERIODICALS

Booklist, March 1, 2005, Gilbert Taylor, review of *Under and Alone: The True Story of the Undercover Agent Who Infiltrated America's Most Violent Outlaw Motorcycle Gang,* p. 1120.

Entertainment Weekly, April 8, 2005, Gregory Kirschling, review of *Under and Alone,* p. 69.
Kirkus Reviews, January 15, 2005, review of *Under and Alone,* p. 110.
Library Journal, March 15, 2005, John R. Vallely, review of *Under and Alone,* p. 98.
People, May 2, 2005, review of *Under and Alone,* p. 47.
Publishers Weekly, March 21, 2005, review of *Under and Alone,* p. 49.*

*   *   *

QUIÑONES, Magaly 1945-
(Marta Magaly Quiñones Perez)

PERSONAL: Born 1945, in Ponce, PR. *Education:* University of Puerto Rico, M.A.

ADDRESSES: Home—P.O. Box 22269, University Station, San Juan, PR 00931-2269. *E-mail*—mquinone@rrpac.upr.clu.edu.

AWARDS, HONORS: PEN award, 1986; Mairena poetry prize, for *Nombrar.*

WRITINGS:

POETRY

Entre me voz y el tiempo, Juan Ponce de León (San Juan, PR), 1969.
Era que el mundo era, illustrated by Antonio Marorell, Nacional (Carolina, PR), 1974.
Zambayllu, [San Juan, PR], 1976.
Cantándole a la noche misma, [San Juan, PR], 1978.
En la pequeña Antilla, Mairena (San Juan, PR), 1982.
Nombrar, Mairena (Rio Piedras, PR), 1985.
Razón de lucha, razón de amor, Mairena (San Juan, PR), 1989.
Sueños de papel, University of Puerto Rico Press (San Juan, PR), 1996.

SIDELIGHTS: Puerto Rican poet Magaly Quiñones's poems include such themes as the preservation of cultural identity and customs and women's issues.

They have appeared in several journals and book collections. In her *Cantándole a la noche misma* the poems examine such topics as the relationship between self and nature, poverty and exploitation, and destruction. Often divided into four sections, Quiñones's collections offer a variety of themes and textures. In *En la pequeña Antilla,* for example, metaphors are used to express intimacy, pain, sadness, death, and time, yet the collection concludes on a more concrete note with poems about the Antilles.

Unlike many of her books, *Entre me voz y el tiempo* is divided into five sections, not four. It is devoted to the poet's voice and era and uses lyrical language to describe traditional ideas. *Era que el mundo era* returns to a four-part organization with a focus on the poet's connection with nature as well as the struggle against solitude. Dedicated to Chile, Peru, and Latin America, *Zambayllu* presents sensitivity and admiration for native culture. Luis Diaz Marquez, a reviewer for *Horizontes,* commended Quiñones for building "tension with quietude and movement; eternity with history; masculinity with femininity; identity with insanity." Marquez also applauded Quiñones for including in her poetry "the contemplation of the individual within history, the collective, and the consequences of the contradictions and dangers."

BIOGRAPHICAL AND CRITICAL SOURCES:

PERIODICALS

Horizontes, October, 1982, Luis Diaz Marquez, "Historia y mito en la poesia de Magaly Quiñones," pp. 19-31.*

*   *   *

QUIÑONES PEREZ, Marta Magaly
See QUIÑONES, Magaly

R

RABIKOVITZ, Dalia 1936-2005
(Dalyah Rabikowitz, Dahlia Ravikovitch, Dalia Ravikovitch)

OBITUARY NOTICE— See index for *CA* sketch: Born November 17, 1936, in Ramat Gan, Palestine (now Israel); died from a suspected suicide attempt, August 21, 2005. Author. Rabikovitz was a prominent Israeli poet associated with the "state generation" of writers who were born just after the country was founded. Her difficult childhood included the death of her father when she was six and several years spent in a much-disliked kibbutz. Unhappy with life in a collective community, she left the kibbutz at the age of thirteen and spent five years in foster homes. Married at the young age of eighteen, Rabikovitz soon went through the first of what would eventually be three divorces. As an Israeli citizen, she next served her compulsory military service, and it was during this time that she began writing poetry. Rabikovitz would go on to attend Hebrew University and, from 1959 to 1963, she worked as a teacher. She would also occasionally work as a journalist. Sometimes called unpatriotic for her controversial opinions, Rabikovitz's verses revealed her concerns for justice, her outrage over the treatment of Palestinians by the Israelis and violence against women and children, and a disdain for secularist, urban Israelites. In addition to her poems, she also was a translator of English-language writers such as Edgar Allan Poe, T.S. Eliot, and *Mary Poppins* author P.L. Travers. She also wrote several children's books and short-story collections. Rabikovitz's work earned her such honors as the 1987 Bialik Prize for poetry and the 1998 Israel Literary Prize. Many of her books have been translated into other languages, including two into English: *A Dress of Fire* (1976) and *The Window: New and Selected Poems* (1989). She was also the editor of *The New Israeli Writers: Short Stories of the First Generation* (1990). Having struggled with depression for many years, her death was suspected to be a suicide.

OBITUARIES AND OTHER SOURCES:

PERIODICALS

Guardian (London, England), August 30, 2005, p. 20.
Independent (London, England), August 24, 2005, p. 32.
Times (London, England), September 5, 2005, p. 52.

* * *

RABIKOWITZ, Dalyah
See RABIKOVITZ, Dalia

* * *

RAMOS, Samuel 1897-1959

PERSONAL: Born June 8, 1897, in Zitácuaro, Michoacán, Mexico; died 1959, in Mexico City, Mexico; son of a physician. *Education:* Attended Colegio de San Nicolás de Hidalgo, c. 1909-17; studied medicine at Medical Military School, Mexico City, Mexico, 1917-19; attended School of Higher Studies,

c. 1919; National Autonomous University of Mexico, Ph.D., 1944; additional study at Sorbonne, College of France, and University of Rome.

CAREER: Philosopher and educator. College of Philosophy and Literature, Mexico, headmaster and dean of humanities and professors, 1944-52; instructor in philosophy for Mexico's national preparatory school; instructor in logic and ethics for Mexico's national teachers college.

WRITINGS:

El caso Strawinsky (title means "The Case of Stravinsky"), Ediciones de la Revista Contemporáneos (Mexico), 1929.

El perfil del hombre y de la cultura en México (title means "The Profile of Mexican People and Culture"), [Mexico], 1934, reprinted, Espasa-Calpe (Mexico City, Mexico), 1991.

Ensayo sobre Diego Rivera, 1935.

Mas allá de la moral de Kant (title means "Further Thoughts on the Moral of Kant"), [Mexico], 1938.

Hacia un nuevo humanismo (title means "Making a New Humanisim"), La Casa de España (Mexico), 1940.

Veinte años de educación en México (title means "Twenty Years of Mexican Education"), 1941.

Historia de la vida artística (title means "History of the Artistic Life"), 1942.

La filosofía de la vida artística (title means "The Philosophy of the Artistic Life"), 1955.

El problema del a priori y la experiencia y las relaciones entre la filosofía y la ciencia (title means "The a priori Problem and the Experience and Relationships between Philosophy and Science"), 1955.

Nuevo esayo sobre Diego Rivera, 1958.

Estudios de estética, UNAM (Mexico City, Mexico), 1963.

Ramos's works were also collectively published as *Obras Completas.*

SIDELIGHTS: Mexican philosopher Samuel Ramos examined the cultural character of the Mexican people, using the scientific method for his approach. That approach was one he learned from his father, a doctor who endowed his son with a wide range of cultural and humanistic interests. Father and son had long talks about the fundamentals of philosophy, and Dr. Ramos read long passages from such works as *Don Quixote* to his son. From an early age, Ramos took an interest in his fellow Mexicans, looking for the hidden meanings behind their gestures, their words, and their expressions. The very role of culture, according to Ramos, was for the creation and perfection of human beings. From these observations he put together a distinctly Mexican philosophy that was tied to the life of his people.

Ramos's point of view was heavily influenced by the works of early twentieth-century psychoanalyst Alfred Adler. In fact, in his writings Ramos proposed psychoanalysis as the only way for the Mexican mind to achieve its full potential. He pointed out that the Mexican attitude toward life is one of ambivalence. He felt that the constitutional chaos that marked the revolutionary period of the early 1830s was a sign of a theoretical rejection of political realities. Ramos further claimed that reality itself was close to taboo in the Mexican psyche of the times. The Mexican "illness," Ramos suggested, was a propensity to view everything outside of oneself as superior and therefore to suffer under a personal and national "sentiment of inferiority." The problem, Ramos observed, came from the "double heritage" of the peoples of the Americas. On the one hand, the values and cultural models of these peoples are a "derivative culture," inherited from the shores of Europe. However, the possessors of these values are not European, because they live in the Americas. In an essay focusing on the psychoanalysis of the Mexican, Ramos contended that this feeling of inferiority leads to the use of masks to cover up this supposed inferiority. These masks include aggression, violence, and dishonesty. Through psychoanalysis, Ramos felt, the Mexican consciousness could be returned to the singularly important value of "sincerity."

BIOGRAPHICAL AND CRITICAL SOURCES:

PERIODICALS

Chasqui, November, 1983, "Luis G. Urbina y la tematica de la soledad," p. 12.

Cuadernos Americanos, May, 1999, Maria Rosa Palazon, "Conocimiento, verdad e illusión en algunas artes," p. 123; May, 1999, Carlos Coria Sanchez, "El Gesticulador," p. 208.

Philosophy Today, Volume 44, 2000, Manuel Vargas, "Lessons from the Philosophy of Race in Mexico," p. 18.

Texto Critico, July, 1995, Esther Hernandez Palacios, "Breves notas sobre el concepto de 'belleza' en la estética mexicana," p. 263.

ONLINE

Wanadoo, http://www1.gratisweb.com/ (June 13, 2005), Miguel Angel Corral Chagolla, "La cultura en Samuel Ramos."*

*   *   *

RAVIKOVITCH, Dahlia
    See RABIKOVITZ, Dalia

*   *   *

RAVIKOVITCH, Dalia
    See RABIKOVITZ, Dalia

*   *   *

RAY, Jean
    See DE KREMER, Raymond Jean Marie

*   *   *

REECE, Spencer 1963-

PERSONAL: Born 1963, in Hartford, CT; son of a doctor (father). *Education:* Wesleyan University, B.A.; University of York (York, England), master's degree; Harvard Divinity School, M.A. (theology), 1990; attended Bowdoin College.

ADDRESSES: Home—Lantana, FL. *Office*—Brooks Brother, 225-C Worth Ave., Palm Beach, FL 33480.

CAREER: Writer, poet, farmer, editor, and manager. Brooks Brothers, Palm Beach, FL, assistant manager. Worked as an editor of medical newsletters and reviewer of medical books.

AWARDS, HONORS: Katharine Bakeless Nason Prize for poetry, Middlebury College and Bread Loaf Writers' Conference, 2003.

WRITINGS:

The Clerk's Tale (poems), Houghton Mifflin (Boston, MA), 2004.

Contributor of poems to periodicals, including *New Yorker,* and to literary journals, including *Boulevard, Poetry Wales,* and *Painted Bride Quarterly.* Sound recording include *The Poet and the Poem from the Library of Congress,* Library of Congress (Washington, DC), 2004, and *Poets on Being,* Library of Congress, 2004.

SIDELIGHTS: With only a few published works to his credit, poet Spencer Reece made an impression on the world of American poetry with his first collection. Penned while the poet was an assistant manager at a Brooks Brothers department store in Florida, *The Clerk's Tale* recalls the Chaucerian story of a marriage, as well as Reece's experiences as a retail clerk. Reece noted in an interview for the *New Yorker* that his "work life is very much like a marriage" like that described in Chaucer's story. "We're together so much, I mean."

Originally harboring plans to enter the ministry, Reece wanted to become a hospital chaplain and follow in the tradition of his literary idols, Elizabethan versifiers George Herbert and John Donne. Instead, he moved to Minnesota to run the family's farm, where he worked for about four years. There, he also worked on his poetry. When his family went bankrupt, the farm was lost, and a rancorous split occurred between family members. "The family fell apart, and I have never seen them since," Reece stated in the *New Yorker* interview. The trauma led to a stay in a mental hospital, and when Reece was released, he went to stay with his nurse, Martha, and her family, who lived in the same small town where Reece's family had once farmed. "I never went back, and I never looked," Reece stated in the *New Yorker* interview. "I had to give away my dog and sell my library, and it just broke me. I really knew what grief was at that point, and I didn't know before."

The Clerk's Tale is a collection of poems "so exquisite, atmospheric, and varied" that they were selected for the Bread Loaf Writers' Conference Bakeless Prize in 2003, noted Barbara Hoffert and Mirela Roncevic in

Library Journal. The "supple, atmospheric, and lucent" collection explores the contrasts between solitude and connection, philosophy and madness, and peace and pain, commented Donna Seaman in *Booklist.* While acknowledging the outside world, Reece turns inward with many of his works, traversing a broad inner landscape of emotion, sorrow and joy, loneliness and togetherness, wistful remembrance and hard knowledge of current reality. In his "marvelous first book of poems," Reece has "crafted a book as neat and tight as an impeccable Windsor tie, while still deftly creating a sweet melancholy," remarked Amy Schroeder in *Antioch Review.* "Reece's striking debut yields new revelations with each reading," observed Seaman.

BIOGRAPHICAL AND CRITICAL SOURCES:

PERIODICALS

Antioch Review, spring, 2005, Amy Schroeder, review of *The Clerk's Tale,* p. 400.
Booklist, April 15, 2004, Donna Seaman, review of *The Clerk's Tale,* p. 1417.
Library Journal, July, 2004, Barbara Hoffert and Mirela Roncevic, review of *The Clerk's Tale,* p. 88.
New Yorker, June 16, 1003, Alice Quinn, "The Poet in the Fitting Room," interview with Spencer Reece.*

*   *   *

RENSHAW, John C. 1952-

PERSONAL: Born October 18, 1952, in London, England; married Maria Graciela, February 4, 1978; children: James Carlos, Henry Eduardo, Elisabeth Jazmin, Mary Ann Margarita. *Education:* Cambridge University, B.A., 1974, Ph.D., 1986.

ADDRESSES: Agent—c/o Author Mail, University of Nebraska Press, 1111 Lincoln Mall, Lincoln NE 68588. *E-mail*—john.renshaw1@virgin.net.

CAREER: Writer.

WRITINGS:

The Indians of the Paraguayan Chaco: Identity and Economy, University of Nebraska Press (Lincoln, NE), 2002.

BIOGRAPHICAL AND CRITICAL SOURCES:

PERIODICALS

Journal of Latin American Studies, May, 2004, Nigel Poole, review of *The Indians of the Paraguayan Chaco: Identity and Economy,* p. 400.

*   *   *

ReVELLE, Charles S. 1938-2005
  (Charles Seymour ReVelle)

OBITUARY NOTICE—See index for *CA* sketch: Born March 26, 1938, in Rochester, NY; died of lymphoma, August 10, 2005, in Baltimore, MD. Environmental engineer, systems analyst, educator, and author. ReVelle was a Johns Hopkins University professor who specialized in creating mathematical models for development planning and natural resources management. His bachelor's degree from Cornell University, earned in 1961, was in chemistry; he then completed a Ph.D. in sanitary engineering in 1967 with a doctoral thesis on how best to allocate medicines in developing countries plagued by tuberculosis. ReVelle taught at Cornell for three years before joining the Johns Hopkins faculty in 1970. In 1975 he was promoted to professor of systems analysis and economics for public decision-making at the university's department of geography and environmental engineering. Over the years ReVelle developed algorithms that would help engineers and designers plan for a variety of projects. These mathematical models related to such diverse projects as hospital development, power grids, nature preserves, tree harvesting, and sewage-treatment plants, to name a few. He was also the coauthor of several college textbooks, including *The Environment: Issues and Choices for Society* (1981) and *Civil and Environmental Systems Engineering* (1997). In recognition of his work, ReVelle earned such honors as the Agamemnon Award from the Constantine Porphyrogenitus Association of Greece in 1995 and the Lifetime Achievement Award in Location Analysis from the Section on Location Analysis of the Institute for Operations Research and Management Science in 1996.

OBITUARIES AND OTHER SOURCES:

PERIODICALS

Grand Rapids Press, August 26, 2005, p. B7.
New York Times, August 25, 2005, p. C17.

ONLINE

Johns Hopkins University Gazette Online, http://www. jhu.edu/~gazette/ (August 22, 2005).

*   *   *

ReVELLE, Charles Seymour
  See ReVELLE, Charles S.

*   *   *

RIEGLE, Rosalie G. 1937-
  (Rosalie Riegle Troester)

PERSONAL: Born February 19, 1937, in Flint, MI; daughter of John L. (a printer) and Eleanor (a volunteer; maiden name, Hines) Riegle; married Edmund M. Troester (divorced); children: Kathryn Marie, Maura Clare, Ann Elizabeth Troester Lennon, Margaret Meagher Troester Murphy. *Ethnicity:* "White." *Education:* St. Mary's College, B.A., 1959; Wayne State University, M.A., 1971; University of Michigan, D.A., 1983. *Religion:* Roman Catholic.

ADDRESSES: Home—1585 Ridge Ave., Ste. 410, Evanston, IL 60201. *E-mail*—rriegle@sbcglobal.net.

CAREER: Writer. Saginaw Valley State University, University Center, MI, professor of English, 1969-2001, Hilda Rush distinguished lecturer, 2000. Member, Catholic Worker Movement.

MEMBER: Oral History Association, Michigan Women's Studies Association (member, board of directors, 1970-85).

AWARDS, HONORS: Landee Award for excellence in teaching, 1993, Ishahara Award for mentoring, 1994, and Daniels Award, 2003, both from Saginaw Valley State University.

WRITINGS:

(Editor, as Rosalie Riegle Troester) *Historic Women of Michigan: A Sesquicentennial Celebration,* Michigan Women's Studies Association (Lansing, MI), 1987.

(Editor, as Rosalie Riegle Troester) *Voices from the Catholic Worker,* Temple University Press (Philadelphia, PA), 1993.
Dorothy Day: Portraits by Those Who Knew Her, Orbis Books (Maryknoll, NY), 2003.

Contributor to periodicals, including *Oral History Review, Fellowship, Feminist Theology, Michigan Voice,* and *Sage: A Scholarly Journal on Black Women.* Contributor to books, including *Dorothy Day and the Catholic Worker Movement: Centenary Essays,* edited by William J. Thorn, Phillip M. Runkel, and Susan Mountin, Marquette University Press (Milwaukee, WI), 2001.

WORK IN PROGRESS: Doin' Time: The Prison Reflections of Nonviolent Activists for Peace, an oral history.

SIDELIGHTS: Rosalie G. Riegle, who has also written as Rosalie Riegle Troester, told *CA:* "I came to oral history by the back door, with no front-door history training, but led by my admiration of Studs Terkel, my interest in the Catholic Worker movement, and some beginning interviewing experience. I'll never forget that summer afternoon when I realized I could combine these influences and write an oral history of the Catholic Worker. I called Mr. Terkel that very day and asked if I could study with him. He said 'no' right away, of course, but it was the most cordial 'no' I ever received. His encouragement and 230 interviews produced my first oral history, *Voices from the Catholic Worker.*

Historian Donald Fleming of Harvard said, 'Research only counts if it's close to the bone.' Well, my research on the Catholic Worker cut deeply, so with two friends I opened a house of hospitality in Saginaw, Michigan. There we worked against the constant wars our country is embroiled in and also provided food, shelter, friendship, and support to homeless women and their children, trying to live the Sermon on the Mount in the way that Catholic Worker cofounder Dorothy Day modeled for us.

Day herself continued to fascinate me and I realized there was a dearth of honest and detailed writing about her life, so I conducted over one hundred more interviews with Catholic Workers, young and old, and wrote *Dorothy Day: Portraits by Those Who Knew Her.* During these years of research, I opened a second Catholic Worker house, this time with two recent graduates of the university where I taught."

BIOGRAPHICAL AND CRITICAL SOURCES:

PERIODICALS

Catholic New Times, May 23, 2004, Peter Dembski, review of *Dorothy Day: Portraits by Those Who Knew Her,* p. 17.
National Catholic Reporter, January 9, 2004, Tim Unsworthy, review of *Dorothy Day,* p. 9.
Oral History Review, summer-fall, 2004, Carole Garibaldi Rogers, review of *Dorothy Day,* p. 111.
Other Side, January-February, 2004, review of *Dorothy Day,* p. 40.

*   *   *

RIEHL, Gene

PERSONAL: Male.

ADDRESSES: Home—La Jolla, CA. *Agent*—c/o Author Mail, St. Martin's Press, 175 5th Ave., New York, NY 10010. *E-mail*—griehl@san.rr.com.

CAREER: Writer, FBI agent, and law enforcement officer. U.S. Federal Bureau of Investigation, federal agent and specialist in undercover work, foreign counterintelligence, and counterespionage; services as on-air terrorism analyst for CBS, NBC, CNN, and Fox television.

WRITINGS:

Quantico Rules (fiction), St. Martin's Minotaur (New York, NY), 2003.
Sleeper (fiction), St. Martin's Press (New York, NY), 2005.

WORK IN PROGRESS: Black Ops: FBI, a television series in development; *Dead Evil,* a third FBI-based thriller novel.

SIDELIGHTS: A former FBI agent, terrorism expert, undercover operative, and counterespionage specialist, Gene Riehl uses his varied law enforcement background to infuse his work with verisimilitude born of experience. As a veteran of more than twenty years with the U.S. Federal Bureau of Investigation, he worked on a variety of federal crimes, "including kidnapping, extortion, bank robbery, major art and jewelry thefts, and organized author's home page. His specialty was undercover operations and foreign counterintelligence, and for four years he worked for an operations group that performed special surveillance, short-term undercover assignments, and wiretap investigations. He has also served as an on-air commentator and counterterrorism analyst for television broadcast networks.

In his debut novel, *Quantico Rules,* Riehl introduces FBI agent Puller Monk, a compulsive gambler with an alcoholic veterinarian girlfriend, an ailing, formerly abusive father suffering from Alzheimer's disease, and a trunkful of childhood traumas only partially stifled by the constant gambling and subsequent perpetual debt. As a member of an FBI Special Inquiries, or SPIN squad, Monk is in charge of an investigation into U.S. Supreme Court nominee Brenda Thompson, the first African-American woman nominated to such a position. Ostensibly a thoroughly professional jurist with a clean record, Thomson seems certain to gain the coveted seat on the bench. However, during the investigation, Special Agent Lisa Sands discovers a troubling discrepancy on Thompson's personal security questionnaire. As the discrepancy snowballs into an outright lie, more lies, complex power relationships, and disturbing secrets are uncovered. Monk and Sands increase the intensity of their investigation, but obstacles block their progress, including a complete suspension from the investigation. Soon a highly skilled hit man is shadowing their every move, threatening to end their lives at the slightest opportunity. The nightmarish scenario becomes one of kill-or-be-killed, as Monk and Sands ponder a relationship and seek to expose the highly placed sources that set a killer on their trail who wants to keep Judge Thompson's secrets unexposed.

"Reading this debut novel is like finding a gold nugget when all you were expecting was a few pretty stones," remarked David Pitt in *Booklist.* Riehl "writes like a pro, and this is one of those thrillers you genuinely wish wouldn't end," Pitt added. "Riehl writes a lean, vigorous prose laced with self-deprecating humor, and as an ex-FBI man he fuels his story with fascinating insider details," commented a *Publishers Weekly* reviewer. "Monk is a great protagonist with flaws and troubles that overwhelm him at times," commented Harriet Klausner in a review for *AllReaders.com.*

Sleeper, Riehl's second "Puller Monk" thriller, pits the troubled agent against a deadly female assassin, born Samantha Williamson but now known as Sung Kim. Kidnapped at a young age and vigorously trained in martial arts and assassination techniques, Sung Kim vexes the FBI agents who seek her out; they do not even know what she looks like, though her signature style of art theft leaves little doubt when she is at large. While Sung Kim is dispatched to the United States to commit murder in the highest level of power, Monk becomes the only agent capable of stopping her. Meanwhile, still under the grip of a gambling addiction, Monk must deal with the death of his father and the realization that he is genetically predisposed to the Alzheimer's disease that killed his sire. A *Publishers Weekly* reviewer remarked that the novel "lacks the substance to support the story's more serious concerns," but commented favorably on the "terrific surprise twist." The book is an "intriguing sequel in which the fascinating character is the villainess," observed Harriet Klausner in *MBR Bookwatch.* Pitt, in another *Booklist* review, called Puller Monk "a fresh, exciting, and dramatic creation."

BIOGRAPHICAL AND CRITICAL SOURCES:

PERIODICALS

Booklist, May 1, 2003, David Pitt, review of *Quantico Rules,* p. 1554; January 1, 2005, David Pitt, review of *Sleeper,* p. 828.
Kirkus Reviews, June 1, 2003, review of *Quantico Rules,* p. 778; January 1, 2005, review of *Sleeper,* p. 17.
MBR Bookwatch, March, 2005, Harriet Klausner, review of *Sleeper.*
Orlando Sentinel, September 16, 2003, Ann Hellmuth, review of *Quantico Rules.*
Publishers Weekly, June 9, 2003, review of *Quantico Rules,* p. 34; February 7, 2005, review of *Sleeper,* p. 42.

ONLINE

AllReaders.com, http://www.allreaders.com/ (July 9, 2005), Harriet Klausner, review of *Quantico Rules*; Harriet Klausner, review of *Sleeper.*
BookLoons, http://www.bookloons.com/ (July 9, 2005), Hilary Williamson, review of *Quantico Rules.**

*   *   *

RIORDAN, Teresa

PERSONAL: Children: two daughters, one son. *Hobbies and other interests:* Collecting buttons.

ADDRESSES: Home and office—P.O. Box 11305, Takoma Park, MD 20913. *E-mail*—tr@inventing beauty.com.

CAREER: Writer. *New York Times,* New York, NY, patents columnist.

AWARDS, HONORS: Knight Science journalism fellowship at Massachusetts Institute of Technology, 2000-01; Alfred P. Sloan Foundation grant.

WRITINGS:

Inventing Beauty: A History of the Innovations That Have Made Us Beautiful, Broadway Books (New York, NY), 2004.

Contributor of articles to periodicals, including *ABCNEWS.com, People, U.S. News & World Report,* and *Washington Post Magazine.*

SIDELIGHTS: Teresa Riordan's *Inventing Beauty: A History of the Innovations That Have Made Us Beautiful* puts forth the thesis that beauty aids such as cosmetics and foundation garments have not oppressed but rather empowered women in their relationships with men. "We can transform beauty, changing it from something we're born with to something we can impose on ourselves," Riordan told *U.S. News & World Report* reporter Nancy Shute. In the book, Riordan also points out that women have often been the creators of beauty products. For instance, during the period covered by the book—the mid-nineteenth century to the mid-twentieth century—women received two-thirds of the patents for devices intended to enhance the bosom. Riordan said that she decided to deal with this era because it begins with the first calls for women's rights in the United States and ends with the rise of the feminist movement in the 1960s. "Inventions that come after the consciousness-raising of the 1960s have to be evaluated through a different lens, I think," she told Martha Henry, an interviewer for the *Massachusetts Institute of Technology* Web site. "Some feminists, especially second wave feminists who generally came of age between the 1960s and the 1980s, have denigrated the pursuit of beauty as being oppressive, as being a kind of male ideal foisted on women," Riordan added. "But now that we're beyond the very important revolution of the Sixties and Seventies, it's time to consider beauty in a more nuanced way."

Some reviewers thought this type of nuance marked Riordan's book. *Inventing Beauty* "is neither a feminist polemic against the beauty industry nor a frivolous celebration of it," commented a *Publishers Weekly* critic. Riordan, the critic added, brings a "brilliant style" and "relish for the minutiae of technological history" to chronicles of such items as eyebrow pencils, nail polish, brassieres, and bustles. Linda V. Carlisle, writing in *Library Journal,* called the book "less social theory than a lighthearted story of inventions and inventors" and praised Riordan's far-ranging research and the book's many illustrations, which include patent-office documents and vintage advertisements. Similarly, *Booklist* contributor Barbara Jacobs noted that "Riordan has completed more than her share of homework." The book she has produced, Jacobs remarked, is "riveting."

BIOGRAPHICAL AND CRITICAL SOURCES:

PERIODICALS

Booklist, September 15, 2004, Barbara Jacobs, review of *Inventing Beauty: A History of the Innovations That Have Made Us Beautiful,* p. 184.
Library Journal, September 1, 2004, Linda V. Carlisle, review of *Inventing Beauty,* p. 174.
Publishers Weekly, July 26, 2004, review of *Inventing Beauty,* p. 45.

U.S. News & World Report, October 18, 2004, Nancy Shute, "The Technology of Feminine Allure," p. 76.

ONLINE

Massachusetts Institute of Technology Web site, http://web.mit.edu/ (June 13, 2005), Martha Henry, interview with Teresa Riordan.
Teresa Riordan Home Page, http://inventingbeauty.com (June 13, 2005).*

*　　*　　*

ROOSEVELT, Kermit 1971-

PERSONAL: Born 1971, in Washington, DC. *Education:* Harvard University, A.B. (summa cum laude), 1993; Yale University, J.D., 1997.

ADDRESSES: Home—Philadelphia, PA. *Office*—University of Pennsylvania Law School, 3400 Chestnut Street, Philadelphia, PA 19104. *E-mail*—krooseve@law.upenn.edu.

CAREER: Lawyer, educator, and novelist. Harvard University, Cambridge, MA, teaching fellow, 1993-94; law clerk for Judge Justice Stephen F. Williams, Washington, DC, 1997-98, and U.S. Supreme Court Justice David H. Souter, 1999-2000; Mayer, Brown & Platt, Chicago, IL, associate, 2000-02; University of Pennsylvania, Philadelphia, assistant professor of law, 2002—. Member of human rights advisory board of Harvard Kennedy School Of Government,1998—; fellow of Information Society Project for Yale Law, 1998—. Senior editor of *Yale Law Journal* and editor of *Yale Journal on Regulation,* 1995.

AWARDS, HONORS: Detur Prize, and Derek Bok Center for Teaching certificate of distinction, both Harvard University; Israel H. Peres Prize, 1997, for best publication in *Yale Law Journal.*

WRITINGS:

In the Shadow of the Law (novel), Farrar, Straus & Giroux (New York, NY), 2005.

Contributor to law journals, including *Michigan Law Review, Emory Law Review, Yale Journal on Regulation, Notre Dame Law Review, Columbia Law Review, Santa Clara Law Review, Connecticut Law Review* and *University of Pennsylvania Law Review.* Contributor to books, including *Exploring Nature on Nantucket,* Kerriemuir Press, 1993, and *Yale Biographical Dictionary of American Law.*

SIDELIGHTS: A lawyer and educator whose interests include conflict of laws, constitutional law, and law and technology, Kermit Roosevelt—the great-great-grandson of U.S. President Theodore Roosevelt—worked for a short time for a law firm before moving on to academia. In his first novel, *In the Shadow of the Law,* Roosevelt tells the story of young attorneys in a high-powered law firm working on two disparate cases. One is a pro-bono case in which the lawyers are defending an individual facing the death penalty. The other case involves a chemical company facing a class-action lawsuit for an industrial accident. "I wanted to look at the different ways that these cases get treated by the legal system—one involving a large corporation, the other a single individual who doesn't have the same sort of resources," Roosevelt told *Legal Intelligencer* contributor Joann Loviglio. "I wanted to give a lot of perspective on the legal system and the roles that people play and the choices they have to make."

As Roosevelt tells the story, readers get a first-hand look at the unique pressure placed on fledgling law firm associates, from the long grueling hours to the sometimes questionable ethical decisions they must make. Mark Clayton is assigned to defend a man sentenced to death, but there is little glory in the assignment. Nevertheless, Mark is an idealist who works hard on his client's behalf. On the other hand, Katja Phillips is helping out on the case defending the Texas chemical company client, whose negligence has led to the death of many of its lower-income workers. When she discovers documents that incriminate the company's high-powered client, Katja faces a moral dilemma. In addition to these cases, Roosevelt focuses on a variety of other people in the firm, including Ryan Grady, a shallow young associate who is only interested in getting ahead, and former U.S. Supreme Court clerk Walker Eliot, who has top credentials and appears to be the star of the group.

Writing in the *Library Journal,* David Keymer called *In the Shadow of the Law* a "superior novel." A *Kirkus Reviews* contributor wrote that it is "an issue-packed first novel." A *Publishers Weekly* reviewer called the book an "outstanding debut"and also noted: "Most of all it's the vividness and complexity of the characters . . . that heralds the arrival of an exciting new voice." Gilbert Cruz, writing in *Entertainment Weekly,* noted that the author "masterfully captures the culture of a legal factory," while *Philadelphia Inquirer* reviewer Carlin Romano wrote that the novel "contains enough harpoon attacks on corporate legal practice to drive impressionable young readers elsewhere . . . even (gulp!) to graduate school in the humanities." "And yet," the reviewer added, "a subtle payoff of Roosevelt's debut are the rays of idealism that creep in by the end."

Roosevelt told *CA:* "I started writing mostly out of a love of language. The interest in plot and characters came later. I started out trying to emulate James Joyce and Vladimir Nabokov. That was a mistake, and the books I wrote then are deservedly unpublished. My more recent work is more influenced by Scott Turow and Jonathan Franzen. I work at night, usually from about ten p.m. to three a.m. There are no distractions.

"The most surprising thing I have learned as a writer is how few copies most books sell.

"I hope that my books will help non-lawyers understand the legal system better, and inspire lawyers to retain independent moral judgment."

BIOGRAPHICAL AND CRITICAL SOURCES:

PERIODICALS

Entertainment Weekly, June 10, 2005, Gilbert Cruz, review of *In the Shadow of the Law,* p. 113.

Kirkus Reviews, April 1, 2005, review of *In the Shadow of the Law,* p. 382.

Legal Intelligencer, June 24, 2005, "New Novel Is by Penn Law Professor with Presidential Ancestry."

Library Journal, April 15, 2005, David Keymer, review of *In the Shadow of the Law,* p. 76.

Philadelphia Enquirer, July 6, 2005, Carlin Romano, review of *In the Shadow of the Law.*

Publishers Weekly, April 25, 2005, review of *In the Shadow of the Law,* p. 37.

Time, June 20, 2005, Lev Grossman, review of *In the Shadow of the Law,* p. 70.

ONLINE

University of Pennsylvania Law School Web site,
http://www.law.upenn.edu/ (September 18, 2005),
information on author's career.

* * *

ROSE, Lee H.

PERSONAL: Married, wife's name Eleanor.

ADDRESSES: Home—Charlotte, NC. *Agent*—c/o
Author Mail, Human Kinetics Publishers, P.O. Box
5076, Champaign, IL 61825-5076.

CAREER: Writer, educator, and basketball coach. Versailles High School, Versailles, KY, teacher-coach,
1958; Transylvania University, coach, 1959; San Antonia Spurs, assistant coach, 1986. Coached college
basketball for University of Cincinnati, University of
North Carolina at Charlotte, Purdue University, and
University of South Florida. National Basketball Association consultant for National Basketball Developmental League coaches.

AWARDS, HONORS: Named *Sporting News* National
Coach of the Year, 1977; inducted into Pioneer Hall of
Fame, Transylvania University, 1993; inducted into
Kentucky Athletic Hall of Fame, 2001; named Coach
of the Year, Kentucky Intercollegiate Athletic
Conference, Sun Belt Conference, and Big Ten
Conference.

WRITINGS:

*The Basketball Handbook: Winning Essentials for
Players and Coaches,* Human Kinetics Publishers
(Champaign, IL), 2004.

SIDELIGHTS: In a professional career spanning forty-
five years, author and basketball coach Lee H. Rose
has worked with ballplayers at three significant levels
of play. In 1958, he began coaching at Versailles High
School; in 1959, he moved to a position at Transylvania University, which led to numerous other college
coaching jobs; and in 1968, he joined the National
Basketball Association (NBA) as assistant coach of the
San Antonio Spurs. In 2003, he retired from the NBA.

Rose's professional accomplishments include leading
the University of North Carolina (UNC) at Charlotte to
the National Invitational Tournament (NIT) finals in
1976 and the NCAA finals in 1977. He also coached
Purdue University to the NIT finals in 1979 and to the
"Final Four" in 1980. His winning record as a college-
level head coach stands at .705 (388-162), with a
record of .800 (72-18) at UNC Charlotte.

In *The Basketball Handbook: Winning Essentials for
Players and Coaches* Rose combines a series of
anecdotes from his coaching career with detailed
instructional material and practical coaching exercises.
He offers an expansive assortment of drills and training activities that help players develop fundamental
skills in shooting, passing, and rebounding, as well as
more advanced abilities such as improving side
defense and executing screens. Rose focuses on physical abilities such as strength, agility, speed, and timing.
He also outlines a performance-rating system designed
to help players and coaches identify players' strengths
and weaknesses. A reviewer in *Coach and Athletic
Director* called Rose's unique rating system "a superb
evaluation tool." *Library Journal* contributor James
Miller commented that Rose's drills and exercises
provide "a wealth of valuable information" for serious
players and coaches.

BIOGRAPHICAL AND CRITICAL SOURCES:

PERIODICALS

Coach and Athletic Director, November, 2004, review
of *The Basketball Handbook: Winning Essentials
for Players and Coaches,* p. 84.
Library Journal, September 15, 2004, James Miller,
review of *The Basketball Handbook,* p. 64.

* * *

ROSEN, Jennifer
(Chotzi)

PERSONAL: Female. *Education:* New York University,
B.A., International Wine Guild, Master Sommelier
certification. *Hobbies and other interests:* Belly
dancing, trapeze, skiing.

ADDRESSES: Home—Denver, CO. *Office*—Rocky Mountain News, 100 Gene Amole Way, Denver, CO 80204. *E-mail*—chotzi@aol.com.

CAREER: Writer, columnist, wine critic, sommelier, ski instructor, horse trainer, and handwriting analyst. Conducts wine seminars for clients including Beaulieu Vineyards, Toastmasters International, Denver Art Museum, and Colorado Symphony Orchestra. Appears regularly on syndicated radio shows, including *Les's Wines and Vines, Pierre Wolfe's Food & Wine,* and *Mike Rosen Show.*

AWARDS, HONORS: Best Drinks Writer Award finalist, Jacob's Creek International, 2003; James Beard Award for Internet Writing on Food, Restaurant, Beverage, or Nutrition, 2005.

WRITINGS:

Waiter, There's a Horse in My Wine: A Treasury of Entertainment, Exploration, and Education by America's Wittiest Wine Critic, Dauphin Press (Denver, CO), 2005.

Author of syndicated wine column for *Rocky Mountain News* and *Denver Post.* Contributor to periodicals, including *Wine Enthusiast, Beverage Network, New Zealand Winepress, Long Island Wine Gazette,* and *Wine Club Newsletter.*

SIDELIGHTS: Writer and columnist Jennifer "Chotzi" Rosen is a wine expert whose wine column appears in newspapers near her native Denver and in a variety of other papers across the country. In addition to being a prolific writer on viticultural subjects, Rosen also conducts educational wine seminars for businesses and vineyards throughout the United States. She has worked with software giant Microsoft to develop wine-related software and interactive blind tasting seminars for business leaders. A frequent radio quest, Rosen also teaches skiing, trains horses, and analyzes handwriting. Able to speak six languages, including French, German, Italian, Arabic, and Spanish, Rosen stays physically active and "works off the job perks with belly dancing and trapeze," as reported on her home page.

Waiter, There's a Horse in My Wine: A Treasury of Entertainment, Exploration, and Education by America's Wittiest Wine Critic is a "chuckle-inducing collec-tion" of works by Rosen, noted a reviewer in *Small Press Bookwatch.* Rosen sets out to make wine easy to understand, even for the most inexperienced, and in doing so, she seeks to disarm wine snobs who interfere with popular enjoyment of the fruit of the vine. She irreverently skewers stolid topics that venerable publications such as *Wine Spectator* cover with near-solemnity. She offers a selection of wine facts and sheds light on misunderstandings. In addition, she debunks some myths and sets the reader straight on a number of wine fallacies related to labeling, content, and quality. Her articles combine humorous travel reporting with wine criticism as she visits notable wine regions around the world. Among the humor, Rosen offers practical guidance for selecting and enjoying wines in an everyday setting. The *Small Press Bookwatch* contributor concluded that the book is a "delightful guide" that is "just plain fun to read."

BIOGRAPHICAL AND CRITICAL SOURCES:

PERIODICALS

Small Press Bookwatch, June, 2005, review of *Waiter, There's a Horse in My Wine: A Treasury of Entertainment, Exploration, and Education by America's Wittiest Wine Critic.*

ONLINE

Associated Content Web site, http://www.associated content.com/ (July 9, 2005), biography of Jennifer "Chotzi" Rosen.
Gallagher's Travels Web site, http://www.gallaghers travels.com/ (July 9, 2005), biography of Jennifer "Chotzi" Rosen.
Jennifer Rosen Home Page, http://www.vinchotzi.com (July 9, 2005).
Midwest Book Review Online, http://www.midwest bookreview.com/ (July 9, 2005), review of *Waiter, There's a Horse in My Wine.* *

*   *   *

ROSENBLATT, Naomi H.
(Naomi Harris Rosenblatt)

PERSONAL: Born in Haifa, Israel; immigrated to United States; married; husband's name Peter. *Education:* Catholic University (Washington, DC), M.S.W.

ADDRESSES: Agent—c/o Author Mail, Miramax Books, 77 W. 66th St., 11th Fl., New York, NY 10023.

CAREER: Writer, lecturer, and psychotherapist. Leader of Bible study groups for senators, congressional representatives, and business professionals in New York and Washington, DC. *Military service:* Served in Israeli Navy.

WRITINGS:

(With Joshua Horwitz) *Wrestling with Angels: What the First Family of Genesis Teaches Us about Our Spiritual Identity, Sexuality, and Personal Relationships,* Delacorte Press (New York, NY), 1995.

After the Apple: Women in the Bible: Timeless Stories of Love, Lust, and Longing, Miramax Books (New York, NY), 2005.

ADAPTATIONS: Author's works have been recorded on audio cassette and released by Bantam Doubleday Dell Publishing Group (New York, NY), 1995.

SIDELIGHTS: A practicing psychotherapist, public speaker, and author, Naomi H. Rosenblatt is known for the Bible study groups she conducts for prominent senators and congressional representatives. In an appreciation on the Library of Congress's *Thomas Web site,* U.S. Senator Larry Pressler commented that Rosenblatt "is a splendid teacher, but more importantly, a fine, insightful person. I wish that time would allow me to attend more of her classes." Her weekly Old Testament classes have attracted many of the nation's most prominent politicians, including senators Pressler and Arlen Specter, as well as journalists such as William Safire and Marvin Kalb, noted Jonathan Groner in the *Washington Post.*

Rosenblatt's published works also deal with religious and biblical themes. *Wrestling with Angels: What the First Family of Genesis Teaches Us about Our Spiritual Identity, Sexuality, and Personal Relationships* evolved from her teaching sessions on Capitol Hill, Groner noted. "It's Rosenblatt's first book, and what a fascinating effort it is; part biblical interpretation, part self-help treatise; a book that adopts an unmistakably Jewish perspective yet remains acces-

sible to readers of all backgrounds," Groner commented. Rosenblatt "presents the biblical stories in a way that a contemporary audience steeped in the drama of talk shows and gossip columns can understand," observed Marci Whitney-Schenck in *Christian Century.* She examines the fundamental stories of Genesis, such as that of Abraham and Sarah, an elderly couple who long for children, and couches their situation in terms of a troubled marriage in need of help. But Sarah is also selfless, as when she offers up her maidservant to be the surrogate mother of the child she and Abraham want so badly. Rosenblatt interprets Jacob's nighttime struggle with the angel to be representative of three segments of his personality; his conflict with his brother Esau, his own darker side, and Jacob's own fear of mortality. Perhaps the most famous biblical story of all, that of Adam and Eve, is interpreted to show Eve not as a temptress, "but an individual who wanted to share her wisdom," Whitney-Schenck commented. In *Wrestling with Angels* readers are "reintroduced to the people that have shaped our lives, only to discover that, as adults, we more clearly understand their strengths and flaws, because we now recognize the same in ourselves," observed a *Publishers Weekly* reviewer. "Rosenblatt's thoughts often echo and extend some of the interpretations already found in Jewish tradition," commented Groner. "The result is as if one were seeing the old stories with new eyes."

After the Apple: Women in the Bible: Timeless Stories of Love, Lust, and Longing contains Rosenblatt's retellings of the stories of fifteen notable women from the Bible. Applying her expertise as a relationship therapist, she offers professional insight into ancient stories that many perceive only as inspiring tales taught in Sunday school. Rosenblatt examines the role of gender in the lives of well-known biblical women and considers the effect of that gender on husbands and sons. Better-known biblical matriarchs such as Eve, Delilah, Jezebel, and Rachel are considered alongside lesser-known women such as Michal, Shulamite, Tamar, Abigail, and the queen of Sheba. "She elaborates on the narratives, placing issues such as rape, polygamy, and genocide in contemporary context," noted *Library Journal* contributor Joyce Smothers. Rosenblatt "dispels the pervasive notion many have that biblical matriarchs were weak and ineffective," observed a *Publishers Weekly* reviewer. Instead, these biblical women were tough risk-takers whose efforts "catapulted the struggling Jewish nation to survival and prominence." The *Publishers Weekly* critic concluded that Rosenblatt "teaches her readers not just to study but to imagine."

BIOGRAPHICAL AND CRITICAL SOURCES:

PERIODICALS

Booklist, September 15, 1995, Ray Olson, review of *Wrestling with Angels: What the First Family of Genesis Teaches Us about Our Spiritual Identity, Sexuality, and Personal Relationships,* p. 115; March 1, 2005, Ellen Loughran, review of *After the Apple: Women in the Bible: Timeless Stories of Love, Lust, and Longing,* p. 1116.
Christian Century, December 6, 1995, Marcy Whitney-Schenck, review of *Wrestling with Angels,* p. 1186.
Kirkus Reviews, January 1, 2005, review of *After the Apple,* p. 43.
Library Journal, March 1, 2005, Joyce Smothers, review of *After the Apple,* p. 93.
Presbyterian Record, September, 1996, review of *Wrestling with Angels,* p. 44.
Publishers Weekly, August 14, 1995, review of *Wrestling with Angels,* p. 29; August 27, 2001, Jon F. Baker, "Bible Women for Burnham at TM," p. 13; February 14, 2005, review of *After the Apple,* p. 72.
Washington Post, October 15, 1995, Jonathan Groner, "The Bible Tells Us So," review of *Wrestling with Angels.*

ONLINE

Thomas Web site, http://thomas.loc.gov/ (October 26, 1995), appreciation of Naomi Rosenblatt.*

*   *   *

ROSENBLATT, Naomi Harris
   See ROSENBLATT, Naomi H.

*   *   *

ROSENZWEIG, Gary 1969-

PERSONAL: Born October, 1969; married May 6, 1999; wife's name Debby; children: Luna. *Education:* Drexel University, B.S., 1992; University of North Carolina at Chapel Hill, M.A., 1994. *Hobbies and other interests:* Playing computer games, camping, road trips, astronomy, bowling, film.

ADDRESSES: Home—Denver, CO. *Office*—CleverMedia, 1022 N. Speer Blvd., Denver, CO 80204. *E-mail*—rosenz@clevermedia.com.

CAREER: Writer, software developer, consultant, engineer, and entrepreneur. Igneus (cable company), multimedia software developer, 1994-96; CleverMedia (multimedia software company), Denver, CO, founder, owner, and chief engineer, 1996—; Attic Bookstore, co-owner, 2001—. Worked for *Baltimore Sun.*

MEMBER: International Game Developer Association (Colorado chapter coordinator).

WRITINGS:

The Comprehensive Guide to Lingo: Creating Interactive Applications with Macromedia Director: For Windows & Macintosh, Ventana (Research Triangle Park, NC), 1996.
The Director Six Book: The Ultimate Handbook for Multimedia Professionals, Ventana (Research Triangle Park, NC), 1997.
Using Macromedia Director Seven, Que (Indianapolis, IN), 1999.
Advanced Lingo for Games, Hayden Books (Indianapolis, IN), 2000.
Using Macromedia Director Eight, Que (Indianapolis, IN), 2000.
Macromedia Flash Five ActionScript for Fun and Games, Que (Indianapolis, IN), 2001.
Macromedia Flash MX ActionScript for Fun and Games, Que (Indianapolis, IN), 2002.
SAMS Teach Yourself Flash MX ActionScript in Twenty-four Hours, SAMS (Indianapolis, IN), 2002.
Special Edition Using Director 8.5, Que (Indianapolis, IN), 2002.
Special Edition Using Macromedia Director MX, Que (Indianapolis, IN), 2003.
(With Jay Shaffer) *MacAddict Guide to Making Music with GarageBand,* Que (Indianapolis, IN), 2004.

SIDELIGHTS: Author, computer consultant, and engineer Gary Rosenzweig is an expert in the development of multimedia games and Internet applications. He is the founder and owner of CleverMedia, a technology consulting firm specializing in creating multimedia games, applications, and utilities using popular commercial software Macromedia Director as well as Flash and Shockwave. He and his wife, Debby, are co-owners of The Attic Bookstore, a used bookstore in Denver, Colorado.

Rosenzweig is also the author of almost a dozen books on using a variety of commercial software applications, including multimedia software Macromedia Director, animation software Macromedia Flash, and music creation and recording software GarageBand. He provides detailed, expert guidance for getting the most out of each application, offering tips and in-depth instruction that benefits both beginners and expert users.

In *MacAddict Guide to Making Music with GarageBand,* written with Jay Shaffer, Rosenzweig covers the many uses of a software application that lets users record, manipulate, and enhance music. Designed for home-grown music groups and the titular garage bands, the software gives users advanced recording features such as the ability to record on multiple tracks, change tempo and key, improve timing and pitch of recordings, and more. Rosenzweig and Shaffer's work offers "beginning to intermediate users more information on the software's uses from a musician's point of view," noted Rachel Singer Gordon in *Library Journal.*

With *SAMS Teach Yourself Flash MX ActionScript in Twenty-four Hours* Rosenzweig gives readers a crash-course in the practical uses of the ActionScript programming language available in Macromedia's popular video and animation software, Flash. The book contains detailed instructions and in-depth explanations of ActionScript's features and abilities and how they can be used by multimedia developers. Rosenzweig concentrates on programming with ActionScript, but the text remains "accessible to those with no programming knowledge," noted Gordon in another *Library Journal* review.

Advanced Lingo for Games covers another programming language, Lingo, used to expand the functions of Macromedia Director into a tool for creating computer games and entertainment applications. Rosenzweig describes in detail how Lingo can be used to create a variety of games, including arcade games, card games, and puzzles. He discusses Lingo's usefulness in creating online multiplayer games as well as adventure and strategy games. Thom Gillespie, writing in *Library*

Journal, observed that Lingo is not an especially easy programming language to learn, but that Rosenzweig's "lucid" guidebook "makes it fun."

Rosenzweig's own area of professional software expertise centers on the use of Macromedia Director, and in *Using Macromedia Director Seven,* he delves into the software application he uses most in his own business. Though he covers many of the basics of Director, the book is geared toward users who are already knowledgeable in using Director and its other features, such as the Lingo programming language. Rosenzweig concentrates on the use of Director in professional application development and discusses issues of concern to the expert developer and object-oriented programmer working in a business or commercial environment. Gillespie noted in another *Library Journal* review that the book is intended for programmers and developers pursuing "serious interactive media design."

BIOGRAPHICAL AND CRITICAL SOURCES:

PERIODICALS

Library Journal, July, 1999, Thom Gillespie, review of *Using Macromedia Director Seven,* p. 126; May 1, 2000, Thom Gillespie, review of *Advanced Lingo for Games,* p. 149; November 1, 2002, Rachel Singer Gordon, review of *SAMS Teach Yourself Flash MX ActionScript in Twenty-four Hours,* p. 125; September 1, 2004, Rachel Singer Gordon, review of *MacAddict Guide to Making Music with GarageBand,* p. 182.

ONLINE

Gary Rosenzweig Home Page, http://www.gary rosensweig.com (June 14, 2005).

Gary Rosenzweig Web Log, http://developerdispatch. com/ (June 14, 2005).*

*   *   *

ROSSNER, Judith 1935-2005
(Judith Perelman Rossner)

OBITUARY NOTICE—See index for *CA* sketch: Born March 1, 1935, in New York, NY; died August 9, 2005, in New York, NY. Author. Rossner was a best-selling novelist who first became famous with the publication of her 1975 book, *Looking for Mr. Goodbar.* Dropping out of City College at the age of nineteen, she married her first husband, from whom she would divorce in 1972. She would later marry and divorce a second time before marrying her third husband, Stanley Leff. After her first divorce, Rossner moved to New York City and supported herself and her family by working as a secretary. In her spare time, she began writing novels. The first to be published was 1966's *To the Precipice.* Two more novels followed before the publication of *Looking for Mr. Goodbar,* which became a best seller and was adapted to film in 1977. By this time, it was clear that Rossner's major literary concern was the poor treatment of women in modern American society, whether it was with regard to sex, marriage, work, or other factors. Her books were often considered disturbing or even depressing by critics and readers alike, though they repeatedly succeeded in touching people's emotions. In addition to a number of short stories, Rossner published nine novels over the years, including the notable *August* (1983).

OBITUARIES AND OTHER SOURCES:

PERIODICALS

Chicago Tribune, August 11, 2005, section 3, p. 9.
Los Angeles Times, August 11, 2005, p. B10.
New York Times, August 11, 2005, p. C18.
Times (London, England), August 12, 2005, p. 56.
Washington Post, August 11, 2005, p. B5.

*   *   *

ROSSNER, Judith Perelman
    See ROSSNER, Judith

*   *   *

ROTBLAT, Joseph 1908-2005

OBITUARY NOTICE—See index for *CA* sketch: Born November 4, 1908, in Warsaw, Poland; died August 31, 2005, in London, England. Physicist, educator, and author. A onetime scientist for the Manhattan Project, Rotblat became an anti-nuclear activist and cofounder of the Pugwash Conferences on Science and World

Affairs. Trained as an electrician as a young man, he was inspired by Albert Einstein's work to study physics. He subsequently completed a master's degree in physics at the Free University of Poland in 1932, followed by a Ph.D. from the University of Warsaw in 1938. Because he won a fellowship to attend Liverpool University the next year, Rotblat was out of the country when Germany invaded Poland. Despite his best efforts, he was unable to return to Poland and rescue his wife, and she became a victim of the Holocaust. Remaining in England, he became a lecturer at Liverpool. During World War II, fears emerged that the Germans were developing a nuclear bomb. Rotblat was convinced that he should become part of the Manhattan Project team that was seeking to develop a nuclear warhead for the Allies. After less than a year on the project, however, he saw that the Allies were winning the war and that a nuclear bomb was no longer necessary. He quit the project in 1944 and returned to England, where he was pursued by American federal agents who accused him of being a spy for the Soviets. Rotblat managed to persuade them that he was innocent, though he was prevented from reentering the United States until 1951. During the late 1940s he served as director of research in nuclear physics at the University of London. After joining the university's Medical College at St. Bartholomew's Hospital in 1949, he led studies on the effects of radiation on living tissue. Rotblat had been horrified by the U.S. bombings of Nagasaki and Hiroshima, Japan, and when the Americans proceeded to bomb Bikini Atoll in the Marshall Islands during a 1954 nuclear test that left its native people homeless, he teamed up with a group of scientists and intellectuals that included Albert Einstein, Bertrand Russell, Linus Pauling, Max Börn, and others, most of whom were or would become Nobel Prize winners. The scientists issued a public statement protesting the production and use of nuclear weapons. They then organized what would become the Pugwash Conference, which first met in Pugwash, Nova Scotia, Canada. The purpose of these meetings was to allow scientists from all over the world to discuss nuclear arms without the political pressures of being representatives of their respective nations. Attended by many of the world's most brilliant scientist, the Pugwash Conferences became a highly effective means of influencing international politics. Today, many historians have credited Pugwash as a key influence in the weapons bans that resulted in such agreements as the Nonproliferation Treaty of 1968, the Anti-Ballistic Missile Treaty of 1972, and the Chemical Weapons Convention of 1993. Though Rotblat and his colleagues were often accused of being Soviet or Communist sympathizers, especially by conservative politicians in the West, their anti-war stand ultimately contributed to a less-militaristic world. As an author, Rotblat published many books on his anti-war views, including *Scientists in the Quest for Peace: A History of the Pugwash Conferences* (1972), *The Arms Race at a Time of Decision* (1984), *Strategic Defense and the Future of the Arms Race* (1987), and *War No More: Eliminating Conflict in the Nuclear Age* (2003). Rotblat, who retired from the University of London in 1976, was honored many times for his activism and contributions to science, including with the 1983 Bertrand Russell Society award, the 1992 Albert Einstein Peace Prize, a 1995 Nobel prize, the Toda peace research prize in 2000, and the 2002 Linus Pauling award. He was also named a commander in the Order of the British Empire in 1965, a fellow of the Royal Society, and was knighted in 1998.

OBITUARIES AND OTHER SOURCES:

PERIODICALS

Chicago Tribune, September 2, 2005, section 3, p. 11.
New York Times, September 2, 2005, p. C14.
Times (London, England), September 2, 2005, p. 72.
Washington Post, September 2, 2005, p. B5.

*   *   *

RUTKOW, Ira M. 1948-

PERSONAL: Born October 13, 1948, in Newark, NJ; son of Al and Bea (Goldberg) Rutkow; married Beth Denise Greenwald, June 11, 1972; children: Lainie Wendy, Eric Ian. *Education:* Union College, B.S., 1970; St. Louis University, M.D., 1975; Johns Hopkins University, M.P.H., 1978, D.P.H., 1981.

ADDRESSES: Home—7 Pamela St., Marlboro, NJ 17746-1621. *Office*—The Hernia Center, 222 Schanck Rd., Ste. 100, Freehold, NJ 07728-2974.

CAREER: Writer, physician, educator, and medical historian. Boston City Hospital, Boston, MA, intern and resident, 1975-77; Johns Hopkins University Hospital, Baltimore, MD, resident, 1977-80; New Jersey Medical School, resident in University Hospital, 1980-82, clinical professor of surgery, 1983; Hernia Center, Freehold, NJ, founder and surgical director, 1984—; University of Medicine and Dentistry of New Jersey, clinical professor of surgery.

MEMBER: American College of Surgeons, Medical Society of New Jersey.

AWARDS, HONORS: Robert Wood Johnson Clinical Scholar, 1977-78; Edwin L. Crosby Memorial fellow, American Hospital Association, 1979-80.

WRITINGS:

(Guest editor) *Symposium on Surgical Health Care Delivery,* Saunders (Philadelphia, PA), 1982.
The History of Surgery in the United States, Norman Pub. (San Francisco, CA), 1988.
(Editor) *Socioeconomics of Surgery,* Mosby (St. Louis, MO), 1989.
Surgery: An Illustrated History, Mosby Year Book/Norman Pub. (St. Louis, MO), 1993.
(With Stanley B. Burns) *American Surgery: An Illustrated History,* Lippincott-Raven Publishers (Philadelphia, PA), 1998.
Bleeding Blue and Gray: Civil-War Surgery and the Evolution of American Medicine, Random House (New York, NY), 2005.

AUTHOR OF INTRODUCTION

John Hooker Packard, *A Manual of Minor Surgery,* Norman Pub. (San Francisco, CA), 1990.
Stephen Smith, *Hand-Book of Surgical Operations,* Norman Pub. (San Francisco, CA), 1990.
William Alexander Hammond, *A Treatise on Hygiene: With Special Reference to the Military Service,* Norman Pub. (San Francisco, CA), 1991.
Joseph Janvier Woodward, *The Hospital Steward's Manual: For the Instruction of Hospital Stewards, Ward-Masters, and Attendants, in Their Several Duties,* Norman Pub. (San Francisco, CA), 1991.
James B. McCaw, *Confederate States Medical and Surgical Journal,* Norman Pub. (San Francisco, CA), 1992.
William Grace, *The Army Surgeon's Manual: For the Use of Medical Officers, Cadets, Chaplains, and Hospital Stewards,* Norman Pub. (San Francisco, CA), 1992.

Joseph Janvier Woodward, *Outlines of the Chief Camp Diseases of the United States Armies: As Observed during the Present War,* Norman Pub. (San Francisco, CA), 1992.

Consulting editor for surgical history, *Archives of Surgery.*

SIDELIGHTS: Author and practicing surgeon Ira M. Rutkow is a medical historian who is considered the "world's leading expert on the history of American surgery," as Eric D. Albright stated in *Library Journal.* His books concentrate primarily on the history of American surgery and on the state of surgery and medical practice during the U.S. Civil War. He is also the author of more than seventy-five technical and scientific papers in the medical field.

In *Surgery: An Illustrated History,* Rutkow traces the development of surgery from primitive practices in Paleolithic times to advanced twentieth-century techniques and equipment. As he describes surgical procedures from various regions of the world, he provides a sense of the cultural influences on developing surgeons around the globe. Rutkow examines the development of professionalism in surgery and how the profession evolved in Europe from practitioners who were frequently despised, to the often-ridiculed barber-surgeons who practiced bloodletting, to the prestigious specialists known today. The book also includes biographical sketches of more than 1,000 well-known and prominent surgeons who have wielded a scalpel through the ages. In many cases, portraits and illustrations of contemporary medical instruments and techniques are also included. Astrid James, writing in *Lancet,* concluded that "there is much here to interest the public and those involved in the care of patients, particularly surgeons."

American Surgery: An Illustrated History narrows the historical focus from the world to the United States. Beginning with surgery as it was practiced in colonial America, Rutkow's text travels chronologically through topics such as the development of anesthesia, the harsh conditions of medical treatment during the U.S. Civil War, the development of the concepts of antisepsis and asepsis, medicine in World Wars I and II, and the rise of medical specialization. He ends with a discussion of modern concepts and controversies, such as Medicare, managed care, and physician

compensation. He provides "excellent biographical accounts of major participants of each era," remarked William Stoney in the *British Medical Journal.* Stoney concluded that "this is an outstanding book and will be the standard by which future historical collections of American surgery will be measured."

Bleeding Blue and Gray: Civil War Surgery and the Evolution of American Medicine offers an in-depth examination of the medical treatment available to the average Civil War soldier—treatment which was the best of its kind at the time, but which by modern standards seems brutal. Rutkow also explores a variety of "political and social changes that had significant impact upon war medicine," such as the work of the U.S. Sanitary Commission's often-thwarted attempts to establish better conditions for wounded soldiers, noted Albright in another *Library Journal* review. Most of Rutkow's sources come from the Union side of the battle, as Confederate resources are notably scarce. Rutkow explains how gunshot wounds often led to amputations; how the lack of antiseptic conditions meant it was more common for soldiers to die from postoperative infections than from actual battlefield wounds; and how communicable diseases spread unchecked through armies on both sides. A *Kirkus Reviews* contributor called the book "an absorbing account of how American medicine was changed forever by the efforts to bring good medical care to men on the battlefields of the Civil War." A *Publishers Weekly* critic concluded that the book is "fast-moving and informative" and "a gritty, compelling story well-told."

BIOGRAPHICAL AND CRITICAL SOURCES:

PERIODICALS

British Medical Journal, April 17, 1999, William Stoney, review of *American Surgery: An Illustrated History,* p. 1082.

Kirkus Reviews, January 1, 2005, review of *Bleeding Blue and Gray: Civil War Surgery and the Evolution of American Medicine,* p. 43.

Lancet, July 2, 1994, Astrid James, review of *Surgery: An Illustrated History,* p. 45.

Library Journal, December, 1997, Eric D. Albright, review of *American Surgery,* p. 138; February 1, 2005, Eric D. Albright, review of *Bleeding Blue and Gray,* p. 109.

Publishers Weekly, February 21, 2005, review of *Bleeding Blue and Gray,* p. 164.*

S

SADLER, Mark
See LYNDS, Dennis

*   *   *

SAGGS, Henry W.F. 1920-2005
(Henry William Frederick Saggs)

OBITUARY NOTICE— See index for *CA* sketch: Born December 2, 1920, in Weeley, Essex, England; died August 31, 2005. Linguist, educator, and author. Saggs was an authority on the ancient Assyrian and Babylonian civilizations and their Akkadian language. After graduating from King's College London with a theology degree in 1942, he joined the Royal Navy and served as an airplane navigator. After recovering from a broken back received in a plane crash, he was assigned to ground duty in Palestine because of his knowledge of Hebrew. It was here that he became interested in Middle Eastern cultures. Returning home after the war, Saggs taught math for a while before finishing a master's degree at King's College. During this time, he learned Akkadian, and this led to his being hired as a lecturer in Assyriology at the University of London School of Oriental and African Studies. He earned his Ph.D. there in 1954, and continued to teach at the University of London until 1966, except for a year spent as a visiting professor at Baghdad University. While still a doctoral student, Saggs gained attention for his work deciphering the inscriptions at the Assyrian capital of Nimrud. He would return to Nimrud several times during the 1950s, and in 1965 he traveled to Iraq to work with David Oates on the Tell al-Rimah excavation. In 1966 Saggs left London to teach at the University of Wales from 1966 until his 1983 retirement. He returned to Iraq as a visiting professor at Mosul University. His last trip to Iraq occurred in 1979; he traveled there to study cuneiform texts. Highly respected for his scholarly work, Saggs was also a prolific author of books for general readers. Among his works are *The Greatness That Was Babylon: A Survey of the Ancient Civilization of the Tigris-Euphrates Valley* (1962; revised edition, 1988), *The Might That Was Assyria* (1984), and *Babylonians* (1995).

OBITUARIES AND OTHER SOURCES:

PERIODICALS

Guardian (London, England), October 6, 2005, p. 33.

*   *   *

SAGGS, Henry William Frederick
See SAGGS, Henry W.F.

*   *   *

SALLIS, Eva 1964-
(Eva Katerina Hornung, Eva Katerina Sallis)

PERSONAL: Born August 21, 1964, in Bendigo, Victoria, Australia; daughter of Richard Hornung and Briar Mitcalfe; married Roger Sallis. *Education:* University of Adelaide, M.A., 1991, Ph.D., 1996.

ADDRESSES: Agent—Lesley McFadzean, Cameron Creswell Agency, 7th Fl., 61 Marlborough St., Surry Hills, New South Wales 2010, Australia.

CAREER: Writer, poet, and novelist. University of Adelaide, visiting research fellow. Australians against Racism, cofounder.

AWARDS, HONORS: Australian/Vogel Literary Award, 1997, and Nita May Dobbie Literary Award, both for Hiam; Steele Rudd Literary Award, 2004, for Mahjar; Asher Literary Award, 2005, for The Marsh Birds.

WRITINGS:

Hiam (novel), Allen & Unwin (Crows Nest, New South Wales, Australia), 1998.
Sheherazade through the Looking Glass: The Metamorphosis of the 1,001 Nights (literary criticism), Curzon, 1999.
(Editor, with others) Painted Words, Wakefield Press (Kent Town, South Australia, Australia), 1999.
(Editor, with Heather Miller) AIR! Australia Is Refugees: Winning Essays and Stories 2002, Australians against Racism (North Fitzroy, Victoria, Australia), 2002.
(Editor with others) Forked Tongues, Wakefield Press (Kent Town, South Australia, Australia), 2002.
The City of Sealions, (novel), Allen & Unwin (Crows Nest, New South Wales, Australia), 2002.
Mahjar (novel), Allen & Unwin (St. Leonards, New South Wales, Australia), 2003.
(Editor, with Sonja Dechian and Heather Miller) Dark Dreams: Australian Refugee Stories, Wakefield Press (Kent Town, South Australia, Australia), 2004.
Fire Fire (novel), Allen & Unwin (Crows Nest, New South Wales, Australia), 2004.
(Editor, with Heather Millar) There Is No Place like Home: Winning Stories 2004, Australians against Racism, 2004.
The Marsh Birds (novel), Allen & Unwin (Crows Nest, New South Wales, Australia), 2005.

Contributor of fiction to periodicals, including Heat, Elle, Joussour, Island, Southerly, Nouvelle Revue Fran‚aise, and Griffith Review. Contributor to publications, including Journal of Arabic and Middle Eastern Literatures, Journal of Semitic Studies, Kalimat, Australian Bookseller & Publisher, Australian Screen Education, and Goodreading. Author of libretto for The Lover and AlieNation.

WORK IN PROGRESS: A modern "Romulus and Remus" story set in Moscow.

SIDELIGHTS: Australian author Eva Sallis is a writer of fiction, nonfiction, and poetry whose works "explore ideas on culture, exile and belonging," as reported on her home page. A frequent traveler to the Middle East, Sallis is fluent in Arabic. She is cofounder of Australians against Racism, an organization that works to increase public awareness and knowledge of the many experiences of refugees and asylum seekers throughout the world.

Sallis served as coeditor, with Sonja Dechian and Heather Miller, of Dark Dreams: Australian Refugee Stories. This anthology of thirty-seven stories, all written by refugees between the ages of eleven and twenty years, is "a melding of fictions, truths, and imagination creating something vital, cellular and unique," commented Chelsea Rodd in the Journal of Australian Studies, "The stories deliver important, rare perspectives and personal insights allowing oft-silenced voices to speak from their hearts." The tales concern a variety of modern refugees, seekers of asylum, and immigrants who fled intolerable circumstances in their homeland for a better chance in Australia. The wave of refugees profiled first began arriving in Australia in 1976, many after dangerous journeys over open waters. Though their lives had been uprooted, and everything and everyone they knew had been left behind, they were readily accepted into Australian society. Modern refugees in Australia face greater difficulties, however, and are often ignored, refused, and marginalized. The book "offers precious insights into the varied experiences of refugees," Rodd noted. "Each story is unique, deeply personal, and powerfully seductive."

In her debut novel, Hiam, Sallis tells the story of Hiam, a young Arab woman, who not only must adjust to a new life in Australia but also deal with the emotional consequences of a once-vibrant relationship that has dissolved. In often-mysterious situations, Hiam ponders the devastation that immigration can visit upon a marriage, upon one's sense of self, and upon one's cultural identity. Hiam's happier years in a lush, satisfying Yemen are contrasted with the dry, desolate Australian landscape she drives through, a setting that in turn mirrors the bleak psychological landscapes Hiam's painful circumstances have created. When she meets a handsome young gas-station attendant on her travels, however, she finds that the exquisite pain of her past may subside, and beauty may finally bloom for her on Australian soil. "The novel is exquisitely woven, stitched together with reminiscences, dreams, and interior monologue, all lonely activities, which only serve to heighten the pervasive sense of alienation and sorrow," commented Cleo Lloyd da Silva in *Antipodes*. Sallis "explores her characters' foibles and vulnerabilities with sensitivity and insight," da Silva observed.

Though many of Hiam's experiences span cultural boundaries, Sallis does not want readers to ignore or diminish the different cultural aspects of Hiam's life. "Sameness and difference have to be acknowledged side by side," she stated in an interview with Paul Best in *AQ*. "I very much wanted to write against the way we generalize about other cultures and simply present that as a given, as something you have to flow with rather than judge and stand back from. The cultural difference can't be erased."

The City of Sealions is set on the coast of South Australia where Lian, daughter of Vietnam refugee Phi-Van and Australian native Nev, works to define her identity even as she struggles to escape from the strong but dysfunctional influence of her mother. Phi-Van is cut off from her own cultural heritage in Southeast Asia, and her longing for it is unassuaged by affable fisherman and upstanding husband Nev. The relationship that develops between mother and daughter is fraught with jealousy, distrust, and rancor, but even when Lian finally breaks away to study abroad in Yemen, her mother's unhappy influence still presses in on her life. However, as she becomes publicly invisible behind the concealing traditional clothing of Yemen's Arabic culture, she finds a closeness in the community of Arabic women that she never had in Australia. The love of religious student Ibrahim offers to take her even further from her stifling homeland. The novel stands as "a timely and thoughtful exploration of contemporary Australia and belonging," remarked Lisa Slater in *Southerly*. A *Kirkus Reviews* critic called Sallis's work "strong and evocative," and named the novel "a gracefully wrought reflection on identity within exile."

Mahjar contains a collection of fifteen interlinking short stories that examine the experiences of Arab im-

migrants in Australia. In the book's first story, a couple on vacation is attacked by a kangaroo; though the Australian husband is savaged by the beast, the Arab wife beats the creature to death with her shoe, all the while shouting "God is great!" The story presents "an allegory for the startling collision between Australian and Arab cultures," observed a *Kirkus Reviews* critic. In another tale, Zein is unhappy at her son's impending wedding to a plain, skinny Australian girl. An insightful observance of the "electric happiness" between her son and future daughter-in-law, however, brings Zein a much-needed epiphany. The stories mix realism, Arabic folklore, and humor to created "an original and pithy book that should be read as much for its laughs as for its insights," commented Ceridwen Spark in the *Sydney Morning Herald*. A reviewer in the Paddington, New South Wales *Bulletin* called it "a book full of wisdom and treasured gentle moments, but also of such anger that it's difficult to reconcile, which is perhaps what Sallis intended."

BIOGRAPHICAL AND CRITICAL SOURCES:

PERIODICALS

Age (Melbourne), February 15, 2003, "A Woman of Many Cultures," profile of Eva Sallis.

Antipodes, December, 1999, Cleo Lloyd Da Silva, "On Loneliness and Exile," review of *Hiam,* p. 125.

AQ, November-December, 1998, Paul Best, interview with Eva Sallis.

Bulletin (Paddington, New South Wales, Australia), April 30, 2003, review of *Mahjar.*

Journal of Australian Studies, September, 2004, Chelsea Rodd, review of *Dark Dreams: Australian Refugee Stories,* p. 142.

Kirkus Reviews, February 1, 2005, review of *The City of Sealions,* p. 145; February 15, 2005, review of *Mahjar,* p. 194.

Pharmacy News, May 18, 2005, "Separation Anxiety: From Homeland to Hurtland, a Refugee Story," review of *The Marsh Birds.*

Southerly, autumn, 2002, Lisa Slater, "Possibilities for Australia," review of *The City of Sealions,* p. 197.

Sydney Morning Herald, April 5, 2003, Ceridwen Spark, review of *Mahjar.*

ONLINE

AussieReviews Online, http://www.aussiereviews.com/ (July 14, 2005), Sally Murphy, reviews of *Fire Fire* and *Mahjar.*

AustLit Web site, http://www.austlit.edu/ (July 14, 2005), biography of Eva Sallis.

Australians against Racism Web site, http://www.australiansagainstracism.org/ (July 14, 2005).

Eva Sallis Home Page, http://www.evasallis.com (July 14, 2005).

*   *   *

SALLIS, Eva Katerina
See SALLIS, Eva

*   *   *

SANKARAN, Lavanya 1968(?)-

PERSONAL: Born c. 1968, in Bangalore, India; married; children: one daughter. *Education:* Attended Bryn Mawr College.

ADDRESSES: Home—Bangalore, India. *Agent*—c/o Author Mail, Dial Press, 1745 Broadway, New York, NY 10019.

CAREER: Writer, investment banker, and financial consultant.

WRITINGS:

The Red Carpet: Bangalore Stories, Dial Press (New York, NY), 2005.

Contributor to periodicals such as *Atlantic Monthly* and *Wall Street Journal.*

WORK IN PROGRESS: A novel for Dial Press.

SIDELIGHTS: Indian author Lavanya Sankaran, a native of Bangalore, began her career as an investment banker, business consultant, and financial professional. Though she worked with figures and statistics, she maintained a close connection to the world of words as well, and wrote articles for the *Wall Street Journal,* "But I wrote fiction on the side," she said in a interview with Meenakshi Reddy Madhavan in *Delhi*

Newswire. Encouraged by writer friends in the United States, she submitted some of her creative writing to agents. On the strength of two short stories—an unusual situation in that agents often prefer to see completed book-length manuscripts—she sparked interest in her fiction among five American agents. Finally, she selected Lane Zachary of the New York agency Zachary Shuster Harmsworth. Zachary told her to "go and write," she related to Madhavan. With this exhortation from her agent, she went to Bangalore and, two years later, emerged with *The Red Carpet: Bangalore Stories,* a collection of short stories and her debut work of fiction. Zachary warned her that the American market for short stories has long been weak. However, Sankaran's book ignited keen interest and sparked a bidding war among nine publishers who vied for the book during a three-day auction.

Sankaran ascribes much of the interest in *The Red Carpet* to reaction to the non-stereotypical subject matter of the stories. "All told me that this is incredibly fresh," she remarked to Sangeeta Barooah Pisharoty in the *Hindu,* and "unlike the misery of women, grinding poverty, or mystery and magic, the subjects that one usually gets to see from India." Instead, the book "deals with India as we know it—socialites, software programmers, convent schools, young modern couples—an India of changing times," observed Madhavan.

The Red Carpet contains eight stories set in modern-day Bangalore that "approach the changing city from eight different angles," commented the *Hindu* reviewer. "It speaks of several worlds and points of view that cohabit a landscape and touch each other, collide with each other, or go their separate ways after brief encounters." In Sankaran's work, the characters, the cities, and the country itself struggle to maintain a connection to their history and traditions while the conveniences and trappings of Western society inexorably infiltrate Indian culture with their modern enticements. In "Bombay This," Ramu, a thirty-year-old software expert, sets his mother the task of finding him a suitable wife. Before she can finish her quest, however, Ramu takes an interest in a vibrant woman from Bombay whose modern ways dismay his mother. The accountant protagonist in "Mysore Coffee," still reeling from her father's suicide, discovers that her work has been wrongfully claimed by a charismatic, handsome, but unscrupulous colleague. Rangappa, a driver for the wealthy Mrs. Choudhary, toils in relative poverty while silently observing the excesses of his employer in "The Red Carpet." Though Mrs. Choudhary is kind to Rangappa and his family, the driver is scandalized by her modern clothing and habits. A well-educated Indian woman who grew up in America feels a cultural obligation to return to India and be "Brown in a Brown Country" in "Alphabet Soup." After living in India for a while, however, the choice to leave or stay is not as clear-cut as she thought it would be. A group of American-educated software professionals, highly sought after for jobs, live the ultimately vapid reality of their childhood fantasies of success fueled by American influences in "Apple Pie, One by Two." In the end, the collection stands as "well-polished, smartly relevant fiction," commented a *Kirkus Reviews* critic.

"Sankaran is an observer of some talent, and in her writing, the flavor of the city and its contemporary character comes through beautifully," according to a reviewer on the *DesliLit* Web site. A *Publishers Weekly* contributor noted that "Sankaran builds tension brilliantly" in her stories, although she "doesn't always offer a climax to balance it." Mini Kapoor, in Bombay's *Indian Express,* observed that "these are often sad stories. Their slick structure is repeatedly unsettled by yearning and nostalgia. But each time Sankaran finds a way of enlarging the idea of the city, of celebrating Bangalore." The collection reveals a "varied, vibrant culture in flux," remarked Aaron Clark in *Newsweek International.*

BIOGRAPHICAL AND CRITICAL SOURCES:

PERIODICALS

Deccan Herald (Bangalore, India), May 15, 2005, "Red Carpet Welcome, Alright!," Priyanka Haldipur, interview with Lavanya Sankaran.
Delhi Newsline, April 29, 2005, Meenakshi Reddy Madhavan, "The Red Carpet Welcome," profile of Lavanya Sankaran.
Entertainment Weekly, April 29, 2005, Nisha Gopalan, review of *The Red Carpet: Bangalore Stories,* p. 153.
Hindu (Chennai, India), May 5, 2005, Sangeeta Barooah Pisharoty, "India That She Knows," review of *The Red Carpet*; May 9, 2005, "Sankaran's Success Story," profile of Lavanya Sankaran.

Indian Express (Bombay, India), May 8, 2005, Mini Kapoor, "The Word: Change Is a Two-Way Street," review of *The Red Carpet.*
Kirkus Reviews, February 15, 2005, review of *The Red Carpet,* p. 15.
Newsweek International, May 16, 2005, "Snap Judgment: Books," review of *The Red Carpet,* p. 63.
Publishers Weekly, April 25, 2005, review of *The Red Carpet,* p. 40.*

*   *   *

SAVIN-WILLIAMS, Ritch C. (Ritch Charles Savin-Williams)

PERSONAL: Male. *Education:* University of Missouri, B.A., 1971; University of Chicago, M.A., 1973, Ph.D., 1977; attended University of Massachusetts.

ADDRESSES: Office—College of Human Ecology, Cornell University, 145 Martha Van Rensselaer Hall, Ithaca, NY 14853-4401. *E-mail*—rcs15@cornell.edu.

CAREER: Psychologist, educator, and writer. Cornell University, Ithaca, NY, chairman of Department of Human Development, 2003—, professor of human development. Served on numerous university boards and committees, as well as in other capacities for numerous regional and national organizations, including consultant for American Civil Liberties Union; curriculum writer for Unitarian Universalist Association, Boston, MA; consultant for Department of Health Resources and Services Administration; investigator for New York State Division for Youth Detention Centers, Attorney General's Office. Consultant for Human Rights Campaign FamilyNet online National Cancer Institute.

MEMBER: American Psychological Association (cochair of Scrivner awards, 1999-2003).

AWARDS, HONORS: Mark Freedman Memorial Award for Outstanding Research Paper on Homosexuality, American Psychological Association, 1986; Award for Distinguished Scientific Contribution, Division 44, American Psychological Association, 2001; grants from Spence Foundation, Sloan-Kettering Cancer Center, New York Division for Youth, and New York Hatch.

WRITINGS:

Adolescence: An Ethological Perspective, Springer-Verlag (New York, NY), 1987.

Gay and Lesbian Youth: Expressions of Identity, Hemisphere (New York, NY), 1990.

(With Tracey Robinson-Harris) *Beyond Pink and Blue: Exploring Our Sterotypes of Sexuality and Gender: A Program for Ages 13 to 15,* Unitarian Universalist Association (Boston, MA), 1994.

(Editor and contributor, with Kenneth M. Cohen) *The Lives of Lesbians, Gays, and Bisexuals: Children to Adults,* Harcourt Brace College (Fort Worth, TX), 1996.

"—And Then I Became Gay": Young Men's Stories, Routledge (New York, NY), 1998.

Mom, Dad, I'm Gay: How Families Negotiate Coming Out, American Psychological Association (Washington, DC), 2001.

The New Gay Teenager, Harvard University Press (Cambridge, MA), 2005.

Also author of *Dominance-Submission Behaviors and Hierarchies in Young Adolescents at a Summer Camp* (microfilm), Library of Congress, 1977. Author or coauthor of numerous articles for professional journals, including the *Journal of Gay and Lesbian Issues in Education, Journal of Adolescence, Current Problems in Pediatric-and Adolescent Health Care, Journal of Family Psychology,* and *Child and Adolescent Psychiatric Clinics of North of America.* Contributor to books, including *Men and Masculinities: A Social, Cultural, and Historical Encyclopedia,* edited by M.S. Kimmel and A. Aronson, ABC-Clio (Santa Barbara, CA), 2004; *Adolescent Boys: Exploring Diverse Cultures of Boyhood,* edited by N. Way and J.Y. Chu, New York University Press (New York, NY), 2004; and *Educating Adolescents: Challenges and Strategies,* edited by T. Urdan and F. Pajaries, Information Age Publishing (Greenwich, CT), 2004. Served on editorial boards, including *Journal of Homosexuality,* 1983—; *Journal of HIV/AIDS Prevention & Education for Adolescents & Children,* 1994-99; *International Journal of Sexuality and Gender Studies,* 1997-2002; *Archives of Sexual Behavior,* 2001—; *Journal of LGBT Family Studies,* 2003—; *Sexuality Research and Social Policy, Journal of NSRC,* 2003—; and *Journal of Gay and Lesbian Issues in Education,* 2003—.

WORK IN PROGRESS: A book titled *". . . And Then I Kissed Her": Young Women's Stories.*

SIDELIGHTS: Ritch C. Savin-Williams is a clinical psychologist whose interests focus on psychosexual development during adolescence, sexual identity development among adolescents and early adults, and sexual minority development. In his book *Gay and Lesbian Youth: Expressions of Identity,* the author reports on his study of more than 300 gay and lesbian youths to learn more about the areas of self-esteem and disclosure. The author discusses a variety of topics, including issues such as research literature on lesbian and gay youth, the idea of poor self-esteem in these youth, and youth coming out as homosexual. "The final Chapter 10, 'Moving the Invisible to Visibility,' is the heart of the book," wrote Richard R. Pleak in the *Archives of Sexual Behavior.* "Here, Savin-Williams explores issues of importance in research involving lesbian/gay youths and in working with these youths." As Pleak went on to note, "The chief importance of the book is its focus on lesbian/gay youths and the author's ability to see this underresearched group in nonpathological terms and challenge the concept that lesbian and gay youths necessarily have low self-esteem."

In *The Lives of Lesbians, Gays, and Bisexuals: Children to Adults,* Savin-Williams and coeditor Kenneth M. Cohen bring together a wide range of researchers and experts to produce an academic book looking at many aspects of homosexuality. In a review in the *Journal of Sex Research,* Scott C. Strader commented that "a significantly different collection is offered than has heretofore been seen in the professional literature: an opportunity to understand even the most 'hard scientific data' in individual, unique, and human terms." Strader went on to note one of the author's own chapters in the book, commenting that Savin-Williams "presents a welcomed ethnology in his chapter on memories of childhood and early adolescent sexual feelings among gay and bisexual boys, demonstrating his vast knowledge of the field."

The author compares the development of gay versus heterosexual youth in *"—And Then I Became Gay": Young Men's Stories,* Based largely on the author's interviews with 180 boys and men aged fourteen to twenty-five, the author presents his belief that there are similarities in the developmental life of gay and heterosexual youths but that there also exist vast differences in their pathways of development. "Previously, psychological research has assumed that the development of sexual identity follows a single pathway, and that individual experiences are simply variations on the same, more inclusive trajectory," William Leap wrote in the *Lambda Book Report.* "So it is refreshing to see that Savin-Williams acknowledges that 'the continuity and discontinuity in individual lives and the turning points that redirect or rechannel the meanings of experiences' are multiple and diverse." Richard Violette, writing in the *Library Journal,* commented that "the sensitive treatment and personal narratives will appeal to well-informed lay readers." *Journal of Sex Research* contributor Strader called the book "thorough and thought-provoking."

Mom, Dad, I'm Gay: How Families Negotiate Coming Out focuses on sexual minority youth and their families and is based on the author's interviews with eighty-six young men and seventy-eight young women. Savin-Williams discusses such issues as how a healthy relationship can be formed between the youth and parents and what the author believes are some general misconceptions about the process of homosexual youths coming out. Writing in the *Archives of Sexual Behavior,* Daniel M. Medeiros commented that the author "has achieved his goal of creating a valuable resource for sexual-minority youths and their families and for those who care for them."

Savin-Williams examines the new and evolving attitudes that gay youngsters have about themselves in his book *The New Gay Teenager.* He points out that many youth look at their sexuality in very different ways than most prior generations, pointing out that they often reject the idea of labeling themselves as either homosexual or heterosexual. The author also discusses how the more liberal outlook toward the conventions of sexuality among youth may impact culture in the future. *Library Journal* contributor David S. Azzolina noted the author's "ability to transmit complicated concepts clearly."

BIOGRAPHICAL AND CRITICAL SOURCES:

PERIODICALS

Archives of Sexual Behavior, June, 1993, Richard R. Pleak, review of *Gay and Lesbian Youth: Expressions of Identity,* p. 282; August, 2001, Domonick J. Wegesin, review of *The Lives of Lesbians, Gays, and Bisexuals: Children to Adults,* p. 450; October, 2003, Daniel M. Medeiros review of *Mom, Dad, I'm Gay: How Families Negotiate Coming Out,* p. 488.

Human Ecology, June, 2004, Metta Winter, "ReConceptualizing the Gay Teen," p. 14.
Journal of Sex Research, winter, 1997, Scott C. Strader, review of *The Lives of Lesbians, Gays, and Bisexuals,* p. 57; February, 1999, Scott C. Strader, review of *"—And Then I Became Gay": Young Men's Stories,* p. 117.
Lambda Book Report, November, 1998, William Leap, review of *"—And Then I Became Gay,"* p. 35.
Library Journal, January, 1998, Richard Violette, review of *"—And Then I Became Gay,"* p. 122; March 1, 2005, David S. Azzolina, review of *The New Gay Teenager,* p. 101.

ONLINE

Cornell University College of Human Ecology Web site, http://www.human.cornell.edu/ (September 19, 2005), faculty profile of author.*

*   *   *

SAVIN-WILLIAMS, Ritch Charles
See SAVIN-WILLIAMS, Ritch C.

*   *   *

SAVITZKAYA, Eugène 1955-

PERSONAL: Born 1955, in Liège (one source says Saint-Nicolas), Belgium; children: one son.

ADDRESSES: Agent—c/o Author Mail, Quale Press, 93 Main St., Ste. 2, Florence, MA 01062.

CAREER: Poet and novelist.

WRITINGS:

Le coeur de schiste, Atelier de l'Agneau (Liège, Belgium), 1974.
Mongolie, plaine sale (also see below), Seghers (Paris, France), 1974.
Rue obscure (also see below), Atelier de l'Agneau (Liège, Belgium), 1975.

L'Empire (also see below), Atelier de l'Agneau (Liège, Belgium), 1976.

Mentir (novel), Éditions de Minuit (Paris, France), 1977.

Un jeune homme trop gors, Éditions de Minuit (Paris, France), 1978.

La traversée de l'Afrique, Éditions de Minuit (Paris, France), 1979.

Les couleurs de boucheries (poetry), C. Bourgois (Paris, France), 1980.

La disparition de maman (novel), Éditions de Minuit (Paris, France), 1982.

Les morts sentent bon (novel), Éditions de Minuit (Paris, France), 1983.

Veulerie, Le Verbe et l'Empreinte (Saint Laurent-du-Pont, France), 1984.

Quatorze cataclysmes, Le Temps Qu'il Fait (Cognac, France), 1985.

Bufo, bufo, bufo (poetry), Éditions de Minuit (Paris, France), 1986.

Capolican: un secret de fabrication, Arcane 17 (Saint-Nazaire, France), 1987.

Sang de chien (novel), Éditions de Minuit (Paris, France), 1988.

La folie originelle, Éditions de Minuit (Paris, France), 1991.

Marin mon coeur (novel), Éditions de Minuit (Paris, France), 1992.

(With Alain le Bras and Philippe Bordes) *Alain le Bras,* Association des Amis d'Alain le Bras (Nantes, France), 1993.

Mongolie, plaine sale; L'empire; Rue obscure, preface by Mathieu Lindon, commentary by Carmelo Virone, Labor (Brussels, Belgium), 1993.

En vie (novel), Éditions de Minuit (Paris, France), 1994.

Jérôme Bosch et Eugène Savitzkaya (catalog), Flohic (Paris, France), 1994.

(With Jean-Dominique Burton) *Ecorces: Jean-Dominique Burton,* Éditions de l'Octogone (Brussels, Belgium), 1994.

Cochon farci, Éditions de Minuit (Paris, France), 1996.

(With Jacques Izoard) *Ketelslegers* (includes "Code des mandarins" by Savitzkaya), illustrated by Robert Ketelslegers, Labor (Brussels, Belgium), 1997.

Cénotaphe: poèmes inédits-1973, Atelier de l'Agneau (Liège, Belgium), 1998.

Mamouze, Atelier de l'Agneau (Liège, Belgium), 1998.

Saperlotte!, Flohic (Paris, France), 1998.

Fou civil, Flohic (Paris, France), 1999.

Célébration d'un mariage improbable et illimité, Éditions de Minuit (Paris, France), 2002.

Exquise Louise (novel), Éditions de Minuit (Paris, France), 2003.

Rules of Solitude (poems; in English and French), English translations by Gian Lombardo, Quale Press (Florence, MA), 2004.

SIDELIGHTS: Comparing Belgian writer Eugène Savitzkaya to such contemporary French autobiographical authors as Patrick Drevet, Pierre Michon, and Pierre Bergounioux, *Times Literary Supplement* reviewer Jeremy Alden commented that Savitzkaya uses unconventional plots and themes in his prose works such as *En vie* and *Marin mon coeur.* Savitzkaya is not "fundamentally concerned with character or family relationships" in his books; rather, the critic observed that the author "is someone who scrutinizes organic life, ever aware of its continuing decay. Apprehending the world . . . means distinguishing one leaf from countless others." While Savitzkaya ultimately suggests that life offers little that is "spiritual," noted Alden, the author also "immerses us in the pleasure we can derive from the Earth and from our houses," posing the question, "Can we honestly hope . . . for anything beyond the mere satisfaction of our primary appetites?"

In addition to his prose writings, Savitzkaya has written poetry collections. In 2004, his first bilingual French/English edition of verse, *Rules of Solitude,* was released. Noting that Savitzkaya uses deceptively simple and sparse language in his poems, *NewPages. com* reviewer Deborah Diemont remarked that he "writes about nothing less complicated than the soul." She added, "These poems blend concrete and abstract in such a way that we never 'get' them, but must approach them again and again like paintings."

BIOGRAPHICAL AND CRITICAL SOURCES:

PERIODICALS

Express International, March 16, 1995, André Clavel, review of *En vie,* p. 64.

Times Literary Supplement, October 6, 1995, Jeremy Alden, "Wear and Tear," review of *En vie,* p. 27.

ONLINE

NewPages.com, http://www.newpages.com/ (May 10, 2005), Deborah Diemont, review of *Rules of Solitude.**

SCHACHTER-SHALOMI, Zalman 1924-
(Zalman Meshullam Schachter-Shalomi)

PERSONAL: Born Zalman Meshullam Schachter, 1924, in Zolkiew, Poland, immigrated to United States, 1941. *Education:* Boston University, M.A., 1956; Hebrew Union College, Ph.D., 1968.

ADDRESSES: Office—Spiritual Eldering Institute, 970 Aurora Ave., Boulder, CO 80302.

CAREER: Rabbi and writer. Founder of B'nai Or Fellowship (formerly B'nai Or Religious Fellowship) and Spiritual Eldering Institute, 1989. World Wisdom Chair at Naropa University, Boulder, CO, until 2000, and full-time teacher until 2004. University of Manitoba, Winnipeg, Canada, former head of Department of Near-Eastern and Judaic Studies; Temple University, Philadelphia, PA, member of faculty, beginning 1975, then professor emeritus.

WRITINGS:

S.J. Agnon's 'Iddo w'Eynam: A Study of a Myth about Myth and Its Symbols, Z.M. Schachter (Cincinnati, OH), 1966.

(With Donald Gropman) *The First Step: A Guide for the New Jewish Spirit,* Bantam Books (New York, NY), 1983, published as *First Steps to a New Jewish Spirit: Reb Zalman's Guide to Recapturing Intimacy & Ecstasy in Your Relationship with God,* Jewish Lights Publishing (Woodstock, VT), 2003.

(With Edward Hoffman) *Sparks of Light: Counseling in the Hasidic Tradition,* Random House (New York, NY), 1983.

(Under name Zalman Meshullam Schachter-Shalomi) *Spiritual Intimacy: A Study of Counseling in Hasidism,* Jason Aronson (Northvale, NJ), 1991.

Paradigm Shift: From the Jewish Renewal Teachings of Reb Zalman Schachter-Shalomi, edited by Ellen Singer, Jason Aronson (Northvale, NJ), 1993.

(With Ronald S. Miller) *From Age-ing to Sage-ing: A Profound New Vision of Growing Older,* Warner Books (New York, NY), 1995.

Wrapped in a Holy Flame: Teachings and Tales of the Hasidic Masters, edited by Nataniel M. Miles-Yepez, Jossey-Bass (San Francisco, CA), 2003.

(With Joel Segel) *Jewish with Feeling: A Guide to Meaningful Jewish Practice,* Riverhead Books (New York, NY), 2004.

Contributor to periodicals, including *Tikkun.*

SIDELIGHTS: Zalman Schachter-Shalomi is a Hassidic rabbi who began developing innovations in Jewish worship and ritual that were not strictly orthodox, such as allowing women more privileges in worship. He also experimented with LSD and wrote about it for the journal *Psychedelic Review.* He eventually expanded his belief that the Jewish religion encompasses the only true knowledge of God. Since that time he has "emerged as one of the most prominent New Age spokespeople within the Jewish community,"as noted by a contributor to *Religious Leaders of America.* Nevertheless, despite his acceptance of other religious thought, the author told Or Rose in an interview for *Tikkun:* "For all of my universalism, I strongly believe that Judaism has unique gifts to offer the world."

Schachter-Shalomi has authored or coauthored numerous books, including *From Age-ing to Sage-ing: A Profound New Vision of Growing Older,* which he wrote with journalist Ronald S. Miller. The book sets forth Schachter-Shalomi's philosophy of both how to approach aging and how to use the wisdom that living many years often provides a person. In a keynote address to the board of directors of the Spiritual Eldering Institute, which the author founded, as posted on the institute's Web site, Schachter-Shalomi noted that he wrote the book when he was approaching his sixtieth birthday. "Using whatever was available to me about the management of consciousness (for a person who is entering in such a life phase), I realized that I was depressed because I didn't switch gears. I was still trying to go up the hill in high gear. I had to switch to a lower gear in order to be able to make that move to the next place."

From Age-ing to Sage-ing discusses how to think differently about aging and how to perceive it not as a sorrowful decline but as a rewarding fulfillment of life that includes spiritual growth and the ability to contribute to society. The book includes an in-depth discussion of the "Spiritual Eldering" program that Schachter-Shalomi founded, which focuses on increased awareness and social activism. The book especially stresses the importance of mentoring, both for the elderly themselves and those they mentor. In addition, the author and his cowriter address death and the dying process and include instructions on achieving a "conscious" death.

Denise Perry Donavin, writing in *Booklist* called *From Age-ing to Sage-ing* "a worthwhile, multicultural look at the value of aging individuals." In a review for *Tikkun,* Thomas R. Cole noted, "Other people have called for a cultural transformation of aging, but Zalman Schachter-Shalomi is the first to develop a program to make it happen." Cole also called the book "a welcome alternative to the mainstream response to the postmodern life course."

In *Wrapped in a Holy Flame: Teachings and Tales of the Hasidic Masters,* Schachter-Shalomi presents the original works of teachers in the Hassidic movement of Judaism and discusses the meaning of the teachings and their value in a modern society. The author also includes brief biographical profiles of each of the teachers. "As an introduction to Hasidism, this is a very useful sourcebook," wrote Herbert E. Shapiro in the *Library Journal.* Roger S. Gottlieb, writing in *Tikkun,* noted that the book "joins . . . distinguished company in pursuing the insights and inspirations of the leaders of the great Hasidic religious revival." Gottlieb also wrote, "Schachter's book is not meant to be a straightforward elucidation of the content of Hasidism, but an adaptation of its inner intentions to what he calls the 'new paradigm' of contemporary spirituality."

Schachter-Shalomi discusses both the traditions and the present-day practice of Judaism in his book *Jewish with Feeling: A Guide to Meaningful Jewish Practice.* The author also reflects on his own experience with doubt in his faith as he presents ancient Hasidic tales and discusses how to become more spiritually active in a way that enables one to practice Judaism as a living religion. A *Publishers Weekly* contributor noted that the author "offers a Judaism with a keen sense of the present infused with the sacredness of the past, yet written with a hopeful eye toward the future." Graham Christian, writing in the *Library Journal,* commented that Schachter-Shalomi bases his beliefs in tradition but that they "are fresh in their emphasis."

BIOGRAPHICAL AND CRITICAL SOURCES:

BOOKS

Religious Leaders of America, 2nd edition, Thomson Gale (Detroit, MI), 1989.

Schwartz, Howard, collector and reteller, *The Dream Assembly: Tales of Rabbi Zalman Schachter-Shalomi,* illustrated by Yitzhak Greenfield, Amity House (Amity, NY), 1988.

Wiener, Shohama Harris, and Jonathan Omer-Man, editors, *Worlds of Jewish Prayer: A Festschrift in Honor of Rabbi Zalman M. Schachter-Shalomi,* J. Aronson (Northvale, NJ), 1993.

PERIODICALS

Booklist, April 15, 1995, Denise Perry Donavin, review of *From Age-ing to Sage-ing: A Profound New Vision of Growing Older,* p. 1459.

Library Bookwatch, May, 2005, review of *Jewish with Feeling: A Guide to Meaningful Jewish Practice.*

Library Journal, April 15, 2003, Herbert E. Shapiro, review of *Wrapped in a Holy Flame: Teachings and Tales of the Hasidic Masters,* p. 93; March 1, 2005, Graham Christian, review of *Jewish with Feeling,* p. 94.

Publishers Weekly, February 28, 2005, review of *Jewish with Feeling,* p. 64.

Tikkun, November-December, 1995, Thomas R. Cole, review of *From Age-ing to Sage-ing,* p. 78; May-June, 2004, Roger S. Gottlieb, review of *Wrapped in a Holy Flame,* p. 75; July-August, 2004, Or Rose, "On the Growing Edge of Judaism: Reb Zalman at Eighty," p. 49.

ONLINE

Integral Naked Web site, http://integralnaked.org/ (September 19, 2005), "Who Is Rabbi Zalman Schachter-Shalomi?"

Spiritual Eldering Institute Web site, http://www.spiritualeldering.org/ (February 16, 2006), profile of author and excerpts from speeches and writings.*

*   *   *

SCHACHTER-SHALOMI, Zalman Meshullam
See SCHACHTER-SHALOMI, Zalman

*   *   *

SCHNEIDER, Elizabeth M.

PERSONAL: Female. Education: Bryn Mawr College, B.A.; London School of Economics and Political Science, M.Sc.; New York University School of Law, J.D.

ADDRESSES: Office—Brooklyn Law School, 250 Joralemon St., Rm. 811, Brooklyn, NY 11201. *E-mail*—liz.schneider@brooklaw.edu.

CAREER: Writer, attorney, and educator. Brooklyn Law School, Brooklyn, NY, Rose L. Hoffer Professor of Law, 1983—. Staff attorney, Rutgers Law School-Newark Constitutional Litigation Clinic and Center for Constitutional Rights; visiting professor, Harvard Law School and Columbia Law School.

MEMBER: American Law Institute.

AWARDS, HONORS: Publishers Book Award, legal category, Professional/Scholarly Publishing Division of Association of American Publishers, 2000, for *Battered Women and Feminist Lawmaking.*

WRITINGS:

Battered Women and Feminist Lawmaking, Yale University Press (New Haven, CT), 2000.
(With Clare Dalton) *Battered Women and the Law,* Foundation Press (New York, NY), 2001.

Contributor to books, including *Woman in Sexist Society: Studies in Power and Powerlessness,* edited by V. Gornick and B. Moran, 1971; *The Prostitution Papers: A Candid Dialogue,* 1972; *Feminist Legal Theory: Foundations,* edited by D. Kelly Weisberg, 1993; *Justice Confronts Race, Domestic Violence, Lawyers, Money, and the Media,* edited by J. Abramson, 1996; and *Women and the United States Constitution: History, Interpretation, and Practice,* edited by S. Schwarzenbach and P. Smith, 2003. Contributor to journals and periodicals such as *New York University Law Review, University of Chicago Legal Forum, De Paul Law Review, Brooklyn Law Review, New England Law Review, Texas Journal of Women and the Law, Columbia Journal of Gender and Law, Georgetown Journal of Gender and Law,* and *Journal of Legal Education.*

SIDELIGHTS: Elizabeth M. Schneider is a legal expert on gender discrimination and violence against women. Schneider has been a pioneer in the attempt to bring greater public awareness to the issues of gender law and domestic violence, both as a practicing attorney

and as a legal thinker and scholar. She has successfully litigated cases on behalf of battered women, including *State v. Wanrow,* in which Native-American woman Yvonne Wanrow was initially convicted for shooting and killing a man who entered her babysitter's home, uninvited, inebriated, and apparently intent on causing harm. At the time of the incident, Wanrow was injured and able to walk only with crutches. The man was physically much larger and stronger than Wanrow, and Schneider maintains that the defendant's deadly use of a firearm constituted an appropriate response to the threat posed by her dangerous opponent. Schneider argued that, in terms of Wanrow's self-defense claim, what constitutes a threat to her person would not be necessarily the same as what would be considered threatening to an average man. Further, Wanrow's concept of "self" included her children, who were under her protection, and her ability to put up a "defense" was hindered by her physical condition. "In articulating Wanrow's perspective, Schneider and the other lawyers who worked on her case helped make the law appreciate that equal treatment did not mean identical treatment," observed Katharine K. Baker in the *Yale Law Journal.*

In *Battered Women and Feminist Lawmaking* Schneider carefully examines the legal, political, and social issues surrounding domestic violence and the system of coercion, control, and subordination that underlies it. She divides the book into four sections. The first looks at the history and social framework of domestic-violence issues. The second section puts forth a number of theoretical notions on legal elements of battering and violence. The third part offers an expert analysis of the law pertaining to domestic violence, while the last section considers the future of feminist lawmaking and legal protection of battered women.

"Schneider has done feminism a great service by writing this book," Baker noted. The author's "analysis is intelligent and persuasive and brings new understanding to the problem," remarked Mary Jane Brustman in *Library Journal.* "We are lucky to have Elizabeth Schneider," observed Mimi Wesson in the *Women's Review of Books,* "and fortunate that she has made her work, of both sorts, accessible to us in this admirable book."

BIOGRAPHICAL AND CRITICAL SOURCES:

PERIODICALS

Library Journal, November 1, 2000, Mary Jane Brustman, review of *Battered Women and Feminist Lawmaking,* p. 112.

Women's Review of Books, December, 2000, Mimi Wesson, review of *Battered Women and Feminist Lawmaking,* p. 29.

Yale Law Journal, June, 2001, Katharine E. Baker, review of *Battered Women and Feminist Lawmaking,* p. 1459.

*   *   *

SCHULTZ, Connie 1958(?)-

PERSONAL: Born c. 1958; daughter of a factory worker and a nurse's aide; married Sherrod Brown; children: two children, two stepdaughters. *Education:* Kent State University, B.A., 1979.

ADDRESSES: Office—Plain Dealer, 2019 Center St., Ste. 200, Cleveland, OH 44113. *E-mail*—cschultz@plaind.com.

CAREER: Writer, journalist, essayist, and columnist. Freelance writer, 1978-93; *Plain Dealer,* Cleveland, OH, columnist, 1993—.

AWARDS, HONORS: American Association of Sunday and Feature Editors Award for best short feature, best in Ohio recognition, 1998, for narrative series, "Losing Lisa"; National Headliner Awards Best of Show, Robert F. Kennedy Award for Social Justice Reporting (domestic), journalism awards from Harvard and Columbia universities, and Pulitzer Prize finalist, all 2003, all for narrative series, "The Burden of Innocence"; James Batten Medal, Foundation for the Batten Medal, 2004, for journalistic work; Pulitzer Prize, Scripps-Howard Award, and National Headliners Award, all 2005, all for commentary; American Society of Newspaper Editors finalist for commentary; named best feature writer in Ohio, Associated Press Society of Ohio.

WRITINGS:

Contributor to periodicals, including Cleveland *Plain Dealer.*

SIDELIGHTS: Pulitzer Prize-winning journalist Connie Schultz is a columnist for the Cleveland *Plain Dealer* newspaper. A winner of multiple awards for her commentary and journalism, Schultz worked as a freelance writer for fifteen years before going to work for the *Plain Dealer.* He readily admits that in her writing she takes a woman's perspective, and she does not try to blunt that approach. "If you saw my column without my name on it, you would still know it's written by a woman," Schultz remarked in a profile by Dave Astor in *Editor & Publisher.*

Schultz grew up in Ashtabula, Ohio, a working-class city near Cleveland, and was the first in her family to attend college, noted a biographer on the *Everything Cleveland* Web site. Schultz's columns often focus on the underprivileged and the underdog."I like to use the column for those who need a voice," Schultz stated in a profile on the *Batten Medal* Web site. "I have no interest in the privileged. They have plenty of people to speak for them."

Schultz's Pulitzer Prize was earned for commentary. She was also a Pulitzer finalist in 2003 for a series titled "The Burden of Innocence," the story of a man wrongly incarcerated thirteen years for a rape he did not commit, but who continued to suffer the stigma of being an ex-convict long after he was exonerated and released from prison. A narrative series on a dying woman, titled "Losing Lisa," was named the best series in Ohio in 1998. Another prize-winning piece focused on the plight of a coat-check worker who was forced to surrender her tip money to management. As a result of Schultz's reporting, the management of that establishment was embarrassed into changing their policy.

Stuart Warner, *Plain Dealer* deputy features editor and writing coach, attributes Schultz's success to "enthusiasm, compassion, ability to connect with working-class readers, and willingness to accept writing advice," Astor reported. As reported on the award's Web site, judges on the Batten Medal panel remarked that "they were impressed with the range of Schultz's work and her ability 'to make stories of ordinary people significant, meaningful, and touching.'"

BIOGRAPHICAL AND CRITICAL SOURCES:

PERIODICALS

Editor & Publisher, May 1, 2005, Dave Astor, "Pulitzers: Connie Keeps It Real in Cleveland."

ONLINE

Batten Medal Web site, http://www.battenmedal.org/ (April 22, 2004), "*Plain Dealer*'s Connie Schultz Wins 2004 Batten Medal."
Everything Cleveland, http://www.cleveland.com/ (April 4, 2005), biography of Connie Schultz.*

* * *

SCHWARTZ, Erika

PERSONAL: Born in Romania; immigrated to United States; naturalized U.S. citizen; married; children: two daughters. *Education:* New York University, B.A.; State University of New York Downstate College of Medicine, M.D. (cum laude); King's County Hospital Center, postgraduate training.

ADDRESSES: Home—Westchester County, NY. *Office*—10 W. 74th St., New York, NY 10023.

CAREER: Writer, physician, television show host, and consultant. Westchester County Medical Center, directory of emergency medicine. *Health Horizons* television show, host, 1995-99. Founder of International Hormone Institute. Member of board of managers, State University of New York Downstate College of Medicine.

MEMBER: Alpha Omega Alpha.

WRITINGS:

(With Carol Colman) *Natural Energy: From Tired to Terrific in Ten Days,* Putnam (New York, NY), 1998.
The Hormone Solution: Naturally Alleviate Symptoms of Hormone Imbalance from Adolescence through Menopause, Warner Books (New York, NY), 2002.
The Thirty-Day Natural Hormone Plan: Look and Feel Young Again without Synthetic HRT, Warner Books (New York, NY), 2004.
The Teen Weight-Loss Solution: The Safe and Effective Path to Health and Self-Confidence, Morrow (New York, NY), 2004.

SIDELIGHTS: Erika Schwartz is an expert in women's health and related issues. Born in Romania, Schwartz was raised in Italy and came to the United States at age fifteen. She became the first woman and the youngest physician ever to direct a major university-hospital trauma center when she became head of the emergency room at Westchester County Medical Center in Valhalla, New York. Schwartz often lectures on medical and health topics and has been a frequent guest on such television programs as *O'Reilly Factor, Hardball with Chris Matthews, The View,* and *CBS Early Show.* For four years, Schwartz herself was a television show host and producer for *Health Horizons,* a program airing in the greater New York metropolitan area and designed to educate patients and to bring doctors and patients closer together.

Schwartz is an advocate for the use of natural hormones in medical care, and is the founder of the International Hormone Institute. Several of her books focus on the use of natural hormone replacement therapy (HRT) in a health-care setting. *The Hormone Solution: Naturally Alleviate Symptoms of Hormone Imbalance from Adolescence through Menopause* addresses problems with hormonal imbalances that can occur in women at any age. Mood swings and acne in teenage girls are caused by hormone problems; migraines and weight gain can be hormone-related for middle-aged women. In her book, Schwartz offers a "clear, accessible account of the role of hormones in health," noted Judy Bass, writing in *Natural Health.* She describes how natural plant-based hormones are identical to the types of hormones produced by the body, and are much more effective than synthetic hormones. Though available only by prescription and sometimes difficult to get—pharmaceutical companies have little profit incentive to produce natural hormones since natural substances cannot be patented—Schwartz continues to recommend close collaboration between doctor and patient in devising an effective treatment plan.

In *The Thirty-Day Natural Hormone Plan: Look and Feel Young Again without Synthetic HRT* Schwartz outlines a program for gradually introducing hormone therapy into a patient's daily lifestyle. She describes a month-long program designed to treat menopausal symptoms with natural hormones. She encourages gradual adoption of more healthful dietary habits while discontinuing the use of sugar, alcohol, processed foods, and caffeine. *Library Journal* reviewer Martha

E. Stone lauded Schwartz's program because she "divides her plan into manageable daily chunks" that can easily fit into a busy lifestyle. A *Publishers Weekly* critic noted that Schwartz's program "will be helpful" to women with hormonal problems "who want to avoid any possible health risks in taking synthetic hormones."

The Teen Weight-Loss Solution: The Safe and Effective Path to Health and Self-Confidence contains Schwartz's expert suggestions for teenage health and wellness through the use of natural hormones. Not restricted solely to weight loss, Schwartz describes how properly regulated hormones can help adolescent girls "feel physically better and mentally clearer," commented Rachel M. Minkin in *Library Journal.* "Losing weight is just an added benefit of regulated hormones," Minkin observed. Acne and a number of emotional issues can be successfully addressed with hormone therapy, Schwartz notes. "Schwartz does cover her territory well when it comes to mothers and daughters," commented a *Publishers Weekly* contributor, who called the book "eye-opening" for parents and teens.

Schwartz told *CA:* "My mission is to improve healthcare by giving women the tools and support necessary to be healthy at all ages. I am an expert in the use of bioidentical hormones and I integrate natural methods with conventional medical wisdom in all my practices. I started writing ten years ago. For me, writing is the ideal way to share my expertise and life experiences with the public.

"My writing grows out of the information that I gather from my patients, the wisdom shared by the professionals and laymen who I encounter in my daily life, and my personal experience and research. The most surprising thing that I have learned as a writer is how desperate we all are to be acknowledged and not alone. My writing gives people hope, strength, and support. When you read my books you learn that you are not alone but rather are part of a community of millions—and our problems can be solved together. My writing offers safe, caring, and compassionate solutions."

BIOGRAPHICAL AND CRITICAL SOURCES:

PERIODICALS

Business Wire, July 5, 2000, "New Natural Hormone Therapy Program Developed by Erika Schwartz, M.D.," p. 2405.

Library Journal, January, 2004, Martha E. Stone, review of *The Thirty-Day Natural Hormone Plan: Look and Feel Young Again without Synthetic HRT,* p. 148; September 15, 2004, Rachel M. Minkin, review of *The Teen Weight-Loss Solution: The Safe and Effective Path to Health and Self-Confidence,* p. 75.

Natural Health, May-June, 2002, Judy Bass, "A Look at a Powerful Remedy: This Doctor's New Book Says Natural Hormones Are Not Just for Menopause," p. 103.

Publishers Weekly, November 10, 2003, review of *The Thirty-Day Natural Hormone Plan,* p. 56; July 5, 2004, review of *The Teen Weight-Loss Solution,* p. 53.

ONLINE

Erika Schwartz Home Page, http://www.drerika.com (June 12, 2005).

*   *   *

SCHWARZSCHILD, Edward 1964-

PERSONAL: Born 1964. *Education:* Boston University, M.F.A.; Washington University, Ph.D. *Religion:* Jewish.

ADDRESSES: Office—Department of English, University at Albany, State University of New York, Humanities 339, 1400 Washington Ave., Albany, NY 12222. *Agent*—Dorian Karchmar, William Morris Agency, 1325 Avenue of the Americas, New York, NY 10019. *E-mail*—schild@Albany.edu; ed@edwardschwarzschild.com.

CAREER: Writer and educator. State University of New York at Albany, assistant professor of English and with New York State Writers Institute. Taught at Sweet Briar College.

AWARDS, HONORS: Boston University, Helen Deutsch fellow in creative writing; Stanford University, Wallace Stegner fellow.

WRITINGS:

Responsible Men (novel), Algonquin Books of Chapel Hill (Chapel Hill, NC), 2005.

Contributor to periodicals such as *Southwest Review, Virginia Quarterly Review, StoryQuarterly, Moment,* and *Yale Journal of Criticism.*

SIDELIGHTS: In addition to writing fiction, Edward Schwarzschild teaches writing and literature at the State University of New York at Albany. During Schwarzschild's early upbringing in Philadelphia, a literature-focused career seemed unlikely: His father, a salesman, discouraged him from entering sales, so the young Schwarzschild directed his attentions toward becoming a doctor. "Medicine seemed the way to go," Dan Pine observed in the *Jewish News Weekly,* "but a stubborn artistic temperament kept getting in the way." Schwarzschild was a constant reader and writer of stories, and three abortive attempts to pass medical school entrance exams finally convinced him that his true interests lay elsewhere. He earned a Ph.D. in American literature and an M.F.A. in creative writing four years later and devoted himself to life as a man of letters.

In Schwarzschild's debut novel, *Responsible Men,* salesman Max Wolinsky has returned to Philadelphia after a year in Florida to attend his son Nathan's bar mitzvah while still reeling from the breakup of his marriage to Nathan's mother Sandy, who left him for the family gardener. Max is a salesman with dubious morals—his deals sometimes veer from unethical to outright criminal, though his own sense of honor dictates that he not physically harm anyone or leave them financially destitute—and shortly after arriving back in Philadelphia he concocts a scam to sell nonexistent real estate to a local couple. To his dismay, some unpleasant former associates want in on the action. In the meantime, Nathan has become a "responsible man" and finds himself joining a kosher Boy Scout group. Scoutmaster Mervyn Spiller has himself concocted a seemingly legitimate scheme to import cheap scout uniforms from China. When Max falls for local woman Estelle, he begins to question his life of dirty dealings and looks for a better way, which Spiller's business deal may provide. Somewhere, somehow, amidst the chaos, Max and Nathan have to come to terms with each other.

"Wrapped up inside this debut novel about a shady salesman is a warm tale of father-son reconciliation," observed a reviewer in *Publishers Weekly. Booklist* contributor Misha Stone noted that "Schwarzschild's accomplished, no-nonsense prose captures one family's attempt at responsibility and reconciliation." *Entertainment Weekly* reviewer Melissa Rose Bernardo called *Responsible Men* a "marvelous debut novel." "From a complicated business deal to a teenager's first kiss, Schwarzschild works with the quiet authority of a master," concluded a *Kirkus Reviews* critic. "This is one terrific debut."

BIOGRAPHICAL AND CRITICAL SOURCES:

PERIODICALS

Booklist, January 1, 2005, Misha Stone, review of *Responsible Men,* p. 823.
Entertainment Weekly, April 8, 2005, Melissa Rose Bernardo, review of *Responsible Men,* p. 71.
Jewish News Weekly, May 6, 2005, Dan Pine, "Novelist Weighs Pros and Cons," profile of Edward Schwarzschild.
Kirkus Reviews, January 15, 2005, review of *Responsible Men,* p. 80.
Publishers Weekly, January 24, 2005, review of *Responsible Men,* p. 218.

ONLINE

Edward Schwarzschild Home Page, http://www.edwardschwarzschild.com (July 14, 2005).
State University of New York at Albany Web site, http://www.albany.edu/ (July 14, 2005), biography of Edward Schwarzschild.

*   *   *

SEIERSTAD, Åsne 1970-

PERSONAL: Born 1970, in Lillehammer, Norway; daughter of Dag Seierstad (a political scientist) and Froydis Guldahl (a writer). *Education:* Attended Oslo University and Moscow University.

ADDRESSES: Agent—c/o Author Mail, Virago Press, Brettenham House, Lancaster Place, London WC2E 7EN, England.

CAREER: Writer, television war correspondent, translator, and journalist.

WRITINGS:

With Their Backs to the Wall: Portraits of Serbia, Virago (London, England), 2000.

Bokhandleren i Kabul: et familiedrama, Cappelen (Oslo, Norway), 2002, translation by Ingrid Christopherson published as *The Bookseller of Kabul,* Little, Brown (Boston, MA), 2003.

Hundre og én dag: en reportasjereise, Cappelen (Oslo, Norway), 2003, translation by Ingrid Christopherson published as *A Hundred and One Days: A Baghdad Journal,* Virago (London, England), 2004.

Author of translations.

The Bookseller of Kabul has been translated more than two dozen languages.

SIDELIGHTS: Norwegian author Åsne Seierstad is a print and television journalist who is well known throughout her native Norway and the Scandinavian countries. Adept at several languages, including Chinese, Russian, and Spanish, she has been a translator and foreign-language reporter for a variety of Scandinavian newspapers. She has covered the Chechen war, the U.S. invasion of Iraq in 2003, the fall of Baghdad, and other conflicts in Serbia, Kosovo, and Afghanistan.

Hundre og én dag: en reportasjereise, published in English translation as *A Hundred and One Days: A Baghdad Journal* in 2004, covers the U.S. invasion of Iraq during the second Gulf War. "Her book focuses far less on the big, dramatic events than on the war's impact on ordinary Iraqis," noted Julie Wheelwright in the London *Independent,* adding that it portrays "the gut-wrenching tragedy of thousands who were—quite literally—caught in the crossfire." She talks to a grieving grandfather whose grandson was killed in a civilian massacre at the el Nasser market. A visit to a morgue results in photographs too graphic and too gruesome to be published. She tells about her translator, Aliya, who longs for Saddam Hussein's return and who fell into a sort of unresponsive state of numbness after the dictator was deposed. While dodging the sanitized view of the country provided by her official handlers, she manages to travel with a child psychologist to look at the war's effect on children. "While more ambitious narratives may provide more context," a *Publishers Weekly* reviewer noted, "this is a valuable impressionistic portrait." *Booklist* reviewer Kristine Huntley called the book "required reading for anyone who truly wants to delve into the complexities of life in Iraq under Saddam and during the war and its aftermath." A *Kirkus Reviews* contributor described Seierstad's reporting as "dispatches scorched by the flames of battle and delivered by Seierstad, to enormous effect, in tense, crisp language."

Bokhandleren i Kabul: et familiedrama, published in English translation as *The Bookseller of Kabul* in 2003, is Seierstad's acclaimed story of the life and household of patriarchal Afghani bookseller Sultan Khan. Seierstad first encountered Khan and his bookshop while she was covering Northern Alliance soldiers during the war in Afghanistan. She was intrigued by the presence of a bookseller in a fundamentalist Taliban country. After she and Khan became friends, he agreed to let her spend some time in his home to report on the status of life in Afghanistan during and after the Taliban regime. With Khan's youngest daughter as an interpreter, Seierstad spent four months living and observing Khan and his family.

In Seierstad's telling, Khan is a complex, often maddeningly contradictory man. Literate, well-traveled, and stoic in the face of adversity and opposition, Khan resolved to continue to sell books that preserve Afghan culture and ideas, even after several instances in which communists or the Taliban raided his shop and burned books deemed offensive or immoral. To preserve his stock, he carefully stashed hundreds of books in dozens of locations throughout Kabul. Yet, while waging a personal war against censorship, Khan upheld the harsh traditions of his homeland in his family life. Seierstad presents tellingly vivid accounts of his tyrannical hold over his household; how he took a sixteen-year-old second wife after his first wife, Sharifa, turned fifty; how Sharifa was expected to teach the new wife how to care for the master of the house; how youngest sister Leila was expected to give up her independence to serve as the household's unpaid perpetual servant; and how even Khan's sons had to bend to Khan's iron will, foregoing education and helping him run his bookselling business. Instead of a story about an enlightened man who championed the continued freedom of thought in a country that tried so hard to repress it, Seierstad found "a world of repression, dirt and crushed hopes, which in her view is symptomatic of the nation as a whole," commented Sheena Gurbakhash in *Asia Africa Intelligence Wire.* Even after the ouster of the repressive fundamentalist Taliban, in Afghanistan, women, in particular, still suffered in the stranglehold of tradition.

"Seierstad presents a vivid, intimate, yet frustrating picture of family life after the Taliban," commented *Library Journal* contributor Lucille M. Boone. The book "allows us a glimpse of Afghan life that transcends the daily news," commented Linda Simon in *World and I. Booklist* reviewer Ellen Loughran called *The Bookseller of Kabul* a "fascinating, thought-provoking look at Afghanistan," while a *Publishers Weekly* critic found it an "astounding portrait of a nation recovering from war, undergoing political flux and mired in misogyny and poverty." Carol Bere, writing in *Women's Review of Books,* concluded that, "whether fiction, nonfiction, or so-called immersion journalism, provocative works like *The Bookseller of Kabul* add to the growing body of literature that explores the situation of Afghan women from historical, social, and cultural perspectives."

BIOGRAPHICAL AND CRITICAL SOURCES:

PERIODICALS

Asia Africa Intelligence Wire, March 3, 2004, Sheena Gurbakhash, review of *The Bookseller of Kabul.*

Booklist, November 1, 2003, Ellen Loughran, review of *The Bookseller of Kabul,* p. 477; March 15, 2004, Kristine Huntley, review of *A Hundred and One Days: A Baghdad Journal,* p. 1261.

Bookseller, July 30, 2004, "A Booksellers' Hit," p. 15.

Contemporary Review, July, 2004, Karen Steele, "The Women behind Kabul's Bookseller," p. 54.

Entertainment Weekly, October 31, 2003, S.L. Allen, review of *The Bookseller of Kabul,* p. 78.

Independent (London, England), December 10, 2004, Julie Wheelwright, "Åsne Seierstad: Behind the Front Lines."

Kirkus Reviews, September 1, 2003, review of *The Bookseller of Kabul,* p. 1116; February 15, 2004, review of *A Hundred and One Days,* p. 220.

Library Journal, December, 2003, Lucille M. Boone, review of *The Bookseller of Kabul,* p. 148.

Mother Jones, May 12, 2005, Lisa Katayama, "A Hundred and One Days; An Interview with Åsne Seierstad."

New Statesman, September 1, 2003, Yvonne Ridley, review of *The Bookseller of Kabul,* p. 37.

Nordic Business Report, September 22, 2003, "Subject of Norwegian Book Considers Memoirs."

Publishers Weekly, September 29, 2003, review of *The Bookseller of Kabul,* p. 55; September 29, 2003, Edward Nawotka, "Sultan Rules the Roost: PW Talks with Åsne Seierstad"; November 22, 2004, John F. Baker, "Basic Books Publisher Liz Maguire Bought a New Book by the Norwegian Author of the Bestselling *Bookseller of Kabul,*" p. 11; March 14, 2005, review of *A Hundred and One Days,* p. 60.

School Library Journal, June, 2004, Jackie Gropman, review of *The Bookseller of Kabul,* p. 182.

Smithsonian, September, 2004, Eliot Marshall, review of *The Bookseller of Kabul,* p. 114.

Spectator, August 30, 2003, Matthew Leeming, review of *The Bookseller of Kabul,* p. 31.

Women's Review of Books, March, 2004, Carol Bere, review of *The Bookseller of Kabul,* p. 16.

World and I, December, 2003, Linda Simon, review of *The Bookseller of Kabul,* p. 235.*

*   *   *

SHANOWER, Eric James 1963-

PERSONAL: Born October 23, 1963, in Key West, FL; son of James Lowell and Karen Elizabeth (Hietanen) Shanower; partner of David Maxine (a record producer, musical theater historian, and artist). *Education:* Jo Kubert School of Cartoon and Graphic Art, graduated 1984.

ADDRESSES: Home—San Diego, CA. *Office*—Hungry Tiger Press, 5995 Dandridge Lane, Ste. 121, San Diego, CA 92115-6575.

CAREER: Independent artist, graphic novelist, cartoonist, and illustrator, 1984—. First Comics, letterer, inker, and illustrator, 1984-90, working on *Warp, Nexus, Badger,* and *Starslayer* comics; DC Comics, illustrator, 1985-90, letterer, penciler, inker, and illustrator, working on *Conqueror of the Barren Earth, Talent Showcase, Who's Who in the DC Universe, Prez: Smells like Teen President,* and others; Epic Comics, illustrator, 1990, working on *The Elsewhere Prince*; Dark Horse Comics, 1992-98, inker and illustrator working on *Dark Horse Presents, Medal of Honor, Star Wars: The Last Command, Harlan Ellison's Dream Corridor, King Tiger & Motorhead,* and others. Founder, with partner David Maxine, of Hungry Tiger Press, San Diego, CA, 1994. *Exhibitions:* Group exhibitions include *Queer Cartoons, A Different Light,* New York, NY, 1995; New Jersey State Council on the Arts Fellowship exhibition, 1996, 1997; and Jersey City Museum, Jersey City, NJ, 1998.

AWARDS, HONORS: Will Eisner Comics Industry Award for Best Writer/Artist, and named to NinthArt Lighthouse Award Roll of Honour for Best Bookshelf Comic, both 2001, both for *Age of Bronze: A Thousand Ships;* special guest at ComicCon International convention, San Diego, CA, 2002; Will Eisner Comics Industry Award for Best Writer/Artist, 2003, for *Age of Bronze* series.

WRITINGS:

GRAPHIC NOVELS; AND ILLUSTRATOR

The Enchanted Apples of Oz, First Comics (Chicago, IL), 1986.

The Secret Island of Oz, First Comics (Chicago, IL), 1986.

The Ice King of Oz, First Comics (Chicago, IL), 1987.

The Forgotten Forest of Oz, First Comics (Chicago, IL), 1988.

The Blue Witch of Oz, Dark Horse Comics (Milwaukie, OR), 1992.

The Giant Garden of Oz, Emerald City Press (New York, NY), 1993.

(With Ed Brubaker) *An Accidental Death,* Fantagraphics Books (Seattle, WA), 1993.

Age of Bronze: The Story of the Trojan War: A Thousand Ships (originally published in comic-book format), Image Comics (Orange, CA), 2001.

The Salt Sorcerer of Oz and Other Stories, Hungry Tiger Press (San Diego, CA), 2003.

Age of Bronze: The Story of the Trojan War: Sacrifice (originally published in comic-book format), Image Comics (Orange, CA), 2004.

ILLUSTRATOR

L. Frank Baum, *The Third Book of Oz: The Collected and Complete Queer Visitors from the Marvelous Land of Oz and the Woggle-Bug Book,* edited by Martin Williams, Armstrong State College Press, 1986, new edition, Buckethead Enterprises of Oz (Albuquerque, NM), 1989.

Virginia Wauchope-Bass and Robert Wauchope, *Invisible Inzi of Oz,* Buckethead Enterprises of Oz (Albuquerque, NM), 1993.

Rachel Cosgrove Payes, *The Wicked Witch of Oz,* International Wizard of Oz Club (Kinderhook, IL), 1993, new edition, Hungry Tiger Press (San Diego, CA), 1999.

(And editor) John R. Neill, *The Runaway in Oz,* Books of Wonder (New York, NY), 1995.

Jack Snow, *Spectral Snow: The Dark Fantasies of Jack Snow,* afterword by David Maxine, Hungry Tiger Press (San Diego, CA), 1996.

Bram Stoker, *Dracula's Guest,* Books of Wonder (New York, NY), 1997.

Edward Einhorn, *Paradox in Oz,* Hungry Tiger Press (San Diego, CA), 2000.

Eloise Jarvis McGraw, *The Rundelstone of Oz,* Hungry Tiger Press (San Diego, CA), 2001.

OTHER

Contributor of stories and illustrations to periodicals, including *Oziana, Baum Bugle, Oz Observer, Ozmapolitan, Bean Home Newsletter,* and others. Contributor of illustration to tribute anthology *Alan Moore: Portrait of an Extraordinary Gentleman,* Abiogenesis Press, 2003. Illustrator and writer for books and coloring books, magazines, non-sports trading cards (including *Wildstorms, Spawn,* and *WildC.A.T.s*), newsletters, apparel, cards, calendars, and catalogs.

WORK IN PROGRESS: Continuing work on *Age of Bronze* series.

SIDELIGHTS: American cartoonist, illustrator, and graphic novelist Eric James Shanower was interested in drawing, comics, and L. Frank Baum's "Wonderful Wizard of Oz" stories from an early age. His parents saw that he took art lessons as often as possible, and, in an online interview with Katherine Keller for *Sequential Tart,* he especially credited teacher Ed Moriarty for helping him develop his talent for drawing comics. He also said the original "Oz" illustrations by John R. Neill were "a factor impossible to underestimate in my attraction to the *Oz* books and as an influence on my career." In an online interview with Smoky Man for *Ultrazine,* Shanower named other influences on his art: the nineteenth-century illustrators Charles Dana Gibson, Maxfield Parish, and Alphonse Mucha, and the cartoonists Winsor McCay, Charles Burns, Milton Caniff, Dave Sim, Walt Kelly, Carl Barks, and others.

On graduation from high school, Shanower entered the Joe Kubert School of Cartoon and Graphic Art in Dover, New Jersey. He began working in the comics industry right after graduation, in 1984, and has since written and/or illustrated for most of the major American comics publishers as an independent artist.

Shanower is best known for his "Oz" comic-book series of graphic novels, written and illustrated between 1986 and 1991, which continue the stories written by Baum, and for his *Age of Bronze* comic-book series, an epic retelling of the Trojan War legends. As of December of 2003, issues 1-9 had been collected into a graphic novel, *Age of Bronze: A Thousand Ships.* Issues 10-18 of Volume 2, *Age of Bronze: Sacrifice* have also been completed. Shanower has also illustrated Oz books by other authors, bringing to new life stories written decades ago. A prolific illustrator, he has also contributed work to magazines and newsletters, advertisements, and other media.

Shanower told Smoky Man that he developed a desire to write and draw "Oz" books after his parents read *The Road to Oz* to him as a six year old. He told Keller that his interest in the stories was sparked by "the strange and exciting adventures, the unusual and grotesque characters, the child protagonists," and by Baum's "ability to gently lead the reader into impossible settings and make them absolutely believable."

The Forgotten Forest of Oz, Shanower's fourth graphic novel in his series continuing Baum's stories, brings Dorothy and her friends into a magical forest after the dryad Nelanthe has married a troll king and war has been declared against the forest wood nymphs. Gregory Walker, in a review for *Booklist,* called Shanower's art "striking" and commented that he has "produced stories closer to the Baum magic than previ-

ous efforts of stage, screen, or prose." In *The Giant Garden of Oz,* sixth in the series, Dorothy's Uncle Henry and Aunt Em find giant vegetables overtaking their garden, and Dorothy discovers that spells cast by the witch Old Magda are responsible for the behemoth crop. All turns out well in the end, however, and Dorothy befriends a cow named Imogene. Patricia A. Dollisch, in a review for *School Library Journal,* found the story line and character development "weak" and the whimsy "forced," although Don D'Ammassa, in *Science Fiction Chronicle,* noted that Shanower captures Baum's tone "reasonably well."

Shanower provided the illustrations for books about the "Oz" world by other authors. Rachel Cosgrove Payes's *The Wicked Witch of Oz,* her second "Oz" book, written half a century before Shanower's newly illustrated 1993 version. It introduces the Wicked Witch of the South, Singra, who wakes after a 100-year nap and plots to turn Dorothy into a piece of cheese. The Scarecrow and other familiar characters are in the story, but Payes also introduces Dorothy's new friends Percy the Giant White Rat and Leon the Neon, who is made from neon tubing. They hope to defeat Singra before she can carry out her plans.

Shanower also illustrated and edited John R. Neill's 1943 manuscript, *The Runaway in Oz,* Neill's fourth "Oz" story. The main character is Scraps, the rambunctious Patchwork Girl of Oz, who, after getting her feelings hurt by Queen Ozma, tries to run away from Oz. She needs a little help from her new friends Popla and Twinkler, though, especially when they encounter Fanny the Weather Witch. Dollisch, in a *School Library Journal* review, commented that the characters "have a great deal of trouble hanging onto the very thin plot," although Shanower does a "competent" job with the black-and-white illustrations.

When the residents of Oz begin aging in Edward Einhorn's *Paradox in Oz,* Ozma consults Glinda the good witch and then begins her adventures to restore the magical land to youth as she travels on the back of the Parrot-Ox Tempus, a sort of flying time machine. She uncovers a secret answer in the witch Mombi and the Man Who Lives Backwards. Dollisch, in *School Library Journal,* described Tempus as "chock-full of personality," the writing as "crisp," and Shanower's art as "charming."

Shanower told Keller that he was inspired to embark on the *Age of Bronze* comic-book series in 1991, after reading the chapter on Troy in Barbara Tuchman's *The*

March of Folly: From Troy to Vietnam. In addition, he had read Greek mythology as a student and had enjoyed Mary Renault's retellings of the Theseus story in the late 1980s, as well as Gore Vidal's historical novels. He had originally planned to do a comic set in ancient Egypt, but when his interest was sparked by the Trojan War, he changed his focus. It took seven years to research and promote the *Age of Bronze* comics, and the first installment appeared in 1998.

In the interview with Keller, Shanower said: "One of the reasons I'm attracted to the Trojan War is because of the range of human drama and human interaction. Anything that happens in anybody's life happens in this story, every situation, every emotion is on display to maximum effect." Shanower remarked that his goal with the series is to show every detail with as much current archaeological accuracy as possible and to blend the many, often conflicting, versions of the Trojan War legend into one seamless version. He also strives to reveal the human concerns that are in conflict and to explore why the characters do what they do. His primary sources for the comic are Homer's *Iliad*, classical Greek and Roman texts, medieval European sources, and Shakespeare's *Troilus and Cressida.* He also relies on archaeological data from ancient Mycenae, Knossos, Pylos, and Troy. His research has been so thorough that he even has college professors advising him on, for example, the appearance of ships from the bronze age. Each issue takes about three months to complete.

The first nine issues of the comic-book series were published together as the Eisner Award-winning graphic novel *Age of Bronze: A Thousand Ships.* The story opens as the young man Paris leaves home to compete in the games at Troy. When he wins the games it is revealed that he is the son of King Priam. The story of the milk-white bull, the kidnapping of Helen, the start of the war, and the introduction of the young Achilles follow. Francisca Goldsmith, of *Booklist,* was pleased with the book's appended material—a genealogy chart, glossary, explanations of variant spelling, and lengthy bibliography. She also thought Shanower's black-and-white artwork "carries the story." A *Publishers Weekly* contributor was equally pleased with Shanower's research and called the result "a fantastically rich narrative" with settings that "look like Bronze Age artifacts" and drawings that evoke "woodcuts and classical paintings."

Kat Kan commented on the sexual element in the *Age of Bronze* comic-book series in a review for *Voice of*

Youth Advocates, saying that "Shanower's tale is very sensual; he doesn't shy away from portraying people's physical lust, managing to convey their almost palpable feelings without graphic detail." In the interview with Keller, Shanower commented on the sexual aspect: "You can't get away from the sex in the Trojan War. I mean, that's why the war happened. . . . I had to show that. It's the human dimension." Sex continues its importance in further installments in the comic-book series, collected in book form as *Age of Bronze: Sacrifice.* Shanower chooses to follow a version of the epic that depicts Achilles and Patroklus as gay lovers before Patroklus is killed by the Trojans, causing Achilles to seek vengeance. In issue 14, they share a first kiss, and Achilles is surprised by what he feels.

Randy Lander, in an online review for the *Fourth Rail,* concluded that *Age of Bronze* "remains a unique book in the industry, both in terms of the subject matter it tackles and the way that the creator handles it." Don MacPherson, also in the *Fourth Rail,* wrote that Shanower's "soft, realistic artwork, meticulous research and remarkable level of accessibility make for a thoroughly satisfying read. . . . This book could easily have been a stilted, yawn-inducing series, but there's a sense of fun, adventure and intelligence to it instead." Classical archaeology professor John G. Younger, in a review for *Archeology,* praised Shanower's research and accurate archaeological detail, down to the artist's decision to make the Trojans an Anatolian people in keeping with findings made during the 1990s excavation at the site of Troy. Younger called the research "almost impeccable," concluding: "Shanower's comic book series is destined, I think, to become a staple in many college courses. Besides being beautifully drawn and intelligently, even intellectually, composed, it is archaeologically accurate—by those qualities it's better than any film I've ever seen on Bronze Age Greece. . . . I have already spent hours pondering some of Shanower's more interesting archaeological choices, and I am eager to be challenged by those yet to come."

In an interview with Michael Cart for *Booklist,* Shanower said he believes comics "are as valid an aesthetic experience as any other art form. What the creator brings to the reader to observe can be as rich and fulfilling as any other aesthetic experience." He continued, "There are some absolute gems that if folks don't experience, their lives will be less rich."

BIOGRAPHICAL AND CRITICAL SOURCES:

PERIODICALS

Archaeology, September, 2001, John G. Younger, "Hoppin' Hittites, Hector! A Comic Book Series Revisits the Trojan War," p. 72.

Booklist, April 1, 1989, Gregory Walker, review of *The Forgotten Forest of Oz,* p. 1372; September 15, 2001, Francisca Goldsmith, review of *Age of Bronze: A Thousand Ships,* p. 214; December 15, 2002, Michael Cart, "Carte Blanche: Got Graphic?," p. 750.

Locus, August, 1993, Charles N. Brown and Scott Winnett, review of *The Giant Garden of Oz,* p. 47.

Publishers Weekly, September 3, 2001, review of *Age of Bronze: A Thousand Ships,* p. 68; September 24, 2001, Douglas Wolk, review of *Age of Bronze* series, p. 26.

School Library Journal, October, 1993, Patricia A. Dollisch, review of *The Giant Garden of Oz,* p. 130; October 5, 1995, Patricia A. Dollisch, review of *The Runaway in Oz,* p. 138; August, 2000, Patricia A. Dollisch, review of *Paradox in Oz,* p. 180.

Science Fiction Chronicle, October, 1993, Don D'Ammassa, review of *The Giant Garden of Oz,* p. 38.

Voice of Youth Advocates, February, 2002, Kat Kan, review of *Age of Bronze: A Thousand Ships,* pp. 430-431.

Wilson Library Bulletin, February, 1988, Patty Campbell, review of *The Ice King of Oz,* p. 81.

ONLINE

Age of Bronze Home Page, http://age-of-bronze.com/ (December 9, 2003), "Issues," "Our Story So Far," "Books."

Eric Shanower Official Home Page, http://www.eric shanower.com (October 2, 2003).

Flooby, http://www.flooby.com/ (August 19, 2003), review of *Age of Bronze,* issues 1 and 2.

Fourth Rail, http://www.thefourthrail.com/ (July 31, 2002), Don MacPherson, review of *Age of Bronze,* issue 13 and *Age of Bronze: Behind the Scenes,* issue 1; (August 21, 2002) Randy Lander, review of *Age of Bronze,* issue 14.

Hollywood Comics Web site, http://www.hollywood comics.com/ (August 19, 2003) "Eric Shanower."

Hungry Tiger Press Web site, http://www.hungrytiger press.com/ (August 19, 2003).

SD Buzz: The Ultimate Gay Guide to San Diego, http://www.sdbuzz.com/ (August 19, 2003), J. Nathaniel Moore, "Comics Come of Age."

Sequential Tart, http://www.sequentialtart.com/ (August 19, 2003) Katherine Keller, "The Wizard of Bronze: An Epic Interview with Eric Shanower."

Ultrazine, http://www.ultrazine.org/ (August 19, 2003), Smoky Man, "An Interview with Eric Shanower: Be Charmed by Myth."*

*   *   *

SHAW, David 1943-2005

OBITUARY NOTICE—See index for *CA* sketch: Born January 4, 1943, in Dayton, OH; died of complications from a brain tumor, August 1, 2005, in Los Angeles, CA. Journalist, critic, and author. Shaw was a Pulitzer Prize-winning media critic and reporter for the *Los Angeles Times.* Interested in journalism from a young age, he first started writing for his high school newspaper and had his first reporting job—with the Huntington Park, California, *Daily Signal*—while still attending the University of California at Los Angeles. After graduating in 1965, he was a feature writer based in Long Beach, California, for two years before joining the *Los Angeles Times* in 1968. During his first few years there, Shaw was a feature writer for the paper. His career took a notable turn when his editor, William F. Thomas, selected him to be the newspaper's media critic. Thomas believed that circulation for the *Los Angeles Times* was declining because readers were losing trust in its reporting. He assigned Shaw to criticize not only other papers and media outlets, but his own paper as well. Thus the public would hopefully regain confidence that the paper was trying to report fairly on issues. With the backing of his editor, Shaw took the job to heart, and felt free to pick apart the work of his fellow journalists for their sloppy research and biased reporting. Naturally, this cost him many friends, but Shaw's articles did, indeed, prove effective in winning readers. After working many years as media critic and winning a 1991 Pulitzer Prize, Shaw gained popularity with a food-and-wine column he began in 2002 called "Matters of Taste." The column shared his knowledge of and love for fine cuisine and wines in Los Angeles and around the world. In addition to his newspaper writings, Shaw was the author of several books, including *Journalism Today: A Changing Press for a Changing America* (1977), *Press Watch: A Provocative Look at How Newspapers Report the News* (1984), and *The Pleasure Police: How Bluenose Busybodies and Lily-Livered Alarmists Are Taking All the Fun out of Life* (1996).

OBITUARIES AND OTHER SOURCES:

PERIODICALS

Chicago Tribune, August 4, 2005, section 3, p. 8.
Los Angeles Times, August 2, 2005, p. B8.
New York Times, August 3, 2005, p. C17.
Washington Post, August 4, 2005, p. B7.

*   *   *

SHELLENBARGER, Sue

PERSONAL: Married (marriage ended). *Hobbies and other interests:* Riding all-terrain vehicles.

ADDRESSES: Office—Career Journal, P.O. Box 300, Princeton, NJ 08543. *E-mail*—sue.shellenbarger@wsj.com.

CAREER: Writer. *Wall Street Journal,* Chicago bureau chief, "Work & Family" columnist, 1991—. Associated Press, financial markets columnist; "Work & Family" (talk-radio program), host.

AWARDS, HONORS: Working Mother Twenty-five citation, *Working Woman* magazine; named among Twenty-five Most Influential Working Mothers by *Working Mother* magazine; Missouri Lifestyle Journalism Award, 2000; National Society of Newspaper Columnists award, 2000; Darrell Sifford Memorial Prize in Journalism; Emma Award; Clarion Award.

WRITINGS:

Work & Family: Essays from the "Work & Family" Column of the Wall Street Journal, Ballantine Books (New York, NY), 1999.

The Breaking Point: How Female Midlife Crisis Is Transforming Today's Women, Henry Holt (New York, NY), 2005.

Parenting magazine, contributing editor.

SIDELIGHTS: Sue Shellenbarger is best known for the "Work & Family" column she has contributed to the *Wall Street Journal* since 1991. Her first book, *Work & Family: Essays from the "Work & Family" Column of the Wall Street Journal,* contains selections from the first decade of Shellenbarger's column. "The theme of how to satisfy competing demands runs through all these thoughtful essays," stated a *Publishers Weekly* reviewer, adding that "these short, sometimes pointed pieces only begin to address the complexities of working families in the postindustrial economy." "Using personal profiles of people in the workplace," a biographer for the *Wall Street Journal Executive Career Site* noted, "Shellenbarger illustrates the issues Americans face in trying to balance their jobs and their home lives."

Some of those issues have to do with the ability of workers to keep those two facets of their lives distinct. Shellenbarger, however, sees the two converging. In an interview with *LiNE Zine* contributor Brook Manville, Shellenbarger said: "I think one big trend is simply the erosion of boundaries between work and family. Technology is assisting this of course with increased use of cell phones and computer technology that allows us to work anytime, anywhere." A key part of this trend lies in the way that online learning allows individuals to blur the lines between their professional and personal lives. "Learning professionals need to think of ways to integrate learning into family lifestyles and look for ways to provide families with some of the same learning opportunities that they are providing to the worker," Shellenbarger told Manville. "And to think in the holistic terms that learning is a value for the family and not just the individual."

Shellenbarger's second book, *The Breaking Point: How Female Midlife Crisis Is Transforming Today's Women,* also draws on her own experience. The motivating factors behind the book, wrote Edward M. Eveld in the *Kansas City Star,* were Shellenbarger's father's death, the end of her marriage, and the maturing of her children. She responded to the stress by turning to riding all-terrain vehicles (ATVs) and then writing about her experiences in the *Wall Street Journal*. "Shellenbarger wrote a column about her ride on the wild side," explained Eveld, "and women bombarded her with messages about their own midlife changes, some turbulent and provoked by circumstances, others quiet and provoked by introspection. She then did her own study of the topic and wrote a book." As Shellenbarger told *Library Journal* interviewer Lynne Maxwell, "Women long overloaded by juggling work and family are at risk." She added, "So are those who carry a lot of emotional baggage from childhood. In the presence of any or several of these circumstances, a woman's inborn drive toward wholeness can easily erupt into crisis."

The Breaking Point is based on interviews Shellenbarger conducted with fifty different women who had gone through midlife transitions of one kind or another. "Of the fifty women in her study," Eveld explained, "she counted thirteen new spouses or partners. She also counted twenty new careers, fourteen new hobbies and fifteen new religious pursuits, plus sixteen women who took up adventure travel and eight who threw themselves into extreme sports." "Contrary to popular wisdom," a *Publishers Weekly* contributor observed, "Shellenbarger says 'the vital juices of joy, sexuality, and self-discovery are bubbling within, more powerfully and compellingly than ever' at midlife." Shellenbarger also identified six different archetypes, each of which may use any one of six different approaches to crisis. "The archetypes came to me in a sort of epiphany," she told Maxwell. "I realized each woman had experienced one of a handful of driving forces that would be readily understandable to anyone living in our culture." In a *Library Journal* review of the book, Maxwell stated, "This powerful, eminently readable book will answer questions women may have about why they feel compelled to forge new life paths with the onset of middle age."

BIOGRAPHICAL AND CRITICAL SOURCES:

PERIODICALS

Booklist, March 15, 1999, David Rouse, review of *Work & Family: Essays from the "Work & Family" Column of the Wall Street Journal,* p. 1266.

Kansas City Star, April 18, 2005, Edward M. Eveld, review of *The Breaking Point: How Female Midlife Crisis Is Transforming Today's Women.*

Library Journal, December 1, 2004, Barbara Hoffert, review of *The Breaking Point,* p. 92; March 1, 2005, Lynne F. Maxwell, review of *The Breaking Point,* p. 101; March 15, 2005, Lynne F. Maxwell, "Q&A: Sue Shellenbarger," p. 100.

People, May 30, 2005, review of *The Breaking Point,* p. 45.

Publishers Weekly, February 22, 1999, review of *Work & Family,* p. 73; March 7, 2005, review of *The Breaking Point,* p. 62.

ONLINE

LiNE Zine, http://www.linezine.com/ (June 25, 2003), Brook Manville, "Weighing the Balance: An Interview with Sue Shellenbarger, *Wall Street Journal*'s 'Work & Family' Columnist" (June 25, 2005).

Wall Street Journal Executive Career Web site, http://www.careerjournal.com/ (June 25, 2005), biography of Sue Shellenbarger.*

*   *   *

SHELTON, Sandi Kahn

PERSONAL: Born in Jacksonville, FL; married Jim Shelton (a reporter); children: three. *Education:* Attended University of California, Santa Barbara; graduated from Southern Connecticut State College.

ADDRESSES: Office—New Haven Register, 40 Sargent Dr., New Haven, CT 06511.

CAREER: Writer. *New Haven Register,* New Haven, CT, humor columnist, 1987—; *Working Mother* magazine, 1989—.

AWARDS, HONORS: Best local column award, New England Associated Press, 1993.

WRITINGS:

You Might as Well Laugh: Surviving the Joys of Parenthood, Bancroft Press (Baltimore, MD), 1997.

Sleeping through the Night—and Other Lies, St. Martin's Press (New York, NY), 1999.

Preschool Confidential, St. Martin's Press (New York, NY), 2001.

What Comes after Crazy (novel), Shaye Areheart Books (New York, NY), 2005.

SIDELIGHTS: Since the late 1980s Sandi Kahn Shelton has written a humor column for the *New Haven Register* on the mixed blessings of parenthood. Her first three books, *You Might as Well Laugh: Surviving the Joys of Parenthood, Sleeping through the Night—and Other Lies,* and *Preschool Confidential,* all deal with the problems parents have to face while caring for young children. "With a breezy style that belies a sophisticated wit, Shelton . . . exaggerates daily life with a baby, but only just a little," wrote a *Publishers Weekly* contributor in a review of *Sleeping through the Night—and Other Lies.* The reviewer added that "readers will need to pay attention to realize when she crosses the line from vaguely absurd reality to hyperbole." Commenting on *Preschool Confidential, Library Journal* contributor Annette V. Janes wrote that the book is "a refreshing look at child rearing, written in short sections that can be read in five to ten minutes."

What Comes after Crazy is Shelton's first foray into fiction. The novel tells the story of Maz Lombard, a woman chasing normalcy after surviving a childhood under the influence of a sex-crazed carnival-fortune-teller mother. Maz's attempts to give her two daughters, ten-year-old Hope and younger sister Abbie, a normal childhod growing up are thwarted by her cheating ex-husband Lenny (recently returned from a year-long stay in New Mexico following an affair with his daughter's nursery-school teacher), and her manic-depressive mother Lucille—now beginning her sixth marriage—who insists on running Maz's life for her. Adding to the confusion are Maz's shy attempts to return to dating, first with a naturopathic doctor, and then with a much younger graduate student. She is also plagued by the boredom and lack of fulfillment stemming from her job as a baker of health-food bread. "When Lenny and Madame Lucille kidnap Hope and whisk her away to Santa Fe," a *Publishers Weekly* critic observed, "Maz realizes she must once and for all find the courage to defy her past in order to protect her future."

Critics acknowledged Shelton's accomplishment in *What Comes after Crazy,* praising her grasp of characterization and the sense of humor revealed in her fiction. "Shelton, author of three parenting books, has a good touch with mother/daughter conflicts and a strong sense of the ambiguities of friendships," noted a *Kirkus Reviews* contributor. "Her Maz is a sympathetic character not in spite of but because of her self-acknowledged flaws." *Library Journal* reviewer Shelley Mosley wrote that "this remarkable fiction debut by the author of several parenting books is both hilarious and poignant." *Booklist* contributor Kristine Huntley concluded, "Shelton's lively novel is perfect for readers who enjoy the antics of quirky characters."

BIOGRAPHICAL AND CRITICAL SOURCES:

PERIODICALS

Booklist, March 1, 2005, Kristine Huntley, review of *What Comes after Crazy,* p. 1139.

Kirkus Reviews, January 1, 2005, review of *What Comes after Crazy,* p. 19.

Library Journal, April 15, 2001, Annette V. Janes, review of *Preschool Confidential,* p. 126; February 15, 2005, Shelley Mosley, review of *What Comes after Crazy,* p. 121.

People, April 11, 2005, review of *What Comes after Crazy,* p. 53.

Publishers Weekly, April 5, 1999, review of *Sleeping through the Night—and Other Lies,* p. 233; February 7, 2005, review of *What Comes after Crazy,* p. 43.*

*   *   *

SHIELDS, Brooke 1965-

PERSONAL: Born May 31, 1965, in New York, NY; daughter of Francis Alexander (a business executive) and Maria Theresia (a manager; maiden name, Schmon) Shields; married Andre Agassi (a professional tennis player; divorced); married Chris Henchy (a television comedy writer), 2001; children (second marriage): Rowan Francis Henchy. *Education:* Princeton University, B.A. (French literature; with honors), 1988.

ADDRESSES: Agent—c/o Kassie Evashevski, Brillstein-Grey Management, 9150 Wilshire Blvd., Ste. 350, Beverly Hills, CA 90212.

CAREER: Writer, actor, television producer, fashion model, entertainer, and public speaker. *Suddenly Susan* (television series), producer, 1996-2000. Actor in motion pictures, including *Communion* (also released as *Alice Sweet Alice*), Harristown Funding, 1976; *King of the Gypsies,* Dino De Laurentis Productions, 1978; *Pretty Baby,* Paramount Pictures, 1978; *Tilt,* Warner Brothers, 1979; *Wanda Nevada,* Hayward-Fonda Productions, 1979; *Just You and Me, Kid,* Columbia Pictures Corporation, 1979; *The Blue Lagoon,* Columbia, 1980; *Endless Love,* PolyGram Filmed Entertainment, 1981; *Sahara,* Cannon Group, 1983; *Wet Gold,* VCL Communications, 1984; *Speed Zone!* (also released as *Cannonball Fever*), Entcorp Communications, 1989; *Brenda Starr,* New World Pictures, 1989; *Backstreet Dreams* (also released as *Backstreet Strays*), Vidmark Entertainment, 1990; *Running Wild* (also released as *Born Wild*), Columbia TriStar Home Video, 1992; *Freaked* (also released as *Hideous Mutant Freekz*), Tommy, 1993; *The Seventh Floor,* Portman Productions, 1994; *Freeway,* August Entertainment, 1996; *The Almost Perfect Bank Robbery,* Hearst Entertainment Productions, 1996; *The Misadventures of Margaret* (also released as *Folies de Margaret*), Granada Productions, 1998; *The Weekend,* Granada Film Productions, 1999; *Black and White,* Bigel/Mailer Films, 1999; *The Bachelor,* New Line Cinema, 1999; *After Sex,* Miracle Entertainment, 2000; *Mariti in Affitto* (also released as *Rent-a-Husband*), Senza Pictures, 2004; (voice) *The Easter Egg Adventure,* Funline Animation, 2005; and *Bob the Butler,* Park Entertainment, 2005.

Actor in television films, including *After the Fall,* Gilbert Cates Productions, 1974; *The Prince of Central Park,* Lorimar Productions, 1977; *The Diamond Trap,* Columbia Pictures Television, 1988; *I Can Make You Love Me* (also released as *Stalking Laura*), Franke Abatemarco Productions, 1993; *Un amore Americano* (also released as *An American Love,* Unione Cinematografica, 1994; *Nothing Lasts Forever* (miniseries), Gerber/ITC Entertainment Group, 1995; *What Makes a Family,* Columbia/TriStar Television, 2001; *Widows* (miniseries), ABC-Greengrass Productions, 2002; (voice) *Miss Spider's Sunny Patch Kids,* Nelvana Limited, 2003; and *Gone but Not Forgotten,* Larry Levinson Productions, 2004.

Actor on television series, including *Suddenly Susan,* Warner Brothers Television, 1996-2000, and *That '70s Show,* Carsey-Werner-Mandelbach Productions, 2004,

and episodes, including: "Leaping of the Shrew—September 27, 1956," *Quantum Leap,* Universal TV, 1992; "The Front," *The Simpsons,* Twentieth Century-Fox Television, 1993; "Came the Dawn," *Tales from the Crypt,* Home Box Office (HBO), 1993; "The One After the Superbowl," *Friends,* Warner Brothers Television, 1996; "The Book," *The Larry Sanders Show,* Columbia Pictures Television, 1997; "Erlene and Boo," *Just Shoot Me,* Universal Network Television, 2001; (voice) "Future Ex-Wife," *Gary the Rat,* Grammnet Productions, 2003; and "Poison Ivy," *I'm with Her,* American Broadcasting Company (ABC), 2004.

Appeared as herself in television productions, including *The Fifty-first Annual Academy Awards,* ABC, 1979; *Circus of the Stars No. 4,* Columbia Broadcasting System, Inc. (CBS), 1979; *Men Who Rate a Ten,* 1980; *Bob Hope for President,* National Broadcasting Company (NBC), 1980; *Circus of the Stars No. 5,* CBS, 1980; *The Bob Hope Christmas Special* (also released as *The Bob Hope Christmas Show and All-Star Comedy Special*), NBC, 1980; *The Bob Hope Anniversary Show,* NBC, 1981; *The Fifty-third Academy Awards,* ABC, 1981; *Spring Fling of Glamour and Comedy* (also released as *Bob Hope's Spring Fling of Glamour and Comedy*), NBC, 1981; *All-Star Salute to Mother's Day,* NBC, 1981; *Bob Hope's All-Start Comedy Birthday Party from West Point,* NBC, 1981; *Circus of the Stars No. 6,* CBS, 1981; *The Bob Hope Christmas Special,* NBC, 1981; *Hollywood's Children,* Wombat Productions, Inc., 1982; *Bob Hope's Women I Love: Beautiful but Funny,* NBC, 1982; *Night of 100 Stars,* ABC, 1982; *Bob Hope's All-Star Birthday Party at Annapolis,* NBC, 1982; *Star-Studded Spoof of the New TV Season, G-Rated, with Glamour, Glitter, and Gags,* NBC, 1982; *Circus of the Stars No. 7,* CBS, 1982; *Circus of the Stars No. 8,* CBS, 1983; *Salute to Lady Liberty,* CBS, 1984; *Bob Hope's USO Christmas in Beirut,* NBC, 1984; *Olympic Gala,* NHK, 1984; *Bob Hope's Unrehearsed Antics of the Stars,* NBC, 1984; *Circus of the Stars No. 9,* CBS, 1984; *Joan Rivers and Friends Salute Heidi Abromowitz,* Rivers-Rosenberg Productions, 1985; *The Bob Hope Christmas Show,* NBC, 1985; *Bob Hope's High-Flying Birthday,* NBC, 1986; *Change of Heart,* Discovery Channel, 1987; *Bob Hope's Winterfest Christmas Show,* NBC, 1987; *Fourteenth Annual People's Choice Awards,* CBS, 1988; *Voices That Care,* Flattery Yukich, Inc., 1991; *Yellow Ribbon Party* (also released as *Bob Hope's Yellow Ribbon Celebration*), NBC, 1991; *Desperately Seeking Roger,* Wonderdog Productions, 1991; *Legends of the West,* Vidmark Entertainment, 1992; *Scratch the*

Surface, Midred Productions, 1997; *Christmas in Washington,* 1998; *AFI's 100 Years . . . 100 Movies,* Smith-Hemion Productions, 1998; *Junket Whore,* 1998; *Fifth Annual Screen Actors Guild Awards,* Jeff Margolis Productions, 1998; *Massholes,* Media Financial Incorporated, 2000; *The Twenty-eigth Annual American Music Awards,* Dick Clark Productions, 2001; *Intimate Portrait: Brooke Shields,* Greif Company, 2001; *Fear No More: Stop Violence against Women,* 2002; *100 Years of Hope and Humor,* Hope Enterprises/Gary Smith Company, 2003; *Mayor of the Sunset Strip,* Caldera Productions, 2003; *Broadway on Broadway,* NBC, 2004; *Macy's Thanksgiving Day Parade,* NBC, 2004; *The Outsider,* Green Room Films, 2005; and *A&E Biography: Brook Shields,* A&E, 2005. Performer in stage productions, including *The Vagina Monologues, Cabaret, Chicago,* and *Wonderful Town.* Guest on television shows *The View, Late Show with David Letterman, The Tonight Show with Jay Leno, The Rosie O'Donnell Show, The Tonight Show Starring Johnny Carson, The Muppet Show,* and *The Barbara Walters Special.*

AWARDS, HONORS: People's Choice Award and Golden Globe Award nomination for best actress in a comedy series, both for *Suddenly Susan.*

WRITINGS:

The Brooke Book, Pocket Books (New York, NY), 1978.

On Your Own, Villard Books (New York, NY), 1985.

(Author of foreword) Bobbi Brown and Annemarie Iverson, *Bobbi Brown Teenage Beauty: Everything You Need to Look Pretty, Natural, Sexy, & Awesome,* Cliff Street Books (New York, NY), 2000.

Down Came the Rain: My Journey through Postpartum Depression (biography), Hyperion (New York, NY), 2005.

SIDELIGHTS: Actor and author Brooke Shields is an award-winning performer in films, on stage, and on television. She has been a high-demand fashion model, a television producer, and frequent celebrity guest on a variety of television programs and specials. She has expressed a keen interest in children's issues and lends her charitable support to the cause of children's welfare and education, noted a biographer on the *Penguin UK* Web site.

Shields's career in front of the camera began early in her life, propelled by her mother and manager, Teri Shields, herself an actress. Before she was a year old, Shields portrayed the "Ivory Snow baby," the cherubic infant that appeared on boxes of the popular household detergent. This role led to Shields being called "the most beautiful baby in the world," noted Sandra Brennan in a biography of Shields on the *Yahoo! Movies* Web site. In great demand as an advertising model, Shields continued working in support of a variety of products during her early childhood.

Her feature film debut came with *Alice Sweet Alice* in 1976, but she ascended to genuine stardom with her role in the controversial *Pretty Baby.* In that movie, Shields stars as a teenage prostitute who becomes the Lolita-like obsession of an older man. Teri Shields was criticized for allowing her daughter to take on such a provocative role, but "the general consensus was that Shields was not exploited in the film," Brennan noted. Much of Shields's professional work in the 1970s and 1980s found her in the "precarious position of simultaneously being idolized as a late-seventies icon of adolescent wholesome virginal innocence and being constantly photographed in manners verging on the mildly pornographic," Brennan observed. A racy ad for Calvin Klein jeans and a starring role alongside teen idol Christopher Atkins in the ostensibly innocuous but ultimately titillating film *Blue Lagoon* fueled this dualism. While not working in film, Shields remained in front of the cameras as a highly sought-after fashion model throughout her teens.

After appearing in director Franco Zeffirelli's 1981 teen romance film *Endless Love,* Shields decided to commence her formal education. She became a student at Princeton University, where, as Brennan reported, she majored in French literature and developed an interest in theatre work. She graduated from Princeton with honors.

Throughout the 1980s and early 1990s Shields was a frequent guest on television programs, including numerous Bob Hope specials, *Circus of the Stars,* and other celebrity-driven presentations. She even appeared as an animated version of herself on the popular program *The Simpsons.* She also frequently appeared on prominent television talk shows such as *Late Show with David Letterman* and *The Tonight Show with Jay Leno.* A marriage to—and subsequent divorce from—volatile tennis champion Andre Agassi fueled her celebrity status.

In 1996, Shields starred in the NBC television situation comedy *Suddenly Susan.* She played the title character, a magazine writer who left her rich fiancée, Kip, at the altar. Susan's work life is complicated by the fact that Kip's brother, Jack, is Susan's boss at *The Gate,* a trendy publication in San Francisco. Over its four-year run, the show followed Susan as she coped with being a single professional, interacted with her coworkers, and rebuilt her romantic life. In addition, the show returned Shields to prominence as an actor and gave her experience as a producer. She has also became a performer on the Broadway stage in productions such as *Chicago, The Vagina Monologues,* and *Cabaret.*

In 2001, Shields married television comedy writer Chris Henchy. In 2003, she took on what she considered her most important role: that of mother to daughter Rowan Francis Henchy. In what appeared to be a perfect personal and professional life, however, deep trouble loomed. During "the first months after Rowan's birth, Brooke struggled with thoughts of suicide and felt completely unable to bond with her baby," reported Kate Coyne in *Good Housekeeping.* A "depression that terrified her" took control almost immediately after her daughter's birth, Coyne noted. "But her determination to muddle through initially prevented her from asking for help," according to Coyne.

Shields did eventually seek help and was diagnosed with and treated for severe postpartum depression and anxiety. She recounts her experience in *Down Came the Rain: My Journey through Postpartum Depression.* Though Shields was confused by the feelings of depression and alienation, she assumed they would pass as she became more attached to her daughter. However, the negative emotions did not go away; they intensified to include guilt and anxiety. Even when Rowan was brought to her to nurse, Shields states that she felt her baby was a stranger, that she had no attachment to her. "Shields pulls no punches in describing her profound detachment from her child," observed a contributor to *Kirkus Reviews.* "She had no desire to pick up or care for Rowan, she admits; what she wanted was to run away." Treatment with Paxil, an anti-depression medication, helped some, but her decision to abruptly stop taking the drug caused more problems. Eventually, Shields regained control of her emotions through a combination of medication and therapy, and forged the deepest of maternal bonds with her daughter. "This brave memoir doesn't shy away from Shields's most difficult moments, including her suicidal thoughts, clearly showing the despair postpartum depression can wreak," commented a *Publishers Weekly* reviewer. To assist others in a similar situation, Shields' book also contains lists of resources, including other books, telephone hotlines, and Web sites.

BIOGRAPHICAL AND CRITICAL SOURCES:

BOOKS

Shields, Brooke, *Down Came the Rain: My Journey through Postpartum Depression,* Hyperion (New York, NY), 2005.

PERIODICALS

Good Housekeeping, May, 2005, Kate Coyne, "Brooke Shields Back from the Brink: After Having Her Baby, She Fell Apart," p. 174.
Kirkus Reviews, March 1, 2005, review of *Down Came the Rain: My Journey through Postpartum Depression,* p. 281.
Publishers Weekly, February 28, 2005, review of *Down Came the Rain,* p. 48.

ONLINE

Internet Movie Database, http://www.imdb.com/ (July 14, 2005), Brooke Shields filmography.
Penguin UK Web site, http://www.penguin.co.uk/ (July 14, 2005), biography of Brooke Shields.*

* * *

SINGLETON, Linda Joy 1957-
(L.J. Singleton, Jamie Suzanne, a house pseudonym)

PERSONAL: Born October 29, 1957; daughter of Edwin D. (a computer technician) and Nina Jean (a square-dance caller; maiden name, Lowes) Emburg; married Corey L. Swaine, 1975 (divorced, 1980); married David G. Singleton (a crane operator), January 2, 1982; children: (second marriage) Melissa, Andrew. *Education:* Telephone Company, Sacramento, CA, operator, 1975, word processor, 1975-82, staff clerk, 1982. *Politics:* Democrat. *Hobbies and other interests:* Square dancing, boating, swimming, walking, reading, collecting series books, cats.

ADDRESSES: Home—P.O. Box 155, Burson, CA 95225. *Agent*—Pesha Rubinstein, 1392 Rugby Rd., Teaneck, NJ 07666. *E-mail*—ljscheer@inreach.com.

CAREER:

MEMBER: Romance Writers of America, Society of Children's Book Writers and Illustrators, Young Adult Writers Network, Sisters in Crime.

AWARDS, HONORS: Romance Writers of America's Silver Diary Award; HOLT Contest finalist; first-place winner, MARA Contest; Young Adult Library Association Quick-Pick Choice, 2001, for "Regeneration" series; Eppie Award for best children book, 2003, for *Twin Again.*

WRITINGS:

Almost Twins, Willowisp Press, 1991.
Opposites Attract ("Sweet Dreams" series), Bantam (New York, NY), 1991.
(As Jamie Suzanne) *Barnyard Battle* ("Sweet Valley Twins" series), Bantam (New York, NY), 1992.
Almost Perfect ("Sweet Dreams" series), Bantam (New York, NY), 1992.
Love to Spare ("Sweet Dreams" series), Bantam (New York, NY), 1993.
Deep in My Heart ("Sweet Dreams" series), Bantam (New York, NY), 1994.
The Saturday Night Bash ("Pick Your Own Dream Date" series), Lowell House, 1994.
Spring Break! ("Pick Your Own Dream Date" series), Lowell House, 1994.
Dreamboat ("Sweet Dreams" series), Bantam (New York, NY), 1995.
Double Vision, Amber Quill Press, 2003.

Author of e-books, including *Mail-Order Monster* and *Melissa's Mission Impossible.* Contributor to *The Whispered Watchword.*

"MY SISTER THE GHOST" SERIES

Twin Again, Avon (New York, NY), 1995.
Escape from Ghostland, Avon (New York, NY), 1995.
Teacher Trouble, Avon (New York, NY), 1996.
Babysitter Beware, Avon (New York, NY), 1996.

"CHEER SQUAD" SERIES

Crazy for Cartwheels, Avon (New York, NY), 1996.
Spirit Song, Avon (New York, NY), 1996.
Stand up and Cheer, Avon (New York, NY), 1996.
Boys Are Bad News, Avon (New York, NY), 1997.
Spring to Stardom, Avon (New York, NY), 1997.
Gimme a C-A-M-P!, Avon (New York, NY), 1997.

"REGENERATION" SERIES; UNDER NAME L.J. SINGLETON

Regeneration, Berkley Jam (New York, NY), 2000.
The Search, Berkley Jam (New York, NY), 2000.
The Truth, Berkley Jam (New York, NY), 2000.
The Impostor, Berkley Jam (New York, NY), 2000.
The Killer, Berkley Jam (New York, NY), 2001.

Also author of *Cloned and Dangerous,* posted on *LJSingleton.com.*

"STRANGE ENCOUNTERS" SERIES

Oh, No! UFO!, Llewellyn (St. Paul, MN), 2004.
Shamrocked!, Llewellyn (St. Paul, MN), 2005.
Sea Switch, Llewellyn (St. Paul, MN), 2005.

"SEER" SERIES

Don't Die Dragonfly, Llewellyn (St. Paul, MN), 2004.
Last Dance, Llewellyn (St. Paul, MN), 2005.
Witch's Ball, Llewellyn (St. Paul, MN), 2006.
Sword Play, Llewellyn (St. Paul, MN), 2006.

SIDELIGHTS: A longtime collector of vintage juvenile novels in the "Nancy Drew," "Trixie Belden," "Judy Bolton," and other series, Linda Joy Singleton eventually translated all that reading into writing. Beginning her writing career penning middle-grade fiction,

Singleton has contributed titles to the ongoing "Sweet Valley Twins," "Sweet Dreams," and "Pick Yourself a Dream Date" series. In 1994 her own series, the "My Sister the Ghost" books—which Singleton described on her home page as "a spooky series about twins"—was released and was followed by her "Cheer Squad" series. In 2000 Singleton shifted genres, moving to science fiction with her popular "Regeneration" books, and she has gone on to produce several other series as well as stand-alone books published both in print and e-book format. Discussing her preference for series novels with Patricia M. Newman in *California Kids!*, Singleton noted: "When you read a series, the characters become your friends. . . . It's nice when a book doesn't stop at the end."

In the "Regeneration" series, Singleton focuses on five children—Varina, Chase, Eric, Allison, and Sandee—who suddenly learn that each of them have been cloned from other individuals, strangers. Realizing that the scientist who created them wishes their destruction, the children team together, and soon they learn that each of them has been given a special power. Each of the "Regeneration" novels, which include *Regeneration, The Search,* and *The Killer,* follows one of the children as they grapple with their power and find adventure. Her "Seer" novels, which include *Don't Die Dragonfly* and *Last Dance,* move into the supernatural as they focus on sixteen-year-old psychic Sabine Rose, who tries to hide her ability to solve crimes but continues to become drawn into mystery.

In *Don't Die Dragonfly* Sabine is haunted by a vision about a girl with a dragonfly tattoo and becomes determined to find and warn her, while *Last Dance* finds her road trip with goth friend Opal veering off course when a restless ghost named Chloe begins to haunt her. Enthusiastic about Singleton's series, *Reviewer's Bookwatch* contributor Charisse Floyd wrote of *Don't Die Dragonfly* that "the surprising twists and page-turning cliffhangers literally pulsate with dramatic tension, and the novel's pace . . . runs full-throttle." While noting that the prose in *Last Dance* is standard genre fare, *School Library Journal* contributor Jessie Platt added that several "sections are quite poetic and help reinforce the eerie mood."

Singleton once commented: "I wrote my first two-hundred-page novel on blue-lined note paper when I was eleven years old. It was a romantic suspense called 'Holiday Terror,' and I was especially proud of the gruesome scene where a body is discovered. I was always reading and writing as a kid. Mostly, I would start a story, write several chapters, get bored with it, and begin a new story. I enjoyed reading my stories aloud to my mother—and I still do. When I was fourteen, I was too young to take a writing course at a college, so my father took it instead. He helped me submit some stories to *American Girl* magazine, which gave me my first rejection experiences. I've learned not to get too upset over rejections; instead I consider each one a step closer to my goal.

"A job, marriages, and two children filled my life until I was twenty-seven—that's when I renewed my childhood dream of writing. I joined Romance Writers of America, attended a weekly critique group, read avidly, and learned as much as I could from writing workshops. Then in 1988, my dream came true—I sold my first book to Willowisp Press! *Almost Twins* is a juvenile story about girls who pretend to be twins. I continued to sell books after that, mostly teen romances for Bantam's "Sweet Dreams" line. But it wasn't until 1994 that my BIGGEST dream came true.

"As a kid, I loved Nancy Drew, Judy Bolton, Penny Parker, and other girl series books. I even corresponded with Judy Bolton's author, Margaret Sutton. More than anything, I wanted a series of my own. And that happened in 1994 when my agent sold 'My Sister, the Ghost' to Avon books for publication in 1995, letting me add my own series books to the thousands of others in my collection." By 2005, according to Newman, Singleton had amassed over four thousand series books, several from the classic girls' series of the 1920s and 1930s.

"Wonderful things can happen if you work hard and hold onto your dreams," Singleton maintains, and she shares this optimistic attitude with others. "I love seeing the world through the heart of a child," she noted on her home page, "where magic is real and every day begins a new adventure. I hope to inspire [readers] . . . to reach for their dreams. Writing for kids is a gift, a responsibility, and an honor."

BIOGRAPHICAL AND CRITICAL SOURCES:

PERIODICALS

California Kids!, January, 2005, Patricia M. Newman, "Who Wrote That? Featuring Linda Joy Singleton."

Daily Times (Ottawa, IL), June 20, 2000, Julia Durango, interview with Singleton.

Kliatt, May, 2005, Sherry Hoy, review of *Don't Die Dragonfly,* p. 36.

Reviewer's Bookwatch, March, 2005, Charisse Floyd, review of *Don't Die Dragonfly* and *Oh No! UFO!*

School Library Journal, July, 2005, Jessie Platt, review of *Last Dance,* p. 108.

Voice of Youth Advocates, August, 1992, p. 170.

ONLINE

Crescent Blues Web site, http://www.crescentblues. com/ (December 1, 2005), Lynne Marie Pisano, review of *Double Vision.*

FictionForum.net, http://www.fictionforum.net/ (November 25, 1005), Bob Rich, interview with Singleton.

Linda Joy Singleton Home Page, http://www. lindajoysingleton.com (December 1, 2005).

*   *   *

SINGLETON, L.J.
See SINGLETON, Linda Joy

*   *   *

SLONCZEWSKI, Joan 1956-
(Joan Lyn Slonczewski)

PERSONAL: Born August 14, 1956 in Hyde Park, NY; Married Michael J. Barich, 1977; children: two sons. *Education:* Bryn Mawr College, A.B. (magna cum laude), 1977; Yale University, Ph.D., 1982.

ADDRESSES: Office—Department of Biology, Higley Hall, Kenyon College, 202 North College Road, Gambier, OH 43022. *E-mail*—slonczewski@kenyon. edu.

CAREER: Biologist, educator, and writer. University of Pennsylvania, Philadelphia, postdoctoral fellow, 1982-1984; Kenyon College, Gambier, OH, assistant professor, 1984-91, associate professor, 1991-2000, chair of biology, 1993-96, professor of biology, 2000—. Princeton University, Princeton, NJ, National Science Foundation visiting professorship for women, 1990-1991; University of Maryland at Baltimore visiting associate professor, 1998-99. Served in administrative positions, including chair of Division K. Microbial Physiology and Metabolism, American Society for Microbiology, 1996-97; director of Elementary School Science Month and Elementary School Scientists program for grades K-6 at elementary and middle schools in Mount Vernon City and Knox County, 1992-94; panelist for NASA Gravitation Ecology and Microbiology, 2002-03; panelist for National Science Foundation, Prokaryotic Genetics Study Section, 1990-95, 2003—; director of Howard Hughes Medical Institute Undergraduate Biological Sciences Education Program Award, 1996—.

AWARDS, HONORS: National Institutes of Health Research Service Award, 1982-84; John Campbell Memorial Award for Best Science-Fiction Novel, 1987, for *A Door into Ocean*; Robert Tomsich Award, for science research, Kenyon College, 1997, 2001; Vector Laboratories Young Investigator Travel Award, 1987, for outstanding research presented at the American Society for Microbiology Annual Meeting; Silver Medal, National Professor of the Year program, Council for the Advancement and Support of Education, 1989; numerous educational and research grants from various organizations, including National Science Foundation and Howard Hughes Medical Institute.

WRITINGS:

SCIENCE FICTION

Still Forms on Foxfield, Ballantine (New York, NY), 1980.

A Door into Ocean, Arbor House (New York, NY), 1985.

The Wall around Eden, Morrow (New York, NY), 1989.

Daughter of Elysium, Morrow (New York, NY), 1993.

The Children Star, Tor (New York, NY), 1998.

Brain Plague, Tor (New York, NY), 2000.

Contributor of short stories to anthology *Year's Best in Science Fiction,* 1986. Author of science-based books *Genomics and SF* and *Future Biology of Reproduction.*

Contributor to numerous periodicals and scientific journals, including *Analog Science Fiction/Science Fact, Kenyon Review, Nature, Science Fiction Research Association Review, Journal of Bacteriology, Journal of Cell Biology,* and *Writer.* Contributor to science books, including *Cellular and Molecular Biology,* American Society for Microbiology Press (Washington DC), 1996; *Methods in Enzymology, Bacterial Pathogenesis Part C,* Academic Press, 2002; and *Microbiology: A Genomic Perspective,* W.W. Norton (New York, NY).

SIDELIGHTS: Joan Slonczewski is a biology professor who uses her knowledge of science to write science-fiction stories and novels focusing on biology, ethics, and politics. In the *St. James Guide to Science-Fiction Writers,* the author noted that her fiction addresses a myriad of questions, including: "What does it mean to be a human being? What do we seek and desire most? Do women and men, and individuals of varied genetic and cultural backgrounds, share the same quest; or do they differ?" For example, in her first novel, *Still Forms on Foxfield,* the author addresses these issues via her story of the United Nations Interplanetary (UNI) culture, which her heroine, Allison, rejects as being necessary for all human cultures because of the violence the UNI perpetuates.

In *A Door into Ocean* Slonczewski presents pacifism as a more powerful force than war as she tells of two worlds: one a traditional patriarchal world and the other, named Shora, a more matriarchal world with no centralized government or sense of hierarchies. A contributor to *St. James Guide to Science-Fiction Writers* called the novel "remarkable for several reasons, including the careful character development and multiple viewpoints." In her novel *The Wall around Eden,* most biological life on Earth has perished after a nuclear holocaust and the surviving humans live in domes created by aliens. "The work is tantalizing for its misdirection," noted the *St. James Guide to Science-Fiction Writers* contributor, pointing out that most of the Earth's inhabitants mistakenly think that the aliens are responsible for the Earth's near destruction.

In *Daughter of Elysium* Slonczewski returns to the world of Shora, which now includes a new society of humans who appear to be almost ageless. When a family comes to the planet to live with the "Elysiums,"

they soon learn that this seemingly advanced society is caught up in universal political intrigues. A *Publishers Weekly* contributor commented that Slonczewski's "settings and alien cultures are rich and detailed, her characters memorable and often extremely endearing." *The Children Star* continues the story of the Elysium and their control of the politics within the confederation of worlds known as the Fold, often in conflict with the Sharers, an environmentally conscientious people. When an Elysian capitalist sets his sights on developing a planet, its ecology and many life forms—including colonists who have been genetically altered—are threatened. A *Publishers Weekly* contributor noted that the book "features enough absorbing material on genetics and planetary ecology to satisfy any aficionado of hard SF." The reviewer added that the author "tackles a wide range of moral issues . . . in a story that is not only exciting but also is filled with memorable characters." Jackie Cassada, writing in *Library Journal,* called the story "imaginative and compelling." In a review for the *New York Times Book Review,* Gerald Jonas wrote that "this novel's fireworks in the final third admirable justify its long, slow fuse."

With her novel *Brain Plague,* Slonczewski further develops the worlds and the story she began in *A Door into Ocean.* The focus this time is on symbiotic, sentient microbes that have distinct personalities and political systems. As a result, sometimes they benefit and sometimes they harm the humans they inhabit. Chrys is a struggling artist, and when she becomes inhabited by the microbes, they help refine her art and make her so successful that she begins to believe she is a god. But the microbes also have their own agenda. Jackie Cassada, writing in *Library Journal,* noted that the novel contains "a quirky humor with deep insights into the human mind." A *Publishers Weekly* contributor wrote that the "narrative . . . is rich in subtle analyses of the relationships between individuals and societies, art and life, the organic and inorganic, health and disease, free will and personal responsibility, and spiritual and scientific aspirations." In a review for *Booklist,* Roland Green felt that the author's "world building is magnificent" and added that the "tale is impossible to dismiss."

BIOGRAPHICAL AND CRITICAL SOURCES:

BOOKS

St. James Guide to Science-Fiction Writers, 4th edition, St. James Press (Detroit, MI), 1996.

PERIODICALS

Booklist, August, 2000, Roland Green, review of *Brain Plague,* p. 2125.

Library Journal, August, 1998, Jackie Cassada, review of *The Children Star,* p. 139; July 2000, review of *Brain Plague,* p. 147.

New York Times Book Review, October 4, 1998, Gerald Jonas, review of *The Children Star,* p. 30; September 3, 2000, Gerald Jonas, review of *Brain Plague,* p. 21.

Publishers Weekly, June 7, 1993, review of *Daughter of Elysium,* p. 57; July 27, 1998, review of *The Children Star,* p. 57; July 31, 2000, review of *Brain Plague,* p. 76.

ONLINE

Kenyon College Department of Biology Web site, http://biology.kenyon.edu/ (August 21, 2005), biographical and career information on author.*

*　　*　　*

SLONCZEWSKI, Joan Lyn
See SLONCZEWSKI, Joan

*　　*　　*

SLOVO, Gillian 1952-

PERSONAL: Born March 15, 1952, in Johannesburg, South Africa; daughter of Joe Slovo (a political activist) and Ruth First (a journalist); children: one daughter. *Education:* Manchester University, B.A., 1974.

ADDRESSES: Agent—c/o Author Mail, A.P. Watt, Ltd., 20 John St., London WC1N 2DL, England.

CAREER: Novelist, journalist, and film producer.

WRITINGS:

Ties of Blood (novel), Morrow (New York, NY), 1990.
Façade (novel), Virago Press (London, England), 1993.

Every Secret Thing: My Family, My Country (autobiography), Little, Brown (Boston, MA), 1997.
Red Dust (novel), Virago Press (London, England), 2000, W.W. Norton (New York, NY), 2002.
Ice Road (historical novel), W.W. Norton (New York, NY), 2005.
(With Victoria Brittain) *Guantanamo: Honor Bound to Defend Freedom* (play), Oberon Books (London, England), 2005.

CRIME NOVELS

Morbid Symptoms, Dembner Books (New York, NY), 1984.
Catnap, Virago Press (London, England), 1985, St. Martin's Press (New York, NY), 1986.
Close Call, Virago Press (London, England), 1986.
Death by Analysis, Women's Press (London, England), 1986, Doubleday (New York, NY), 1988.
Death Comes Staccato, Women's Press (London, England), 1987, Doubleday (New York, NY), 1988.
The Betrayal, Virago Press (London, England), 1992.

Contributor to publications, including the *Guardian.*

SIDELIGHTS: South African writer Gillian Slovo was born in Johannesburg in 1952, the daughter of Joe Slovo, leader of the South African Communist Party, and Ruth First, like her husband an anti-apartheid activist. (Also a journalist, First would be killed by a letter bomb in 1982.) Slovo moved to England in 1964, where she received her education and went on to work as a journalist, novelist, and film producer. *Morbid Symptoms,* her first book, starts a series of crime novels, many of which feature female detective Kate Baeier. Set in London, the story follows journalist-turned-investigator Baeier as she investigates the death of a man found at the bottom of an elevator shaft, and answers the question of whether he jumped or was pushed. When the case is revealed to be one of murder, Baeier discovers that it reveals a far broader mystery involving apartheid and the racist program's English supporters.

Death by Analysis takes place during the summer of 1981, while England celebrates the marriage of Prince Charles and Lady Diana. Meanwhile, political intrigue points toward serious problems for the nation, and the death of a psychoanalyst with a political past might be a warning to anyone believing their own past to be dead. In *Death Comes Staccato* Baeier is hired to protect a young musical prodigy from a stalker, but finds that the greatest threats sometimes come from within one's own family. The case forces her to deal with drug runners and corrupt police, putting her in the same danger as her client.

Slovo has written novels outside of the crime genre as well. With *Red Dust,* she mines her experiences in her native South Africa. The story follows Sarah, an attorney originally from South Africa who is now working in New York City as a prosecutor. Her mentor requests that she return home and she finds herself the legal advisor to a young black man, Alex, who has been asked to testify before the government's Truth and Reconciliation Commission. Alex does not want to return to his hometown where he was previously jailed and tortured, but agrees to go in order to help the parents of a friend who has been murdered discover the truth about his death. Claire Rosser, in a review for *Kliatt,* wrote that "Slovo is unrelenting—she shows how injustice, violence, and humiliation affect personalities, relationships, and a culture." Writing for *World Literature Today,* Ursula Barnett commented that Slovo "shows much of her skill in unveiling a mystery," but added that "elements of drama, excitement, and detection, however, do not sit altogether easily with the philosophical and psychological examination of truth, guilt, revenge, forgiveness, and justice triggered by the Truth and Reconciliation Commission." Melanie Kaye, in an article for *Women's Review of Books,* wrote that Slovo's work "opens into deep questions of guilt and innocence, the relationship between truth and justice. Does truth heal? Is justice essential or possible? Every overthrow of massive oppression, dictatorship, brutality, has to reckon with what to do with those who oppressed and tortured. How to heal a society fractured by hate and violence." A contributor for *Publishers Weekly* remarked that "this powerful novel—full of legal and emotional twists and turns—strips bare the torment forever ingrained in victim and jailer alike, a torment that runs through all segments of post-apartheid society."

In *Ice Road,* Slovo turns away from South African politics and instead looks at the USSR under Stalin. Set in Leningrad in the winter of 1933, the book fol-lows the lives of various characters as the promises of the Russian Revolution crumble under political reality. A contributor for *Kirkus Reviews* wrote that "Slovo risks melodrama, but on the whole her tale is smart and poignant, exploring some of the same moral territory as Nikita Mikhalkov's film *Burnt by the Sun.* A big idea well handled."

Examining another, quite different political situation, Slovo coauthored the play *Guantanamo: Honor Bound to Defend Freedom* with Victoria Brittain. The play addresses the U.S. military's acquisition of young Muslims of various nationalities from Afghanistan and other places, and the transport of these detainees to a base at Guantanamo Bay, Cuba, where they were held in violation of humanitarian laws. Richard Norton-Taylor, reviewing the work for *New Statesman,* remarked of viewing the play that "my confidence in drama as an effective vehicle for exploring current affairs was confirmed."

Slovo has also written an autobiography that focuses on her experiences as a child in South Africa and on the effect her parents' political convictions and work as activists had on her. *Every Secret Thing: My Family, My Country* pays homage to her parents' lives and achievements, and includes personal as well as political information. The volume garnered criticism for being anti-communist, and Slovo was accused of revealing too many details that should have remained private, but the book's honesty reflects her attempt to remain at least partly impartial. Melanie Kaye called the work "a dazzling and essential book," and remarked that reading it "reinforces one's sense of the essential dignity of the struggle against apartheid and the value of her parents' lives." Hazel Rochman, writing for *Booklist,* stated of Slovo that, "fueled by anger and by love, her writing is lyrical and intelligent and open."

BIOGRAPHICAL AND CRITICAL SOURCES:

BOOKS

Slovo, Gillian, *Every Secret Thing: My Family, My Country,* Little, Brown (Boston, MA), 1997.

PERIODICALS

Booklist, April 15, 1997, Hazel Rochman, review of *Every Secret Thing: My Family, My Country,* p. 1378; December 15, 2001, Hazel Rochman, review of *Red Dust,* p. 704.

Kirkus Reviews, October 1, 2001, review of *Red Dust,* p. 1390; March 1, 2005, review of *Ice Road,* p. 257.

Kliatt, July, 2003, Claire Rosser, review of *Red Dust,* p. 27.

Library Journal, October 1, 2001, Christine Perkins, review of *Red Dust,* p. 144.

Nation, May 12, 1997, Vivian Gornick, review of *Every Secret Thing,* p. 46.

New Internationalist, January-February, 2001, review of *Red Dust,* p. 46.

New Statesman, June 7, 2004, Richard Norton-Taylor, "Spirit of Inquiry," review of *Guantanamo: Honor Bound to Defend Freedom,* p. 39.

Publishers Weekly, November 5, 2001, review of *Red Dust,* p. 39.

Race and Class, October-December, 1997, Barbara Harlow, review of *Every Secret Thing,* p. 95.

Women's Review of Books, July, 2002, Melanie Kaye, "The Price of Heroism," reviews of *Red Dust* and *Every Secret Thing,* p. 30.

World Literature Today, April-June, 2003, Ursula Barnett, review of *Red Dust,* p. 88.*

*   *   *

SMITH, Sarah Harrison

PERSONAL: Female. *Education:* Oxford University, B.A., Columbia University, M.A.

ADDRESSES: Agent—New York Times Magazine, 229 W. 43rd St., New York, NY 10036.

CAREER: Writer, researcher, and fact checker. *New Yorker,* New York, NY, former fact checker; *New York Times Magazine,* New York, NY, began as head of research/checking, managing editor, 2005—.

WRITINGS:

The Fact Checker's Bible: A Guide to Getting It Right, Anchor Books (New York, NY), 2004.

SIDELIGHTS: Writer, researcher, and professional fact-checker Sarah Harrison Smith was head of research and checking at the *New York Times Magazine* before becoming a managing editor there. Previously a fact checker at the *New Yorker,* she has made a career out of "getting it right" and finding the correct answers when she needs them.

With *The Fact Checker's Bible: A Guide to Getting It Right,* Smith offers a reference work for other word-wrights and editorial professionals who need to get the facts straight as quickly and efficiently as possible. In a book designed for practicing journalists, freelance writers, editors, and researchers, Harrison explains the intricacies and inside tricks of the craft of research and fact-checking. She encourages skeptical reading, the development of a sense of whether a written work is credible, persuasive, and factual. She describes the process of fact-checking at a number of prominent publications and offers a listing of reliable resources on a variety of general topics. Real-world examples illustrate the need for fact-checking, how to identify potential factual errors, and what resources to consult when scouring source material. Harrison also discusses issues of libel, plagiarism, outright fabrication, and malice as they apply to professional publishing and the duties of a fact checker. *Library Journal* contributor Ann Schade called *The Fact Checker's Bible* "invaluable" and "an excellent resource for researchers, writers, and fact checkers."

BIOGRAPHICAL AND CRITICAL SOURCES:

PERIODICALS

Library Journal, September 15, 2004, Ann Schade, review of *The Fact Checker's Bible: A Guide to Getting It Right,* p. 66.

*   *   *

SMITH, Tara Bray 1970-

PERSONAL: Born 1970, in HI; daughter of Karen Morgan. *Education:* Dartmouth College, received degree; Columbia University, M.F.A., 2003.

ADDRESSES: Home—Brooklyn, NY. *Agent*—Alexis Welby, Senior Publicist, Simon & Schuster, 1230 6th Ave., 12th Fl., New York, NY 10020. *E-mail*—tara@ tarabraysmith.com.

CAREER: Writer.

WRITINGS:

West of Then: A Mother, a Daughter, and a Journey Past Paradise (memoir), Simon & Schuster (New York, NY), 2004.

Also author of *Why Won't the Landlord Take Visa?: The Princeton Review's Crash Course to Life after Graduation.* Contributor to periodicals, including *Granta.*

SIDELIGHTS: Tara Bray Smith was born and raised in Hawaii, and in her memoir, *West of Then: A Mother, a Daughter, and a Journey Past Paradise* she returns to the islands as a lush but ironic backdrop to the story of her difficult relationship with her mother, Karen Morgan. Bray intertwines a detailed history of Hawaii with the story of her early years and return, as an adult, to Honolulu to find her mother, who disappeared long ago and is feared dead.

West of Then is "a daughter's memoir both appalling and inspiring, in which Tara Bray Smith tells the story of her mother's addiction to drugs," noted reviewer Susanna Moore in *Vogue.* Bray was born in 1970 into a family with deep local connections. They had long been plantation owners who had once been wealthy business owners with interests in sugar and real estate. Changing economic times and diverse interests of new generations had shuttered the lucrative farms before Smith was born, but the family still retained a sense of being "local nobility," Moore observed. Perhaps worse than the family's reduced fortunes was the drug-fueled atmosphere of the 1960s and 1970s that forged Bray's mother's personality. Karen Brewster Morgan was a fifth-generation white Hawaiian, a genuine descendent of the *Mayflower,* and a physically beautiful women. She was also a heroin addict who was prone to debilitating drug binges and to simply forgetting about her children. Smith was abandoned by Morgan at age seven and was raised by her father and stepmother. Long after reaching adulthood, Smith received a frantic call from a sister who said that their mother had been missing for weeks. With no hesitation, Smith left her life in New York City to search for the homeless, hopeless Morgan.

"The search for her mother is, in truth, a search for herself, and she rebuilds her past by mining her memories" of a contradictory childhood long gone, and a mother's love she still longs for, commented a *Kirkus Reviews* contributor. "Smith writes with grace of the contradictions of childhood; the confusing rages and humiliations; the longing for order; the delicate pleasures; the misunderstandings occasioned by innocence," Moore observed. She "blends reportorial objectivity with the baring of her soul to sublime effect," concluded *Booklist* reviewer Carol Haggas.

Smith is also the author of a practical guidebook for new college graduates, *Why Won't the Landlord Take Visa?: The Princeton Review's Crash Course to Life after Graduation.* The book offers advice for newly minted graduates' thoughts on finding a job, creating a satisfying social life with little money, and adjusting to the demands of life after college.

BIOGRAPHICAL AND CRITICAL SOURCES:

PERIODICALS

Booklist, September 1, 2004, Carol Haggas, review of *West of Then: A Mother a Daughter, and a Journey Past Paradise,* p. 27.
Chicago Tribune, May 1, 2005, Kera Bolonik, "An Elusive Memoirist in Search of a Mother-Daughter Bond," review of *West of Then.*
Kirkus Reviews, August 1, 2004, review of *West of Then,* p. 733.
Library Journal, September 15, 2004, Pam Kingsbury, review of *West of Then,* p. 65.
People, October 18, 2004, Lynne Andriani, review of *West of Then,* p. 50.
Vogue, October, 2004, Susanna Moore, "A Love Adrift: In a Lyrical Memoir of Her Hawaiian Childhood, Tara Bray Smith Searches for a Mother Who Is All but Lost to Her," review of *West of Then,* p. 264.

ONLINE

Columbia University Web site, http://www.columbia.edu/ (June 19, 2005), "With Her Debut Book, Tara Bray Smith (SoA, '03) Joins Growing List of Recently Published Columbians."
Tara Bray Smith Home Page, http://www.tarabraysmith.com (June 19, 2005).*

                              *   *   *

SPRATFORD, Becky Siegel

PERSONAL: Female. *Education:* Amherst College, B.A., 1997; Dominican University, M.L.I.S., 2001.

ADDRESSES: Office—Berwyn Public Library, 2701 Harlem Ave., Berwyn, IL 60402.

CAREER: Dominican University, River Forest, IL, adjunct faculty member in Graduate School of Library and Information Science; Berwyn Public Library, Berwyn, IL, readers' advisory librarian and reference librarian.

WRITINGS:

(With Tammy Hennigh Clausen) *The Horror Readers' Advisory: The Librarian's Guide to Vampires, Killer Tomatoes, and Haunted Houses,* American Library Association (Chicago, IL), 2004.

SIDELIGHTS: Librarian Becky Siegel Spratford is a readers' advisory librarian in Illinois who helped create her library's readers' advisory section in 2000, noted a biographer on the *American Library Association* Web site. As part of her duties, she advises readers and patrons on types and availability of selections and helps them pick fiction and nonfiction appropriate to their tastes and age level. Spratford expanded her advisory counsel to a wider audience with the publication of her *The Horror Readers' Advisory: The Librarian's Guide to Vampires, Killer Tomatoes, and Haunted Houses.* In the book, Spratford and coauthor Tammy Hennigh Clausen offer a detailed overview of the horror genre in both literature and film. It is comprehensive enough to give librarians unfamiliar with the horror genre enough of a grounding to successfully advise readers on book and literature choices. The guide "does not just advise on advising but does a dissection of the literary devices in horror and allows the librarian to understand what this literature is about," commented *Kliatt* reviewer Joseph DeMarco. Writing from a horror lover's perspective, Spratford and Clausen address the needs of librarians, but also of readers "who believe that they've read it all," noted Lynn Evarts in *School Library Journal.*

The authors "give credible explanations as to what makes horror appealing and why horror fiction has become so mainstream," remarked Karan Jones in *Australian Library Journal.* They outline a brief history of horror and how it relates to, and has been affected in popular perception by, horror films. Spratford and Clausen are careful to explain that horror is more than just deranged killers and splattered guts; the genre also consists of quieter, more-thoughtful fare such as subtle ghost stories, creepy atmospheric pieces, and elegantly written tales of the weird. Horror sub-genres are covered, including themes such as witches, ghosts and haunted houses, werewolves, mummies, vampires, biomedical horror, demonic possession, and psychological horror. They explore seven basic factors that motivate people to read horror, such as readers' desires to find a place to confront their own fears or to explore the psychology of horror. The authors include aids such as summary lists, book descriptions, and comprehensive suggestions for finding additional horror resources. They also devote an entire chapter to the readers' advisory interview and what librarians can expect when advising patrons on horror choices. Librarians can find practical advice on marketing their horror collections to both new and old readers.

Kenley Neufeld, writing in *Teacher Librarian,* concluded that *The Horror Readers' Advisory* is "the right book for any novice or experienced horror reader who needs to buy, read or recommend horror fiction." Evarts also noted, "Librarians will find this book invaluable" in advising patrons seeking darker reading and viewing options.

BIOGRAPHICAL AND CRITICAL SOURCES:

PERIODICALS

American Libraries, May, 2004, 'Scared Silly," review of *The Horror Readers' Advisory: The Librarian's Guide to Vampires, Killer Tomatoes, and Haunted Houses,* p. 64.
Australian Library Journal, February, 2005, Karan Jones, "The Fascination of the 'Orrible," review of *The Horror Readers' Advisory,* p. 95.
Kliatt, July, 2004, Joseph DeMarco, review of *The Horror Readers' Advisory,* p. 36.
Library Journal, September 1, 2004, Jennifer Baker, "Fresh Meat for Horror Fans," review of *The Horror Readers' Advisory,* p. 195.
School Library Journal, July, 2004, Lynn Evarts, review of *The Horror Readers' Advisory,* p. 135.
Teacher Librarian, October, 2004, Kenley Neufeld, "Funding and Advocacy for the School Library," review of *The Horror Readers' Advisory,* p. 38.

ONLINE

American Library Association Web site, http://www.ala.org/ (June 19, 2005), biography of Becky Siegel Spratford.

STABINER, Karen

PERSONAL: Married Larry Dietz; children: Sarah. *Education:* Attended Syracuse University for one year; University of Michigan, B.A.

ADDRESSES: Home—Santa Monica, CA. *Agent*—c/o Author Mail, Little, Brown & Company, 1271 Avenue of the Americas, New York, NY 10020. *E-mail*—info@ karenstabiner.com.

CAREER: Journalist and writer. Santa Barbara *News and Review,* cofounder and art editor; worked for various publications in Los Angeles, CA, including *Mother Jones* and *New West;* freelance writer.

WRITINGS:

Limited Engagements (novel), Seaview Books (New York, NY), 1979.
Courting Fame: The Perilous Road to Women's Tennis Stardom, Harper & Row (New York, NY), 1986.
Inventing Desire: Inside Chiat/Day; The Hottest Shop, the Coolest Players, the Big Business of Advertising, Simon & Schuster (New York, NY), 1993.
To Dance with the Devil: The New War on Breast Cancer, Delacorte Press (New York, NY), 1997.
(With Piero Selvaggio) *The Valentino Cookbook,* photographs by Patricia Williams, Villard (New York, NY), 2001.
All Girls: Single-Sex Education and Why It Matters, Riverhead Books (New York, NY), 2002.
My Girl: Adventures with a Teen in Training, Little, Brown (New York, NY), 2005.

Contributor to periodicals, including *Mother Jones, Vogue, O, Los Angeles, Travel and Leisure, Gourmet,* and *NewWest.*

SIDELIGHTS: California-based writer Karen Stabiner earned a B.A. in English with honors from the University of Michigan, then went on to found the Santa Barbara *News and Review,* a weekly newspaper for which she was the arts editor and film critic for four years. She moved to Los Angeles and worked for a number of publications before deciding to become a freelance writer, focusing primarily on health, women's

and family issues, and food. Stabiner is the author of several books on topics ranging from advertising to sports to education, as well as a novel, *Limited Engagements.*

Stabiner's roots in journalism are reflected in the majority of her books. In *Inventing Desire: Inside Chiat/Day; The Hottest Shop, the Coolest Players, the Big Business of Advertising* she delves into the world of a major advertising agency that was known for its cutting-edge, hip style in the late 1980s, but underwent a radical change in fortune when several major clients took their business elsewhere. Stabiner spent a year at the Venice, California offices, speaking with employees and observing them at work. Joanne Kaufman, in a review for *People,* called the book "a riveting account of the firm's transition from halcyon days to, so to speak, Halcion days."

To Dance with the Devil: The New War on Breast Cancer addresses the political machinations behind advances in medical treatment, focusing specifically on how legislation and political positioning affect progress in the fight against breast cancer. Stabiner followed University of California, Los Angeles surgeon Susan Love, observing her methods and the ways in which they affected her patients. In an article for *Women's Review of Books,* Lundy Braun commented that "Stabiner's book is an interesting one, but her narrative lacks a clear focus," while Francine Prose, reviewing for *People,* wrote that "although the stories of some patients are harrowing, Stabiner's account of Dr. Love's near-visionary dedication is uplifting." A contributor for *Publishers Weekly* called the book a "disturbing look at a field where cost-benefit analyses have become more important than human life," while *Town and Country* reviewer Stacey Okun remarked that Stabiner's work "in many parts, reads like a novel—but whose compelling subject is all too real."

All Girls: Single-Sex Education and Why It Matters takes a look inside two all-girls schools in an attempt to show what the positives and the drawbacks are to single-sex education for women. Stabiner visited a public girls' school in Harlem and a private girls' school in Los Angeles, examining the daily lives of the girls, both in school and in their homes. She also spent time with teachers and administrators. In a review for *Booklist,* Gillian Engberg called the book "moving, intimate, and revealing," and remarked that it "raises larger questions about how success is measured." Charlotte Hays, writing for *Women's Quarterly,* remarked that "this book is a must read for anyone who cares about the fate not only of single-sex education but of education in general. In Stabiner's hands, the material becomes a rip-roaring adventure-tale." Stabiner herself, in an article for *Daughters* in which she explained her decision to write the book and what she learned in the process, summed up by noting: "In a good girls' school there are high expectations communicated by the teachers that the girls just sop up. If you put your daughter somewhere people have expectations of her competence and abilities, she will respond to that."

My Girl: Adventures with a Teen in Training is about Stabiner's daughter Sarah and the changes in the mother-daughter relationship as Sarah grew from little girl to teenager. Always close to her daughter, Stabiner had heard horror stories about what would happen as the girl approached her teen years, both from books on parenting and from her own friends. So Stabiner kept track for herself, and with her book offers a different view of this transitional period in a girl's life. A contributor for *Kirkus Reviews* pointed out that the majority of the volume focuses on Sarah's sixth-grade year, when she was still fairly young, and also that Stabiner's affluence hardly makes them a typical example; "she seems not to realize readers may blink at her descriptions of Sarah's posh private school." Gillian Engberg, writing for *Booklist,* called the book a "vivid, intimate memoir."

BIOGRAPHICAL AND CRITICAL SOURCES:

PERIODICALS

Booklist, April 1, 1997, William Beatty, review of *To Dance with the Devil: The New War on Breast Cancer,* p. 1272; June 1, 2002, Gillian Engberg, review of *All Girls: Single-Sex Education and Why It Matters,* p. 1653; March 1, 2005, Gillian Engberg, review of *My Girl: Adventures with a Teen in Training,* p. 1121.
Daughters, January-February, 2004, Karen Stabiner, "Karen Stabiner on All-Girls Schools," p. 1; May-June, 2005, Karen Stabiner, "The Girls Are Alright, Alright?" p. 15.
Kirkus Reviews, January 15, 2005, review of *My Girl,* p. 112.

Library Journal, April 1, 1997, Cress-Ingebo, review of *To Dance with the Devil,* p. 116; March 15, 2001, Judith Sutton, review of *The Valentino Cookbook,* p. 102; August, 2002, Terry Christner, review of *All Girls,* p. 114; May 1, 2005, Kay Hogan Smith, "Mama's Got a New Bag," review of *My Girl,* p. 104.
People, June 28, 1993, Joanne Kaufman, review of *Inventing Desire: Inside Chiat/Day; The Hottest Shop, the Coolest Players, the Big Business of Advertising,* p. 31; June 23, 1997, Francine Prose, review of *To Dance with the Devil,* p. 31.
Publishers Weekly, April 7, 1997, review of *To Dance with the Devil,* p. 83; February 5, 2001, review of *The Valentino Cookbook,* p. 84; June 3, 2002, review of *All Girls,* p. 75.
Town and Country, May, 1997, Stacey Okun, review of *To Dance with the Devil,* p. 46.
Women's Quarterly, summer, 2002, Charlotte Hays, interview regarding *All Girls,* p. 11.
Women's Review of Books, December, 1997, Lundy Braun, review of *To Dance with the Devil,* p. 21.

ONLINE

Karen Stabiner Home Page, http://www.karenstabiner. com (July 11, 2005).*

*   *   *

STACE, Wesley 1965-
(John Wesley Harding, Wesley Harding Stace)

PERSONAL: Born October 22, 1965, in Hastings, England; son of Christopher (an educator) and Molly (an opera singer and educator) Townson. *Education:* Jesus' College, Cambridge, B.A.; graduate study in political and social theory. *Politics:* "Imaginative" *Religion:* Methodist, but "all the gods are in Hollywood."

ADDRESSES: Home—Brooklyn, NY. *Agent*—c/o Jennifer Rudolph Walsh, William Morris Agency, 1325 Avenue of the Americas, New York, NY 10019. *E-mail*—Wesley@wesleystace.com.

CAREER: Musician and novelist. Folk musician, recording and touring as opening act in United Kingdom and United States.

WRITINGS:

(As John Wesley Harding) *Collected Stories: 1990-1991* (song lyrics), Warner Brothers, 1991.

(Author of introduction) Charles Dickens, *The Haunted House,* Modern Library (New York, NY), 2004.

Misfortune (novel), Little, Brown (New York, NY), 2005.

Contributor to periodicals, including *Bomb, Post Road, Creem, Raygun, L.A. Style, Stereophile, Telegraph, Stranger* and *Los Angeles Times.*

SOUND RECORDINGS; LYRICIST UNDER NAME JOHN WESLEY HARDING

It Happened One Night, Demon Records, 1988.

God Made Me Do It: The Christmas LP, Sire/Reprise, 1989.

Here Comes the Groom, Sire/Reprise, 1990.

Just Say Da (compilation) Sire/Reprise, 1990.

Where the Pyramid Meets the Eye (compilation), Sire/Reprise, 1990.

The Name above the Title, Sire/Reprise, 1990.

Just Say Anything (compilation), Sire/Reprise, 1991.

Why We Fight, Sire/Reprise, 1992.

John Wesley Harding's New Deal, Rhino, 1996.

Awake (reissue), Appleseed, 1998.

Trad Arr Jones (reissue), Appleseed, 1999.

Confessions of St. Ace, Mammoth, 2000.

Adam's Apple, DRT, 2004.

SIDELIGHTS: Singer/songwriter and novelist Wesley Stace was born in Hastings, England, the son of two school teachers. Stace inherited his musical talent from his mother, who started her career as an opera singer, though his own interests ran to folk rock. After studying English at Jesus' College, Cambridge, under the name John Wesley Harding, he went on to record a number of albums with artists from various bands, including the bassist and drummer from the Attractions, Elvis Costello's group. He later collaborated with several other artists, including Bruce Springsteen and Iggy Pop. Critics compared his music to both Elvis Costello and Bob Dylan, and Stace himself credits both Dylan and Joan Baez as influences. Stace released a volume of lyrics, *Collected Stories: 1990-1991,* in 1991.

Misfortune, Stace's first novel, is based on the lyrics to his song, "Miss Fortune." The book is about a middle-aged man who, lacking an heir, takes in an abandoned baby girl he finds on the streets of London while he is out for a carriage ride. The girl reminds him of his own sister, who has died, and he determines she will be his daughter. However, the baby is actually a boy. Reminiscent of the sprawling Victorian-era novels of Charles Dickens and Anthony Trollope, the book examines what happens to the child, Rose, as it grows to maturity. In an interview with Dave Weich for *Powells.com,* Stace explained his approach to writing the book: "I tried to make one of those novels that tell a whole story and create a whole world, a bildungsroman, a coming-of-age story—but with a subject matter they couldn't have written about in the nineteenth century. That was my initial idea, after I'd written the song." Stace's novel differs from that of the authors who influenced him, however, as he takes a contemporary approach to his work, despite the period setting. As Stace told Weich: "I determined very early on not to have it be a pastiche of nineteenth century literature; I wanted it to be a modern novel set in the past. It's narrated in 1918, which is basically modern."

Laura Miller, in a review for *Salon.com,* wrote that "for the many readers who don't care about the proper allocation of periwigs and hansom cabs, Stace has concocted a big, cheesy amusement completely unafraid to resort to the most outrageous stunts and caricatures to hold their attention. Historically, it's about as unreliable as one of Stace's beloved ballads, but on the upside, as a pastime, it's also as fun." A contributor for *Publishers Weekly* remarked that "Rose's original narrative voice is engaging from the get-go: smart, funny, observant, and even hip." Reporting for the London *Guardian,* Colin Greenland noted of Stace that "there is something musical, almost symphonic, about the sweep of his novel, its single-minded pursuit of themes through sections strongly distinct in mood and approach." In an article for *Kirkus Reviews,* a contributor stated that the book's "abundant cleverness sometimes slips into preciousness, but the narrative is full of surprises," concluding that it is "a most promising debut."

BIOGRAPHICAL AND CRITICAL SOURCES:

PERIODICALS

Booklist, February 15, 2005, Michael Gannon, review of *Misfortune,* p. 1037.

Bookseller, February 4, 2005, review of *Misfortune,*
p. 30.

Entertainment Weekly, April 15, 2005, Gilbert Cruz,
"Double the Fun: The Cult Folksinger Takes Back
His Birth Name," review of *Misfortune,* p. 84.

Kirkus Reviews, January 1, 2005, review of *Misfortune,*
p. 19.

Library Journal, December 1, 2004, Barbara Hoffert,
review of *Misfortune,* p. 88; February 1, 2005,
Henry L. Carrigan, Jr., review of *Misfortune,* p. 71.

Publishers Weekly, January 24, 2005, Suzanne Mantell,
review of *Misfortune,* p. 113; January 31, 2005,
review of *Misfortune,* p. 47.

ONLINE

Elle Web site, http://www.elle.com/ (July 10, 2005),
"Wesley Stace."

Guardian Online, http://books.guardian.co.uk/ (July
10, 2005), "Wesley Stace."

John Wesley Harding Home Page, http://www.
johnwesleyharding.com (July 10, 2005).

Powells Web site, http://www.powells.com/ (July 10,
2005), "Wesley Stace."

Salon.com, http://www.salon.com/ (July 10, 2005),
"Wesley Stace."

Washington Post Online, http://www.washingtonpost.
com/ (July 10, 2005), "Wesley Stace."

Wesley Stace Home Page, http://www.wesleystace.com
(July 10, 2005).

* * *

STACE, Wesley Harding
  See STACE, Wesley

* * *

STANLEY, Julian Cecil, Jr.
  See STANLEY, Julian C., Jr.

* * *

STANLEY, Julian C., Jr. 1918-2005
  (Julian Cecil Stanley, Jr.)

OBITUARY NOTICE—See index for *CA* sketch: Born
July 9, 1918, in East Point, GA; died of pneumonia,
August 12, 2005, in Columbia, MD. Psychologist,

educator, and author. A retired psychology professor,
Stanley was best known for his groundbreaking
research with mathematically gifted children and for
helping to establish ways to better meet their educational needs. After finishing a B.S. in 1937 at what is
now Georgia Southern College, he taught high-school
math for five years. He then went to Harvard University to earn a master's degree in 1946 and a doctorate
in experimental and educational psychology in 1950.
Stanley was an associate professor at George Peabody
College for Teachers until 1953, and he joined the
University of Wisconsin—Madison faculty that year.
At Madison, he was a professor of educational
psychology and directed the laboratory of experimental
design from 1961 to 1967. He specialized in quantitative psychology in these early years, but his focus
changed shortly after transfering to a position at Johns
Hopkins University in 1967. An encounter with a brilliant thirteen-year-old boy who was gifted in math led
Stanley to worry that the educational system did not
foster such talents well. He set out to find a way to
test young children and find out which ones were
mathematically gifted; thus began the Study of
Mathematically Precocious Youth at Johns Hopkins.
Stanley used tests based on college-level exams to
identify the most intelligent children, and he used his
data to convince the university to start a program cater-
ing to these students. Johns Hopkins consequently
founded the Center for Talented Youth, which offers
challenging weekend and summer classes for gifted
kids. Initially, Stanley believed that such children
should be allowed to attend regular college classes,
but he later changed his opinion, saying that young
teens were not emotionally prepared for such a
challenge. Stanley continued to teach at Johns Hopkins until retiring in 1999. In appreciation for his work
with gifted children, Mensa presented him with a
lifetime achievement award in 2000. Stanley wrote and
edited numerous scholarly books over the years,
including *Statistical Methods in Education and Psychology* (1970), *Mathematical Talent: Discovery,
Description, and Development* (1974), *Academic
Precocity: Aspects of Its Development* (1983), and
Intellectual Talent: Psychometric and Social Issues
(1996).

OBITUARIES AND OTHER SOURCES:

PERIODICALS

Chicago Tribune, August 16, 2005, section 3, p. 9.
New York Times, August 15, 2005, p. A19.

ONLINE

Johns Hopkins University Center for Talented Youth Web site, http://www.jhu.edu/~gifted/ (August 31, 2005).

*   *   *

STEELE, Henry Maxwell
See STEELE, Max

*   *   *

STEELE, Max 1922-2005
(Henry Maxwell Steele)

OBITUARY NOTICE— See index for *CA* sketch: Born March 30, 1922, in Greenville, SC; died August 1, 2005, in Chapel Hill, NC. Educator and author. Steele was a University of North Carolina creative writing professor and award-winning author of novels and short stories. After attending several different universities and serving in the U.S. Army Air Forces during World War II, he earned a B.A. from the University of North Carolina in 1946. He then continued his studies in France at the Sorbonne and the Academie Julienne. Returning to the United States, he lectured at his alma mater for two years and taught at the Bread Loaf Writers Conference in 1956. Teaching at the University of North Carolina, he rose to the post of full professor of creative writing in 1972 and directed the writing program from 1968 to 1988, when he retired. Steele not only taught writing; he was an accomplished fiction author himself. His work includes the novel *Debby* (1950; retitled *The Goblins Must Go Bare*), which won the Harper Prize; short stories—two of which earned him O. Henry prizes; and three children's books. He was also an editor for *Story* magazine.

OBITUARIES AND OTHER SOURCES:

PERIODICALS

Los Angeles Times, August 8, 2005, p. B9.

ONLINE

Herald Sun Online, http://www.heraldsun.com/ (August 5, 2005).
University of North Carolina Web site, http://www.unc.edu/ (August 5, 2005).

STEIN, Garth 1965(?)-

PERSONAL: Born c. 1965, in Los Angeles, CA; married; children: two sons. *Education:* Columbia University, B.A., 1987, M.F.A., 1990.

ADDRESSES: Home—Seattle, WA. *Agent*—c/o Author Mail, Soho Press Inc., 853 Broadway, New York, NY 10003.

CAREER: Worked variously as filmmaker, producer, and stage manager. Theatre Guild, New York, NY, assistant to Philip Lagner and stage manager for "Theatre at Sea" cruises. Film work includes: (director) *What's Wrong with This Building?*; (producer) *The Lunch Date*; (coproducer) *When Your Head's Not a Head, It's a Nut;* (coproducer) *The Last Party* coproducer; and (director) *Philadelphia Burning.*

AWARDS, HONORS: Academy Award for Live-Action Short, 1991, for *The Lunch Date.*

WRITINGS:

Raven Stole the Moon (novel), Pocket Books (New York, NY), 1998.
How Evan Broke His Head and Other Secrets (novel), Soho Press (New York, NY), 2005.
Brother Jones (play), produced in Los Angeles, CA, 2005.

WORK IN PROGRESS: Raven Steals the Sun, a sequel to *Raven Stole the Moon.*

SIDELIGHTS: Writer and filmmaker Garth Stein was raised in Seattle, Washington, prior to moving to New York City, where he earned both his B.A. and his M.F.A. at Columbia University. His diverse ethnic background—his mother is part Irish and part Tlingit Indian, and his father is an Austrian Jew—and his ties to his family help to shape his outlook on society and have influenced some of his films and writing projects. Stein worked at various jobs after graduating from school, including as a director on the documentary film, *What's Wrong with This Building?,* which chronicles the controversy over whether to add a new wing to the Whitney Museum of Art, and as a producer on *The Lunch Date,* a short film that went on to win a

1991 Academy Award for best live-action short. Other projects include *When Your Head's Not a Head, It's a Nut,* a film about his sister's brain surgery to help her epilepsy, coproducing *The Last Party,* and directing *Philadelphia Burning,* and a number of music videos. Stein also served as an assistant to Philip Lagner, the head of Broadway's Theatre Guild, for four years.

Raven Stole the Moon, Stein's first novel, is heavily steeped in the stories of his Tlingit ancestors. Stein wanted to incorporate the tale of the kushtaka, shapeshifters that can steal human souls, and who exist between the worlds of the living and the dead. The book tells the story of Jenna Rosen, a young woman who, mourning the death of her small son two years before, leaves her husband behind in Seattle and goes to Wrangell, Alaska, to visit her Tlingit grandmother. Wrangell is located near Thunder Bay, where her son drowned, and though her purpose is to lay the past to rest, Jenna finds herself involved in something much less comforting as she comes to believe that her son's spirit has been taken by the kushtaka. V. Louise Saylor, in a review for *Library Journal,* called the book "richly textured" and "layered with vivid descriptions and characters." A contributor for *Publishers Weekly* observed that "Stein's restrained prose is a good vehicle for Jenna's examination of the nature of religious faith and belief."

How Evan Broke His Head and Other Secrets is the story of Evan, a thirty-one-year-old musician with epilepsy who suddenly finds himself responsible for a son he is never met—now aged fourteen—when the boy's mother dies. The relationship is complicated by the fact that Evan's own maturity level is hardly higher than his son's. A contributor for *Kirkus Reviews* found it "an unconvincing second outing," while a reviewer for *Publishers Weekly* remarked that the book "is littered with life lessons that Stein weaves into the narrative with honesty and compassion."

Stein is also the author of a play, *Brother Jones,* about a boat builder named Jones Riddell who returns home after twenty-four years to attend his sister's wedding. The work debuted in Los Angeles, California, in January of 2005.

BIOGRAPHICAL AND CRITICAL SOURCES:

PERIODICALS

Booklist, February 28, 1998, Mary Ellen Quinn, review of *Raven Stole the Moon,* p. 901; March 15, 2005,

Joanne Wilkinson, review of *How Evan Broke His Head and Other Secrets,* p. 1267.
Kirkus Reviews, February 15, 2005, review of *How Evan Broke His Head and Other Secrets,* p. 195.
Library Journal, January, 1998, V. Louise Saylor, review of *Raven Stole the Moon,* p. 145.
Publishers Weekly, December 8, 1997, review of *Raven Stole the Moon,* p. 53; March 28, 2005, review of *How Evan Broke His Head and Other Secrets,* p. 57.

ONLINE

Garth Stein Home Page, http://www.garthstein.com (July 10, 2005).
Plays 411, http://www.plays411.com/ (July 10, 2005), "Garth Stein."
Raven Moon Web site, http://www.ravenmoon.com/ (July 10, 2005).
Writers Write Web site, http://www.writerswrite.com/ (July 10, 2005), "Garth Stein."*

*   *   *

STEIN, Sara Bonnett 1935-2005

PERSONAL: Born October 7, 1935; died of lung cancer, February 25, 2005, in Vinalhaven, ME; daughter of Earl Clough (an insurance medical examiner) and Sara (a psychoanalyst) Bonnett; married Martin Stein (an architect), 1959; children: Aram, Joshua, Rafael, Lincoln. *Education:* Attended Cornell College; New School for Social Research (now New School University), B.A. *Hobbies and other interests:* Gardening.

CAREER: Writer and illustrator. During early career, worked as a toy designer.

AWARDS, HONORS: Noah's Garden: Restoring the Ecology of Our Own Back Yards named among 75 Great American Garden Books, American Horticultural Society.

WRITINGS:

(Editor) *New Parents' Guide to Early Learning,* introduction by Ira J. Gordon, New American Library (New York, NY), 1976.

Learn at Home the Sesame Street Way, Simon & Schuster (New York, NY), 1979.

(And illustrator) *A Family Dollhouse,* photographs by Jon Naso, Viking (New York, NY), 1979.

(Editor) *Soviet Almanac,* Harcourt (New York, NY), 1981.

Girls & Boys: The Limits of Nonsexist Childrearing, Scribner (New York, NY), 1983.

My Weeds: A Gardener's Botany, illustrated by Ippy Patterson, Harper (New York, NY), 1988.

(With Carol Greenberg) *Pretend Your Nose Is a Crayon, and Other Strategies for Staying Younger Longer,* Houghton (Boston, MA), 1991.

(And illustrator) *Noah's Garden: Restoring the Ecology of Our Own Back Yards,* Houghton (Boston, MA), 1993.

Planting Noah's Garden: Further Adventures in Backyard Ecology, Houghton (Boston, MA), 1997.

Noah's Children: Restoring the Ecology of Childhood, North Point Press (New York, NY), 2001.

(Author of foreword) Zeva Oelbaum, *Flowers in Shadow: A Photographer Rediscovers a Victorian Botanical Journal,* Rizzoli (New York, NY), 2002.

FOR CHILDREN

A Piece of Red Paper, illustrated by Otto David Sherman, Small World Press (Princeton, NJ), 1973.

About Dying: An Open Family Book for Parents and Children Together, photographs by Dick Frank, Walker (New York, NY), 1974.

A Hospital Story: An Open Family Book for Parents and Children Together, photographs by Gilbert W. Kliman, Walker (New York, NY), 1974.

The New Baby: An Open Family Book for Parents and Children Together, photographs by Dick Frank, Walker (New York, NY), 1974.

About Handicaps: An Open Family Book for Parents and Children Together, photographs by Dick Frank, Walker (New York, NY), 1974.

Making Babies: An Open Family Book for Parents and Children Together, photographs by Doris Pinney, Walker (New York, NY), 1974.

The Kids' Kitchen Take-over, Workman Publishing (New York, NY), 1975.

How to Raise a Puppy, photographs by Robert Weinreb, Random House (New York, NY), 1976.

How to Raise Mice, Rats, Hamsters, and Gerbils, photographs by Robert Weinreb, Random House (New York, NY), 1976.

Great Pets!: An Extraordinary Guide to Usual and Unusual Family Pets, Workman Publishing (New York, NY), 1976.

How to Raise Goldfish and Guppies, photographs by Robert Weinreb, Random House (New York, NY), 1976.

A Child Goes to School, photographs by Don Connors, Dolphin Books (Garden City, NY), 1978.

The Adopted One: An Open Family Book for Parents and Children Together, Walker (New York, NY), 1979.

About Phobias: An Open Family Book for Parents and Children Together, photographs by Erika Stone, Walker (New York, NY), 1979.

On Divorce: An Open Family Book for Parents and Children Together, Walker (New York, NY), 1979.

The Science Book, Workman Publishing (New York, NY), 1979.

Cat, illustrated by Manuel Garcia, Harcourt (San Diego, CA), 1985.

Mouse, illustrated by Manuel Garcia, Harcourt (San Diego, CA), 1985.

(And illustrator) *The Evolution Book,* photographs by Rona Beame, Workman Publishing (New York, NY), 1986.

(And illustrator) *The Body Book,* Workman Publishing (New York, NY), 1992.

Oh, Baby!, illustrated by Holly Ann Shelowitz, Walker (New York, NY), 1993.

SIDELIGHTS: Sara Bonnett Stein was best known as a writer of nonfiction books for children, as well as three books for adults about ecologically minded gardening. Stein initially earned a degree in Russian studies from the New School for Social Research, but after she married and began a family, her mind turned to other subjects. First, she found work as a toy designer and even constructed a doll house that was exhibited at the Museum of the City of New York, and became the subject of her 1979 book *A Family Dollhouse.* Then her interest turned to writing nonfiction for children. Notable among these titles is her series that addresses serious issues, such as death, adoption, hospitalization, phobias, and divorce, in a way that young readers can understand. Books such as *Making Babies: An Open Family Book for Parents and Children Together* and *On Divorce: An Open Family Book for Parents and Children Together* are written specifically so that parents can sit down with their children and discuss these issues with the assistance of Stein's text. Stein also wrote juvenile nonfiction on such subjects as taking care of one's pets and scientific subjects such as evolution and human anatomy.

Some of Stein's books about children are intended for adults. Her *Girls & Boys: The Limits of Nonsexist Childrearing,* for example, tries to dispel some misconceptions parents may have about gender identity. Although some psychologists have held that gender roles in children are largely learned through their environment, Stein pointed out that there is also a strong biological basis for how a boy or girl behaves. In fact, the author goes so far as to assert that parents are misguided if they try to avoid gender stereotyping in their child-rearing practices. "*Girls & Boys* is a triumph of femininity over fanaticism," Joseph Sobran concluded in the *National Review* praising the book as a "seamless blend of experience and scholarship." Noting that the author's position will invite some criticism from those who do not share her views, the reviewer attested that there is much "wisdom" in the work and that Stein "has done a lovely thing" in writing it.

An amateur gardener, Stein had long worked in her backyard to produce a beautiful vista incorporating flowers and ornamental plants. However, as she cleared away native species of flora, she noticed that her home was visited less and less frequently by birds, butterflies, and other endemic animals. Eventually, she realized that her "gardening" was destroying the native environment. This led her to study ecology and write a series of books about how gardening can affect the environment, beginning with *Noah's Garden: Restoring the Ecology of Our Own Back Yards.* This book urges people to become better stewards of the land, and to plant flowers, shrubs, herbs, and grasses that will attract wildlife by providing them with food and shelter. "The book is an account of her reeducation," according to *Horticulture* contributor Christopher Reed. "It is filled with personality, and among its other virtues it is entertaining reading." *Countryside & Small Stock Journal* reviewer Robert Di Falco praised how the "author explains land and vegetation and habitat in a way that is easily understood."

In her follow-up book, *Planting Noah's Garden: Further Adventures in Backyard Ecology,* Stein talks about her experiences on the lecture circuit after she published *Noah's Garden,* and she further develops her explanations on how to create natural backyard habitats. Camille LeFevre, writing in a *Horticulture*

review, observed some flaws in Stein's ideas about conservation, noting that advocating collecting certain plant species from the wild and replanting them in one's own garden is sure to "infuriate conservationists." LeFevre also did not agree with Stein's suggestions that mixing native and non-native species is fine, yet at the same time strongly indicting the "public nonchalance about invasive exotic species." On the other hand, a *Library Journal* contributor felt that *Planting Noah's Garden* "will surely become a bible for anyone interested in a rehabilitation project."

With *Noah's Children: Restoring the Ecology of Childhood* Stein combined her interest in gardening with her concern for children in a book about the necessity of exposing children to nature in order for them to better develop healthy bodies and minds. Stein maintains that city children who spend most of their time indoors, and children who live in the suburbs but are surrounded by an unnaturally manicured landscape that is largely bereft of wildlife, are denied sensory experiences that can enhance creativity and problem-solving skills. While critic Laura Sessions Stepp commented in a *Washington Post Book World* review that Stein's arguments can be flawed by their sense of nostalgia for the old, pre-suburbia days, she added that "Stein does a great service by reminding us how the pieces of a child's environment should fit together." A *Publishers Weekly* contributor concluded that "Stein's rambling style, her observations and philosophy are consistently engrossing."

BIOGRAPHICAL AND CRITICAL SOURCES:

PERIODICALS

Booklist, March 1, 1994, Stephanie Zvirin, review of *Oh, Baby!,* p. 1261.

Chicago Tribune, August 5, 2001, Joanne Trestrail, interview with Sara Bonnett Stein, p. 5.

Countryside & Small Stock Journal, May-June, 1994, Robert Di Falco, review of *Noah's Children: Restoring the Ecology of Childhood,* p. 72.

EPA Journal, winter, 1995, review of *Noah's Children,* p. 27.

Horticulture, October, 1993, Christopher Reed, review of *Noah's Garden: Restoring the Ecology of Our Own Back Yards,* p. 70; February, 1998, Camille LeFevre, review of *Planting Noah's Garden: Further Adventures in Backyard Ecology,* p. 60.

Library Journal, April 15, 1997, Beth Clewis Crim, review of *Planting Noah's Garden,* p. 106; June 1, 2001, review of *Noah's Children,* p. 198.

National Review, March 23, 1984, Joseph Sobran, review of *Girls & Boys: The Limits of Nonsexist Childrearing,* p. 46.

Publishers Weekly, March 8, 1993, review of *Noah's Garden,* p. 58; September 20, 1993, review of *Oh, Baby!,* p. 70; May 28, 2001, review of *Noah's Children,* p. 70; June 23, 2003, review of *Great Pets!: An Extraordinary Guide to Usual and Unusual Family Pets,* p. 70.

School Library Journal, December, 1993, Jacqueline Elsner, review of *Oh, Baby!,* p. 109.

Washington Post Book World, July 11, 2001, Laura Sessions Stepp, review of *Noah's Children,* p. 9.

ONLINE

Wild Ones Web site, http://www.for-wild.org/ (June 28, 2004), Cindy Crosby, "A Conversation with Sara Stein."

OBITUARIES

PERIODICALS

Los Angeles Times, March 14, 2005, p. B7.
New York Times, March 9, 2005, p. A23.*

*   *   *

STELLA, Leslie

PERSONAL: Married; children: one son. *Education:* Graduated from Marquette University.

ADDRESSES: Home—Chicago, IL *Agent*—c/o Author Mail, Three Rivers Press, 1745 Broadway, New York, NY 10019.

CAREER: Journalist and novelist. *Lumpen* (zine), Chicago, IL, founder and editor, 1992-98.

WRITINGS:

Fat Bald Jeff, Grove Press (New York, NY), 2001.

The Easy Hour, Three Rivers Press (New York, NY), 2003.

Unimaginable Zero Summer, Three Rivers Press (New York, NY), 2005.

Contributor of short fiction to periodicals, including *Mississippi Review, Adirondack Review, Bust,* and *Easy Listener,* and to anthology *Book of Zines,* Henry Holt (New York, NY), 1997.

SIDELIGHTS: Writer Leslie Stella was raised in Milwaukee, Wisconsin, and attended Marquette University before moving to Chicago and starting the zine, *Lumpen* for which she served as editor and co-publisher. The magazine was issued once or twice a year between 1992 and 1998, and focused on culture and political commentary. Stella then moved on to writing novels, starting with *Fat Bald Jeff,* is a humorous look at job dissatisfaction and the struggle to find one's place in the world. Heroine Addie Prewett is the product of wealthy grandparents and drop-out, hippie parents, and her greatest wish is to find the perfect life, complete with house, garden, and a servant. Instead she shares a plain apartment and works as an underpaid copy editor at the fictional National Association of Libraries. Michael Cart, in a review for the *San Francisco Chronicle,* remarked that "Addie has an often-askew take on reality, but her misinterpretations are as comically transparent to readers as a freshly washed window," and concluded that "there are so many funny lines . . . that even librarians may like it." Danise Hoover, reviewing the novel in *Booklist,* commented that, "although as subtle as a sledgehammer, this is a fun, harmless, and quick read." A contributor for *OnMilwaukee.com* wrote of the book: "fresh, fast-paced and laugh-out-loud funny, it marks Stella as an author to watch."

Stella's follow-up book, *The Easy Hour,* returns to the theme of the workplace. The novel recounts the story of Lisa Galisa, who works at a Chicago store selling sportswear to fisherman, and is desperate to change her lot in life. A reviewer for *Publishers Weekly* wrote that "this sparkling novel probes the humiliations and class divisions of the workplace with intelligence and wit." A contributor for *Kirkus Reviews* called the book "a good-natured comedy about social climbing as a nice girl from Chicago's South Side gets taken up by the glitterati," concluding that it was "a pleasant take on the vanity of human wishes: well conceived, nicely wrapped up." Amanda Taylor, in a review for *USA Today.com*, remarked that "wacky plot twists peppered with witty dialogue keep the story entertaining. There's never a dull moment."

In *Unimaginable Zero Summer* Stella introduces Verity Presti, an overweight young woman who loves thrift stores and crocheted beer hats, and who is distressed at the approach of her fifteen-year high school reunion. Stella follows Verity as she tries to take stock of her life, and eventually reveals to the reader the truth behind Verity's unhappiness. Katie Haegele, in a review for the *Philadelphia Inquirer*, remarked that "Stella's novel is about a lot of things—grief, growing older, fear of failure, Scandinavian death metal, and getting over it, whatever *it* happens to be. But it's also a moving portrait of the squirrelly ways we all have of dealing with those things." A contributor for *Kirkus Reviews* called the book "a comforting if sometimes cartoonish riff on Gen-X lives."

Stella is also the author of a number of short stories. Her fiction has appeared in such publications as the *Mississippi Review*, *Adirondack Review*, and *Easy Listener*, and was nominated for the Pushcart Prize in 2004.

BIOGRAPHICAL AND CRITICAL SOURCES:

PERIODICALS

Booklist, February 1, 2001, Danise Hoover, review of *Fat Bald Jeff*, p. 1041.
Kirkus Reviews, March 1, 2003, review of *The Easy Hour*, p. 344; February 15, 2005, review of *Unimaginable Zero Summer*, p. 196.
Publishers Weekly, February 26, 2001, review of *Fat Bald Jeff*, p. 58; January 27, 2003, review of *The Easy Hour*, p. 233.

ONLINE

Adirondack Online, http://adirondackreview. homestead.com/ (July 12, 2005), "Leslie Stella."
Leslie Stella Home Page, http://www.lesliestella.com (July 12, 2005).

OnMilwaukee.com, http://www.onmilwaukee.com/ (July 12, 2005), "Leslie Stella."
Philadelphia Inquirer Online, http://www.macon.com/ (July 12, 2005), "Leslie Stella."
San Francisco Chronicle Online, http://www.sfgate. com/ (July 12, 2005), "Leslie Stella."
USA Today Online, http://www.usatoday.com/ (July 12, 2005), "Leslie Stella."*

*   *   *

STOCKLEY, Philippa

PERSONAL: Female.

ADDRESSES: Home—London, England. *Office*—Evening Standard, Northcliffe House, 2 Derry St., Kensington, London W8 5TT, England. *Agent*—c/o Rogers, Coleridge & White, 20 Powis Mews, London W11 1JN, England.

CAREER: Writer and painter. *Evening Standard*, London, England, deputy editor.

WRITINGS:

FICTION

The Edge of Pleasure, Abacus (London, England), 2002.
A Factory of Cunning, Harcourt (Orlando, FL), 2005.

SIDELIGHTS: Philippa Stockley is a painter and a deputy editor for London's *Evening Standard* newspaper, as well as a novelist. Stockley's debut novel, *The Edge of Pleasure*, focuses on Gilver, a successful young English artist who lives a decadent life and is famous for his over-the-top parties and good looks as much as for his paintings. Though his lavish lifestyle gradually causes a decrease in productivity, he fails to curtail his spending and finds himself, at nearly forty, nearly broke. When Gilver meets Alice, he takes advantage of her good will as well as her feelings for him, but inevitably Alice's strength of character wins out. A contributor for *Kirkus Reviews* called the book a "brazenly romantic debut" and concluded that "while Stockley can be catty . . . she is seldom glib and never dull. Repellent characters [are] redeemed by saucy, vivid writing."

Stockley's sophomore effort, *A Factory of Cunning,* is an historical novel that picks up where French novelist Choderlos de Laclos's *Les liasions dangereuse* left off. It tells the story of how the marquise is forced to leave France after causing the deaths of two people and the ruin of a young girl. The noblewoman takes on the name of Mrs. Fox and flees to London. As de Laclos did with his own work, Stockley tells the entire story through letters and excerpts from diaries. She follows "Mrs. Fox" during her time in London, revealing that she has learned nothing from her tragic experiences in France as she continues to toy with people's lives simply to entertain herself. In a review for the *Spectator,* Andrew Barrow called Stockley's novel "a squelchingly well-researched period piece with sex, lust, over-ripeness and what one character calls the 'odour' of the scholar permeating every paragraph," also describing it as "a remarkable tour de force, jam-packed with poetry, verbal fireworks, vitality and charm." Cynthia Johnson, writing for *Library Journal,* praised the novel by calling it "a compellingly complex tale of seduction, betrayal, and manipulation," and a contributor for *Publishers Weekly* stated that it is "narrated with wit and sexually provocative detail." In an article for the *Independent Online,* D.J. Taylor wrote that. "If Stockley's accomplished second novel has a flaw it is the thought that, amid lashings of cruelty and moral turpitude, nothing very serious is at stake." Jessica Mann, in an online review for the London *Telegraph,* stated that "the scene is convincingly set; the action keeps the audience's attention; and in the end the outcome of Fox and the earl's devious machinations is about as credible, or incredible, as a traditional melodrama's final corpse-strewn stage." London *Observer* online contributor Laura Baggaley remarked that "Stockley spins a romantic yarn of travel, murder, intrigue and adventure while resolutely rejecting the sentiment of romance. This is a cracking tale of depravity, our avaricious heroine fiercely committed to life and survival—too awful to like but too fascinating to hate."

Stockley told *CA:* "Writing and painting are things I have always done, interchangeably. The act or art of describing—for so they both are—is gripping, consuming, exciting. It would be too simple to say that one feeds into the other, but it IS true that one restores the other. When I can write no longer, I can paint, and vice versa. I consider this the greatest good fortune."

BIOGRAPHICAL AND CRITICAL SOURCES:

PERIODICALS

Kirkus Reviews, November 1, 2003, review of *The Edge of Pleasure,* p. 1293; January 1, 2005, review of *A Factory of Cunning,* p. 20.
Library Journal, December 1, 2004, Barbara Hoffert, review of *A Factory of Cunning,* p. 88; March 1, 2005, Cynthia Johnson, review of *A Factory of Cunning,* p. 81.
Publishers Weekly, February 7, 2005, review of *A Factory of Cunning,* p. 38.
Spectator, March 12, 2005, Andrew Barrow, "Lady into Urban Fox," p. 48.

ONLINE

Bookpage, http://www.bookpage.com/ (July 12, 2005), "Philippa Stockley."
Curled up with a Good Book, http://www.curledup.com/ (July 12, 2005), "Philippa Stockley."
Independent Online, http://enjoyment.independent.co.uk/ (July 12, 2005), D.J. Taylor, review of *A Factory of Cunning.*
Observer Online, http://books.guardian.co.uk/ (July 12, 2005), Laura Baggaly, review of *A Factory of Cunning.*
Telegraph.co.uk, http://www.telegraph.co.uk/ (July 12, 2005), Jessica Mann, review of *A Factory of Cunning.*

*   *   *

STONE, David Lee 1978-

PERSONAL: Born 1978, in Margate, Kent, England; son of Barbara Anne Stone and Henry Cooke. *Hobbies and other interests:* Role-playing games.

ADDRESSES: Home—Kent, England. *Agent*—c/o Author Mail, Hodder Headline, 338 Euston Rd., London NW1 3BH, England.

CAREER: Novelist. Blockbuster Video, clerk, then assistant manager, 1999-2001; freelance writer.

AWARDS, HONORS: Three Dover District Festival of Literature prizes, 1988.

WRITINGS:

The Ratastrophe Catastrophe ("Illmoor Chronicles"), Hodder Children's Books (London, England), 2003, Hyperion Books for Children (New York, NY), 2004.

The Yowler Foul-Up ("Illmoor Chronicles"), Hodder Children's Books (London, England), 2004.

The Shadwell Shenanigans ("Illmoor Chronicles"), Hodder Children's Books (London, England), 2005.

Contributor to periodicals, including *Xenos* and *SFX.* Short fiction included in anthology *Knights of Madness,* edited by Peter Haining, Souvenir Press, 1998.

ADAPTATIONS: The Ratastrophe Catastrophe was adapted as an audiobook, read by Robert Llewellyn, Listening Library, 2004.

SIDELIGHTS: A fan of fantasy literature and role-playing games, British writer David Lee Stone knew that he wanted to be a writer from an early age, and was inspired by the works of Douglas Adams (his literary idol), Terry Pratchett, Mervyn Peake, and Fritz Leiber. Leaving secondary school at age sixteen after an admittedly irregular attendance record, he worked as a freelance writer for several years. He had several stories published in *Xenon* magazine, but became so discouraged with his novel-length efforts that he tossed away his second full-length manuscript. Thanks to his mother, who fished the manuscript out of the trash and mail it to a literary agent, Stone has since become a published author: his first novel, *The Ratastrophe Catastrophe,* was published in 2003 as the first volume of Stone's "Illmoor Chronicles," a fantasy series that had been in the works for much of its author's life. Praising Stone's brand of fantasy in *Kliatt,* Michele Winship wrote that the novel serves up "a healthy dose of sarcasm and one-liners that fly by quickly."

The Ratastrophe Catastrophe introduces readers to the slightly askew city of Dullitch in the land of Illmoor. Dullitch residents proudly engage in thievery in addition to other unethical modes of behavior, all guided by an egomaniacal duke. In addition to all its societal corruption, Dullitch also happens to be plagued by rats. Diek Wustapha, a young shepherd, seems to be the solution to the citizens' plight: he possesses a magical mouth organ that is able to lead the rats out of the city, much as did the legendary Pied Piper of Hamlin. However, after this particular de-ratting, when Diek goes to collect his payment due from the city council, his request is refused. In revenge, the angered young man plays a new tune, this time leading Dullitch children away into hidden caves and forests. Worried for the town's youth, Duke Modeset commissions the quick-witted and well-connected Jimmy Quickstint, along with a dwarf comrade, to track the children down, promising a healthy reward in return. Larry Cooperman commented in *School Library Journal* that "*The Ratastrophe Catastrophe* comes crackling to life with humor, danger, and adventure," while in *Horn Book* Anita L. Burkham called Stone's prose "lighthearted" and his protagonists "outsized and colorful."

The Ratastrophe Catastrophe was followed by *The Yowler Foul-Up* and *The Shadwell Shenanigans,* both of which continue to chronicle the events ongoing in and around Dullitch. In *The Yowler Foul-Up* a sect takes root in the corrupt city, making it even more unpleasant than ever. Rising to fight this growing menace are Jimmy Quickstint as well as a less-than-enthusiastic Duke Modeset and a half-vampiric resident. Further events are covered in *The Shadwell Shenanigans,* as a pair of local looters run amuck while citizens demand that the duke take action. Remarking on his own long relationship with reading, Stone was quoted as remarking on the British Literacy Trust Web site: "Reading is fun and exciting, and there's nothing better than a really good book. Films allow you to explore other people's imaginations, but books allow to explore YOUR OWN."

BIOGRAPHICAL AND CRITICAL SOURCES:

PERIODICALS

Booklist, November 1, 2004, Kay Weisman, review of *The Ratastrophe Catastrophe,* p. 486.

Bookseller, April 11, 2003, p. 11.

Bulletin of the Center for Children's Books, January, 2005, Timnah Card, review of *The Ratastrophe Catastrophe,* p. 228.

Horn Book, January-February, 2005, Anita L. Burkam, review of *The Ratastrophe Catastrophe,* p. 99.

Kirkus Reviews, September 15, 2004, review of *The Ratastrophe Catastrophe,* p. 921.

Kliatt, November, 2004, Michele Winship, review of *The Ratastrophe Catastrophe,* p. 11; May, 2005, Carol Reich, review of *The Ratastrophe Catastrophe,* p. 59.

Library Media Connection, February, 2005, Sherry Hoy, review of *The Ratastrophe Catastrophe,* p. 74.

M2 Best Books, March 26, 2003.

Publishers Weekly, November 8, 2004, review of *The Ratastrophe Catastrophe,* p. 56.

School Library Journal, January, 2005, Farida S. Dowler, review of *The Ratastrophe Catastrophe,* p. 137; February, 2005, Larry Cooperman, review of *The Ratastrophe Catastrophe,* p. 74.

Voice of Youth Advocates, December, 2004, review of *The Ratastrophe Catastrophe,* p. 410.

ONLINE

British Broadcasting Corporation Web site, http://www.bbc.co.uk/ (November 6, 2005), "David Lee Stone."

David Lee Stone Home Page, http://www.illmoorchronicles.com (November 6, 2005).

Infinity Plus Web site, http://www.infinityplus.co.uk/ (January 29, 2005), Caleb Woodbridge, review of *The Ratastrophe Catastrophe.*

Literacy Trust Web site, http://www.literacytrust.org.uk/ (November 6, 2005), "Reading Champions: David Lee Stone."

Write Away! Web site, http://www.improbability.ultralab.net/writeaway/ (April 8, 2005), Tom Costello, interview with Stone.

*   *   *

STRAND, Ginger
(Ginger Gail Strand)

PERSONAL: Female. *Education:* Princeton University, Ph.D., 1992.

ADDRESSES: Home—New York, NY. *Agent*—c/o Author Mail, Simon & Schuster, 1230 Avenue of the Americas, New York, NY 10020. *E-mail*—email@gingerstrand.com.

CAREER: Author, freelance communications consultant, and copywriter. Part-time instructor at New York University, New York, NY, and Fordham University, New York, NY. Has also worked as a roadhouse waitress, advertising agency secretary, copywriter for a consultant firm, test-question writer, film critic, studio assistant for an artist, medical transcriber, theatre box-office manager, and restaurant hostess.

AWARDS, HONORS: Awarded fiction residencies at Yaddo and Virginia Center for the Creative Arts; Sewanee Writers' Conference Tennessee Williams scholarship; MacDowell Colony fellowship.

WRITINGS:

Flight (novel), Simon & Schuster (New York, NY), 2005.

Author of short stories. Contributor to numerous magazines, including *Swink Online, Poets & Writers, Believer, Iowa Review, Carolina Quarterly, Raritan, Gettysburg Review, Review: Literature and Arts of the Americas, Mississippi Review, Harper's,* and *New England Review.*

SIDELIGHTS: Although trained as an academic, Ginger Strand found her calling writing fiction. She wrote and published numerous short stories before producing her first novel, *Flight.* The novel is greatly influenced by Strand's own father, who was employed as a pilot for TransWorld Airlines. In the book, the protagonist, Will Gruen, is a commercial airline pilot who also works on his family farm in Michigan. Will struggles with his career as he nears a forced, age-related retirement, while his wife, Carol, is unhappy and looking for her own career path. Meanwhile, the couple's two daughters deal with their own life issues: Margaret's marriage is falling apart, while Leanne is about to be married.

A critic writing in *Publishers Weekly* noted that "Strand writes convincingly, if not scintillatingly, of the Gruen family as they face down their demons and reach out for their dreams in this solid debut." Other critics were also enthusiastic. *Library Journal* contributor Patrick Sullivan calling *Flight* "impressive" and stating: "This powerfully engaging novel is enthusiastically recommended."

Strand told *CA:* "I've always wanted to be a writer, because I've always enjoyed reading more than anything else in life. I love everything from Virgil to Virginia Woolf to *Vogue* magazine. Sometimes I have to stop reading, because I tend to hear the voices of other authors in my head when I'm writing. A little bit of that is okay, but not too much. In an ideal world my own writing would be like a hallway, taking you in its own direction, but with everything I've ever read echoing down it."

BIOGRAPHICAL AND CRITICAL SOURCES:

PERIODICALS

Booklist, April 1, 2005, review of *Flight,* p. 1345.
Kirkus Reviews, March 1, 2005, review of *Flight,* p. 258.
Library Journal, April 1, 2005, Patrick Sullivan, review of *Flight,* p. 89.
Publishers Weekly, March 21, 2005, review of *Flight,* p. 36.

ONLINE

Ginger Strand Home Page, http://www.gingerstrand. com (June 29, 2005).

*   *   *

STRAND, Ginger Gail
  See STRAND, Ginger

*   *   *

STRATTON, William Kip
  See STRATTON, W.K.

*   *   *

STRATTON, W.K.
  (William Kip Stratton)

PERSONAL: Married; wife's name, Luscaine.

ADDRESSES: Home—Austin, TX. *Agent*—c/o Author Mail, Harcourt, 6277 Sea Harbor Dr., Orlando, FL 32887.

CAREER: Freelance newspaper and magazine journalist.

WRITINGS:

Backyard Brawl: Inside the Blood Feud between Texas and Texas A & M, Crown Publishers (New York, NY), 2002.
(Editor, with Jan Reid) *Splendor in the Short Grass: The Grover Lewis Reader,* University of Texas Press (Austin, TX), 2005.
Chasing the Rodeo: On Wild Horse Rides, Broken Hearts and Broken Bones, and One Man's Search for the West, Harcourt (Orlando, FL), 2005.

Contributor to various periodicals, including *Sports Illustrated, Gentleman's Quarterly, Outside,* and *Southern.*

SIDELIGHTS: Texas-based writer W.K. Stratton worked for years as a journalist, both on newspapers and for magazines, before writing his first book, *Backyard Brawl: Inside the Blood Feud between Texas and Texas A & M.* The book examines the legendary rivalry between the two universities' football teams in an attempt to discover what is at the foundations of their long-time feud. He focused on the cultures of each locale, not just the history of the games, in order to give a new view of the ongoing rivalry. A contributor to *Kirkus Reviews* remarked that the book is "good-natured, intelligent, funny, and less bombastic than the title suggests," and Wes Lukowsky, reviewing for *Booklist,* called it "funny, intelligent, insightful, and just a little Texas crazy."

Splendor in the Short Grass: The Grover Lewis Reader collects Texas journalist Grover Lewis's magazine articles and a number of other short works into a single volume. Stratton served as coeditor on the work, along with Jan Reid. Chris Chang, writing for *Film Comment,* called the collection "a gloriously cracked mirror reflecting a not-so-golden age."

Chasing the Rodeo: On Wild Horse Rides, Broken Hearts and Broken Bones, and One Man's Search for the West examines the lives and experiences of the men and women who work on the rodeo circuit. Stratton's own father, whom he barely knew, was a rodeo rider, a connection that prompted Stratton to take on the topic. He covers the history of the sport as well as offering colorful descriptions of the events and the people involved. A *Publishers Weekly* contributor called the book "a lively, earnest portrayal" that "demonstrates rodeo's rich tradition, and . . . vividly illuminates the trials both inside and outside the ring."

BIOGRAPHICAL AND CRITICAL SOURCES:

PERIODICALS

Booklist, September 15, 2002, review of *Backyard Brawl: Inside the Blood Feud between Texas and Texas A & M,* p. 193.

Film Comment, March-April, 2005, Chris Chang, review of *Splendor in the Short Grass: The Grover Lewis Reader,* p. 77.

Kirkus Reviews, June 15, 2002, review of *Backyard Brawl,* p. 869; February 15, 2005, review of *Chasing the Rodeo: On Wild Horse Rides, Broken Hearts and Broken Bones, and One Man's Search for the West,* p. 221.

Library Journal, September 1, 2002, William O. Scheeren, review of *Backyard Brawls,* p. 184.

Publishers Weekly, March 7, 2005, review of *Chasing the Rodeo,* p. 57.

Texas Monthly, March, 2005, Mike Shea, review of *Chasing the Rodeo,* p. 72.

ONLINE

W.K. Stratton Home Page, http://www.wkstratton.com (July 11, 2005).*

*   *   *

STRODTBECK, Fred L. 1919-2005
(Fred Louis Strodtbeck)

OBITUARY NOTICE— See index for *CA* sketch: Born June 10, 1919, in Middletown, OH; died of Parkinson's disease-related heart failure, August 7, 2005, in Chicago, IL. Sociologist, educator, and author. Strodtbeck was a retired University of Chicago professor who was best known for his work studying group dynamics and how groups of people choose their leaders. His undergraduate studies were done at Miami University, where he earned a B.A. in 1940; he then earned a master's degree from Indiana University in 1942. With his studies interrupted by World War II, he served in the U.S. Army as a researcher. After returning to civilian life, Strodtbeck taught for two years at the University of California at Los Angeles before finishing his Ph.D. at Harvard University in 1950. During the early 1950s, he was an assistant professor at Yale University. He then joined the University of Chicago faculty in 1953, and he remained there for the rest of his academic career, retiring in 1989. While at the University of Chicago Strodtbeck served as the director of the Social Psychology Laboratory and as founding director of the Inter-university Project for Behavioral Science Training. His interest in the ways that people interact with one another led to several important studies, including one on how juries select a foreman (he was director of experimental research at the university law school's American Jury Project from 1953 to 1959). He also researched how family members relate to one another and how street gangs pick their leaders. The jury study concluded that several factors are involved when juries pick a spokesman, including gender, age, occupation, and even where people sit around a table. Strodtbeck, furthermore, was codeveloper of the values orientation theory, which is still used by sociologists conducting cross-cultural research. A contributor to many professional journals, encyclopedias, and books, he was the author or coauthor of such titles as *Group Process and Gang Delinquency* (1965) and *A Study of Husband-Wife Interaction in Three Cultures* (1980).

OBITUARIES AND OTHER SOURCES:

PERIODICALS

Chicago Tribune, August 21, 2005, section 4, p. 9.

ONLINE

University of Chicago News Office Web site, http://www-news.uchicago.edu/ (August 17, 2005).

*   *   *

STRODTBECK, Fred Louis
See STRODTBECK, Fred L.

STUART, Gary L. 1939-

PERSONAL: Born October 8, 1939, in Gallup, NM; son of Arthur Lester and DeAva (Cato) Stuart; married August 31, 1962; wife's name, Kathleen Ann; children: Gregory Lester, Kara Stuart Lewis, Tosh Forrest. *Education:* Attended St. Michael's College (Santa Fe, NM), 1961-62; University of Arizona, B.S., J.D., 1967.

ADDRESSES: Office—Gary L. Stuart, P.C., 2039 East Glenn, Phoenix, AZ 85020-5647. *E-mail*—gstuart@ keyed.com.

CAREER: Lawyer, writer, lecturer, and educator. Jennings, Strouss & Salmon, Phoenix, AZ, associate, 1967-71, partner, 1971-98, of counsel, 1998—; practices law part time; University of Arizona James E. Rogers College of Law, Arizona State University College of Law, adjunct law professor. Chairman of ethics committee for Arizona Bar, Phoenix, 1976-86; faculty member of Arizona College Trial Advocacy, 1987; chairman of Arizona Advisory Commission on Litigation, 1989.

MEMBER: Arizona Bar Foundation (founding fellow), American Board of Trial Advocates (faculty member, 1976, president, 1986).

WRITINGS:

The Ethical Trial Lawyer, Arizona State Bar (Phoenix, AZ), 1994.
Ethical Litigation, Lexis-Nexis Publishing, 1998.
The Gallup 14 (novel), University of New Mexico Press (Albuquerque, NM), 2000.
Miranda: The Story of America's Right to Remain Silent (nonfiction), foreword by Janet Napolitano, University of Arizona Press (Tucson, AZ), 2004.

Editor of the *Arizona Law Review* while attending law school.

SIDELIGHTS: Gary L. Stuart, a practicing lawyer and an expert in trial advocacy and professional ethics, has written several books pertaining to the law, including a novel about a 1935 riot of mineworkers that resulted in the murder of a sheriff in Gallup, New Mexico. *The Gallup 14,* recounts the real-life historical episode

through two fictitious narrators: a member of the defense team named Billy Wade and Wade's lover, Mary Ann Shaughnessy, who is a schoolteacher. The people charged with the sheriff's murder are Mexican workers who rioted because of low pay and mistreatment while working in the town's nearby coal fields. Further complicating the plot is the ongoing struggle to see who will lead the miners: the National Miners Union, which was backed by a communist organization, or the United Mine Workers, led by the famous John L. Lewis. A *Publishers Weekly* contributor noted that the book "provide[s] fascinating insights into the moral schisms of New Mexico's political-legal-judicial hierarchy of the day." The reviewer went on to note that the author's "painstakingly constructed novel stands as telling social/moral commentary."

Stuart's book *Miranda: The Story of America's Right to Remain Silent* is a nonfiction look at the famous case that led to the legal requirement that law officers read criminals their rights, beginning with, "You have the right to remain silent." The *Miranda* case stems from the 1963 arrest and conviction of an uneducated Latino for various crimes committed in Phoenix. The American Civil Liberties Union eventually took on the case and argued before the U.S. Supreme Court that Miranda did not know about a person's right not to incriminate himself. The court ultimately issued the Miranda warning statement that is now required to be read to people accused of crimes. In addition to the right to remain silent, the other three points to be made in the statement are to inform arrested persons that anything they said can be used in a court of law during their trial, that they have a right to a lawyer during questioning, and that a lawyer can be appointed to them if they cannot afford one. In his book, Stuart delves into the many facts of the case and the court proceedings. He then discusses the relation between the *Miranda* case and civil liberties, including a discussion of the potential assaults on civil liberties following the September 11, 2001, terrorist attacks.

In a review of *Miranda* on the *Z Mag* Web site, William Lengeman noted that many books have been written about the case and its aftermath but added: "Something Stuart brings to the table, that many of his predecessors did not, is a familiarity with the case and many of the principals from the legal and law enforcement communities in Arizona, where the Miranda case played out." David Pitt, writing in *Booklist,* called the book "interesting, timely, and important." *Legal Times* contributor Seth Stern noted, "Lay readers get a primer on criminal procedure. Students of the law see how a case percolates to the Supreme Court, owing less to a deficient defense attorney than to a nudge from a local lawyer from the American Civil Liberties Union." John Shelton Lawrence noted in the *Journal of American Culture* that the author "contributes notably to understanding the maze of issues and emotions embedded in Miranda," and Lawrence added that "Stuart offers a balanced discussion of whether Miranda has impeded law enforcement, citing predictably conflicting opinions."

BIOGRAPHICAL AND CRITICAL SOURCES:

PERIODICALS

Booklist, September 1, 2004, David Pitt, review of *Miranda: The Story of America's Right to Remain Silent,* p. 31.

Business Journal (Phoenix, AZ), October 15, 1999, Tara Teichgraeber, "Long-Time Valley Lawyer Tapped for Regents Board," p. 19.

Journal of American Culture, June, 2005, John Shelton Lawrence, review of *Miranda,* p. 241.

Legal Times, October 4, 2004, Seth Stern, review of *Miranda.*

Publishers Weekly, February 7, 2000, review of *The Gallup 14,* p. 65.

ONLINE

Gallup 14 Web site, http://www.thegallup14.com/ (August 22, 2005).

Gary L. Stuart Home Page, http://www.garylstuart.com (August 22, 2005).

Z Mag Online, http://zmagsite.zmag.org/ (August 22, 2005), William Lengeman, review of *Miranda.**

*   *   *

STURGES, Philemon

PERSONAL: Married; wife's name, Judy Sue; children: three daughters. *Hobbies and other interests:* Cooking.

ADDRESSES: Home—Boston, MA; Princeton, MA. *Agent*—c/o Author Mail, HarperCollins Children's Books, 1350 Avenue of the Americas, New York, NY 10019.

CAREER: Architect and children's writer. *Military service:* U.S. Navy, served four years.

WRITINGS:

CHILREN'S BOOKS

The Gift of Christmas, illustrated by Holly Berry, North-South Books (New York, NY), 1995.

Ten Flashing Fireflies, illustrated by Anna Vojtech, North-South Books (New York, NY), 1995.

Rainsong/Snowsong, illustrated by Shari Halpern, North-South Books (New York, NY), 1995.

What's that Sound, Woolly Bear?, illustrated by Joan Paley, Little, Brown (Boston, MA), 1996.

(Reteller, with Anna Vojtech) *Marushka and the Month Brothers: A Folktale,* illustrated by Anna Vojtech, North-South Books (New York, NY), 1996.

Bridges Are to Cross, illustrated by Giles Laroche, G.P. Putnam (New York, NY), 1998.

Crocky Dilly, illustrated by Paige Miglio, Museum of Fine Arts (Boston, MA), 1998.

(Reteller) *The Little Red Hen Makes a Pizza,* illustrated by Amy Walrod, Dutton Children's Books (New York, NY), 1999.

I Love Trucks!, illustrated by Shari Halpern, HarperCollins (New York, NY), 1999.

Sacred Places, illustrated by Giles Laroche, G.P. Putnam (New York, NY), 2000.

(With Bonnie Lass) *Who Took the Cookies from the Cookie Jar?,* illustrated by Ashley Wolff, Little, Brown (Boston, MA), 2000.

I Love Trains!, illustrated by Shari Halpern, HarperCollins (New York, NY), 2001.

I Love Planes!, illustrated by Shari Halpern, HarperCollins (New York, NY), 2003.

I Love School!, illustrated by Shari Halpern, HarperCollins (New York, NY), 2004.

She'll Be Comin' 'Round the Mountain, Little, Brown (Boston, MA), 2004.

Down to the Sea in Ships, illustrated by Giles Laroche, G.P. Putnam (New York, NY), 2004.

I Love Bugs!, illustrated by Shari Halpern, HarperCollins (New York, NY), 2005.

This Little Pirate, illustrated by Amy Walrod, Dutton Children's Books (New York, NY), 2005.

Waggers, illustrated by Jim Ishikawa, Dutton Children's Books (New York, NY), 2005.

I Love Tools!, illustrated by Shari Halpern, HarperCollins (New York, NY), 2006.

ADAPTATIONS: She'll Be Comin' 'Round the Mountain, was adapted as a video, Nutmeg Media, 2005.

SIDELIGHTS: Philemon Sturges left behind his career as an architect so he could focus all his energies on writing children's books. "Everything is new to kids," Sturges noted on his home page. "It is an honor to introduce them to things—plus, it's fun." In one of his first books, *Ten Flashing Fireflies,* Sturges tells the story of a little boy and girl catching fireflies and putting them in a glass jar. The book enables the young reader to count from one to ten as each firefly is captured. At the end of the story the young children count down as they watch the fireflies fly away. In a review in *Booklist,* Lauren Peterson commented, "This most unusual counting book captures the charm and innocence of a favorite summertime activity." A *Publishers Weekly* contributor called the book "makes a memorable entry in a heavily populated picture-book category."

Sturges focuses on the holiday season in *The Gift of Christmas,* which a *Publishers Weekly* contributor noted "catalogues with delight the sights, sounds and smells" of Christmas. In *Rainsong/Snowsong* the author tells various stories through rhyme as a boy and a girl marvel at the rain and snow. "The fun of it all is captured in the buoyant double-page illustrations," noted Leone McDermott in *Booklist.*

What's That Sound, Woolly Bear? guides young readers through a list of various insects. "A final spread gives interesting additional information on each insect, including a way to tell temperature by counting chirps," noted Susan Dove Lempke in *Booklist.* A *Publishers Weekly* contributor also commented that the "final spread successfully blends succinct information and colorful fun facts."

The author recounts an old Czechoslovakian folktale in *Marushka and the Month Brothers: A Folktale.* Like the tale of Cinderella, the story revolves around a young girl living with her evil stepmother and stepsister. As the story progresses, the girl is sent out into a blizzard to retrieve food and is only able to make it back safely through the help of the twelve Month brothers. Eventually, the evil stepmother and stepsister disappear into a storm conjured up by the brothers. Hazel Rochman, writing in *Booklist,* called the book "a freshly told version" of the tale, while a *Publishers Weekly* contributor noted the book's "lyrical narrative."

Sturges describes amazing bridges from around the world, such as the rope suspension bridge in the Andes mountains of Peru, in *Bridges Are to Cross.* "In just two or three sentences, Sturges . . . explains how each particular bridge works within its environment," noted a contributor to *Publishers Weekly.* Susan Dove Lempke, writing in *Booklist,* commented that the book "is guaranteed to make most readers look at bridges with new eyes."

Sturgess is also the author of a series of rhyming books that began with *I Love Trucks!,* which *Booklist* contributor Carolyn Phelan commended for its inclusion of women truck drivers, noting that the "text is as direct and purposeful as its subject." In *I Love Trains!* a little boy describes the various trains he watches passing by on the tracks. "Toddlers will enjoy making the hoot, roar, and rumble sounds and identifying the various cars," noted Hazel Rochman in *Booklist. I Love Planes!* includes descriptions of technical terms associated with planes and flying as a little boy talks about flying in planes, gliders, and balloons. "Young flight enthusiasts will soon be taking off on solo reading jaunts," wrote a *Kirkus Reviews* contributor. Julie Cummins, writing in *Booklist,* called the book "a high-flying treat for children."

Sturges takes on education in *I Love School!* as he leads readers through a day at school as described by a group of children. A *Kirkus Reviews* contributor called the book "a soothing, bright-as-noon introduction to school that ought to help chase away any shim-shams" felt by young children who may be going to school for the first time. *School Library Journal* contributor Phyllis M. Simon felt it is a "good choice for family sharing." *I Love Bugs!* follows a little boy on a safari in his backyard and was called "engaging as well as informative," by *Booklist* contributor Connie Fletcher.

Sturges presents a new take on another old story in *The Little Red Hen Makes a Pizza,* which recounts a hen's hankering for a pizza and her recruitment of other animals to help her get the ingredients and make one. A *Publishers Weekly* contributor noted that the book "exudes charm, thanks to conversational narration." In *Who Took the Cookies from the Cookie Jar?* the author tells the story of a search for the animal that snatched the cookies. "Children will enjoy the challenge of solving the mystery and astute observers will notice the clues provided on the front cover and title page," noted Tim Wadham in *School Library Journal.*

The author addresse a timely topic in his book *Sacred Places,* as he talks about different religions and religious practices around the world. "The text is simple and stately," noted *Booklist* contributor Ilene Cooper. Patricia Lothrop-Green, writing in *School Library Journal,* called the book a "striking tour of 28 religious sites around the world" and also noted that "Sturges's open-minded view of religious aspirations is a worthy one."

In *Waggers,* Sturges recounts an old folk tale about dogs sniffing each other. As the story goes, the practice is left over from bygone days when dogs misplaced their tails after hanging them up during a meeting on how to get rid of cats once and for all. Unknown to the dogs, a cat also attended the meeting. When it dispersed by calling out "Fire!," the dogs ran for their lives, grabbing whatever tail they could, and have spent the rest of their days checking to see if they have the right ones. "Sturges's saucy rhyme and imaginative plot will tickle the fancy of children," wrote Marge Loch-Wouters in *School Library Journal.*

Nautical themes are the basis for *Down to the Sea in Ships* and *This Little Pirate. School Library Journal* contributor Teresa Pfeifer called the first "a seamless collection of finely honed but telling histories." Linda Staskus, also writing in *School Library Journal,* noted that *This Little Pirate* is a "wacky, imaginative nautical tale . . . filled with action and adventure."

BIOGRAPHICAL AND CRITICAL SOURCES:

PERIODICALS

Appleseeds, March, 2002, Sheila Wilensky, review of *Sacred Places,* p. 32.

Booklist, June 1, 1995, Lauren Peterson, review of *Ten Flashing Fireflies,* p. 1789; November 1, 1995, Leone McDermott, review of *Rainsong/Snowsong,*

p. 478; April 15, 1996, Susan Dove Lempke, review of *What's That Sound, Woolly Bear?,* p. 1447; October 15, 1996, Hazel Rochman, review of *Marushka and the Month Brothers: A Folktale,* p. 429; December 15, 1998, Susan Dove Lempke, review of *Bridges Are to Cross,* p. 747; February 1, 1999, Carolyn Phelan, review of *I Love Trucks!,* p. 978; April 1, 1999, Susan Dove Lempke, review of *Crocky Dilly,* p. 1422; November 15, 1999, Marta Segal, review of *The Little Red Hen Makes a Pizza,* p. 639; October 1, 2000, Ilene Cooper, review of *Sacred Places,* p. 360; October 15, 2000, Todd Morning, review of *Who Took the Cookies from the Cookie Jar?,* p. 445; July, 2001, Hazel Rochman, review of *I Love Trains!,* p. 2022; February 1, 2003, Julie Cummins, review of *I Love Planes!,* p. 1002; August, 2004, Hazel Rochman, review of *I Love School!,* p. 1949; August, 2004, Jennifer Mattson, review of *She'll Be Comin' 'Round the Mountain,* p. 1940; March 1, 2005, Connie Fletcher, review of *I Love Bugs!,* p. 1206.

Horn Book, March-April, 1997, Ann A. Flowers, review of *Marushka and the Month Brothers,* p. 207.

Kirkus Reviews, February 1, 2003, review of *I Love Planes!,* p. 240; June 15, 2004, review of *I Love School!,* p. 582; March 1, 2005, review of *Waggers,* p. 296; April 1, 2005, review of *I Love Bugs!,* p. 426; April 15, 2005, review of *Down to the Sea in Ships,* p. 483; May 15, 2005, review of *This Little Pirate,* p. 596.

Publishers Weekly, June 5, 1995, review of *Ten Flashing Fireflies,* p. 61; September 18, 1995, review of *The Gift of Christmas,* p. 98; April 29, 1996, review of *What's That Sound, Woolly Bear?,* p. 71; November 11, 1996, review of *Marushka and the Month Brothers,* p. 74; November 9, 1998, review of *Bridges Are to Cross,* p. 74; August 16, 1999, review of *The Little Red Hen Makes a Pizza,* p. 83; October 2, 2000, review of *Who Took the Cookies from the Cookie Jar?,* p. 83; October 30, 2000, review of *Bridges Are to Cross,* p. 78; June 25, 2001, review of *I Love Trucks!,* p. 75; December 16, 2002, review of *I Love Planes!,* p. 69; June 28, 2004, review of *I Love School!,* p. 52; February 28, 2005, review of *Waggers,* p. 65.

School Library Journal, October, 2000, Tim Wadham, review of *Who Took the Cookies from the Cookie Jar?,* p. 128; December, 2000, Patricia Lothrop-Green, review of *Sacred Places,* p. 136; June, 2001, Melinda Piehler, review of *I Love Trains!,*

p. 130; March, 2003, Bina Williams, review of *I Love Planes!,* p. 208; July, 2004, Bina Williams, review of *She'll Be Comin' 'Round the Mountain,* p. 96; August, 2004, Phyllis M. Simon, review of *I Love School!,* p. 96; December, 2004, Ginny Gustin, review of *She'll Be Comin' 'Round the Mountain,* p. 59; March, 2005, Marge Loch-Wouters, review of *Waggers,* p. 188; April, 2005, Be Astengo, review of *I Love Bugs!,* p.113; June, 2005, Teresa Pfeifer, review of *Down to the Sea in Ships,* p. 187; July, 2005, Linda Staskus, review of *This Little Pirate,* p. 82.

Teacher Librarian, March, 1999, Shirley Lewis, review of *Bridges Are to Cross,* p. 44.

ONLINE

BookLoons, http://www.bookloons.com/ (August 22, 2005), Hilary Williamson, review of *She'll Be Comin' 'Round the Mountain.*

Philemon Sturges Home Page, http://www.philemon sturges.com (August 22, 2005).*

*   *   *

SUZANNE, Jamie
See SINGLETON, Linda Joy

*   *   *

SZEJNMANN, Claus-Christian W. 1965-

PERSONAL: Born April 5, 1965, in Munich, West Germany (now Germany). *Education:* University of London, B.A., Ph.D.

ADDRESSES: Office—University of Leicester, University Rd., Leicester LE1 7RH, England. *E-mail*—ccws1@leicester.ac.uk.

CAREER: Middlesex University, London, England, lecturer in modern European history, 1995-2000; University of Leicester, Midlands, England, lecturer in modern European history, 2000—.

WRITINGS:

Nazism in Central Germany: The Brownshirts in "Red Saxony," Berghahn Books (New York, NY), 1999.

Von Traum zum Alptraum: Sachsen Während der Weimarer Republik, Kiepenheuer Verlag (Leipzig, Germany), 2000.

Contributor to *The Rise of National Socialism and the Working Classes in Weimer Germany,* edited by Conan Fischer, Berghahn Books (Oxford, England), 1996, and *Saxony in German History: Culture, Society, and Politics, 1830-1933,* edited by J. Retallack, University of Michigan Press (Ann Arbor, MI), 2000. Contributor to *German History.*

SIDELIGHTS: Claus-Christian W. Szejnmann's *Nazism in Central Germany: The Brownshirts in "Red Saxony"* "fills a major void in the literature on the rise of National Socialism in central Germany," according to *History: Review of New Books* contributor Johnpeter Horst Grill. As Szejnmann, a professor of history at Leicester University, stated on his faculty Web site, he tries in the book to answer specific questions: "Why did anyone from a comparatively modern society support such a radical and brutal movement as the Nazi movement?"; "How did Nazism gain mass support?" Szejnmann focuses his book on the German state of Saxony during the rise of Nazism. His interest in this area is based on the fact that Saxony was, as he explained, "one of the earliest strongholds of the movement," as well as being "the most industrialised and urbanised" area in Germany at that time and the "cradle of the labour movement."

The Weimar Republic, under which an attempt was made to shore up a debilitated Germany after its defeat in World War I, slowly disintegrated between 1919 and 1933. Szejnmann studies how the Nazis were able to capitalize on the weaknesses of the republic and bring various German factions together. He does this by analyzing the history of Saxony between the late nineteenth century and the Nazi's rise to power. During this time, there were significant conflicts between the country's social democrats, communists, and more affluent bourgeoisie. The republic was not strong enough to stop the polarization that developed between the working class and the bourgeoisie that controlled most of the land and all of the industry.

Interior pressures, Szejnmann shows, were not the only factor in the deterioration of Weimar power. There were the harsh realities of having lost the war and having to comply with Allied demands for monetary reparation. At the same time, between 1929 and 1933 Germany felt the effects of the Great Depression, which increased the number of unemployed to more than six million people. The economic depression also impacted the bourgeois, cutting into their economic stability and making them more inclined to look to someone who might lead them out of their financial difficulties. On July 30, 1933, Adolf Hitler took office, thus ending the Weimar Republic.

Szejnmann shows how the Nazis were able to gain popular support in both the working-class and nationalist bourgeois populations. On his Web site, he concluded: "*Nazism in Central Germany* demonstrates the ways in which deep-rooted local traditions determined the success or failure of Nazism among the local population." The rise of Nazism should be a lesson to everyone that "the survival of a peaceful, pluralistic and democratic system depends on the ability of all groups in society to enter a serious dialogue, to make compromises and to treat each other with respect," he added

As Grill noted, Szejnmann incorporates material from newly opened archives into his study, which the critic considered a "solid work" that "confirms much of what we know . . . . from other regional studies of the party." *Choice* contributor R.V. Pierard found the book to be "an insightful, well-documented, and convincing study."

BIOGRAPHICAL AND CRITICAL SOURCES:

PERIODICALS

Book Watch, August, 1999, review of *Nazism in Central Germany: The Brownshirts in "Red Saxony,"* p. 3.
Choice, January, 2000, R.V. Pierard, review of *Nazism in Central Germany,* p. 1004.
History: Reviews of New Books, fall, 1999, Johnpeter Horst Grill, review of *Nazism in Central Germany,* p. 22.

ONLINE

H-Net Reviews in the Humanities and Social Sciences, http://www.h-net.org/ (June, 2000), Michael C. Schneider, review of *Nazism in Central Germany.*
University of Leicester Web site, http://www.le.ac.uk/ (August 20, 2005).*

T

TAKAHAMA KYOSHI 1874-1959

PERSONAL: Born February 22, 1874, in Matsuyama, Japan; died April 8, 1959, in Kamakura, Japan.

CAREER: Writer. Editor of *Hototogisu,* beginning 1898.

WRITINGS:

Haikaishi (novel; title means "Haiku Master"), 1909.
Susumubeki haiku no michi (title means "The Proper Direction for Haiku"), 1918.
Sōseki-shi to watakushi/Takahama Kyoshi cho/kaisetsu Inoue Yuriko (correspondence), Arusu (Tokyo, Japan), 1918.
Kunikki, six volumes, 1936–60.
Haiku no gojūnen, 1947.
Kyoshi shōsoku (correspondence and reminiscences), 1948.
Kyoshi kyōyū kuroku, 1948.
Kaki futatsu, 1948.
Kyoshi jiden (biography), 1948.
Teihon Kyoshi zenshū, Sogensha, Showa (Tokyo, Japan), 1948.
Kijuen, 1950.
Bashō (literary criticism), 1951.
Kyoshi jisen kushū, Sogensha, Showa (Tokyo, Japan), 1951.
Haiku-dokuhon, Sogensha, Showa (Tokyo, Japan), 1951.
Haiku no tsukuriyō, 1952.
Haiku e no michi, 1955.

Gendai shasei bunshū (short stories), 1955.
Hototogisu zatsuei senshu, 1962.
Kyoshi haiwa, edited by Toshio Takahama, 1963.
Kyoshi no meiku, edited by Toshiro Kyosaki, 1967.
Gohyakku, 1969.
Haiku tokuhon, 1972.
Takahama Kyoshi zenhaiku shu (title means "The Complete Haiku Poems of Takahama Kyoshi"), two volumes, 1980.
Takahama Kyoshi (collected works), edited by Toshihiko Matsui, Nihon Tosho Senta (Tokyo, Japan), 1994.

Contributor to anthologies, including *Masaoka Shiki, Takahama Kyoshi, Nafatsuka Takashi, Isikawa Takuboku shū,* 1978, and *Kyoshi, Toshio Teiko sandai bokuhitsu shū,* 1980.

SIDELIGHTS: Japanese poet Takahama Kyoshi was a major contributor to the development of the modern haiku form. A devoted student of haiku master Masaoka Shiki, in 1898 he took over editorship of the haiku magazine Masaoka had founded, titled *Hototogisu.* After his master's death, Takahama quarreled with his old friend, the poet Kawahigashi Hekigoto, who sought to invigorate haiku by disregarding the form's traditional pattern of syllables. Takahama firmly disagreed with this development and further argued that haiku should continue to focus on realistic descriptions of nature.

In addition to his many volumes of haiku, Takahama wrote several novels, as well as books of criticism. His *Susumubeki haiku no michi,* for one, is an argument for what he considered to be the proper direction for modern haiku; he also wrote a study of sixteenth-century poet Bashō Matsuo, who is considered the greatest haiku poet in Japanese literary history.

BIOGRAPHICAL AND CRITICAL SOURCES:

BOOKS

Miyasaka Shiuzo, *Kyoshi no Komoro,* Kashinsha (Tokyo, Japan), 1995.*

* * *

TALTY, Stephan 1965(?)-

PERSONAL: Born c. 1965, in Buffalo, NY. *Education:* Graduate of Amherst College (magna cum laude).

ADDRESSES: Agent—PFD, Drury House, 34-43 Russell St., London WC2B 5HA, England.

CAREER: Worked as a critic for *Time Out New York* and as an editor for *Details.*

WRITINGS:

Mulatto America: At the Crossroads of Black and White Culture: A Social History, HarperCollins (New York, NY), 2003.

Contributor to periodicals, including *Men's Journal, Irish Times, Chicago Review, Gentleman's Quarterly,* and the *New York Times* magazine.

SIDELIGHTS: Stephan Talty is a journalist who frequently writes about racial issues. His *Mulatto America: At the Crossroads of Black and White Culture: A Social History* is a study of the intermingling of blacks and whites beginning in the U.S. antebellum era, and includes accounts of whites who were kidnapped or sold into slavery. Using personal papers and court memoirs, he finds that there were about thirty such cases a year, primarily involving children who had no way to prove their race. Once

they were designated as black, neither their appearances nor their own statements recording their family were considered. A slave trader admitted on his deathbed to having purchased Irish natives in 1774 that he advertised as being light-skinned blacks. He sold these people in the South, where they brought a higher price than they would have as indentured servants. During the same period, Harriet Beecher Stowe sold light-skinned mulatto children at auction in order to raise money to free them.

The topic of black conversion to Christianity in the antebellum South is also discussed, including the fact that black converts felt they would become white upon entering heaven. A *Kirkus Reviews* contributor said that "an essay on interracial relationships rediscovers wonderful stories of whites drinking their paramours' blood in order to circumvent the 'one-drop' rule." *Library Journal* contributor Paula N. Arnold wrote that "Talty suggests that now blacks and whites have choices, allowing the personal finally to trump the social and historical."

New City Chicago writer Nathaniel Zimmer stated that the book "is chock-full of intriguing tidbits on everything from white slavery to Marvin Gaye's fondness for Perry Como." Talty gives examples of how both whites and blacks have copied each other's styles and cultures, from the melding that took place within the New Orleans jazz scene and society up to and including the rap performed by white performers such as Eminem, both instances of whites emulating blacks. He writes of mixed-race celebrities like Paul Robeson and Dorothy Dandridge, who crossed the color barrier and were accepted as "honorary whites," as well as blacks, such as boxer Mohammad Ali and singer Sam Cooke who crossed that same line on their own terms. Talty covers black intellectual life at the turn of the twentieth century with its emphasis on European culture and notes that figures of that time, including W.E.B. Dubois, were admired and respected by whites. He also writes of the rejection of white culture by blacks in the 1960s and the widespread popularity of black sports figures in the 1970s.

In a *Washington Post Book World* review, Jabari Asim noted that Talty's essay on the 1960s is particularly effective. "He astutely identifies the association of overt racism during that period with the white underclass, a linkage that left the elite free to inflict harm in their own ingenious style." Talty implies that

Southern rednecks took the heat for being up front with their racism while the upper classes were rewarded for their discretion. Asim said that Talty "implies that semiliterate mobs and their supportive sheriffs were merely enforcing the policies legislated by their superiors, whose talons extended all the way to the highest levels of state and federal power. It's consoling to imagine racism as the province of the unwashed and uneducated, but Talty knows that the facts have always suggested otherwise." A *Publishers Weekly* reviewer called *Mulatto America* "an informed, occasionally inspired work that pulls its historical examples under a broad view of biracialism—as a phenomenon of memes as well as genes." *BookPage* contributor Arlene McKanic called the book "an intelligent and accessible analysis of race in this country."

BIOGRAPHICAL AND CRITICAL SOURCES:

PERIODICALS

Booklist, January 1, 2003, Vernon Ford, review of *Mulatto America: At the Crossroads of Black and White Culture: A Social History,* p. 818.

Kirkus Reviews, November 15, 2002, review of *Mulatto America,* p. 1682.

Library Journal, March 1, 2002, Paula N. Arnold, review of *Mulatto America,* p. 108.

Los Angeles Times Book Review, March 30, 2003, Kate Manning, review of *Mulatto America,* p. 3.

Publishers Weekly, December 2, 2002, review of *Mulatto America,* pp. 44-45.

St. Louis Post-Dispatch, February 5, 2003, Lorraine Kee, review of *Mulatto America,* Everyday section, p. E1.

Washington Post Book World, January 28, 2003, Jabari Asim, review of *Mulatto America,* p. 8.

ONLINE

BookPage.com, http://www.bookpage.com/ (August 16, 2005), Arlene McKanic, review of *Mulatto America.*

New City Chicago Online, http://www.newcitychicago. com/ (January 29, 2003), Nathaniel Zimmer, review of *Mulatto America.**

*   *   *

TELLERMANN, Esther 1947-

PERSONAL: Born 1947, in Paris, France. *Education:* Graduate of École Normale Supérieure.

ADDRESSES: Agent—c/o Author Mail, Flammarion, 26 rue Racine, Paris 75278, France.

CAREER: Educator and poet. Teacher in Paris, France.

WRITINGS:

POETRY, EXCEPT AS NOTED

Première apparition avec épaisseur (title means "First Appearance with Thickness"), Flammarion (Paris, France), 1986.

Trois plans inhumains (title means "Three Inhuman Plans"), Flammarion (Paris, France), 1989.

Distance de fuite (title means "Outdistance Escape"), Flammarion (Paris, France), 1993.

Pangéia, Flammarion (Paris, France), 1996.

Guerre extrême (title means "Extreme War"), Flammarion (Paris, France), 1999, selections translated by Keith Waldrop published as *Mental Ground,* Burning Deck Press (Providence, RI), 2002.

Encre plus rouge (title means "Redder Ink"), Flammarion (Paris, France), 2003.

Une odeur humaine (prose; title means "A Human Odor"), Farraro Léo Scheer, 2004.

Work represented in anthologies, including *Anthologie de la poésie française au XVIIIème au XXème siècle* (title means "Anthology of French Poetry from the Eighteenth to the Twentieth Century"), Gallimard (Paris, France). Contributor to literary journals, including *Banana Split, Poésie, Action Poétique, Ralentir Travaux, Scherzo, Nouveau Recueil, Nioques, Étrangère,* and *Moriturus.* Member of editorial board, *Célibataire.*

SIDELIGHTS: Esther Tellermann is a French poet and educator who also has an interest in psychoanalysis, which she applies as editor of the journal *Célibataire.* In reviewing her third collection, *Distance de fuite,* in *World Literature Today,* Michael Bishop called Tellermann "a poet at once ethically and ontologically very much focused upon her experience of the concrete world," as well as "a fine and discreetly urgent poetic voice that should be heard and meditated."

The poems collected as *Pangéia* refer to the events of the Holocaust, although nowhere in the volume is that dark point in history directly mentioned. The first section of the book, "Train sans paysages," offers images of people being transported like cattle in boxcars without windows. The poems portray suffering and burial, and at the conclusion of the section promise redemption for those who have survived. The second part, titled "Tentation," focuses on a new Exodus across the desert to an unnamed sea. That sea has been crossed in the last section, named for the collection's title; Tellermann writes of a new beginning, or Genesis, on the eighth day, when the earth becomes renewed through sound and sight. Mechthild Cranston wrote in *World Literature Today* that, "moving between 'le vide et l'évènement,' as sand would, blown by the wind, Tellermann's poetry arrives at a presence that subsists . . . above and beyond the fissures in the texture of the earth and the text of language."

Bishop reviewed *Guerre extrême*, saying that "Tellermann continues her dense and fragmented narrative quest in the at once pugnacious and tautly serene poems" of this collection. A number of these poems were translated and published in English by Burning Deck Press as *Mental Ground*.

In a review of Tellerman's *Encre plus rouge*, Bishop described the poet as "an important and distinctive voice." The critic asserted that, with the publication of this 2004 collection, "the long, patient, exploded poetic narrative of Esther Tellermann continues to evolve and even dramatically surprise."

BIOGRAPHICAL AND CRITICAL SOURCES:

PERIODICALS

World Literature Today, winter, 1994, Michael Bishop, review of *Distance de fuite,* p. 83; winter, 1997, Mechthild Cranston, review of *Pangéia,* pp. 109-110; summer, 2000, Michael Bishop, review of *Guerre extrême,* p. 632; May-August, 2004, Michael Bishop, review of *Encre plus rouge,* p. 85.

ONLINE

Burning Deck Press Web site, http://www.burningdeck. com/ (July 12, 2005), profile of Tellermann.

French Embassy, Chicago Web site, http://www. consulfrance-chicago.org/ (July 12, 2005), profile of Tellermann.*

*   *   *

TRACY, Kathleen

PERSONAL: Female.

ADDRESSES: Agent—c/o Mitchell Lane Publishers, P.O. Box 196, Hockessin, DE 19707. *E-mail*—zrunt@ aol.com.

CAREER: Journalist and author of nonfiction. Has worked as a portrait photographer for ten years and as a photojournalist.

WRITINGS:

BIOGRAPHIES

(With Earl Greenwood) *The Boy Who Would Be King,* Dutton (New York, NY), 1990.
(With Earl Greenwood) *Elvis—Top Secret: The Untold Story of Elvis Presley's Secret FBI Files,* Signet (New York, NY), 1991.
(With Jeff Rovin) *Ellen DeGeneres Up Close: The Unauthorized Biography of the Hot New Star of ABC's Ellen,* Pocket Books (New York, NY), 1994.
(With Jeff Rovin) *Kelsey Grammer: The True Story,* HarperPaperbacks (New York, NY), 1995.
(With Jeff Rovin) *The Essential Jackie Chan Sourcebook,* Pocket Books (New York, NY), 1997.
Home Brewed: The Drew Carey Story, Boulevard Books (New York, NY), 1997.
Antonio Banderas, Tor Books (New York, NY), 1997.
Jerry Seinfeld: The Entire Domain, Carol Publishing Group (Secaucus, NJ), 1998.
The Girl's Got Bite: An Unofficial Guide to Buffy's World, Renaissance Books (Los Angeles, CA), 1998, revised as *The Girl's Got Bite: The Original Unauthorized Guide to Buffy's World, Completely Revised and Updated,* St. Martin's Press (New York, NY), 2003.
Matt Damon, St. Martin's Paperbacks (New York, NY), 1998.

Ellen: The Real Story of Ellen DeGeneres, Carol Publishing Group (Secaucus, NJ), 1999.

Ricky Martin: Red-Hot and on the Rise!, Kensington Publishing (New York, NY), 1999.

Imus: America's Cowboy, Carroll & Graf (New York, NY), 1999.

Jennifer Lopez, ECW Press (Toronto, Ontario, Canada), 2000.

Neve Campbell, ECW Press (Toronto, Ontario, Canada), 2000.

Daytime Divas: The Dish on Dozens of Daytime TV's Great Ladies, Renaissance Books (Los Angeles, CA), 2000.

Angelina Jolie, ECW Press (Toronto, Ontario, Canada), 2001.

Regis!: The Unauthorized Biography, ECW Press (Toronto, Ontario, Canada), 2001.

Welcome to the Dixie Chicks Photo Biography, ECW Press (Toronto, Ontario, Canada), 2004.

Diana Rigg: The Biography, BenBella Books (Dallas, TX), 2004.

"UNLOCKING THE SECRETS OF SCIENCE" SERIES; FOR CHILDREN

Barbara McClintock: Pioneering Geneticist, Mitchell Lane (Bear, DE), 2002.

Marc Andreessen and the Development of the Web Browser, Mitchell Lane (Bear, DE), 2002.

William Hewlett: Pioneer of the Computer Age, Mitchell Lane (Bear, DE), 2003.

Willem Kolff and the Invention of the Dialysis Machine, Mitchell Lane (Bear, DE), 2003.

"LATINOS IN AMERICAN HISTORY" SERIES; FOR CHILDREN

Lorenzo de Zavala, Mitchell Lane (Bear, DE), 2003.

Mariano Guadalupe Vallejo, Mitchell Lane (Bear, DE), 2003.

Cesar Chavez, Mitchell Lane (Bear, DE), 2004.

"BLUE BANNER BIOGRAPHY" SERIES; FOR CHILDREN

Mary-Kate and Ashley Olsen, Mitchell Lane (Bear, DE), 2004.

Clay Aiken: From Second Place to the Top of the Charts, Mitchell Lane (Hockessin, DE), 2004.

Queen Latifah, Mitchell Lane (Hockessin, DE), 2005.

Avril Lavigne, Mitchell Lane (Hockessin, DE), 2005.

Beyoncé, Mitchell Lane (Hockessin, DE), 2005.

Lindsay Lohan, Mitchell Lane (Hockessin, DE), 2005.

Justin Berfield, Mitchell Lane (Hockessin, DE), 2005.

Mario, Mitchell Lane (Hockessin, DE), 2005.

"UNCHARTED, UNEXPLORED, AND UNEXPLAINED" SERIES; FOR CHILDREN

Robert Koch and the Study of Anthrax, Mitchell Lane (Hockessin, DE), 2005.

Pierre and Marie Curie and the Discovery of Radium, Mitchell Lane (Hockessin, DE), 2005.

Friedrich Miescher and the Story of Nucleic Acid, Mitchell Lane (Hockessin, DE), 2005.

Henry Bessemer: Making Steel from Iron, Mitchell Lane (Hockessin, DE), 2005.

"BIOGRAPHY FROM ANCIENT CIVILIZATIONS" SERIES; FOR CHILDREN

The Life and Times of Homer, Mitchell Lane (Hockessin, DE), 2005.

The Life and Times of Constantine, Mitchell Lane (Hockessin, DE), 2005.

The Life and Times of Confucius, Mitchell Lane (Hockessin, DE), 2005.

"CLASSIC STORYTELLERS" SERIES; FOR CHILDREN

John Steinbeck, Mitchell Lane (Hockessin, DE), 2005.

Judy Blume, Mitchell Lane (Hockessin, DE), 2005.

"MONUMENTAL MILESTONES" SERIES; FOR CHILDREN

Top Secret: The Story of the Manhattan Project, Mitchell Lane (Hockessin, DE), 2005.

The Fall of the Berlin Wall, Mitchell Lane (Hockessin, DE), 2005.

OTHER

The Complete Idiot's Guide to Portrait Photography, Alpha (Indianapolis, IN), 2002.

The Secret Story of Polygamy, Sourcebooks (Naperville, IL), 2002.

(With Tess Crebin) *It Shouldn't Happen to a Journalist,* Xlibris, 2002.

Also contributor to periodicals, including *A&E Biography* and *Film News International.*

SIDELIGHTS: In the early 1990s, Kathleen Tracy, a former photojournalist turned entertainment journalist, began writing celebrity biographies. The first of these was a book about Elvis Presley, *The Boy Who Would Be King,* written with Presley's cousin, Earl Greenwood. The book concentrates primarily on the death at birth of Elvis Presley's twin brother, his youthful poverty and strong attachment to his alcoholic mother, and his sex life and history of drug abuse. Tracy has since gone on to reveal the lives of other celebrities, including actors, comedians, and television hosts. In *Jerry Seinfeld: The Entire Domain,* for example, she writes about the comedian whose long-running show ended after nine years while it was still experiencing high ratings. She follows his life and success as a stand-up comic before beginning the series and also the lives and careers of his costars, Jason Alexander, Julia Louis-Dreyfus, and Michael Richards. *Booklist* contributor Brad Hooper wrote that Tracy "effectively separates the real Jerry from the television Jerry."

Ellen: The Real Story of Ellen DeGeneres is Tracy's biography of the comedian who "came out" in her television sitcom, revealing that she was a lesbian. The author writes that DeGeneres made the decision because she lacked "a consistent voice for her character, which at times still exuded a vagueness that translated into a feeling that something was missing." Ellen's intention was not to become a flag bearer or role model for lesbian women, but to bring her true character to the show. Whether it was the conservative opposition to the show that caused it to fail or a combination of factors, including cast changes, cannot be absolutely determined, but *Ellen's* ratings dropped after her revelation, and the show was cancelled. Kelli N. Perkins noted in *Library Journal* that in providing the details "Tracy remains neutral. . . . We are left with an awareness of DeGeneres's enduring humor."

Another celebrity who became the focus of a Tracy biography is Don Imus, the caustic radio personality whose New York program has been syndicated on more than one hundred stations. In *Imus: America's Cowboy* Tracy follows the career of the controversial disk jockey who worked at a number of jobs and served for a decade with the U.S. Marines before his star began its rise in the 1960s. Tracy includes many of Imus's most notable comments and interchanges with public figures, including President Bill Clinton. A *Kirkus Reviews* writer described the book as a "breezy biography."

Tracy has also written a number of biographies for young readers about their favorite pop culture stars, including actresses Mary-Kate and Ashley Olsen. In other biographies, she focuses on historic figures, including Homer, Constantine, and Confucius in the "Biography from Ancient Civilizations" series. She has also written about well-known writers and notable Hispanics and about significant events in the past. In addition, as a contributor to a number of academic series, she has profiled pioneers in science and technology, including geneticist Barbara McClintock. In *Marc Andreessen and the Development of the Web Browser* she explains how ARPANET, the predecessor of the Internet, was created as a communication tool during the cold war. She follows Andreessen's life from childhood and his obsession with computers, which led him to take part in the creation of the Mosaic Web browser at the University of Illinois, and his subsequent creation of the Netscape Navigator browser. *School Library Journal* reviewer May Mueller wrote that Tracy "is admiring of her subject, emphasizing his creativity and philanthropy."

Among Tracy's nonbiographical works is *The Secret Story of Polygamy,* which focuses on the 1998 trial of Mormon John Daniel Kingston, who beat his daughter due to her refusal to become the fifteenth wife of her own brother. The author asserts that although polygamy was renounced by the Mormon church in 1890, it continues to flourish in Western states, particularly Utah. Tracy points out that the practice puts women in the position of being breeders, servants, and generators of welfare benefits for their families, and that they suffer from sexual and other abuses. In an interview posted on the Sourcebooks Web site, she writes that it will help the reader understand "how underage girls are being victimized under the guise of religious freedom and why the polygamous environment is a fertile ground for such abuses of civil liberties."

With Tess Crebin, Tracy wrote *It Shouldn't Happen to a Journalist,* in which the two authors talk about their careers and candidly reveal the positive and negative aspects of their chosen field. They are donating ten percent of the proceeds from the sales of the book to Dorset Victim Support, which helps those who have lost a loved one to murder, and another ten percent to Crime Victims for a Just Society. Rachel Newcombe, who reviewed the volume online for *Absolute Write,* felt that, "whether you're a journalist or not, it's a compelling read and is sure to have you turning the pages with interest until the very end."

BIOGRAPHICAL AND CRITICAL SOURCES:

BOOKS

Tracy, Kathleen, and Jeff Rovin, *Ellen DeGeneres Up Close: The Unauthorized Biography of the Hot New Star of ABC's Ellen,* Pocket Books (New York, NY), 1994.

PERIODICALS

Booklist, October 15, 1998, Brad Hooper, review of *Jerry Seinfeld: The Entire Domain,* p. 370; May 1, 1999, Mike Tribby, review of *Ellen,* p. 1556; October 15, 2004, Todd Morning, review of *The Life and Times of Homer,* p. 415.
Kirkus Reviews, June 1, 1999, review of *Imus: America's Cowboy,* pp. 873-874.
Library Journal, May 15, 1999, Kelli N. Perkins, review of *Ellen,* p. 98; November 15, 2001, Tim Delaney, review of *The Secret Story of Polygamy,* p. 88.
Publishers Weekly, July 13, 1990, Genevieve Stuttaford, review of *The Boy Who Would Be King,* p. 47; June 28, 1999, review of *Imus: America's Cowboy,* p. 65; November 26, 2001, review of *The Secret Story of Polygamy,* p. 54.
School Library Journal, January, 2002, Mary Mueller, review of *Marc Andreessen and the Development of the Web Browser,* p. 168; February, 2002, Maren Ostergard, review of *Barbara McClintock: Pioneering Geneticist,* p. 139; December, 2002, Carol Fazioli, review of *Willem Kolff and the Invention of the Dialysis Machine,* p. 165; December, 2004, Anne M. Holcomb, review of *The Life and Times of Homer,* p. 170; January, 2005, Mary Mueller, review of *John Steinbeck,* p. 140; March, 2005, Deanna Romriell, review of *Robert Koch and the Study of Anthrax,* p. 236.

ONLINE

Absolute Write, http://www.absolutewrite.com/ (July 14, 2005), Rachel Newcombe, review of *It Shouldn't Happen to a Journalist.*
Sourcebooks Web site, http://www.sourcebooks.com/ (July 14, 2005), interview with Tracy.*

* * *

TRAVERSI, Derek A. 1912-2005
(Derek Antona Traversi)

OBITUARY NOTICE— See index for *CA* sketch: Born November 7, 1912, in Caersws, Montgomeryshire, Wales; died August 25, 2005, in Richmond, Surrey, England. Educator and author. Traversi was a respected Shakespearean scholar who spent many years as a lecturer for the British Council. He earned an M.A. in 1934 and a B.Litt. in 1937, both from Oxford University. He then earned a B.A. in Italian from University College London in 1938. Traversi had spent some years growing up in Italy and was fond of its language and culture, and after finishing this last degree he joined the British Institute of Rome. At the time, fascist dictator Benito Mussolini was in power, and Traversi found himself in conflict with the authorities. He thus decided to return to England. Found unfit for active duty as World War II heated up, he continued his association with the British Institute and moved to Madrid to lecture. In Madrid he met the woman who would become his wife and also became friends with the director of the Madrid Institute. In 1944 Traversi was promoted to director of the Madrid Institute in Bilbao and then Barcelona. Over the next decades he continued to travel around the world as a lecturer and cultural director. He returned to Europe in 1959 as the cultural relations director in Madrid and, from 1966 to 1970, in Rome, Italy. The last part of his career was spent as a professor of English teaching at Swarthmore College from 1970 to 1983. Though he wrote on other authors and literary subjects, including T.S. Eliot, Chaucer, and Dante, Traversi was best known for his Shakespearean studies. Among his books are *An Approach to Shakespeare* (1938; 3rd edition, 1969), *Shakespeare: The Roman Plays* (1963), *T.S. Eliot: The Longer Poems* (1976), and *Chaucer: The Earlier Poetry* (1987).

OBITUARIES AND OTHER SOURCES:

PERIODICALS

Guardian (London, England), September 15, 2005, p. 37.
Independent (London, England), September 27, 2005, p. 34.
Times (London, England), September 16, 2005, p. 75.

*   *   *

TRAVERSI, Derek Antona
    See TRAVERSI, Derek A.

*   *   *

TROESTER, Rosalie Riegle
    See RIEGLE, Rosalie G.

*   *   *

TUFARIELLO, Catherine 1963-

PERSONAL: Born 1963, in Ithaca, NY; married; children: one daughter. *Education:* State University of New York, Buffalo, B.A.; Cornell University, Ph.D.

ADDRESSES: Home—IN. *Office*—Department of English, Valparaiso University, Huegli Hall, 1800 Chapel Dr., Valparaiso, IN 46383. *E-mail*—Catherine. Tufariello@valpo.edu.

CAREER: Educator and poet. Taught at various colleges and universities, including Cornell University, College of Charleston, and University of Miami; Valparaiso University, Valparaiso, IN, instructor in English.

AWARDS, HONORS: Finalist, Book Prize in Poetry, *Los Angeles Times,* Editor's Choice selection, *Booklist,* and Walt McDonald First Book Poetry Prize, all 2004, all for *Keeping My Name.*

WRITINGS:

Keeping My Name, Texas Tech University Press (Lubbock, TX), 2003.

Author of chapbooks *Free Time,* published by Robert L. Barth, and *Annunciations,* published by Aralia Press. Contributor of poetry to anthologies, including *Poetry, a Pocket Anthology,* edited by R.S. Gwynn, Penguin Academics, 2001; *The Poetry Anthology: 1912-2002,* edited by Joseph Parisi and Stephen Young, Ivan R. Dee, 2002; and *The Zoo Anthology of Younger American Poets,* edited by David Yezzi, Zoo Press, 2004. Contributor to periodicals, including *Poetry, Hudson Review,* and *Yale Italian Poetry.*

SIDELIGHTS: Poet and educator Catherine Tufariello was born in Ithaca, New York, and raised in Amherst, in upstate New York. She studied English at the State University of New York at Buffalo, and earned her doctorate in American literature from Cornell University, writing her thesis on the poetry of Emily Dickinson and Walt Whitman. She has taught English and writing at several universities, including Cornell, the College of Charleston, the University of Miami, and Valparaiso University. Her own poems have appeared in various periodicals, including *Poetry, Hudson Review,* and *Yale Italian Poetry,* and have been collected in two chapbooks.

Tufariello's first book of poems, *Keeping My Name,* won the Walt McDonald First Book Poetry Prize, and was a finalist for the *Los Angeles Times* Book Prize in poetry for 2004. The poems have appeared individually both in periodicals and anthologies. Most of her poems are metrical and rhymed, and she has also done translations of medieval Italian love poets. Referring to an image of a girl dancing at a wedding in one of the poems, Ruby Olson, a contributor for *Booklist,* wrote that Tufariello "conjures such common-enough scenes so vividly that one's mind and heart are fully engaged." In an interview for the Valparaiso University Web site, Tufariello explained her work by saying: "One of the reasons I like to work in meter and rhyme is that it helps me to get some aesthetic distance on my experiences and make them accessible to others. A young woman recently told me after a reading that she found consolation in the poems because they confronted grief and doubt, but were ultimately affirmative and hopeful. That's one of the nicest compliments I've ever gotten."

Tufariello told *CA:* "When I was very young, in elementary school, I wanted to be a fiction writer. I loved reading stories, and the idea of creating my own imaginary worlds grew naturally from the pleasure of reading. Now and then I wrote fan letters to authors and most were generous enough to write back, which was very exciting. Getting their replies showed me that authors were real people, and that being a writer when I grew up was an ambition I could have. But in high school I started to recognize that plotting was not a strong suit. Nothing much ever happened in my stories; they were all about the characters' interior lives. And at age thirteen or so I fell in love with poetry in a serious way—Emily Dickinson, Robert Frost, and Ralph Waldo Emerson were early favorites—and turned my attention in that direction.

"The core or catalyst of a new poem is always words. I begin with a key phrase, or a line or two, rather than a subject or idea. And I never begin with the intention that I'm going to write a sonnet, or a poem in couplets, or in any other form. Rather, the first line or two (which often aren't the first lines of the poem) narrow down the infinity of possible forms to a few, and I feel my way from there. Occasionally a poem comes quickly and doesn't need much revision, and that's exciting. But usually the process is very slow. It often takes me months or years between the first inspiration and the finished poem, and I end up discarding a lot of drafts or partial drafts that don't work. It's a good thing the flights of inspiration are so much fun, because the rest of the process is often like working a fiendishly difficult puzzle. Of course, that has its own satisfactions.

"I've learned that form itself brings surprises, that the commitment to it is (when the poem is working, at least) liberating rather than confining. Rhyme, for example, brings an element of arbitrariness and serendipity into the writing process. The need to find appropriate rhymes often forces me away from my usual habits of thinking, conjuring up fresh images, carrying me farther afield than I would otherwise go. Poems, for me, are by nature cranky, recalcitrant, full of surprises, and insistent on being who they are. You can't do anything you like with them, any more than a parent can with a child.

"Since I began to publish my work, in the late 1990s, I've been happily surprised by the way it has connected me with other poets and with readers. Writing is by nature a solitary occupation. I never took creative-writing courses or belonged to workshops, and often it was hard to imagine that my poems could exist in the world as well as in my head. But soon after publishing my first poems in literary periodicals, in the late 1990s, I began forming a network of poet friends with whom I could informally share new work. I began to feel part of an artistic community, and that was very helpful after several years of working in isolation. And since the book was published, I've begun to make contact with readers as well. Doing readings has given me a better sense of which poems are most and least successful, and I feel privileged to be able to talk to readers and hear their stories. While the audience for poetry is small in relative terms, it does exist, and the people who love poetry care passionately about it. That's been very heartening to me. So what began as an avocation that drew me out of the world, into the privacy of my own mind, has in the end brought me back into it."

BIOGRAPHICAL AND CRITICAL SOURCES:

PERIODICALS

Booklist, April 1, 2004, Ruby Olson, review of *Keeping My Name*, p. 1342; January 1, 2005, review of *Keeping My Name*, p. 768.
Dark Horse, summer, 2005, Kathleen McDermott, review of *Keeping My Name*, p. 92.
Hudson Review, winter, 2005, R.S. Gwynn, review of *Keeping My Name*, p. 685.
Poetry, February, 2005, Brian Phillips, review of *Keeping My Name*, p. 403.

ONLINE

Poems Daily, http://www.poems.com/ (July 10, 2005), "Catherine Tufariello."
Poem Tree, http://www.poemtree.com/ (July 10, 2005), "Catherine Tufariello."
University of Portland Web site, http://lewis.up.edu/ (July 10, 2005), "Catherine Tufariello."
Valparaiso University Web site, http://www.valpo.edu/ (July 10, 2005), "Catherine Tufariello."

U-V

UPTON, Charles 1948-

PERSONAL: Born December 13, 1948, in San Francisco, CA; married Jenny Doane. *Education:* Attended University of California, Davis. *Religion:* Sufism.

ADDRESSES: Home—100 Sycamore Ave., San Anselmo, CA 94960. *E-mail*—cupton@sbcglobal.net.

CAREER: Poet and writer.

WRITINGS:

Panic Grass (poems), City Lights Books (San Francisco, CA), 1968.
Time Raid (poems), Four Seasons Foundation (San Francisco, CA), 1969.
(Editor, with Robert Starfire and others) *Because You Talk: Poetry and Prose,* Other Voices Literary Society (San Francisco, CA), 1976.
(Translator) *Doorkeeper of the Heart; Versions of Rabi'a,* Threshold Books (Putney, VT), 1988.
Hammering Hot Iron: A Spiritual Critique of Bly's Iron John, Quest Books (Wheaton, IL), 1993.
The System of Antichrist: Truth and Falsehood in Postmodernism and the New Age, Sophia Perennis (Ghent, NY), 2001.
Cracks in the Great Wall: The UFO Phenomenon and Traditional Metaphysics, Sophia Perennis (Hillsdale, NY), 2004.
Legends of the End: Prophecies of the End Times, Antichrist, Apocalypse, and Messiah from Eight Religious Traditions, Sophia Perennis (Hillsdale, NY), 2004.

SIDELIGHTS: Charles Upton's first book of poems, *Panic Grass,* created a sensation when the nineteen-year-old author gave a public reading of it in San Francisco in 1968. The long poem was viewed as the record of a deeply spiritual search and the work of a dedicated visionary of the apocalypse. Upton had been interested in poetry since the age of ten, when he discovered the work of the Beat poets. While still in high school, he began writing his own poetry. "It was a poetry of fervent, sincere emotion whose symbology was drawn from fundamentally Christian sources which, mixed with the images of direct experience, expressed an unfettered, idealistic spirituality," wrote Pat Nolan in the *Dictionary of Literary Biography.*

Panic Grass was inspired by a cross-country road trip Upton took with a friend in 1967. As he explained in an article posted on the *Serious Seekers* Web site, he rejected his privileged background—which included descent "from many European kings," including Charlemagne and Alfred the Great—and became active in political protests and countercultural activities. He "hitchhiked around the country, rode freight trains, took psychedelic drugs, wrote poetry, visited gurus, dabbled in yoga and meditation, and delved into comparative religion and mythology." During this period he met Beat poet Lew Welch, who helped him publish a book of juvenilia, *Time Raid,* as well as the long poem *Panic Grass.*

According to Nolan, *Panic Grass* is "Upton's synthesis of [Allen Ginsberg's] *Howl* and [Jack] Kerouac's *On the Road.*" It describes late-twentieth-century America on the verge of apocalypse as Vietnam-era protests and race riots engulfed the country, and it ends with an image of a burning sky. As Nolan pointed out, Upton employs the long line and the natural language of his major poetic influences, Walt Whitman and Ginsberg. *Panic Grass* elicited significant praise. Indeed, according to Nolan, the poem "probably reflected the sentiment of its time more accurately than any other poem of that era; it was straight from the gut."

Despite the success of *Panic Grass,* which catapulted Upton to fame, the young poet quickly withdrew from the literary spotlight. As he noted on the *Serious Seekers* Web site, "at 19 I was 'the youngest member of the Beat Generation' . . . with absolutely nothing more to say. So I withdrew. I hid out. I never did a public reading of *Panic Grass* after it was published. My poetry fell apart, became corny or sentimental or eerily thin. I had no idea who I was or what I was supposed to do with my life." Upton moved to Canada, "commune-hopping" to various parts of British Columbia but returned to California, shortly before his father's death. After a fire destroyed the house in which he grew up, Upton and his mother moved to a small apartment, and the poet began to drink heavily. At the same time he continued his exploration of mystical spiritual traditions. Eventually, Upton and his wife became followers of Sufism.

His conversion enabled Upton to stop drinking and to focus more specifically on his study of metaphysical themes. His book *Hammering Hot Iron: A Spiritual Critique of Bly's Iron John,* which he described as his "first work of 'metaphysics and social criticism,'" explores the psychological insights and "dangerous Neo-Pagan tendencies" in Bly's notable work about male spirituality. A more recent book, *The System of Antichrist: Truth and Falsehood in Postmodernism and the New Age,* considers the "dangers and errors of the New Age movement."

BIOGRAPHICAL AND CRITICAL SOURCES:

BOOKS

Dictionary of Literary Biography, Volume 16: *The Beats: Literary Bohemians in Postwar America,* Thomson Gale (Detroit, MI), 1983, pp. 517-520.

ONLINE

Charles Upton Home Page, http://www.systemofanti christ.com (August 24, 2005).

Serious Seekers, http://www.seriousseekers.com/ (June 18, 2003), "Charles Upton."
Sophia Perennis Books Web site, http://www.sophia perennis.com/ (August 24, 2005).*

* * *

VAILLANT, John 1963(?)-

PERSONAL: Born c. 1963; married; wife an anthropologist and potter); children: two.

ADDRESSES: Home—Vancouver, British Columbia, Canada. *Agent*—c/o Author Mail, W.W. Norton and Company, 500 5th Ave., New York, NY 10110.

CAREER: Writer and freelance journalist.

WRITINGS:

The Golden Spruce: A True Story of Myth, Madness, and Greed, W.W. Norton (New York, NY), 2005.

Contributor to periodicals, including *New Yorker, Atlantic Monthly, National Geographic—Adventure, Outside,* and *Men's Journal.*

SIDELIGHTS: Writer and freelance journalist John Vaillant lives in Vancouver, British Columbia, Canada with his wife and their two children. His writing has appeared in various publications, including the *New Yorker, Atlantic Monthly,* and *Outside.* His first book, *The Golden Spruce: A True Story of Myth, Madness, and Greed,* was developed out of an article he originally wrote for the *New Yorker* about a rare three-hundred-year-old Sitka spruce tree growing in British Columbia. The tree, which stood one hundred-sixty-five feet high, was cut down by Grant Hadwin, a logger who had become an activist. After felling the tree, Hadwin left his clothes and belongings along the shore of a river in Queen Charlotte Islands and jumped into the water while still carrying his chainsaw. Not only had the tree been an ancient part of the forest, but it had spiritual and symbolic meaning for the local Haida natives, representing a golden child from their mythology. Even logging companies had respected the old tree, including it as one of those traditionally spared when they were cutting through the forest. Had-win disappeared soon after he chopped down the spruce, but continued to receive death threats and to be sought after for his crime. Vaillant includes a history of the tree, as well as addressing environmentalism as it affects the native Canadians, loggers, and environmentalists themselves.

According to John Marshall, a reviewer for the *Seattle Post-Intelligencer,* the book relates far more than a simple story about the chopping down of a tree; it delves into history, science, and even meteorology. Marshall commented that "Vaillant's greatest accomplishment is that he not only ranges so far and wide, he weaves his disparate plot elements into a compelling narrative that is never less than fascinating. Even seemingly arcane or dense topics come resonantly alive in his masterful account with its creative comparisons, surprising insights and engaging phrasing." In a review for the *Canadian Broadcasting Corporation* Web site, Andrea Curtis wrote that "what makes the book so brilliant and unusual is that it's not a typical adventure story at all. Out of what is essentially the tale of a man and a tree, Vaillant manages to create enormous narrative tension."

Entertainment Weekly contributor Wook Kim called Vaillant's book a "scrupulously researched narrative," and Donna Seaman, writing for *Booklist,* remarked that Vaillant has "a firm grasp of every confounding aspect of this suspenseful and disturbing story." As a contributor for *Publishers Weekly* observed, "Vaillant paints a haunting portrait of man's vexed relationship with nature." Comparing Vaillant's writing to that of nature-based adventure writers Jon Krakauer and Sebastian Junger, Curtis called *The Golden Spruce* "Canada's first great new adventure book."

BIOGRAPHICAL AND CRITICAL SOURCES:

PERIODICALS

Booklist, March 1, 2005, Donna Seaman, review of *The Golden Spruce: A True Story of Myth, Madness, and Greed,* p. 1124.

Entertainment Weekly, April 29, 2005, Wook Kim, review of *The Golden Spruce,* p. 153.

Kirkus Reviews, February 15, 2005, review of *The Golden Spruce,* p. 222.

Library Journal, February 15, 2005, Ilse Heidmann, review of *The Golden Spruce,* p. 155.

Publishers Weekly, December 23, 2002, John F. Baker, "Tale of a Tree," p. 12; February 14, 2005, review of *The Golden Spruce,* p. 60.

Science News, May 7, 2005, review of *The Golden Spruce,* p. 303.

Seattle Post-Intelligencer, May 13, 2005, John Marshall, review of *The Golden Spruce.*

ONLINE

Canadian Broadcasting Corporation Web site, http://www.cbc.ca/ (July 15, 2005), Andrea Curtis, review of *The Golden Spruce.*

Manchester News Online (Manchester, VT), http://www.manchestervermont.com/ (July 15, 2005), "John Vaillant."

Straight.com, http://www.straight.com/ (July 15, 2005), Alexander Varty, review of *The Golden Spruce.**

*   *   *

VALA, Katri 1901-1944
[A pseudonym]
(Karin Alice Heikel, Pecka)

PERSONAL: Born September 11, 1901, in Muonio, Finland; died of tuberculosis, April 28, 1944, in Eksjö, Sweden; daughter of Robert Waldermar (a forest officer) and Alexandra Frederika (Mäki) Wadenström; married Armas Heikel (a chemist), 1930; children: Mauri Henrik. *Education:* Graduated from teacher's training school, 1922.

CAREER: Worked as a teacher.

WRITINGS:

Kaukainen puutarha (poems), Söderström (Porvoo, Finland), 1924.

Sininen ranta (poems), Söderström (Porvoo, Finland), 1926.

Maan laiturilla, 1930.

Paluu (poems), Söderström (Porvoo, Finland), 1934.

Pesäpuu palaa, 1942.

Henki ja aine eli yksinäisen naisen pölyimuri, Mikkeli, 1945.

Kootut runot, Söderström (Porvoo, Finland), 1948.

Valikoima runoja, Söderström (Porvoo, Finland), 1958.

Suorasanaista: 30-luvulta ja-luvusta, Kansankulttuuri (Helsinki, Finland), 1981.

Contributor to *Hurmioituneet kasvot,* 1925; contributor to periodicals, including *Nuori Voima;* contributor of articles, under pseudonym Pecka, to *Tulenkantajat.* Work represented in translation in anthologies, including *Voices from Finland,* edited by E. Tompuri, 1947; *Twentieth-Century Scandinavian Poets,* edited by Martin S. Allwood, 1950; *Singing Finland,* edited by K.V. Ollilainen, 1956; *Finnish Odyssey,* edited by Robert Armstrong, 1975; and *Salt of Pleasure,* edited by Aili Jarvenpa, 1983.

ADAPTATIONS: Heikel's poems were set to music by Joonas Kokkonen and published, with musical scoring, as *Illat,* Fazer Musiikki (Helsinki, Finland), 1977.

SIDELIGHTS: Karin Alice Heikel was a Finnish writer who produced collections of poetry under the pseudonym Katri Vala during the years between the two world wars. Heikel trained as a teacher, and she eventually worked in elementary schools situated in some of Finland's more remote regions. She produced her first poetry collection, *Kaukainen puutarha,* in 1924, and readily showed herself to be a significant writer. In this volume, as well as in *Sininen ranta,* which appeared two years later, her romantic, free-verse poems, frequently set in exotic lands, prove the norm. Likewise, Heikel's contributions to *Hurmioituneet kasvot,* an anthology featuring the verse of writers known collectively as "Tulenkantajat," revel in exoticism and free-verse expression.

Even as Heikel succeeded in establishing herself as a proficient poet, she also managed to devote herself to leftist causes. Her political beliefs are expressed in her 1934 collection, *Paluu,* as well as in articles and essays published in various periodicals, including, under the pseudonym Pecka, in *Tulenkantajat,* for which her brother served as publisher.

Heikel, who contracted tuberculosis in the late 1920s, was eventually compelled, by both her declining health and the lack of acceptance accorded her radicalism, to move to Sweden, where her brother had earlier relocated. She died there, in a sanatorium, in 1944.

BIOGRAPHICAL AND CRITICAL SOURCES:

PERIODICALS

Bonnieres Literara Magasin, September, 1988, Ann Jäderlund, "Katri Vala: Sju dikter" p. 248.

ONLINE

Pegasos, http://www.kirjasto.sci.fi/kvala.htm/ (June 30, 2005), Katri Vala.*

*   *   *

VANDERBURG, Willem H. 1944-

PERSONAL: Born August 3, 1944, in the Netherlands; immigrated to Canada; became naturalized citizen; married Rita Endhoven, July 11, 1970; children: Esther, David. *Education:* University of Waterloo, B.A.Sc., 1966, M.A.Sc., 1968, Ph.D., 1973.

ADDRESSES: Home—120 Neville Park Blvd., Toronto, Ontario M4E 3P8, Canada. *Office*—University of Toronto, Department of Civil Engineering, 35 Saint George St., Toronto, Ontario M5S 1A4, Canada. *E-mail*—bill.vanderburg@utoronto.ca.

CAREER: Writer. University of Toronto, Toronto, Ontario, Canada, professor of civil engineering, environmental studies, and sociology, 1978—, director, Center for Technology and Social Development, 1986—. Ontario Audio Library Services, vice president, 1983-90; Canadian National Institute for the Blind, Ontario Division, director, 1991-95; McMaster University, Hamilton, Ontario, John W. Hodgins Memorial lecturer, 1992; Colorado School of Mines, Golden, Hennebach visiting professor, 1997-98; P.A.L. Reading Services, president.

MEMBER: National Association for Science, Technology, and Society, Society for Philosophy and Technology, Jacques Ellul Society, Société pour la Philosophie de la Technique.

AWARDS, HONORS: NATO postdoctoral fellowship; Faculty of Applied Science and Engineering Teaching Award, 1985-86; named among top twenty-five leading researchers in Canada, Canadian Foundation for Innovation, 2002.

WRITINGS:

(Editor) *Perspectives on Our Age: Jacques Ellul Speaks on His Life and Work,* Seabury Press (New York, NY), 1981, 2nd edition, House of Anansi Press (Toronto, Ontario, Canada), 2004.

The Growth of Minds and Cultures: A Unified Theory of the Structure of Human Experience, University of Toronto Press (Toronto, Ontario, Canada), 1985.

The Labyrinth of Technology, University of Toronto Press (Toronto, Ontario, Canada), 2000.

(With Namir Khan) *Healthy Cities: An Annotated Bibliography,* Scarecrow Press (Lanham, MD), 2001.

(With Namir Khan) *Sustainable Energy: An Annotated Bibliography,* Scarecrow Press (Lanham, MD), 2001.

(With Namir Khan) *Sustainable Production: An Annotated Bibliography,* Scarecrow Press (Lanham, MD), 2001.

(With Namir Khan and Nina Nakajima) *Healthy Work: An Annotated Bibliography,* Scarecrow Press (Lanham, MD), 2005.

Living in the Labyrinth of Technology, University of Toronto Press (Toronto, Ontario, Canada), 2005.

Editor-in-chief, *Bulletin of Science, Technology, and Society,* 2000—.

WORK IN PROGRESS: A project on the meaning of Christianity in modern technological society.

SIDELIGHTS: Willem H. Vanderburg told *CA:* "When I was completing a doctoral thesis in engineering in the early 1970s, I became increasingly convinced that I was ill prepared to teach engineering in a world profoundly shaped by the interactions between technology, society, and the biosphere, since my professional 'world' was full of technology and little else. I decided to continue my study of technology via the social sciences and humanities with the French thinker Jacques Ellul, with the support of a NATO postdoctoral fellowship. The intellectual 'worlds' I then entered were full of people, communities, and ecosystems, but little or no technology. No wonder our industrial civilization was not making much headway in confronting its difficulties. With the kind of intellectual and professional division of labor developed in the twentieth century, we were lost before we started.

"My response to this situation was to embark on an intellectual journey to discover where we had taken science and technology and where these creations were taking us. I began by writing *The Growth of Minds and Cultures: A Unified Theory of the Structure of Human Experience* to better understand how people made sense of and lived in the world before science and technology began to change all this. Next, in *The Labyrinth of Technology,* I examined how modern technology functions, and how this simultaneously produces our spectacular successes and our equally spectacular failings. I sought to uncover the deep structural roots of our difficulties and to develop a new kind of intellectual and professional division of labor based on what I call preventative approaches. The Canada Foundation for Innovation recognized it as one of twenty-five important Canadian innovations in 2002. We were about to begin plans to advise the province of Ontario on how to restructure all professional education in order to create a new kind of technological and economic growth with a superior ratio of desired to undesired effects, when a newly elected government ended all that. A somewhat similar federal initiative to redirect the teaching and research culture of the Canadian university was also stillborn.

"On the positive side, I had time to complete *Living in the Labyrinth of Technology,* which is a narrative of our journey with science and technology during the last 200 years. What is absolutely essential is not only to understand how people have changed technology but how technology has simultaneously changed people. As we transformed our social and physical surroundings, the experiences from which subsequent generations 'grew' their minds and cultures were an integral part of how we not only changed our moorings in the earth through the borrowing of matter and energy but also our moorings in the heavens. We again created what cultural anthropologists call myths, on which we built new religious forms, including the secular political religions that ravaged the twentieth century. In all this, the mentorship of Jacques Ellul was invaluable. I sought to bring his intellectual gift to many by helping to create an Ideas programme for the Canadian Broadcasting Corporation, which became the book *Perspectives on Our Age: Jacques Ellul Speaks on His Life and Work.* In my search for solutions, I compiled many potential components for annotated bibliographies dealing with materials, energy, work, and the urban habitat. All these writings are my small part in helping to create a more livable, just, and sustainable world.

"When I became editor-in-chief of the *Bulletin of Science, Technology, and Society,* I sought to make it a vehicle for bringing together people who are thinking deeply about our journey with science and technology, where it is taking us, and how we ought to change this journey if we are to have a future worth living. Having gradually lost my sight (becoming legally blind as a teenager), I have also been very involved in integrating people with disabilities into our colleges, universities, and communities. A project that I am still working on is a reflection on the meaning Christianity has for a civilization dominated by a scientific and technical rationality."

*   *   *

van NIJLEN, Jan 1884-1965

PERSONAL: Born November 10, 1884, in Antwerp, Belgium; died August 14, 1965, in Vorst, Belgium.

CAREER: Poet. Worked in banking; Ministry of Justice, Brussels, Belgium, staff member, beginning 1919.

WRITINGS:

POETRY

Het aangezicht der aarde: Verzen, Hijjan, Stenfert Kroese & Van der Zande (Arnhem, Netherlands), 1923.
De lokstem, A.A.M. Stols (Maastricht, Netherlands), 1925.
De vogel Phoenix, 1928.
Geheimschrift, 1934.
Het oude kind, 1938.
Gedichten, 1904-1938, A.A.M. Stols (Maastricht, Netherlands), 1938.
De dauwtrapper, A.A.M. Stols (the Hague, Netherlands), 1947.
Verzamelde gedichten, 1904-1948, A.A.M. Stols (The Hague, Netherlands), 1948.
Te laat voor deze wereld, Van Oorschot (Amsterdam, Netherlands), 1957.
Verzamelde gedichten, 1903-1964, van Oorschot (Amsterdam, Netherlands), 1964.

Bedeesd maar onbedaard, verzameld en ingeleid, edited by C. Bittremieux, Heideland (Hasselt, Belgium), 1977.

OTHER

Uren met Montaigne (essays), 1915.
Francis Jammes (essays), Sijthoff (Leiden, Netherlands), 1918.
Charles Péguy (essays), Sijthoff (Leiden, Netherlands), 1919.
Herinneringen aan E. du Perron, van Oorschot (Amsterdam, Netherlands), 1955.
Druilende burgerij: Jeugdherinneringen van een eenzelvig man, van Oorschot (Amsterdam, Netherlands), 1982.

SIDELIGHTS: Flemish writer Jan van Nijlen was known as a romantic poet whose verses often dealt with the emotions of loneliness and unfulfilled longing. In addition to his poems, many of which are collected in *Verzamelde gedichten, 1903-1964,* van Nijlen published the scholarly works *Uren met Montaigne, Francis Jammes,* and *Charles Péguy.*

BIOGRAPHICAL AND CRITICAL SOURCES:

PERIODICALS

Dietsche Warande en Belfort, 1966, Eugene van Itterbeek, "Péguy in Vlaanderen: Van Jan van Nijlen tot Richard Minne," pp. 64-69; 1967, P.G. Buckinx, "Jeugdherinneringen van Jan van Nijlen," pp. 309-311.
Nieuwe Taalgids, September, 1982, Anne Marie Musschoot, "'In de enge cel van 't middelmatig lot': Op zoek naar de poetica van Jan van Nijlen," pp. 428-443.
Tirade, September-December, 1985, Pierre H. Dubois, "De literaire familie van Jan van Nijlen," pp. 653-671.*

*   *   *

VANTREASE, Brenda Rickman 1945-

PERSONAL: Born 1945, in White County, TN; daughter of Barney and Arlene Rickman; married Don Vantrease. *Education:* Belmont University, B.A., 1967; Middle Tennessee State University, Ph.D.; attended London School of Economics. *Hobbies and other interests:* Travel.

ADDRESSES: Home—Nashville, TN. *Agent*—c/o Author Mail, St. Martin's Press, 175 5th Ave., New York, NY 10010.

CAREER: Writer. Metro-Nashville School System, TN, librarian and English teacher, 1966-91.

WRITINGS:

The Illuminator, St. Martin's Press (New York, NY), 2005.

Contributor of short stories and essays to periodicals, including *VeriTales, Thelma,* and *Coast to Coast.*

WORK IN PROGRESS: Sequel to *The Illuminator.*

SIDELIGHTS: Novelist Brenda Rickman Vantrease was born and raised in Tennessee, where she earned her undergraduate degree in English from Belmont University and her doctorate from Middle Tennessee State University. She taught and worked as a librarian in the Metro-Nashville School District for twenty-five years prior to turning to a full-time career as a writer. She attended writer's conferences across the country and was published in several periodicals before writing her first novel.

The Illuminator is set in fourteenth-century England and combines both historical and fictional characters. The story centers upon the widowed Kathryn of Blackingham, who takes in two borders to help support herself during a violent period of war, plague, and religious differences as the Normans began to adopt English as their main language. In an interview with Wilda Williams for *Library Journal,* Vantrease explained that she chose the time period because "I have always liked English history, and I am also interested in church history. The 1300s appealed to me because it was such a period of transformation. The feudal system was breaking down, the church was in crisis, and the English language was emerging."

Booklist reviewer Elizabeth Dickie called the book "a richly detailed story of love, political intrigue, and religious tyranny." Though a *Kirkus Reviews* critic found it "long, lax, [and] chatty," *Library Journal* reviewer Mary K. Bird-Guilliams remarked that

Vantrease "depicts this complex period with imagination and care, realistically presenting actual historical figures." Lauren F. Winner, writing for *Publishers Weekly,* commented that the book "reads like historical fiction of the old school—grand, sweeping, big." Winner noted, "this is not just a debut novel, but a breakout novel."

BIOGRAPHICAL AND CRITICAL SOURCES:

PERIODICALS

Booklist, February 15, 2005, Elizabeth Dickie, review of *The Illuminator,* p. 1062.
Kirkus Reviews, January 15, 2005, review of *The Illuminator,* p. 82.
Library Journal, March 1, 2005, Wilda Williams, "Q&A: Brenda Rickman Vantrease," p. 77; Mary K. Bird-Guilliams, review of *The Illuminator,* p. 81.
Publishers Weekly, February 7, 2005, review of *The Illuminator,* p. 41; March 28, 2005, Lauren F. Winner, "Brenda Rickman Vantrease: Illuminated," p. S17; April 4, 2005, review of *The Illuminator,* p. 21.

ONLINE

Bookreporter.com, http://www.bookreporter.com/ (July 15, 2005), Curtis Edmonds, review of *The Illuminator.*
Brenda Rickman Vantrease Home Page, http://www. brendarickmanvantrease.com (July 15, 2005).
Mostly Fiction, http://www.mostlyfiction.com/ (July 15, 2005), Jana Kraus, review of *The Illuminator.*
Romantic Times Web site, http://www.romantictimes. com/ (July 15, 2005), Kathe Robin, review of *The Illuminator.**

*   *   *

VERISSIMO, Luis Fernando 1936-

PERSONAL: Born September 26, 1936, in Porto Alegre, Brazil.

ADDRESSES: Agent—c/o Author Mail, New Directions Publishing Company, 80 8th Ave., New York, NY 10011.

CAREER: Writer. Writes a column for *Veja*. Also plays saxaphone in a jazz band.

WRITINGS:

Bits and Pieces, translated from the Portuguese by Ana Beatriz Davi Borges Duarte, Riocell (Porto Alegre, Brazil), c. 1970.

O popular; crônicas; ou coisa parecida, J. Olympio (Rio de Janeiro, Brazil), 1973.

As cobras, Editora Milha (Porto Alegre, Brazil), 1975.

A grande mulher nua: crônicas, Livraria J. Olympio Editora (Rio de Janeiro, Brazil), 1975.

Amor brasileiro: crônicas, Livraria J. Olympio (Rio de Janeiro, Brazil), 1977.

Brazilian Writer Luís Fernando Veríssimo Reading from His Work (sound recording), Archive of Hispanic Literature on Tape, Library of Congress, (Washington, DC), 1977.

As cobras & outros bichos, inclusive o homem, L&PM Editores (Porto Alegre, Brazil), 1977.

O rei do rock: crônicas RBS/Editora Globo (Porto Alegre, Brazil), 1978.

As cobras do Veríssimo, Editora Codecri (Rio de Janeiro, Brazil), 1979.

Ed Mort e outras histórias, L&PM Editores (Porto Alegre, Brazil), 1979.

Sexo na cabeça (articles), L&PM Editores (Porto Alegre, Brazil), 1980, reprinted, Objetiva (Rio de Janeiro, Brazil), 2002.

O analista de Bagé L&PM Editores (Porto Alegre, Brazil), 1981.

O gigolô das palavras: crônicas, edited by Maria da Gloria Bordini, L&PM Editores (Porto Alegre, Brazil), 1982.

A mesa voadora: crônicas de viagem e comida, L&PM Editores (Porto Alegre, Brazil), 1982.

Outras do analista de Bagé, L&PM Editores (Porto Alegre, Brazil), 1982.

(With Edgar Vasques) *O analista de Bagé: em quadrinhos,* L&PM Editores (Porto Alegre, Brazil), 1983.

A velhinha de Taubaté, L&PM Editores (Porto Alegre, Brazil), 1983.

A mulher do Silva, L&PM Editores (Porto Alegre, Brazil), 1984.

Aventuras da família Brasil, L&PM Editores (Porto Alegre, Brazil), 1985.

(With Miguel Paiva) *Ed mort em procurando o Silva,* L&PM Editores (Porto Alegre, Brazil), 1985.

A mãe do Freud, L&PM Editores (Porto Alegre, Brazil), 1985.

O marido do Dr. Pompeu, L&PM Editores (Porto Alegre, Brazil), 1987.

Zoeira, edited by Lucia Helena Verissimo and Maria da Glória Bordini, L&PM Editores (Porto Alegre, Brazil), 1987.

O jardim do diabo, L&PM Editores (Porto Alegre, Brazil), 1988.

Glauco Rodrigues, Salamandra (Rio de Janeiro, Brazil), 1989.

(With Miguel Paiva) *Ed mort em conexão nazista,* L&PM Editores (Sao Paulo, Brazil), 1989.

Orgias, L&PM Editores (Porto Alegre, Brazil), 1989.

Peças íntimas, L&PM Editores (Porto Alegre, Brazil), 1990.

(With Joaquim da Fonseca) *Traçando New York,* Artes e Ofícios (Porto Alegre, Brazil), 1991.

(With Jô Soares and Millôr Fernandes) *Humor nos tempos do Collor,* L&PM Editores (Porto Alegre, Brazil), 1992.

O suicida e o computador, L&PM Editores (Porto Alegre, Brazil), 1992.

Traçando Paris, Artes e Ofícios (Porto Alegre, Brazil), 1992.

Aventuras da família Brasil. Parte II, L&PM Editores (Porto Alegre, Brazil), 1993.

Traçando Roma, Artes e Ofícios (Porto Alegre, Brazil), 1993.

América (articles and essays), illustrated by Eduardo Reis de Oliveira, Artes e Ofícios (Porto Alegre, Brazil), 1994.

Comédias da vida privada: 101 crônicas escolhidas, L&PM Editores (Porto Alegre, Brazil), 1994.

(With Joaquim da Fonseca) *Traçando Porto Alegre,* Artes e Ofícios (Porto Alegre, Brazil), 1994.

Comédias da vida pública: 266 crônicas datadas (articles), L&PM Editores (Porto Alegre, Brazil), 1995.

Novas comédias da vida privada: 123 crônicas escolhidas, L&PM Editores (Porto Alegre, Brazil), 1996.

A versão dos afogados: novas comédias da vida pública (articles), L&PM Editores (Porto Alegre, Brazil), 1997.

Aquele estranho dia que nunca chega (articles), Objetiva (Rio de Janeiro, Brazil), 1999.

A eterna privação do zagueiro absoluto (articles), Objetiva (Rio de Janeiro, Brazil), 1999.

Histórias brasileiras de verão (articles), Objetiva (Rio de Janeiro, Brazil), 1999.

(With Luiz Pilla Vares and J. Luiz Marques) *Marcos Faerman, profissão repórter,* organized by João Batista Marçal, Corag (Porto Alegre, Brazil), 1999.

(With others) O desafio ético, organized by Ari Roitman, Garamond (Rio de Janeiro, Brazil), 2000.

Borges e os orangotangos eternos, (fiction), Companhia das Letras (São Paulo, Brazil), 2000, published as *Borges and the Eternal Orangutans,* translated by Margaret Jull Costa, New Directions (New York, NY), 2005.

O clube dos anjos, (novel), Objetiva (Rio de Janeiro, Brazil), 2002, translated by Margaret Jull Costa as *The Club of Angels,* New Directions (New York, NY), 2002.

Banquete com os deuses (articles), Objetiva (Rio de Janeiro, Brazil), 2003.

Contributor to *Oito ou nove ensaios sobre o Grupo Corpo* (essays), Cosac & Naify (São Paulo, Brazil), 2001. Also contributor to numerous periodicals, including *Americas.*

SIDELIGHTS: A popular writer in his native Brazil who is known for his satirical columns, Luis Fernando Verissimo is also an accomplished novelist. His first novel to be translated into English, *The Club of Angels,* is about a group of wealthy Brazilians who call themselves the Beef Stew Club and who meet once a month for a gastronomical feast prepared by one of their members. When the club's leader, Ramos, dies from AIDS, his place is taken by the mysterious Lucidio. The feasts that Lucidio prepares rank among the best. However, it does not take long for members to become aware that after each one of Lucidio's meals, one of their members dies. The remaining club members do not banish Lucidio and refuse to eat his meals. Rather, they keep on gathering as always, their taste buds strangely tantalized by the knowledge that the delicious meal will mean death for one of them when the final extra serving is handed out.

Writing in the *Review of Contemporary Fiction,* Chad W. Post noted that the author really "doesn't answer the question of why these members allow themselves to be poisoned, a question that lends a certain allegorical weight to the novel." A *Publishers Weekly* contributor wrote that, "on the way to his maniacal conclusion, Verissimo serves up a critique of male bonding . . . along with a withering probe into the motivations of his eccentric characters." The reviewer also noted the book's "witty and deft illustrations by Verissimo himself."

In *Borges and the Eternal Orangutans* Verissimo pens another mystery that includes famed writer Jorge Luis Borges as a character. The novel's narrator, Vogelstein, attends a Buenos Aires meeting of devotees to the works of Edgar Allan Poe. When a German Poe expert at the conference is killed inside a locked room, Vogelstein teams up with Borges, who is also attending the conference, to try and solve the mystery. At the heart of the murder are a series of growing disputes among some of the Poe scholars, including a belief by one that Poe had encrypted the *Necronomicon,* a famous mystical book of the dead, into his stories and writings. When one of the Poe scholars announces his intention to make a presentation on this topic, another vows to stop him. Verissimo's book contains many overt and subtle references to Poe's works. He borrows the basis for the story's plot from Poe's *Murders in the Rue Morgue,* in which a woman is found murdered in a locked room. The title of Verissimo's book also refers to Poe's tale, which involved an orangutan, and the name of the local detective assigned to the case, Cuervo, means "raven" in Spanish. The book is also replete with many other literary references as well as references to magic and the occult.

In a review in the *Los Angeles Times,* Thomas McGonigle called *Borges and the Eternal Orangutans* "a perfect novel," and added that "the reader will mourn because the novel is so short." James Francken, writing in London's *Sunday Telegraph,* noted that "detective fiction excited Borges's imagination." "Verisimmo's elegantly constructed caper works in Borges's enthusiasm," Francken added, "and ratchets up the tension before its final, fateful disclosure." *Washington Post Book World* contributor Melvin Jules Bukiet called the novel "an authentic whodunit as well as a loving homage to its eponymous detective and a serious meditation on the truths that Borges himself lived to reveal, intuit and invent." In a review that appeared in the *Philadelphia Enquirer,* Carlin Romano wrote: "Try combining three especially artful forms . . . the detective tale, Borgesian philosophical story, and 'Small World' takeoff of academic life . . . and only masters need apply. Treat yourself, then, to Luis Fernando Verissimo." Romano went on to note that the author "makes lovely music from all the literary strings it strums, keeping a smile on your face throughout." A *Kirkus Reviews* contributor called the novel "an exquisite feat of literary legerdemain," while another reviewer, writing in *Publishers Weekly,* commented: "Borges claims that one 'write[s] to remember,' but Verissimio . . . demonstrates that one also writes to pay homage, to provide pleasure and to have fun."

BIOGRAPHICAL AND CRITICAL SOURCES:

PERIODICALS

Kirkus Reviews, March 15, 2005, review of *Borges and the Eternal Orangutans,* p. 316.

Los Angeles Times, July 3, 2005, Thomas McGonigle, review of *Borges and the Eternal Orangutans.*

Philadelphia Enquirer, June 8, 2005, Carlin Romano, review of *Borges and the Eternal Orangutans.*

Publishers Weekly, April 8, 2002, review of *The Club of Angels,* p. 202; April 11, 2005, review of *Borges and the Eternal Orangutans,* p. 32.

Review of Contemporary Fiction, fall, 2000, Chad W. Post, review of *The Club of Angels,* p. 159.

Sunday Telegraph (London, England), June 27, 2004, James Francken, review of *Borges and the Eternal Orangutans.*

Washington Post Book World, June 5, 2005, Melvin Jules Bukiet, review of *Borges and the Eternal Orangutans,* p. 7.*

W

WALL, Judith Henry
(Anne Henry)

PERSONAL: Born in IN; children: three. *Hobbies and other interests:* Travel, University of Oklahoma sports, health and fitness, environmental issues, talking about books.

ADDRESSES: Home—Norman, OK. *Agent*—c/o Author Mail, Simon & Schuster, 1230 Avenue of the Americas, New York, NY 10020.

CAREER: Writer.

MEMBER: Sierra Club.

WRITINGS:

NOVELS

A Chain of Gold, 1987.
Love and Duty, Viking (New York, NY), 1988.
Handsome Women, Viking (New York, NY), 1990.
Blood Sisters, Viking (New York, NY), 1992.
Love and Glory, HarperCollins (New York, NY), 1992.
Death Eligible, Bantam (New York, NY), 1995.
Mother Love, Bantam (New York, NY), 1995.
If Love Were All, Simon & Schuster (New York, NY), 1998.
My Mother's Daughter, Simon & Schuster (New York, NY), 2000.

The Girlfriends Club, Simon & Schuster (New York, NY), 2002.
A Good Man, Simon & Schuster (New York, NY), 2005.

Also author of eleven romance novels under pseudonym Anne Henry.

ADAPTATIONS: Mother Love was adapted as a television movie titled *A Family Divided.*

WORK IN PROGRESS: The Surrogate, a novel, expected 2006.

SIDELIGHTS: Author Judith Henry Wall was raised in a military family. One of her earlier novels, *Handsome Women,* reflects this background. In the book, two sisters raised in a military family both marry military men themselves. The plot focuses on the sisters' relationships with their husbands and families. Reviewing the book in *Publishers Weekly,* Sybil Steinberg wrote that the novel "possesses an entertaining immediacy."

Wall's book *If Love Were All* focuses on middle-aged Charlotte Haberman. The recent death of Charlotte's husband allows her to travel after selling the family home in Nebraska. However, her efforts to move on upset her adult children. By the novel's end, Charlotte comes to realize that she has to make her own happiness. Praising Wall's "simple prose," a *Publishers Weekly* critic remarked that "The moral of this gentle tale . . . goes down easily." Diana Tixier Herald, writing in *Booklist,* called the novel a "solid, womanly story."

Strong female friendships are explored in Wall's *The Girlfriends Club*. In the book, four adult women who have been friends since elementary school share a vacation cottage in Kansas. A secret is kept by three of the friends to protect the fourth friend, Mary Sue, who is already suffering from cancer. *The Girlfriends Club* explores issues facing middle-aged women such as marriage, divorce, dating, and family, and a reviewer writing in *Publishers Weekly* noted that "the neat twist that ends this suspenseful, highly readable tale is appropriate, credible and satisfying."

The idea for Wall's next novel, *A Good Man,* came from an observation of Wall's nephew, Grant McFarland, that his aunt's novels feature more negative male characters than positive ones. Set in Texas and New York City, *A Good Man* focuses on the complicated friendship shared by three women. One of the friends is married to a man who has many good qualities although he is constantly overlooked. A *Kirkus Reviews* critic noted that the book contains "less-than-convincing apologias for good but dull husbands before getting to the genuinely intriguing questions." However, Harriet Klausner, writing in *Best Reviews,* stated that "Wall paints a powerful family drama."

BIOGRAPHICAL AND CRITICAL SOURCES:

PERIODICALS

Booklist, June 1, 1995, Denise Perry Donavin, review of *Mother Love,* p. 1732; July 1998, Diana Tixier Herald, review of *If Love Were All,* p. 1862; May 1, 2000, Danise Hoover, review of *My Mother's Daughter,* p. 1654.

Kirkus Reviews, March 15, 2002, review of *The Girlfriends Club,* p. 365; March 1, 2005, review of *A Good Man,* p. 258.

Library Journal, June 15, 1998, Barbara E. Kemp, review of *If Love Were All,* p. 109; May 10, 2000, Marianne Fitzgerald, review of *My Mother's Daughter,* p. 127; March 15, 2002, Marianne Fitzgerald, review of *The Girlfriends Club,* p. 110.

Publishers Weekly, January 26, 1990, Sybil Steinberg, review of *Handsome Women,* p. 405; June 8, 1998, review of *If Love Were All,* p. 45; May 1, 2000, review of *My Mother's Daughter,* p. 51; April 29, 2002, review of *The Girlfriends Club,* p. 42.

ONLINE

Best Reviews, http://www.thebestreviews.com/ (June 29, 2005), Harriet Klausner, review of *A Good Man.*

Judith Henry Wall Home Page, http://www.judith henrywall.com (June 29, 2005).

*   *   *

WALLS, Jeannette 1960(?)-

PERSONAL: Born c. 1960; daughter of Rex and Rose Marie (an artist) Walls; married John Taylor (a writer). *Education:* Barnard College, B.A., 1984.

ADDRESSES: Home—New York, NY; and Long Island, NY. *Agent*—c/o Author Mail, Scribner, Simon & Schuster, 1230 Avenue of the Americas, New York, NY 10020.

CAREER: Journalist. *New York Magazine,* New York, NY, gossip columnist, 1987-93; *Esquire,* New York, NY, gossip columnist, 1993-98; *MSNBC.com,* gossip columnist, 1998—.

WRITINGS:

Dish: The Inside Story on the World of Gossip, Spike (New York, NY), 2000.
The Glass Castle: A Memoir, Scribner (New York, NY), 2005.

SIDELIGHTS: New York-based writer Jeannette Walls is a popular gossip columnist for magazines such as *New York* and *Esquire,* and online for *MSNBC.* Her first book, *Dish: The Inside Story on the World of Gossip,* analyzes the role of gossip in media and public perception, and traces its history from the 1950s up through its explosion in the 1990s. The book includes revealing tidbits as well, showing how Walls gained her reputation as a top gossip columnist. Charles Winecoff, writing for *Entertainment Weekly,* remarked that the book "is at its best when detailing the often-ignominious backgrounds of some of today's most ubiquitous news figures." Winecoff added, however, that it "never delivers any real bombshells, and its relentlessly garrulous tone eventually becomes anesthetizing." *Library Journal* contributor Kelli N. Perkins called Walls' book "both an entertaining insider's look and a solid history of gossip." Jonathan Bing, writing for *Variety*, stated that "Walls proves the quintessential insider, and a highly entertaining one at that. Her accounts of dueling Hollywood gossips Hedda Hopper and Louella Parsons, tabloid TV icons like Barbara Walters and Geraldo Rivera, and high-flying editrix Tina Brown, lay bare the inner workings of the major gossip outlets in their ongoing efforts to somehow balance dish, cronyism and actual news."

In *The Glass Castle: A Memoir* Walls applies her fascination with people's lives to herself, revealing her own painful, deprived childhood and a life she once viewed as a shameful secret. Told from Walls' point of view as a child, the book describes her alcoholic father and artist mother, parents who seemed more intent on their next adventure than on providing basic necessities for their children. At the age of three, Walls caught her dress on fire while attempting to cook a hotdog because her mother was too busy painting to fix her a meal. The family often skipped town in the dead of night to avoid bill collectors or paying back rent on apartments that lacked heat or running water. When they ended up in Welch, Virginia, the small mining town where Walls' father grew up, the children could add their grandmother's abuse to their list of hardships. At age seventeen, Walls finally escaped to New York City with her older sister, and the two struggled to support themselves with jobs in the service industry while living in an apartment in the South Bronx. Eventually, Walls graduated from Barnard College, a degree paid for with scholarships, loans, and her own hard-earned money, then went on to a career in journalism.

The Glass Castle describes not only the hardships Walls overcame, but the guilt associated with improving her lot in life. When her parents moved to New York, they became squatters in lower Manhattan, digging through dumpsters and refusing to acknowledge that they needed assistance, their lives a sharp contrast to Walls' own successful Park Avenue existence. *Spectator* reviewer Olivia Glazebrook remarked that Walls' memoir "is full of astonishing episodes, but the book is a success beyond its ability to shock. Jeannette Walls . . . has managed to balance her account with great precision: as she and her siblings did, we must both love and hate her parents." In an *Entertainment Weekly*

review of the memoir, Nicolas Fonesca noted, "it's safe to say that none of her scoops could outshine the blunt truths on these pages." *Booklist* reviewer Stephanie Zvirin commented: "shocking, sad, and occasionally bitter, this gracefully written account speaks candidly, yet with surprising affection." A contributor for *Kirkus Reviews* observed that Walls' "tell-it-like-it-was memoir is moving because it's unsentimental; she neither demonizes nor idealizes her parents, and there remains an admirable libertarian quality about them, though it justifiably elicits the children's exasperation and disgust."

In an interview with *Entertainment Weekly* contributor Karen Valby, Walls explained her reluctance to tell people about her past: "I never set out to deceive anybody," the journalist maintained. "I'm a bad liar. I just didn't want to be 'Oh, the girl with the homeless mom.'"

BIOGRAPHICAL AND CRITICAL SOURCES:

BOOKS

Walls, Jeannette, *The Glass Castle: A Memoir,* Scribner (New York, NY), 2005.

PERIODICALS

Booklist, February 1, 2000, Ilene Cooper, review of *Dish: The Inside Story on the World of Gossip,* p. 995; October 1, 2000, Candace Smith, review of *Dish,* p. 367; February 1, 2005, Stephanie Zvirin, review of *The Glass Castle,* p. 923.
Columbia Journalism Review, July, 2000, Andie Tucher, review of *Dish,* p. 66.
Entertainment Weekly, March 10, 2000, Charles Winecoff, review of *Dish,* p. 64; March 11, 2005, Nicholas Fonseca, review of *The Glass Castle,* p. 107; March 18, 2005, Karen Valby, "Coming up for Air: In Her Blistering New Memoir, *The Glass Castle,* Gossip Columnist Jeannette Walls Dredges up Her Own Long-Buried Secrets and Lies," p. 32.
Kirkus Reviews, December 15, 2004, review of *The Glass Castle,* p. 1195.
Library Journal, April 1, 2000, Kelli N. Perkins, review of *Dish,* p. 119; February 15, 2005, Gina Kaiser, review of *The Glass Castle,* p. 141.

Newsweek, March 7, 2005, Barbara Kantrowitz, review of *The Glass Castle,* p. 55.

People, April 4, 2005, Edward Nawotka, review of *The Glass Castle,* p. 45.

Psychology Today, May-June, 2005, review of *The Glass Castle,* p. 36.

Publishers Weekly, May 1, 2000, review of *Dish,* p. 32; January 17, 2005, review of *The Glass Castle,* p. 41; February 7, 2005, Bridget Kinsella, "Media Flocks to Scribner's *The Glass Castle,*" p. 20.

Spectator, April 30, 2005, Olivia Glazebrook, review of *The Glass Castle,* p. 38.

Vanity Fair, April, 2005, Jim Windolf, review of *The Glass Castle,* p. 184.

Variety, June 5, 2000, Jonathan Bing, review of *Dish,* p. 31.

ONLINE

MSNBC.com, http://www.msnbc.com/ (July 16, 2005), Denise Hazlick, review of *The Glass Castle.*

Village Voice Online, http://www.villagevoice.com/ (July 16, 2005), Joy Press, review of *The Glass Castle.**

*   *   *

**WANNISKI, Jude 1936-2005
(Jude Thaddeus Wanniski)**

OBITUARY NOTICE— See index for *CA* sketch: Born June 17, 1936, in Pottsville, PA; died of heart failure, August 29, 2005, in Morristown, NJ. Economist, journalist, consultant, and author. Wanniski was a famous and influential economic theorist best remembered for devising the theory of supply-side economics. Interestingly, he came from a family of dedicated communists, though Wanniski would become a much more conservative thinker. He attended the University of California at Los Angeles, where he earned a B.A. in political science in 1958 and an M.S. in journalism in 1959. During the early 1960s, he was a political columnist for the *Las Vegas Review Journal.* Moving to Washington, DC, he reported for the *National Observer* from 1965 to 1972. In 1972 he formulated his theory of supply-side economics, postulating that when tax breaks are given to wealthy individuals and businesses, the money saved is reinvested into the economy to the benefit of everyone. This theory was soon adopted by many conservative politicians, especially during the administration of U.S. President Ronald Reagan in the 1980s, but Democrats on occasion also accepted the theory. After joining the *Wall Street Journal* staff in 1972, Wanniski worked there for the next six years, but was fired in 1978 for overtly campaigning for a Republican candidate. That year, Wanniski founded his economic consulting firm, Polyconomics, in Morristown, New Jersey. He also published his influential book *The Way the World Works* (1978; revised edition, 1983), which defends classical economics and explains the causes of the 1929 stock market crash. In his later years Wanniski began to moderate his views, proposing a new single-tax-rate theory in 1996. What was even more shocking to those who knew him was his support in the 1990s of Nation of Islam leader Louis Farrakhan, and, less controversially, Democratic candidate John Kerry in the 2004 presidential elections. Wanniski also later published the book *The Last Race of the Twentieth Century* (1999).

OBITUARIES AND OTHER SOURCES:

PERIODICALS

Los Angeles Times, August 31, 2005, p. B11.
New York Times, August 31, 2005, p. C16.
Polyconomics Web site, http://www.polyconomics.com/ (November 8, 2005).
Washington Post, August 31, 2005, p. B6.

*   *   *

**WANNISKI, Jude Thaddeus
See WANNISKI, Jude**

*   *   *

WASHBURN, Jennifer

PERSONAL: Female.

ADDRESSES: Home—Brooklyn, NY. *Office*—New America Foundation, 1630 Connecticut Ave. NW, 7th Fl., Washington, DC 20009. *E-mail*—Washburn@ newamerica.net.

CAREER: Writer. Freelance journalist, 1995—; New School for Social Research, World Policy Institute, New York, NY, senior research associate in Arms Trade Resource Center; Open Society Institute, New York, NY, fellow; New America Foundation, Washington, DC, fellow; Project on Government Oversight, Washington, DC, investigator.

AWARDS, HONORS: Science-in-Society award, National Association of Science Writers, 2000, for "The Kept University."

WRITINGS:

University, Inc.: The Corporate Corruption of American Higher Education, Basic Books (New York, NY), 2005.

Contributor to periodicals, including *Atlantic Monthly, Washington Post, Nation, Newsday, Washington Times,* and *Mother Jones.*

SIDELIGHTS: Jennifer Washburn began working as a freelance writer in 1995 and has served as a research fellow for several public-policy think tanks, including New America Foundation and the Open Society Institute. While working for the latter, she investigated the increasing frequency with which government agencies contract services to privately owned corporations and, more specifically, how this trend affects universities. This research resulted in an award-winning cover article for *Atlantic Monthly,* coauthored with Eyal Press and published as "The Kept University." It also served as the basis for Washburn's first book, *University, Inc.: The Corporate Corruption of American Higher Education.*

In this book Washburn maintains that universities are structuring themselves more and more like major corporations, instead of merely allowing outside companies to oversee their research. She cites the Bayh-Dole Act, passed by Congress in 1980, as a turning point in this trend. Under the act, universities that conduct research are awarded intellectual property rights to any research that is funded by the taxpayers. Unfortunately, this also provides the universities with a profit motive that Washburn believes draws their attention away from students and pure research. Little of the money earned through research is ever funneled back into improving the quality of education for the students. Washburn cites the details of various relationships between universities and corporations to illustrate her point.

Gary Greenberg, writing for *Mother Jones,* called the book "a painstakingly detailed chronicle of how the free market has penetrated the inner sanctum of higher learning." He added that Washburn "illustrates just what is at stake here: not only public health but the 'knowledge commons' that once was one of the greatest achievements of modernity." A *Kirkus Reviews* contributor called Washburn's effort "a heartfelt, well-documented expose of a major rip-off that debases education in several important ways." While noting that "Washburn offers a few modest and thoughtful prescriptions for saving higher education," however, a *Publishers Weekly* contributor observed that "this book is more likely to be read for the illnesses it lucidly diagnoses."

Washburn told an online interviewer for *CorpWatch* that "people who are on these college campuses must look into where industry money is playing a big role." She added, "Increasingly, universities are signing contracts that allow industry to dictate the terms of the research in ways that violate academic freedom. The only ways those contracts can become public is if someone starts to raise questions and insists on openness."

BIOGRAPHICAL AND CRITICAL SOURCES:

PERIODICALS

Kirkus Reviews, January 1, 2005, review of *University, Inc.: The Corporate Corruption of American Higher Education,* p. 45.
Mother Jones, March-April, 2005, Gary Greenberg, review of *University, Inc.,* p. 81.
Publishers Weekly, January 31, 2005, review of *University, Inc.,* p. 63.

ONLINE

Clemson University Web site, http://www.clemson.edu/ (July 18, 2005), biography of Jennifer Washburn.

CONTEMPORARY AUTHORS • Volume 242

CorpWatch, http://www.corpwatch.org/ (July 18, 2005), Jennifer Borden, interview with Jennifer Washburn.

New America Foundation Web site, http://www.newamerica.net/ (July 18, 2005), biography of Jennifer Washburn.

UT Watch Web site, http://www.utwatch.org/ (July 18, 2005), Nick Schwellenbach, interview with Jennifer Washburn.*

*   *   *

WATSON, Jules 1969(?)-

PERSONAL: Born c. 1969, in Perth, Western Australia, Australia; married Alistair Watson (a musician). *Education:* University of Western Australia, B.A.; Edith Cowan University, graduate diploma in public relations, 1995.

ADDRESSES: Agent—c/o Author Mail, Orion Publishing Group, Orion House, 5 Upper Saint Martin's Lane, London WC2H 9EA, England. *E-mail*—jules@juleswatson.com.

CAREER: Novelist. Formerly worked as an archeologist. Freelance writer.

WRITINGS:

NOVELS; "DALRIADA" TRILOGY

The White Mare, Orion (London, England), 2004.
The Dawn Stag, Orion (London, England), 2005.

WORK IN PROGRESS: The Boar Stone, volume three of the "Dalriada" trilogy.

SIDELIGHTS: Jules Watson was born in Perth, Western Australia, and studied archaeology at the University of Perth before completing a second degree in public relations. She worked various jobs as an archeologist and freelance writer before turning to fiction. Watson and her husband, Alistair Watson, lived in England from 1999 to 2002 while he pursued his interest in songwriting and she worked at her writing. When Watson received a book contract for a trilogy of novels, she and Alistair returned to Australia.

The White Mare, Watson's first novel and debut volume in her "Dalriada" trilogy, tells the story of Rhiann, a Scottish princess who, upon the death of her uncle, the king, is forced to make a political marriage in order to have a child that can serve as heir to the throne. Jackie Cassada, in a review for *Library Journal,* observed that the "historic detail and the addition of a touch of magic and prophecy make this a strong fantasy debut." A *Publishers Weekly* reviewer wrote that "Watson deftly blends fact and fancy, action and romance." Likewise, a *Kirkus Reviews* contributor commended Watson's mix of realism and fantasy: "she's done her homework, boning up on Tacitus for historical detail and verisimilitude, but there's imagination here, too, and the work's all the better for it."

BIOGRAPHICAL AND CRITICAL SOURCES:

PERIODICALS

Kirkus Reviews, January 15, 2005, review of *The White Mare,* p. 90.
Library Review, February 15, 2005, Jackie Cassada, review of *The White Mare,* p. 123.
Publishers Weekly, February 7, 2005, review of *The White Mare,* p. 46.

ONLINE

Aussiereviews.com, http://www.aussiereviews.com/ (July 18, 2005), Sally Murphy, review of *The White Mare.*
Beatrice.com, http://www.beatrice.com/ (July 18, 2005), "Author2Author: Juliet Marillier and Jules Watson."
Jules Watson Home Page, http://www.juleswatson.com (July 18, 2005).

*   *   *

WEBB, Nick 1959-

PERSONAL: Born 1959; married; wife's name Sue.

ADDRESSES: Home—Hackney, England. *Agent*—c/o Author Mail, Ballantine Books, 1745 Broadway, New York, NY 10019.

CAREER: Writer. Pan Books, London, England, former senior fiction editor.

WRITINGS:

(Editor, with Emma Barker and Kim Woods) *The Changing Status of the Artist,* Yale University Press (New Haven, CT), 1999.

(Editor, with Peter Elmer and Roberta Wood) *The Renaissance in Europe: An Anthology,* Yale University Press (New Haven, CT), 2000.

Wish You Were Here: The Official Biography of Douglas Adams, Headline (London, England), 2003, Ballantine Books (New York, NY), 2005.

SIDELIGHTS: In the 1970s Nick Webb was a fiction editor for Pan Books, a successful publishing company located in England. A series of radio plays titled *The Hitchhiker's Guide to the Galaxy* piqued Webb's interest and in 1978 he approached the show's writers, Douglas Adams and John Lloyd, about committing the series to the page. Pan bought the rights to the first book in 1979, and the "Hitchhiker" series of novels—written solely by Adams—went on to become hugely successful. Although Webb soon moved on to work for other publishing companies, he maintained a close friendship with Adams until the author's death in 2001. Armed with Adams' personal files and access to family members, friends, and colleagues for interviews, Webb set out to chronicle the author's life story. The resulting work is *Wish You Were Here: The Official Biography of Douglas Adams,* published in the United Kingdom in 2003 and the United States in 2005.

Carl Hays, writing for *Booklist,* called *Wish You Were Here* "easily the best of several existing Adams biographies" and "a fascinating, witty portrait of a cultural icon." *Library Journal* contributor Kathryn R. Bartelt remarked that "Webb's informal, intimate writing style works well, and his insights are rendered with a great deal of affection." *MBR Bookwatch* reviewer Harriet Klausner described the book as a "masterful job," further commenting: "The well-written biography is parts irreverent (Mr. Adams must have provided divine guidance for that inclusion) and parts insightful." "If only all biographies could be this much fun," remarked a *Kirkus Reviews* contributor, who called the biography "a warm and humorous exploration of a generation's answer to Vonnegut—and Einstein." Greg

Stepanich, writing in the *Palm Beach Post,* deemed *Wish You Were Here* "a chatty, dazzling, beautifully written eulogy for a friend" and "a flat-out joy to read."

BIOGRAPHICAL AND CRITICAL SOURCES:

PERIODICALS

Booklist, March 1, 2005, Carl Hays, review of *Wish You Were Here: The Official Biography of Douglas Adams,* p. 1132.

English Historical Review, February, 2001, Stephen Bowd, review of *The Renaissance in Europe: An Anthology,* p. 208.

Library Journal, March 1, 2005, Kathryn R. Bartelt, review of *Wish You Were Here,* p. 86.

MBR Bookwatch, March, 2005, Harriet Klausner, review of *Wish You Were Here.*

Palm Beach Post, June 26, 2005, Greg Stepanich, "'Hitchhiker's' Biography Celebrates His Journey."

Publishers Weekly, January 17, 2005, review of *Wish You Were Here,* p. 43.

ONLINE

Douglas Adams Continuum, http://www.douglasadams. se/ (July 16, 2005), interview with Nick Webb.*

*   *   *

WEI, Chuxiong
  See WEI, C.X. George

*   *   *

WEI, C.X. George 1952-
  (Chuxiong Wei, George Wei)

PERSONAL: Born January 15, 1952, in Shanghai, China; immigrated to United States; naturalized U.S. citizen; children: Shuting. *Ethnicity:* "Chinese" *Education:* Washington University (St. Louis, MO), M.A., 1991, Ph.D., 1996.

ADDRESSES: Office—Susquehanna University, Department of History, Selinsgrove, PA 17870. *E-mail*—wei@susqu.edu.

CAREER: Educator and historian. Shanghai Academy of Social Sciences, Shanghai, China, assistant professor of history, 1983-88; Washington University, St. Louis, MO, instructor, 1993-94; University of Toledo, Toledo, OH, visiting assistant professor, 1994-96, adjunct member of graduate faculty, 1995-2001; Whitman College, Walla Walla, WA, visiting assistant professor, 1996-97; Susquehanna University, Selingsgrove, PA, assistant professor, 1997-2001, associate professor of history, 2001—, history department chair, 2004—.

MEMBER: Phi Alpha Theta (director of Susquehanna University chapter, 2000—).

AWARDS, HONORS: Pacific Cultural Foundation (Taiwan) research grant, 1994-95, 1997-99; guest professor, Institute of History Research, Shanghai Academy of Social Sciences, 1999; Arthur Vining Davis Award, Susquehanna University, 2002, 2003.

WRITINGS:

Sino-American Economic Relations, 1944-1949, Greenwood Press (Westport, CT), 1997.

(Editor, with Xiaoyuan Liu) *Chinese Nationalism in Perspective: Historical and Recent Cases,* Greenwood Press (Westport, CT), 2001.

(Editor, with Xiaoyuan Liu) *Exploring Nationalisms of China: Themes and Conflicts,* Greenwood Press (Westport, CT), 2002.

Contributor to *Nations under Siege: Globalization and Nationalism in Asia,* edited by Roy Starrs, Palgrave (New York, NY), 2002. Contributor of articles and book reviews to periodicals, including *Pacific Historical Review, Journal of Asian Studies, Education About Asia, Peoria Journal Star, Roanoke Times, Sunday Times* (Central Contra Costa, GA), *Daily Local News* (PA), *Joplin Globe* (MO), *Daily Messenger* (Canandaigua, NY), and *Patriot News* (PA). Also contributor of articles to Chinese-language books and periodicals. Susquehanna University Press, editorial board member, 1997—.

BIOGRAPHICAL AND CRITICAL SOURCES:

ONLINE

Susquehanna University Department of History Web site, http://www.susqu.edu/history/ (May 30, 2005), author profile.

*   *   *

WEI, George
  See WEI, C.X. George

*   *   *

WEINER, Ellis 1950-

PERSONAL: Born October 31, 1950; married; children: two. *Education:* University of Pennsylvania, graduated 1972.

ADDRESSES: Home—PA. *Agent*—c/o Author Mail, Chronicle Books, 85 2nd St., 6th Fl., San Francisco, CA 94105.

CAREER: Writer. *National Lampoon,* Los Angeles, CA, editor, 1976-78.

WRITINGS:

The Great Muppet Caper (based on a screenplay by Tom Patchett and others), Bantam Books (New York, NY), 1981.

National Lampoon's Doon, Pocket Books (New York, NY), 1984.

Decade of the Year, Dutton (New York, NY), 1987.

The Dream Team (novel; based on a screenplay by Jon Connolly and David Loucka), Berkley Books (New York, NY), 1989.

(With Sydney Biddle Barrows) *Mayflower Manners: Etiquette for Consenting Adults,* Doubleday (New York, NY), 1990.

Letters from Cicely: A Book (based on the television series *Northern Exposure*), Pocket Books (New York, NY), 1992.

The Northern Exposure Cookbook: A Community Cookbook from the Heart of the Alaskan Riviera, Contemporary Books (Chicago, IL), 1993.

The Joy of Worry, illustrated by Roz Chast, Chronicle Books (San Francisco, CA), 2004.

(With Barbara Davilman) *Yiddish with Dick and Jane,* illustrated by Gabi Payn, Little, Brown (New York, NY), 2004.

Santa Lives! Five Conclusive Arguments for the Existence of Santa Claus, Riverhead (New York, NY), 2005.

"PETE INGALLS" MYSTERY SERIES

Drop Dead, My Lovely, New American Library (New York, NY), 2004.

The Big Boat to Bye-Bye, New American Library (New York, NY), 2005.

Contributor to periodicals, including *National Lampoon, Spy, New Yorker, Paris Review,* and *New York Times Magazine.*

SIDELIGHTS: Since the early 1980s, former *National Lampoon* editor Ellis Weiner has published both fiction and nonfiction, his subject matter ranging from the benefits of worry and the existence of Santa Claus to Yiddish slang and Alaskan cooking.

In 2004 Weiner published the first novel in a series of mock detective stories featuring Pete Ingalls, a bookstore clerk who turned private investigator after a skull-crushing run-in with a pile of books. In *Drop Dead, My Lovely* Weiner shares the story of the fateful accident that led Ingalls to set up shop as a character straight out of his favorite detective novels, and follows him as he bungles his way through his first cases. *Allreaders.com* contributor Harriet Klausner called the book "an outstanding reading experience," adding, "the best part of Ellis Weiner's novel is the dialogue. Pete sounds like an anachronistic Phillip Marlow clone in a twenty-first-century context and that makes for a hilarious novel." Kevin Burton Smith, writing for *Mystery Scene,* called *Drop Dead, My Lovely* "the stuff that comedic dreams are made of" and commended Weiner for giving readers "an honest-to-goodness mystery to solve."

Weiner's second book in the "Pete Ingalls" series, titled *The Big Boat to Bye-Bye,* has Ingalls tackling a blackmail case in which lewd photographs of the pup-

pet stars of a children's television show are held for ransom. In an *MBR Bookwatch* review, Klausner remarked, "The blackmail turning into a homicide investigation is cleverly conceived so that fans of Hollywood Noir receive an enjoyable often amusing one reel tale." A reviewer for *Publishers Weekly* commented that Weiner "uses a rapid-fire technique that sprays gags and gimmicks—some wildly off-target, some dead-on—in a parody of the hard-boiled PI novel."

Yiddish with Dick and Jane, which Weiner coauthored with television writer Barbara Davilman, parodies the "Dick and Jane" series of reading primers from the mid-twentieth century. Also published in 2004, Weiner's *The Joy of Worry,* illustrated by Roz Chast, pokes fun at the national pastime of worrying, revealing the "secrets" of harnessing worry to lose weight, become a more effective parent, and make more money. Weiner sets out to prove the existence of Father Christmas once and for all in *Santa Lives! Five Conclusive Arguments for the Existence of Santa Claus,* released in 2005.

Several of Weiner's earlier works include *National Lampoon's Doon,* a spoof on Frank Herbert's *Dune* series, in which a sugar-coated planet is found to harbor the much-treasured resource: beer; *Mayflower Manners: Etiquette for Consenting Adults,* a guide to good manners during erotic encounters, written with Sydney Biddle Barrows; and two books inspired by the popular early 1990s television series *Northern Exposure: Letters from Cicely: A Book,* excerpts from letters written by the show's fictional characters, and *The Northern Exposure Cookbook: A Community Cookbook from the Heart of the Alaskan Riviera,* with recipes and commentary from the show.

BIOGRAPHICAL AND CRITICAL SOURCES:

PERIODICALS

Entertainment Weekly, January 14, 1994, Erica Kornberg, review of *The Northern Exposure Cookbook: A Community Cookbook from the Heart of the Alaskan Riviera,* p. 49.

MBR Bookwatch, March, 2005, Harriet Klausner, review of *The Big Boat to Bye-Bye.*

Publishers Weekly, January 19, 2004, review of *Drop Dead, My Lovely,* p. 56; February 28, 2005, review of *The Big Boat to Bye-Bye,* p. 45.

ONLINE

Allreaders.com, http://www.allreaders.com/ (July 14, 2005), Harriet Klausner, review of *Drop Dead, My Lovely.*
Mystery Scene, http://www.mysteryscenemag.com/ (July 14, 2005), Kevin Burton Smith, review of *Drop Dead, My Lovely.**

*   *   *

WELCH, Michelle M. 1971-

PERSONAL: Born July 12, 1971, in Tucson, AZ; daughter of Roger and Chestine Welch. *Ethnicity:* "Caucasian." *Education:* Arizona State University, B.A., 1995; University of Arizona, M.A., 1997.

ADDRESSES: Agent—Christine Cohen, Virginia Kidd Agency, 538 E. Hartford St., P.O. Box 278, Milford, PA 18337. *E-mail*—madwrtr@netzero.net.

CAREER: Writer. Maricopa County Library District, Phoeniz, AZ, library assistant and librarian, 1994-2000; Chandler Public Library, AZ, reference librarian, 2000—.

MEMBER: Arizona Library Association, Society for Creative Anachronism.

WRITINGS:

FANTASY NOVELS

Confidence Game, Bantam Books (New York, NY), 2003.
The Bright and the Dark, Bantam Books (New York, NY), 2004.
Chasing Fire, Bantam Books (New York, NY), 2005.

Contributor of short story "Charon" to *Reader's Break,* Pine Grove Press (Jamesville, NY), 1995.

SIDELIGHTS: Michelle M. Welch told *CA:* "When asked how long I've been writing, I usually say 'since they put the fat pencil in my hand in kindergarten.' I started writing stories then and never stopped. Publication seemed like the next logical step in the process, and I began marketing my short stories in the early 1990s, until I distracted myself by starting to write novels. While my short stories tend to have an element of unreality to them and can best be described as magic realism, my novels have always been strictly fantasy.

"As a fantasy writer, I've always been conscious of how the genre is perceived, both in the literary world and by some science fiction readers who deride fantasy as unrealistic and trivial. My background in English literature has given me a particular attitude toward the fantasy genre, a belief in its strength as allegory and its ability to communicate truths about the human condition that might be taken for granted if presented in a more mainstream fashion. In my novels I am less concerned with presenting conventional fantasy elements such as magic than with portraying how these elements affect the characters."

*   *   *

WHITE, Gary W. 1966-

PERSONAL: Born February 2, 1966, in Orrville, OH; son of Dallas (self-employed) and Bonnie (a homemaker) White. *Education:* Youngstown State University, B.S. (magna cum laude), 1988; Kent State University, M.L.S., 1991; University of Akron, M.B.A., 1995.

ADDRESSES: Home—1251 S. Garner St., State College, PA 16801. *Office*—Pennsylvania State University, 309 Paterno Library, University Park, PA 16802. *E-mail*—gww2@psu.edu.

CAREER: Writer. Pennsylvania State University, Schreyer Business Library, head librarian, 1992—.

MEMBER: American Library Association (chair of business reference and services section, 2003-04).

WRITINGS:

(With Gregory A. Crawford, Huijie J. Chen, and Lisa R. Stimatz) *Using Microsoft PowerPoint: A How-to-Do-It Manual for Librarians,* Neal-Schuman (New York, NY), 1998.

(Editor) *Help Wanted: Job and Career Information Resources,* American Library Association (Chicago, IL), 2003.

(Editor) *The Core Business Web: A Guide to Key Information Resources,* Haworth Information Press (New York, NY), 2003.

* * *

WHITE, Max E. 1946-

PERSONAL: Born May 19, 1946, in Cornelia, GA; married Jeanne Vosecky (a teacher), September 5, 1970; children: Douglas, David. *Education:* University of Georgia, B.A., 1968, M.A., 1970; Indiana University, Ph.D., 1980. *Religion:* Baptist.

ADDRESSES: Office—Piedmont College, Department of Social Science, Demorest, GA 30535. *E-mail*—mwhite@piedmont.edu.

CAREER: Writer. Piedmont College, Demorest, GA, professor, 1989—. Member, Southeastern Archaeological Conference.

MEMBER: Southern Anthropological Society, Sons of Confederate Veterans, Sons of the American Revolution.

WRITINGS:

Georgia's Indian Heritage: The Prehistoric Peoples and Historic Tribes of Georgia, W.H. Wolfe Associates (Roswell, GA), 1988.

The Archaeology and History of the Native Georgia Tribes, University Press of Florida (Gainesville, FL), 2002.

* * *

WHITSON, Audrey J. 1957-

PERSONAL: Born August 28, 1957, in Edmonton, Alberta, Canada; daughter of Douglas (Tim) Izod (a farmer) and Theresa (Schermann) Whitson; married Willaim Nichols (an organizational change consultant), July 24, 1999. *Education:* University of Calgary,

B.S.W., 1981; Graduate Theological Union-Franciscan School of Theology, M.A., 1989. *Politics:* "Left of center." *Religion:* Roman Catholic. *Hobbies and other interests:* Singing, gardening, bird-watching, photography, reading, genealogy.

ADDRESSES: Home—10782 One Hundred Sixty-five St., Edmonton, Alberta T59 3T5, Canada. *Office*—Tortoise Press, Inc., P.O. Box 1492 Station Main, Edmonton, Alberta T59 2N7, Canada. *E-mail*—awhitson@spiritlinks.org.

CAREER: Editor, educator, and writer. Spirit Links, Edmonton, Alberta, Canada, proprietor and workshop facilitator, 1991—; St. Joseph's College, Edmonton, lecturer in theology, 1992-94, 2003; St. Stephen's College, Edmonton, lecturer in theology, 1997-2000; Company's Coming, Edmonton, proofreader, 2001-02; self-employed writer, editor, and Web editor, 2002-03. Tortoise Press, Inc., Edmonton, editor-in-chief, 2003—. Other Voices Publishing Society, Edmonton (editorial collective), reviews coordinator, 2001-03.

MEMBER: Writer's Guild of Canada, Editors' Association of Canada (voting member, 2001—), Writers' Guild of Alberta (Edmonton branch; member of writing retreats committee, 1994-99), Edmonton Labyrinth Society (founding chair, 1998-2001).

WRITINGS:

Teaching Places, Wilfrid Laurier University Press (Waterloo, Ontario, Canada), 2003.

Contributor of articles to periodicals, including *Journal of Feminist Studies in Religion, Edmonton Journal, National Bulletin on Liturgy, Catholic New Times, Canadian Woman Studies, Vox Feminarum, Grail, Quest, Way of St. Francis, Creation Spirituality, Rags,* and *FreeFall.*

WORK IN PROGRESS: Work in multiple genres, including short fiction, a novel, poetry, and essays. Research on several topics, including "the relationship between children's games and contemporary and ancient ritual; medieval music and instruments, especially monastic chant; Plato and other early philosophers and their views on women; the works of Sor Juana Ines de la Cruz; and medieval European pilgrimage and shrine lore, especially as related to women."

SIDELIGHTS: Audrey J. Whitson told *CA:* "I've been writing creatively since I could print. As a child it was my way of finding my place in the world, of knowing the world—still is. I think of myself as a woman writer. And so I especially read women writers in English, though I do read several male writers in Spanish. I have also been part of a spoken poetry movement here in Edmonton and that has broken open the experience of poetry from many perspectives.

"I'm inspired at odd times—when I'm on a walk, about to go to sleep at night, in my dreams, or when I first wake up in the morning. New experiences also often jolt me into new awareness. (I had a writing instructor who said once it was better to take any course but writing—because it opened you to new experiences.) I've learned to obey the voice inside, the voice that says 'write this down.' I take a notebook and a pen with me wherever I go. I sleep with a journal close at hand. I have kept a journal since I was a teenager (about thirty years). It is one of my most important spiritual practices.

"Nature has been a part of my life since I was a very small child. I grew up on a farm and nature was my first experience of spirit. Nature is my spiritual source and the more time I can spend there, the more and clearer my writing on any subject. That's why I garden and bird-watch a lot in the city and get out to the country whenever I can."

BIOGRAPHICAL AND CRITICAL SOURCES:

ONLINE

Audrey Whitson Home Page, http://www.spiritlinks.org (May 30, 2005).

*   *   *

WILSEY, Sean 1970-

PERSONAL: Born 1970, in San Francisco, CA; son of Al Wilsey (a businessman) and Pat Montandon (a gossip columnist); married Daphne Beal; children: Owen.

ADDRESSES: Office—McSweeney's, 826 Valencia St., San Francisco, CA 94110.

CAREER: Editor and writer. *McSweeney's Quarterly,* San Francisco, CA, editor-at-large. Former editorial assistant at *New Yorker,* fact checker at *Ladies' Home Journal,* letters correspondent at *Newsweek,* and apprentice gondolier in Venice, Italy.

WRITINGS:

Oh the Glory of It All (memoir), Penguin Press (New York, NY), 2005.

Articles have appeared in the *London Review of Books, Los Angeles Times,* and *McSweeney's Quarterly.*

SIDELIGHTS: Sean Wilsey turned to his own life and his parents' messy divorce for his first book, the memoir *Oh the Glory of It All.* In recounting his life up to his early twenties, Wilsey reveals how, when he was nine years old, his family life played out in newspaper headlines after his wealthy father, an entrepreneur, filed for divorce from his gossip-columnist mother so he could marry his mother's best friend. After the divorce, his mother became suicidal and, for a time wanted her son to join her in a leap to death from her apartment balcony. His father, cold and distant, eventually disowned Wilsey, and the boy's new stepmother seemed to hate him as she tried to maniacally control his life. Wilsey began to exhibit problem behaviors that led him to get repeatedly expelled from various schools. Although his parents were self-obsessed, Wilsey credits his mother for becoming a peace activist, which activity eventually led to mother and son meeting some of the political giants of the day, including Soviet leader Mikhail Gorbachev and Indian Prime Minister Indira Gandhi.

"Wilsey details the trials of his particular brand of teenage life in an engrossing, entertaining, and often hilarious memoir," noted Ronald Ray Ratliff in *Library Journal.* Bill Goldstein, writing in *People,* called the memoir "touching" and "a book worth reading." In a review in *Artforum International,* Jenifer Berman wrote: "Wilsey's narrative, told against the backdrop of the haute echelons of San Francisco society, is a classic tale of excess and redemption," while a *Publish-*

ers *Weekly* contributor called the book "a startlingly honest tale" and added that the "writing . . . is vivid, detailed, deep and filled with fresh metaphors."

BIOGRAPHICAL AND CRITICAL SOURCES:

BOOKS

Wilsey, Sean, *Oh the Glory of It All,* Penguin Press (New York, NY), 2005.

PERIODICALS

Artforum International, summer, 2005, Jenifer Berman, review of *Oh the Glory of It All,* p. S53.
Entertainment Weekly, May 20, 2005, Jennifer Reese, review of *Oh the Glory of It All,* p. 80.
Kirkus Reviews, April 1, 2005, review of *Oh the Glory of It All,* p. 410.
Library Journal, June 1, 2005, Ronald Ray Ratliff, review of *Oh the Glory of It All,* p. 144.
People, June 6, 2005, Bill Goldstein, review of *Oh the Glory of It All,* p. 52.
Pittsburgh Post-Gazette, July 3, 2005, Kristofer Collins, review of *Oh the Glory of It All.*
Publishers Weekly, May 2, 2005, review of *Oh the Glory of It All,* p. 184.

ONLINE

New York Metro Online, http://newyorkmetro.com/ (August 26, 2005), Boris Kachka, "Conversation: Francine du Plessix Gray and Sean Wilsey."*

*　　*　　*

WILSON, Leslie 1952-

PERSONAL: Born 1952, in Nottingham, England; married; children: Jo, Kathy. *Education:* Durham University, graduated. *Hobbies and other interests:* Gardening, photography, Chinese martial arts.

ADDRESSES: Home—Berkshire, England. *Agent*—Sarah Molloy, A.M. Heath and Co. Ltd., 6 Warwick Ct., London WC1R 5DJ, England. *E-mail*—cornelius wilson@btinternet.com.

CAREER: Writer and writing tutor. Former translator.

AWARDS, HONORS: Guardian Children's Fiction Award shortlist, 2004, and Branford Boase Award, 2005, both for *Last Train from Kummersdorf.*

WRITINGS:

FOR ADULTS

Mourning Is Not Permitted, Women's Press, 1990.
Malefice, Pantheon Books (New York, NY), 1992.
The Mountain of Immoderate Desires, Weidenfeld & Nicolson (London, England), 1994.

FOR YOUNG ADULTS

Last Train from Kummersdorf, Faber & Faber (London, England), 2004.

SIDELIGHTS: One of British author Leslie Wilson's first awards came during childhood: a package of Cadbury creme eggs, won for the budding author's prize story about the origin of Easter eggs. In the years since, Wilson has balanced jobs in adult education and as a translator with her writing career. She published her first adult novel in 1990, and *Last Train from Kummersdorf,* her first novel for young-adult readers, was released in 2005.

Inspired by the memories of Wilson's mother, *Last Train from Kummersdorf* brings readers back to 1945 Germany, during the days leading up to the end of World War II. In this highly acclaimed novel, two streetwise teens, sixteen-year-old Hanno and communist resistance-fighter Effi, meet while hiding in rural Germany and find themselves on the run as Hitler's Reich crumbles around them. With no family and no home, the teens rely on their wits and what the land will provide. In an amoral world full of desperate people, where laws no longer exist, they find that threats can lurk in the most unlikely places. As Geraldine Bedell noted in her review of the book for the London *Observer,* Wilson's "beautifully written" novel brings to life the terror felt by "two teenagers who have lost almost everything, but hold on doggedly, somehow, to the exuberance and optimism of their youth."

Geared for older readers, Wilson's novel *Malefice* takes place in seventeenth-century England and follows the last days of a doomed woman who is ultimately executed for witchcraft by her fellow villagers. The narration alternates back and forth between Alice Slade as she sits in her jail cell and the thoughts of her friends, family and fellow villagers leading up to her dreary fate. "Wilson's lean, uncluttered prose evokes this distant era with the earthy resonance of folktales," commented a *Publishers Weekly* reviewer.

BIOGRAPHICAL AND CRITICAL SOURCES:

PERIODICALS

Observer (London, England), April 11, 2004, Geraldine Bedell, "Reality Check."
Publishers Weekly, April 12, 1993, review of *Malefice,* p. 48; October 31, 1994, review of *The Mountain of Immoderate Desires,* p. 45.
School Librarian, spring, 2004, review of *Last Train from Kummersdorf,* p. 49.

ONLINE

Guardian Unlimited, http://books.guardian.co.uk/ (October 12, 2004), Claire Armitstead, review of *Last Train from Kummersdorf.*
Leslie Wilson Web site, http://www.lesliewilson.co.uk (December 11, 2005).

*   *   *

WILSON, William Scott 1944-

PERSONAL: Born 1944; children: Matthew, Michelle. *Education:* Dartmouth College, B.A. (political science); Monterey Institute of Foreign Studies, B.A. (Japanese language and literature); University of Washington, M.A. (Japanese language and literature), 1979.

ADDRESSES: Home—Miami, FL. *Agent*—Kodansha International, Otowa YK Building, 1-17-14 Otowa, Bunkyo-ku, Tokyo 112-8652, Japan.

CAREER: Author and translator.

WRITINGS:

(Translator and author of introduction) *Ideals of the Samurai: Writings of Japanese Warriors,* edited by Gregory N. Lee, Ohara Publications (Burbank, CA), 1982.
(Translator) Hung Ying-ming, *The Roots of Wisdom: Saikontan,* Kodansha International (New York, NY), 1985.
(Translator) Takuan Sōhō, *The Unfettered Mind: Writings of the Zen Master to the Sword Master,* Kodansha International (New York, NY), 1986.
The Lone Samurai: The Life of Miyamoto Musashi, Kodansha International (New York, NY), 2004.

SIDELIGHTS: While an undergraduate student at Dartmouth College, William Scott Wilson was invited by a friend to take a kayak trip for three months along the coast of Japan. The trip, which was later chronicled in *National Geographic,* was his first experience with the Asian country and it ultimately altered the course of his studies. After studying Japanese language and literature in college, Wilson then traveled to Nagoya, Japan, where he began researching Edo period philosophy at the Aichi Prefectural University. He later earned a master's degree in Japanese language and literature from the University of Washington. These studies provided Wilson with a broad range of knowledge concerning Japanese culture, literature, and history, with an emphasis on the samurai. In an interview posted on the Kodansha International Web site, he talked about bushido, a Japanese way of life: "Bu comes from two radicals meanings 'stop' and 'spear.' So even though the word now means 'martial' or 'military affair,' it has the sense of stopping aggression. Shi can mean 'samurai,' but also means 'gentleman' or 'scholar.' Looking at the character, you can see a man with broad shoulders but with his feet squarely on the ground. Do, with the radicals of head and motion, originally depicted a thoughtful way of action. It now means a path, street or way. With this in mind, we can understand Bushido as a way of life, both ethical and martial, with self-discipline as a fundamental tenet." Regarding the modern culture of Japan, he stated that "it impressed me that the company had sort of taken the place of a feudal lord, and that the stipend of the samurai had become the salary of the white-collar worker." Wilson has translated several texts from Japanese to English and is also the author of *The Lone Samurai: The Life of Miyamoto Musashi.*

The Lone Samurai tells the story of Miyamoto Musashi, who many consider to have been the finest Japanese swordsman ever. The seventeenth-century samurai eventually became an artist, but he is best remembered for his superb fighting skills and technique. A reviewer for *Library Bookwatch* remarked that the author "draws upon his considerable expertise as a preeminent translator of classic samurai texts to write an original biography." A *Publishers Weekly* contributor commented that Wilson "integrates a considerable amount of Japanese history and culture into a short, dense book with lots of specialized information."

BIOGRAPHICAL AND CRITICAL SOURCES:

PERIODICALS

Kirkus Reviews, September 1, 2004, review of *The Lone Samurai: The Life of Miyamoto Musashi,* p. 857.
Library Bookwatch, November, 2004, review of *The Lone Samurai.*
Library Journal, September 1, 2004, John Jaeger, Charles W. Hayford, review of *The Lone Samurai,* p. 167.
Newsweek International, November 29, 2004, Hideko Takayama, review of *The Lone Samurai,* p. 73.
Publishers Weekly, October 11, 2004, review of *The Lone Samurai,* p. 68.

ONLINE

Kodansha International Web site, http://www.kodansha-intl.com/ (June 21, 2005), "William Scott Wilson."
University of Washington Web site, http://faculty.washington.edu/ (June 21, 2005), "William Scott Wilson."*

*   *   *

WITCOVER, Paul

PERSONAL: Born in Zurich, Switzerland; son of Jules Witcover (a political columnist). *Education:* Clarion Science-Fiction and Fantasy Writers' Workshop, Michigan State University, graduated 1980.

ADDRESSES: Home—New York, NY. *Agent*—c/o Author Mail, Eos, 10 E. 53rd St., 7th Fl., New York, NY 10022. *E-mail*—stilskin@sff.net.

CAREER: Writer. Freelance editor and novelist.

WRITINGS:

Zora Neale Hurston (biography), Chelsea House (New York, NY), 1991.
Waking Beauty (novel), HarperPrism (New York, NY), 1997.
Tumbling After (novel), Eos (New York, NY), 2005.

Also creator, with Elizabeth Hand, of *Anima* comic-book series for DC Comics.

SIDELIGHTS: Paul Witcover knew from an early age that he wanted to become a writer, and his endeavors were strongly influenced by his parents; his father is political columnist Jules Witcover, and his mother was an English teacher and editor. A 1980 graduate of the renowned Clarion Science-Fiction and Fantasy Writers' Workshop, Witcover has worked as a freelance writer and editor. His first book, a biography of African-American author Zora Neale Hurston, was published in 1991.

Witcover's first fantasy novel, *Waking Beauty,* was conceived as a retelling of the story of Sleeping Beauty from a feminist perspective. A reviewer for *Publishers Weekly* called the book "rich and ambitious," adding that "this is a striking first novel, a find for those who want more than the same old fantasy worlds and comfortable adventures." *Rambles.net* contributor Donna Scanlon described *Waking Beauty* as "a lush and sensuous first novel . . . highly descriptive, emphasizing and appealing to the senses." In a *Fantastic Metropolis* online review, Jeff Topham wrote that "*Waking Beauty* is one of the most distinctive and meticulously-rendered fantastic visions of the [1990s] . . . , a violent and erotic reimagining of the story of Sleeping Beauty." He added, "Relentlessly ambitious and often strikingly beautiful, it's an imaginative achievement of wonderful originality and intensity."

On his official Web site, Witcover described his second novel, *Tumbling After,* as "a novel about growing up, about playing games, about what is and isn't real. It's a novel of sexual awakening and magical transformation." The novel involves two parallel storylines, one set in 1977 and involving a twelve-year-old boy who seemingly gains the ability to alter reality after a near-tragic accident and the other set far in the future and involving a seventeen-year-old mutant caught in the battle between the "mutes" and normal humans. *Washington Post* contributor Bill Sheehan called Witcover "a gifted, fiercely original writer whose genre-bending fiction deserves the widest possible attention," and further commented: "Witcover has made something powerful and strange out of familiar materials. The story is dauntingly dense, though satisfying. The prose is clean and precise, lending an aura of understated authority to the entire enterprise." "It is a fully realized novel by a significant new voice," Sheehan added. "I hope it finds the audience it deserves." Jackie Cassada, in a review for *Library Journal,* remarked that Witcover "evokes the painful emotions of preadolescence and awakening adulthood in this cross-world fantasy that should appeal to fans of role-playing and general fantasy." A *Publishers Weekly* reviewer described *Tumbling After* as "compelling" and "a winning, entertaining cross-genre roll." *Booklist* reviewer Regina Schroeder found the book "a nifty take on parallel worlds and superhuman power" and "a ripping yarn with particular appeal to horror fans."

BIOGRAPHICAL AND CRITICAL SOURCES:

PERIODICALS

Booklist, March 15, 2005, Regina Schroeder, review of *Tumbling After,* p. 1276.
Kirkus Reviews, January 1, 2005, review of *Tumbling After,* p. 26.
Library Journal, March 15, 2005, Jackie Cassada, review of *Tumbling After,* p. 75.
Publishers Weekly, January 20, 1997, review of *Waking Beauty,* p. 398; January 17, 2005, review of *Tumbling After,* p. 39.
Washington Post Book World, March 13, 2005, Bill Sheehan, review of *Tumbling After,* p. 13.

ONLINE

Fantastic Metropolis, http://www.fantasticmetropolis.com/ (October 28, 2001), Jeff Topham, "Blood and Roses: A Reflection on Paul Witcover's *Waking Beauty*"; (June 19, 2005) Jeffrey Ford, "An Interview with Paul Witcover."

Paul Witcover Home Page, http://www.sff.net/people/stilskin (March 17, 2005).
Rambles.net, http://www.rambles.net/ (July 17, 2005), Donna Scanlon, review of *Waking Beauty.**

*   *   *

WOLFE, Lisa M.

PERSONAL: Children: two. *Education:* Associate degree in exercise science. *Hobbies and other interests:* Motorcycles, climbing, martial arts, reading.

ADDRESSES: Agent—Wish Publishing, P.O. Box 10337, Terre Haute, IN 47801.

CAREER: Fitness instructor and personal trainer; gym owner.

WRITINGS:

YogaBand: An Exciting and Challenging New Yoga Workout, Wish Publishing (Terre Haute, IN), 2004.
Enjoy the Ride: A Fitness Guide for Motorcyclists, Bristol Fashion Publications (Rockledge, FL), 2004.
Off the Wall: Exercises for Climbers, Equilibrium Books (Terre Haute, IN), 2005.
Save Time with Circuit Training, Wish Publishing (Terre Haute, IN), 2005.

Contributor of fitness articles to various periodicals. Creator of video workouts based on her books.

SIDELIGHTS: Lisa M. Wolfe holds an associate degree in exercise science and is certified as an American Council on Exercise (ACE) personal trainer, an ACE group fitness instructor, and a Yoga-Fit instructor. In addition to working as a personal trainer and fitness instructor, she previously owned a gym and has contributed various articles on fitness to a range of magazines. Her book *YogaBand: An Exciting and Challenging New Yoga Workout* offers a challenging workout routine that Wolfe created based on more than a decade of experience in the fitness field. The goal of the workout is to enable the exerciser to build muscle tone, increase flexibility, and reduce stress using special exercise bands for added resistance and aid positioning. Wolfe includes a brief explanation of the origins of each exercise prior to explaining the exercises themselves. She also includes tips on preparing to do the routine, including safety information, breathing exercises, and advice on things to keep in mind when performing any form of exercise. Elaine M. Lasda remarked in a review for *Library Journal* that "Wolfe touches on the relaxation portion, but her emphasis is on yoga's physical fitness aspects." A contributor to *Small Press Bookwatch* called the book "a welcome and highly recommended addition to personal and professional yoga exercise program reference collections."

BIOGRAPHICAL AND CRITICAL SOURCES:

PERIODICALS

American Fitness, September-October, 2004, review of *YogaBand: An Exciting and Challenging New Yoga Workout,* p. 36.
Library Journal, December, 2003, "Accessible Yoga for Every Body" (video review), p. 181; September 15, 2004, Elaine M. Lasda, review of *YogaBand,* p. 75.
Reviewer's Bookwatch, September, 2004, Sharon Stuart, review of *YogaBand.*
Small Press Bookwatch, September, 2004, review of *YogaBand.*

*   *   *

WOODING, Chris 1977-

PERSONAL: Born February 28, 1977, in Leicester, Leicestershire, England. *Education:* Attended University of Sheffield. *Hobbies and other interests:* Watching movies, backpacking in foreign countries, touring with his band.

ADDRESSES: *Home*—London, England. *Agent*—Carolyn Whitaker, London Independent Books, 26 Chalcot Crescent, London NW1 8YD, England.

CAREER: Full-time writer.

AWARDS, HONORS: Smarties Book Prize, 2001, *Horn Book* Notable Book designation, *School Library Journal* Best Books designation, and American Library Association Best Book For Teens designation, all 2004, all for *The Haunting of Alaizabel Cray;* Lancashire Children's Book of the Year Award, and Dracula Society Children of the Night Award for best gothic novel, both 2004, and Children's Book Council Outstanding International Book Award, 2005, all for *Poison.*

WRITINGS:

YOUNG-ADULT NOVELS

Crashing, Scholastic (London, England), 1998, Scholastic/Push (New York, NY), 2003.
Catchman, Scholastic (London, England), 1998.
Kerosene, Scholastic (London, England), 1999.
Endgame, Scholastic (London, England), 2000.
The Haunting of Alaizabel Cray, Scholastic (London, England), 2001, Orchard (New York, NY), 2004.
Poison, Scholastic (London, England), 2003, Orchard Books (New York, NY), 2005.
Storm Thief, Orchard (New York, NY), 2006.

"BROKEN SKY" SERIES; FANTASY; FOR CHILDREN

Broken Sky: Part One, illustrated by Steve Kyte, Scholastic (London, England), 1999.
Broken Sky: Part Two, illustrated by Steve Kyte, Scholastic (London, England), 1999.
Broken Sky: Part Three, illustrated by Steve Kyte, Scholastic (London, England), 1999.
Broken Sky: Part Four, illustrated by Steve Kyte, Scholastic (London, England), 1999.
Broken Sky: Part Five, illustrated by Steve Kyte, Scholastic (London, England), 1999, published as *Defy It,* Scholastic (New York, NY), 2000.
Broken Sky: Part Six, illustrated by Steve Kyte, Scholastic (London, England), 1999.
Broken Sky: Part Seven, illustrated by Steve Kyte, Scholastic (London, England), 2000.
Broken Sky: Part Eight, illustrated by Steve Kyte, Scholastic (London, England), 2000.
Broken Sky: Part Nine, illustrated by Steve Kyte, Scholastic (London, England), 2000.

"BRAIDED PATH" SERIES; FANTASY; FOR ADULTS

The Weavers of Saramyr, Gollancz (London, England), 2003.

The Skein of Lament, Gollancz (London, England), 2004.

The Ascendancy Veil, Gollancz (London, England), 2005.

OTHER

Halflight (adult fantasy novel), Gollancz (London, England), 2006.

WORK IN PROGRESS: The screenplays *Nursery,* a horror film, for director Michael Radford, and *Fusion,* a cartoon series for Canada's Nelvana television; *Pandemonium,* a graphic novel, for Scholastic's Grafix imprint, due 2008.

SIDELIGHTS: Chris Wooding achieved success as an author at a very young age. His first novel, *Crashing,* was written and accepted for publication while he was still a teenager, and by the time he graduated from college at age twenty-one he was making a living as a full-time writer. Being published so young "was brilliant, obviously," Wooding told a *Push* online interviewer, "but more because I had finally achieved what I'd been trying for all my life up till then. I had a frighteningly sharp focus on what I wanted to do and be ever since I can remember."

Wooding's first few books, including *Crashing* and *Kerosene,* are realistic novels about teenagers struggling with love and bullies. In *Crashing,* protagonist Jay is a teenager at the end of his last year of high school. His parents have gone out of town, giving him the chance to throw a party for his friends to celebrate the end of exams and have one last get-together before they all head off into adulthood. He also hopes that the party will give him a chance to get closer to Jo, a girl on whom he has long had his eye. However, things do not go as planned, and Jay and his friends soon find the party devolving into a clash with a drunken lout named Stew and Stew's gang of buddies. The book "captures the essence of being a high school boy, yearning for first love, and wanting to impress your friends," Sarah Applegate wrote in *Kliatt,* while a

Publishers Weekly contributor concluded that "the character study of friends on the verge of adulthood has a pleasing, cinematic energy."

Kerosene is the story of Cal, an almost pathologically shy sixteen-year-old boy. Two of the popular girls at his school, Emma and Abby, team up to torture Cal just for fun, and to cope with his frustration he begins setting fires—first small ones, then larger and larger blazes. Although some reviewers were unhappy with the book's resolution, *School Library Journal* contributor Sharon Rawlins noted that Cal's "feelings of alienation and inadequacy are believably portrayed." "Although Cal himself realistically suffers from being overwrought, the story is not, but rather is a gripping and insightful psychological adventure," Francisca Goldsmith noted in *Kliatt.*

The Haunting of Alaizabel Cray differs from Wooding's earlier works. This supernatural novel, which won the prestigious British Smarties Book Prize, is set in an alternate London full of magic and strange monsters. Most people in this city fear that if they go out at night they will be in danger from the wyches, but some, including seventeen-year-old Thaniel Fox, bravely set out to hunt the creatures instead. While out hunting one night, Thaniel finds Alaizabel Cray, a half-mad, seemingly possessed young woman whom the wyches find strangely attractive. "This is dark fare, often graphically violent," Jennifer Mattson noted in *Booklist,* adding that "Wooding delivers characters to care about." Reviewers praised many aspects of *The Haunting of Alaizabel Cray.* A *Kirkus Reviews* contributor commented on the "complex plotting and structure[, which] combine with rich, atmospheric world-building in a fast-paced, tension-filled read." Another critic, writing in *Publishers Weekly,* wrote that "the tactile quality of the prose will make readers feel as if they can touch and smell the dank sewers of the city." Wooding "fuses together his best storytelling skills—plotting, atmosphere, shock value—to create a fabulously horrific and ultimately timeless underworld," Hillias J. Martin concluded in *School Library Journal.*

BIOGRAPHICAL AND CRITICAL SOURCES:

PERIODICALS

Booklist, July, 2002, Todd Morning, review of *Kerosene,* p. 1838; August, 2004, Jennifer Mattson, review of *The Haunting of Alaizabel Cray,* p. 1925.

Bookseller, December 7, 2001, "Three Take Gold Smarties," p. 6; February 4, 2005, review of *The Ascendancy Veil,* p. 32.

Girls' Life, October-November, 2004, review of *The Haunting of Alaizabel Cray,* p. 42.

Horn Book, November-December, 2004, Anita L. Burkam, review of *The Haunting of Alaizabel Cray,* p. 719.

Kirkus Reviews, August 15, 2004, review of *The Haunting of Alaizabel Cray,* p. 815.

Kliatt, July, 2002, Francisca Goldsmith, review of *Kerosene,* p. 26; May, 2004, Sarah Applegate, review of *Crashing,* p. 25; July, 2004, Michele Winship, review of *The Haunting of Alaizabel Cray,* p. 13.

Publishers Weekly, February 18, 2002, review of *Kerosene,* p. 98; December 15, 2003, review of *Crashing,* p. 75; September 13, 2004, review of *The Haunting of Alaizabel Cray,* p. 80.

School Librarian, autumn, 1999, review of *Kerosene,* p. 158; winter, 2000, review of *Endgame,* p. 215; autumn, 2001, review of *The Haunting of Alaizabel Cray,* p. 161; autumn, 2003, review of *Poison,* p. 161.

School Library Journal, July, 2002, Sharon Rawline, review of *Kerosene,* p. 128; August, 2004, Hillias J. Martin, review of *The Haunting of Alaizabel Cray,* p. 132; April, 2005, review of *The Haunting of Alaizabel Cray,* p. 72.

Voice of Youth Advocates, June, 2004, Ed Sullivan, review of *Crashing,* p. 138.

ONLINE

British Broadcasting Corporation Web site, http://www.bbc.co.uk/blast/ (November 6, 2005), "Blast: Chris Wooding."

Chris Wooding Home Page, http://www.chriswooding.com (November 6, 2005).

Fantastic Fiction Web site, http://www.fantasticfiction.co.uk/ (November 6, 2005), "Chris Wooding Bibliography."

Push Web site, http://www.thisispush.com/ (November 6, 2005), interview with Wooding.

ScifiDimensions.com, http://www.scifidimensions.com/ (November 6, 2005), Chris Coppeans, review of *The Skein of Lament.*

Y-Z

YARMON, Morton 1916-2005

*OBITUARY NOTICE—*See index for *CA* sketch: Born March 8, 1916, in New York, NY; died of complications following a stroke, August 3, 2005, in New York, NY. Journalist, public relations executive, philanthropist, and author. Yarmon was a former newspaper editor and public relations manager who in later life was a major benefactor to Beth Israel Medical Center in New York City. Graduating from what is now the City College of the City University of New York when he was eighteen, he received a B.S. in journalism in 1935. While serving in the U.S. Army in Paris as a captain, he published his first book, the coauthored *How to Get a Defense Job* (1941), which was quickly followed by *Opportunities in the Armed Forces* (1942). After working briefly for the *New York Herald Tribune,* Yarmon joined the staff at the *New York Times* as a foreign editor assistant until 1956. He next became involved in public relations as a director of creative services for the firm Ruder & Finn, and for four years was associate managing editor for *Parade* magazine. With this experience behind him, he was hired as director of public education and information for the American Jewish Committee in 1962, and remained there until his retirement in 1991. After retiring, Yarmon and his wife began donating to Beth Israel. Having invested wisely over the years (he was the author of 1961's *Invest Smartly*), the Yarmons had become millionaires, and they eventually donated over five million dollars to the hospital. Yarmon was also the author of such books as *Early American Antique Furniture* (1952) and *Opportunities in Civil Service* (1957).

OBITUARIES AND OTHER SOURCES:

PERIODICALS

New York Times, August 6, 2005, p. B14.

*   *   *

YBARRA, Michael J.

PERSONAL: Male. *Education:* Attended University of California at Los Angeles; University of California at Berkeley, M.A.

ADDRESSES: Home—San Francisco, CA. *Agent*—Steerforth Books, 25 Lebanon St., Hanover, NH 03755.

CAREER: Former staff reporter for *Wall Street Journal;* freelance writer.

WRITINGS:

Washington Gone Crazy: Senator Pat McCarran and the Great American Communist Hunt, Steerforth Press (Hanover, NH), 2004.

Contributor to periodicals, including *New York Times, Los Angeles Times, Washington Post,* and *New Republic.*

SIDELIGHTS: Former *Wall Street Journal* reporter Michael J. Ybarra is the author of *Washington Gone Crazy: Senator Pat McCarran and the Great American Communist Hunt.* A biography of Senator McCarran, it reminds the reader that Senator Joseph McCarthy, though highly visible and vocal during the anti-Communist campaigns of the 1950s, was not the only power behind the now-notorious "Red Scare" era. In fact, McCarran was the actual motivator behind the government's activities during that period. In a review for the *New York Times,* David Greenberg remarked that, "as important as the recent archival disclosures about Communist espionage may be, Ybarra's painstakingly drawn study of this dyspeptic, power-hungry titan . . . shows that it was gratuitous persecutions at home, waged in the name of the hunt for those spies, that sowed panic, ruined lives and stained America indelibly." *Booklist* reviewer Bryce Christensen pointed out that, "though far from sympathetic with McCarran's objectives, Ybarra marvels at his skill in dominating Congress." A contributor to *Publishers Weekly* wrote that, "by favoring careful documentation over demonization, Ybarra's hefty account offers a welcome new perspective on the origins of the Cold War."

BIOGRAPHICAL AND CRITICAL SOURCES:

PERIODICALS

Booklist, September 1, 2004, Bryce Christensen, review of *Washington Gone Crazy: Senator Pat McCarran and the Great American Communist Hunt,* p. 31.

Library Journal, September 1, 2004, Ed Goedeken, review of *Washington Gone Crazy,* p. 170.

New York Times, October 31, 2004, David Greenberg, "Nativist Son," review of *Washington Gone Crazy.*

Publishers Weekly, August 23, 2004, review of *Washington Gone Crazy,* p. 47.

ONLINE

History News Network, http://hnn.us/ (June 22, 2005), "Michael J. Ybarra."*

*   *   *

YEE, Sienho

PERSONAL: Male. *Education:* Brandeis University, B.A., 1989; Columbia University, J.D., 1993; attended Oxford University, 1997-2001.

ADDRESSES: Office—University of Colorado, School of Law, 401 UCB, Boulder, CO 80309. *E-mail*—yee@ sienhoyee.org.

CAREER: Educator and attorney. U.S. Circuit Court of Appeals, Third Circuit, Trenton, NJ, law clerk, 1993-94; United Nations international criminal tribunal for former Yugoslavia, the Hague, Netherlands, law clerk in appeals chamber, 1995-96; University of Colorado, Boulder, associate professor of law, 2001—. Instructor of international law at University of London, Northwestern University, and St. Hugh's College, Oxford; International Monetary Fund, counsel in legal department. *Chinese Journal of International Law,* editor-in-chief, 2001—.

WRITINGS:

(Editor, with Wang Tieya) *International Law in the Post-cold War World: Essays in Memory of Li Haopei,* Routledge (New York, NY), 2001.

(Editor) *International Crime and Punishment: Selected Issues,* Volume 1, University Press of America (Lanham, MD), 2003, Volume 2, 2004.

Toward an International Law of Co-Progressiveness, Martinus Nijhoff Publishers (Boston, MA), 2003.

Contributor of articles to periodicals, including *International Law, Columbia Law Review, European Journal of International Law, German Yearbook of International Law, International and Comparative Law Quarterly,* and *Max Planck Yearbook of the United Nations.*

SIDELIGHTS: Sienho Yee told *CA:* "When I grew up my parents instilled in me a sense of responsibility and I somehow cultivated in myself a sense of curiosity about things and an urge to improve upon things. I think these two are the most important."

BIOGRAPHICAL AND CRITICAL SOURCES:

ONLINE

Sienho Yee Home Page, http://www.sienhoyee.org (May 30, 2005).

YELLIN, Tamar 1963-

PERSONAL: Born 1963, in Leeds, England; married Bob Tasker. *Education:* Graduated from Oxford University.

ADDRESSES: Home—Yorkshire, England. *Agent*—c/o Author Mail, Howard Morhaim, 11 John St., Ste. 407, New York, NY 10038. *E-mail*—tamar@oivas.com.

CAREER: Writer. Worked variously as a supermarket clerk, primary school teacher, college lecturer in Judaism, and Jewish faith advisor to schools.

WRITINGS:

The Genizah at the House of Shepher, Toby Press (New York, NY), 2005.

Contributor to periodicals, including *London, Stand, Jewish Quarterly, Panurge, Writing Women, Metropolitan, Leviathan Quarterly, Iron, Third Alternative, Big Issue, Staple,* and *Nemonymous.* Contributor to anthologies, including *Slow Mirror and Other Stories: New Fiction by Jewish Writers,* edited by Sonja Lyndon and Sylvia Paskin, Five Leaves (Nottingham, England), 1996; *Leviathan 3,* edited by Jeff Vandermeer, Prime Books (Holicong, PA), 2002; *Mordecai's First Brush with Love: New Stories by Jewish Women in Britain,* edited by Laura Phillips and Marion Baraitser, Loki Press (London, England), 2004; and *Best Short Stories.*

SIDELIGHTS: Author Tamar Yellin studied Hebrew at Oxford University and began publishing short stories in respected literary journals at age thirty. Her first novel, however, was fifteen years in the making. The story behind *The Genizah at the House of Shepher* began in 1987, when Yellin, then age twenty-four, traveled from her native England to her grandparents' Jerusalem home for a final visit before the building's scheduled demolition. Hidden in the attic among an impressive collection of historical papers was a notebook, missing since 1915, that proved to be of vital importance in recreating an ancient Biblical text lost in a 1947 fire. Yellin soon began work on a fictional narrative based on nearly 150 years of her family's history, a project that took until 2005 to complete and publish. In an interview with *Yorkshire*

Post Today reporter Sheena Hastings, Yellin remarked, "I wish the book hadn't taken up so much of my life, but nor was I ever going to give up on it."

In a review for *Booklist,* Debi Lewis called Yellin's debut novel "impossible to put down," adding that the book's story is infused with "beauty, deep love, and a timelessness that will likely make it a classic." A contributor to *Publishers Weekly* called the work "novel is warm and engrossing, rich with historical detail and unmet yearning." *Library Journal* reviewer Molly Abramowitz remarked that, "Filled with myth, mystery, and history, this novel gives the flavor of Jerusalem neighborhoods through the modern era." A *Kirkus Reviews* contributor described the book as "a warmly portrayed, densely researched fictional history of a scattered Jewish clan migrated to Jerusalem" and "a fascinating, labyrinthine journey."

BIOGRAPHICAL AND CRITICAL SOURCES:

PERIODICALS

Booklist, March 1, 2005, Debi Lewis, review of *The Genizah at the House of Shepher,* p. 1143.
Kirkus Reviews, January 15, 2005, review of *The Genizah at the House of Shepher,* p. 82.
Library Journal, March 1, 2005, Molly Abramowitz, review of *The Genizah at the House of Shepher,* p. 81.
Publishers Weekly, February 7, 2005, review of *The Genizah at the House of Shepher,* p. 38.

ONLINE

Fantastic Metropolis, http://www.fantasticmetropolis. com/ (October 17, 2005), author interview.
Tamar Yellin Home Page, http://www.tamaryellin.com (June 22, 2005).
Yorkshire Post Today Online, http://www.yorkshire today.co.uk/ (May 4, 2005), Sheena Hastings, "A Secret in the Attic and a Mystery That Spans the Years."

*   *   *

ZALOOM, George

PERSONAL: Born in Brooklyn, NY. *Education:* University of Southern California, graduated from School of Cinema-Television.

ADDRESSES: Agent—Don Buchwald & Associates, 6500 Wilshire Blvd., Ste. 2200, Los Angeles, CA 90048; fax: 323-655-7470.

CAREER: Cofounder of ZM Productions. Executive producer of films, including *H-E Double Hockey Sticks,* 1999. Producer of films, including *2010: The Odyssey Continues,* 1984; (with Les Mayfield) *Hearts of Darkness: A Filmmaker's Apocalypse,* Triton, 1991; *Encino Man,* Buena Vista, 1992; and *Wildfire 7,* 2004. Executive producer and producer of videos, including *Under Pressure: Making The Abyss,* 1993; *The Making of Jurassic Park,* 1995; *Saturday Morning Cartoons' Greatest Hits,* 1995; and *William Shatner's Star Trek Memories,* 1995. Executive producer of television movies and programs, including (as co-executive producer) *"What'z up?"* (series), 1994; *The Computer Wore Tennis Shoes,* American Broadcasting Companies (ABC), 1995; *Freaky Friday,* ABC, 1995; *Escape to Witch Mountain,* ABC, 1995; *The Barefoot Executive,* ABC, 1995; (as co-executive producer) *Encino Woman,* ABC, 1996; *The Cape,* 1996; *Tower of Terror,* ABC, 1997; *The Love Bug,* ABC, 1997; *Images of Life,* 1998; *Beverly Hills Family Robinson,* Disney Channel/ABC, 1998; *Frank Capra, an American Legend,* 1998; *The Making of Terminator 2: 3-D,* 2000; *The Sports Pages,* Showtime, 2001; and *Buried Alive,* 2002. Producer of television movies and programs, including *The Secrets of the Back to the Future Trilogy,* 1990; (with Mayfield) *Psycho IV: The Beginning,* National Broadcasting Company (NBC), 1990; *All in the Family: 20th Anniversary Special,* 1991; and *The Shaggy Dog,* 1994. Director of *The Whole Shebang,* 2001. Assistant editor of *The Magnificent Major,* Viacom, 1977. Played a janitor in *Psycho IV: The Beginning,* NBC, 1990. Contributor to sound production for *The Making of Indiana Jones and the Temple of Doom,* 1984, and *Indiana Jones: Making the Trilogy,* 2003.

WRITINGS:

SCREENPLAYS

(With Shawn Schepps) *Encino Man,* Buena Vista, 1992.
(With Z.A. K.) *Dogmatic,* Spectacor, 1999.
(With Jeff Rothberg) *The Whole Shebang,* 2K Media, 2001.

Also author of series pilots and episodes for *The Cape,* 1996; and episode for *The Sports Pages,* Showtime, 2001.

SIDELIGHTS: George Zaloom has a long list of credits as a producer for both films and television programs, as well as for his writing and occasional acting parts. With Les Mayfield, he founded ZM Productions, which has produced such films as *Psycho IV: The Beginning,* in which Zaloom also played the part of the janitor. Written by Joseph Stefano, who wrote the original screenplay, and starring Anthony Perkins, who reprises his role as Norman Bates, the film examines the childhood (the young Norman is played by Henry Thomas) and horrors of the man who, in the original *Psycho* directed by Alfred Hitchcock, famously slashed actress Janet Leigh in the shower. Olivia Hussey plays the mother who psychosexually torments her young son in this television film. Rick Kogan, reviewing the film in the *Chicago Tribune,* noted that this follow-up "is less a horror film—fewer knives and chills—than it is a rather disturbing portrait of emotional terror."

Hearts of Darkness: A Filmmaker's Apocalypse is documentary film produced by ZM Productions that examines the difficulties involved with making Francis Ford Coppola's epic film *Apocalypse Now.* The film was supposed to be shot in sixteen weeks, but it stretched out to thirty-four, and the budget nearly tripled. Actor Harvey Keitel was fired, and Martin Sheen, who replaced him, suffered a heart attack. Marlon Brandon came to the set overweight and difficult to work with. The movie, which portrays the Vietnam conflict, was shot in close proximity to battles then being fought in a very similar war in the Philippines, and some of the sets were destroyed by a monsoon. The film draws from nearly sixty hours of footage shot by Coppola's wife, Eleanor, during the making of the 1976 film; it also relies on interviews with the stars, who included Dennis Hopper, as well as the Coppolas, John Milius, and director George Lucas, who also worked on the film. Michael Wilmington wrote in the *Los Angeles Times* that the film is "an almost hypnotic document. All the interviewees are salty and unsparing, of themselves especially. Milius is bearish and hilarious; Eleanor idealistic, precise; Coppola nakedly open."

Zaloom also produced and cowrote the screenplay for *Encino Man.* The film stars Sean Astin as Dave and Pauly Shore as Stoney, two teens who discover Cro-Magnon Brendan Fraser frozen in a glacier. They defrost him and pass him off as Link, an exchange student, in their California high school, where the cave man tries to adapt to their culture. Of this comedy, Caryn James said in the *New York Times* that "Fraser plays Link as an endearing caveman, suggesting some of the guileless charm of Tom Hanks." Another comedy Zaloom directed is *The Whole Shebang,* starring Stanley Tucci as Giovanni, an Italian who has had a recent romantic breakup and accepts an offer by his cousin to come to New Jersey to help run his fireworks business.

BIOGRAPHICAL AND CRITICAL SOURCES:

PERIODICALS

Chicago Tribune, November 9, 1990, Rick Kogan, review of *Psycho IV: The Beginning,* p. 1.
Los Angeles Times, January 24, 1992, Michael Wilmington, review of *Hearts of Darkness: A Filmmaker's Apocalypse,* p. F1; April 2, 1995, Ed Dwyer, "The Tube Masters of Nostalgia," Magazine section, p. 18.
New York Times, May 22, 1992, Caryn James, review of *Encino Man.*
Pantagraph, June 6, 1992, Dan Craft, "Wit Extinct in 'Encino Man,'" p. B7.
Times-Picayune (New Orleans, LA), May 22, 1992, David Baron, "Neanderthal Happenings," p. L21.
Variety, September 3, 2001, Eddie Cockrell, review of *The Whole Shebang,* p. 41.
Washington Post, May 22, 1992, Desson Howe, review of *Encino Man.*

ONLINE

Internet Movie Database, http://imdb.com/ (June 16, 2005), career information on George Zaloom.
Writers Boot Camp, http://www.writersbootcamp.com/ (June 16, 2005), interview with George Zaloom.*

*   *   *

ZIHALA, Maryann 1959-

PERSONAL: Born October 1, 1959. *Education:* University of Maryland, B.A., 1986; Catholic University, M.A.; Southern California University, Santa Ana, J.D., 2003.

ADDRESSES: *Agent*—c/o Author Mail, University Press of America, 4501 Forbes Blvd., Ste. 200, Lanham, MD 20706. *E-mail*—zihala@msn.com.

CAREER: Writer. Professor of political science and criminal justice at Central Florida Community College, Lecanto, 1993-94, Santa Fe Community College, Gainesville, FL, 1994-97, Lake City Community College, FL, 1995-97, Butler Community College, El Dorado, KS, 1997-98, Southwest Missouri State University, Springfield, 1998-2000, Ozarks Tech Community College, Springfield, MO, 1998-2004, and Crowder Community College, Neosho, MO, 2000-04. Republic Communications, Inc., owner, 1992-97. *Military service:* U.S. Air Force, 1981-92, intelligence research analyst and cryptologic linguist.

WRITINGS:

Edith Wharton's Old New York Society, University Press of America (Lanham, MD), 2002.
(Editor and author of introduction) *Democracy: The Greatest Good for the Greatest Number,* University Press of America (Lanham, MD), 2003.
Lieutenant Joey Tucker (fiction), JoNa Books (Indianapolis, IN), 2004.
Rights, Liberties, and the Rule of Law, University Press of America (Lanham, MD), 2004.

Contributor of articles to periodicals, including *Washington Times, Springfield News-Leader, Fort Myers News-Press, Gainesville Sun, Tampa Tribune, Impact,* and *Republic.*

WORK IN PROGRESS: *Galactic Americana,* a work of fiction, expected 2005.

BIOGRAPHICAL AND CRITICAL SOURCES:

ONLINE

Maryann Zihala Home Page, http://www.zihala.com (May 30, 2005).

*   *   *

ZILVERSMIT, Arthur 1932-2005

OBITUARY NOTICE—See index for *CA* sketch: Born July 5, 1932, in The Hague, Netherlands; died of kidney and bowel failure, August 22, 2005, in Vorhees, NJ. Historian, educator, and author. Zilversmit was a retired professor of history at Lake Forest College who was noted as an innovative teacher and authority on African-American history. Brought to America by his family at age six to avoid the German invasion of Holland, he grew up in New York City and attended Cornell University. After graduating with a B.A. in 1954, he went on to finish an M.A. at Harvard University the next year. While teaching at Williams College, he earned a Ph.D. from the University of California at Berkeley in 1962. Zilversmit joined the Lake Forest faculty in 1966 as an assistant professor of history. He was promoted to full professor by 1973, was a department chair for a time, and was named distinguished service professor of history in 1994. An accomplished teacher, he developed new courses for his students, including the college's African-American history curriculum, and was awarded an Outstanding Teacher Award. He retired as professor emeritus in 1998. Zilversmit published two books on history, *The*

First Emancipation: The Abolition of Slavery in the North (1967) and the edited *Lincoln on Black and White: A Documentary History* (1971), as well as the work *Changing Schools: Progressive Education Theory and Practice, 1930-1960* (1993).

OBITUARIES AND OTHER SOURCES:

PERIODICALS

Chicago Tribune, September 5, 2005, section 4, p. 10.

ONLINE

Lake Forest College Web site, http://www.lakeforest.edu/ (January 6, 2006).